AFFAIRS OF STATE

AFFAIRS OF STATE

Public Life in Late
Nineteenth Century America

Morton Keller

THE BELKNAP PRESS
OF HARVARD UNIVERSITY PRESS
Cambridge, Massachusetts, and
London, England   1977

Library of Congress Cataloging in Publication Data

Keller, Morton.
  Affairs of State.

  Includes bibliographical references and index.
  1. United States—History—1865–1898.
I. Title.
E661.K27   973.8   76–21676
ISBN 0–674–00721–2

For Oscar Handlin
and to the memory
of Mary Handlin

I SUPPOSE I am not by nature disposed to think so much as most people do, of "institutions." The Americans think and talk very much of their "institutions." I am by nature inclined to call all this sort of thing *machinery* . . . But the more I see of America, the more I find myself led to treat "institutions" with increased respect. Until I went to the United States I had never seen a people with institutions which seemed expressly and thoroughly suited to it.

—Matthew Arnold, *Civilization in the United States: First and Last Impressions of America* (Boston, 1888), 114–115.

Preface

THE MOST ACUTE visitors to the nineteenth century United States—Alexis de Tocqueville, James Bryce, Matthew Arnold—agreed that the essence of that strange and unsettling society lay in its public institutions. Party politics and elections, political thought and public issues, legal doctrines and court decisions, the work of legislatures and public officials made up in sum a substantial and evocative part of American life. The character of the nation's public experience from the Civil War to the end of the nineteenth century is the topic of this book.

Politics and government were the chief—almost the sole—subjects of American historical writing before the twentieth century. History is past politics, politics is present history: this was the prevailing belief. But in more recent times there emerged a broader vision of the past, embracing intellectual, economic, and social history. What Americans thought, how they got and spent, how they lived seemed more important than how they were governed.

Now, in these Bicentennial years, it appears once again that the utility and legitimacy of American politics, law, and government have great social importance. Clearly it is time to take fresh stock of the nation's public life. But to do so in a tendentious, adversary manner—the currently fashionable style—is as inadequate as the celebratory historical writing of the past. What is needed, rather, is analysis of the sort that has been lavished on the nation's social and economic systems, and on its dominant modes of thought.

That is what I have sought to do here. I examine late nineteenth century American politics, law, and government as the components of a national public life, an American *polity*. I have in mind the dictionary definition of the word as "the general or fundamental system of organization of a government, . . . its relation to the people, their political and civil rights, etc." In this view the polity like the economy is a major component of the American social system, creating and allocating power as the economy creates and allocates wealth.

If the idea of a polity defines the content of this book, then the theme of historical generations defines its form. The philosopher Ortega y Gasset spoke of generations as states of "historical coexistence," in which the major events of a time determine the character of a society's attitudes, actions, and institutions. It has been suggested that a decisive politically relevant experience determines the parameters of a political generation. In this sense the years from 1865 to around 1880 may be seen as the time of the postwar polity, when government, politics, and law were caught up in the task of dealing with the consequences of the Civil War. The confrontation with industrialism emerges as the major theme of American public life during the 1880s and 1890s: the time of the industrial polity.

This notion of political generations makes possible a treatment of public life that accords with the rapid pace of American social experience. (It is worth recalling that Justice Oliver Wendell Holmes knew both John Quincy Adams and Alger Hiss.) At the same time, it allows one to take due account of the underlying continuities that interplay with the forces of change. Indeed, a major theme of this book is the way in which tensions as old as America herself—between equality and liberty, between the desire for freedom and the need for social order, between dependence on government and hostility to the state, between localism and nationalism—persisted through the tumultuous decades of the late nineteenth century. These were not so much years of governmental lethargy and subservience to vested interests—the customary view—as a time of intense conflict between old values and the pressures generated by massive change.

Americans in 1865 had just gone through the bloodiest war of the nineteenth century. By 1900 they had experienced the most extensive industrialization in modern history. What was the impact of those traumatic events on the nation's public life? How did American politics, law, and government respond to the Civil War and then to the rise of a new social and economic order? These are the questions that I have tried to answer.

I want to thank a number of individuals and institutions for their help—exempting all, of course, from responsibility for what I did with their time, ideas, and money.

Aida Donald, David Donald, David Fischer, Oscar Handlin, Andrew Kaufman, Phyllis Keller, David Landes, David Rothman, Stephan Thernstrom, Robert Weibe, and C. Vann Woodward read and helpfully commented on some or all of the text.

Ina Malaguti and Irene Topalian bravely took on much of the burden of typing.

Grants from the American Council of Learned Societies, the American Philosophical Society, the Charles Warren Center for Studies in American History, the National Endowment for the Humanities, and the Rockefeller Foundation furthered my research and writing. Brandeis University was good about leave, and provided its own special air of intellectual stimulation.

I owe a great debt of gratitude to the faculty and staff of the Harvard Law School. They most generously provided office space, instruction in legal niceties, and the use of their magnificent library. As always, Harvard's Widener Library and Brandeis's Goldfarb Library were indispensable to my work.

M.K.

Contents

Tables

AFFAIRS OF STATE

CHAPTER 1

The Weight of the War

MORE THAN A century after the event, the Civil War remains the great watershed in the history of the American nation. On its far side is the young Republic: agrarian, decentralized, living still under the spell of the Revolution and the Founding Fathers, burdened by slavery but exhilarated by the lure of the great undeveloped West. And on its near side is modern America: a nation of cities, factories, immigrants; a society whose controlling realities are not simplicity and underdevelopment but complexity and maturity.

Yet by most indices of social change, the Civil War worked no great revolution in American life. If anything, it slowed economic development.[1] Nor did the war fundamentally alter American social patterns. Other forces governed the great movements of people into the nation, and within it. And while the end of slavery appeared to promise a profound change in the status of American Negroes, the freedmen in fact continued to be caught in a web of social and economic repression.

Finally, the war did not transform the American system of gov-

1. Ralph Andreano, ed., *The Economic Impact of the American Civil War* (Cambridge, Mass., 1962); David T. Gilchrist and W. David Lewis, eds., *Economic Change in the Civil War Era* (Greenville, Del., 1965); Stanley L. Engerman, "The Economic Impact of the Civil War," *EEH*, 2d ser., 3 (1966), 176–199; Harry N. Scheiber, "Economic Change in the Civil War Era: An Analysis of Recent Studies," *CWH*, 11 (1965), 396–411. See Jeffrey G. Williamson, "Watershed and Turning Points: Conjectures on the Long-Term Impact of Civil War Financing," *JEH*, 34 (1974), 636–661.

ernment. The triumph of nationalism, and of the political power of the North, were part of the main current of nineteenth-century American historical development. The war affected its pace but not its character. The party system, the forms of government, the structure of law underwent no sudden sea change because of the conflict.

Nevertheless, Americans of the Civil War generation had a profound sense of living through events that changed their world. For a while at least, men thought and acted as though they had been sharply detached from their past. Henry James believed that Americans got from the war "a certain sense of proportion and relation, of the world being a more complicated place than it had hitherto seemed." The historian George Ticknor wrote in 1869 that the war left a "great gulf between what happened before it in our century and what has happened since, or what is likely to happen hereafter. It does not seem to me as if I were living in the country in which I was born."[2]

This was the ambiguous inheritance of the Civil War: aside from the end of slavery and the defeat of secession, no profound alteration of American society; yet for many of that generation, a sense of vast and sudden change. The contradiction inherent in this legacy set the tone of the nation's postwar public life.

A War for Nationality

At first the Civil War seemed to be a striking exception to the trend toward national unity in the mid-nineteenth century Western world. Precisely in the decade when Italy and Germany were unified, the United States was rent in two. During the war's early years, much northern as well as southern opinion concluded that the ultimate destiny of the North American continent was a congeries of independent states. Even Abraham Lincoln speculated in July 1861: "Is there in all republics this inherent and fatal weakness? Must a government, of necessity, be too *strong* for the liberties of its own people, or too *weak* to maintain its own existence?" He

2. Henry James quoted in George M. Fredrickson, *The Inner Civil War: Northern Intellectuals and the Crisis of the Union* (New York, 1965), 1; Ticknor, *Life, Letters, and Journals* (Boston, 1877) II, 485.

was not inclined to answer those questions affirmatively. But that he felt called upon to ask them was testimony to their force.[3]

A considerable body of British opinion was quick to write off the experiment of the American Union. Gladstone thought in 1862 that "Jefferson Davis and other leaders of the South . . . have made a nation"; the novelist Edward Bulwer-Lytton predicted that four or more governments would emerge from the wreckage of the United States. In 1863 the English historian Edward A. Freeman published the first volume of his chillingly titled *History of Federal Government from the Foundation of the Achaian League to the Disruption of the United States*. He anticipated that by 1869 an established Confederacy and a truncated United States would exchange ambassadors. The Virginian Charles Fenton Mercer's *The Weakness and Inefficiency of the Government of the United States of America* had titillated its English audience when it appeared in 1845. It was reprinted in 1863 with an introduction that observed: "Recent events have verified his clear discernment of the future; and strengthens our confidence in his judgment . . . that the government of the United States of America is inherently bad and deficient."[4]

Southern hopes often fed on chiliastic predictions of violence in northern cities and a triumphant Confederacy. An apocalyptic literature that dwelt on the inevitable dismemberment of the Union had a vogue in the North as well. In 1861 William B. Wedgwood, professor of law at the University of the City of New York, recommended that the United States be divided into three or four republics, loosely bound together in a Hapsburglike "Democratic Empire."[5]

3. Lincoln in *MP*, VII, 3224. See also David M. Potter, "Civil War," in C. Vann Woodward, *The Comparative Approach to American History* (New York, 1968), 135–145.

4. Ephraim D. Adams, *Great Britain and the American Civil War* (New York, 1925), I, 277; Allan Nevins, *The War for the Union* (New York, 1959), II, 242 ff; Freeman, *History* (London, 1863); Mercer, *Weakness* (London, 1863), ix–x.

5. Wedgwood, *The Record of the Government of the United States of America: A Democratic Empire Advocated, and an Imperial Constitution Proposed* (New York, 1861). See also James Williams, *The Rise and Fall of the 'Model Republic'* (London, 1863); Harold M. Hyman, *A More Perfect Union: The Impact of the Civil War and Reconstruction on the Constitution* (New York, 1973), ch. 3.

But the course of the war soon created a very different frame of mind. It became apparent that the conflict in fact was a major episode in the development of nineteenth century Western nationalism, not a detour into disunion. The war compelled the most influential northern intellectuals, publicists, and politicians to subscribe to the ideal of a powerful, unified, purposeful nation. Even anti-institutional democrats such as Wendell Phillips and Walt Whitman (who in 1856 had declared: "We want no *reforms*, no *institutions*, no *parties*") were swept along. It was difficult to sustain an Emersonian skepticism toward public institutions when Emerson himself served on an official visiting committee to West Point, and welcomed Lincoln's 1864 electoral victory as evidence "that a nation shall be a nation, . . . that a nation cannot be trifled with."

Not since the time of Alexander Hamilton had men of education and intellectual influence reveled so openly in the potentialities of an active, powerful state. The Unitarian minister Henry Bellows exulted: "The state is indeed divine, as being the great incarnation of a nation's rights, privileges, honor and life." A "strong government" appealed to the New York lawyer and diarist George Templeton Strong. The historian John Lothrop Motley, vicariously fighting the war from his post as minister in Vienna, thought that "no individual is anything in the midst of this great revolution." At the end of 1863 Edward Everett Hale published the most widely read piece of wartime fiction, "The Man Without a Country." The horror of an existence without national identification caught the imagination of his audience. A vast wartime pamphlet literature dwelt on the theme of national strength and purpose. As a speaker at Williams College put it, "We at the North, all learned that there was in our . . . Government a power of which we never dreamed."[6]

Organized religion did much to strengthen this mood. The re-

6. Fredrickson, *Inner Civil War*, 21, 178; Edward W. Emerson and Waldo E. Forbes, eds., *Journals of Ralph Waldo Emerson* (Boston, 1914), X, 82; Allan Nevins and Milton H. Thomas, eds., *The Diary of George Templeton Strong* (New York, 1952), III, 66; George W. Curtis, ed., *The Correspondence of John Lothrop Motley* (New York, 1889), II, 182, 188; Hale, "The Man Without a Country," *AM*, 12 (1863), 666–679; Alexander H. Bullock, *The Relations of the Educated Man with American Nationality* (Boston, 1864). See also Frank Freidel, ed., *Union Pamphlets of the Civil War, 1861–1865* (Cambridge, 1967).

ligious exhortations of the war years at first dwelt on the sanctity of the Union. But as the war went on a bolder imagery appeared: an imagery of guilt and atonement, centering on the national crime of slavery. John Brown's prophetic vision ("the sin of slavery is one of which it may be said that without the shedding of blood there is no remission") was fulfilled on dozens of sodden battlefields. But with atonement came salvation. In the words of a religious paper, "it became the general sense that we were passing through an ordeal of purification rather than destruction." The war would "reinvigorate and recover the republic, its institutions and functions of civil government, and its political and social character, from the decay and degeneracy of national virtue, and . . . replenish the life of the nation with increased moral vigor and purity." The religious no less than the secular perception of the war fostered an optimistic, activist nationalism.[7]

A final measure of the war's impact lay in its character as an event of international significance. For the most part, Europeans had given pre-Civil War Americans little reason to regard themselves as other than amusing provincials. Now the war, as no event since the Revolution, thrust America into the full consciousness of the Atlantic community. The conflict came to be viewed everywhere as a major confrontation between separatism and nationalism, oppression and freedom, oligarchy and democracy: "a contest," said the British historian and publicist Goldwin Smith, "between the great parties that divide mankind,—the party of justice and of the future, the party of privilege and of the past." Charles Francis Adams, the wartime minister to Great Britain, observed in January 1865: "It cannot be doubted that the aristocracy feel this

---

7. B. F. Morris, *Christian Life and Character of the Civil Institutions of the United States, Developed in the Official and Historical Annals of the Republic* (Philadelphia, 1864), 682, 670. See also William W. Sweet, *The Methodist Episcopal Church and the Civil War* (Cincinnati, 1912); Chester F. Dunham, *The Attitude of The Northern Clergy toward the South 1860–1865* (Toledo, 1942); Lewis G. Vander Velde, *The Presbyterian Churches and the Federal Union 1861–1869* (Cambridge, Mass., 1932). An example of the more extreme forms of religious expression untapped by the war is [J. Hunt], *The American Union Shown to be the New Heaven and the New Earth, and Its Predicted Restoration to Life within Four Years from Its Death* (New York, 1865), which explains that the Civil War is the trial out of which the Resurrection will come.

struggle to be one that may affect very deeply the permanence of their own privileges." Karl Marx called the Civil War "a world upheaval." His International Workingmen's Association predicted that "as the American war of independence initiated a new era of ascendancy for the middle class, so the American anti-slavery war will do for the working classes."[8]

Americans, too, saw the war in more than national terms. Secretary of State William H. Seward at first wanted his emissaries abroad to stress the conservative nature of the Union effort. If the United States failed, he warned, "anarchy must come upon the earth . . . Does France or Great Britain want to see a social revolution here, with all its horrors, like the slave revolution in San Domingo?" But as the war went on, and Seward's confidence in its outcome grew, his tone changed. Increasingly he stressed the positive moral and political significance of the war. The future United States would be "a homogeneous, enlightened nation, virtuous and brave, inspired by lofty sentiments to achieve a destiny for itself that shall, by its influence and example, be beneficient to mankind." By 1865 he believed that "the United States regard their cause in the present conflict . . . as the cause of human nature."[9]

The message that Seward carried to the world reflected the view of much of the North's intellectual, religious, and political leadership. It was by no means a universal attitude. There was widespread popular resistance throughout the war to the government and its policies. Forty-five percent of the North's voters in 1864 supported the Democratic candidate and platform, which read no such meaning into the war. Nevertheless, the rhetoric of wartime nationalism foreshadowed views that were to have a major impact on the character of the postwar American policy.

8. Goldwin Smith quoted in Adams, *American Civil War*, II, 300; Adams to Seward, Jan. 26, 1865, U.S., *FR* (1865–1866), I, 100; Karl Marx and Frederick Engels, *The Civil War in the United States*, 3d ed. (New York, 1961), 258, 281. See also Joseph M. Hernon, Jr., "British Sympathies in the American Civil War: A Reconsideration," *JSH*, 33 (1967), 356–367; Belle Becker Sideman and Lillian Freedman, eds., *Europe Looks at the Civil War* (New York, 1960); Harold Hyman, ed., *Heard Round the World: The Impact Abroad of the Civil War* (New York, 1969).

9. Seward to Anson Burlingame (Vienna), April 13, 1861, to Charles Francis Adams (London), Feb. 17, 1862, to William L. Dayton (Paris), June 20, 1862, to Adams, Jan. 9, 1865, U.S., *FR* (1861–1865).

The Spurs of Voluntarism

The war had major practical as well as ideological consequences. Resources were utilized, public opinion influenced, the power of government exercised in forceful new ways. The conflict opened the door to bold experiments in voluntary association for public ✓ ends. But at the same time it imposed counterdemands for centralized organization and control. The resulting tension was an important factor in wartime and postwar public life.

The most dramatic new venture in voluntary association was the Confederacy itself; and nowhere was the clash between voluntarism and sovereignty keener. Most white southerners were devoted to their experiment in national independence. The self-reliant southerners were tough and resourceful soldiers. But they were disinclined to make the sacrifices of individual and local independence necessary to create a viable new nation. The Confederacy was a strange and halting state, never fully realized. Its judicial system retained the dockets, the rules of law, and the precedents of the Union. The Confederate constitution differed from its federal model only in details: slavery, not government, was the distinguishing characteristic of the new state.[10]

The states' rights localism that made the Confederacy possible ultimately made it unviable. Vice President Alexander H. Stephens never accepted the centralism imposed by war, and often was deeply at odds with President Jefferson Davis. Robert Barnwell Rhett of South Carolina, a founding father of the Confederacy, attacked Davis's government for refusing to guarantee the right of secession. States' rights lay at the heart of the Confederacy's creed; and much of its brief history was a tale of state politicos and legislatures at odds with the Richmond government and with each other. Generals, congressmen, and bureaucrats acted more frequently as spokesmen of separate sovereignties—or of no sovereignty but themselves—than as members of a new national entity. Political parties and a patronage system in the civil service, devices essential to viable nineteenth century American government, never gained a foothold in the wartime South.

10. William M. Robinson, Jr., *Justice in Grey: A History of the Judicial System of the Confederate States of America* (Cambridge, 1941); William R. Leslie, "The Confederate Constitution," *MQR*, 2 (1963), 153–165.

Secession inexorably led to the government intervention that it was designed to avert. Conscription, a wildly inflated currency, presidential authority to suspend the writ of habeas corpus, government power to requisition property, and taxes on land and slaves were among the expedients adopted by the Confederacy out of wartime necessity. The ultimate irony came at the war's end. Davis and General Robert E. Lee proposed that slaves be conscripted into the army—and that their emancipation follow in due course. Georgia Governor Joseph E. Brown saw the implications of that policy: "We cannot expect them to fight well to continue the enslavement of their wives and children, and it is unreasonable to demand it of them. When we establish the fact that they are a military people, we destroy our own theory that they are unfit to be free, and when we arm them we abandon slavery."[11]

The wartime North found things easier insofar as it was committed to the preservation, not the diminution, of national sovereignty. But there too the very nature of the Civil War brought forth a mass of claimants to the instruments of power, and the resolution of these claims did not prove to be an easy matter.

Much of the initial war effort was of necessity in private, voluntary hands. Regiments often were created by aspiring politicians or prominent citizens acting on no man's authority but their own. The idiosyncratically uniformed Zouaves of the war's early days were a product of this military localism. So too were the complex jurisdictional disputes that arose over the essentially political business of recruiting and commissioning. Massachusetts Democratic politician

11. James Z. Rabun, "Alexander H. Stephens and Jefferson Davis," *AHR*, 58 (1953), 290–321; James F. Rhodes, *History of the United States from the Compromise of 1850* (New York, 1900), V, ch. 28; Eric L. McKitrick, "Party Politics and the Union and Confederate War Efforts," in William H. Chambers and Walter D. Burnham, eds., *The American Party Systems* (New York, 1967), 117–151; Paul P. Van Riper and Harry N. Scheiber, "The Confederate Civil Service," *JSH*, 25 (1959), 448–470; on Lee and Negro troops, Rhodes, *History*, V, 80–81; on Brown, "Georgia," *AC* (1865). See also Thomas B. Alexander and Richard E. Beringer, *The Anatomy of the Confederate Congress: A Study of the Influence of Member Characteristics on Legislative Voting Behavior, 1861–1865* (Nashville, 1972), a statistical demonstration of the lack of a party—or, indeed, a national—sense in the Confederate legislature; May S. Ringold, *The Role of the State Legislatures in the Confederacy* (Athens, Ga., 1966); Wilfred B. Yearns, *The Confederate Congress* (Athens, Ga., 1960); Charles R. Lee, Jr., *The Confederate Constitutions* (Chapel Hill, 1963); Robert F. Durden, *The Gray and the Black: The Confederate Debate on Emancipation* (Baton Rouge, 1972).

(and now militia brigadier general) Benjamin F. Butler clashed sharply with Governor John A. Andrew over the right to commission officers. The general obtained a Washington order creating a "Department of New England" which put the region's six states under his command for recruiting purposes. Andrew refused to commission Butler's Massachusetts officer list. Finally, Secretary of War Edwin M. Stanton resolved the controversy in Andrew's favor.[12]

The Union's propaganda effort also had an extragovernmental base. The Loyal Publication Societies of New York and New England and the Board of Publications of the Philadelphia Union League distributed millions of pamphlets defending the Union cause—or, more precisely, their version of that cause. They jousted with the Democrats' Society for the Diffusion of Useful Knowledge, which harped on the inferiority of Negroes and called for a negotiated peace. Members of the Loyal Publication Society encouraged William Conant Church to establish the *Army and Navy Journal* in 1863 as an organ "of unquestionable loyalty" which would provide a public forum for that suddenly powerful branch of government, the military.

The Loyal Publication Society gave men such as the merchant and railroad investor John Murray Forbes and the editor–essayist Charles Eliot Norton a strong sense of participation in the war effort. Forbes wanted "a committee of correspondence upon the rigorous prosecution of the war" to exert pressure on the administration. He worked closely with Governor Andrew to strengthen Massachusetts's contribution to the war, was active in recruiting and organizing Negro regiments, and participated in a consortium to build a cruiser that would be a match for the Confederate raider *Alabama*. The lack of clear distinction between the public and the private sectors of American life allowed an influential individual such as Forbes to range widely without a government position.[13]

12. Fred A. Shannon, *The Organization and Administration of the Union Army, 1861–1865*, 2 vols. (Cleveland, 1928); on Butler and Andrew, William B. Hesseltine, *Lincoln and the War Governors* (New York, 1955), 186–191. Allan Nevins, *The War for the Union* (New York, 1959–1971) is the most complete discussion of the Union war effort.

13. Frank Freidel, "The Loyal Publication Society: A Pro-Union Propaganda Agency," *MVHR*, 26 (1939), 359–376; Edith E. Ware, "Committees of Public Information, 1863–1866," *HO*, 10 (1919), 65–67; Freidel, ed., *Union Pamphlets*, I, 1–9, 14–15; Donald N. Bigelow, *William Conant Church and the Army and Navy Journal* (New York, 1952), 100–102; on Forbes, Rhodes, *History*, V, 243.

The most potent quasi-public organization of the war years was the United States Sanitary Commission, established in 1861 by leading citizens of Boston, New York, and Philadelphia. Initially designed to care for sick and wounded Union troops, the Commission became "a great teacher . . . showing the value of order, and the dignity of work," and schooled many of the nation's elite in the possibilities of public power. Frederick Law Olmsted, the landscape architect who served as executive secretary of the Commission, and president Henry W. Bellows were as interested in political influence as they were in good works. Bellows, a New York Unitarian minister, played an important part in the founding of the city's Union League Club and in later movements for municipal and civil service reform. The Sanitary Commission, he later recalled, "acted not merely as a Board of Military Health, but as a kind of Cabinet & Council of War—boldly seizing anomalous power, advising the Government, & seeking to influence the men, military and otherwise who command the position."[14]

The Union League Clubs of New York and Philadelphia drew from the same social circles that dominated the Sanitary Commission, and were more overtly political. They fought against those who wanted a negotiated peace, encouraged thousands to join the Union army, worked for the Union Republican party in elections, and attempted to "urge upon public attention large and noble schemes of national advancement." Another important association, the United States Christian Commission, was composed of elements —YMCAs, Bible and temperance societies, Sunday schools—that

14. Katherine P. Wormeley, *The United States Sanitary Commission: A Sketch of Its Purposes and Its Work* (Boston, 1863), 253; William Q. Maxwell, *Lincoln's Fifth Wheel: The Political History of the United States Sanitary Commission* (New York, 1956); Bellows quoted in Fredrickson, *Inner Civil War*, 108. See also Edward E. Hale, "The United States Sanitary Commission," *AM*, 19 (1867), 416–429; Thomas Evans, *La commission sanitaire des Etats-Unis* (Paris, 1865), xi ("It is the grandest act of philanthropy that mankind has ever conceived of or accomplished. By its influence, the whole of American society has been altered."); Clifford E. Clark, Jr., "Religious Beliefs and Social Reforms in the Gilded Age: The Case of Henry Whitney Bellows," *NEQ*, 43 (1970), 59–78.

The National Academy of Sciences, established in 1863, evoked a similar euphoria. Senator Henry Wilson of Massachusetts welcomed it as "an element of power" that would help to make the nation "one and indivisible." A. Hunter Dupree, *Science in the Federal Government* (Cambridge, 1957),

gave it a broader social base than the business and professional men of the Sanitary Commission and the Union League Clubs.[15]

The war opened new opportunities for economic interests as well. Wartime entrepreneurs got a thorough schooling in the possibilities —and drawbacks—of doing business with the government. Thomas A. Scott, vice president of the Pennsylvania Railroad, served as assistant secretary of war in the early days of the conflict. He had much to do with the organization of government and private railroad lines for the North's military effort. Henceforth he would be keenly sensitive to the uses of federal charters and subsidies in railroad construction and consolidation. He was not alone; William H. Osborn, president of the Illinois Central, joined hundreds of midwestern business and political leaders in a wartime quest for a ship canal to reduce East-West transportation costs. A transcontinental railroad, the great federally aided enterprise of the nineteenth century, got under way during the war years.

The war's daily lessons in the value of organization spurred a variety of economic groups to seek ways by which their interests might be better served. The first national trade associations—among them the American Bureau of Shipping, the National Association of Wool Manufacturers, and the National Paper Manufacturers' Association—were wartime creations. Farmers and workers, too, were encouraged to pool their interests. Charles D. Bragdon, editor of the influential *Rural New Yorker*, urged farmers to organize. Wool marketing associations and cooperative cheese factories were some among many wartime cooperative agricultural enterprises. Four national labor unions had been created before 1861; eleven new ones were founded during the war years.[16]

Large numbers of Americans, then, ranging from secessionist

135–146. See also Ralph L. Rush, ed., *The Letters of Ralph Waldo Emerson* (New York, 1939), V, 396.

15. Union League Club of New York, *Address of the President, June 23, 1866* (New York, 1866); statement in Henry W. Bellows, *Historical Sketch of the Union League Club of New York* (New York, 1879); Robert H. Bremner, "The Impact of the Civil War on Philanthropy and Social Welfare," *CWH*, 12 (1966), 293–303; Rev. Robert Patterson, *Christ in the Army: A Selection of Sketches of the Work of the United States Christian Commission* (Philadelphia, 1865); Timothy L. Smith, *Revivalism and Social Reform* (New York, 1957), 76–78; "Christian Commission," *AC* (1864).

16. Samuel R. Kamm, *The Civil War Career of Thomas A. Scott* (Philadelphia, 1940); on ship canal, Paul W. Gates, *Agriculture and the Civil*

southerners to nationalist northern intellectuals, from civic-minded business and professional men to workingmen, farmers, and entrepreneurs, were spurred by the war to create new forms of voluntary association. This wartime experience was important because it schooled potent groups in the possibilities or organization, and left them restive under a polity that did not readily satisfy their demands.

The war that fostered these associations also brought them into conflict with a central government more and more aware of its own power and prerogatives. Secretary of War Stanton was bitterly hostile to the Sanitary Commission, on the ground that it challenged the primacy of the administration. (Lincoln, in his ironic way, referred to the Commission as "a fifth wheel to the coach" of the war effort.) Increasing pressure brought the Sanitary Commission, the Union League Clubs, and the Loyal Publication Societies to serve the needs of the government and of Lincoln's Union Republican party.[17]

Only the central government could provide the leadership and authority that the war ultimately demanded. The American Freedmen's Aid Societies of Boston, New York, and Philadelphia, concerned about the condition of Negroes freed by the advancing Union armies, told Lincoln in December 1863 that "the question is too large for anything short of Government authority, Government resources, and Government ubiquity to deal with. The plans, the means, the agencies within any volunteer control are insignificant in their inadequacy to the vastness of the demand." They asked for "a regularly constituted government bureau, with all the machinery

---

War. (New York, 1965), 349–351, and Leonard P. Curry, *Blueprint for Modern America: Nonmilitary Legislation of the First Civil War Congress* (Nashville, 1968), 136–146; on trade associations, Emerson D. Fite, *Social and Industrial Conditions in the North during the Civil War* (New York, 1910), 164–168; on Bragdon, Gates, *Agriculture*, 354–355; on labor unions, Fite, *Social and Industrial Conditions*, 204–205, and David Montgomery, *Beyond Equality: Labor and the Radical Republicans, 1862–1872* (New York, 1967), ch. 3. See also Arthur C. Cole, *The Irrepressible Conflict 1850–1865* (New York, 1934), ch. 13; Nevins, *War for the Union*, passim.

17. Allan Nevins, "The United States Sanitary Commission and Secretary Stanton," *MHS Proceedings,* 67 (1941–1944), 402–419; Benjamin P. Thomas and Harold M. Hyman, *Stanton: The Life and Times of Lincoln's Secretary of War* (New York, 1862), 367–368. Stanton also—but less successfully—opposed challenges to his authority by the *Army and Navy Journal.* Bigelow, *Church,* 105.

and civil powers of the government behind it." With the establishment of the Bureau of Freedmen, Refugees, and Abandoned Lands in March 1865 they got their wish.[18]

The Force of Arms

The transformation of the military was the most conspicuous (and ephemeral) instance of the war's expansive effect on the power of the state. Before 1861 the army was a neglected arm of the government, with little money and less status. It would be so again after 1865. But for a few years millions of men belonged to an organization whose size, power, and administrative complexity were unmatched in nineteenth century American—indeed, Western—history.

At first the headlong growth of the army outstripped the capacity of its leaders to control it. The corruption and incompetence of the early days of the Union war effort had causes more basic than Secretary of War Simon Cameron's stunted sense of public duty. The flow of men and supplies faltered because the expertise to handle this vast new organization had not yet emerged.

The Army of the Union initially was a congeries of national, state, and local units. The act of July 24, 1861, authorizing a volunteer army of half a million men, depended on the recruiting, commissioning, and outfitting powers of the states and localities. Governors had the right to commission officers to the rank of general; and the law initially required that lesser officers be selected by their men. Through the course of the war most Union troops entered as local volunteers organized into state regiments.

When in 1863 the government turned to conscription, there was violent resistance to so great an extension of federal authority. Riots occurred in a number of cities. The most spectacular, in New York during July 1863, cost scores of lives. Habeas corpus proceedings were instituted to secure the release of drafted men. Towns and cities, counties and states competed in offering bounties—over half a billion dollars' worth in sum—for volunteers so as to avoid con-

18. James M. McPherson, *The Struggle for Equality: Abolitionists and the Negro in the Civil War and Reconstruction* (Princeton, 1964), 189; on the affiliated United States Union Commission, headed by Lyman Abbott, see *AC* (1864), 803–805.

scription. Well-off individuals could purchase a substitute if they were unfortunate enough to be drafted. Congressman James G. Blaine defended the practice as necessary to protect "the great 'middle interest' of society—the class on which the business and prosperity of the country depend."[19]

The early conduct of the struggle reveals how far mid-nineteenth century Americans were from the twentieth century conception of total war. After the fighting started, southern religious leaders asked their northern brethren for prayer books and church tracts to distribute among the Confederate troops. These materials were sent, and the government allowed them to pass through the lines. The American Letter Express Company, chartered in Tennessee in 1861, used special messengers to carry correspondence between the warring sections.

Military service did not stop Americans from giving free rein to their entrepreneurial instincts. A substantial exchange of southern cotton and northern manufactured goods was fostered and controlled by congressional statute, presidential proclamation, and Treasury regulations. Ben Butler, in command of the Union-occupied city of New Orleans, announced in a businesslike way in July 1862: "I will assure safe-conduct, open market, and prompt shipment of cotton and sugar sent to New Orleans, and the owner were he [Confederate leader John] Slidell himself, should have the pay for his cotton if sent here under this assurance." In January 1864 the exasperated army medical director in Baton Rouge reported: "The officials one and all are *so* engrossed by thoughts of speculation and making money that they can not except by *repeated* urging attend to the legitimate business of their respective offices. What think you of 15 Government Teams passing out one night to supply the rebels with goods?"[20]

19. A. Howard Meneely, *The War Department, 1861: A Study in Mobilization and Administration* (New York, 1928); on bounties, James G. Randall, *Constitutional Problems under Lincoln* (Urbana, 1951) 249–250; on Blaine, Shannon, *Organization and Administration,* II, 32. See also Adrian Cook, *The Armies of the Streets: The New York City Draft Riots of 1863* (Lexington, Ky., 1974).

20. On religious materials, Rhodes, *History,* V, 468; on American Letter Express Company, John B. McMaster, *A History of the People of the United States during Lincoln's Administration* (New York, 1927), 159; on cotton trade, Rhodes, *History,* V, 277–286, 411–420, Nevins, *War for the Union,*

Much of the North's early military leadership had a halfhearted attitude toward the war. Generals Henry B. Halleck and George B. McClellan saw it as essentially a massive police action—and they had considerable sympathy for the views of the lawbreakers. McClellan had only a tenuous loyalty to his commander-in-chief. He told his wife in August 1861: "The people call on me to save the country . . . The President is nothing more than a well meaning baboon." Announcing the Emancipation Proclamation to his troops, he added his own exegesis: "the remedy for errors . . . is to be found only . . . at the polls."

Unsympathetic to the idea of a war to end slavery, reared in a tradition of defensive tactics, the early Union generals let their ambivalent attitude toward the conflict influence their military performance. Ulysses S. Grant later recalled: "The trouble with many of our generals in the beginning was that they did not believe in the war. I mean that they did not have the complete assurance in success which belongs to good generalship. They had views about slavery, protecting rebel property, State rights—political views that interfered with their judgments." The abolitionist general John C. Frémont was no less indifferent to Lincoln's authority. He announced in August 1861 that his differences with the governor of Missouri made it necessary for him to "assume the administrative powers of the State," and he proceeded to impose martial law and confiscate slaves without consulting, or even informing, the President.[21]

But the evolution of the war into a massive struggle, in which the end of slavery as well as the preservation of the Union was at stake, gave a new character to the military effort. Allan Nevins has summed up the process: "the old individualism yielded in a hundred ways to disciplined association." A milestone in the change was Edwin M. Stanton's appointment as secretary of war in January 1862. This dedicated, hard-minded lawyer brought "order, regular-

---

III, 348 ff, Z. C. McDonnell to Doolittle, Jan. 5, 1864, Doolittle Mss, LC. See also Ludwell H. Johnson, "Northern Profit and Profiteers: The Cotton Rings of 1864–1865," CWH, 12 (1966), 101–115.

21. McClellan quoted in Nevins, War for the Union, II, 230–231; David Donald, "Refighting the Civil War," Lincoln Reconsidered, 2d ed. (New York, 1961), 82–102; Grant quoted in John R. Young, Around the World with General Grant (New York, 1879), II, 289–290; on Frémont, William E. Parrish, Turbulent Partnership: Missouri and the Union 1861–1865 (Columbia, Mo., 1963), 60.

ity, and precision" to his department. His quartermaster-general, Montgomery C. Meigs, oversaw the development of a massive system of transportation, equipment, and supplies that made the Union army an awesome instrument by the end of the war. In September 1862 Joseph Holt became the first judge advocate general, responsible for military jurisdiction in (and, as it developed, outside) the war zone. Colonel James B. Fry was appointed provost-marshal-general in March 1863. With a large staff of local provost marshals he organized recruiting, enforced conscription, and rounded up deserters. In early 1863 the political theorist Francis Lieber drew up General Orders 100 for the Department of War: "Instructions for the Government of the Armies of the United States." This, the first code of rules governing land warfare, sought to reduce the independence of generals acting under martial law.

The use of Negro troops was eloquent testimony to the changing character of the war effort. As the war dragged on, white hostility to the use of black soldiers declined. An army private summed up the new attitude. "They've as much right to fight for themselves as I have to fight for them." By the war's end about 180,000 Negro troops had served.[22]

McClellan was the representative general in the first phase of the war; Grant and William T. Sherman dominated the later conflict. Trading with the enemy ceased when they came into command. They insisted, in Sherman's words, on "war pure and simple, with no admixture of civil compromise." All means were appropriate to preserve the Union: "so important a thing as the self-existence of a great nation should not be left to the fickle chances of war." The purpose of his march through Georgia, Sherman said, was to make the South "feel that war and individual ruin are synonymous terms . . . This may not be war but rather statesmanship." War, he be-

22. Nevins, *War for the Union*, II, viii, III, ch. 8, "The Sweep of Organization"; Hyman and Thomas, *Stanton*, 161, 184; Russell F. Weigley, *Quartermaster-General of the Union Army: A Biography of M. C. Meigs* (New York, 1959); on Holt and Fry, Hyman and Thomas, *Stanton*, 234, 285, and Hugh G. Earnhart, "The Administrative Organization of the Provost Marshal General's Bureau in Ohio, 1863–1865," *NOQ*, 37 (1965), 87–99; Frank Freidel, "General Orders 100 and Military Government," *MVHR*, 32 (1946), 541–556; Dudley T. Cornish, *The Sable Arm: Negro Troops in the Union Army, 1861–1865* (New York, 1956), 93. See also Hyman, *More Perfect Union*, chs. 9–10, 12–13.

lieved, "is simply power unrestrained by constitution or compact."

Grant was less outspoken than Sherman, but his generalship reflected similar views. He came to be widely regarded as the incarnation of that powerful machine the Union army. The lawyer-novelist Richard Henry Dana, Jr., met Grant and mused afterward: "How war, how all great crises bring us to the one-man power!"[23]

The Wartime State

The war created new possibilities of power for civilian as well as military authority. Men in public office, traditionally hamstrung by localism, individualism, and hostility to the state, now found it possible to assert themselves as never before.

The judiciary at first was an exception to this rule. The courts were inherently at odds with the fast-paced, activist character of wartime government. And the apex of the judicial system, the Supreme Court, was headed by Roger B. Taney, who opposed the war's purposes, indeed its very existence. His Dred Scott decision of 1857 proclaimed slavery to be a national institution, denied free as well as slave Negroes the right of citizenship, and held that Congress could not legislate on slavery even in the territories. Taney told former President Franklin Pierce in June 1861 of his hope that the North as well as the South "will see that a peaceful separation with free institutions in each section—is far better—than the union of all the present states under a military government and a reign of terror." Old and petulant, he denied the legality of the wartime acts of Lincoln and the Congress: legal tender, the income tax, the suspension of the writ of habeas corpus.

Lincoln was quick to suggest that Taney's Court had abdicated its power. In his first Inaugural he declared: "if the policy of the government is to be irrevocably fixed by the decisions of the Su-

23. Sherman quoted in Russell F. Weigley, *Towards an American Army: Military Thought from Washington to Marshall* (New York and London, 1962), 85–89, and Rhodes, *History,* V, 30n; Samuel Shapiro, *Richard Henry Dana, Jr. 1815–1882* (East Lansing, 1961), 129. See also John B. Walters, "General William T. Sherman and Total War," *JSH,* 14 (1948), 447–480, and the discussion of the Grant and Sherman memoirs in Edmund Wilson, *Patriotic Gore: Studies in the Literature of the American Civil War* (New York, 1962), chs. 4, 5.

preme Court . . . the people will have ceased to be their own rulers."
The wartime Congress, too, turned on its sister institution. The Senate Committee on the Judiciary was directed in December 1861 to look into the "expediency and propriety of abolishing the present judicial system of the United States." In 1863 Taney despondently wondered whether the Court would "ever be again restored to the authority and rank which the Constitution intended to confer upon it."[24]

But in the four years of his presidency Lincoln was able to make five appointments to the Court, more than enough to assure that it would accept the government's conduct of the war. The wartime Court did not interfere with newspaper censorship, the military's arrest and imprisonment of civilians, the naval blockade of the South, the draft, or even emancipation of the slaves. In the Prize Cases of 1863, which upheld the legality of the blockade, Justice Robert C. Grier declared: "They cannot ask a court to affect a technical ignorance of the existence of a war, which all the world acknowledges to be the greatest civil war known in the history of the human race, and thus cripple the arm of the government and paralyze its power by subtile definitions and ingenious sophisms." Meanwhile the federal courts became an increasingly powerful arm of the national government, setting themselves against recalcitrant state tribunals and enforcing the nation's wartime measures.

In October 1864 the eighty-seven year old Taney died. Charles Sumner hailed this as "a victory for Liberty and for the Constitution." Charles Francis Adams expected now to see "the Executive, Legislative, Judiciary and Army of this country working in one harmonious whole like the strands of a cable. It is a pleasant vision."[25]

While the onset of war initially lessened the power of the Court, it had the opposite effect on state governors. Of necessity they bore

24. Taney to Pierce in David M. Silver, *Lincoln's Supreme Court* (Urbana, 1956), 33; Charles Warren, *The Supreme Court in United States History* (Boston, 1923), III, 94–96.

25. Prize Cases, 67 U.S. 459, 477 (1863); Sumner in Silver, *Supreme Court*, 199; Adams to Henry Adams, Oct. 15, 1864, in Worthington C. Ford, ed., *A Cycle of Adams Letters* (Boston, 1920), II, 206. See also Stanley I. Kutler, *Judicial Power and Reconstruction Politics* (Chicago, 1968), chs. 1–2; Randall, *Constitutional Problems*; Hyman, *More Perfect Union*, chs. 6, 14.

much of the brunt of the early war effort; and an office that for decades before had been held down by popular suspicion and legislative hostility dramatically increased its authority. Strong state executives such as John Andrew of Massachusetts, Oliver Morton of Indiana, and Andrew Curtin of Pennsylvania "were war ministers as truly as Cameron at Washington."

During the war Lincoln appointed governors in Arkansas, Tennessee, North Carolina, and Louisiana. As the chief executives of war-torn states, these men acted with great vigor. They often removed local officials, and strictly regulated the activity of schools and churches. George Shepley, Louisiana's 1862 governor, ordered all eligible electors to vote in the first election held under Union auspices. "Indifference," he warned, "will be treated as a crime and faction as treason." Andrew Johnson's similarly firm performance in Tennessee secured him the 1864 nomination as Lincoln's vice presidential running mate.[26]

Oliver Morton's conduct in Indiana was an instructive example of the wartime expansion of gubernatorial power. He sent the reformer Robert Dale Owen abroad as a state agent to purchase arms for Indiana troops. An Indiana Sanitary Commission tended to the wants of the state's soldiers (and, it need hardly be said, feuded with the United States Sanitary Commission). Faced in 1863 with a hostile Democratic legislature, Morton organized his own Bureau of Finance, raised funds through federal and local loans, gifts, and the sale of arms from the state arsenal to the Department of War, and disbursed over a million dollars without the legislature's authorization.

A number of governors or their representatives met in Cleveland in May 1861, and then in Altoona, Pennsylvania in September 1862, to seek a greater voice in the direction of the war. As Curtin explained to Andrew: "the time has come to give the war a definite aim and end, and . . . the Governors of the loyal states should take prompt united and decided action in the matter." Andrew was more than sympathetic. He told a correspondent: "Besides doing my proper work, I am sadly but firmly trying to help organize some movement, if possible to save the Prest. from the infamy of ruining his country."

26. Randall, *Constitutional Problems*, 413; Shepley quoted in A. H. Carpenter, "Military Government of Southern Territory, 1861–1865," *AHA Annual Report*, I (1900), 478.

But the centralizing tendency of the war put limits on the governors similar to those imposed on voluntary organizations. The recruitment of men and supplies increasingly came under the control of Stanton's War Department. State authority did not fare well in a war for the Union. As Stanton put it in 1863, "If the national Executive must negotiate with state executives in relation to the execution of an Act of Congress, then the problem which the rebellion desires to solve is already determined."[27]

The ambiguities inherent in a major war effort by a free society affected the character of Abraham Lincoln's presidency as well. He defined the war as "a struggle for maintaining ... that form ... of government whose leading object is to elevate the condition of men, ... to afford all an unfettered start and a fair chance in the race of life." Americans now had "to demonstrate to the world that those who can fairly carry an election can also suppress a rebellion." But to maintain by military force a nation whose people so highly valued individualism, localism, and freedom from government was to pose an almost unresolvable conflict of means and ends.

Edmund Wilson has compared Lincoln to Bismarck and Lenin as a ruthless architect of national unity. This view ignores the context of cultural and institutional restraints in which a mid-nineteenth century American President worked. Lincoln's achievement was not so much to resolve the conflict between localism and centralism as to keep that conflict from fatally crippling the war effort.[28]

From a twentieth century standpoint he was a conspicuously trammeled chief executive. He had neither the national constitu-

27. On Morton, Kenneth M. Stampp, *Indiana Politics during the Civil War* (Indianapolis, 1949), 100 ff; on Altoona meeting, Hesseltine, *War Governors*, 253–262; Thomas and Hyman, *Stanton*, 283, 319. See also Fred A. Shannon, "States Rights and the Union Army," *MVHR*, 12 (1925–1926), 51–57; Carl R. Fish, "Social Relief in the Northwest during the Civil War," *AHR*, 22 (1917), 309–324; John C. Haugland, "Politics, Patronage, and [Alexander] Ramsey's Rise to Power, 1861–1863," *MinnH*, 37 (1961), 324; Jean J. L. Fennimore, "Austin Blair: Civil War Governor," *MH*, 49 (1965), 193–227, 344–369; Catherine Y. Pickering, *Richard Yates: Civil War Governor* (Danville, Ill., 1966); and William B. Weeden, *War Government Federal and State in Massachusetts, New York, Pennsylvania, and Indiana* (Boston, 1906).

28. Lincoln in *MP*, VII, 3231; Wilson, *Patriotic Gore*, xvi; on Lincoln's presidency, James G. Randall, *Lincoln the President* (New York, 1945).

ency nor the bureaucratic apparatus of a Franklin D. Roosevelt. But the war did give new authority to the presidency. Lincoln was the first chief of state since Andrew Jackson to win a second term; the first since Martin Van Buren even to seek it. When he came into office he conducted the most complete sweep of federal employees known to that time: of 1,520 holders of presidential appointments, 1,195 were removed. By 1865 he presided over a civil service that had almost 200,000 employees (as compared to about 40,000 in 1861). Presidential proclamations declared that war in fact existed, established the blockade, expanded the army, provided for the first large-scale military expenditures, suspended the writ of habeas corpus, and ordered the end of slavery in the occupied portions of the Confederacy. Lincoln installed a form of "presidential justice" in occupied territory by creating provisional courts with unlimited jurisdiction. He maintained his authority over balky cabinet members Seward and Chase, over assertive state governors, even over Grant (in March 1865 he told the Union commander: "you are not to decide, discuss or confer upon any political questions"). More than any President since Jackson, Lincoln was criticized for "assertions of transcendent executive power," for "military despotism."

Lincoln was not the mystical, brooding President of American folklore any more than he was an oligarch. Rather, he was a man whose perceptions, in his law partner William Herndon's words, were "slow—cold—precise and exact—not sharp. Every thing came to him in its precise shape and color." That description with equal facility may be applied to the other great figure of the wartime North, Ulysses S. Grant. Their dual success lay in the fact that they adeptly wielded the centralized power that the war required, while preserving the democratic qualities of style and personality that mid-nineteenth century Americans demanded of their leaders.[29]

The political malaise of the prewar years had substantially reduced Congress's effectiveness as an instrument of government. During the 1850s it became a cave of the winds, in which the vent-

29. Harry J. Carman and Reinhard H. Luthin, *Lincoln and the Patronage* (New York, 1943) 331; Paul P. Van Riper and Keith A. Sutherland, "The Northern Civil Service, 1861–1865," *CWH*, 11 (1965), 351–369; Lincoln to Grant quoted in Thomas and Hyman, *Stanton*, 348; Benjamin R. Curtis, *Executive Power* (Cambridge, 1862); William H. Herndon, "Analysis of the Character of Abraham Lincoln," *ALQ*, 1 (1941), 361.

ing of sectional passions supplanted the business of legislation. The machinery of the institution all but broke down under the weight of these animosities; members came armed and inflicted bodily harm upon each other.

But the Republican victory of 1860, the departure of the southerners, and the weight of the war transformed the national legislature. The Joint Committee on the Conduct of the War, created in December 1861, attempted to guide the administration on war policy, investigated military disasters, and sought the removal of generals it deemed incompetent. As one of the committee's members, Senator Henry Wilson of Massachusetts, put it: "we should teach men in civil and military authority that the people expect that they will not make mistakes, and that we shall not be easy with their errors."

Inevitably the leaders of a more powerful Congress clashed with a more powerful President. Charles Sumner spoke for many of his associates: "I claim for Congress all that belongs to any government in the exercise of the rights of war." The President, he declared, was "only the instrument of Congress." Even Lyman Trumbull of Illinois, a congressional moderate and an old friend of Lincoln's, said of him: "He is just as subject to our control as if we appointed him, except that we cannot remove him and appoint another in his place."[30]

It is instructive to compare the legislative output of the wartime Congress with prewar sessions (table 1). These figures portray a wartime legislature that was less disposed to pass private acts, was more concerned with affairs of general, public moment, and adopted a substantially larger proportion of the legislation put before it than did prewar Congresses.

One set of bills—the Confiscation Acts of 1861 and 1862, the Militia Acts, and the Enrollment Acts—provided the men and authority necessary for the initial prosecution of the war. And a variety of legislative expedients—income, inheritance, sales, and

30. William W. Pierson, Jr., "The Committee on the Conduct of the Civil War," *AHR*, 23 (1918), 550–576; Hans L. Trefousse, "The Joint Committee on the Conduct of the War: A Reassessment," *CWH*, 10 (1964), 5–19; Wilson quoted in Louis Smith, *American Democracy and Military Power* (Chicago, 1951), 197; Nevins, *War for the Union*, II, 198; Hyman, *More Perfect Union*. ch. 11.

TABLE 1. Congressional legislation, 1857–58 to 1863–64

| Congress | Legislation proposed | | | Legislation passed | | Total number and percent passed |
	Acts	Joint resolutions	Total	Public acts and resolutions	Private acts and resolutions	
35th (1857–58)	1,544	142	1,686	129	183	312 (20)
36th (1859–60)	1,595	151	1,746	157	213	370 (23)
37th (1861–62)	1,370	291	1,661	428	93	521 (38)
38th (1863–64)	1,402	306	1,708	411	104	515 (37)

Source: HS, 690.

corporation taxes; loans, bank notes, and legal tender; a national banking system—furnished the financial sinews for the war effort.

Powerful interests opposed or had reservations about these fiscal innovations. Jacksonian hard-money men (including Treasury Secretary Salmon P. Chase), eastern bankers who wanted interest-bearing Treasury notes to serve as legal tender, and gold-rich Californians had no enthusiasm for the government's unsecured greenbacks. State bankers in general, and western bankers profitably engaged in the bank note business in particular, objected to a national banking system. But the war's disastrous impact on the existing currency and credit system could not be ignored. Massive business failures followed on the cessation of southern trade, and western bank currencies based on southern securities collapsed. The need for heavy taxation and for nationalized currency and banking was clear. Public opinion and the war's sudden and enormous fiscal demands brooked no delay, and Congress acted accordingly.[31]

31. On fiscal legislation, Robert T. Patterson, "Government Finance on the Eve of the Civil War," *JEH*, 12 (1952), 35–44; Bray Hammond, *Sovereignty and an Empty Purse: Banks and Politics in the Civil War* (Princeton, 1970); Joseph Ellison, "The Currency Question on the Pacific Coast during the Civil War," *MVHR*, 16 (1929), 50–66; Leonard P. Curry, *Blueprint for Modern America: Nonmilitary Legislation of the First Civil War Congress* (Nashville, 1968), 185–199. See also Allan G. Bogue, "The Radical Voting

This legislation was not the product of strong executive leadership. Rather, a relatively few congressmen and special interests were responsible for enacting measures to whose principles there was general assent. Justin Morrill said of his 1861 tariff bill that it was "but coldly received by manufacturers, who always and justly fear instability." But Republicans generally agreed on the utility of the tariff as a source of revenue. And few seemed to be concerned that a handful of highly organized interests—most notably, wool and iron producers—were bending tariff legislation to their own ends. A tariff revision in 1864 conspicuously served the wool and iron interests; yet it too passed quickly, with relatively little debate.[32]

The Land Grant College Act followed a similar pattern. It was not proposed in the 1860 Republican platform. And there was considerable railroad and western opposition to a bill that removed substantial portions of the national domain from such toothsome uses as railroad aid and devoted it to the rather remote purposes of higher education. What was more, the state grants under the act were based on population, thus benefiting the more densely peopled eastern commonwealths. Yet Justin Morrill of Vermont and Thaddeus Stevens of Pennsylvania, who championed the bill for ideological and local interest reasons, were able to put it through the House without debate.[33]

The Pacific Railroad Act met a demand long present in national politics; and it appeared in a blaze of rhetoric about "public purpose" and a "grand national enterprise." Yet the act initially envisaged an interlocking network of "pet roads" rather than a single

Dimension in the U.S. Senate During the Civil War," *JIH*, 3 (1973), 449–474 and "Some Dimensions of Power in the Thirty-Seventh Senate," in William O. Aydelotte and others eds., *The Dimensions of Quantitative Research in History* (Princeton, 1972), 285–317.

32. Edward Stanwood, *American Tariff Controversies in the Nineteenth Century* (Boston, 1903), 128. See also Reinhard Luthin, "Abraham Lincoln and the Tariff," *AHR*, 49 (1944), 609–629; Richard Hofstadter, "The Tariff Issue on the Eve of the Civil War," *AHR*, 44 (1938), 50–55; Thomas M. Pitkin, "Western Republicans and the Tariff in 1860," *MVHR*, 27 (1940), 401–420.

33. John Y. Simon, "The Politics of the Morrill Act," *AH*, 37 (1963), 103–111; Paul W. Gates, "Western Opposition to the Agricultural College Act," *IMH*, 37 (1941), 103–136, *Agriculture and the Civil War*, 253, 285; Curry, *Blueprint*, 108–114.

transcontinental system. By threatening to divert men and material, it was positively counterproductive to the war effort. Again, it was the work primarily of a few congressmen and a few interests: James Rollins of Missouri and the Leavenworth, Parnee and Western Railroad Company; Thaddeus Stevens and the Pennsylvania iron industry.[34]

The war (and the departure of the southern members) gave Congress no less than the other branches of government new scope for the assertion of its authority. Yet here too the diversity and localism of American political culture limited the degree to which that newfound power could be concentrated and applied.

The war altered party politics as it did the more formal instruments of government. At first the party fragmentation of the 1850s continued unabated. The Democrats sharply divided into War and Peace wings. Conservative Republicans who wanted the war fought for the preservation of the Union alone clashed with their more abolitionist-minded colleagues. Party labels were as fluid as the groupings they identified. Republicans in Pennsylvania, Indiana, and New York took the name of the People's party in 1860; two years later the same label was used by antiwar Democrats in Massachusetts.

Gradually the polarizing effect of the war made itself felt. Lincoln sought to isolate his opposition by fostering a Union party coalition of Republicans and War Democrats. Secure state organizations, such as those of Iowa and Michigan, opposed the idea. But embattled Republicans, as in New Jersey, eagerly approved, arguing that "when the Government shall be rescued from danger of annihilation, then only will it be time to remember our party names." The reorganized Republicans became "more and more a national Lincoln party and less a federation of state organizations."

Within both the Union Republican coalition and the Democracy, those who had strong views on the war and its purposes tended to prevail. Many Republican conservatives were defeated by their

34. Wallace D. Farnham, "The Pacific Railroad Act of 1862," *NH*, 43 (1962), 141–167; Robert W. Fogel, *The Union Pacific Railroad: A Case Study in Premature Enterprise* (Baltimore, 1960); Curry, *Blueprint*, 121–135; Robert R. Russel, *Improvement of Communication with the Pacific Coast as a Factor in American Politics, 1783–1864* (Cedar Rapids, 1948).

Democratic opponents in 1862, or declined to run because of local disapproval. A growing number of organizations—the Union League Clubs, the Loyal League, the National Union Clubs, the Loyal National Leagues, the Strong Bands—helped to identify the administration and the Union Republican party with total victory and the end of slavery. These clubs—often secret and quasi-military—may have had as many as a million members. In May 1863, with the establishment of the National Federation of Union Leagues, they came under more centralized administration control.[35]

The wartime Democratic party underwent a similar development. The powerful antiwar, prosouthern wing of the party came to be known as Copperheads: a term that probably derived from Pennsylvania politics in the 1840s, when hard-money Democrats wore copper pennies around their necks. The major sources of Copperhead strength were German and Irish Catholics clustered in the cities, and rural counties with a long tradition of adherence to the old Jacksonian antibank, low tariff party faith. Such a place was Mercer County, Ohio, intellectually and economically isolated and fundamentalist in religion; or Dutch-German Bergen County, New Jersey. Peace Democrats were especially active in Irish New York City and in the lower Midwest, where the influence of migrants from Virginia and the Carolinas was strong.[36]

Societies such as the Knights of the Golden Circle, the Sons of Liberty, and the Order of American Knights were the clandestine, antiwar Democratic equivalents of the Republican Union League

35. William D. Mallam, "Lincoln and the Conservatives," *JSH*, 28 (1962), 31–45; on party labels, Olynthus D. Clark, *Politics of Iowa during the Civil War and Reconstruction* (Iowa City, 1911), 173, 199; Charles M. Knapp, *New Jersey Politics during the Period of the Civil War and Reconstruction* (Geneva, N.Y., 1924), 128; Guy J. Gibson, "Lincoln's League: The Union League Movement during the Civil War," Ph.D. diss., University of Illinois, 1957. See also T. Harry Williams, *Lincoln and the Radicals* (Madison, 1941); Nevins, *War for the Union*, III, ch. 12.

36. Charles H. Coleman, "The Use of the Term 'Copperhead,' During the Civil War," *MVHR*, 25 (1938), 263–264; Robert Rutland, "The Copperheads of Iowa: A Re-Examination," *IJH*, 52 (1954), 1–30; Eugene H. Roseboom, "Southern Ohio and the Union in 1863," *MVHR*, 39 (1952), 29–44; Paul Kleppner, *The Cross of Culture: A Social Analysis of Midwestern Politics 1850–1900* (New York, 1970), 104–108; Frank L. Klement, *The Copperheads in the Middle West* (Chicago, 1960). Klement argues that the midwestern Copperheads were the forerunners of postwar agrarian radicalism, a view challenged in Ronald P. Formisano and William G. Shade, "The Concept of Agrarian Radicalism," *MAm*, 52 (1970), 3–30.

Clubs. They fostered a prosouthern, Negrophobic, states' rights creed. The password of the Order of American Knights was Nuohlac (Calhoun reversed); the oath of membership began with their own modification of the Declaration of Independence: "All men are endowed by their Creator with certain rights—equal only as far as there is equality in the capacity for the appreciation, enjoyment, and exercise of these rights."[37]

The ideology of the Peace Democrats hardened in an atmosphere of accusation and repression. Just as the character of the war strengthened the hand of the more radical elements in the Union Republican coalition, so the Democrats became stauncher advocates of a negotiated peace, states' rights, and resistance to emancipation. Democratic senators' unity increased; the gulf that separated them from the Republicans widened. Massachusetts Republican George S. Boutwell said of this time: "I do not recall the name of one man who favored emancipation as a policy and adhered to the Democratic Party. When a man reached the conclusion that negroes should be free, he could not do otherwise than join the Republican party."[38]

The election of 1864 demonstrated the wartime growth of party centralization and ideological polarization. Lincoln far more than in 1860 was the actual as well as the nominal head of his party. His victory over Democratic candidate George McClellan (who was forced to repudiate a peace plank in his party's platform) rested on a broad base of popular northern support. And the strongly Republican Congress that was elected with him would enact the policies of Reconstruction.[39]

37. Mayo Fesler, "Secret Political Societies in the North during the Civil War," *IMH*, 14 (1918), 225, 228; Wood Gray, *The Hidden Civil War* (New York, 1942).

38. Leonard P. Curry, "Congressional Democrats, 1861–1863," *CWH*, 12 (1966), 213–229; Boutwell, *Reminiscences of Sixty Years of Public Affairs* (New York, 1902), II, 43. See also Allan G. Bogue, "Bloc and Party in the United States Senate: 1861–1863," *CWH*, 13 (1967), 221–241; Robert H. Abzug, "The Copperheads: Historical Approaches to Civil War Dissent in the Midwest," *IMH*, 66 (1970), 40–55; Frank L. Klement, *The Limits of Dissent: Clement L. Vallandigham and the Civil War* (Lexington, Ky., 1970).

39. William F. Zornow, *Lincoln and the Party Divided* (Norman, Okla., 1954); Harold M. Dudley, "The Election of 1864," *MVHR*, 18 (1932), 500–518; James P. Jones, "John A. Logan and the Election of 1864 in Illinois," *MAm*, 42 (1960), 219–230.

The wartime surge of government activism reached its climax in the Thirteenth Amendment to the Constitution, which ended Negro slavery in the United States. The story of presidential and congressional caution on the subject of emancipation is a familiar one. Lincoln for some time toyed with schemes of colonization and of gradual, compensated emancipation before issuing his Proclamation of January 1, 1863, which freed the slaves in Confederate-held territory. Congress too moved slowly and incrementally, abolishing slavery (with compensation to loyal owners) in the District of Columbia and in the territories, calling on the border slave states to accept compensated emancipation, ratifying a treaty with Great Britain to suppress the African slave trade, repealing the fugitive slave laws (this not until June 28, 1864), permitting Negro testimony in federal courts, removing the law that forbade Negroes from carrying the mail. This was what Kentucky Democrat John C. Breckinridge had predicted would occur: "a loosing of all bonds."

A constitutional amendment proposed as a last, desperate alternative to secession in early 1861 had declared: "No amendment shall be made to the Constitution which will authorize or give the Congress the power to abolish or interfere within any State with the domestic institutions thereof including that of persons held to labor or service by the laws of said state." Two-thirds of the House approved of that amendment a week before Lincoln's inauguration; the legislatures of Ohio and Illinois ratified it even after the war began; Lincoln had "no objection" to it. Now, four years later, Congress considered a very different addition to the nation's fundamental law: "Neither slavery nor involuntary servitude, except as a crime whereof the party shall have been duly convicted, shall exist within the United States, or any place subject to their jurisdiction."[40]

Lincoln had justified his 1863 Emancipation Proclamation as "warranted by the Constitution upon military necessity." But a more solid legal underpinning was necessary if slavery was to be banished permanently from the nation. Only a constitutional amendment had the appropriate finality.

40. Breckinridge quoted in Henry Wilson, *History of the Antislavery Measures of the Thirty-Seventh and Thirty-Eighth United States Congresses, 1861–1864* (Boston, 1864), 4; on 1861 amendment, Arthur Bestor, "The American Civil War as a Constitutional Crisis," *AHR,* 69 (1964), 334.

It was not easily attained. Intense anti-Negro sentiment in the North made the end of slavery a far less attractive cause than the preservation of the Union. But here the war had its most profound impact on American public policy. The identification of the Confederacy with its peculiar institution, and of the Union war effort with the cause of human freedom, gradually became a necessary justification for the bloodshed and suffering.

The case of the lawyer-politician-soldier Ben Butler of Massachusetts suggests how the North moved inexorably to emancipation. Butler was a delegate to the 1860 Democratic convention, and voted persistently for Jefferson Davis as his party's nominee. But on September 29, 1864, after observing an attack by Negro troops at New Market, Virginia, he mused:

> Poor fellows, they seem to have so little to fight for in this contest, with the weight of prejudice loaded upon them, their lives given to a country which has given them not yet justice, not to say fostering care. To us, there is patriotism, fame, love of country, pride, ambition, all to spur us on, but to the negro, none of all these for his guerdon of honor. But there is one boon they love to fight for, freedom for themselves and their race forever, and may my "right hand forget her cunning" but they shall have that.[41]

The final debate over the emancipation amendment came in January 1865, when the war was approaching its end. Congressman Glenni W. Scofield of Pennsylvania voiced what had come to be the prevailing sentiment: "Slavery in the end must die ... The only question is, shall it die now, by a constitutional amendment ... or shall it linger in party warfare through a quarter or half a century of acrimonious debate, patchwork legislation, and conflicting adjudication?" Given the mood of the wartime Congress, there could be only one answer.

Nevertheless, the opposition of House Democrats (which, if unanimous, would be enough to block the two-thirds vote necessary for passage) made political strategy necessary. Lincoln and Charles

41. Butler, *Private and Official Correspondence of General Benjamin F. Butler* (Norwood, Mass., 1917), V, 192. On wartime anti-Negro sentiment see Forrest G. Wood, *Black Scare: The Racist Response to Emancipation and Reconstruction* (Berkeley and Los Angeles, 1968); V. Jacques Voegeli, *Free But Not Equal: The Midwest and the Negro during the Civil War* (Chicago, 1967).

Sumner may have gained critical New Jersey Democratic votes by satisfying some of the demands of the Camden and Amboy Railroad; Secretary of State Seward, a group of lobbyists, and antislavery New York Democrats worked on lame duck Democratic congressmen, who provided fourteen of the sixteen Democratic votes for the amendment; Confederate relatives of wavering congressmen got releases from prisoner-of-war camps; patronage was discreetly used.

On January 31 the House passed the amendment. George Julian of Indiana described the scene:

> The cheering in the hall and densely packed galleries exceeded anything I ever saw and beggared description. Members joined in the shouting and kept it up for some minutes. Some embraced one another, others wept like children . . . I have felt, ever since the vote, as if I were in a new country.

During the next few days a Negro minister delivered the daily sermon before the House of Representatives, and with Sumner's sponsorship a black lawyer was admitted to practice before the Supreme Court. Changes had come to the citadels of American government that would have been inconceivable a few years before. But whether Julian's "new country" would be an apt description of postwar America remained to be seen.[42]

1865

The end of the war sharply focused the changes in northern public opinion wrought by four years of civil conflict. The emotional release of Lee's surrender at Appomattox—on Palm Sunday—and the sudden tragedy of Lincoln's assassination—on Good Friday—shook a still religious generation to its core. "Not often in human history,"

---

42. Scofield in U.S., *CG*, 38th Cong., 2d sess. (Jan. 6, 1865), 144; David F. Trask, "Charles Sumner and the New Jersey Railroad Monopoly during the Civil War," *NJHS Proceedings*, 75 (1957), 259–275; Fawn M. Brodie, *Thaddeus Stevens* (New York, 1959), 204; LaWanda Cox and John H. Cox, *Politics, Principle, and Prejudice, 1865–1866* (New York, 1963), 24; George W. Julian, *Political Recollections, 1840–1872* (Chicago, 1884), 250, 252. See also David H. Donald, *Charles Sumner and the Rights of Man* (New York, 1970), 193–194.

John Lothrop Motley observed, "has a great nation been subjected to such a sudden conflict of passions."

Exultation and weariness went hand in hand. The fall of Richmond was greeted in the North by celebration and rejoicing—and by solemn processions in towns and cities intoning "Praise God from Whom All Blessings Flow." The victory of the Union was right and necessary: "God's purpose is accomplished," a Philadelphia minister announced. But the pain and suffering of the war was the price paid by the nation for the sin of slavery. General David S. Stanley's victory announcement to the Fourth Army Corps in Tennessee included the observation: "Let us reflect, and we may profit by so doing, that great national, as great personal sin, must be atoned for by great punishment."

Many found satisfaction in the idea of national purification and the promise of the American future rather than in the defeat of a hated enemy. Horace Greeley's *New York Tribune* declared on Good Friday, April 14: "The dispensation is over; the new era begun! . . . A new world is born." James Russell Lowell wrote to Charles Eliot Norton: "the news, my dear Charles, is from Heaven. I felt a strange and tender exaltation. I wanted to laugh and I wanted to cry, and ended by holding my peace and feeling devoutly thankful. There is something magnificent in having a country to love."[43]

And then came the crime at Ford's Theatre, the near slaying of Seward, the abortive attempt on the life of Grant: a time of rumors, of fear that the Confederates sought to gain by assassination what they had lost on the battlefield. On April 15, the day Lincoln died, a letter from John Wilkes Booth was made public: "I have ever held the South were right . . . This country was formed for the *white*, not for the black man." When the war ended General Sherman had favored easy terms for the South. Now he issued a special field order: "*We have met every phase which this war has assumed, and must now be prepared for it in its last and worst shape, that of assassins and guerillas; but woe unto the people who seek to expend their wild passions in such a manner for there is but one dread result.*"

43. Motley to Seward, April 30, 1865, U.S., FR (1865–1866), III; Henry Boardman, *The Peace-Makers. A Sermon Preached in the Tenth Presbyterian Church, Philadelphia, . . . April 9, 1865* (Philadelphia, 1865); Stanley quoted in Edmund N. Hatcher, *The Last Four Weeks of the War* (Columbus, 1891), 232; Lowell quoted in Rhodes, *History*, V, 132.

Calls for vengeance became as commonplace as the solemn thanksgiving of a week before. The Philadelphian Sidney George Fisher predicted: "The feelings of good will and conciliation, which were spreading thro the North at the hopes of a speedy peace, will now be checked and converted in the hearts of many into resentment and rage." The North became a land of flags withdrawn, then hung again festooned in black; of joyous release turned suddenly to bitterness. George Templeton Strong reported on the prevailing attitude in New York City: " 'No more compromise! No more forgiveness!' is the one earnest expression upon thousands of quivering lips." In Trinity Church on Easter Sunday—"Black Easter," when great numbers of Americans thronged the churches to hear sorrowing (and often vindictive) sermons—Strong suddenly thought: "Perhaps Lincoln had done his appointed work . . . Perhaps the time had come . . . for vengeance and judgment." The *Chicago Tribune* grimly observed: "Yesterday we were, with the late President, for lenity; . . . to-day we are with the people for Justice." A report from Sherman's troops in North Carolina declared that "the whole current of feeling in the army has been changed by this crowning act of villainy."[44]

Religious spokesmen echoed and reinforced these sentiments. The Presbyterian New School Assembly met five weeks after Lincoln's assassination, and with Calvinist precision examined its meaning: "we recognize the same wise Providence, which, looking far above our feeble vision, permitted the existence of Slavery and the rise of this Rebellion, and which, in this last act of baffled and defeated despotism, has illustrated its debased and malignant spirit so as to excite the loathing, horror and abhorrence of the world." The *Episcopal Recorder*, the voice of a less pietistic and passionate denomination, expressed similar sentiments: "It is good and great to forgive sin. But it is evil to forgive it in such a manner as to diminish a sense of its enormity . . . Where there is no penance, and no sense, and no acknowledgment of wrong, it is not for us to hurry forward with a forgiveness which is not asked, and will be despised."

A final ceremony of sorrow riveted the assassination onto the memory of a generation. Lincoln's funeral procession took twenty

44. Wilkes letter in Hatcher, *Last Four Weeks*, 258; Sherman order ibid., 280; Edward C. Carter, "The Diary of Sidney George Fischer," *PMHB*, 89 (1965), 211; Strong, *Diary*, III, 585–586; Hatcher, *Last Four Weeks*, 273.

days to pass in a great sweep of the North from Washington to Springfield. It moved on a wave of grief, as millions participated in this national rite of mourning. The most eloquent voices of the day—Emerson, Holmes, Bancroft, Beecher, Sumner, Bryant, Melville, Whitman—eulogized the martyred President. And always intertwined with the sorrow and eulogy was the theme of vengeance:

> There is sobbing of the strong
> And a pall upon the land;
> But the people in their weeping
> Bare the iron hand;
> Beware the People weeping
> When they bare the Iron Hand.

Powerful mechanisms of mass psychology—of grief, anger, guilt—were unleashed by the war's climacteric. They came after years of sorrow and worry over the killed, the sick and wounded, the captured rotting in southern prisons. And they coincided with a surge of political and governmental power unmatched in the nation's previous history. Countervailing forces—parochialism and conflicting interest, fading memory and new concerns—quickly lessened the war's impact on American public life. But the shape and substance of the postwar polity cannot be understood without constant reference to the war experience.[45]

45. Vander Velde, *Presbyterian Churches*, 352; *Episcopal Recorder* quoted in Theodore B. Wilson, *The Black Codes of the South* (University, Ala., 1965), 123–124; Lloyd Lewis, *Myths After Lincoln* (New York, 1919), 78 ff; Herman Melville, "The Martyr," in Hennig Cohen, ed., *The Battle Pieces of Herman Melville* (New York, 1963), 130.

PART ONE

The Postwar Polity
1865-1880

EVERY SECTOR OF the postwar American polity went
through a strikingly similar evolution during the years that followed
the Civil War. At first the wartime legacy of active, expanded
government and a broader view of civil equality left its mark
everywhere: in Congress and the courts, in the victorious North as
well as the defeated South, in a broad range of social and economic
policies. Then in the 1870s this tendency was widely repudiated. ✓
Social values and attitudes toward the state that were more typical
of nineteenth century America—racism, localism, laissez-faire
—rapidly reasserted themselves.

This was the central dynamic of postwar American public life.
Of course the appearance and then the rejection of public policies
that lacked the social underpinning necessary to make them
viable hardly was unique to the post-Civil War United States. But
rarely has there been so striking an encounter of new views of
government with opposing social realities. That the contrast was
so vivid in the years after 1865 is a measure of the degree to which
the Civil War altered the terms of public discourse. It is also a revealing commentary on the intractability of the American civic
culture.

CHAPTER 2

The Politics
of Reconstruction

AMERICAN PUBLIC LIFE in the immediate post-Civil War years was dominated by the effort to reconstruct the defeated South. A convulsive struggle between President Andrew Johnson and a Republican-controlled Congress resulted in the Fourteenth and Fifteenth Amendments to the Constitution, a number of laws designed to set the terms of governance in the South, and the near-successful impeachment of the President. Party politics and Supreme Court decisionmaking also were caught up in this massive effort to deal with the issues that flowed from the North's military victory and the end of slavery. Indeed, in its passion and intensity the politics of Reconstruction seemed at times to invert Clausewitz's maxim: to be the continuation of war by other means.

Reconstruction policy took form in an atmosphere charged with polar beliefs as to the nature of government, race relations, and American citizenship—beliefs subsumed under the labels of Radicalism and Conservatism. Majoritarian Republican sentiment moved substantially in the direction of the Radicals' insistence on southern black suffrage and a strong federal hand in the reconstruction of the ex-Confederacy. But the specifics of Reconstruction policy were determined by "moderates": politicians who were not unalterably in either ideological camp. In this sense the politics of Reconstruction exemplified the process that went on in every sector of the postwar polity: the interplay between the war-born ideals of strong central government and race-blind citizenship, and more traditional American beliefs in localism, limited government, and racial inequality.[1]

The New Nationalism and the Old

For most northern Americans the Civil War was a grim, grey weariness, punctuated finally by the satisfaction of victory and the shock of Lincoln's assassination. But many of the North's more vocal spokesmen read a larger meaning into these events. On April 14, 1865, the American flag was raised again over the ruins of Fort Sumter. Ministers Henry Ward Beecher and Theodore Tilton, abolitionist crusader William Lloyd Garrison, and Congressman William D. Kelley of Pennsylvania commemorated with appropriate oratory this symbolic restoration of national sovereignty. The Fourth of July in this year of victory had special meaning, and evoked frequent contrasts of the dismal past with the glorious future—"a future too grand for my feeble portrayal; a development of the resources of nature, a growth of manufactures, commerce, civilization, and Christianity, which shall be the glory of the New World and the wonder of the Old."

In the summer of 1865 a group including Samuel Bowles, editor of the influential *Springfield Republican*, and House Speaker Schuyler Colfax, undertook a journey to California. Bowles sententiously told Colfax that "our party were almost the first who had ever

1. Modern studies of the Reconstruction controversy that stress the importance of radical and conservative ideology are W. R. Brock, *An American Crisis: Congress and Reconstruction, 1865–1867* (New York, 1963) and David Montgomery, *Beyond Equality: Labor and the Radical Republicans 1862–1872* (New York, 1967), ch. 2. See also Hans Trefousse, *The Radical Republicans* (New York, 1969) and Harold M. Hyman, ed., *The Radical Republicans and Reconstruction, 1861–1870* (Indianapolis, 1967). On the prewar antecedents of postwar radicalism, see Margaret Shortreed, "The Antislavery Radicals: From Crusade to Revolution, 1840–1868," *PP*, 16 (1959), 65–87, and Eric Foner, *Free Soil, Free Labor, Free Men: The Ideology of the Republican Party before the Civil War* (New York, 1970).

Critiques of this radical-conservative distinction, which stress the shared Negrophobia of the two camps, include C. Vann Woodward, "Seeds of Failure in Radical Race Policy," in his *American Counterpoint* (Boston, 1971), 163–183; William S. McFeely, *Yankee Stepfather: General O. O. Howard and the Freedmen* (New Haven, 1968), and Michael L. Benedict, *A Compromise of Principle: Congressional Republicans and Reconstruction, 1863–1869* (New York, 1974).

traveled Across the Continent simply to see the country, to study its resources, to learn its people and their wants, and to acquaint ourselves more intelligently, thereby, each in our duties to the public,—you in the government, and we as journalists." The lesson of the seven weeks' trip turned out to be the lesson of the Civil War. Arriving in San Francisco, Bowles rhapsodized: "Greater the wonder grows at the extent of the Republic; but larger still our wonder at the mysterious but unmistakable homogeneity of its people."[2]

References to "the Nation" and "the great Republic" filled the public prints of the time. Publicists, intellectuals, and politicians indulged in a rhetoric of triumphant nationalism. When a group of abolitionists established a postwar magazine designed to carry on in the spirit of Garrison's *Liberator*, *The Nation* seemed an eminently appropriate name. College oratory—as always, given to exaggerated renderings of fashionable ideas—dwelt on the nationalist theme. Students at Williams were told to "think how great a thing a nation is . . . The organism of a nation! It enfolds and blesses races; it perpetuates traditions, ideas, examples, principles."[3]

Postwar political theory celebrated the restoration of national unity. Its quality has rightly earned it a place in the dustbin of American political thought (not in any case a distinguished genre since the time of the founders). Nor can this body of writing be said to have had a profound or lasting influence on American public life. But its assertions, and what it left unsaid, reflected the mood of the postwar polity.

Antebellum political thought had dwelt on the interrelationship

2. Rev. Jacob M. Manning, "Peace under Liberty, " in *The Celebration of the Eighty-Eighth Anniversary of the Declaration of Independence, July 4th, 1865. At Virginia and Gold Hill, Nevada* (San Francisco, 1965), 53; Samuel Bowles, *Across the Continent. A Summer's Journey to the Rocky Mountains, the Mormons, and the Pacific States, with Speaker Colfax* (Springfield, Mass., 1865), iii–iv, 159. Other contemporary works that dwell on the nation's size and newly won unity include A. D. Richardson, *Beyond the Mississippi* (Hartford, 1867), and James D. McCabe, Jr., *The Great Republic: A Descriptive, Statistical and Historical View of the States and Territories of the American Union* (Philadelphia, 1871).

3. William M. Armstrong, "The Freedmen's Movement and the Founding of the *Nation*," *JAH*, 53 (1967), 708–726; Alexander H. Bullock, *The Relations of the Educated Man with American Nationality* (Boston, 1864), 4–5. See also J. Arthur Partridge, *The Making of the American Nation or the Rise and Decline of Oligarchy in the West* (London, 1866); William H. Barnes, *The Body Politic* (Cincinnati, 1866); Charles Sumner, "Prophetic Voices About America. A Monograph." *AM*, 20 (1867), 275–306.

of state and federal authority, and on natural rights and natural law. But these concerns had no important place in postwar political theory. The Union victory settled once and for all the nation's supremacy over its parts. And natural law no longer was an important concept when human rights had been secured by force of arms, and institutions appeared to be so responsive to men's devices. Instead, "the authority of the State, allegiance to the State, protection of the State" was the primary concern of postwar theorists. But they had little to say about the policy implications of a triumphant national sovereignty. Theirs was a celebration of things settled, not of possibilities opened.[4]

Such was the case with the writings of Francis Lieber, the dean of mid-century American political theorists. He came to the United States in 1827, schooled in the Germanic tradition of natural law. The inherent social conservatism of that doctrine won him some success in Calhoun's South Carolina. But Lieber's nationalism (and his ambition) led him to the North in 1856 and to active support of the Union cause. While he busied himself with wartime work for the Loyal Publication Society, two sons fought for the Union—and one fought and died for the Confederacy. Lieber expected that a refreshed national authority would end the divisiveness "not only of the states, but of a thousand institutions." But he had no wish to see an active, reformist polity. He positively feared the legislative branch; he opposed an elected judiciary; he favored educational qualifications for voting; he had little interest in the protection of Negro civil rights.[5]

Boston lawyer John C. Hurd's *The Theory of our National Exis-*

4. Benjamin F. Wright, *American Interpretations of Natural Law* (Cambridge, 1931), 276–277; quotation from Albert B. Hart, "Growth of American Theories of Popular Government," *APSR*, 1 (1907), 554–555. See also Paul C. Nagel, *This Sacred Trust: American Nationality 1798–1898* (New York, 1971), 195 ff; Merle Curti, *The Roots of American Loyalty* (New York, 1946), 173–181.

5. Lieber quoted in Bernard E. Brown, *American Conservatives* (New York, 1951), 83; Lieber, *Miscellaneous Writings* (Philadelphia, 1881), 197, 204. See also C. B. Robson, "Francis Lieber's Nationalism," *JP*, 8 (1946), 57–73; Merle Curti, "Francis Lieber and Nationalism," *HLQ*, 4 (1941), 263–292; Frank Freidel, *Francis Lieber: Nineteenth-Century Liberal* (Baton Rouge, 1947), ch. 17. Elisha Mulford's *The Nation* (New York, 1870) was a uniquely Hegelian—and notably turgid—treatment of the postwar republic as a "moral organism."

tence, as Shown by the Action of the Government of the United States since 1861 (1881) splendidly illustrates the difficulty that postwar theorists had in applying their nationalism to the realities of governance and public policy. With a lack of specificity quite in keeping with what was to follow, Hurd dedicated his book "in homage to the Sovereign: whoever he, she, or they, may be." He offered up elaborate juristic variations on the theme that sovereignty resides in the *political* people: that is, those who were involved in some direct way with the state. But he had no readily discernible notion as to what the state might *do.*[6]

Hurd's work was strongly influenced by Orestes Brownson's *The American Republic* (1866). This onetime Jacksonian radical, who moved from Unitarianism to Roman Catholicism, celebrated the triumph of the Union on metaphysical grounds. He proclaimed that "the American Republic . . . has a mission, and is chosen of God for the realization of a great idea." But that idea turned out to be "not so much the realization of liberty" as "the sovereignty of the people without social despotism, and individual freedom without anarchy." Brownson championed the Union cause "on legal and conservative, not on radical and revolutionary principles." He feared that the "humanitarian democracy" of the abolitionists, having defeated the "personal democracy" of the South, might spur a "tendency to exaggerate the social element, to overlook the territorial basis of the state, and to disregard the rights of individuals."[7]

A few theorists were bolder, calling for a new "national constitution" to replace the existing document, or for the concentration of

6. Hurd, *Theory of Our National Existence* (Boston, 1881). See also Charles E. Larson, "Nationalism and States' Rights in Commentaries on the Constitution after the Civil War," *AJLH,* 3 (1959), 360–369; Philip S. Paludan, *A Covenant with Death: The Constitution, Law, and Equality in the Civil War Era* (Urbana, 1975); William A. Dunning, "American Political Philosophy," *YR,* 4 (1895–1896), 153; Harold M. Hyman, *A More Perfect Union: The Impact of the Civil War and Reconstruction on the Constitution* (New York, 1973), chs. 24–25.

7. Brownson, *The American Republic: Its Constitution, Tendencies, and Destiny* (New York, 1866), 4–5, 351, 354; "Are the United States A Nation?" *BQR, National Series,* 1 (1864), 385–419, and "Politics at Home," *BQR, Last Series,* 1 (1873), 95–111; Arthur M. Schlesinger, Jr., *A Pilgrim's Progress: Orestes A. Brownson* (Boston, 1939, 1966), 260–262. See also William G. Dix, *The American State and American Statesmen* (Boston, 1876), a Catholic call for "a national constitution, which shall equally recognize the organic, pervading, indestructible laws of civil government."

government power in a single, national legislative chamber. The German radical Karl Heinzen wanted a "common center, where the universal will may manifest itself, and be put into action . . . In the State, in the democratic State, there can exist but *one* supreme interest, that of the *whole* people, represented in the central government." But even Heinzen's concept of the "people" was limited to men of property.[8]

In sum postwar political theorists failed to do more than celebrate the triumph of American nationalism in abstract terms. Their modes of analysis—juristic, metaphysical, German Idealist—had little relevance to the realities of postwar American life. This failure presaged the experience of the polity at large. For the two great legacies of the Civil War—a stronger and more active state and an expanded definition of civil equality—ultimately were impossible to implement.

The prevailing imagery in postwar discussions of the American future was of the nation's rebirth—and of its power. The hardheaded New York lawyer George Templeton Strong declared that "the people has (I think) just been bringing forth a new American republic—an amazingly big baby—after a terribly protracted and severe labor." John W. Draper, chemist, historian, and champion of science in its nineteenth century warfare with religion, dwelt on the "future grandeur of the Great Republic . . . An Imperial power has come into existence before our eyes." The contrast between past and future could not be more dramatic:

> I turn from the hideous contemplation of a disorganization of the Republic, each state, and county, and town setting up for itself, and the continent swarming with the maggots bred from the dead body politic. I turn from that to a future I see in prospect—an imperial race organizing its intellect, concentrating it, and voluntarily submitting to be controlled by its reason.[9]

8. Heinzen, *What Is Real Democracy?* (Indianapolis, 1871), 11, 20. See also Moncure D. Conway, *Republican Superstitions as Illustrated in the Political History of America* (London, 1872); Montgomery, *Beyond Equality,* 73.

9. Allan Nevins, ed., *The Diary of George Templeton Strong* (New York, 1952), IV, 56; Draper, *Thoughts on the Future Civil Policy of America* (New York, 1865), 9, 252, *History of the American Civil War* (New York, 1870), III, 657, 664.

The clergy—Draper's antagonists, and the group that perhaps most profoundly influenced public opinion—had strikingly similar views. To the secular nationalism of the intellectuals they added the vision of postwar America as a New Jerusalem. One minister advised the nation's youth to "learn that the day of a wilful individualism, that prides itself on sectional and local peculiarities, is passing away."

Prominent in postwar clerical thinking was the idea that the church had a proper—indeed, a necessary—role to play in public life. The *American Presbyterian and Theological Review* warned that "the loyal churches of the North form a large army and wield a good deal of political influence." December 7, 1865, designated a National Day of Thanksgiving, released a flood of religious nationalism. The Episcopal Bishop of Delaware thanked God for "the accomplishment of a great moral and social revolution—the glory of our age and country, and the marvel of the civilized world." The chaplain of the House of Representatives told the newly convened Thirty-Ninth Congress that the war "was the grandest vindication of free institutions, the resistless might of free intelligence, the world has seen." Before the war there was "no definite and well-compacted political structure," no "one mighty national life." But now "a new nation has been born—a nation that embodies ... the spirit of the Gospel."[10]

Jesse T. Peck's *The History of the Great Republic, Considered from A Christian Stand-Point* (1868) was the major statement of this postwar Christian nationalism. Peck argued that the American Republic had been called into existence by God *"to advance the human race beyond all its precedents in intelligence, goodness, and power,"* and that *"religion is the only life-force and organizing power of liberty."* The war had taught the American people that slavery was not merely a misfortune but an "enormous individual and national crime." But God in his mercy "determined to extend

10. Rev. Amory D. Mayo, *East and West* [Cincinnati, 1865], 31; George L. Prentiss, "The Political Situation," *APTR*, 4 (1866), 331; Alfred Lee, *The Great National Deliverance: A Sermon Preached ... in St. Andrews's Church* [Wilmington, 1865]; C. B. Boynton, *National Thanksgiving Sermon before the House of Representatives* [Washington, 1865]. See also Gilbert Haven, *National Sermons* [Boston, 1869] and Timothy L. Smith, *Revivalism and Social Reform in Mid-Nineteenth Century America* [New York, 1957], 234–238.

to the nation the regeneration which had long been recognized as the privilege of the individual only." The United States had passed through a sequence of stages—Preparation, Independence, Development, Emancipation—to its current (and final) one of Mission. Strengthened by universal suffrage and education, by an "American Church" freed from the curse of slavery, the nation now could become "the grandest missionary of progress ever known among men."[11]

This sense of living in a time of special promise was widely shared by postwar intellectuals. George W. Curtis, editor of the influential magazine *Harper's Weekly*, told lecture audiences in the winter of 1864–1865: "we are mad if the blood of the war has not anointed our eyes to see that all reconstruction is vain that leaves any question too brittle to handle. Any system, any policy, any institution that may not be debated will overthrow us, if we do not overthrow it." Charles Eliot Norton, discussing "American Political Ideas" in 1865, thought that the great lesson of the war was that "politics are a subordinate branch of morals, . . . and that the government is but a device . . . for the attainment of certain ends."[12]

Influential British friends of the Union cause shared this euphoria. John Bright called the North's victory "the event of the age. The friends of freedom everywhere should thank God and take courage." William H. Dixon, an English journalist, reported in his book *New America* (1867) that "the tide of Union" had replaced the prewar "rage for *separation*, for independence, for individuality." He thought that "the negro is here the coming man." Charles Dickens returned to the United States in 1868 after more than twenty years' absence, found "amazing changes, . . . changes moral, changes physical," regretted the anti-Americanism of *Martin Chuzzlewit*, and wrote an apology to be placed in all future editions of the book.

---

11. Peck, *Great Republic* (New York, 1868), viii, 679, 686–710. See also John Weiss, *The Political Exigencies of Political Submission* (Boston, 1865) and John Taffe, *An Address to the Churches of Christ in Kentucky, and Other Loyal States, in Regard to the Treatment of Church-Members Who Have Been Engaged in the Rebellion* (Cincinnati, 1866). For a more modest statement of the church's political role see "The *Princeton Review* on the State of the Country and of the Church," *PR*, 37 (1865), 627–657.

12. Edward Cary, *George William Curtis* (Boston, 1894), 187; Norton, "American Political Ideas," *NAR*, 101 (1865), 559. See also George S. Hillard, *The Political Duties of the Educated Classes* (Boston, 1866).

John Stuart Mill struck a particularly evocative note in May 1865: "The great concussion which has taken place in the American mind must have loosened the foundations of all prejudices and secured a fair hearing for impartial reason on all subjects such as it might not otherwise have had for many generations."[13]

When Thomas Carlyle skeptically analyzed the implications of the North's victory in "Shooting Niagara" (1867), Walt Whitman rose to the defense of the postwar nation. In a series of essays that became *Democratic Vistas* (1871) he attempted to reconcile individualism, nationalism, and democracy. Whitman did not "gloss over the appalling dangers of universal suffrage in the United States," nor did he deny that American government was "saturated in corruption, bribery, falsehood, mal-administration." But he rejected the easy alternative of government by "the merely educated classes." The experience of the 1860s was proof "that popular democracy, whatever its faults and dangers, practically justifies itself beyond the proudest claims and wildest hopes of its enthusiasts."[14]

Intellectuals—particularly younger ones—readily assumed that they had an important part to play in the postwar polity. Harvard law professor Joel Parker predicted: "There is, or is to be a new epoch . . . The opinions of men *under thirty* are to be the ruling opinions. They were educated by the war, and have lived a *deeper life* than falls to the lot of ordinary sluggish generations." E. L. Godkin excitedly wrote to Frederick Law Olmsted during the war: "I am duly thanking Heaven that I live here and in this age." He turned

---

13. George M. Trevelyan, *Life of John Bright* (London, 1913), 325; Dixon, *New America* (Philadelphia, 1867), 451, 467; Edgar Johnson, *Charles Dickens* (New York, 1952), II, 1093; Mill to Godkin, May 24, 1865, in Hugh S. R. Elliot, ed., *Letters of John Stuart Mill* (London, 1910), II, 36. See also "Bright-Sumner Letters, 1861–1872," *MHS Proceedings*, 46 (1912–1913), 93–164; Charles W. Dilke, *Greater Britain: A Record of Travel in English-Speaking Countries during 1866 and 1867* (New York, 1869), 30, 53; and William L. Barrington, *Reflections on Some of the Results of the Late American War* (Dublin, 1866). Robert Kelley in *The Transatlantic Persuasion: The Liberal-Democratic Mind in the Age of Gladstone* (New York, 1969) argues that English Liberals and American Democrats were ideological brothers. Over the course of the century this may well have been so. But English Radicals and Liberals clearly were sympathetic to the precepts of Radical Republicanism.

14. Edward F. Grier, "Walt Whitman, The Galaxy, and *Democratic Vistas*," *ALit*, 23 (1951–1952), 332–350; Whitman, *Democratic Vistas* (Washington, 1871), 5, 62, 71, 73.

in 1865 (when he was thirty-four) to the editorship of the *Nation* with the hope of wielding the journalistic influence that Garrison of the *Liberator* and Greeley of the *Tribune* had before him. Initially he supported Radical Republican policies and defended American democracy from English critics such as Carlyle.

Henry Adams, twenty-seven years old in 1865, felt the same stirrings. He wrote to a friend during the war: "We want a national set of young men like ourselves or better, to start new influences not only in politics, but in literature, in law, in society, and throughout the whole social organism of the country—a national school of our own generation." The twenty-four year old Oliver Wendell Holmes, Jr., fitted this mold precisely. He had come close to death three times in eighteen months on Civil War battlefields; in 1865 he threw himself into the work of the law. The historian John Lothrop Motley met Holmes in 1867 and thought that he was "one of the fellows who have got to prove to the world that America means Radicalism —that America came out of chaos in order to uproot, not to conserve the dead and polished productions of former ages."[15]

In a few years this euphoria was gone; and Godkin, Adams, and Holmes would be among the more critical observers of late nineteenth century American democracy. But in the wake of the war American intellectuals shared a rare mood of optimism—a mood that left its mark on every sector of the postwar polity.

The issue that most strongly engaged postwar intellectuals was the reconstruction of the South. Emerson feared that "the high tragic historic justice which the nation . . . should execute, will be softened and dissipated and toasted away at dinner-tables." James Russell Lowell revived his *Biglow Papers*, poems which had aided the antislavery cause before the war:

15. Parker, *The Three Powers of Government* (New York, 1869), 76; Godkin to Olmsted, n.d., Godkin Mss, HL; E. L. Godkin, *Problems of Modern Democracy*, ed. Morton Keller (1896; Cambridge, 1966), Introduction; Godkin, "Aristocratic Opinions of Democracy," ibid., 1–67; Ernest Samuels, *The Young Henry Adams* (Cambridge, 1967), 145–146; Mark DeWolfe Howe, *Justice Oliver Wendell Holmes: The Shaping Years, 1841–1870* (Cambridge, 1957); Motley to Holmes, March 12, 1867, in George W. Curtis, ed., *The Correspondence of John Lothrop Motley* (New York, 1889), II, 255. On Holmes's wartime idealism see Saul Toster, "In Search of Holmes from Within," *VLR*, 18 (1965), 437–472.

Make 'em Amerikin, an' they'll begin
To love their country ez they loved their sin;
Let 'em stay Southun, an' you've kep' a sore
Ready to fester ez it done afore.

Curtis declared in *Harper's Weekly:* "The policy which truly con-serves the principle and spirit of a free system is that which is called Radicalism." Theodore Tilton's Congregationalist *Independent*, the most influential religious periodical of its time, adamantly pro-claimed: "There is one, and only one, sure and safe policy for the immediate future, namely: *the North must remain the absolute Dictator of the Republic until the spirit of the North shall become the spirit of the whole country.*"[16]

These views were given still wider circulation by two popular commentators on postwar political life: the humorist David Ross Locke and the cartoonist Thomas Nast. Neither had been active in the antislavery movement. Their postwar views were a product of the war and the change in public sentiment that it brought about. Their work had much in common: the cast of self-taught, native talent; a vigorous, passionate, sardonic tone.

Locke's great creation was Petroleum Vesuvius Nasby, an arche-typal Copperhead Democrat: "illiterate, hyprocritical, cowardly, loafing, lying, dissolute." He placed Nasby in hotbeds of Demo-cratic sentiment: small, isolated towns in southern Ohio, New Jersey, Kentucky, Maryland, and in New York City. After the war Nasby settled down to a postmastership, granted by President An-drew Johnson, in "Confedrit Xroads," Kentucky. Nasby wrote "letters" filled with the anti-Union, Negrophobic sentiments of his political creed. Originally written for the *Toledo Blade*, the Nasby letters soon appeared in newspapers throughout the North.

In some ways Nasby resembled his creator: "Nasby was what . . . Locke might have been had he not possessed a gnawing conscience." But Locke believed that "government is the most important matter on this earth," and said of the situation of the freedmen: "Knowing how deep the prejudice is against the race, knowing how low down in our very natures its roots have struck, I demand, in our renewed

16. Edward W. Emerson and Waldo E. Forbes, eds., *Journals of Ralph Waldo Emerson* (Boston, 1914), X, 93; Lowell, *Biglow Papers*, no. XI (April 1866), in Lowell, *Poetical Works*, II, *Writings* (Boston, 1892); *HW*, 10 (1866), 242; *Independent*, 17 (May 4, 1865), 4.

and purified republic, the abrogation of all laws discriminating against them."[17]

Nast's powerful cartoons supported black suffrage and other Radical Republican positions, and brutally stigmatized Andrew Johnson, Negrophobic white southerners, and the Democrats. In 1872 he illustrated a collection of Locke's Nasby letters, and Charles Sumner wrote an introduction to the book. The senator said of its contents: "They have an historic character from the part they performed in the war with slavery, and in advancing reconstruction . . . each letter was like a speech, or one of those songs which stir the people"—or like one of Thomas Nast's cartoons.[18]

A similar tone characterized influential northern newspapers such as Horace Greeley's *New York Tribune*, John W. Forney's *Philadelphia Press*, and Samuel Bowles's *Springfield Republican*. Local newspapers in Indiana spoke of "a different people," "a new stage of being" emerging from the war. The United States, they told their readers, would "from the crucible of war and the sacrifice of blood present a more perfect civilization . . . than the world has yet seen."

A final, revealing instance of the entry of Radical views into the political thinking of the postwar years was the ideological odyssey of the New York lawyer–observer George Templeton Strong. In September 1865 Strong still was uncommitted on the touchstone issue of Negro suffrage: "It would not be easy now to draw a line between Democrats and Republicans, Conservatives, and Radicals, unless in regard to Negro suffrage—and that's a question to be left to the Southern States themselves, and not a national issue." But in January 1866 he noted that "almost every one has changed a little during the last six months, and become a little more Radical or Conservative." Faced with the choice, Strong decided: "On the whole, I think I am a 'Radical.' "[19]

17. James C. Austin, *Petroleum V. Nasby* (New York, 1965), 28, 47–51; John M. Harrison, "David Ross Locke and the Fight on Reconstruction," *JQ*, 39 (1962), 491–499, and *The Man Who Made Nasby, David Ross Locke* (Chapel Hill, 1969).

18. Albert B. Paine, *Thomas Nast; His Period and His Pictures* (New York, 1904); Morton Keller, *The Art and Politics of Thomas Nast* (New York, 1968); [David Ross Locke], *The Struggles (Social, Financial and Political) of Petroleum V. Nasby* (Boston, 1872).

19. Howard K. Beale, *The Critical Year: A Study of Andrew Johnson and Reconstruction* (New York, 1930), 315–329; Kenneth M. Stampp, *Indiana Politics during the Civil War* (Indianapolis, 1949), 186; Nevins, ed., *Strong*, IV, Sept. 8, 1865, Jan. 19, Sept. 12, 1866.

The Radical temper that emerged from the Civil War faced a self-conscious Conservative opposition. New York lawyer Vine W. Kingsley's *Reconstruction in America* (1865) set down the principal themes of the Conservative creed. He called for the restoration rather than the reconstruction of the South; criticized the Radical ideal of a homogeneous nation; and championed white supremacy.[20]

Few important intellectuals, publicists, or clerics promoted these views in the postwar years. But they had wide popular—and hence political—appeal. Conservatism spoke for those who had the smallest stake in the war, or were least in sympathy with its outcome: white southerners, hardscrabble northern farmers, Irish Catholic laborers, merchants whose interests lay with the prewar economy; Baptists, Lutherans, and Old School Presbyterians skeptical of human perfectibility. They made up, in Carl Schurz's words, "essentially a party of the past."

Conservatism found its voice in journals closely linked to the Democratic party, or in the platforms and oratory of the party itself. *The Old Guard*, a monthly "Devoted to the Principles of 1776 and 1789," appeared from 1862 to 1870. It was fiercely anti-Radical (and anti-Lincoln), anti-New England, Negrophobic, sympathetic to slavery and secession. The most influential Conservative newspaper was the *New York World*. Manton Marble, its editor, was the leading Democratic journalist of his generation.[21]

There was a Conservative equivalent to David Ross Locke: Marcus M. ("Brick") Pomeroy. His work first appeared in the La Crosse, Wisconsin *Democrat*, and won the paper a circulation of 100,000 by 1868. For the next two years Pomeroy published the *New York Democrat* with Tammany boss William Marcy Tweed's encouragement. His crude, often scatological political humor was bitterly

20. Kingsley, *Reconstruction in America* (New York, 1865). See Joel Parker, *Revolution and Reconstruction* (New York, 1866) and *The Three Powers of Government* (New York, 1869); S. S. Nicholas, *Conservative Essays*, III–IV (Louisville, 1867–1869); Alonzo Alverez, *Progress and Intelligence of Americans* (New York, 1865); James A. Stewart, *Conservative Views. The Government of the United States: What Is It?* (Atlanta, 1869); Charles G. Loring, *Reconstruction* (Boston, 1866).

21. Montgomery, *Beyond Equality*, 59–72; Mary C. Phelan, *Manton Marble of the New York World* (Washington, 1957); George T. McJimsey, *Genteel Partisan: Manton Marble, 1834–1917* (Ames, Iowa, 1971).

Negrophobic, antireform, hostile to active government: the obverse of the Radical creed.[22]

States' rights and the iniquity of active, centralized government were major Conservative themes. New York Democrats called for a return to the "old-fashioned, time-honored regard for the relations and rights of the States and the Federal Government," and warned that "the centralization of power in this State, no less than in the Union, is fatal to the harmony of our political system." The *World* spoke longingly of the "old Democratic doctrine . . . to permit the town to do nothing which the school district could not as well do; the county nothing which the town could do; the State nothing which the county or city could do; and the federal government nothing the State could as completely and safely accomplish." Lewis D. Campbell, a prewar Whig, wartime Union Republican, and by the 1870s a Democrat, saw a fundamental difference between Radicalism and Conservatism: "There are two conflicting elements in human nature always operating in society. One seeks to acquire power—the other is fearful and jealous of it." Augustus W. Clason in *The American Conflict* (1866) warned: "The principle of the Union is no longer justice, but force," and predicted that a new struggle between "liberty and despotism" would replace the old one over sectionalism and slavery.[23]

This was an attractive appeal, speaking to a localism, an identification of privilege with centralized power, that was deeply embedded in the American political consciousness. It lent itself to attacks on the "money power," on "this mystic Babylon, this vast trellis-work of Banks and Bonds," on Republican policies designed

22. Montgomery, *Beyond Equality*, 49–50; Frank L. Klement, " 'Brick' Pomeroy: Copperhead and Curmudgeon," *WMH*, 35 (1951), 106–113, 156–157; Mary Eliza P. Tucker, *Life of Marcus M. Pomeroy* (New York, 1868; reprinted 1970); Pomeroy, *Nonsense, or Hits and Criticisms on the Follies of the Day* (New York, 1868) and *Soliloquies of the Bondholder, the Poor Farmer, the Soldier's Widow, the Political Preacher, the Poor Mechanic, the Freed Negro, the "Radical" Congressman, the Returned Soldier, the Southerner* (New York, 1866). Artemus Ward (Charles Farrar Browne) was a prewar humorist who shared Pomeroy's political and social outlook. John Q. Reed, "Artemus Ward," *MQ*, 7 (1966), 241–251.

23. Democratic platform in "New York," *AC* (1865); *World*, March 7, 1865, quoted in Brock, *American Crisis*, 63; *Speech of Hon. Lewis D. Campbell, at Delaware, Ohio, Sept. 7, 1870, in Reply to Sen. John Sherman* (n.p., 1877); Clason, *American Conflict* (New York, 1866).

"to please the preacher and the politician, the servile ministers of bond-aristocracy." From this point of view the Civil War was "simply a conflict for power between king cotton and king monopoly." The popular appeal of that perspective contributed to the postwar Democratic recovery in the North. In the long run it was an ideological link between the antimonopoly rhetoric of the Jacksonian Democrats and the anti-big business appeal of William Jennings Bryan.[24]

Postwar Conservatives put special stress on the evil consequences of Negro emancipation. White southerners, marginal northern farmers, and Irish immigrants, so varied in other respects, responded warmly to the argument that "To change nature's laws, to thwart the decrees of Heaven, to make the black man white, and the white man black" was to bow one last and terrible time to the Radical temper. Restoration—the central tenet of the Conservative faith—had an especially strong appeal when it was linked to white supremacy. Representative Andrew J. Rogers of New Jersey, speaking to the House on "A White Man's Government," asked: "Shall the brave soldiers of our army be now, by any kind of extreme and radical legislation, put upon equality with the very men whom they fought to free?" To do so, he warned, was to betray the immigrants who came to the United States assuming equality among whites— and the inferiority of the blacks. An 1868 Democratic campaign pamphlet, "White Men Must Rule America!" spoke of the hideous transformation of the South, "where the Sumners, Wades, Butlers, Stevenses, and the balance of the Mongrel hordes who administer this government, have set up nigger monarchies, turning that once beautiful region into a social and political hell." It promised in the event of a Democratic victory to "maintain the supremacy of the white race at all hazards, and restore negroes to that condition where they can exist in accordance with the laws of their being, and where they will become in the future, as they were in the past, the happiest and most valuable race of subordinates on earth."

While not many Americans shared the Radical belief in civil

24. [A. C. Harness], *The Genius of Democracy; or, the Fall of Babylon* [Philadelphia, 1873]. See also Ransom H. Gillet, *Democracy in the United States. What It Has Done, What It Is Doing, What It Will Do* [New York, 1868], and Horatio Seymour, "The Government of The United States," *NAR*, 127 [1878], 359–374.

equality for blacks, the Negrophobia of the Conservatives had a special edge. Hinton R. Helper of North Carolina, whose *Impending Crisis* (1857) indicted slavery from the viewpoint of the South's poor whites, fiercely assaulted the freedmen during the postwar years. His clumsily titled novel *Nojoque* (1867) was explicit enough in its intent: "the primary purpose of this work is to write the negro out of existence." In *The Negroes in Negroland* (1868), used by the Democrats as a campaign tract, and in *Noonday Exigencies in America* (1871), Helper with pathological fervor dwelt on the black threat to white racial purity.[25]

Before the war *DeBow's Review* was the voice of the large cotton planters that Helper so bitterly opposed. Revived in 1866, the magazine accepted the end of slavery, and was as one with Helper in rejecting Negro civil equality. It gave space to longtime expositors of black racial inferiority such as the sociologist George Fitzhugh and the ethnologist Josiah C. Nott ("The history of the negro race is simply a page of natural history, because God has not endowed it with the faculties necessary to preserve written records."). Poor white and planter in the South were on common ground in their racial views.

Northern Democratic state platforms echoed these assumptions. The Ohio party in 1865 called Negro suffrage "an insidious attempt to overthrow popular institutions by bringing the right to vote into disgrace"; Pennsylvania Democrats declared in 1866: "The white race alone is entitled to the control of the Government of the Republic." In the 1867 election campaign, Ohio Democrats paraded young girls dressed in white, carrying banners inscribed: "Fathers, Save Us from Negro Equality."[26]

Few Democrats were pure Conservative ideologues (although the great majority were in sympathy with its major tenets); few Republicans adhered to all of the assumptions of Radicalism. Never-

25. Rogers in U.S., *CG*, 39th Cong., 1st sess. (Jan. 11, 1866), 203; Helper, *Nojoque: A Question for a Continent* (New York, 1867), v; Hugh C. Bailey, *Hinton Rowen Helper: Abolitionist Racist* (University, Ala., 1965), 153.

26. Otis C. Shipper, *J. D. B. De Bow, Magazinist of the Old South* (Athens, Ga., 1958); *De Bow's Review*, 1 (1866), 273; "Ohio," *AC* (1865), "Pennsylvania," *AC* (1866). See also Forrest G. Wood, *Black Scare: The Racist Response to Emancipation and Reconstruction* (Berkeley and Los Angeles, 1968).

theless, in the wake of the Civil War (as in the 1790s and the 1930s), the normal fuzziness and indeterminacy of American political life was affected by the presence of conflicting polar ideologies. Nowhere was this more evident than in the politics of Reconstruction.

Republicans, Unionists, Democrats

Important economic interests interlaced with ideological concerns over Reconstruction policy. Northern merchants, middlemen, and investors had a substantial stake in the revival of southern cotton production. Chief Justice Salmon P. Chase called President Andrew Johnson's hostility to Negro suffrage "a moral, political and financial mistake" likely to cost over $50,000,000 in lost productivity because of a discontented black labor force. Horatio Seymour spoke for many Democrats when he identified congressional Reconstruction with the interests of a particular section: New England. The "leading minds" there, he said, "who shape the policy of the Radicals have in view . . . Power to give them wealth—Power to throw upon other sections of the country the load of taxation . . . The question of Tariffs and Taxes are the real questions . . . The vast commerce and carrying trade of New York is in danger." The *Commercial and Financial Chronicle,* which represented New York City mercantile interests, argued that Andrew Johnson's policies would restore "the Southern communities at the earliest possible day to their normal relations of production and consumption with the rest of the republic."[27]

But it would be a mistake to ascribe congressional Reconstruction, as one historian has, to a "system of tariff, drawbacks, tax reductions, bounties, and government-organized exploitation of the Southern region, sponsored by the Boston-Philadelphia-Northwestern merchant-dominated political alliance." Midwestern and Middle Atlantic Republicans, who did most to shape Reconstruction policy, often were sharply at odds on economic issues with their party fellows from New England. Economic interests in fact were

27. Chase to Joseph W. Schuckers, June 25, 1865, Chase Mss, LC; Seymour to Montgomery Blair, Jan. 3, 1866, Blair Family Mss, LC; *CFC,* 1 (1865), 259.

too localized and diverse to determine the character of Reconstruction.[28]

Rather, the conflict over Reconstruction policy that dominated national politics and policymaking during the late 1860s was the product of a complex interplay of economic and political identities of interest with the larger emotional inheritance of the Civil War. As *Harper's Weekly* observed:

> The airy gentlemen who think that half a nation can be alienated from the other half for forty years, and after appealing to a tremendous civil war, which rages for four years, tearing up the industrial and political system of half a continent by its roots, and after one party is vanquished in the field and still remains hostile at heart, can conjure a settlement and reunion in a few weeks or months by a free use of the word "conciliation," will have an opportunity of learning wisdom from events.

Gideon Welles, Lincoln's secretary of the navy and a supporter of Andrew Johnson, also knew what was at stake: "This question of negro suffrage, together with a proscription of the Southern whites, soon became a party test, and with it came in the old distinction in regard to State rights and central power." The war had opened a Pandora's box of issues: the distribution of sovereignty and the extent of government power; the character of party politics; the place of the freedmen in American life. That box would not be quickly or easily closed.[29]

As was so often the case in American history, a major national controversy quickly took the form of a party issue: between Republicans, who more and more made Reconstruction policy a

28. George R. Woolfolk, *The Cotton Regency: The Northern Merchants and Reconstruction, 1865–1880* (New York, 1958), 76; Glenn M. Linden, " 'Radicals' and Economic Policies: The Senate, 1861–1873," *JSH*, 32 (1966), 189–199. See also B. P. Galloway, "Economic Determinism in Reconstruction Historiography," *SSSQ*, 46 (1965), 244–254; Peter Kolchin, "The Business Press and Reconstruction, 1865–1868," *JSH*, 33 (1967), 183–196; Stanley Coben, "Northeastern Business and Radical Reconstruction: A Re-Examination," *MVHR*, 46 (1958), 67–90; for an older economic determinist view, Howard K. Beale, "The Tariff and Reconstruction," *AHR*, 35 (1930), 276–294.

29. *HW*, 10 (1866), 82; Albert Mordell, comp., *Selected Essays by Gideon Welles: Civil War and Reconstruction* (New York, 1959), 204.

measure of party identity, and an opposition composed of a nascent National Union party led by Andrew Johnson and, more important, the Democrats.

Lincoln's wartime Union Republican party, a mixed bag of War Democrats, Conservative or moderate Republicans, and Radicals, held together because its members agreed on the goals of preserving the Union and ending slavery. But after those ends were achieved, the party threatened to come unstuck. Intramural divisions—especially between former Democrats and former Whigs—flared up everywhere.

In most states, control of postwar Republican organizations passed into the hands of men who were more favorably disposed than their wartime predecessors to the Radical position on southern Reconstruction and Negro rights. Charles P. Smith of the Trenton Union League took party leadership in New Jersey; Reuben Fenton and Roscoe Conkling deposed Thurlow Weed, William H. Seward, and Henry J. Raymond in New York; Conservative Unionists in Pennsylvania lost out to Radicals Thaddeus Stevens, William D. Kelley, and John White Geary. Lincoln himself felt this pressure in the months before his death. He said of Missouri's Radicals, who were embroiled in factional warfare with the state's Conservative Unionists, "They are nearer to me than the other side in thought and sentiment, though bitterly hostile personally."[30]

The most consistent Republican exponents of Radical ideas were a small but dedicated group, led by Charles Sumner in the Senate and Thaddeus Stevens in the House. They were committed not only to Negro suffrage but also to a national authority that directly safeguarded the rights of citizenship. Sumner announced that hence-

30. Charles M. Knapp, *New Jersey Politics during the Period of the Civil War and Reconstruction* (Geneva, N.Y., 1924); on New York, La Wanda Cox and John H. Cox, *Politics, Principle, and Prejudice, 1865–1866* (New York, 1963) and James C. Mohr, *The Radical Republicans and Reform in New York during Reconstruction* (Ithaca, 1973), ch. 1; Erwin S. Bradley, *The Triumph of Militant Republicanism: A Study of Pennsylvania and Presidential Politics, 1860–1872* (Philadelphia, 1964); Lincoln quoted in William E. Parrish, *Turbulent Partnership: Missouri and the Union, 1861–1865* (Columbia, Mo., 1963), 166. See also Benedict, *Compromise of Principle*, 60 ff; Felice A. Bonadio, *North of Reconstruction: Ohio Politics, 1865–1870* (New York, 1970), 17–18; on Michigan, George M. Blackburn, "Radical Republican Motivation: A Case History," *JNH,* 54 (1969), 109–126.

forth "the states will exercise a minute jurisdiction required for the convenience of all; the Nation will exercise that other paramount jurisdiction required for the protection of all." Senator Timothy Howe of Wisconsin argued: "it is not the business of the national Government to sway States ... It is the business of this Government to control people." A few Radicals went further, and looked to national power to create a society free of racism and class distinctions. Representative Jehu Baker of Illinois asserted: "once for all we should have done with class rule and aristocracy as a privileged power before the law."[31]

In style as well as content the Radicals were what Wendell Phillips (who was one of them) called "the earnest men of the times." They considered themselves to be the moral trustees of a war for political nationalism and human freedom. Sumner dismissed pro-Johnson Secretary of State William H. Seward with the scornful judgment: *"He never understood our war."* Historians have pointed to psychological sources of the Radicals' fervor, such as Sumner's sexual difficulties and the trauma he suffered from his caning by South Carolina Congressman Preston Brooks in 1857, or Stevens's emotional compensations for his club foot. But the verbal excesses of the Radicals were matched by their Conservative opponents: Montgomery Blair of Maryland for one, and Andrew Johnson himself. Strong language was part of the prevailing political culture. James A. Garfield's friend Burke Hinsdale acutely observed: "Most Republicans now in public life [he could have added Democrats as well] have been trained in a school little calculated to create either calmness of mind or moderation of speech." An English visitor was struck by the widespread "vocabulary of abuse" in political controversy.

Change in party affiliation also was an important part of the postwar Republican political ambiance. Massachusetts Radical Ben Butler had supported Jefferson Davis (and then southern Democratic candidate John C. Breckinridge) for President in 1860. Secretary of War Edwin M. Stanton was attorney general in the prewar admin-

31. Sumner, *Are We A Nation: Address to the Young Men's Republican Union,* ... *Nov. 19, 1867* [New York, 1867, NYPL]; Howe in U.S., *CG,* 39th Cong., 1st sess. (Jan. 10, 1866), 163–170; Baker ibid. (Dec. 18, 1865), 69. On the division of congressional Republicans into radicals, centrists, and conservatives see Benedict, *Compromise of Principle,* ch. 1.

istration of Democrat James Buchanan. John Logan of Illinois backed Copperhead leader Clement Vallandigham for speaker of the 36th Congress before the war, and did not become a Republican until 1864. George S. Boutwell, James M. Ashley, and Oliver Morton, important figures in the politics of Reconstruction, originally were Democrats. Sumner, especially, had a political style that was so personal as to all but exclude the idea of party. He once defined politics as "the application of morals to the administration of public affairs."[32]

Some of the more conspicuous proponents of Radical Reconstruction would later set out on new political paths: to Liberal Republicanism, to the Greenback and Labor Reform movements, back to the Democrats. But most postwar Republican leaders stayed with their party. A persisting tension existed between those Republicans for whom ideology was most important, and those (the majority, and the more influential) for whom Radical ideology was secondary to factional and partisan political considerations.

It is not surprising that Andrew Johnson emulated his great predecessor by attempting to create a National Union party coalition to sustain his policies. The experience of the past decade had taught that party identification was fluid and ephemeral, and that political reorganization was the appropriate response to new conditions.

As the war drew to a close, there was much talk of political realignment. *Herald* editor James Gordon Bennett hoped to see "A Great Conservative National Party" based on "a reconciliation of State and national parties upon different principles than those of Northern abolitionists and Southern fire-eaters." Other wartime Union Republicans—Welles, Seward, Hugh McCulloch, and Edward Bates of Lincoln's cabinet, Governor Jacob D. Cox of Ohio, Congressman John Kasson of Iowa, Thurlow Weed of New York

32. David Donald, *Charles Sumner and the Rights of Man* (New York, 1970), 280, and *Charles Sumner and the Coming of the Civil War* (New York, 1960); Fawn M. Brodie, *Thaddeus Stevens* (New York, 1959); Mary L. Hinsdale, ed., *Garfield-Hinsdale Letters* (Ann Arbor, 1949), 408; Samuel Smith, *Reflections Suggested by a Second Visit to the United States of America* (Liverpool, 1867), 22; Sumner quoted in Walter T. Mills, *The Science of Politics*, rev. ed. (New York, 1881), 186.

—were ready to provide the state and national leadership for a new political organization.

Conservative Union Republicans and Democrats had a substantial community of interest on major issues. One of these was centralized government power. Edward Bates, Lincoln's attorney general, feared "that our fierce, progressive radicals are . . . taking the one short step from the Republic to the Empire," as France had done twice before. Another was acceptance of Negro civil rights. Few Republicans favored full black civil equality. Indeed, they were spread over a spectrum of opinion that reached to the unabashed Negrophobia of most Democrats. Seward, for all his hostility to slavery, readily adopted the view that the freedmen were "God's poor . . . They will find their place . . . The North must get over this notion of interfering with the affairs of the South."[33]

The hopes of Johnson and his supporters for a new political party centered on the congressional elections of 1866. A Philadelphia convention in August formally launched the National Union party under the slogan "Restoration and Peace." Johnson vigorously wielded his presidential patronage, replacing over a thousand post office employees. Tennessee Republican leader William F. Brownlow reported that " 'Johnson Clubs' are being organized, and they have money as they need it . . . The patronage of the Federal Government is bestowed upon rebels and copperheads alone." In fact, Johnson used patronage to win the support of local politicos regardless of their previous political coloration.[34]

But Johnson's National Union experiment only increased Republican party cohesion. Postmaster General William Dennison, Secretary of the Interior James Harlan, and Attorney General James Speed resigned from his cabinet. Speed complained that the Philadelphia convention "tends . . . to form a party for sustaining, not the Government entire . . . but a department of the Government." Republican supporters of congressional Reconstruction created a

33. Cox and Cox, Politics, 98, 33–40; Bates to Sen. James Doolittle, Oct. 10, 1865, Doolittle Mss, WSHS; Seward quoted in Brodie, Stevens, 285.

34. Thomas Wagstaff, "The Arm-in-Arm Convention," CWH, 14 (1968), 101–119; on patronage, Dorothy G. Fowler, The Cabinet Politician: The Postmaster General 1829–1909 (New York, 1943), 131–135, Bonadio, North of Reconstruction, 123–131; Brownlow to Chase, June 20, 1866, in Diary and Correspondence of Salmon P. Chase, AHA Annual Report, II (1902), 515; Benedict, Compromise of Principle, 69.

political apparatus of their own for the 1866 election. They held conventions in Philadelphia and Pittsburgh, and attacked the "Johnson Party," the "Seward-Johnson Reaction."[35]

In the lean days that followed the end of the war, Democrats were ready enough to let Johnson's party-building proceed. Horatio Seymour of New York told Montgomery Blair that in the Philadelphia National Union convention "good policy demands that conservative Republicans *lead off* . . . we of Democratic antecedents must readily 'fall in.' " Almost all Democratic congressmen embraced the National Union program. Oldtime Democrats George Bancroft, Jeremiah S. Black, David Dudley Field, and Robert J. Walker helped the President with his veto messages and prepared legal challenges to Radical Reconstruction.

But they exacted an ideological and political price for their support. "Jere" Black set the terms: full southern participation in the national government; no enforcement of Negro suffrage; a white man's government in the South; reduction of the federal army. A Democratic publicist told National Unionist Senator James R. Doolittle in February 1866: "In politics we have doubtless disagreed before now. But now, we stand on the same platform, *Johnson, and the Union* as it was—with *none of the states out.*"[36]

The Democrats were quick to claim patronage and other perquisites. A Missouri correspondent assured Montgomery Blair: "I have talked enough with Prest. Johnson to know that all we want is a bold push to get possession of the Departments." New York Democratic leader Samuel J. Tilden warned that the President "can not . . . work out the problems of his administration by *an exclusive reliance on the republican machine.*"

The obstacles to Johnson's political third force became clear in

35. Speed quoted in "United States," *AC* (1866); Mark M. Krug, *Lyman Trumbull: Conservative Radical* (New York, 1965), 244; E. P. Whipple, "The Johnson Party," *AM*, 18 (1866), 374–381; James R. Lowell, "The Seward-Johnson Reaction," *NAR*, 103 (1866), 520–549. See also George S. Boutwell, "The Usurpation," *AM*, 18 (1866), 506–513.

36. Seymour to Blair, July 19, 1866, Blair Family Mss, LC; John H. Cox and La Wanda Cox, "Andrew Johnson and His Ghost Writers," *MVHR*, 48 (1961), 460–479; on Black's terms, Benjamin P. Thomas and Harold M. Hyman, *Stanton: The Life and Times of Lincoln's Secretary of War* (New York, 1962), 521; Marcus M. Pomeroy to Doolittle, Feb. 5, 1866, Doolittle Mss.

the 1866 election. Many Republicans broadened their appeal by supporting a moderate Reconstruction policy; most of the National Union congressional candidates were Democrats. The Republicans won a sweeping victory. The next Congress would have an over-whelming Republican preponderance of 42 to 11 in the Senate, 143 to 49 in the House. The minority was not National Unionist but hard-line Democratic: from border states Delaware, Maryland, and Kentucky; from urban Democratic strongholds of the foreign-born (New York, San Francisco, Buffalo); from traditional Democratic counties (Pike, York, Luzerne, Montgomery, and Berks in Pennsyl-vania; Warren and Monmouth in New Jersey; Dearborn and Floyd in Indiana).

Johnson's National Union coalition had little chance in postwar America. He attempted to win popular support with a personal "Swing Around the Circle" during the 1866 campaign. As he tra-versed the arc of the North from Washington to Chicago, he re-sorted to more and more intemperate language in responding to the hecklers that dogged his trail, which only added to his unpopular-ity. But Johnson's failure had a deeper cause: his increasing un-willingness to accept even a moderate program of southern Reconstruction. To speak of Peace, Union, and the Constitution was not enough in the climate of the postwar polity, as became clear in his confrontation with Congress over the policies of Re-construction.[37]

Congress Confronts the President

The 39th and 40th Congresses, in session (with interruptions) from December 4, 1865 to March 4, 1869, shaped the policies of Recon-struction. The acerb Polish Count Adam Gurowski, resident in Washington during the 1860s, thought that the postwar Congress would have "a majority for *good* such as there never was in all the

37. Thomas Noell to Blair, Jan. 8, 1866, Tilden to Blair, March 10, 1866, Blair Mss; on 1866 election, Benedict, *Compromise of Principle,* 195 ff, Eric McKitrick, *Andrew Johnson and Reconstruction* (Chicago, 1960), ch. 13, Charles D. Cashdollar, "Andrew Johnson and the Philadelphia Elec-tion of 1866," *PMHB*, 92 (1968), 365–383; congressional election returns in *The Tribune Almanac for the Years 1838 to 1868* (New York, 1868), II, "Tribune Almanac for 1867."

history of parliamentary and representative government ... [Its] power ... will be enormous and unprecedented." John Greenleaf Whittier paid the 39th Congress the unique homage of an ode:

> O PEOPLE-CHOSEN! are ye not
> Likewise the chosen of the Lord,
> To do his Will and speak his Word?

The young Georges Clemenceau, observing postwar politics as a reporter for a Paris newspaper, spoke admiringly of congressional Reconstruction as "the great American revolution."[38]

Over half the members of the 39th Congress, elected with Lincoln in 1864, were first-termers. This was not unusual in the period, but it ensured a high congressional sensitivity to the current popular mood. William M. Fishback, sent to the Senate by the Arkansas legislature but denied his seat by the Republican Senate majority, told Andrew Johnson:

> The present attitude of Congress is, I think, hardly to be wondered at—Elected during the darkest period of our Civil War and under the influence of the passions of Such an hour, it had been out of the usual Course of Events, if these men had not brought to the Legislation of the Country views representing the New phase of public sentiments ensuing upon the Cessation of hostilities.

As congressional Reconstruction policy unfolded, from the Wade-Davis bill of 1864 to the Enforcement Acts of 1870–1871, the influence of Radical attitudes toward black civil rights and strong central government was strikingly evident. It is true that the specifics of Reconstruction policy were determined primarily by moderate Republican leaders such as Senators Lyman Trumbull and William P. Fessenden and Congressmen John A. Bingham, James A. Garfield, and James G. Blaine. And it is true that their inclinations were to hasten rather than delay southern political reintegration; to do little to change the economic and social structure of the post-

---

38. Gurowski, *Diary: 1863–'64–'65* (Washington, 1866), III, 393; Whittier Ode in *Nation*, 1 (1865), 714; Clemenceau, *American Reconstruction* (New York, 1928), 79. See also William H. Barnes, *History of the Thirty-Ninth Congress of the United States* (Indianapolis, 1867); Henry Wilson, *History of the Reconstruction Measures of the Thirty-Ninth and Fortieth Congresses 1865–1868* (Hartford, 1868); J. B. Mansfield and D. M. Kelsey, *Personal Sketches of Members of the Fortieth Congress* (Baltimore, 1867).

war South; to limit the degree to which the federal government interceded to protect the civil rights of the freedmen. But the intransigence of Andrew Johnson and most white southerners, along with the moral and ideological pressure of postwar Radicalism, moved congressional Republicans to adopt policies affecting the freedmen and southern government which, while not meeting Radical goals in full, went far beyond most wartime expectations as to what Reconstruction would entail.[39]

Three strands of conflict reinforced each other in the struggle between Congress and President over Reconstruction. One was the *ideological* clash between the Radical and Conservative approaches to the postwar South, involving issues such as Confederate disfranchisement, the extent of social and economic reconstruction, and the capacity of the federal government to enforce Negro suffrage. At the same time Congress and the President were caught up in complex and fluid *political* considerations. Johnson's uncertain political base, the erosion of the wartime Union Republican coalition, and year-by-year election results—the Republican congressional victory of 1866, Democratic state triumphs in 1867—substantially affected the course of Reconstruction. Finally, events were shaped by an *institutional* struggle between the executive and legislative branches of government. Quite apart from ideology and politics, Congress and President clashed over the question of their powers and prerogatives.

Radicals at first welcomed Johnson's assumption of the presidency. The *Chicago Tribune* expected that his "little finger will prove thicker than were Abraham Lincoln's loins"; B. Gratz Brown of Missouri rejoiced "that God in His providence has called you to complete the work of rebuilding this nation that it might be stamped with the idea of radical democracy in all its parts." Even Karl Marx, watching American affairs from London, noted approvingly that "*Johnson* is stern, inflexible, revengeful and as a former Southern white has a deadly hatred of the oligarchy."[40]

39. Fishback to Johnson, Dec. 26, 1865, Johnson Mss, LC. See also Benedict, *Compromise of Principle;* McKitrick, *Johnson and Reconstruction;* David Donald, *The Politics of Reconstruction 1863–1867* (Baton Rouge, 1965).
40. *Chicago Tribune,* April 18, 1865; Norma L. Peterson, *Freedom and Franchise: The Political Career of B. Gratz Brown* (Columbia, Mo., 1965),

But during the spring and summer of 1865 the President rapidly ✓ restored the south to full participation in political affairs. By December, when the 39th Congress convened, every southern state had its own government, and most had elected representatives to the national legislature. Marx's enthusiasm for the new President had waned by June: "Johnson's policy disquiets me. Ridiculous affectation of severity against single persons [such as Jefferson Davis]; up to the present extremely vacillating and weak in substance."

Treasury Secretary Hugh McCulloch defended Johnson's southern policy to Sumner as an experiment in leniency and nothing more. If it failed, Johnson

> will then be at liberty to pursue a sterner policy and the country will sustain him in it. Rebels and enemies will not be permitted to take possession of the Southern States, or to occupy seats in Congress or to form coalitions with the Northern Democracy for the repudiation of the national debt or the restoration of slavery.

But by December it seemed as if precisely these prospects were in the offing. Confederate leaders were prominent in the delegations sent to Congress. Southern state "Black Codes" preserved much of the restrictive apparatus of slavery days. When Congress asked Johnson for a report on the state of affairs in the South, he provided the sanguine observations of Ulysses S. Grant, who spent two days in Charleston and one day each in Raleigh, Savannah, and Augusta. But he suppressed the far more pessimistic picture drawn by Carl Schurz after a three month tour of South Carolina, Georgia, Alabama, Mississippi, and Louisiana.[41]

A mix of ideological, political, and personal considerations led Johnson to a stand on Reconstruction that alienated moderate as well as Radical Republicans. His belief in black racial inferiority was shared by the great majority of his contemporaries. But the Negrophobia of this onetime slaveholder from southern poor white origins had an ugly, rasping edge to it. After meeting with a group of Negro spokesmen led by Frederick Douglass, Johnson said to his

---

150; Marx and Frederick Engels, *The Civil War in the United States*, 3d ed. (New York, 1961), 275.

41. Marx and Engels, *Civil War*, 276; McCulloch to Sumner in James F. Rhodes, *History of the United States from the Compromise of 1850* (New York, 1904), V, 531; on tours, ibid., 552, McKitrick, *Johnson and Reconstruction*, 164.

secretary: "I know that d—d Douglass; he's just like any nigger, & he would sooner cut a white man's throat than not."

It has been argued that Johnson's background made him susceptible to the flattery of postwar southern leaders. He told a large Virginia delegation in September 1865: "I know that I am of the Southern people, and I love them." But his need for southern support was as much political as it was psychological. His position in American public life was a peculiarly isolated one. He failed to inherit Lincoln's wartime Union Republican coalition; the northern Democrats never accepted him as one of their own; his National Union party proved to be unviable. Johnson's attitude toward the presidential records in the White House summed up the character of his presidency: "I found nothing here when I came, and I am going to leave nothing here when I go."[42]

Congress and the President clashed first over the status of the freedmen. In early 1866 Congress passed a bill strengthening and extending the life of the Freedmen's Bureau and a Civil Rights Act that guaranteed the legal and civil (but not the political) rights of Negroes as citizens.

Radical Republicans wanted stronger guarantees, and far more change in the South, than these bills provided. Thaddeus Stevens called for large-scale confiscation of slave plantations and the creation of forty-acre homesteads for the freedmen. George W. Julian's Southern Homestead Act, passed in June 1866, made large purchases of southern lands illegal. His ideal was a South of small farms, free schools, stable communities, and political freedom: the classic Republican ideal of the good society. "Nationalizing the South," he said, "would tend powerfully to make our whole country homogeneous." Nevertheless, the Freedmen's Bureau and Civil Rights Acts were striking testimony to the government activism and broadened conception of black civil rights that came out of the war.

42. Hans L. Trefousse, *Impeachment of a President: Andrew Johnson, the Blacks, and Reconstruction* (Knoxville, Tenn., 1975), 15; James G. Blaine, *Twenty Years of Congress* (Norwich, Conn., 1884), II, 68–70; William H. Crook, *Through Five Administrations* (New York, 1910), 147. See also Curtis P. Nettels, "Andrew Johnson and the South," *SAQ*, 25 (1926), 55–64; McKitrick, *Johnson and Reconstruction*, ch. 4.

Less idealistic considerations also lay behind these bills, which were the work of Republican moderates led by Lyman Trumbull of Illinois. They were intended not only to protect the freedmen, but also to secure a contented black labor force whose productivity was high and who stayed in the South. A Boston merchant told his city's Board of Trade that southern labor "can be . . . provided for by the government, and at the present moment, by it only."[43]

For all this, Johnson vetoed the two bills. He called the Freedman's Bureau Act an attempt to transform a wartime expedient into "a permanent branch of the public administration, with its powers greatly enlarged." The Civil Rights Act, too, was a stride "toward centralization and the concentration of all legislative power in the National Government." Most of all he sought to make an issue of the place of Negroes in postwar American life. Johnson appealed to the deepest racial fears of whites: "if Congress can abrogate all State laws of discrimination between the two races in the matter of real estate, of suits, and of contracts generally Congress may . . . also repeal the State laws as to the contract of marriage between the two races."

This was a compelling argument. Most northern whites (and Republican congressmen) believed Negro racial inferiority to be a fact. But the threat to Republican hegemony posed by a Johnson-Democratic alliance, the institutional conflict between Congress and President, and the ideological challenge that Johnson laid down, combined to weaken his position. His Freedmen's Bureau and Civil Rights vetoes shocked the powerful moderate Republican senator from Maine, William P. Fessenden, into a heightened concern for congressional prerogatives. Fessenden reluctantly concluded: "I have tried hard to save Johnson, but I am afraid he is beyond hope. His 'policy' has driven all sense and direction out of him." John Sherman, also an important Republican moderate, observed that "Johnson is suspicious of every one, and I fear will drift into his old party relations." Lyman Trumbull, too, believed that "the President is daily separating further and further from Congress and getting closer and closer to the democrats." Oliver Morton told

43. Stevens in U.S., *CG*, 40th Cong., 1st sess. (March 19, 1867), 203; Julian quoted in Brock, *American Crisis*, 189–190; Woodward, "Seeds of Failure"; Woolfolk, *Cotton Regency*, 51. See also Benedict, *Compromise of Principle*, 147 ff.

Johnson that acceptance of the Civil Rights Act was essential if he wanted to preserve his Union Republican party identification. When Johnson responded with talk of his National Union coalition, Morton grimly replied: "all roads out of the Republican party lead into the Democratic party."[44]

The Reconstruction controversy took further shape with the passage of the Fourteenth Amendment. The first article of the amendment defined American citizenship in language that reflected the struggles to end slavery and preserve the Union:

> All persons born or naturalized in the United States, and subject to the jurisdiction thereof, are citizens of the United States and of the State wherein they reside. No State shall make or enforce any law which shall abridge the privileges or immunities of citizens of the United States; nor shall any State deprive any person of life, liberty or property, without due process of law; nor deny to any person within its jurisdiction the equal protection of the laws.

Just what was meant by these phrases would be the major issue in American constitutional law for the next century and more. The weight of evidence suggests that the drafters did not intend to create a strong new category of national citizenship, as the Radicals wanted, but rather to limit the degree to which the states could inhibit the basic rights of the freedmen as new American citizens. Even so, the amendment made possible a federal interposition in state affairs, and proposed a race-blind conception of the rights of citizenship, that would have been inconceivable before 1860.[45]

The Fourteenth Amendment notably neglected to require Negro suffrage. Sumner favored a suffrage requirement; Stevens was wary of Negroes voting while the southern states were run by Conserva-

44. *MP*, 3598–3599, 3611, 3604–3605; Charles A. Jellison, *Fessenden of Maine: Civil War Senator* (Syracuse, 1962), 199–200; Sherman quoted in Rhodes, *History*, V, 583; Krug, *Trumbull*, 236; William D. Foulke, *Life of Oliver P. Morton* (Indianapolis, 1899), I, 467.

45. For interpretations that stress the broad citizenship purpose of the amendment see Jacobus tenBroek, *The Antislavery Origins of the Fourteenth Amendment* (Berkeley and Los Angeles, 1951), and Howard J. Graham, *Everyman's Constitution* (Madison, 1968), 157–241. Hyman, *More Perfect Union*, ch. 26 ("a virtually machineless machine," p. 468) and Benedict, *Compromise of Principle*, ch. 8, stress its more restricted intent. See also Charles Fairman, "Does the Fourteenth Amendment Incorporate the Bill of Rights? The Original Understanding," *StLR*, 2 (1949), 5–139.

tive whites; most congressional Republicans were aware of (and shared) their constituents' hostility to black suffrage. The matter was further complicated by conflicting northern interests over voting and congressional apportionment. Stevens of Pennsylvania and Roscoe Conkling of New York favored congressional representation according to the number of qualified voters within a state. But New Englanders opposed this. Their section had a smaller percentage of adult males than the rest of the country, and educational qualifications for voting further limited their electorate. And other problems arose: were nonnaturalized immigrants to be counted? Or Indians? Or the Chinese in the West?

The amendment's apportionment article was redolent with the smell of compromise. The South was given the choice of allowing Negroes to vote or losing the electoral votes and congressional seats that counting the black population would give to the region. New England and states with large numbers of immigrants were assuaged by the provision that apportionment otherwise would be based on "the whole number of persons in each State, excluding Indians not taxed." When Sumner complained that the amendment failed to provide a national guarantee of Negro suffrage, even Thaddeus Stevens denounced "the united force of self-righteous Republicans and unrighteous copperheads."[46]

But Johnson and the white South maintained their intransigent opposition to the terms of congressional Reconstruction. Encouraged by the President, every southern state but Tennessee ✓ rejected the Fourteenth Amendment. Massacres of black and white southern Republicans in New Orleans and Memphis strengthened northern belief in the unregeneracy of the South. And the Republican victory in the 1866 congressional elections encouraged those who wished (in Frederick Douglass's words) to "render the rights of the States compatible with the sacred rights of human nature."

The First Reconstruction Act of March 2, 1867, like the Fourteenth Amendment, was the work primarily of moderate rather than Radical Republicans. The latter wanted not only black suffrage but broad changes in the South's social structure as well.

46. McKitrick, *Johnson and Reconstruction*, ch. 11; Stevens quoted in Rhodes, *History*, V, 595. See also George P. Smith, "Republican Reconstruction and Section Two of the Fourteenth Amendment," *WPQ*, 23 (1970), 829–853.

At one point Sumner came close to having the Senate make racially integrated public schools a condition of Reconstruction. Stevens sought the substantial disfranchisement of ex-Confederates and large-scale land confiscation and redistribution. But the act provided for only limited disfranchisement and made no provision for educational or land reform.

Its impact lay rather in the scale of government reorganization that it imposed on the South, and in its insistence on black suffrage as a condition of southern reintegration into the Union. The ten unregenerate Confederate states were divided into five military districts, subject to martial law. (E. L. Godkin later recalled that in the postwar years "there was hardly any political observer who did not look for the permanent retention among us of the military spirit, . . . and for an increased disposition to use [the army] . . . for the more complete and peremptory assertion of a strong central authority.") Normal civilian government would resume after the Fourteenth Amendment was ratified and new state constitutions guaranteed Negro suffrage. For many Republicans this was a way of assuring that the reconstructed Union would not be substantially changed. With the vote, the freedmen presumably would be able to fend for themselves without the constant intercession of the national government.[47]

The Fifteenth Amendment, forbidding federal or state abridgment of the right to vote "on account of race, color, or previous condition of servitude," came before Congress in January 1869 as "the last . . . of a series of great measures growing out of the rebellion, and necessary for the reorganization and pacification of the country, with which the Republican party . . . has been charged." Like its predecessors, the amendment had its limitations. It did not cover officeholding or forbid other forms of voter disqualification; it relied on negative injunctions rather than positive obligations to secure Negro suffrage.

Nevertheless, the differences between the Republican and Democratic views of government fully emerged in the debate over the amendment. Democrat Charles A. Eldredge of Wisconsin

47. Frederick Douglass, "Reconstruction," *AM*, 18 (1866), 762; McKitrick, *Johnson and Reconstruction*, ch. 14; Godkin, "A Retrospect," *Nation*, 51 (July 3, 1890), 4; Benedict, *Compromise of Principle*, chs. 10–11.

warned: "Every step in the direction of this bill . . . is a step toward centralization and consolidation." James B. Beck of Kentucky frankly questioned "the idea that this is a nation . . . We are in no sense a nation, and whenever we become so we will be a centralized despotism in some form." When Willard Saulsbury of Delaware made a similar point, Oliver Morton took him on:

> The Senator told us to-day frankly that we are not one people. He said . . . after the culmination of a war that cost this nation six hundred thousand lives, that we are not a nation . . . He gave us to understand that he belonged to the tribe of the Delawares, an independent and sovereign tribe living on a reservation . . . near the city of Philadelphia . . . I assert that we are one people . . . we are one nation.

The Fifteenth Amendment was based on the principle of a single, all-encompassing American nationality. But like the Fourteenth Amendment before it, this attempt to define the rights of national citizenship raised a host of problems. Educational, property, and sex restrictions on voting came under assault. Senator Henry W. Corbett of Oregon proposed that the right to vote be denied to "Chinamen" and women; the National Woman Suffrage Association opposed an amendment that did not make provision for female voting. Wendell Phillips feared that advocates of a more inclusive amendment endangered the core objective of ensuring Negro voting rights: "For the first time in our lives we beseech them to be a little more *politicians*—and a little less *reformers.*"

Yet once Congress approved, the Fifteenth Amendment was accepted by the necessary majority of state legislatures with relatively little difficulty. Republican state organizations wheeled into line behind it. And many Democrats acquiesced in a measure which promised to speed the return of the South to political life. When the amendment became part of the Constitution in 1870, it was widely held that the goals of the Civil War had been met. President Ulysses Grant declared that ratification "completes the greatest civil change and constitutes the most important event that has occurred since the nation came into life." According to George W. Julian, the amendment "perfectly consummated the mission of the Republican party, and left its members untrammeled in dealing with new questions." A number of former abolitionist groups disbanded on the assumption that now, finally, their work was done.[48]

The political challenge of Johnson's National Union coalition was checked by the Republican victory in the 1866 congressional elections. The ideological challenge of his Conservatism was met by congressional Reconstruction, which represented a substantial radicalization of mainstream Republican opinion, although it fell short of the desires of the Radicals. And the institutional tension between Congress and an increasingly assertive President culminated in the chief executive's impeachment.

√ The impeachment of Andrew Johnson is testimony to the strains that afflicted the postwar American polity. Newspapers in those years frequently dwelt on the danger of the resumption of civil war. A number of Republican leaders—Massachusetts Congressman George S. Boutwell, Secretary of War Stanton, Benjamin Butler—feared that Johnson planned to use the army to unseat the Republican congressional majority. Representative John A. Logan of Illinois made arrangements for units of the Union army veterans' organization, the Grand Army of the Republic, to rally in aid of Congress at Stanton's signal.[49]

Institutional conflict between Congress and the President steadily mounted in 1867 and early 1868. Senators John B. Henderson of Missouri and Lyman Trumbull of Illinois—no Radicals—suffered from Johnson's patronage policies, and sought to withhold salaries from presidential appointees until they were confirmed by Congress. The size of the Supreme Court was reduced, in effect cutting off Johnson's chance of selecting new justices. The Command of the Army and Tenure of Office Acts, passed on the same day as the First Reconstruction Act, limited the President's control

48. U.S., *CG*, 40th Cong., 3d sess. (Jan. 23, 27, 28, Feb. 3, 8, 1869), 555 (Boutwell), 643 (Eldredge), 687 (Beck), 990 (Morton), 828 (Corbett); Phillips quoted in George S. Boutwell, *Reminiscences of Sixty Years in Public Affairs* (New York, 1902), II, 52; George W. Julian, *Political Recollections* (Chicago, 1883), 330. See also William Gillette, *The Right to Vote: Politics and the Passage of the Fifteenth Amendment* (Baltimore, 1965).

49. Boutwell, *Reminiscences*, II, 79; on Logan, William B. Hesseltine, *Ulysses S. Grant, Politician* (New York, 1935), 629–656; Thomas and Hyman, *Stanton*, 493. See also George S. Boutwell, "The Usurpation," *AM*, 18 (1866), 506–513; William A. Russ, Jr., "Was There Danger of a Second Civil War during Reconstruction?," *MVHR*, 25 (1938–1939), 39–58.

over army personnel and forbade him from dismissing executive officeholders.

Democratic successes in the off-year elections during the fall of 1867 revealed that there was considerable northern popular disapproval of Negro suffrage and other Reconstruction policies. This encouraged Johnson to heighten his confrontation with Congress. His annual message in December 1867 emotionally denounced black suffrage: "Of all the dangers which our nation has yet encountered, none are equal to those which must result from the success of the effort now making to Africanize the half of our country."

Johnson chose to do battle on the issue of Congress's capacity to hobble his power of appointment and removal. In February 1867 he challenged the Tenure of Office Act by trying to remove Secretary of War Stanton and replace him with the more malleable Adjutant General Lorenzo Thomas. At first it seemed as if nothing could have been more misconceived. On February 24, 1868 the House of Representatives by a vote of 124 to 6 (Republicans unanimously in favor) impeached the President for refusing to obey the Tenure of Office Act. Then, by the terms of the Constitution, the matter went to the United States Senate sitting as a high court, with Chief Justice Salmon P. Chase its presiding officer.

Important voices of northern opinion favored Johnson's removal: Horace Greeley's *Tribune* and E. L. Godkin's *Nation*, the regular Republican press, most of the army's leading generals. Many saw in the President's course the rebirth of secessionism. Governor John White Geary of Pennsylvania told Senator Simon Cameron, the state's Republican leader: "The spirit of 1861 seems again to pervade the Keystone State. Troops are rapidly tendering their services to sustain the laws. Let Congress stand firm."[50]

On May 16, 1868 the Senate made its decision. By one vote (with several more in readiness if necessary) it failed to sustain Johnson's impeachment. One reason for this result was that many members of a political generation absorbed in affirming govern-

50. Johnson in *MP*, VIII, 3764; Trefousse, *Impeachment*, chs. 4–9; McKitrick, *Johnson and Reconstruction*, ch. 15. See also Michael L. Benedict, *The Impeachment and Trial of Andrew Johnson* (New York, 1973); Raoul Berger, *Impeachment: The Constitutional Problems* (Cambridge, 1973), ch. 9; and James E. Sefton, "The Impeachment of Andrew Johnson: A Century of Writing," *CWH*, 14 (1968), 120–147.

mental legitimacy and the viability of American institutions came to see impeachment as a threat to both. There was an extremist quality to the act of removing a President that was altogether too reminiscent of secession itself. As Senator William P. Fessenden put it: "The office of President is one of the great co-ordinate branches of the government ... Anything which conduces to weaken its hold upon the respect of the people, to break down the barriers which surround it, to make it the mere sport of temporary majorities, tends to the great injury of our government, and inflicts a wound upon constitutional liberty." David Davis of Illinois disliked the fact that "party men are trying the President, men whose trade is politics." With revealing imagery he added: "If there is any Slavery in the known world—slavery of the soul—equal to that demanded by party, I don't know where it is."[51]

Impeachment failed, too, because of widespread unease with the man who would replace Johnson in the White House. Benjamin Wade of Ohio had been elected president *pro tem* of the Senate at the beginning of the 40th Congress. The 1868 Republican convention was due to open four days after the Senate vote on impeachment, and Wade as the incumbent President would have a strong claim on the nomination. He was an outspoken proponent of an eight-hour day for labor and women's suffrage; he was supposed to have the marginally respectable Ben Butler in mind for his secretary of state; he was regarded (in James A. Garfield's words) as "a man of violent passions, extreme opinions, and narrow views." This and Wade's high tariff, soft money positions encouraged the *New York Times*, the *New York Evening Post*, and the *Chicago Tribune* to turn against Johnson's impeachment at the last moment.[52]

The failure to remove the President, along with the inability of the Radicals to secure laws changing the South's social and economic structure, reveal the constraints that worked on the

51. Fessenden quoted in Benedict, *Impeachment and Trial*, 179; Willard L. King, *David Davis, Lincoln's Manager* (Cambridge, 1960), 258.

52. Hans L. Trefousse, "Ben Wade and the Failure of the Impeachment of Johnson," *HPSO Bulletin*, 18 (1960), 241–252; Garfield quoted in Benedict, *Impeachment*, 134. See also Trefousse, *Impeachment*, ch. 11, and Michael L. Benedict, "Preserving the Constitution: The Conservative Basis of Radical Reconstruction," *JAH*, 61 (1974), 65–90.

politics of Reconstruction. But within those limits there had occurred a remarkable evolution of public policy regarding southern governance and the rights of the freedmen. In retrospect congressional Reconstruction is perhaps most notable for its striking testimony to the force of the new ideas about government and race bequeathed by the Civil War to the postwar polity.

The Supreme Court and Reconstruction

The tension between new and old attitudes toward government dominated the work of the postwar Supreme Court as well. While Congress expanded the jurisdiction of the federal judiciary during the war, the Court only gradually recovered from the disabilities of the Dred Scott decision and Taney's chief justiceship. The members of the postwar Court had little collegiality or sense of institutional responsibility. Senators Roscoe Conkling, Oliver P. Morton, and Timothy Howe, as well as Secretary of State Hamilton Fish, declined Supreme Court appointments during the decade after the Civil War. They preferred the more compelling life of public affairs outside.[53]

Radical Republicans sought to deny the postwar Court the power to review congressional Reconstruction. In early 1868 Thaddeus Stevens wanted to strip the tribunal of its jurisdiction over the Reconstruction acts. Senator Charles D. Drake of Missouri went further, insisting that no federal court had the right to review congressional legislation. A spate of proposed Constitutional amendments sought to transfer the selection of Supreme Court judges from the President to Congress; to set limits on the justices' terms; and to bar them from other federal offices.[54]

53. Charles Fairman, *Reconstruction and Reunion, 1864–1888, Part One* (New York, 1971), 26, 70, 662, 1452–1453, chs. 17, 18; Charles Warren, *The Supreme Court in United States History* (Boston, 1923), III, 275–283. See also John P. Frank, "The Appointment of Supreme Court Justices: Prestige, Principles and Politics," *WLR* (1941), 172–210, 343–379, 461–512.

54. Drake in U.S., *CG*, 41st Cong., 2d sess. (Dec. 13, 1869), 87–93; Stanley I. Kutler, *Judicial Power and Reconstruction Politics* (Chicago, 1968), chs. 3–5. Stuart S. Nagel, "Court-Curbing Periods in American History," *VLR,* 18 (1965), 925–944, finds that of the 165 anti-Supreme Court bills filed in Congress between 1802 and 1959, 22 came in the 1858–1869 period, more than in any other comparable span of years.

But most Republicans had no desire to make such substantial alterations in the distribution of powers. And under the leadership of Chief Justice Salmon P. Chase (1864-1873), the Supreme Court functioned in the postwar years as a coequal branch of government. Chase in some ways resembled Andrew Johnson. His strong presidential ambitions led him constantly to seek a political base. And as chief justice he was highly sensitive to the prerogatives of the Supreme Court. But his political skill—his ability to adapt to the exigencies of the Reconstruction controversy— saved the Court from a direct confrontation with Congress. His judicial model was John Marshall the political jurist, not Joseph Story the legal scholar; he readily conceded that "my own mind is executive rather than judicial."[55]

The general inclination of the Chase Court was to accept the major consequences of the war: the superiority of national over state authority, the end of slavery, the legitimacy of congressional Reconstruction. It struck down state attempts to tax federal bonds and sustained the right of the national government to levy a confiscatory tax on state bank notes. Justice Samuel F. Miller in Crandall v. Nevada (1868) voided a state head tax on railroad and stagecoach passengers on the ground that "the people of these United States constitute one nation."

It is true that the Court found ten acts of Congress to be unconstitutional between 1865 and 1873, as compared to two such instances in its entire previous history. But most of these were minor laws; and the Court was reviewing a vastly expanded body of congressional legislation, much of it reflecting the unusual stresses of the Civil War era. The more significant tendency of the postwar Court was its readiness to let both national and state legislatures act. Chase in Veazie Bank v. Fenno (1869) conceded that "the Judicial cannot prescribe to the Legislative Department of the Government limitations upon the exercise of its acknowledged powers."

At the same time Chase's Court sought with some success to maintain itself as a coequal branch of government. Chase refused

55. Albert B. Hart, Salmon P. Chase (Boston, 1899), 361. See also David F. Hughes, "Salmon P. Chase: Chief Justice," VLR, 18 (1965), 569–614, and the discussions in Fairman, Reconstruction and Reunion, Warren, Supreme Court, and Kutler, Judicial Power.

to open the southern federal circuit courts until "all possibility of claim that the judicial is subordinate to the military power is removed." He declared in September 1868: "I do not believe in military government for American States, . . . nor in the subversion of the Executive and Judicial Departments of the General Government by Congress."[56]

It was in this spirit that the Court dealt with the touchy, intensely political litigation that came before it in the postwar years. In *Ex parte* Milligan (1866) it had to pass on the jurisdiction of wartime military tribunals. Lambdin P. Milligan was an active midwestern Copperhead, a participant in various antiwar conspiracies. Even Andrew Johnson approved of his sentence to death for treason by an Indiana military court. But a unanimous Supreme Court voided the conviction on the ground that that tribunal had no standing to function in a state where the federal courts were operating.[57]

In Cummings v. Missouri and *Ex parte* Garland (1867), majority opinions written by Stephen J. Field rejected some of the bolder applications of Radical Reconstruction. The Cummings decision struck down a Missouri law requiring priests, lawyers, and teachers to take loyalty oaths. The Garland decision voided a wartime act of Congress that exacted a similar oath from lawyers who practiced before the federal courts. The Cummings case was especially sensitive, for it was deeply enmeshed in the politics of Reconstruction. The Missouri test oath law was a major issue in that state's 1866 election. Father John A. Cummings, in whose name the oath requirement was challenged, was a pro-Confederate priest. Francis P. Blair, a leading Missouri Democrat, called on his brother Montgomery (who was active in Maryland Democratic politics) to interest himself in the case: "It will be a great political occasion in which you can serve yourself with the great body of Catholics in Maryland and the whole country."

56. Crandall v. Nevada, 6 Wall. 35 (1868); Veazie Bank v. Fenno, 8 Wall. 533, 548 (1870); Chase to Gerrit Smith, May 31, 1866, Chase Mss, LC; Warren, *Supreme Court*, III, 206n. On findings of unconstitutionality, Kutler, *Judicial Power*, 115–125; Fairman, *Reconstruction and Reunion*, 1426–1431.
57. *Ex parte* Milligan, 4 Wall. 281 (1866); on Milligan, Harry J. Sievers, *Benjamin Harrison* (Chicago, 1968), II, 35–45; on case, Kutler, *Judicial Power*, 89–95, Fairman, *Reconstruction and Reunion*, ch. 5.

Republicans on and off the Court reacted no less strongly to the Garland and Cummings decisions. Miller's Garland dissent dwelt on the country's need for a loyal bar: "To suffer treasonable sentiments to spread here unchecked, is to permit the stream on which the life of the Nation depends, to be poisoned at its source." He defended the "right of the legislatures of the Nation, and of the state" to exclude from public life those who supported the rebellion. *Harper's Weekly* attacked the Garland decision as "another proof of the disposition of the Court to withstand the National will and reverse the results of the war."[58]

Chase—and the majority of his colleagues—had no intention of going so far. In 1869 the Court agreed to review *Ex parte* McCardle, a case similar to Milligan but this time involving a military court functioning in Mississippi. Congress moved to restrict the Court's jurisdiction in actions of this sort. Field wanted to hand down a decision before the limiting bill passed. But Chase drew back from so sharp a challenge to Congress: "We are not at liberty to inquire into the motives of the Legislature . . . judicial duty is not less fitly performed by declining ungranted jurisdiction than in exercising firmly that which the Constitution and the laws confer."[59]

Similarly, when Georgia and Mississippi brought suit in 1867 to block the enforcement of congressional Reconstruction, the chief justice declined to interfere. If the Court ordered the President to refuse to enforce the Reconstruction acts, he warned, "a collision may occur between the Executive and Legislative Departments of the Government." Justice David Davis in private was more direct: "The Court—Grier and Field dissenting—thought it was unjudicial to run a race with Congress."[60]

58. Cummings v. Missouri, 4 Wall. 277 (1867); *Ex parte* Garland, 4 Wall. 333 (1867); Thomas S. Barclay, "The Test Oath for the Clergy in Missouri," *MoHR*, 18 (1924), 345–381; William E. Smith, *The Francis Preston Blair Family in Politics* (New York, 1933), II, 351; Miller at 4 Wall. 386, 382; *HW* quoted in Warren, *Supreme Court*, III, 173–174. See also Fairman, *Reunion and Reconstruction*, 240–248.

59. *Ex parte* McCardle, 7 Wall. 506, 514–515 (1869); Sever L. Eubank, "The McCardle Case: A Challenge to Radical Reconstruction," *JMissH*, 18 (1956), 111–127; Stanley Kutler, "*Ex parte* McCardle: Judicial Impotency? The Supreme Court and Reconstruction Considered," *AHR*, 72 (1967), 835–851; Fairman, *Reconstruction and Reunion*, ch. 10.

60. Georgia v. Stanton, 6 Wall. 50 (1868); Mississippi v. Johnson, 4 Wall. 475, 501 (1867); King, *Davis*, 264.

Texas *v.* White (1869) gave Chase and his associates the opportunity—or imposed the necessity—of making a major judicial
statement on the scope and legitimacy of congressional Reconstruction. The point at issue was the power of Texas's Confederate
government to transfer title to federal bonds in its possession.
George W. Paschal, a Republican and financial agent for the Reconstruction government of the state, sought to recover the bonds.
His ground for doing so was that Texas had remained a state even
though its government was in secessionist hands. Thus the state's
title to the bonds never had been relinquished. This argument
implicitly invited the Court to join with Congress in declaring that
a wide range of Confederate governmental activity was invalid,
and that in consequence the rebel states were legitimate objects of
congressional Reconstruction.

An opposing group including George W. White, a friend and
political supporter of Andrew Johnson, argued that the wartime
bond transfer was valid. They admitted that Texas "is held and
governed by the other States as a conquered province," but suggested that the Court was not "bound to be governed by the action
and decision of the political power of the government." The Court,
in other words, was asked not only to legitimate the action of
Texas's Confederate authorities but to set itself against congressional Reconstruction.

Chase's majority opinion was complex—and politic. He denied
the validity of the wartime bond transfer. That action was designed to aid the rebellion, and was to be distinguished from Confederate measures (such as marriage contracts and property laws)
"necessary to peace and good order." Chase then took up the
sticky, near-metaphysical question of what happened to Texas's
statehood during her Confederate years. He concluded that Texas
continued to be a state—but one whose government had no "constitutional relations with the Union." It was proper, then, for Congress to create a new Texas government: not merely to revive the
old order of things, but to take into account "the new conditions
created by emancipation, and afford adequate security to the people of the State."

In this manner Chase avoided a commitment to the "conquered
province" theory held both by Radicals (who argued that it justified congressional Reconstruction) and by Conservatives (who

argued that the status existed but was unconstitutional). The Court's staunchest Republicans—Miller and Noah Swayne—dissented. Even to permit Texas to maintain an original suit, argued Swayne, was to assume a degree of existing statehood that Congress was not yet ready to grant. The Democrat Robert Grier was equally unhappy with Chase's sophistry. Clearly Texas had been out of the Union during the Confederate years: "This is to be decided as a political fact, not a legal fiction. This Court is bound to know and notice the public history of the nation."

But Chase was making a point of present relevance, not of past accuracy. By arguing that a state's identity persisted through an interlude such as the Confederacy—or, by implication, the military rule of Reconstruction—he accepted the reality of congressional Reconstruction while rejecting the conquered province theory of the Radicals. What was more, Chase retained for the Court the power to determine when a state had been restored to a normal condition of governance.[61]

Hepburn v. Griswold (1870) was Chase's boldest attempt to imprint his political views on the constitutional law of his time. But now he went too far, and ran afoul of powerful ideological, political, and economic forces in postwar America.

At stake in the Hepburn case was the validity of the government's wartime legal tender as a medium for the payment of debts incurred before the passage of the Legal Tender Acts of 1862 and 1863. Debtor-creditor relationships would be profoundly affected by the Court's decision. New York Democrat S. L. M. Barlow anxiously wrote to former Supreme Court Justice Benjamin R. Curtis: "Can you give me an idea as to the probable result of the legal tender cases . . . I owe about $50,000 of old mortgages. If they are likely to be held to be payable in gold I should try to pay them now." Railroads with heavy prewar obligations also were concerned lest they be forced to pay their debts in gold. The president of one line warned President Grant: "How do you suppose the Railroads of the country are to pay their interest in gold and re-

61. Texas v. White, 7 Wall. 700, 720–736 (1869); William W. Pierson, Jr., "Texas v. White," SHQ, 18 (1915), 341–367; Kutler, Judicial Power, 108–111; Fairman, Reconstruction and Reunion, ch. 13; Hyman, More Perfect Union, 517 ff.

ceive only a depreciated currency for their revenue, limited as they are by their charters to a fixed price?"[62]

The issue also had great political importance. More than seventy judges in sixteen state supreme courts ruled on the validity of the Legal Tender Acts before the Hepburn decision. Every Republican jurist but one found in their favor; almost all Democratic judges held against them. Chase himself as Lincoln's secretary of the treasury reluctantly supported the acts as a wartime necessity. But hostility to paper money was an integral part of his Democratic heritage. Speaking for the majority of a closely divided Court, Chase invalidated the Legal Tender Acts. He took pains to explain away his different wartime view: "The time was not favorable to considerate reflection upon the constitutional limits of legislative or executive authority . . . Some who were strongly averse to making government notes a legal tender felt themselves constrained to acquiesce." But "abundant evidence" since had made it clear that the usefulness of legal tenders was "far more than outweighed by the losses of property, the derangement of business, the fluctuations of currency and values, and the increase of prices to the people and the government."

Miller's dissent paid comparable attention to the public policy implications of the case. He dwelt on the role that legal tender played in "supporting the government in the crisis of its fate." Chase's argument that the Legal Tender Acts violated the spirit of the Constitution was

> too abstract and intangible . . . It substitutes our ideas of policy for judicial construction, an undefined code of ethics for the Constitution, and a court of justice for the National Legislature . . . Such is not my idea of the relative functions of the legislative and judicial departments of the government. Where there is a choice of means the selection is with Congress, not the Court.

Battle was fairly joined between opposing views of the proper role of government, of Congress, of the Court. And because the stakes at issue were so large, and the intensity of postwar public life so

---

62. Hepburn v. Griswold, 8 Wall. 603 (1870); Barlow to Curtis, Dec. 14, 1868, Curtis Mss, LC; Hart, *Chase,* 397.

keen, politics entered into the final disposition of this matter with a directness rarely seen in American constitutional history.[63]

Congress in 1869 increased the Court's membership from eight to nine. At the same time, the senile Grier was induced to resign. This gave newly elected President Ulysses S. Grant two Court seats to fill. Grant first chose Edwin L. Stanton and Attorney General E. Rockwood Hoar to fill the two available seats. But Stanton suddenly died and the Senate rejected Hoar. Then, on the same day (February 7, 1870) that the Hepburn decision was handed down, the President nominated William Strong of Pennsylvania and Joseph P. Bradley of New Jersey to the Court. They were duly confirmed; and in November the Court reconsidered the constitutionality of the Legal Tender Acts in Knox v. Lee—a necessary step, said *Harper's Weekly*, because the issue at stake was "the very essence of the war power."[64]

New York Democratic lawyer Clarkson Potter, who argued against the Legal Tender Acts in the Hepburn case, now did so again. He predicted that if the Court once more ruled against the acts, "then this wave of centralization will be rolled back; and to a sound and permanent, because moderate and legitimate, prosperity, you will have added the resource of that system of localized and limited government, in which alone true liberty can be found."

But in May 1871 the Court reversed its Hepburn decision. Strong and Bradley made the difference; and they wrote the opinions for the new Court majority. Strong argued that the reinvigorated national sovereignty of the war period made the Legal Tender Acts constitutionally acceptable. He thought it "a most unreasonable construction of the Constitution" to deny the government "the right to employ freely every means, not prohibited, necessary for its preservation, and for the fulfillment of its acknowledged duties."

Bradley, like Strong, emphasized the right of government to use

63. See analyses in Kutler, *Judicial Power*, 120–124, Warren, *Supreme Court*, III, 220–249, Fairman, *Miller*, 149–174, and *Reconstruction and Reunion*, ch. 14.

64. Knox v. Lee, 12 Wall. 457 (1871); Charles Fairman, "Mr. Justice Bradley's Appointment to the Supreme Court and the Legal Tender Cases," *HLR*, 54 (1941), 977–1034, 1128–1155; *HW*, 14 (1870), 242.

those devices—the sword, the purse—"absolutely essential to independent national existence." It was not for the Court to decide whether, or when, such instruments should be discarded: "Questions of political expediency belong to the legislative halls, not to the judicial forums."

Grant has been accused (most notably by Henry Adams) of "packing" the Court in order to reverse the Hepburn decision. Certainly the President was aware of his appointees' views on the legitimacy of the legal tender. But broader considerations underlay their appointments. Chase's skillful leadership threatened to make the Supreme Court a bastion of anti-Republican policies and attitudes. Treasury Secretary George S. Boutwell summed up the administration's attitude in 1873: "A court without political opinions is a myth . . . and as the Supreme Court must be political let it be right politically rather than wrong." With the accession of Strong and Bradley—and, in 1874, of Chief Justice Morrison Waite—the Supreme Court appeared to be in solid accord with postwar Republican attitudes toward legislative activism and public policy.[65]

The Election of 1868

Postwar presidential politics was caught up in the same conflict over governance that dominated Reconstruction policymaking and judicial review. The off-year state elections of 1867 made clear the popular hostility to black suffrage in the North. The Republicans lost or suffered sharply reduced majorities in Massachusetts, Connecticut, New York, Pennsylvania, Ohio, and California. This political warning blunted Radical Reconstruction and the Johnson impeachment. It affected the party's choice of a presidential candidate in 1868 as well.[66]

That candidate, Ulysses S. Grant, personified the struggle to preserve the Union. But his relationship to congressional Recon-

65. Henry Adams, "The Session," NAR, 111 (1870), 46–54; Boutwell quoted in Sidney Ratner, "Was the Supreme Court Packed by President Grant?," PSQ, 50 (1935), 353.

66. Michael L. Benedict, "The Rout of Radicalism: Republicans and the Election of 1867," CWH, 18 (1972), 334–344; Martin E. Mantell, Johnson, Grant, and the Politics of Reconstruction (New York, 1973), ch. 4.

struction—and indeed to the Republican party—was more equivocal. Benjamin Butler, who had been on bad terms with Grant since wartime, said of him: "so far as any political principles that he has evinced [are concerned,] he may equally well go with either." As late as 1867, a number of Democrats looked on Grant as a possible candidate of their party. Editor Manton Marble of the Democratic *New York World* correctly believed that "the Radical Republicans distrust [Grant] ... & think him not in sympathy with them."

But the exigencies of the struggle between Congress and the President moved Grant into the Republican camp. Thaddeus Stevens drily remarked: "Now we will let him into the Church." The 1868 Republican convention readily nominated the general, with a platform that strongly endorsed congressional Reconstruction—and avoided any commitment to black suffrage outside of the South. The theme of the Republican campaign was that the edifice of Reconstruction was complete.[67]

The Democrats as the minority party were more susceptible to the dictates of Conservative ideologues. But some Democratic spokesmen sought a more moderate course. *World* editor Marble in 1867 wanted to woo northern Negro votes. George H. Pendleton of Ohio, a wartime Copperhead, sought the Democratic nomination on the basis of his "Ohio idea" that greenbacks be issued to redeem wartime government bonds. Chief Justice Chase, too, discerned "the development of a popular desire for a new political departure to be represented by my name ... I hold my old faith in universal suffrage, in reconstruction upon that basis, in universal amnesty, and in inviolate public faith [regarding the wartime debt]; but I do not believe in military government for American States, ... nor in the subversion of the executive and judicial departments of the general government by Congress."

Chase offered in essence an updated Jacksonianism; indeed, his platform was written by Martin Van Buren's son John. The chief

67. Butler to Col. J. M. Cunningham, in Benjamin F. Butler, *Private and Official Correspondence of Gen. Benjamin F. Butler during the Period of The Civil War* (n.p., 1917), V, 714; Marble to Sen. James R. Doolittle, Dec. 29, 1867, Doolittle Mss; Brodie, *Stevens*, 333; Benedict, *Compromise of Principle*, 265–270. See also Louis T. Merrill, *General Benjamin F. Butler and the Campaign of 1868* (Chicago, 1939).

justice assumed that the party fluidity of the past generation would continue and that the ideological polarization of the Civil War years was over and done with. But this was a chimerical hope. As the New York lawyer and diarist George Templeton Strong observed of Chase's candidacy: "It would be equivalent to a reforming of parties—a renunciation by the 'Democrats' of all their cherished platforms and principles, and a repudiation of the Copperhead element." Chase soon conceded that few delegates to the New York Democratic convention shared his wish for a "new departure."[68]

Instead, the doctrines of Conservatism prevailed. Men with secessionist or Copperhead pasts dominated the convention, not despite but because of their views. Horatio Seymour, the party's presidential nominee, had been a prominent antiwar Democrat; his running mate, Francis P. Blair of Missouri, was passionately opposed to congressional Reconstruction. A Democratic administration, Blair promised, would "declare these acts null and void, compel the army to undo its usurpations at the South, disperse the carpet-bag State governments, allow the white people to reorganize their own governments and elect Senators and Representatives." The Democratic platform called congressional Reconstruction "unconstitutional, revolutionary, and void," and promised to abolish "all political instrumentalities designed to secure negro supremacy."[69]

Grant won a comfortable majority of electoral votes. But only 13 of 213 eastern and 43 of 559 midwestern counties shifted from the Democrats to the Republicans between 1864 and 1868. Grant's margin of 300,000 out of 5,700,000 votes cast was 100,000 more than the combined total of the Republican state tickets. Without

68. David P. Thelen and Leslie H. Fishel, Jr., "Reconstruction in the North: *The World* Looks at New York's Negroes, March 16, 1867," *NYH*, 49 (1968), 405–440; on Pendleton, Frank L. Klement, *The Copperheads in the Middle West* (Chicago, 1960), 262, 266; Nevins, ed., *Strong*, IV, 216; Hart, *Chase*, 364. See also Edward S. Perzel, "Alexander Long, Salmon P. Chase, and the Election of 1868," *CincHS Bulletin*, 23 (1965), 3–18.

69. Francis to Montgomery Blair, July 1, 1868, Blair Family Mss, LC; Smith, *Blair Family*, II, 348; "United States," *AC* (1868). See also George B. Woods, "The New York Convention," *NAR*, 57 (1868), 445–465; Democratic Party of New York State, *The Conservative Triumph* (New York, 1868; NYPL); Mantell, *Politics of Reconstruction*, ch. 8.

Grant, and without black votes in the South, the national Republican political majority was by no means secure.

Still, it is hard to imagine any other outcome in the aftermath of the Civil War. Democrats and Republicans substantially differed over the meaning of the war and the character of government, and for a time at least the Republican view was the dominant one. David G. Croly of the Democratic *New York World* perceptively analyzed that contrast before the 1868 election. The Democrats once had been "the movement party." But "during the great slavery agitation and the ensuing war it had become the conservative party." As a result, "it necessarily embraces all the stolid and ignorant voters, especially such as are influenced by the prejudice of race." The Republican party, he conceded, "has placed itself in accord with the spirit of the age."[70]

70. Mantell, *Politics of Reconstruction*, 143–145; David G. Croly, "The Political Outlook," *Galaxy*, 5 (1868), 41–46.

CHAPTER 3

Postwar Governance

THE IMPACT OF the Civil War on the American polity went far beyond the issues of Reconstruction. For a while it seemed as if every level of government was a beneficiary of the wartime legacy of an active state. The federal government lay claim to new powers and responsibilities. States and municipalities, too, shared in the quickened pace of public life.

But the postwar expansion of government was constrained by powerful countervalues: localism, cultural diversity, a widespread belief in laissez-faire. During the 1870s these facts of American life overcame the governmental inheritance of the war.

The World Outside

National self-confidence generated by the victory over secession and slavery inevitably affected postwar foreign policy. Cleansed of slavery, its unity confirmed, the United States with greater justification could resume its traditional role as the exemplar of republicanism and liberalism. Charles Francis Adams, wartime minister to London, observed in July 1865: "The progress of the liberal cause, not in England alone, but all over the world, is, in a measure, in our hands ... In respect to its capabilities of future social development, now that slavery is removed, there is a universal conviction that no such country can be found elsewhere on the globe." House Foreign Affairs Committee Chairman Nathaniel P.

Banks defined the coming American role in world affairs: "to be the grand disturber of the right divine of kings, the model of struggling nations, the best hope of the independence of states and of national liberty."[1]

Radical Republicans in Congress sought a greater role in the conduct of foreign affairs. The House in December 1864 accepted Henry Winter Davis's resolution that it "has a constitutional right to an authoritative voice in declaring and prescribing the foreign policy of the United States." Sumner in 1867 gave new life to an old issue when he induced Congress to bar American ministers from wearing uniforms or court dress unless they were specifically ordered to do so. In 1874 the legislature forbade American diplomats from accepting presents or titles. Informed that Protestant public worship was forbidden in Rome, Congress in 1867 refused to appropriate funds for the American legation there.[2]

The close relationship of foreign to domestic policy attitudes appeared in the American response to the great European event of the postwar decade, the Franco-Prussian War. There was widespread sympathy for a Germany newly unified, vigorous, and dynamic, seemingly committed to an anti-Papal liberalism. Minister to Prussia George Bancroft expected the new German empire to be "the most liberal government on the continent of Europe . . . In one sense . . . the new government is the child of America; but for our success in our civil war it could not have been established. Our victory in that strife sowed the seeds of the regeneration of Europe." Secretary of State Hamilton Fish agreed: "the tendency in the German nationalities to assimilate their constitution and government to the liberal principles which have so well stood the test of our own experience, will excite profound admiration among the American people."

1. Adams to Hunter, July 13, 1865, *FR* (1865–1866), I, 417; Banks report in Seward to Charles F. Adams, July 30, 1866, *FR* (1866–1867), I, 162. See also E. P. Whipple, "The Causes of Foreign Enmity to the United States," *AM*, 15 (1865), 372–376.

2. Glyndon G. Van Deusen, *William Henry Seward* (New York, 1967), 368–369; Robert R. Davis, Jr., "Republican Simplicity: The Diplomatic Costume Question, 1789–1867," *CWH*, 15 (1969), 19–29; 43rd Cong., 1st sess. (June 17, 1874), ch. 294; Leo F. Stock, ed., *United States Ministers to The Papal States: Instructions and Despatches 1848–1868* (Washington, 1933), 413 ff; Anson P. Stokes, *Church and State in the United States* (New York, 1950), I, 95.

Republican organs such as the *Nation* and *Harper's Weekly* were strongly pro-German and anti-French when war broke out between those countries in 1870. Republican party platforms (especially in states with substantial German-American populations) quickly took sides: "We cannot forget that in our late war the sympathies and material aid of the German state were freely given us, and we do not hesitate to declare our unqualified sympathy with the earnest efforts of the Germans to maintain and defend their national unity." French Emperor Louis Napoleon was identified with autocracy, Catholicism, reaction—and a pro-Confederate stance during the Civil War. *Harper's Weekly* condemned the "French Caesarism" that opposed republicanism elsewhere in the Western world.[3]

Democrats—the *New York World*, Samuel J. Tilden, the Massachusetts state party—supported the French. Diarist George Templeton Strong found that the "New York Fenians are swaggering to the side of France," and speculated that their attitude "may drive the whole German vote away from the Democratic party." *Harper's Weekly* belabored the Democratic press for its inability to see that "the cause of Germany is that of liberty and justice," and concluded that the Democracy "has no sympathy with liberty in Europe because it has been the relentless enemy of liberty in the United States."

But these sentiments had no evident impact on American diplomacy. For all its pro-Germanism, *Harper's Weekly* thought that the war resulted from "the ambition of one crowned head and the obstinacy of another." The rapid success of German arms was sobering; and the establishment of France's Third Republic was warmly received. Grant commented on that event in his December 1870 message to Congress: "While we make no effort to impose our institutions upon the inhabitants of other countries, and while we adhere to our traditional neutrality in civil contests elsewhere, we can not be indifferent to the spread of American political ideas in a great and highly civilized country like France." Unilateral in-

3. Bancroft to Fish, Nov. 29, 1870, Fish to Bancroft, Dec. 16, 1870, *FR* (1871), 358–360; John G. Gazley, *American Opinion of German Unification, 1848–1871* (New York, 1926), 320 ff; Eugene N. Curtis, "American Opinion of the French Nineteenth-Century Revolutions," *AHR*, 29 (1924), 249–270; *HW*, 13 (1869), 435.

volvement was unlikely when a self-satisfied nation took credit both for Bismarck's Germany and for the French Third Republic.[4]

It is not surprising that in the wake of a war fought to end slavery and sustain the Union, American diplomacy displayed an active concern for the rights of citizenship. Secretary of State William H. Seward thought that the problems of naturalized citizens were the most important responsibility of the Department of State. Chief among these was the status of foreign-born American citizens who returned to their homelands: peacefully (as in the case of German-Americans who were subjected to their fatherland's conscription laws) or not so peacefully (as with Irish-Americans who came to the British Isles to strike a blow—or set off a bomb—for Home Rule). Seward called on Bismarck to "recognize the principle of naturalization as a natural and inherent right of manhood," and to stop the conscription of German-Americans into the Prussian army. A number of treaties protecting the rights of naturalized American citizens were secured with European states. Congress in 1868 guaranteed the protection of naturalized citizens abroad, and in 1870 the naturalization laws were amended to allow aliens of African birth or descent to become citizens.[5]

The Fenians, an Irish nationalist group organized in New York in 1858, were a special problem. In 1866 and 1867 a number of Fenians were arrested for terrorism in Ireland and England. Three were executed; several were sentenced to life imprisonment. Seward instructed a reluctant Charles Francis Adams to express his government's concern, especially since many of those punished had fought "in the defense of the United States in a war with public enemies." Congress considered a bill authorizing the Presi-

4. "Massachusetts," *AC* (1870); Allan Nevins and Milton H. Thomas, eds., *The Diary of George Templeton Strong* (New York, 1952), IV, 298; *HW*, 14 (1870), 610, 482; *MP*, IX, 4051. See also Charles Sumner, *The Duel between France and Germany, with its Lesson to Civilization* (Boston, 1870).

5. Seward to Charles F. Adams, March 7, 1868, to Reverdy Johnson, July 20, 1868, *FR* (1868), I, 158–159, 328; U.S., Department of State, *Opinions of the Principal Officers of the Executive Departments, . . . Relating to Expatriation, Naturalization, and Change of Allegiance* (Washington, 1873); C. Munde, *Bancroft Naturalization Treaties with German States* Würzburg, 1868); U.S., 40th Cong., 2d sess., ch. 249 (June 27, 1868), 41st Cong., 2d sess., ch. 254 (June 14, 1870).

dent to arrest a British subject in the United States for every Irish-American imprisoned in Great Britain.[6]

Yet another group of citizens—the freedmen—made calls on postwar American diplomacy. Seward protested in 1866 when Spain required that black American sailors going ashore in Cuba post a bond: "The great change of the political relations between the races in this country has made it the duty of this government to see that no unjust or unnecessary discriminations are made in foreign countries between citizens of the United States of different birth, extraction, or color." Freed of its own incubus of slavery, the government criticized the persistence of that institution elsewhere in the New World. Seward's successor Hamilton Fish took note of the special concern of black Americans over the continued existence of slavery in Cuba, and found the sentiment "universal as it is natural and just. It rests upon the instincts of humanity, and is the recognition of those rights of man which are now universally admitted." When Spain freed some thousands of Cuban slaves in a mollifying move in 1873, Fish responded with characteristic rhetoric:

> Ten thousand chains struck from human limbs, ten thousand chattels made men,... this is a noble record ... The rapid increase of the means of communication throughout the globe have brought into almost daily intercourse communities which hitherto have been aliens and strangers to each other, so that now no great social and moral wrong can be inflicted on any people without being felt throughout the civilized globe. All powers interested in the adornment and happiness of the human race, and the spread of peaceful and Christian influences, are watching the noble efforts of Spain to disembarrass herself of the institution of human slavery.

These attitudes also led Fish to protest the treatment of Rumanian Jews in 1870 and 1872, and inspired congressional resolutions in favor of the revolt of the Cubans against Spain and the Cretans against Turkey.[7]

6. William D'Arcy, *The Fenian Movement in the United States: 1858–1866* (Washington, 1947); Brian Jenkins, *Fenians and Anglo-American Relations During Reconstruction* (New York, 1969); "Fenian Brotherhood," *AC* (1868), 332–334; Seward to Adams, March 22, 1866, *FR* (1866), I, 88, May 15, 1867, *FR* (1867), I, 87–88.

7. Seward to John P. Hale (Spain), July 9, 1868, *FR* (1868), II, 9; Fish to Daniel E. Sickles (Spain), Oct. 29, 1872, *FR* (1872), 580–584, April 30,

√   But American diplomacy had neither the will nor the where-
withal to do much more than utter high-sounding sentiments.
Nor should the rhetoric of freedom and equality obscure the strong
commitment of most American leaders to social and political stability. With rare exceptions (a few Irish Catholics, Wendell Phillips,
some labor reformers), the major voices of American public opinion condemned the Paris Commune of 1871. Seward's interest in
republican regimes in Latin America had much to do with his
fear of the alternative: "disorganization, disintegration, and anarchy throughout the American continent." While *Harper's Weekly*
admitted that "every nation seems unwilling to move in radical
reforms until it is roughly seized and shaken," it nevertheless
condemned "The Fenian Folly" of violence and terrorism. Charles
Francis Adams argued from England: "our own indignation is too
fresh yet in America against people from here who yielded assistance to our insurgents, for me to entertain great sympathy with
similar attacks made from our side against the public peace of this
kingdom."[8]

Supporters of American territorial and commercial expansion
tried to tie their ambitions to the triumph of the Union. The *New
York Tribune* optimistically declared in 1867: "The progress and
expanding power of a great, active, and ambitious nation cannot
be restrained." House Foreign Affairs Committee Chairman Nathaniel Banks was the most outspoken congressional expansionist.
His days were filled with plans for the annexation of Canada,
Cuba, Santo Domingo; for leaseholds, protectorates, spheres of influence, military and diplomatic intervention; for the expansion of
American trade, investment, ideas. "This great nation," he intoned, "was intended to hold . . . liberty in trust for all mankind

1873, *FR* (1873), 966; on Jews, Fish to E. J. Morris (Turkey), June 4, 1870,
to Benjamin Peixotto, April 10, 1872, to John Jay (Austria), July 22, 1872,
FR (1872), 650, 688, 55; on Cubans, U.S., *CR*, 41st Cong., 1st sess., House
(April 9, 1869), 711–712; on Cretans, *CR*, 40th Cong., 1st sess., House, Resolution 41 (July 20, 1867).

8. Curtis, "French Nineteenth-Century Revolutions"; Samuel Bernstein,
The First International in America (New York, 1962), ch. 5; Bernstein,
"The Impact of the Paris Commune in the United States," *MR*, 12 (1971),
435–446; Seward to Alvin P. Hovey (Peru), May 7, 1868, *FR* (1868), II,
863–864; *HW*, 12 (1868), 2, 14 (1870), 370; Adams to Seward, Sept. 3, 1867,
FR (1867), I, 133.

... It is destined to enlighten and civilize the rest of the world." Banks's views, implicitly anti-British, appealed to his heavily Irish working class constituency. The *Boston Voice*, a labor newspaper, said of his expansionism: "It lifted us out of the passions ... of the hour, and linked the Great Republic's destiny with the ever-widening progress of humanity."[9]

Secretary of State Seward, too, championed an expansionist post-war foreign policy. He wrote into President Johnson's annual message to Congress in December 1868: "Comprehensive national policy would seem to sanction the acquisition and incorporation into our Federal Union of the several adjacent continental and insular communities." Seward had held such views for decades; and the course of events in the 1860's reinforced them. In 1866 the Russians offered the territory of Alaska for purchase. It was accepted by Seward—and ultimately by Congress—as a step toward "extending national jurisdiction and republican principles in the hemisphere." Seward also supported the Mexicans in their struggle against the French-backed regime of the Emperor Maximilian. A self-governing Latin America, he argued, "offers to mankind the speediest and surest means of rendering available ... the natural treasures of America."[10]

Seward constantly encouraged American entrepreneurs to play a more vigorous role abroad. He called the relaid Atlantic cable "tributary to an expansion of our national commerce, and ultimately of our political institutions, both of which I think are important forces in the progress of civilization." He prodded reluctant capitalists Peter Cooper and William H. Vanderbilt to build a Panama canal, and sought (also without success) to secure and ratify canal treaties with Nicaragua and Colombia. When Perry M. Collins, the head of Western Union, came forward with an ambitious plan for telegraph lines linking the United States to

9. *Tribune* quoted in Theodore C. Smith, "Expansion after the Civil War, 1865–1871," *PSQ*, 16 (1901), 432; Fred H. Harrington, *Fighting Politician: Major General N. P. Banks* (Philadelphia, 1948), 176–177. See also Joe P. Smith, *The Republican Expansionists of the Early Reconstruction Era* (Chicago, 1933).

10. *MP*, VIII, 3886; Victor J. Farrar, *The Annexation of Russian America to the United States* (Washington, 1937), 110; Seward to William L. Dayton, April 24, 1863, *FR* (1863), 663. See also Frank A. Golder, "The Purchase of Alaska," *AHR*, 25 (1920), 411–425; Thomas A. Bailey, "Why the United States Purchased Alaska," *PHR*, 3 (1934), 39–49.

Russia and the Far East, Seward spoke of the government's "deep interest" in the project and instructed the appropriate emissaries abroad to offer what assistance they could.[11]

But postwar commercial expansionism was notable more for its bombast than for its accomplishments. The ventures that sought the aid of American diplomacy were minor and marginally respectable, or were grandiose schemes that existed primarily in the vivid imaginations of their promoters. And even those interests most directly concerned with American overseas commerce did not speak with a single voice on foreign policy. The *Commercial and Financial Chronicle* did not share Seward's enthusiasm for Latin American independence. Better, it said, that Mexico and Cuba be "prosperous and orderly" colonies of European powers than unstable republics.

Seward himself could not ignore the constraints that limited diplomatic assistance to overseas ventures. When the journalist-diplomat James Watson Webb tried to involve the government in a steamship line linking Brazil and the United States, the secretary of state was wary. "The people who go to these regions and encounter great risks in the hope of great rewards," he observed, "must be regarded as taking all the circumstances into consideration, and cannot with reason ask their government to complain that they stand on a common footing with native subjects." He saw no need "to encourage the employment of American capital abroad by extending to it any protection beyond what is due of the strictest obligation."

Seward's postwar diplomacy was hobbled, too, by his identification with the Conservative wing of postwar American politics. He agreed with Charles Francis Adams in 1867 on the need "for an early restoration of constitutional peace, law, order and progress among ourselves," and feared that "centralization, consolidation and [domestic] imperialism" would result from a Radical Republican triumph.[12]

11. Seward to Western Union, March 28, 1867, FR (1867), I, 385–388; on Cooper and Vanderbilt, Van Deusen, *Seward*, 517; Seward to Cassius M. Clay (Russia), Sept. 24, 1864, FR (1864), III, 297.

12. *CFC*, 1 (June 15, 1865), 130–131; Seward to Allan A. Burton (Colombia), April 27, 1866, FR (1866–1867), Part 3, 522–523; Seward to Adams, Aug. 26, 1867, FR (1867), I, 130; Van Deusen, *Seward*, 428–430. Ernest N. Paolino, *The Foundations of American Empire: William Henry Seward and*

The replacement of Johnson by Grant and Secretary of State Seward by Hamilton Fish in 1869 did not suddenly alter the character of postwar foreign policy. Grant offered an expansionist view in his December 1869 message to Congress: "Self-interest... teaches us ... the necessity of looking to other markets for the sale of our surplus. Our neighbors south of us, and China and Japan, should receive our special attention." But there remained a wide gap between rhetoric and reality, as the postwar American experience in Canada, Latin America, and the Far East amply demonstrated.

The annexation of Canada, an attractive prospect to many Americans since the early days of the nineteenth century, had new appeal after the Civil War. Seward included Canada in his vision of hemispheric hegemony, and sent the oldtime filibusterer Robert J. Walker to propagandize for annexation in Montreal. Republicans Edwin M. Stanton, Zachariah Chandler, Benjamin Butler, and Charles Sumner succumbed to the allure of the vast territory to the north. Henry Adams decided that the absorption of Canada by the United States was a historical necessity, and the *Nation*, while rejecting any tie with the "semi-barbarous populations" of Cuba and Santo Domingo, was willing to add Canada to the Union— if the Canadians approved.

But the appeal of Canadian annexation was limited to the upper Midwest and New England, and to politicians with large Irish (and hence anti-British) constituencies. When in 1870 a group of Fenians launched an armed assault on Canada, the Grant administration had to weigh the ambitions of the annexationists against the international consequences of government support and general American disinterest in the enterprise. The choice was clear; and federal authorities helped to break up the Fenian expedition.[13]

U.S. Foreign Policy (Ithaca, 1973), fails to distinguish between Seward's commercial expansionism and end-of-the-century territorial imperialism.

13. *MP*, IX, 3991; Joe P. Smith, "American Republican Leadership and the Movement for the Annexation of Canada in the Eighteen-Sixties," *CHA Report for 1935*, 67–75; Henry Adams, "The Session," *NAR*, 111 (1870), 54–55; "The Annexation Fever," *Nation*, 8 (1869), 289–290; Donald F. Warner, *The Idea of Continental Union: Agitation for the Annexation of Canada to the United States 1849–1893* (Lexington, Ky., 1960), 96, 98, 136; Allan Nevins, *Hamilton Fish: The Inner History of the Grant Administration* (New York, 1936), 217–220, 296–300, 385–399.

Cuba erupted into rebellion against Spanish rule in 1868, thus providing an attractive cause of national independence—and tempting prospects of financial gain from the bonds, commercial charters, and concessions of a new Cuban republic. These lures induced many Republican and some Democratic leaders to call for the recognition of the Cuban belligerents.

Secretary of State Fish refused to take such a step. He agreed that as part of "the inexorable logic of events" Cuba "ought to belong to the great family of American republics." But the taint of jobbery that attached to the American supporters of the insurrection, improved relations with a Spain newly (and briefly) a republic, and the possibility that the United States might wind up in possession of what *Harper's Weekly* called "a people wholly alien from us in principles, language, and traditions, a third of whom are barbarously ignorant," worked against American involvement. The rebellion collapsed in 1878 without having won formal American support.[14]

The movement for American annexation of Santo Domingo was a classic instance of interested parties seeking to shape American diplomacy for financial gain. Speculators and marginal political men such as Grant's private secretary Orville Babcock and Ben Butler took the lead in this venture. The prime advocate of annexation came to be Grant himself. The prospect of American naval bases on the island, economic advantages (Santo Domingo, he predicted, "will become a large consumer of the products of Northern farms and manufacturers"), and humanitarian benefit to the people of the island appealed to him. In 1870 Grant proposed an annexation treaty to Congress, arguing that this would advance the end of slavery (though none existed on the island) and further "the welfare of a down-trodden race . . . The people of San Domingo are not capable of maintaining themselves . . . They yearn for the protection of our free institutions and law, our progress and civilization."

But the scheme ran into a buzzsaw of opposition. Secretary of State Fish nominally supported annexation, but only as a *quid pro quo* for Grant permitting him to oppose intervention in Cuba. In fact he had little taste for the Santo Domingo project. A number of

14. Nevins, *Fish*, chs. 9, 15; Fish to Caleb Cushing (Spain), Feb. 2, 1874, *FR* (1874), 859–863; *HW*, 14 (1870), 434.

former abolitionists opposed annexation because it threatened the independence of the black Republic of Haiti on the same island. As Sumner put it: "To the African belongs the equatorial belt and he should enjoy it undisturbed." Democrats objected on partisan and racial grounds. In 1870 the Senate rejected Grant's treaty.[15]

The weakness of postwar expansionism was evident, too, in American relations with the Far East. The attitude of J. Ross Browne, Seward's last minister to China, who wanted the United States to introduce the railroad and telegraph to that country by force if necessary, was not typical of his successors. Rather, it was Anson Burlingame who set the tone for America's Far East dealings during the Grant-Fish years. Burlingame was a passionately anti-slavery congressman from Massachusetts who went to Peking in 1863 as Lincoln's minister to China. His aim was to establish a "co-operative policy" that was "based upon justice and freed from prejudice of race" as against the prevailing "Caucasian doctrine" of Western exploitation.

Burlingame had a healthy regard for the benefits of trade and commerce. But he thought that they could best be served by respecting Chinese national sovereignty and cultural sensibilities. In 1867 he became the representative of the Chinese government to the Western nations and concluded an agreement—the Burlingame Treaty—in which Seward pledged the United States to respect Chinese sovereignty and permit free bilateral immigration, in return for trading rights.[16]

Hamilton Fish favored this approach. He sought "to pursue a policy of *moral* force—to encourage material development, and the increase of trade." His emissaries to China—Frederick F. Low (1868–1874) and George F. Seward (1876–1880), nephew of the former secretary—shared these views. George Seward wrote to Fish in 1870, when he was consul at Shanghai: "It is easy to deride the

15. Grant in *MP*, IX, 4015–4016; Sumner in Nevins, *Fish*, 322; Democrats in "Ohio," *AC* (1871). See also Charles C. Tansill, *The United States and Santo Domingo, 1798–1873* (Baltimore, 1938).

16. Paul H. Clyde, "The China Policy of J. Ross Browne, American Minister at Peking, 1868–1869," *PHR*, 1 (1932), 312–323; *HW*, 12 (1868), 348; "Anson Burlingame," *DAB*, II, 290; Richard J. Hinton, "A Talk with Mr. Burlingame about China," *Galaxy*, 6 (1868), 613–623; Frederick W. Williams, *Anson Burlingame and the First Chinese Mission to Foreign Powers* (New York, 1912).

advanced liberalism of the age, and to stigmatize the policy which acknowledges broadly the right of any people to work out its destiny freely and independently, as a deliberate sinking of practical ideas and methods . . . But the fact remains that one of the doctrines of the political faith of the age is that all intervention is harmful and should be avoided." He questioned, too, the racism that distorted Western dealings with China: "we are likely to be deceived by appearances, and to attribute to differences of stock peculiarities which might be explained by . . . differing circumstances."[17]

Finally, self-interest and ideology tempered the most sensitive area of postwar American diplomacy, relations with Great Britain. Numerous voices called for a hard line in postwar dealings with England. Democrats appealing to Irish sentiment kept up a drumfire attack. Charles Sumner called for compensation for indirect as well as direct damages resulting from the depredations of the *Alabama* and other British-built Confederate commerce raiders. Grant, Butler, and Chandler were inclined to settle the *Alabama* claims question by seizing Canada. The Senate in 1869 overwhelmingly rejected the Johnson-Clarendon Convention, which sought to have this and other Anglo-American disputes settled by arbitration.

But the major thrust of Anglo-American diplomacy was toward negotiation and compromise. The 1868 triumph of Gladstone and the Liberals eased the way to *rapprochement*. As *Harper's Weekly* observed, "there is a great party in England—a party which now controls the British government—whose political philosophy is that of the great party which controls the Government of the United States, a philosophy which not only recognizes justice and intelligence as the necessary conditions of national welfare, but which substantially agrees as to the methods by which they may best be secured."

17. Fish, *Diaries*, Nov. 3, 1869, LC; Fish to Secretary of the Navy George M. Robeson, April 4, 1870, FR (1870), 331 ff; Clyde, "Frederick F. Low and the Tientsin Massacre," PHR, 2 (1933), 100–108, "Attitudes and Policies of George F. Seward, American Minister at Peking, 1876–1880," PHR, 2 (1933), 387–404; George F. Seward to Fish, April 27, 1870, FR (1870), 347, to Acting Secretary J. C. B. Davis, Aug. 22, 1871, FR (1871), 167. See also Richard J. Hinton, "The Race for Commercial Supremacy in Asia," Galaxy, 8 (1869), 180–194; Tyler Dennett, "Seward's Far Eastern Policy," AHR, 28 (1922), 45–62, Americans in Eastern Asia (New York, 1922).

The Treaty of Washington of May 8, 1871 provided for arbitration of outstanding claims by a Joint High Commission. Insurance, fishing, Canadian annexationist, and Irish spokesmen opposed the settlement, but the Senate ratified the treaty. New Jersey Senator Frederick T. Frelinghuysen celebrated its passage in language that would be more and more typical of elite Americans: "It is a noble thing for the two great protestant Christian nations of the earth to settle by a *tribunal* difficulties and differences . . . It is a great thing for the course of . . . civilization that while the Latin races and the Germans are consolidating their nationality, the Anglo-Saxons are strengthening themselves and their influence by establishing more intimate relations."[18]

The course of foreign policy in the postwar years suggests how narrow in fact was the range of action open to government policy-makers. Despite the ideological and political gulf between the administration of Johnson and Seward and the administration of Grant and Fish, the continuities in their foreign policies were far more striking than the discontinuities.

(For all the postwar rhetoric of expansion and of America's destiny as a world power, powerful forces worked against an activist foreign policy. A widespread popular hostility to military adventurism; the pressure of internal demands on capital and organizing energy; ideological objections to empire-building; strong and persistent American traditions of individualism, localism, and xenophobia; anti-Grant genteel reformers: all tended to mute and restrict the outward thrust of American diplomacy.)

The memory of southern slaveholder designs on Cuba and other Latin American territories could not easily be erased. The *Chicago Tribune* argued in the summer of 1866: "The best mode of propagating Republicanism among other nations is by teaching them that our own Republic is . . . intent on securing the welfare of its own people." The Radical Republican *Charleston Courier* advised: "Let the Government and people of this country look at home. Let them first reconstruct these States upon the basis of constitutional equality before they venture abroad."

18. Nevins, *Fish*, ch. 20; Daniel H. Chamberlin, *Charles Sumner and the Treaty of Washington* (Worcester, Mass., 1902); *HW*, 12 (1868), 770; Frelinghuysen to Joseph P. Bradley, April 27, 1871, Bradley Mss, NJHS.

An imposing list of decisions not to act documents the government's reluctance to undertake an expansionist foreign policy. The Senate refused to ratify a Hawaiian reciprocity treaty proposed by Seward in 1867. It rejected treaties for the purchase of the Virgin Islands (1867), the annexation of Santo Domingo, the building of a Nicaraguan canal (1870), and the annexation of Samoa (1872). The House in 1867 resolved not to appropriate funds for territorial purchases beyond Alaska. Postwar territorial expansion was confined to the purchase of Alaska and the navy's occupation of remote and uninhabited Midway Island.[19]

Grant and Fish, says one American diplomatic historian, were "important links in the chain of economic expansion running from Seward to Theodore Roosevelt and beyond." Another prefers to link postwar foreign policy "to the pre-Civil War type of imperialism." But these views ignore the variability of American foreign policy and the ties that bind it to the ambiance of a particular time. For all its rhetorical flourishes, postwar American diplomacy ultimately was halting and unassertive. In this sense it faithfully reflected the ambivalence toward the use of governmental power that pervaded the postwar American polity.[20]

Washington

The most visible expression of America's rejuvenated postwar nationalism was the transformation of the nation's capital. Before the Civil War Washington was a slovenly, indolent, half-finished

19. Newspapers quoted in Donald M. Dozer, "Anti-Expansionism during the Johnson Administration," *PHR*, 12 (1943), 256–257. See also William M. Armstrong, *E. L. Godkin and American Foreign Policy 1865–1900* (New York, 1957), ch. 5; Robert L. Beisner, "Thirty Years before Manila: E. L. Godkin, Carl Schurz, and Anti-Imperialism in the Gilded Age," *Historian*, 30 (1968), 561–577; Jeannette P. Nichols, "The United States Congress and Imperialism, 1861–1897," *JEH*, 21 (1961), 526–538.

20. Walter LaFeber, *The New Empire: An Interpretation of American Expansion 1860–1898* (Ithaca, 1963), 32; Marilyn Young, "American Expansion, 1870–1900," in Barton E. Bernstein, ed., *Towards a New Past: Dissenting Essays in American History* (New York, 1968), 182. See also William A. Williams, *The Roots of the Modern American Empire* (New York, 1969) and Paolino, *Foundations of American Empire*. For a view that pays closer attention to changes in foreign policy attitudes over time see Ernest R. May, *American Imperialism* (New York, 1968).

city, its social life (such as it was) dominated by the mores of the Old South: the physical embodiment of the American distaste for centralized government. The war brought new vigor and a vastly expanded scale to the federal bureaucracy and muted the city's southernism for a while. But it only added to the vista of mud-filled streets, scattered public buildings in the midst of squalor, and a disregarded (and now swollen) Negro underclass.

Physically the capital city was the antithesis of the Great Republic; and physically it changed in the postwar years. An English visitor predicted in 1867: "As the political centre of the Union [Washington] . . . typifies exactly the weakness and incoherence of the Federal Government, as it existed before the war. Perhaps, now that the Congress is assuming higher functions and the influence of the several States is proportionately declining, Washington itself may acquire a more solid and business like tone." A number of midwesterners wanted a more dramatic gesture: the removal of the capital to St. Louis or Cincinnati as sites more appropriate to a unified, continental nation. But the emotional associations and material interests attached to the old federal city were too strong. Instead, Washington underwent dramatic structural and political alterations after 1865.[21]

The city became a testing ground for the precepts of Radical Republicanism. Black suffrage was instituted by Congress over Johnson's veto in 1866, after white voters rejected it by a vote of 6,591 to 35. Relief funds were allocated for the destitute freedmen; a federal act in 1869 eliminated the word "white" from the city's charter and statutes. The city directory (to the regret of future historians) dropped the designation "Colored" from its pages. Clerical jobs for Negroes in government departments increased substantially, as did black businesses and schooling. There was even a halfhearted attempt at school desegregation. A mayor responsive to

21. James S. Young, *The Washington Community 1800–1828* (New York, 1966); James H. Whyte, *The Uncivil War: Washington During the Reconstruction* (New York, 1958); [John Walter], *First Impressions of America* (London, 1867), 118; on removal, William H. Barnes, *The Body Politic* (Cincinnati, 1866), L. U. Reavis, *A Change of National Empire; or Arguments in Favor of the Removal of the National Capital from Washington City to the Mississippi Valley* [St. Louis, 1869]; Olynthus B. Clark, "The Bid of the West for the National Capital," *MVHA Proceedings,* 3 (1909–1910), 214–290.

Negro rights (and votes), Sayles J. Bowen, was elected in 1868; blacks served on the city council and the school board.[22]

Congress in 1871 made the District of Columbia a federal territory, thus enabling it to have home rule through a territorial government. But political power rested in the Board of Public Works, which had charge of a massive program of civic improvement. The board's strongman was Alexander R. Shepherd—"Boss Shepherd"— an editor, businessman, and politician who had been president of the Washington Common Council since 1862. He was close to President Grant and to many congressional Republican leaders, who welcomed both the sweep of his plans to improve the city and his readiness to arrange construction contracts to their advantage.

House Appropriations Committee Chairman James A. Garfield, unhappy because too small a paving contract had been awarded to a Chicago bidder whose cause he championed, told Shepherd: "In matters of this magnitude and importance the bold and comprehensive policy is the most successful and if I understand the nature of your mind, this is according to your own taste and judgment." Garfield's perception was accurate. Shepherd spent large sums for street improvements, sidewalks, sewers, and schools, transforming Washington into a modern city. As New York Republican Congressman Thomas C. Platt put it: "we are here to make this capital city exemplify the civilization of our country." Postwar Washington displayed something of the spirit—and the corruption—that attended Baron Haussmann's rebuilding of Paris during the mid-century decades.[23]

This time of change did not last long. In 1874 Congress ended

22. Constance M. Green, *Washington: Village and Capital* (Princeton, 1962), chs. 13–14, *The Secret City: A History of Race Relations in the Nation's Capital* (Princeton, 1967), chs. 5–6.

23. Garfield to Shepherd, June 18, 1872, Thomas C. Platt to Shepherd, June 3, 1876, Shepherd Mss, LC; David Pinkney, *Napoleon III and the Rebuilding of Paris* (Princeton, 1958). A curious instance of Congress's involvement in the improvement of Washington was Joint Resolution #1, 41st Cong., 2d sess. (Dec. 12, 1869), which designated a committee to select a site for a new State Department building, "*Provided,* That the committee should reach the conclusion that the present site of that department is the most suitable." Ultimately, however, the massive State, War, and Navy building—Henry Adams called it an "architectural infant asylum"—rose on a different site, south of the White House.

territorial self-government and restored the District to its traditional subservience to the national legislature. Thereafter a House of Representatives that more often than not was Democratic controlled the city's affairs. Blacks were reduced to the servile, politically impotent status that would be their lot for a century to come. An investigation of Shepherd's affairs demonstrated that Washington's physical transformation had come at the cost of considerable corruption and extravagance. But the physical achievement remained: a monument to the Civil War legacy of a strengthened American nationalism.

A Japanese visitor to Washington observed in 1871: "It is . . . claimed by the best thinkers that the American Government was never more powerful and influential for good than it is at the present time." In 1874 a French observer, predicting "threatening attempts at centralization," published the first of four projected volumes on the departments and functions of the national government. And a British commentator had the impression that "the central departments of the Government are upon a much more complete footing, with larger and more various establishments, than anything of the kind that we have. All these centralized departments are the creation of the last few years."

A number of handbooks and guides described a strengthened postwar federal bureaucracy. New departments—Agriculture in 1862 and Justice in 1870—were created; State and Post Office were reorganized by Hamilton Fish and John A. J. Creswell. A variety of new agencies and offices came into being: the National Academy of Sciences (1863), the Commissioner of Immigration (1864), the Bureau of Statistics and the Bureau of Education (1866), the United States Weather Bureau (1870), the Office of the Commissioner of Fish and Fisheries (1871).[24]

24. Mori Arinori, *Life and Resources in America* (Washington, 1871), 39; M. A. de Chambrun, *The Executive Power in the United States: A Study of Constitutional Law* (Lancaster, Pa., 1874), 236; George Campbell, *White and Black: Outcome of a Visit to the United States* (New York, 1879), 274. Typical of the descriptive literature of the time are Ransom H. Gillet, *The Federal Government: Its Officers and their Duties* (New York, 1872); William B. Wedgwood, *Wedgwood's Government and Laws of the United States* (New York, 1868); William H. Barnes, *The American Government*, 3 vols. (New York, 1875–1876); and the magnificently prac-

While interest payments on the wartime debt absorbed the lion's share of the national budget, other forms of federal expenditure rose markedly in the postwar decade. James A. Garfield estimated that spending for the civil service, Indian affairs, and other functions (excluding the military and debt servicing) increased from 1866 to 1872 at a rate about 10 percent higher than the overall rise in government spending. Federal expenditure in 1869 was a higher proportion of national income (4.6 percent) than would be the case for the remainder of the century.[25]

But the most significant changes were qualitative rather than quantitative. There was, for example, a substantial improvement in government data-gathering after the Civil War. The Bureau of Statistics began its work as a branch of the Treasury Department in 1866. In 1878 the *Statistical Abstract of the United States* first appeared: evidence of the new importance placed on full and accurate data, and of the assumption that the national government had a special responsibility to provide that information.

The census, traditionally a slipshod and casual operation, became a more accurate and compendious enterprise in 1870 and especially in 1880 under Superintendent Francis A. Walker. Garfield, Walker's chief congressional supporter, wanted the Census Bureau to be a major fact-finding agency, staffed by trained data collectors. Under his prodding, Congress in 1879 passed a law that ended the inadequate system of using federal marshals to collect census data. Instead, paid enumerators directed by 150 census supervisors, in theory appointed "without reference to their political or party affiliations," were to do the job. It was New York Democratic Representative S. S. Cox's belief that "we are putting

---

tical George W. Raff, *The War Claimant's Guide. A Manual of Laws, Regulations, Instructions, Forms, and Official Decisions, Relating to Pensions, Bounty, Pay, Prize Money, Salvage, Applications for Artificial Limbs, Compensation for Steamboats, Cars, Horses, Clothing, Slaves, and Other Property Lost or Damaged, Commutation of Rations, Travel, etc., and the Prosecution of All Claims Against the Government Growing Out of the War of 1861–1865* (Cincinnati, 1866).

25. *HS*, 710, 718; Garfield cited in David A. Wells, "On the Ratio of Increase in Our National Expenditures," *Nation*, 15 (1872), 54–56; Paul B. Trescott, "Federal Government Receipts and Expenditures, 1861–1875," *JEH*, 26 (1966), 206–222; M. Slade Kendrick, *A Century and a Half of Federal Expenditure* (New York, 1955), 10.

together . . . a species of refined automatic mechanism, for grand political, economical and moral results."[26]

In what Henry Adams later called "almost its first modern act of legislation," Congress in 1867 appropriated funds for a geologi- ✓ cal and topographical exploration of the territory that lay between the Rockies and the Sierras. The geologist Clarence King, then only twenty-five years old, was chosen to head this enterprise. King was one of those figures whose career seems to typify a generation. His close friends Henry Adams and John Hay thought him the brightest and most representative man of his time. King's career in government-directed science was an apt denotation of the active postwar state. In 1879 he briefly served as the first director of the United States Geological Survey. He shared, too, in the sympathetic perception of other races that was part of the postwar environment. Adams said that King was a Republican "chiefly [from] love of archaic races; sympathy with the negro and Indian and corresponding dislike of their enemies." (That sympathy ultimately took the form of having five children with a mulatto mistress.) King was emblematic as well in his turn during the 1880s from public service to moneymaking and a love-hate relationship to material success (like that of Mark Twain) that dogged him to his death in 1901.[27]

King's was not the only postwar effort to chart the Great West. The army, deprived of more martial functions, launched a Corps of Engineers survey that lasted from 1869 to 1879. The Smithsonian Institution supported John Wesley Powell's bold explorations of the Grand Canyon region. Jurisdictional conflicts rose among the King survey, the Corps of Engineers, and the Interior Department's Land Office. Finally Congress in 1879 created a consoli-

26. On Bureau of Statistics, Herbert R. Ferlager, *David A. Wells and the American Revenue System*, 1865–1870 (New York, 1942), 100; Carroll D. Wright, "The Census: Its Methods and Aims," *IR*, 9 (1880), 405–418; Cox in U.S., *CR*, 46th Cong., 3d sess., House (Feb. 18, 1879), 1535. See also "The Importance of Reliable and Full Statistics," *CFC*, 1 (1865), 484–486; Francis A. Walker, "Some Results of the Census," *JSS*, 5 (1873), 71–95; A. Hunter Dupree, *Science in the Federal Government* (Cambridge, 1957), 277–278.

27. Henry Adams, *The Education of Henry Adams* (Boston, 1918), 312; Dupree, *Science*, ch. 10; Thurman Wilkins, *Clarence King* (New York, 1958), 204 ff.

dated Geological Survey, and Powell took over from King as its director in 1881.

Powell made the Survey the greatest American scientific enterprise of the nineteenth century. This gifted, self-trained scientist, explorer, ethnographer, and government bureaucrat had lost an arm at Shiloh. He shared with Francis Walker of the Census Bureau a passion for the scientific collection of data and a readiness to do his work within the framework of a government agency. With these men there may be seen the beginnings of the American bureaucratic style. It is appropriate that the sociologist Lester Ward, one of the shapers of modern social science, was on the staff of the Geological Survey. Ward wrote *Dynamic Sociology*, a pioneering call for social planning, in that supportive ambiance, and dedicated the book to Powell.[28]

Two departments in particular—Justice and Interior—reveal something of the tone and scope of federal governance in the postwar years. The government's legal work before 1870 was scattered over half a dozen divisions and agencies. Lawyers serving the Treasury, Interior, State, and Post Office departments acted independently of the attorney general, and kept the federal government from speaking with a single legal voice. Often the government's argument in Supreme Court cases was presented by private attorneys engaged for the purpose.

Federal legal work increased enormously in the wake of the Civil War. Litigation mounted over wartime claims, Reconstruction policies, and fiscal and revenue matters. The attorney general prepared only ten opinions on government policy questions from 1789 to 1865; from 1865 to 1881 his office prepared forty such opinions.

A group of Republican congressmen led by William Jenckes of Rhode Island set out in 1867 to create "a law department equal to the present emergencies of the law business of the country." In 1870 Congress created the Department of Justice, composed of the attorney general, the legal officers of other departments, and a new official, the solicitor general, whose primary duty was to represent

28. Wallace Stegner, *Beyond the Ninetieth Meridian: John Wesley Powell and the Second Opening of the West* (Boston, 1954); William C. Darrah, *Powell of the Colorado* (Princeton, 1951).

the government before the Supreme Court. The new department was charged also to approve the plans of public buildings, codify the federal statutes—and, as it turned out, to oversee the Grant administration's efforts (weak as they were) to safeguard black voting in the South. Attorney General George H. Williams was known as Grant's "Secretary of State for Southern Affairs"; he and his predecessor A. T. Akerman advised on the deployment of federal troops, marshals, and deputies in the South.[29]

Interior, "the Department of the Great Miscellany," became the repository of a wide range of postwar federal activities. Within its jurisdiction was Howard University, established in 1867 to offer higher education to the freedmen; the Auditor of Railroad Accounts (in 1881 renamed the Commissioner of Railroads), who supervised the government's investment in the Union Pacific; the Patent Office; the Land Office, which handled the disposal of the public domain; the Census Bureau; the Geological Survey; and the Bureau of Pensions. Here in one department was much of the apparatus of an active national state.[30]

Territorial administration also gained new vigor in the postwar years. Control of the territories—once the source of divisive sectional conflict, now a symbol of the reunited nation's future—appropriately moved from the State Department to the Department of the Interior on March 1, 1873. Republicans viewed these lands as places for political colonization (and economic exploitation) not unlike the defeated South. More than 400 officials were sent to the territories in the postwar years. James M. Ashley, a leading Radical Republican congressman, went to Montana as governor in January 1870 "for the express purpose of making this stronghold of de-

29. "Letter from the Attorney-General of the United States, Transmitting a List Embracing All the Publications of the Department . . . ," U.S., 47th Cong., 1st sess., Senate, Exec. Doc. 109; Jenckes quoted in A. G. Langeluttig, *The Department of Justice of the United States* (Baltimore, 1927), 11; on Williams, "The Inflation of the Attorney General," *Nation*, 19 (1874) 214–215. See also Homer Cummings and Carl MacFarland, *Federal Justice: Chapters in the History of Justice and the Federal Executive* (New York, 1937), 219–276; on southern activities, Executive and Congressional Letterbooks, Office of the Attorney General, NA, Ross A. Webb, "Benjamin H. Bristow: Civil Rights Champion, 1866–1872," *CWH*, 15 (1969), 39–53.

30. Leonard D. White, *The Republican Era, 1869–1901: A Study in Administrative History* (New York, 1958), 175–181.

mocracy, Republican." Oliver P. Morton's brother-in-law John B. Burbank sought in Dakota to better the fortunes of both the territorial Republican party and himself.[31]

Utah in particular felt the force of Republican territorial administration. Vermont Senator Justin Morrill proposed an antipolygamy bill in 1862 which would have placed that Mormon-dominated territory under federal control similar to that of conquered portions of the South. Morrill's bill failed to pass, but in 1869 Senator Shelby Cullom of Illinois led a successful effort in Congress to forbid polygamy in the territories. Federal courts and territorial officials enforced the statute, and Presidents Grant, Hayes, and Garfield attacked polygamy in messages to Congress, Hayes declaring that "the sanctity of marriage and the family are the cornerstones of our American society and civilization."[32]

But party politics, localism, and the prevalence of laissez-faire beliefs worked in the 1870s against the development of a strong and self-contained national state. *The U.S. Blue Book* (1881), a guide for those seeking federal employment, stressed the value of political connections rather than professional expertise. Henry Adams decided in 1870: "The government does not govern. Congress is inefficient, and shows itself more and more incompetent . . . to wield the enormous powers that are forced upon it, while the Executive is . . . practically deprived of its necessary strengths by the jealousy of the Legislature." Henry W. Bellows, the key figure in the wartime Sanitary Commission and an apostle of the active state, concluded in the late seventies: "We can see now, that we have demanded and expected too much from the Central Gov-

---

31. On officials, Earl S. Pomeroy, "Carpet-Baggers in the Territories, 1861 to 1890," *Hist*, 2 (1939), 53; on Ashley, Pomeroy, *The Territories and the United States 1861–1890: Studies in Colonial Administration* (Philadelphia, 1947), 63; W. Turrentine Jackson, "Dakota Politics During the Burbank Administration, 1869–1873," *NDH*, 12 (1945), 111–134. See also Howard Lamar, *Dakota Territory 1861–1889* (New Haven, 1956) and "Carpetbaggers Full of Dreams: A Functional View of the Arizona Pioneer Politician," *AW*, 7 (1965), 187–206; Vincent G. Legeder, "Lincoln and the Territorial Patronage: The Ascendancy of the Radicals in the West," *MVHR*, 35 (1948–1949), 77–90; Lawrence R. Murphy, "Reconstruction in New Mexico," *MVHR*, 43 (1968), 99–115.

32. Robert J. Dwyer, *The Gentile Comes to Utah: A Study in Religious and Social Conflict* (Washington, 1941); *MP*, X, 4458.

ernment, and have made administrations responsible for evils they could not manage or remove."[33]

Congress's Joint Select Committee on Retrenchment, which functioned from 1867 to 1871, testified to the desire for economy and reduction in scale. The wartime tax structure was gradually dismantled. The federal inheritance tax ended in 1870, most sales and occupation taxes in 1871, the income tax (after 1867 and 1870 reductions) in 1872. A few officials—Treasury Secretary George S. Boutwell among them—opposed the repeal of the income tax, but they were rare. Most agreed with Thaddeus Stevens, who saw "no reason why a man should be punished in this way because he is rich." Horace Greeley opposed an income tax because it encouraged "a majority of the legal voters to authorize large expenditures for public enterprises of questionable merit."[34]

A revealing measure of the ultimate weakness of postwar government was the lack of strong federal control over the territories. Territorial administration languished under Interior secretaries more interested in party politics and patronage than in setting and implementing policy. The federal judicial system in the territories was slow to develop, and there was little national control of territorial expenditures.

Attempts have been made to equate American territorial government with imperialism and colonialism, but (except for the treatment of the Indians) they are not convincing. The facts of territorial life—the inexorable march to statehood, the lack of a numerically strong or culturally dominant native population—meant that the public life of the territories was intimately entwined with that of the nation at large. Territorial party politics quickly formed along national lines. Everywhere the first stage of control by federal appointees gave way to vigorous two-party conflict. The territorial parties vied with one another in calling for

33. John H. Soulé, The U.S. Blue Book, A Register of Federal Offices and Employment, 3d ed., (Washington, 1881); Adams, "The Session," NAR, 111 (1870), 60; Henry W. Bellows, Historical Sketch of the Union League Club of New York (New York, 1879), 109.

34. Elmer Ellis, "Public Opinion and the Income Tax, 1860–1900," MVHR, 27 (1940), 227–235; Stevens in U.S., CG, 38th Cong., 1st sess., House (April, 26, 1864), 1876; Greeley quoted in Sidney Ratner, American Taxation (New York, 1942), 112 ff. See also Harry E. Smith, The United States Federal Internal Tax History from 1861 to 1871 (Cambridge, 1914).

home rule and statehood; the 1884 Republican national platform declared that territorial officers should be residents of the lands they governed.[35]

Congress was the most important branch of the postwar national government. Grant explicitly conceded the policymaking supremacy of the legislature when he called the President a "purely administrative officer." Congressmen dominated the state and national party organizations; if they were Republicans they controlled the federal patronage.

Cabinet members and bureau chiefs had little discretion over the allocation of funds. The 1871 Appropriations Act for executive departments, the "high-water mark of congressional dictation by itemization," spread itself over twenty-one pages of the *United States Statutes.* This vigor appeared also in the sheer scope of congressional lawmaking. During the 1855–1865 decade an average of about 1,700 bills and resolutions was introduced in each Congress; about 430 became law. During the next ten years the average introduced was around 4,800, almost three times as many, and an average of 824 was passed. Postwar legislative activity reached its peak when the 42nd Congress (1871–1872) enacted 1,012 laws and resolutions.[36]

Congress's institutions matured as its work expanded. The *Congressional Globe,* a privately produced record of Senate and House proceedings published since 1833, gave way in December 1873 to a government document, the *Congressional Record.* An 1871 law codified the forms for drafting and enacting congressional bills. Guides and reference works multiplied. Edward McPherson, Clerk of the House from 1863 to 1875, published a compendious annual *Handbook of Politics* from 1868 to 1894, and newspaperman Benjamin Perley Poore compiled catalogues of public documents and edited an official *Congressional Directory* from 1865.

The postwar Congress paid special attention to the existing laws of the United States. It authorized consolidations of the federal

35. James E. Eblen, *The First and Second United States Empires: Governors and Territorial Government, 1784–1912* (Pittsburgh, 1968); William M. Neil, "The American Territorial System since the Civil War: A Summary Analysis," *IMH,* 60 (1964), 219–240.

36. White, *Republican Era,* 23; *HS,* 690. See also "Lobbying at Washington,"*ALR,* 9 (1874–1875), 696.

bankruptcy, pension, and postal service statutes. In 1870 three commissioners were entrusted with the codification of the entire body of federal laws, hopefully to create *"the starting-point, the mould, the type of all future national legislation."* Three years later they produced *The Revised Statutes of the United States*, a thousand-page monument to the belief that this was a watershed period in the history of American government.[37]

Congress sought also to systematize the manner in which its members were elected. An 1866 law laid down the rules governing the procedure whereby state legislatures chose United States senators. James G. Blaine called this a prime example of the postwar attitude that "everything which may be done by either nation or state may be better and more securely done by the nation." Congress in 1872 made the Tuesday after the first Monday in November the standard date for federal elections (except in Maine, whose constitution specified the second Monday in September). It required also that representatives be chosen by popular ballot, not by the state legislature.[38]

A similar desire for system and order led the postwar Congress to alter its internal organization. House Speakers Blaine (1869–1875) and Samuel J. Randall (1876–1881) made important changes in House procedure. In 1865 many of the fiscal responsibilities of the House Committee on Ways and Means were shifted to the Committee on Banking and Currency and the newly created Committee on Appropriations. A number of new committees were created: Coinage, Weights, and Measures (1864); Mines and Mining (1865); Pacific Railroads (1865); Education and Labor (1867); Revision of the Laws (1868); War Claims (1873); Expenditures in the Department of Justice (1874); Levees and Improvements of the Mississippi River (1875); Alcoholic Liquor Traffic (1879). Under the vigorous chairmanship of James A. Garfield (1871–1875), the House Appropriations Committee watched closely over departmental expenditures and determined congressional spending pol-

37. On drafting of bills, 41st Cong., 3d sess., ch. 71 (Feb. 25, 1871); *Revised Statutes*, 18 Stat. pts. 1, 2; "The Revision of the United States Statutes," *ALR*, 6 (1871–1872), 215.

38. James G. Blaine, *Twenty Years of Congress: From Lincoln to Garfield* (Norwich, Conn., 1886), II, 160; George H. Haynes, *The Senate of the United States: Its History and Practice* (Boston, 1938), I, 82 ff; Everett S. Brown, "Maine's Election Date," *APSR*, 29 (1935), 437–441.

icy. Key congressional functions now came under much more precise and sophisticated oversight than had been the case before.[39]

In 1880 the Committee on Rules became a standing rather than a select committee: part of a rise to dominance that reached its apogee in the late nineteenth century. The ascendancy of Rules over Appropriations in the hierarchy of House committees nicely symbolized the growth of tactical and organizational considerations in the work of Congress. That change was reflected too in the decline of legislation: from the postwar high of more than 1,000 acts in the 42d Congress (1871–1873) to an average of about 700 per Congress for the remainder of the seventies. Finally, Congress's power of investigation, an important instrument in the Reconstruction years, was restricted by the Supreme Court in Kilbourn v. Thompson (1881), which severely limited the power of the House to look into "the private affairs of individuals who hold no office under the government." When the young scholar Woodrow Wilson commented in 1879 on the "despotic authority" of Congress, it was the despotism of party—of patronage and corruption—and not of overweening legislative power that troubled him.[40]

Commonwealth and Municipality

The rise and fall of active government in the postwar years was not limited to the federal branch. State and local government, too, went through a cycle of expansion and contraction. State taxation and expenditure sharply increased in the Civil War decade: from three to six times in most northern commonwealths. Heavier spending went hand in hand with a dramatic rise in the sheer scale of state legislation. The Illinois legislature passed 392

39. M. F. Follett, *The Speakers of the House of Representatives* (New York, 1896), 100–101; Albert V. House, Jr., "The Contributions of Samuel J. Randall to the Rules of the National House of Representatives," *APSR*, 29 (1935), 837–841; George R. Brown, *The Leadership of Congress* (Indianapolis, 1922), 71–83; Lauros G. McConachie, *Congressional Committees* (New York, 1898); George B. Galloway, "Development of the Committee System in the House of Representatives," *AHR*, 65 (1959), 17–30.

40. Nelson W. Polsby, "The Institutionalization of the U.S. House of Representatives," *APSR*, 62 (1968), 146; Kilbourn v. Thompson, 103 U.S. 377 (1881); Thomas Woodrow Wilson, "Cabinet Government in the United States," *IR*, 7 (1879), 146–163.

public and private acts in 1859 and over 2,000 in 1869; Pennsylvania's total increased from 753 to more than 1,200. In New York hundreds of private or local bills came up as omnibus measures for a single—and invariably affirmative—vote.

A breakdown of Pennslyvania's 1872 laws throws light on the character of postwar northern state legislation. There were 214 authorizations to local governments to tax, borrow, build, and incorporate; 158 internal improvements acts; 270 acts of private incorporation; 81 laws dealing with education, charity, public health, and labor; and a scattering of statutes concerning the courts (37), elections (41), and government appointments (29). Private bills dealt with matters as precise and personal as divorces (11) and a change of name (1); one law enabled a married woman to buy a sewing machine without her husband's authorization.[41]

The postwar years saw much rewriting of northern state charters. Between 1864 and 1879, thirty-seven new state constitutions were written and ratified. In addition, practically every state considered (and often adopted) numerous constitutional amendments. There were two stages to the process of postwar constitutional revision. The first of these was an effort to bring state charters into accord with new attitudes toward government, race relations, and the like: "the work of the politics of the war" led to "great organic changes in all the old commonwealths." Then in the 1870s the main thrust was to put limits on legislative and other forms of governmental power.

The Michigan constitutional convention of 1867—a gathering authorized by a popular vote of four to one—suggests the tone of postwar northern constitutionmaking. Among the proposals considered by the delegates were an increase in the salaries of state officers, annual instead of biennial legislative sessions, four- instead of two-year terms for state senators, authorization for cities and

41. On expenditure increase, Clifton K. Yearley, The Money Machines: The Breakdown and Reform of Governmental and Party Finance in the North, 1860–1920 (Albany, 1970), 12; on state legislation, AC (1865) et passim; on New York omnibus bills, ALR, 1 (1867), 578–579; Acts of Pennsylvania (1872). See also Luther S. Cushing, Lex Parliamentaria Americana. Elements of the Law and Practice of the Legislative Assemblies in the United States of America, 2d ed. (Boston, 1863); Stefan A. Riesenfeld, "Law-Making and Legislative Precedent in American Legal History," MinnLR, 23 (1949), 103–144.

townships to borrow up to 10 percent of their assessed valuation for railroad aid, support for an agricultural college, the elimination of racial bars to voting and the affirmation of other civil rights, the prohibition of liquor sales, and women's suffrage. Similar provisions were considered—and some adopted—by constitutional conventions in New York (1867) and Ohio (1873). The 1871 Nebraska constitution provided for compulsory education, the taxation of church property, and local government aid to railroads. Even Delaware Republicans called—with little hope—for a new constitution in 1874 "as a means of securing the reforms that are so much needed in the organic law of the State, and of keeping pace with the enlightened progress of the age, and with our sister States."[42]

But voters rejected the new Michigan, New York, Ohio, and Nebraska constitutions. The ultimate thrust of constitutional revision after the Civil War was not to enhance the power of the state, but rather "a grand design to reduce the field of state law and withhold from it every subject which it is not necessary to concede." New and revised constitutions in the 1870s substantially reduced legislative authority. Illinois forbade its legislature to act in twenty items of local or private concern, Pennsylvania in forty, California in thirty-three. The areas enjoined covered a wide range of government functions: social (name changes, divorce, adoption, minors' rights, inheritance); economic (interest rates, tax exemption, special incorporation acts, local indebtedness); and political (county seats, town incorporation, the conduct of elections, the powers of local officials, grand juries, municipal improvements). The judiciary became the determining authority in most of these instances. A number of states also gave their governors the power to veto specific items in appropriations bills, lengthened guberna-

42. Quotations from Simeon E. Baldwin, "Recent Changes in Our State Constitutions," JSS, 9 (1879), 136, Galaxy, 4 (1867), 371–372; Harriette M. Dilla, The Politics of Michigan 1865–1878 (New York, 1912), 75–91; Charles Z. Lincoln, The Constitutional History of New York (Rochester, 1906), II, 241 ff; James C. Mohr, The Radical Republicans and Reform in New York during Reconstruction (Ithaca, 1973), ch. 7; Ruth M. Stanley, "N. K. Griggs and the Nebraska Constitutional Convention of 1871," NH, 46 (1965), 39–65; "Delaware," AC (1874). See also John A. Jameson, The Constitutional Convention: Its History, Powers, and Modes of Proceeding (New York, 1867).

torial terms, and widened executive discretion in matters such as criminal pardons and claims against the state.[43]

The pacesetting Illinois constitution of 1870 abounded "in negative rather than positive provisions, provisions rather calculated to hedge in powers which have been abused than to establish new ones." With an attention to detail more appropriate to a code than a constitution, Illinois's new charter took up fifty printed pages, and descended to such specifics as forbidding the covert mixing of two grades of grain in the same elevator.

A wide-ranging coalition lay behind the similar Pennsylvania constitution of 1873. Business, agricultural, and political interests were unhappy with the wave of particularistic laws emerging from the postwar legislature and with the growing power of the Pennsylvania Railroad and Simon Cameron's Republican machine. Pittsburgh Republicans wanted general incorporation laws and railroad regulation; the Philadelphia Union League sought checks on the cost and corruption of government; Republicans from Democratic counties favored proportional representation in local offices. They joined with Democrats to secure a charter whose primary purpose was to constrain legislative activism.[44]

The California constitution of 1879 was the most extreme northern reaction to postwar public policy. It was drafted by a convention dominated by Democrats and Dennis Kearney's Workingman's party—and by farmer-labor discontent fed by the depression of the 1870s. The constitution subjected banks, railroads, and mining companies to stringent taxation and regulation; it included severe anti-Chinese provisions; state aid was limited to

43. Baldwin, "Recent Changes," 140; ALR, 5 (1870–1871), 110–112; Henry Reed, "Some Late Efforts at Constitutional Reform," NAR, 121 (1875), 1–36; James Q. Dealey, Growth of American State Constitutions (Boston, 1915), 71–88; James Schouler, Constitutional Studies, State and Federal (New York, 1897), 264–265 ff; Charles C. Binney, Restrictions upon Local and Special Legislation in State Constitutions (Philadelphia, 1894), 130.

44. On Illinois, ALR, 5 (1870–1871), 110–112; Mahlon H. Hellerich, "The Origin of the Pennsylvania Constitutional Convention of 1873," PH, 34 (1967), 158–186, and "Railroad Regulation in the Constitutional Convention of 1873," PH, 26 (1959), 35–53; William A. Russ, "The Origin of the Ban on Special Legislation in the Constitution of 1873," PH, 11 (1944), 260–275.

primary schools (there was even some sentiment in the convention to prohibit public secondary schools); a free textbook provision failed to pass. So strong was the sentiment against legislative activism that a Workingman's party delegate proposed an article declaring: "There shall be no legislature convened from and after the adoption of this Constitution, . . . and any person who shall be guilty of suggesting that a Legislature be held, shall be punished as a felon without the benefit of clergy."[45]

State government during the 1870s shrank in practice as well as principle. Everywhere the scope and quantity of lawmaking declined as constitutional and popular constraints took hold. Pennsylvania and Illinois statutes abruptly fell from over a thousand to fewer than a hundred per session. The Maine legislature passed less than half as many laws during the late seventies as in the decade's early years; Vermont's lawmakers passed a third as many.

State budgets, debts, and taxes similarly declined. New York's indebtedness was $51,800,000 in 1866, $9,200,000 in 1877. So strong was the popular sentiment against direct state taxes in Pennsylvania that by 1878 almost the entire revenue of the commonwealth came from a tax on corporations. Everywhere the tax system was riddled with loopholes and inequities. But reform efforts such as New York's Tax Commission of 1870–1871 got nowhere. By the end of the seventies taxation was as localized and ineffective as were most instruments of American government.

State government entered into a period of atrophy that did not end until the last years of the century. "Legislatures," said one observer, "have ceased to create or concentrate public sentiment; they have become clearing houses for the adjustment of claims." The depression of the 1870s contributed substantially to this development, as did the growing number of state Democratic administrations. And behind these economic and political reasons was a localism and hostility to government that worked against the active state in the North as in the South.[46]

45. Carl B. Swisher, *Motivation and Political Technique in the California Constitutional Convention, 1878–79* (Claremont, Calif., 1930); Noel Sargent, "The California Constitutional Convention of 1878–9," *CalLR*, 6 (1917), 12.

46. "Maine," *AC* (1878); "Vermont," *AC* (1874); "Pennsylvania," *AC* (1878); B. U. Ratchford, *American State Debts* (Durham, 1941), 249, 256; Yearley, *Money Machines*, 6, 172–174; Albert B. Hart, "Growth of American Theories of Popular Government," *APSR*, 1 (1907), 555.

It is difficult to sum up the governmental experience of the thousands of townships, villages, cities, and counties in post-Civil War America. But there were structural uniformities that imposed some patterns. All urban places and many minor civil divisions had state charters; they were in fact municipal corporations and thus subject to legislative and judicial supervision. The New England township and the Virginia county were prototypes for local government in the regional flows of westward settlement. And in the postwar years county and municipal governments no less than their state and federal counterparts were caught up in the tension between war-born centralization and activism on the one hand, and deeply ingrained localism and laissez-faire on the other.[47]

Much of the state legislation that flowed so freely after the war fostered more active local government. Counties, townships, and municipalities subsidized railroads and street railways on a grand scale; towns and cities added to their streets, sewers, schools, and public relief; minor civil divisions elaborated upon an already complex structure of government. The New York legislature between 1867 and 1870 passed more municipal laws than did the British Parliament from 1835 to 1888. When a legislative committee consolidated New York City's statutes in 1882, the result was a seven hundred-page document, longer than the Civil Code of France. John F. Dillon's majestic treatise, *Commentaries on the Law of Municipal Corporations*, appeared in 1872 as a guide to the labyrinthine law that defined the corporate functions of towns and cities. "We have popularized and made use of municipal institutions to such an extent," Dillon observed, "as to constitute one of the most striking features of our government."[48]

Another measure of the quickened pace of local government was the expansion of its debt. In 1861 the nation's townships, villages, cities, and counties had obligations of about one hundred million dollars; in 1870 over five hundred million; in 1880—

47. Albert Shaw, "Local Government in America," *FRev*, 32 (1882), 485–495; John A. Fairlie, *Local Government in Counties, Towns and Villages* (New York, 1906); Herman G. James, *Local Government in the United States* (New York, 1928).

48. On New York legislature, Ernest S. Griffith, *The Modern Development of City Government in the United Kingdom and the United States*, 2 vols. (Oxford, 1927), I, 22n–23n; John A. Fairlie, *Municipal Administration* (New York, 1901), 86 ff; Dillon, *Municipal Corporations*, 4th ed. (Boston, 1890), xi.

TABLE 2. Percentage increases in the population, valuation, taxation, and indebtedness of selected cities, 1860–1875

City	Population	Valuation	Taxation	Indebtedness
Baltimore	63.6	68.4	110.4	83.9
Boston	37.9	148.6	241.2	298.9
Brooklyn	82.7	114.1	313.4	356.9
Chicago	261.9	720.7	1445.6	487.3
Cincinnati	71.3	95.5	377.5	300.8
Detroit	122.0	147.5	384.8	139.8
Louisville	83.7	162.8	318.9	86.3
Milwaukee	123.2	315.1	326.6	127.1
Newark	65.2	251.5	558.8	2658.2
New York	28.5	100.2	430.9	504.1
Philadelphia	30.6	207.2	317.8	152.3
Providence	98.7	99.8	443.3	529.8
St. Louis	183.7	174.8	301.9	257.4
San Francisco	377.5	609.9	538.2	45.8

Source: Simon Sterne, "The Administration of American Cities," IR, 4 (1877), 640.

despite the pressure for reduction in the seventies—over eight hundred million. Elizabeth, New Jersey in 1879 carried a debt that was one half of the city's assessed valuation. Municipal debt and taxation in the postwar decade substantially outstripped other indices of growth (table 2).[49]

In one sense this spending was apolitical: the lure of public improvements (and private profits) transcended party and ideological lines. But the issues that pervaded the other sectors of the postwar polity appeared in municipal affairs as well.

A case in point was the metropolitan commission movement. Before the Civil War, New York's Republican legislature assumed control over the police commissioners of Democratic New York City. In 1866 it created a Metropolitan Fire District and the nation's first Metropolitan Board of Health: both run by the state rather than the city government. By the late 1860s the City Council

49. "City Debt," NJLJ, (1879), 90–92. See also Henry C. Adams, Public Debts: An Essay in the Science of Finance (New York, 1887), 343–346.

controlled less than a sixth of New York's municipal expenditures.

Postwar legislatures imposed state-run police commissioners on a number of other cities: Detroit (1865), Cleveland (1866), New Orleans (1868), Kansas City (1874). Massachusetts's Republican legislature set up boards of street, health, fire, and parks commissioners for Democratic Boston. The 1870 Pennsylvania legislature created a state committee to oversee the construction of Philadelphia's new city hall. New Jersey's 1866 Republican legislature put the Jersey City police under the control of a state commission. Democratic city officials refused to accept the arrangement; and for a time two hostile police forces confronted each other, at the cost of much civic disorder.

In other ways, too, state legislatures tightened their control over the cities. Municipal codes designed to increase state authority over urban affairs by ending special or local legislation were enacted in Ohio (1869), Pennsylvania (1874), and Illinois (1875). Restrictions on municipal debt became common in the seventies, usually setting a limit of 5 percent of assessed property valuation.

Closely related was the postwar effort of professionals, businessmen, and civic reformers to centralize city government and thus lessen the power of local politicians. The schools were a special object of concern: ward or other neighborhood trustees often controlled texts, teachers, and expenditures. By 1870 every large city except Philadelphia had a superintendent of schools, although local trustee and political power remained stubbornly resistant to consolidation.[50]

The clash between state-run or citywide instruments of government and local control was ideological as well as political. Advocates of metropolitan commissions dwelt on the need to bring efficiency, intelligence, and expertise to the business of running a city. Henry Bellows of the wartime Sanitary Commission explained the rationale for New York City's Board of Health: "The general ob-

50. Griffith, *Modern Development*, I, 23–24; Fairlie, *Municipal Administration*, 86–90; Raymond B. Fosdick, *American Police Systems* (New York, 1921), 77–96; James Richardson, *The New York Police* (New York, 1970), chs. 5–7; William R. Grace, "The Government of Cities in the State of New York," *HM*, 67 (1883), 609–616; on Jersey City police, Pangbourn v. Young, 32 N.J. Rep. 29 (1866). See also Jon Teaford, "City versus State: The Struggle for Legal Ascendancy," *AJLH*, 17 (1973), 51–65.

ject was to secure an improved and efficient sanitary system for New York City and vicinity by putting responsibility and power into the hands of a Board, free from political influence and directed by adequate scientific skill and executive ability." *Nation* editor E. L. Godkin called commission government "the next great political revolution in the western world," one that "will place men's relations in society where they never yet have been placed, under the control of trained human reason." The civil service reformer Simon Sterne wanted New York's Board of Aldermen to represent those portions of the community "having intellectual affinities, instead of mere geographical propinquity." His fellow reformer Dorman B. Eaton argued for citywide rather than district voting for city offices:

> A little man seems large enough for a little district ... All the elements and agencies of reform are opposed to the influence of the small district system ... They appeal to that high and instructed public opinion which scorns partisan and small caucus's manipulation, which rests on principle, which speaks through the public press, which demands that the interests of the city shall be comprehended and represented as a whole.

Charles Francis Adams, Jr., discussing Boston's government in 1868, stressed the need for "a System,—a plan with an end, and a concentration of energies to that end." This was no easy thing to attain in America, but "concentration of thought, permanence of system, and broadness of view, the virtues of centralized governments, must, by some device, be infused into democracies ... centralization is necessary; diffusion insures failure." In a similar spirit Frederick Law Olmsted expected his great creation Central Park to exert a "harmonizing and refining" influence on New York's lower classes; and Comptroller Andrew Green wanted large-scale planning in the development of New York's upper West Side.[51]

This perspective was reinforced by the urban problems of the

51. Bellows, *Union League Club*, 90; E. L. Godkin, "The Prospects of the Political Art," *NAR*, 110 (1870), 417, and "Legislation and Social Science," *JSS*, 3 (1871), 115–132; Simon Sterne, "The Administration of American Cities," *IR*, 4 (1877), 642; Eaton, "Municipal Government," *JSS*, 5 (1873), 19–20; Charles F. Adams, Jr., "Boston," *NAR*, 106 (1868), 15; Olmsted, "Public Parks and the Enlargement of Towns," *JSS*, 3 (1871), 34; Seymour J. Mandelbaum, *Boss Tweed's New York* (New York, 1965), 60 ff.

seventies. The inability of city government to cope with disasters such as the Chicago fire of 1871 and the Boston fire of 1873; the continuing influx of immigrants; the labor unrest and human suffering of the depression years after 1873; the growing power of city machines: all added to a sense of urban crisis that would be part of the reformer mentality for a century to come. It led to a continuing stress on efficiency, centralization, and government by educated professionals; to what the sociologist Scott Greer has called "the Morality Plays of American Civic Life": elaborate and usually short-lived attempts at civic purification by the educated and the affluent.[52]

The analogue of the municipal with the private corporation attracted those who wished to take politics out of civic affairs. Dorman B. Eaton warned: "We shall never govern a great city well or rightly comprehend it, until we consider its administration as involving a large amount of business done by businessmen, rather than a large mass of politics to be managed by partisans." Simon Sterne argued that "a city is not a government, but a corporative administration of property interests in which property should have a leading voice." James A. Garfield opposed universal suffrage in the cities, where the poor outvoted the propertied: "In all other business corporations, the member votes in proportion to the amount of his stock."[53]

In the mid-seventies New York Governor Samuel J. Tilden appointed a commission to study the "decay of municipal government" in the state. William M. Evarts, a distinguished Republican lawyer soon to be secretary of state, headed the group; Godkin and Sterne were among its members. The commission's 1877 report assaulted the existing system of urban politics, equated municipal with business corporations, criticized the profligate spending of the city machines, and proposed that a Board of Finance, elected by rent and tax payers, be empowered to determine city taxation and expenditure. But these proposals got nowhere. Neither the post-

52. A. P. Peabody, "Fires in American Cities," *IR*, 1 (1874), 17–34; James M. Bugbee, "Fires and Fire Departments," *NAR*, 117 (1873), 108–141; Scott Greer, *Metropolitics: A Study of Political Culture* (New York, 1963).

53. Eaton, "Municipal Government," 10; Sterne, "Administration of American Cities," 635; Mary L. Hinsdale, ed., *Garfield-Hinsdale Letters* (Ann Arbor, 1949), 314.

war stress on state control nor the civic reformer goal of elite, efficient, economy-minded rule was destined to shape the character of late nineteenth century American urban government.[54]

The cities no less than other areas of the polity turned away during the 1870s from the government centralism and activism of the war period. New "home rule" charters designed to reduce state authority were secured by a number of municipalities. This was a cause to which city machines fighting Republican legislative domination and civic reformers fearful of legislative extravagance repaired with equal enthusiasm. Business and professional leaders joined with boss Tweed to support a home rule charter for New York City in 1870.

Democratic electoral victories in the seventies led often to the abolition of state boards and commissions. And the courts, increasingly hostile to active (and independent) government agencies, lent their support. Influential decisions by Thomas M. Cooley and James V. Campbell of the Michigan Supreme Court severely limited the powers of Detroit's state-controlled Water and Park Commissions.[55]

The machine politicians understood better than the municipal reformers that cities were a congeries of neighborhoods, classes, and interests, and that government had to reflect this social reality. But they were not better equipped to cope with the problems posed by the tumultuous growth and the social disorder of American urban life. Housing, welfare, urban development, harbor use were all but untouched by public policy.

An unmanageable social complexity bred an unmanageable political complexity. Elaborate, unwieldy systems of patronage were necessary to the survival of political machines. Tweed's Tammany had an estimated 60,000 jobs to dispose of; there were 12-15,000 city employees in Philadelphia during the late seventies, serving the needs of the machine more than of the city. The consequence was high and rising urban budgets, often spectacular

54. Yearley, *Money Machines*, 129; Mandelbaum, *Boss Tweed's New York*, 129–130, ff. See also David A. Wells, "The Reform of Local Taxation," *NAR*, 122 (1876), 357–403.

55. On home rule, Griffith, *Modern Development*, II, 23, 106, Fairlie, *Municipal Administration*, 92 ff, Dillon, *Municipal Corporations*, I, 24–25; People v. Hurlbut, 24 Mich. 44 (1871), People v. Detroit, 28 Mich. 228 (1873).

corruption, and continuing conflict between reformers and politicos, between taxpayers and the poor.

The condition of city government was aptly summarized in 1877 by newspaper editor Samuel Bowles: "In this extreme of individuality, this cutting up of representative government into local bits, with its accompanying multiplication of organization and expenditure, the fundamental weakness of our modern municipal system may fairly be said to lie." Much the same could be said of the polity at large. New paths in postwar foreign affairs and in federal, state, and local government turned out to be cul-de-sacs, not the road of the future. From the war years there emerged not a Bismarckian state but rather what Leonard White has called "the culmination of Jacksonian theory and practice": a system of government dominated by localism and laissez-faire.[56]

56. Mandelbaum, *Boss Tweed's New York*, passim; Alexander B. Callow, Jr., *The Tweed Ring* (New York, 1966); Thomas H. Speakman, *The People versus the Politicians* [Philadelphia, 1878]; Samuel Bowles, "The Relations of State and Municipal Government and the Reform of the Latter," *JSS*, 9 (1878), 140–141; White, *Republican Era*, viii.

CHAPTER 4

The Quest for a Good Society

THE TRAUMATIC EVENTS of the 1860s reinforced an old American inclination to look to the state for social reform. Through the first half of the nineteenth century, government dealt with the sale and consumption of liquor; the status of aliens and Catholics; the care of the sick, the insane, and the criminal; the rights of women; the problem of slavery. Pre-Civil War social reform had deep roots in an evangelical Protestantism that identified salvation with the removal of sin from the world. This view was strengthened by the belief that a democratic society had the authority—and the capacity—to deal with mankind's ills. The Civil War schooled a generation in the uses of government power to effect social change and in the ideal of civil equality.

A powerful set of beliefs thus fueled social reform in postwar America. But the urge to transform society was tempered by comparably potent social values: racism, localism, hostility to active government, a growing fear of social change itself. As a result, postwar social policy went through a sequence of action and reaction that was part of the larger experience of the postwar American polity.

Good Works and Social Control

Science, system, organization: these concepts had an important place in postwar social thought. In 1865 the American Social

Science Association, modeled on an English prototype, came into being. The new organization made education, health ("Sanitary Reform"), economics ("Social Economy"), and jurisprudence its chief areas of concern. It sought to be not only a deliberative body but one that shaped public policy; and it attracted men of energy, ability, and public influence. Henry Villard, its first secretary, had a notable wartime career as a journalist, and would later be the organizer of the Northern Pacific Railroad. Frank B. Sanborn, who ran the Association through the late nineteenth century, was a former abolitionist, amateur social scientist, and professional reformer. He was joined by the economist-bureaucrats David Ames Wells, Carroll D. Wright, and Francis A. Walker, who emerged from the war with a strong belief in the capacity of social science and active government to effect social change. Many of the most prominent politicians of the day lent their names to this attempt to apply science, organization, and expertise to reform. John Stuart Mill, active in the British Association for the Promotion of Social Science, told the American group in 1870:

> reason and right feeling on any public subject has a better chance of being favourably listened to, and of finding the national mind open to comprehend it, than at any previous time in American history. This great benefit will probably not last out the generation which fought in the war; and all depends on making the utmost use of it, for good purposes, before the national mind has time to get crusted over with any fresh set of prejudices.

The economist David Ames Wells observed in 1875: "never before in the history of our country has so much attention been given to the investigation and comprehension of the principles which underlie human society, and the application of which tends to ameliorate the condition of mankind."[1]

The prospect for an organized approach to social problems was particularly promising in the field of public health. After years of pressure by prominent citizens, New York City's pioneering

1. Henry Villard, "Historical Sketch of Social Science," *JSS*, 1 (1869), 5–10; Luther Lee Bernard and Jessie Bernard, *Origins of American Sociology: The Social Science Movement in the United States* (New York, 1943), 527 ff; Harold M. Hyman, *A More Perfect Union: The Impact of the Civil*

Metropolitan Sanitary District and Board of Health were created in 1866. The board's immediate success in holding down a cholera epidemic encouraged other states to follow New York's lead. The Ohio legislature in 1867 established boards of health in the state's cities; state boards appeared in Massachusetts (1869), Minnesota (1872), Michigan (1873), and other commonwealths. Congress in 1866 considered giving the secretary of war the authority to enforce quarantines at ports of entry and, if necessary, to set up internal sanitary cordons. The states substantially increased their hospital and public welfare appropriations. Iowa, for example, spent $210,000 for this purpose in 1859–1861 and $1,240,000 ten years later; Ohio's human services expenditures went from $290,665 in 1860 to $997,552 in 1870: this in a decade when the price index rose by about 50 percent.[2]

Similar attitudes and actions affected the treatment of the poor. New York City had a Board of Charity in 1860, and in 1863 Massachusetts created the first state board. A number of states followed suit during the remainder of the decade. Most states spent twice as much money to aid paupers in 1870 as they did ten years before. The guiding spirit of the Massachusetts Board of Charity was Samuel Gridley Howe, longtime benefactor of the poor and the blind and during the war an active member of the United States

War and Reconstruction on the Constitution (New York, 1973), ch. 18; Mill in *JSS*, 5 (1873), 138; public letter by Wells, June 26, 1875, Wells Mss, NYPL. On prewar reform see John L. Thomas, "Romantic Reform in America, 1815–1865," *AQ*, 17 (1965), 656–681; Clifford S. Griffin, "Religious Benevolence as Social Control, 1815–1860," *MVHR*, 44 (1957), 423–444. See also Mary O. Furner, *Advocacy & Objectivity: A Crisis in the Professionalization of American Social Science, 1865–1905* (Lexington, Ky., 1975), ch. 1.

2. Edward R. Dalton, "The Metropolitan Board of Health of New York," *NAR*, 106 (1868), 351–375; Charles E. Rosenberg, *The Cholera Years: The United States in 1832, 1849, and 1866* (Chicago, 1962), 187; James C. Mohr, *The Radical Republicans and Reform in New York During Reconstruction* (Ithaca, 1973), chs. 3–4; John Duffy, *A History of Public Health in New York City 1625–1866* (New York, 1968), 540 ff; "Ohio," *AC* (1867); Michael L. Benedict, "Contagion and the Constitution: Quarantine Agitation from 1859–1866," *JHM*, 25 (1970), 177–193; Ivan L. Pollock, "State Finances in Iowa during the Civil War," *IJH*, 16 (1918), 53–107; Ernest L. Bogart, *Financial History of Ohio* (Urbana-Champaign, 1912), 136–138. See also Harold D. Kramer, "Effect of the Civil War on the Public Health Movement," *MVHR*, 35 (1948–1949), 449–462; Hyman, *More Perfect Union*, ch. 19.

Sanitary Commission. Howe set down the assumptions that governed the work of his board: "the existence of whole classes of defectives, of paupers, and of criminals is not among the essentials, but the accidents of a highly civilized state; ... the number and condition of those classes is largely under human control." The board's reports paid relatively little attention to the moral improvement of the poor, a common prewar concern. It concentrated instead on the prevention, correction, and social sources of poverty and crime.[3]

A continuum of social attitudes linked handling of criminals with care for the sick and the poor. If crime was a product of the "disharmony" of social forces, it was as remediable as slavery, intemperance, disease, or poverty. In Massachusetts, Michigan, and other states, charity boards supervised prisons as well. Michigan's governor in 1873 blamed crime on pauperism, and stressed the need for reformation rather than corporal punishment. Crime would diminish, it was thought, with "the harmonizing of labor and capital; compulsory education; legislative control of the idle, the vagrant, and the helpless; a prompt and rigid prosecution and punishment of the capitalists and caterers of crime, and an enlarged and enlightened application of the law of kindness to prison discipline." Democratic leader Horatio Seymour declared that criminals "are men who in a great degree are moved and directed by the impulses around them. It is a hard thing to draw an indictment against a criminal which is not in some respects an indictment of the community in which he has lived."[4]

The National Prison Association, designed to encourage more

3. F. B. Sanborn, "Poverty and Public Charity," *NAR*, 110 (1870), 349; Howe in Massachusetts State Board of Charity, *2nd Annual Report* (1866), xi, xiii, xxii–xxiii, xxxii. See also Sanborn, "The Poor Laws of New England," *NAR*, 106 (1868), 484–514; Theodore D. Dwight, "The Public Charities of the State of New York," *JSS*, 2 (1870), 69–91. For comparable currents in the care of the insane see William A. Hammond, "The Treatment of the Insane," *IR*, 8 (1880), 225–241, and John Ordronaux, *Commentaries on the Lunacy Laws of New York, and on the Judicial Aspects of Insanity at Common Law and in Equity* (Albany, 1878), vi; Gerald N. Grob, *Mental Institutions in America: Social Policy to 1875* (New York, 1973), chs. 7–8.

4. *Pauperism and Crime in Michigan in 1872–1873. Message of Gov. John J. Bagley, and Official Reports and Documents* (Lansing, 1873); quotation from J. B. Bittinger, "Responsibility of Society for the Causes of Crime," *PR*, 43 (1871), 36; Seymour, "On the Causes of Crime," *ALRec*, 1

professional management of penal institutions, was organized in 1870. Postwar state and county prisons were the subjects of frequent investigation—most notably by commissioners of the New York Prison Association, who in 1866 looked into the penal systems of eighteen states. No subject was more important, they declared, "in all the wide range of social science, in all the varied fields of inquiry which commend the study of the friends of human happiness and progress."

Various states instituted procedural reforms in the handling of criminals. Illinois in 1869 designated youthful offenders wards of the court, and assigned to specific courts the task of dealing with them. As many juvenile reformatories—institutions designed to separate youthful offenders from older criminals—were built between 1865 and 1875 as in the previous history of the nation. A prewar movement to end capital punishment revived after 1865. Illinois (1867) and Iowa (1870) abolished the death penalty; New York (1873) made it more difficult for juries to find for murder in the first degree; Ohio (1875) specified that if an inquest found a convicted murderer to be insane, the death sentence could not be imposed.[5]

American social reform always was the product of a complex mix of often conflicting desires: to create a new society, to preserve the existing one, to recapture a utopian past. The postwar years were no exception.

The belief that American society was threatened by unwanted

(1872–1873), 538. See also Ellen E. Guillot, *Social Factors in Crime as Explained by American Writers of the Civil War and Post Civil War Period* (Philadelphia, 1943), and Blake McKelvey, *American Prisons: A Study in American Social History Prior to 1915* (Chicago, 1936), 53–71.

5. Enoch C. Wines and Theodore W. Dwight, *Report on the Prisons and Reformatories of the United States and Canada, Made to the Legislature of New York, January, 1867* (Albany, 1867), 49; on Illinois, James W. Hurst, *The Growth of American Law: The Law Makers* (Boston, 1950), 155; S. J. Burrows, ed., *The Reformatory System of the United States* (Washington, 1900), 277–278; David B. Davis, "The Movement to Abolish Capital Punishment in America, 1787–1861," *AHR*, 63 (1957), 23–46; "Ohio," *AC* (1875). See also E. S. Nadel, "The Rationale of the Opposition to Capital Punishment," *NAR*, 116 (1873), 138–150; F. B. Sanborn, "American Prisons," *NAR*, 103 (1866), 383–412; "The Reformation of Prison Discipline," *NAR*, 105 (1867), 555–591; Roscoe Pound, *Criminal Justice in America* (New York, 1930), 158–162.

change, and that a prime function of government was to maintain the status quo, intertwined with more forward-looking postwar social attitudes. New York City's Board of Health came into being in part because the 1863 draft riots revealed to a shocked middle class the poverty and unrest fermenting in the Irish slum population. The American Social Science Association espoused "a science conservative of all that is now good in social life, . . . repressing the evils which now exist, . . . adding stability to the rights of labor and property, stimulating a healthy individual ambition, promoting a pure morality."

Events in the 1870s gave protection of a threatened social order precedence over the hope of creating a new one. The Paris Commune of 1871; the unemployment and labor unrest of the 1873–1878 depression; extensive political corruption; widely publicized scandals such as the Beecher-Tilton affair, in which the country's best-known preacher stood trial for adultery: all reinforced the notion that restoration, not change, should be the primary purpose of social policy.[6]

The traditional view of the poor—that they had their own failings to blame for their condition, that charity too readily bestowed sapped the morality of the recipient—overrode more sympathetic attitudes. Charles Loring Brace, a pioneer in providing aid for homeless children, called the idea that the poor had a right to charity a "communistic impression." *Nation* editor E. L. Godkin had similar reservations: "Hospitals, almshouses, and asylums for the poor and infirm are among the marks of a superior civilization . . . but it cannot be said that society owes even these to its weaker members."[7]

Similar attitudes strangled prison reform. The crime rate appeared to be on the increase in the postwar years. Rehabilitation and prison reform gave way to harsher treatment of tramps,

6. On New York Board of Health, Duffy, *Public Health,* 552; "Introductory Note," *JSS,* I (1869), 7; William Strong, "The Study of Social Science," *JSS,* 4 (1871), 1–7; on Commune, "Paris Under the Commune," *PR,* ns, 1 (1872), 115–136, D. A. Wasson, "The International," *JSS,* 5 (1873), 109–121, Samuel Bernstein, "The Impact of the Paris Commune in the United States," *MR,* 12 (1971), 435–446.

7. Brace, "Pauperism," *NAR,* 120 (1875), 316; Godkin quoted in Ernest Samuels, *Henry Adams: The Middle Years* (Cambridge, 1958), II, 19. See also Marvin Gettleman, "Charity and Social Classes in the United States, 1874–1900," *AJES,* 22 (1963), 313–329, 417–426.

vagrants, and other offenders. An attempt to abolish the use of the gag in Massachusetts prisons failed in 1878; and Iowa restored capital punishment for first degree murder. Almost all state legislatures in the mid-seventies modified the criminal law to make a witness's interest in the case no ground for objecting to his competency. At the same time prisons, like other public institutions, suffered severely from reduced government expenditures.[8]

What Georges Clemenceau called the strain of "Puritan intolerance" in American life fed postwar attempts (which became far more extensive later in the century) to restrict social behavior. Michigan and Ohio prescribed prison terms for prizefighters. Antilottery legislation was passed by the federal government (1868, 1876) and by California (1872). An 1873 congressional act tightened Post Office control over the mailing of obscene publications and contraceptive devices, thereby marking the entry of that pioneer professional moralist Anthony Comstock into the singular world of purity reform. Comstock's New York Society for the Suppression of Vice was active in the 1870s, and under pressure from the Massachusetts branch of the Society, Massachusetts and Connecticut in 1879 passed laws forbidding the dissemination of birth control implements.[9]

It is not surprising that temperance and prohibition were the reform issues that made the most insistent claim on the postwar American polity. The attempt to reduce the alcoholic consumption of the American people had been an important prewar reform. Fourteen states passed regulatory or prohibitory laws between 1851

8. James H. Kettner, "The Civil War and Crime: American Attitudes toward War Demoralization," senior thesis, Harvard University, 1966; "Massachusetts," AC (1878); "Iowa," AC (1878); H. S. K., "The Defendant as a Witness in Criminal Cases," CLJ, 5 (1877), 399–400. See also "Justice and Magistracy in the United States," LT, 50 (1871), 496, and "The Criminals and the Law," Nation, 8 (1869), 106–108, for accusations of leniency in the treatment of criminals. The costs of criminal prosecution in one Iowa county increased from $133,846.38 in 1874 to $401,659.39 in 1879. ALR, 14 (1880), 150.

9. Georges Clemenceau, American Reconstruction (New York, 1918), 97; "Michigan," AC (1869); "Ohio," AC (1868); John S. Ezell, Fortune's Merry Wheel: The Lottery in America (Cambridge, 1960), 234–241; Anthony Comstock, Traps for the Young, ed. Robert H. Bremner (1883; Cambridge, 1967); Carol F. Brooks, "The Early History of Anti-Contraceptive Laws in Massachusetts and Connecticut," AQ, 18 (1966), 3–23. See also "Obscene Literature," ALJ, 12 (1875), 37–38; "Sexual Litigation," ALJ, 14 (1876), 384–385.

and 1855, until the antislavery movement and the struggle to preserve the Union turned attention elsewhere. But the tensions and social laxity of the war years appeared to increase liquor consumption; and the 1862 Internal Revenue Act, which licensed and taxed the liquor industry, bolstered the respectability of that enterprise.

The National Temperance Society, organized in 1865, sought to purify further a Republic cleansed of slavery and secession. "The abolition of slavery and the preservation of our Union having been accomplished," Massachusetts prohibitionists announced, "there is no issue now before the country equal to that of prohibition." Maine, Massachusetts, and Rhode Island established state constabularies—the first state police—to provide quasi-military enforcement of their prewar prohibition laws. The Massachusetts Constabulary Act of 1865 came after legislative hearings in which local resistance to prohibition was compared to southern secession. The creation of a state constabulary reflected also a widespread distrust of the cities—"the common sewers of the states"—whose police were supinely subject "to the lawlessness of the mob and the will of the populace." Massachusetts's constabulary was composed of Union army veterans, and its activities were described in a terminology—"raids," "troops," "assaults," "skirmish lines"—drawn from the battlefield. This legion of morality mounted 630 forays in Suffolk County (Boston) alone in 1867; its spoils of war were 100,000 gallons of liquor.[10]

Postwar legislatures frequently sought to limit the sale and consumption of alcohol. Typically, Pennsylvania in 1867 prohibited saloons from staying open after midnight or selling to minors or habitual drunkards. The New York Excise Law of 1866 forbade Sunday liquor sales and set up a state licensing system. Wisconsin's Graham Law of 1872 licensed the sale of liquor, made intoxication an offense, and penalized those responsible for a customer's drunkenness—a provision adopted by a number of other states as well.

The judiciary upheld these controls. The Supreme Court decided that liquor dealers were not protected from prohibition legislation

10. John A. Krout, *The Origins of Prohibition* (New York, 1925); "Massachusetts," *AC* (1870); on Massachusetts constabulary, ibid. (1865–1871), Roger Lane, *Policing the City: Boston, 1822–1885* (Cambridge, 1967), 130–139.

by the contract clause of the Constitution and rejected a similar appeal to the privileges and immunities clause of the Fourteenth Amendment.[11]

But varying religious and cultural beliefs, localism, and hostility to active government worked against restrictive social regulation. The attempt to pass a national quarantine law was blocked by a coalition of state and local boards of health and congressmen hostile to increased federal power. A "Social Evil Ordinance" enacted in 1871 provided for the medical inspection of St. Louis prostitutes. But the Missouri legislature, responding to widespread protests against condoning vice, ended this experiment in 1874. Antiprohibitionists championed "personal liberty against fanatical intermeddling" and warned of the "menacing attitude of temperance and Sabbatarian fanatics." John A. Andrew, wartime governor of Massachusetts and an advocate of a conciliatory Reconstruction policy, passionately denied *"the right of government . . . to pass into the domestic and private sphere."*[12]

Opposition to prohibition and other forms of social control had considerable political potency, even in the high noon of postwar Republicanism. An antiprohibition People's party appeared in Iowa in 1867, and Kansas Germans in the same year organized politically against Sabbatarian and prohibition legislation. A People's party slate opposed to the enforcement of Sunday laws swept Chicago in 1873, and at a Milwaukee convention the American Constitutional Union spoke out against the regulation of social habits.

The Democratic party recovered rapidly in the postwar North as in the South by capitalizing on this sentiment. Democratic victories in the mid-seventies led to the repeal of antiliquor legislation

11. *AC*, states and years cited; Thomas M. Cooley, *A Treatise on the Law of Torts*, 2d ed. (Chicago, 1888), 241–262; Beer Co. v. Mass., 97 U.S. 989 (1878); Bartemeyer v. Iowa, 18 Wall. 129 (1874).

12. Benedict, "Contagion and the Constitution"; John C. Burnham, "Medical Inspection of Prostitutes in America in the Nineteenth Century: The St. Louis Experiment and Its Sequel," *BHM*, 45 (1971), 203–218; "Indiana," *AC* (1880); Andrew, *The Errors of Prohibition. An Argument Delivered in the Representatives' Hall, Boston, April 3, 1867* (Boston, 1867), 128. See also "The Social Evil and Its Remedy," *Nation*, 4 (1867), 153; Rev. W. Silsbee, "Sumptuary Laws," *NAR*, 103 (1876), 88; "Prohibitory Legislation in the United States," *FRev*, ns, 10 (1871), 166–179.

in Massachusetts, Pennsylvania, Michigan, Indiana, and Wisconsin. The party's state platforms often criticized the Republican tendency "to regulate the moral ideas, appetites, or innocent amusements of the people by legislation." New York Democratic Congressman S. S. Cox, speaking at the dedication of the new Tammany Hall on July 4, 1867, goaded his audience: "Why do you allow the dyspeptic Radicalism of Boston to tell you what to drink, and when and how you must behave on Sunday?" He pledged the party to the support of "personal, commercial, industrial, municipal, and constitutional freedom."[13]

What to do with society's sick, its poor, and its criminals were issues as old as American public life. But a civil conflict that ended slavery and led government to new heights of organized effort inevitably left its mark on social reform. The post-Civil War years saw new calls on the state to enter into good works appropriate to a purified Republic.

Other realities of American life quickly eroded this effort. Widespread hostility to active government of any sort weakened the popular base for social reform. And during the troubled 1870s there was growing pressure on government to enforce social stability rather than to further social change.

The Uses of Education

A similar course of development occurred in postwar educational policy. The goal of universal education had powerful appeal. A well-schooled citizenry, many believed, offered the best hope of fostering national unity, of securing the good society. Schooling was "the chief unifying process on which we can rely for a permanent peace"; the *Princeton Review* warned that "our national life hangs upon our common schools."[14]

13. *AC*, states and years cited; Democratic platform quoted in "Indiana," *AC* (1870); *Proceedings of the Tammany Society ... on Laying the Corner-Stone of their New Hall ...*, July 4th, 1867 (New York, 1867).

14. Francis Gillette, *The School and the Commonwealth* (Hartford, 1865); "Common Schools," *PR*, 38 (1866), 39. See also Rush Welter, *Popular Education and Democratic Thought in America* (New York, 1962), 141 ff.

Federal aid to education became an active issue in the postwar years: testimony to the schools' importance as instruments of social policy. Precedents already existed. Portions of the public domain had been reserved to help finance common schools since the Northwest Ordinance of 1785. The Morrill Land Grant College Act of 1862 gave new support to state universities, besides aiding established eastern institutions. Daniel Coit Gilman, secretary of Yale's Sheffield Scientific School and soon to be the first president of Johns Hopkins, spoke in 1867 of the Morrill-assisted colleges as "National Schools of Science," an "assertion of the power of the people, acting through the general government, to secure for themselves benefits which cannot proceed from the action of independent states." In the same spirit, an attempt was made in the postwar years to bring to fruition the old idea of a national university in Washington. And Howard University was chartered by Congress in 1867 as an institution designed primarily for Negroes.[15]

In the same year Congress established a federal Department of Education. Its proponents put their case in terms of an invigorated nationalism: "Our experiment of republican institutions is not upon the scale of a petty municipality or state, but it covers half a continent and embraces people of widely diverse interests and conditions, who are to continue one and inseparable." An early historian of the department was still more explicit as to its purpose:

> When the war closed a great change had come over the land; many of the best and bravest of the people were gone forever, and their places were but poorly filled by the ignorant and superstitious from other countries or from the lower depths of southern social life who came into prominence. Until these elements were thoroughly elevated and harmonized, there could be no real peace for the nation as a whole; until the various parts of the Union understood and adopted the new social, industrial, and legal relations produced by the war,

15. Gilman, "Our National Schools of Science," *NAR*, 105 (1867), 495; A. Hunter Dupree, *Science in the Federal Government* (Cambridge, 1957); David Madsen, *The National University: Enduring Dream of the USA* (Detroit, 1966); George N. Rainsford, *Congress and Higher Education in the Nineteenth Century* (Knoxville, 1972), 23. See also Charles K. Adams, "State Universities," *NAR*, 121 (1875), 365–408, and Andrew D. White, "The Relation of the National and State Governments to Advanced Education," *ON*, 10 (1874), 475–495.

progress could be only uncertain, and politics not a scientific pursuit but a game won by fraud or brute force.[16]

Similar considerations led many Republicans to work for a federal policy on common schools. Charles Sumner considered schooling to be a crucial part of Reconstruction and almost succeeded in making public school systems a requirement for the readmission of the southern states under the First Reconstruction Act. Thaddeus Stevens endorsed the scheme of creating a model school system, based on European educational ideas, in the District of Columbia. Congressmen James A. Garfield, George S. Boutwell, and Ignatius Donnelly argued that a National Bureau of Education, with the power to set minimum standards for school systems, was (in Donnelly's words) an "essential and permanent part of any system of reconstruction." As Garfield put it: "We must make [the freedmen] . . . intelligent, industrious, patriotic citizens or they will drag us and our children down to their level."[17]

In 1870, George Frisbie Hoar of Massachusetts offered a bill designed "to compel by national authority the establishment of a thorough and efficient system of public instruction throughout the whole country." His plan called for the federal government to appoint school superintendents and inspectors, build schools, and distribute standardized textbooks. President Grant declared in 1875 that "the education of the masses becomes of the first necessity for the preservation of our institutions," and proposed a constitutional amendment guaranteeing a free education to all Americans.[18]

But education in postwar America, as before, remained almost exclusively a state and local concern. Northern common schools varied greatly in quality and extent, and postwar state legislation

---

16. Charles Warren, *Answers to Inquiries about the United States Bureau of Education, Its Work and History* (Washington, 1883); John C. Eaton, Jr., *The Relation of the National Government to Public Education* [Cleveland, 1870], 13. See also Donald R. Warren, *To Enforce Education: A History of the United States Office of Education* (Detroit, 1975).

17. George F. Hoar, "Charles Sumner," *NAR*, 126 (1878), 24; Fawn Brodie, *Thaddeus Stevens* (New York, 1959), 321; Donnelly quoted in Gordon C. Lee, *The Struggle for Federal Aid* (New York, 1949), 24; Garfield in U.S., *CG*, 39th Cong., 1st sess. (June 8, 1866), 3049.

18. Hoar in U.S., *CG*, 41st Cong., 2d sess. (Feb. 25, 1870), 1568; Grant in *MP*, 4288. See also Hyman, *More Perfect Union*, 387 ff.

frequently sought to improve them by consolidating and centralizing school systems. By 1880 twenty-four commonwealths had
state boards of education, twenty-nine had county school superintendents.

New York's Free School Law of 1867 provided for fully tax-
supported common schools in place of the existing rate bill system,
in which parents were billed according to the number of days
that their children attended school. A Republican-dominated
Assembly passed the act, to the plaudits of the party press: "With
free soil, free schools, a free press, and free men, the future is full
of hope and promise." The 1870 Illinois constitution prescribed "a
thorough and efficient system of free schools."

State school aid increased as well. Wisconsin in 1867 authorized
notably liberal school expenditures, and Pennsylvania substantially expanded its educational plant. Normal schools rapidly
expanded in size and numbers to meet the growing need for
teachers. Public expenditure on education (in current dollars)
increased from 19.9 million in 1860 to 61.7 million in 1870 and
(more slowly) to 81.5 million in 1880. In sum, this was a period of
major expansion in the history of American education—one that
reflected the special attitudes and aspirations of the postwar years.[19]

But there were strong counterweights to these trends. Democrats
often resisted educational expenditures, championed local over
centralized school systems, and remained unmoved by the ideal
of a unified, homogeneous American citizenry. Maine Democrats
in 1873 opposed "all attempts made to introduce into an American
system of schools for the masses, the Prussian system of compulsory education." Efforts to establish compulsory school attendance failed in Illinois (1870), Oregon (1876), and Pennsylvania
(1878).[20]

Localism, diverse interests, and hostility to active central govern-

19. Edward H. Reisner, *Nationalism and Education since 1789* (New
York, 1922), ch. 17; James C. Mohr, "The Free School Law of 1867," *NYHS
Quarterly*, 53 (1969), 248, and *Radical Republicans and Reform*, ch. 6;
"Illinois," *AC* (1870); "Wisconsin," *AC* (1867); "Pennsylvania," *AC* (1868,
1871); on expansion, Albert Fishlow, "Levels of Nineteenth-Century Amer-
ican Investment in Education," *JEH*, 26 (1966), 418–436.

20. *AC*, states and years cited. See also "Compulsory Education," *ALJ*,
4 (1871), 278–279, "Compulsory Education and Cremation," *ALJ*, 9 (1874),
298–299.

ment sapped the vitality of the postwar movement for a federal role in education. Harvard president Charles W. Eliot led a successful assault by private colleges on the scheme for a national university. Senator Timothy Howe of Wisconsin acidly observed that "the president of Harvard University insists that the Government of the United States must be listless." But in fact there was little public or political support for a government-sponsored university. Similarly, the Department of Education was downgraded in 1869 to a bureau in the Interior Department, with a reduced appropriation. Thereafter it was little more than a data-gathering agency. In part this was the result of pressure from state superintendents of education, who had no wish for a potent federal agency.[21]

A no less potent coalition of interests hamstrung federal aid to common schools. The National Education Association spoke out against the idea in 1871. Critics of Senator Hoar's scheme argued that it encroached on local standards and prerogatives, that it was an example of "over-legislation." Catholics denounced federal aid as calculated "to suppress Catholic education, gradually extinguish Catholicity in this country, and to form one homogeneous American people after the New England Evangelical type."

There was widespread opposition to the centralization and increased funding of school systems in the seventies. An 1875 Michigan law abolished county superintendents of schools and delegated their powers to township superintendents and boards of school inspectors. Popular pressure for cost-cutting was reinforced by the hard times of the 1870s and by repeated instances of official fraud and corruption. Nebraska's governor was accused in 1871 of appropriating part of the school fund for his own use; in 1875 the state treasurer of Kansas was shown to have engaged in illegal school bond transactions. Educational "reformers" in Boston and Quincy, Massachusetts struck a popular note with a "New Departure" that promised to diminish the schools' bureaucracy and reduce their costs.[22]

21. Eliot, "A National University," *PSM*, 3 (1873), 691–692; Howe, "Some Remarks on the Report of President Eliot upon a National University," *Rep*, 2 (1874), 29.
22. On Catholics, Lee, *Struggle for Federal Aid*, 47; Charles R. Starring and James O. Knauss, *The Michigan Search for Educational Standards*

In education as in other realms of postwar social policy, there was a distinct pattern of expansion and contraction. Schooling was an important part of the effort to secure national and social unity. But countering social and political realities—cultural diversity, localism, hostility to active, centralized government—quickly blunted that postwar thrust.

Church and State

The end of slavery, the preservation of the Union, and the postwar ideal of a Great Republic often were linked to a religious ethic. The National Association to Secure the Religious Amendment of the Constitution, established in 1864, wanted a constitutional amendment that overtly identified the United States as a Christian nation. The National Reform Association sought "to maintain existing Christian features in the American government." Charles Eliot Norton thought in 1868 that "the [Protestant] Church might ... become the complete expression, and afford the most effective organization of the moral order which underlies the political system."

This religiosity was reflected in church membership and organization. An estimated 54,009 congregations in 1860 grew to 72,459 in 1870. An observer in 1876 called attention to the "drift of American religious sentiment towards the formation of compact and powerful religious organizations." It was possible, he thought, that the "increasing fluctuation" of American political life "may have disposed some to look with more favor upon stable ecclesiastical forms." Inevitably, that growth led to the intrusion of religious issues into the postwar polity.[23]

(Lansing, 1969), 53; "Nebraska," AC (1871); "Kansas," AC (1875); Michael Katz, "The Emergence of Bureaucracy in Higher Education: The Boston Case, 1850–1884," HEQ, 8 (1968), 319–357, "The 'New Departure' in Quincy, 1873–1881: The Nature of Nineteenth Century Educational Reform," NEQ, 40 (1967), 3–30. See also Richard G. White, "The Public-School Failure," NAR, 131 (1880), 537–550; David Tyack, "Education and Social Unrest, 1873–1878," HER, 31 (1961), 194–212.

23. Edward McPherson, The Political History ... of Reconstruction (Washington, 1880), 506; National Reform Association quoted in Manfred Jonas, "The American Sabbath in The Gilded Age," Jahrbuch für Amerikastudien, 6 (1961), 99; Norton, "The Church and Religion," NAR, 106 (1868), 393–394; HS, 228; J. L. Diman, "Religion in America, 1776–1876," NAR, 122 (1876), 37, 31.

Religious organizations themselves generated controversies that came to the courts for resolution. But in Watson v. Jones (1872) the Supreme Court severely limited the degree of court intervention in such matters. Disagreement during the 1860s over slavery and secession led to a number of schisms within border state Presbyterian congregations. In the Watson decision the Court held that it would accept the view of the highest denominational authority as to which group constituted the legitimate congregation. In doing so, the Court favored those church members who had taken the Unionist, antislavery position. In this sense its decision was "born of the nationalism of 1871." But in a larger perspective the Watson decision had the effect of affirming the Court's desire to avoid involvement in religious controversy.[24]

By far the most substantial religious issue of the postwar years was the place of Roman Catholicism in American life. The Catholic church was widely perceived to be a major threat to the society. Irish Catholics in particular, whose politics were overwhelmingly Democratic, whose Negrophobia was raw and overt, and whose concentration in cities and heavy use of alcohol were sources of social concern, irritated Protestant Republican sensibilities.

The Vatican's policies also fed postwar American anti-Catholicism. This was the period of the Papacy's clashes with the burgeoning national states of Italy and Germany; of Pius IX's explicit repudiation (in the 1864 Syllabus of Errors) of liberalism, science, and nationalism; of the Pope's claim (in the Vatican Council of 1869–1870) to infallibility in a wide range of moral and political matters. Men throughout the West who accounted themselves liberals (such as Gladstone in Great Britain) or nationalists (such as Victor Emmanuel in Italy or Bismarck in Prussia) reacted against the Pope's challenge to the most progressive and dynamic currents of the time.

These anxieties merged into the general postwar Republican concern for the quality and texture of "National Life." John Jay,

---

24. Watson v. Jones, 13 Wall. 679 (1872); Mark D. Howe, *The Garden and the Wilderness: Religion and Government in American Constitutional History* (Chicago, 1965), 90; Charles Fairman, *Reconstruction and Reunion, 1864–1868, Part One* (New York, 1971), 895–917. See also "Naturalization—Religious Tests," *CLJ*, 2 (1875), 198; A. W. Pitzer, "The Taxation of Church Property," *NAR*, 131 (1880), 362–374.

president of the New York Union League and in 1869 United States minister to Austria, warned of the "political claims of the Romish church" and called Pius IX's papacy "the institution which proposes to substitute despotism for republicanism in this country." *Harper's Weekly*, whose pages often were given over to the anti-Catholic articles of Eugene Lawrence and cartoons of Thomas Nast, bitterly condemned the papacy as an obstacle to human progress: "In the breaking of chains, in the increase of knowledge, in the higher welfare of the greater number of human beings, in the emancipation of civilization from the mortmain of ecclesiasticism, the Pope sees only the ravages of Satan."[25]

Congress in 1867 ended American representation at the Vatican in response to reports that the Papacy had closed down Rome's Protestant churches. Democratic congressmen sought to restore the United States mission. A sharp debate ensued, punctuated by Democratic condemnations of "the Puritan element" and Republican assaults on the Syllabus of Errors. *Harper's Weekly* observed that the affair "shows how considerable and inflammable an element Roman Catholicism is becoming in our politics." Sharp controversies arose, too, in New York and Ohio over the issue of Catholic religious instruction in prisons and reform schools.[26]

Education was by far the most explosive issue: for Republicans who regarded the schools as the major instrument by which to enact their postwar social ideals, and for Catholic leaders trying to sustain the faith of a rapidly expanding American constituency. The primary battleground was the common school. Catholics sought to counter the overtly Protestant nature of the schools, while at the same time benefiting from publicly supported education. Catholic clerics devised the Poughkeepsie Plan in 1873, which allowed parochial schools to become part of the city's public school

25. Jay, *Rome in America* (New York, 1869); *HW*, 14 (1870), 34. See also John Jay, "The Roman Catholic Question," *IR*, 8 (1880), 185–198, 287–307; Samuel T. Spear, *Religion and the State* (New York, 1876); [Joseph W. Alden], *Vaticanism Unmasked, or, Romanism in the United States* (Cambridge, 1877); Anon., *Roman Catholicism in the United States* (New York, 1879); E. P. Hurlburt, *A Secular View of Religion in the State* (Albany, 1870); Rev. Joseph P. Thompson, *Church and State in the United States* (Boston, 1873); William A. Russ, Jr., "Anti-Catholic Agitation during Reconstruction," *ACHS Records*, 45 (1934), 312–321.

26. Anson P. Stokes, *Church and State in the United States* (New York, 1950), II, 95; *HW*, 14 (1870), 354–355.

system but to offer religious instruction after school hours. A number of New York communities adopted the plan. But it was not acceptable to Protestants fearful of any conjunction of church and school, or to the Catholic hierarchy, committed after 1875 to the Papal doctrine that Catholic parents had an obligation to send their children to parochial schools.

State aid to Catholic schools became an issue of considerable political consequence. New York had supported Catholic schools until the Irish influx of the 1840s and the 1850s elicited widespread Protestant protests. In 1868, during the heyday of New York City's Irish-supported Tweed Ring, legislation was passed allocating about a fifth of the state's education tax income to private—primarily Catholic—schools. An attempt in the following year to give state support to all free schools, public or private, with two hundred or more pupils was defeated by a unanimous Republican opposition. "The Democratic ring wishes to destroy the present common school system of the city, and the Romish party support the attempt," thundered *Harper's Weekly*. In a number of other communities—Buffalo, New Haven, Springfield, Chicago, San Francisco, Cincinnati—aid to parochial schools was a political issue during the seventies.[27]

The place of Bible reading in the public schools was an issue of comparable sensitivity. Catholic spokesmen attacked the use of the King James version in the Cincinnati schools, claiming that it allowed the public schools to act as Protestantizing institutions. In 1869 the city's board of education banned Bible reading in the schools on the ground that it violated the Ohio constitution. In addition, the board sought to merge the public and parochial school systems. Both Protestants and Catholics successfully opposed the merger; but the restriction on Bible reading continued. Protestants petitioned the Cincinnati Superior Court for an in-

27. On Poughkeepsie Plan, Rev. Richard J. Gabel, *Public Funds for Church and Private Schools* (Washington, 1937), 493; Vincent P. Lawnie, "Alienation in America: The Immigrant Catholic and Public Education in Pre-Civil War America," *RP*, 32 (1970), 503–521; *HW*, 19 (1875), 354 et passim. See also A Cosmopolitan [Charles H. Pullen], *Miss Columbia's Public School; or, Will it Blow Over?* (New York, 1871), illustrated by Thomas Nast; William T. Harris, "The Division of School Funds for Religious Purposes," *AM*, 38 (1876), 171–184; and Timothy L. Smith, "Protestant Schooling and American Nationality, 1800–1850," *JAH*, 53 (1967), 679–695.

junction against the Bible prohibition. This was granted after hearings that attracted national attention. But in 1873 the Ohio Supreme Court upheld the board's right to exclude Bible reading from the public schools. The controversy had a distinct political coloration, with prominent Republicans leading the attack on the board and Democrats and Liberal Republicans conspicuous in its defense.[28]

This was not an isolated instance. The Long Island City Board of Education required in 1872 that Bible readings be part of the school day's opening exercises and expelled Catholic students who refused to participate. The state Superintendent of Public Instruction held that religious training was not within the purview of the public schools, and reversed the board.

But other jurisdictions, especially in Puritan-Republican New England, held differently. The Massachusetts Supreme Judicial Court in 1866 sustained the Woburn school committee's Bible reading requirement. And the Vermont Supreme Court permitted Brattleboro's school authorities to expel over a hundred Catholic pupils whose parents insisted on their right to keep their children home on Corpus Christi Day.[29]

Traditional anti-Catholicism and the special considerations of postwar political life combined to inject the church–school dispute into national politics as well. Observers thought that the issue was "beginning to stir the American mind as nothing else has since the bombardment of Sumter"; that "parties are forming and marshalling for a contest on this subject, which for depth and earnestness has seldom been paralleled in the history of the nation." Henry W. Bellows, the Unitarian minister who had been the guiding force in the wartime Sanitary Commission, warned

28. *The Bible in the Public Schools. Arguments and Opinions in the Case of the Cincinnati Board of Education, before the Superior Court of Cincinnati* (Cincinnati, 1870); Bernard Mandel, "Religion and the Public Schools of Ohio," *OSAH Quarterly*, 58 (1949), 185–207; Harold M. Helfman, "The Cincinnati 'Bible War,' 1869–1870," *OSAH Quarterly*, 60 (1951), 369–386; Robert Michaelsen, "Common School, Common Religion? A Case Study in Church-State Relations, Cincinnati, 1869–70," *CH*, 38 (1969), 201–217.

29. "New York," *AC* (1872); Spiller v. Inhabitants of Woburn, 94 Mass. 127 (1866); "Vermont," *AC* (1876); Ferriter v. Tyler, 48 Vt. 444 (1876) and discussion in *CLJ*, 3 (1876), 700–701; Finley Burke, *A Treatise on the Law of Public Schools* (New York, 1880), 98–101.

Catholics that "if they continue to press their claim to break up our national system of public schools" they would "bring on a civil war, in which they and their churches will be swept, as by a whirlwind, from the land."[30]

As the saliency of wartime and Reconstruction issues faded and the hard times of the seventies sapped Republican strength, party leaders became more outspokenly anti-Catholic. The Indiana Republican platform of 1876 declared: "It is incompatible with American citizenship to pay allegiance to any foreign power, civil or ecclesiastical, which asserts the right to include the action of civil government within the domain of religion and morals." Rutherford B. Hayes, locked in a tight and nationally significant contest for governor of Ohio in 1875, made the question of Catholic influence in the public schools an important part of his campaign. He explained to James G. Blaine why this was necessary: "We have been losing strength in Ohio for several years by emigration of Republican farmers and especially of the young men who were in the Army. In their place have come Catholic foreigners . . . We shall crowd [the Democrats] . . . on the school and other state issues." James A. Garfield struck a similar note in campaign speeches supporting Hayes: "It is evident that the Catholic Church is moving along the whole line of its front against modern civilization and our fight in Ohio is only a small portion of the battlefield." These former soldiers (and future Presidents) were joined by Ulysses S. Grant. In September 1875, a week before the Ohio balloting, the chief executive warned that the next great struggle in America would be between "patriotism and intelligence on the one side, and superstition, ambition, and ignorance on the other." In his December 1875 message to Congress, Grant called for the outright prohibition of public aid to church-related schools. James G. Blaine sponsored a constitutional amendment designed to implement Grant's proposal. The House approved by a margin of 180 to 7, but the Senate vote of 28 to 16 (on strict party lines) fell short of the two-thirds margin necessary to send the amendment on to the states.

30. "Recent Publications on the School Question," PR, 43 (1871), 315, 325. See also Lyman H. Atwater, "Civil Government and Religion," PR, ns, 5 (1876), 195–236; Daniel C. Gilman, "Education in America, 1776–1876," NAR, 122 (1876), 205–207.

Inevitably the issue entered into the presidential campaign of 1876. The Republican convention nominated Hayes and endorsed the Blaine amendment. The Democrats dutifully endorsed "the two-fold separation of church and state, for the sake alike of civil and religious freedom," but took the Republicans to task for "the false issue with which they would enkindle sectarian strife in respect to the public schools, of which the establishment and support belong exclusively to the several States."[31]

Federal prohibition of public aid to parochial schools met with no greater success than did national support for public school education. But church-state questions continued to be an important battleground of the conflict between social unity and cultural diversity.

Civil Rights and Wrongs

One strand of postwar social policy dealt with functional problems of American society: crime, poverty, illness, intemperance, illiteracy. Another dealt with the structure of the society itself; with the status of the people who made up the postwar nation.

By far the most important of these concerns was with the rights of Negroes in American life. This question had a central place in the postwar polity, and it involved the nation at large as well as the Reconstruction South. The North did not have to rid itself of the special burden of slavery in 1865. But it did have to deal with the conflict between the Republican ideal of equal citizenship and the reality of racial discrimination deeply rooted in law and custom.

31. "Indiana," AC (1876); Forrest W. Clonts, "The Political Campaign of 1875 in Ohio," OSAH Quarterly, 31 (1922), 38–97; Hayes quoted in Sr. Marie C. Klinghamer, "The Blaine Amendment of 1875: Private Motives for Political Action," CHR, 42 (1956), 21; Garfield in Harry Barnard, Rutherford B. Hayes and His America (Indianapolis, 1954), 274; Grant in "United States," AC (1875) and MP, IX, 4288; Kirk H. Porter and Donald B. Johnson, National Party Platforms, 2d ed. (Urbana, 1961), 49, 51. See also Politics and the School Question. Attitudes of the Republican and Democratic Parties, in 1876 (n.p., 1876); Paul Goda, "The Historical Background of California's Constitutional Provisions Prohibiting Aid to Sectarian Schools," CHS Quarterly, 46 (1967), 149–171.

At the war's end eighteen of the twenty-five northern states forbade Negro suffrage; and restrictions on Negro education, residence, occupation, and mobility existed almost everywhere. White supremicist attitudes pervaded northern life. Even Massachusetts Republicans in 1865 had "no theories to promulgate in relation to the right of suffrage." The Maine party convention in that year endorsed Negro suffrage, but rejected a resolution calling for an end to "all tests, disabilities, and discrimination based on color or race."[32]

Prominent Republican senators—Lyman Trumbull of Illinois, John Sherman of Ohio, Henry Wilson of Massachusetts—accepted black inferiority as a fact of life. Indeed, the desire to keep Negroes from moving North by improving their condition in the South was one of the rationales for congressional Reconstruction. Republican lawyer Robert G. Ingersoll expressed a widely held attitude when he observed in 1868: "It would be unwise to allow the negro to vote in Illinois and not in the South. The result of that would be to make Illinois a negro Mecca. They would come here in droves. Allow them to vote everywhere and then they would remain where they are and where the climate suits them." Roscoe Conkling of New York and George S. Boutwell of Massachusetts justified their support for the Civil Rights Act of 1866 with similar reasoning.[33]

Republicans seemingly had a large political stake in black suffrage. The South's freedmen were the backbone of the party's strength in that region. Negroes could be an important voting bloc in the border states and the lower North as well. Boutwell estimated that the 146,000 potential black voters in Kentucky, Maryland, Delaware, New York, Pennsylvania, Ohio, and Missouri might make the difference in close elections. As one proponent of Negro suffrage wryly put it: "The highest requirements of abstract justice coincide with the lowest requirements of political prudence."

32. Forrest G. Wood, *Black Scare: The Racist Response to Emancipation and Reconstruction* (Berkeley and Los Angeles, 1968); "Massachusetts," "Maine," *AC* (1865).

33. Eva I. Wakefield, ed., *The Letters of Robert G. Ingersoll* (New York, 1951), 149; C. Vann Woodward, "Seeds of Failure in Radical Race Policy," in his *American Counterpoint* (Boston, 1971), 163–183.

But was this in fact the case? To champion equal suffrage was to risk large-scale northern white opposition. The danger was real enough. Republican attempts to win popular support for black suffrage were defeated in Colorado, Connecticut, the District of Columbia, Kansas, Michigan, Minnesota, Missouri, New York, Ohio, and Wisconsin. The party's 1867 election losses in a number of northern states were blamed primarily on popular hostility to Negro voting.[34]

Nevertheless, Republican support of equal suffrage and other Negro civil rights increased during the postwar years. New York's Union League Club celebrated the passage of the 1866 Civil Rights Act with a hundred-gun salute and the declamation of club president John Jay: "We have renounced before the law Slavery and Caste; we have repudiated, in determining the personal rights of citizens, aristocracy of color and classification of race." When Johnson's veto of the bill was overridden, House Speaker Schuyler Colfax intoned: "being born on American soil, means something now for everyone, high and low, rich and poor, haughty and humble, even for . . . those whom God has destined to be born with a darker skin than you and I." The sincerity of these sentiments was questionable, as subsequent developments made clear. But for a season the character of the war and the end of slavery committed many Republicans to the view that Negroes should share in an expanded national citizenship, and that limits on the rights implicit in that citizenship unconscionably strained the ideal of one nation, one people. Republican state platforms in the late sixties reveal the degree to which these assumptions became part of the common currency of postwar Republicanism: "the first and highest duty of our free Government is to secure to all its citizens, regardless of race, religion, or color, equality before the law, equal protection from it, equal responsibility to it; and to all that have proved their loyalty by their acts, an equal voice in making it"

34. Quotation from E. P. Whipple, "Reconstruction and Negro Suffrage," *AM*, 16 (1865), 247; La Wanda Cox and John H. Cox, "Negro Suffrage and Republican Politics: The Problem of Motive in Reconstruction Historiography," *JSH*, 33 (1967), 303–330; Martin E. Mantell, *Johnson, Grant, and The Politics of Reconstruction* (New York, 1973), ch. 4. See also William Gillette, *The Right to Vote: Politics and the Passage of the Fifteenth Amendment* (Baltimore, 1965), 43, 46–47, 32n–33n; Glenn M. Linden, "A Note on Negro Suffrage and Republican Politics," *JSH*, 36 (1970), 411–420.

(Iowa, 1866); "[we] scout and scorn . . . that political blasphemy which says, 'This is the white man's Government.' It is God's Government made for man!" (Michigan, 1866); "the measure of a man's political rights should be neither his religion, his birthplace, his race, his color, nor any merely physical characteristics" (Minnesota, 1865).[35]

Northern Negroes, too, spoke with increasing vigor in their own cause. There was an initial inclination to be cautious. An Indianapolis Negro meeting in 1866 declared: "we do not ask for social equality . . . Because men go to the polls and vote on equal terms, is no reason that they should associate together, unless they choose to do so." But expectations soared in postwar America. Numerous black state and city conventions sought "to thoroughly canvass the subject of the disabilities, educational and political, that dwell on persons of color . . . impeding their rightful progress, and to devise and set in motion effective agencies for the permanent removal of the same." Kansas Negroes formed an equal rights association, and planned civil rights clubs which would put pressure on the legislature to repeal discriminatory laws. Illinois Negroes identified their cause with the English Reform Act of 1867, Garibaldi and the unification of Italy, Bismarck and the modernization of Prussia, and the end of Russian serfdom. The present, they declared, "is peculiarly the age of IDEAS . . . The institutions of the old world, founded upon a political class distinction, in society, are being eliminated by the progress of liberal ideas, and by the sword."[36]

These beliefs had a sizable impact on legal discrimination (if not on popular attitudes) in the North. Indiana Republican leader Oliver P. Morton demanded in 1867 that the discriminatory clauses in his state's constitution be removed "as an act of public decency." A Pennsylvania law in the same year forbade discrimination on street railways: Republican legislators "who, two years

35. Union League Club of New York, *Address of the President* [New York, 1866], 10; Willard H. Smith, *Schuyler Colfax* (Indianapolis, 1952), 233; *AC*, states and years cited. See also G. Galin Berrier, "The Negro Suffrage Issue in Iowa—1865–1868," *AI*, 39 (1968), 241–261.

36. "Indiana," *AC* (1866); Illinois State Convention of Colored Men, *Proceedings* (Chicago, 1867); "Kansas," *AC* (1872). See also National Equal Rights League, *Proceedings of the First Annual Meeting* (Philadelphia, 1865); Joseph E. Holliday, "Freedmen's Civil Societies in Cincinnati, 1862–1870," *CincHS Bulletin*, 22 (1964), 169–185.

ago, could not be induced to take a bill to prevent exclusion out of committee and bring it before the House, this year could not be persuaded to hold such a bill back."

State civil rights acts began to challenge social discrimination against blacks. Massachusetts passed the first such statute in 1865, covering hotels, restaurants, and public transportation. A flurry of similar laws appeared in the mid-seventies, in tandem with the national Civil Rights Act of 1875.[37]

That bill stands as a lonely monument to the postwar ideal of equal rights—and to the forces that drained the ideal of social meaning. Massachusetts Senator Charles Sumner appropriately enough was its great champion. His chief aim was to secure a federal guarantee of desegregated education. But he sought also a cluster of protective provisions covering jury duty, churches, cemeteries, restaurants, hotels, and public conveyances.

Sumner's all-inclusive civil rights bill ran into broad Republican congressional opposition during the early seventies. Blaine, Dawes, and Garfield (who privately agreed with his Democratic colleague Jeremiah Black that Negroes were "untempered mortar in the national temple") were cool to the act. Trumbull of Illinois was among the many who opposed a federal guarantee of integrated schools; Fessenden of Maine and Anthony of Rhode Island took exception to the ban on segregated churches; Carpenter of Wisconsin objected to the jury clause; Burrows of Michigan opposed the hotel clause. Many feared that the act too greatly extended federal authority, interfered with local government, threatened private rights. Democrats of course denounced it as an unconstitutional attempt "to regulate the association, companionship, tastes and feelings of the people."

The emasculated civil rights act that finally passed in 1875 (schools, cemeteries, churches, and juries were excluded) was the product of elaborate behind-the-scenes compromises, in many ways resembling the settlement of 1877 that made possible the election of Rutherford B. Hayes as President. It was part of a legis-

37. "Indiana," AC (1867); Ira V. Brown, "Pennsylvania and the Rights of the Negro, 1865–1867," PH, 28 (1961), 45–57; Massachusetts, Acts (1865), ch. 277; "The New York Civil Rights Bill," ALJ, 8 (1873), 3–4; Gilbert T. Stephenson, Race Distinctions in American Law (New York, 1910), 120–122; Frederic J. Stimson, American Statute Law (Boston, 1886), 5–6, 662–663.

lative package that included an amnesty act for disfranchised white southerners, Texas & Pacific Railroad bonds, and an army appropriations bill. Even so, only the votes of a number of lame duck Republican congressmen defeated in the 1874 election (about 90 of the 162 in favor) made possible the measure's passage.[38]

The preamble of the act began: "Whereas it is essential to just government *we recognize the equality of all men before the law, and hold that it is the duty of government in its dealings with the people to mete out equal and exact justice to all, of whatever nativity, race, color, or persuasion, religious or political;* and it being the appropriate object of legislation to enact great fundamental principles into law . . ." This was a classic statement of the postwar Republican social ideal. Yet the italicized portion was an almost exact quotation from the 1872 *Democratic* platform. The general view was that the bill was a meaningless composite of empty ideals and tawdry political maneuvering: "a mere piece of legislative sentimentality"; "amusing . . . tea-table nonsense." It was thought that about thirty congressmen voted for the act "merely from a regard for the memory of Mr. Sumner" (who had died in 1874). Another thirty, "who wish all State lines obliterated, and all state governments absorbed by the Federal power," remained as a hard core of Radicals. The rest of the bill's supporters presumably were interested in the legislative package of which the 1875 Civil Rights Act was a part.[39]

To a limited degree the courts added their weight to the postwar movement for Negro civil rights. Circuit court decisions by Chase,

---

38. Garfield, Diaries, May 24, 1873, LC; Democratic quote in Bertram Wyatt-Brown, "The Civil Rights Act of 1875," *WPQ*, 18 (1965), 765; Alfred H. Kelly, "The Congressional Controversy over School Segregation, 1867–1875," *AHR*, 64 (1959), 537–563; John S. Ezell, "The Civil Rights Act of 1875," *MAm*, 50 (1968), 251–271; James M. McPherson, "Abolitionists and the Civil Rights Act of 1875," *JAH*, 52 (1965), 493–510. See also Ronald B. Jager, "Charles Sumner, the Constitution, and the Civil Rights Act of 1875," *NEQ*, 42 (1969), 350–372; David Donald, *Charles Sumner and the Rights of Man* (New York, 1970), 531–539, 541–547, 586–587.

39. On preamble, Kelly, "Congressional Controversy," 562; Charles Warren, *The Supreme Court in United States History* (Boston, 1923), III, 334–337; John M. Leavitt to Thomas Cooley, April 10, 1875, Cooley Mss, MHS. See also William A. Cocke, "Constitutionality of the Civil Rights Law," *SLR*, ns, 1 (1875), 192–209.

Swayne, and Bradley upheld applications of the 1866 Civil Rights Act. The Supreme Court occasionally applied the Fourteenth Amendment and even the 1875 Civil Rights Act in decisions affirming Negro rights.[40]

A scattering of state court decisions upheld equal access to public conveyances, theaters, and restaurants. A few jurisdictions—most notably Michigan in 1869—sustained state laws that forbade segregated schools. The Kansas and Iowa Supreme Courts went further, opposing segregation and discrimination on grounds of public policy. They spoke of "the tendency of our institutions and policy of the government to organize into one harmonious *people*, with a common country and stimulated with the common purpose to perpetuate and spread our free institutions for the development, elevation and happiness of *mankind*"; warned that separation by race implied the power to separate by nationality; and asked: "Is it not better for the grand aggregate of human society, as well as for individuals, that all children should mingle together and learn to know each other?"[41]

But these were rare sentiments, with little support in the public opinion of the time. And even pro-civil rights decisions often reflected prevailing racial views: "The colored race, as a race, was abject and ignorant, and in that condition was unfitted to command the respect of those who had superior intelligence. Their training had left them mere children, and as such they needed the protection which a wise government extends to those who are unable to protect themselves." Chief Justice Beck of the Iowa Supreme Court upheld the claim of a Negro woman to unsegregated accommodations on a river boat. But he thought it necessary to observe that "by her spirited resistance and her defiant words, as well as by her pertinacity in demanding the recognition of her

40. Charles S. Mangum, Jr., *The Legal Status of the Negro* (Chapel Hill, 1940), 27; United States v. Rhodes, 27 Fed. Cas. 785 (C. C. D. Kent. 1866); Strauder v. West Virginia, 100 U.S. 303 (1880); Neal v. Delaware, 103 U.S. 370 (1880); Railroad Company v. Brown, 17 Wall. 445 (1873); Joseph v. Bidwell, 27 La. Ann. 382 (1876): U.S. v. Newcomer, 27 Fed Cas. 127 (E.D. Pa. 1876).

41. People v. Board of Education, 18 Mich. 400 (1869); Lewis G. Vander Velde, "The Michigan Supreme Court Defines Negro Rights, 1866–1869," *MAQR*, 63 (1957), 277–294; Clark v. Board of Directors, 24 Iowa 266, 276 (1868); Board of Education v. Tinnon, 26 Kan. 1, 19 (1881).

rights and in vindicating them, she has exhibited evidence of the Anglo-Saxon blood that flows in her veins."[42]

The major thrust of the postwar courts was to narrow the scope of Negro citizenship and, often on explicitly racial grounds, to resist the principle of equal rights. The Kentucky Supreme Court declared in 1867 that the Thirteenth Amendment did not elevate Negroes "to social or political equality with the white race," and warned that congressional enforcement of equal rights might "legalize intermarriages between the two races deteriorating to the Caucasian blood, and destructive of the social and legislative decorum of States." The words of a Pennsylvania Supreme Court judge, upholding the right of a railroad to provide separate accommodations for blacks and whites, often were cited by other courts: "The natural law which forbids their intermarriage and that social amalgamation which leads to a corruption of races, is as clearly divine as that which imparted to them different natures."[43]

State supreme courts had no difficulty in upholding laws that permitted—or required—segregated schools. As the Kentucky court explained, "It is for the legislature and not for the courts to determine the time, and the manner in which the imperfections in our school-system, growing out of the change in the civil and political condition of the negro, are to be remedied." Nevada's Supreme Court held in 1872: "While [segregation] . . . may be, and probably is, opposed to the spirit of the [Constitution and laws of Nevada and the United States], . . . it is not obnoxious to their letter." A number of other jurisdictions—California, Indiana, Ohio, New York—did not encounter even this doctrinal difficulty. They agreed that the citizens of a state were entitled to equal but not identical rights and privileges.[44]

42. Justice Strong in Strauder v. West Virginia, 100 U.S. 303, 306 (1880); Beck in Coger v. North West Union Packet Company, 37 Iowa 145, 149 (1873). See also Philip Paludan, "Law and the Failure of Reconstruction: The Case of Thomas Cooley," *JHI*, 33 (1972), 597–614.

43. Bowlin v. Commonwealth, 2 Bush (Ky.) 5, 8–9 (1867); Justice Agnew in West Chester and Philadelphia Railroad Company v. Miles, 55 Pa. 209, 213 (1867).

44. Marshall v. Donovan, 10 Bush (Ky.) 681, 694 (1874); State v. Duffy, 7 Nev. 342, 346 (1872); Ward v. Flood, 48 Cal. 36 (1874); Cory v. Carter, 48 Ind. 327 (1874); State v. McCann, 21 Ohio St. 198 (1871); People v. King, 93 N.Y. 438 (1883). See also Lyndon A. Smith, "Recent School Law Decisions," U.S., Bureau of Education, *Circulars of Information*, no. 4 (Washington, 1883).

Racial intermarriage was the most sensitive of black–white social relations and evoked from the courts their most explicit commitment to racial separation. An Indiana Supreme Court justice, upholding his state's anti-intermarriage law in 1871, acidly observed: "If the people of other states desire to permit a corruption of blood, and a mixture of races, they have the power to adopt such a policy." The Fifth Circuit Court in 1879 upheld a Texas act penalizing the white more heavily than the black partner in such a marriage. The court argued that the former, with the advantage of racial superiority, was chiefly to blame. But four years later the United States Supreme Court validated an Alabama law because the parties were subject to the same penalties.[45]

The Supreme Court was less blatant than many of the lesser tribunals, but the ultimate effect of its civil rights decisions was the same. For one thing, it steadily narrowed the scope of the Reconstruction amendments. Chief Justice Morrison R. Waite and others concluded that the Fifteenth Amendment conferred no right to vote per se: "It is only when the wrongful refusal . . . is on account of race, color or previous condition of servitude, that Congress can interfere." The Fourteenth and Fifteenth Amendments were held to apply only to state action, thus ending the hope that individual violators of Negro civil rights might be brought to justice. "With respect to obstacles to the enjoyment of rights arising from other causes," declared Justice Stephen J. Field, "persons of the colored race must take their chances . . . with the rest of the community."[46]

Procedural as well as substantive considerations limited the Supreme Court's enforcement of Negro civil rights. Errors in pleading, for example, served this purpose. Dissenters complained that the Court was "too narrow, too technical and too forgetful of the liberal objects" of the civil rights laws; that the majority had brought "to an impotent conclusion the vigorous amendments on the subject of slavery."

During the late seventies and early eighties the Court went still

45. Justice Buskirk in State v. Gibson, 36 Ind. 389, 404 (1871); *Ex parte* François, 3 Wood 367 (5th Circ. Tex. 1879); Pace v. Alabama, 106 U.S. 583 (1882).

46. Waite in U.S. v. Reese, 92 U.S. 214, 218 (1875); Field in Virginia v. Rives, 100 U.S. 313, 333 (1880).

further in refusing to support equal rights. In Hall v. DeCuir (1877) the justices unanimously struck down a rare survival from Reconstruction: a Louisiana statute that forbade discrimination on public conveyances. Chief Justice Waite argued that the law interfered with the right of Congress to regulate interstate commerce: "If the public good requires such legislation, it must come from Congress and not from the States." Clifford's concurring opinion went much further. He found positive good in a policy of segregation. It was undesirable to mix people "who would be repulsive or disagreeable to each other."[47]

The ultimate Court rejection of the postwar ideal of equal rights came in the Civil Rights Cases (1883), which voided most of the 1875 Civil Rights Act. There was a weary, empty quality to these cases, as indeed there was to the cause of civil rights itself. The defendants offered no briefs; the argument of Solicitor General S. F. Phillips for the 1875 Act was weak and unconvincing. Justice Joseph P. Bradley, who in the Slaughterhouse case a decade before had argued that the Fourteenth Amendment was designed to safeguard the rights of Negro national citizenship, now reduced that purpose to inconsequence. Congress, he argued, cannot legislate a "code of municipal law for the regulation of private rights." Bradley drew the suggestive parallel of Congress's incapacity to pass a law affecting the enforcement of contracts; all that it could do was prevent state impairment. Interpersonal relationships were, by analogy, comparable to the workings of the marketplace. And in both cases the presumption was that laissez-faire should prevail. Beyond this, Bradley justified his stand by dwelling on the social desirability of Negro self-reliance: "When a man has emerged from slavery, and by the aid of beneficent legislation has shaken off the inseparable concomitants of that state, there must be some stage in the progress of his elevation when he takes the rank of a mere citizen, and ceases to be the special favorite of the laws."

John Marshall Harlan's long and powerful dissent was steeped in the postwar ideal of equal national citizenship. The nation had created new rights for its black citizens and had the power to de-

47. Bradley dissent in Blyew v. U.S., 13 Wall. 581, 599 (1872); Hunt dissent in U.S. v. Reese, 92 U.S. 214, 253 (1875); Hall v. DeCuir, 95 U.S. 485, 490, 504 (1877); C. Peter Magrath, *Morrison R. Waite: The Triumph of Character* (New York, 1963), 140–141.

fend those rights. He bitterly concluded "that the substance and spirit of the recent Amendments of the Constitution have been sacrificed by a subtle and ingenious verbal criticism."

But Harlan's view had little ideological or political appeal. *Harper's Weekly* thought it natural that after a "long and terrible Civil War . . . the tendency to magnify the National authority should have been very strong." But now, "in a calmer time, the laws passed under that humane impulse are reviewed, and when found to be incompatible with strict constitutional authority, they are set aside." A black lawyer offered a different and more painfully accurate conclusion: "The old-fashioned sin is being committed over again, in the new American way."[48]

The failure of legislatures and courts to accord any meaningful protection to the civil rights of Negroes reflected the fact that, for all the ideological impact of the war and the end of slavery, the prevailing racial assumptions of nineteenth century America condemned blacks to not much more than a civil demi-freedom. Northern Negro leadership in the seventies, rent by class, color, and age divisions, could do little in response. Popular racism found ready expression in the Democratic party and in mass culture. When Wendell Phillips told a Faneuil Hall audience in 1875: "My anxiety is for the hunted, tortured, robbed, murdered" blacks in Louisiana, a heckler shouted: "That's played out." By the late seventies, *Uncle Tom's Cabin* was not a spur to popular indignation over the mistreatment of blacks by whites, but a half-minstrel, half-circus theatrical entertainment.[49]

Many journalists, intellectuals, reformers, and men of letters who had supported the postwar ideal of a unified and equal na-

48. Civil Rights Cases, 109 U.S. 3, 11, 25, 26 (1883); Warren, *Supreme Court*, III, 336; The Brotherhood of Liberty, *Justice and Jurisprudence: An Inquiry Concerning the Constitutional Limitations of the Thirteenth, Fourteenth, and Fifteenth Amendments* (Philadelphia, 1889), 38. See also Michael J. Horan, "Political Economy and Sociological Theory as Influences upon Judicial Policy-Making: The *Civil Rights Cases* of 1883," *AJLH*, 16 (1972), 71–86.

49. Leslie H. Fishel, Jr., "Repercussions of Reconstruction: The Northern Negro, 1870–1883," *CWH*, 14 (1968), 325–345; Irving Bartlett, *Wendell Phillips* (Boston, 1961), 328; Edmund Wilson, *Patriotic Gore* (New York, 1962), 4. See also George M. Fredrickson, *The Black Image in the White Mind: The Debate on Afro-American Character and Destiny, 1817–1914* (New York, 1971), ch. 6.

tional citizenry succumbed to racism. In part they did so because of their frustrations with a political system dominated by professional politicians. While many Republican regulars adhered to the rhetoric of equal rights, their reformer critics linked the incapacity of Negroes to the evils of machine politics. The biographer James Parton declared that undeveloped races and immature individuals "should be withdrawn from the reach of the politician."

But the science-authenticated racism of the nineteenth century was the ultimate determinant of their views. James Russell Lowell warned: "it is clearly bad policy to urge the inferior into positions which make it hateful to the superior race, and for which it is necessarily unfit." The *Independent* was confident that the best hope for the Negro lay in "his readiness to adopt the sentiments and practices of the superior race." Charles Francis Adams, Jr., too, thought that the southern Negro had best "assume, as quietly and speedily as he can, those natural relations to which, in spite of everything, he must at last come with the community in which his lot is cast." The ubiquity of white supremacist attitudes by the 1870s was a national and not just a southern phenomenon.[50]

White and Red, White and Yellow, Male and Female

Postwar Indian policy, too, was the product of underlying racial hostility tempered by the ideal of equal national citizenship. The government traditionally dealt with the Indian tribes by treaty, as though they were primitive foreign nations. But the flow of white settlement westward made a mockery of the idea that the United States and Indian "nations" could coexist. And the postwar commitment to a unified country further weakened the acceptability of Indian separateness.[51]

50. Parton, "Antipathy to the Negro," *NAR*, 127 (1878), 491; Lowell, "A Look Before and After," *NAR*, 108 (1869), 271; *Independent*, 31 (1879), 16; Adams, "The 'Independents' in the Caucus," *NAR*, 123 (1876), 436. See also John G. Sproat, *"The Best Men": Liberal Reformers in The Gilded Age* (New York, 1968), 29–36; Richard H. Dana, Jr., "Points in American Politics," *NAR*, 124 (1877), 1–30; William H. Trescot, "The Southern Question," *NAR*, 123 (1876), 249–280.

51. Roy H. Pearce, *The Savages of America* (Baltimore, 1953); Loring B. Priest, *Uncle Sam's Stepchildren: The Reformation of United States Indian Policy, 1865–1887* (New Brunswick, 1942).

Important differences of condition distinguished Indians from Negroes. Most red men lived in places where federal authority did not clash with the states, and there was little organized pressure for Indian citizenship. Nevertheless, postwar Indian relations evolved in close cadence with Negro policy. As an adjunct of its increasing concern with the status and condition of the freedmen, Congress in March 1865 created a special joint committee to look into Indian affairs. That committee's report in 1867 summed up the causes of the present state of the Indian: whiskey, smallpox, cholera, measles, syphilis, and "the irrepressible conflict between a superior and an inferior race when brought in [the] presence of each other." The *Nation* in 1867 asked "What Shall We Do With the Indians?" and concluded that they would have to be absorbed into the national population: "What is wanted is a Bureau of Civilization, with enough force at its disposal to gather in the remnants of the tribes on the Plains and settle them somewhere on farms, and teach them to live by labor . . . if they cannot bear civilization, it will at least kill them decently."[52]

But a more humanitarian concern also surfaced in the postwar years. *Harper's Weekly*, condemning a massacre of Piegan Indians by federal troops, scored "Our Indian Policy of Extermination" as "inhuman and unworthy of the United States" and called instead for "a policy of peace." The first tangible expression of a new policy was the 1867 Act to Establish Peace with Certain Hostile Indian Tribes. Congress created a civilian-military peace commission to arrive at a settlement with the tribes of the West "such as will most likely insure civilization for the Indians and peace and safety for the whites." Obviously influenced by the model of congressional Reconstruction, the commissioners proposed that the Office of Indian Affairs be transferred from the Interior to the War Department. Not the reservation but the federal territory was to be the governmental framework for future Indian settlement. Education in the agricultural and mechanical arts would be fostered; and

52. Report quoted in Laurence F. Schmeckebier, *The Office of Indian Affairs* (Baltimore, 1927), 50; *Nation*, 5 (1867), 356, 7 (1868), 544–546. See also Henry E. Fritz, *The Movement for Indian Assimilation, 1860–1890* (Philadelphia, 1963), 28–30; "The New Indian Commonwealth," *CFC*, 1 (1865), 419–420.

"each head of a family should be encouraged to select and improve a homestead."[53]

In 1869 Congress established a Board of Indian Commissioners —ten men "eminent for their intelligence and philanthropy"— who until 1874 served as watchdogs over the Indian Service. President Grant made a wartime aide, the Seneca Ely S. Parker, commissioner of Indian affairs. And with much fanfare Grant embarked on a "Peace Policy" designed to alter the character of white-Indian relations: "A system which looks to the extinction of a race is too horrible for a nation to adopt without entailing upon itself the wrath of all Christendom and engendering in the citizen a disregard for human life and the rights of others, dangerous to society."

Grant proposed that Indians be gathered into large reservations which eventually would be organized into territories, with the inhabitants settled as landowning farmers. Meanwhile, he transferred the administration of many reservations from often corrupt Indian agents to missionaries from the major Christian denominations. Indian Affairs expenditures were doubled to $3,700,000 in 1869. An 1875 law allowed Indians to file for land under the Homestead Act if they left their tribes.

Substantial self-interest lay behind this policy. Gathering the Plains Indians into reservations would ease the building of the transcontinental railroads. And a number of influential westerners—traders, agents, supply men, farmers—had a stake in a policy of peace (and subsidies) rather than extermination. But it also reflected the postwar nationalist ideal of a unified American people. The House of Representatives sought to end Indian separatism in its general appropriation act of March 3, 1871, when it specified that "hereafter no Indian nation or tribe within the territory of the United States shall be acknowledged or recognized as an independent nation, tribe, or power, with whom the United States may contract by treaty."[54]

53. HW, 14 (1870), 178, 210; on peace commission, Fritz, Movement, 62–66.

54. Grant quoted in MP, IX, 3993; Elsie M. Rushmore, Indian Policy during Grant's Administration (Jamaica, N.Y., 1914); Laurie Tatum, Our Red Brothers and the Peace Policy of President Ulysses S. Grant (Philadelphia, 1899); R. Pierce Beaver, Church, State, and the American Indians (St. Louis, 1966); Peter J. Rahill, The Catholic Indian Missions and Grant's

The postwar change in Indian policy had the same ephemeral quality as the movement for Negro civil and social rights. The Fourteenth Amendment did not grant Indians citizenship; no legislation defined their civil rights. If anything, the social gap was widening between the tribes and a white society in the throes of industrialization. And the intellectual respectability of racism worked against Indian assimilation as readily as against Negro integration. James A. Garfield's view was a common one: he thought it best "to let the Indian races sink as gently and easily as possible in oblivion, for there they will go in spite of all efforts."

Francis A. Walker, Parker's successor as commissioner of Indian affairs in 1871, worked out a rationale for Indian subordination closely akin to that for black segregation. Walker considered a humane policy to be safer and cheaper than warfare. But Indians in his view were fixed in savagery. He proposed a "policy of seclusion with more or less of individual constraint" in permanent, isolated reservations. There they would be subject to "moral and economical correction and instruction ... until the lawless, indolent, and wasteful habits of a nomadic life are completely uprooted." The alternative—"hastening the time when all these tribes shall be resolved into the body of our citizenship, without seclusion and without restraint, letting such as will go to the dogs" —was the policy of those who "are not likely to hesitate in extending to the Indians citizenship and the ballot ... After Negro suffrage, any thing."[55]

Postwar sensitivity to the implications of racial and ethnic diversity extended to the Chinese as well. Large numbers of Chinese laborers, driven by the threat of starvation at home and lured by the labor needs of American mining and railroad building, came to the West Coast during the 1850s and the 1860s. Popular feeling against them was strong. But their utility as cheap labor and the Republican creed of a nation of equals afforded them some protec-

---

Peace Policy, 1870–1884 (Washington, 1953); Howard Lamar, *Dakota Territory 1861–1889* (New Haven, 1956), 103–106; on 1871 act, Fritz, *Movement*, 84.

55. Garfield, Diaries, Jan. 12, 1872; Walker, *The Indian Question* (Boston, 1874), 134, 123, "The Indian Question," *NAR*, 116 (1873), 375, 382. See also James D. Cox, "The Indian Question," *IR*, 6 (1879), 617–634; Gene M. Gressley, ed., "A Cattleman Views Indian Policy—1875," *Mont*, 17 (1967), 2–11.

tion. In 1868 Congress ratified the Burlingame treaty, which permitted unrestricted Chinese immigration to the United States. California Democratic Senator Aaron A. Sargent later recalled: "The 'enthusiasm of humanity' was a great moving power in the nation . . . when the Burlingame treaty was ratified. The national exaltation growing out of the emancipation of a race and the sorrowful events of the civil war, had its climax in the opening of our gates to all mankind." The California Republican platform of 1869 approved of Chinese immigration, and publicists spoke of the ease with which the new arrivals could be Americanized. *Harper's Weekly* observed: "in the discussion of the Chinese question, it must not be forgotten that one of the most progressive steps in civilization is the perception of the essential identity of men and races."[56]

But underlying racial animosities and a declining need for Chinese labor fed anti-Chinese sentiment in the seventies. The fact that many came as temporary sojourners through a contract labor system was distressing. *Harper's Weekly* warned that "a cooly trade . . . into a country in half of which slavery has recently been the universal system of labor, should be plainly seen to be a very great peril." Feelings ran high in the West, and anti-Chinese violence mounted. About twenty Chinese were killed in an 1871 Los Angeles riot. California Democratic Governor William Irwin declared in 1876: "an irrepressible conflict between the Chinese and ourselves—between their civilization and ours—has already been initiated." West Coast Republican platforms vied with their Democratic counterparts in anti-Chinese sentiment. States and localities passed numerous restrictive laws; the California constitution of 1879 imposed especially harsh restraints; a federal circuit court held in 1878 that the Chinese were not subject to naturalization.

Congress in 1879 passed a law that in effect abrogated the Burlingame treaty. President Hayes vetoed this action as an insult to

---

56. Gunther P. Barth, *Bitter Strength: A History of the Chinese in the United States, 1850–1870* (Cambridge, 1964); Stuart C. Miller, *The Unwelcome Immigrant: The American Image of the Chinese, 1785–1882* (Berkeley and Los Angeles, 1969); Sargent quoted in Elmer C. Sandmyer, *The Anti-Chinese Movement in California* (Urbana, 1939), 82; HW, 14 (1870), 546–547. See also Raphael Pumpelly, "Our Impending Chinese Problem," *Galaxy*, 8 (1869), 22–33; William M. Armstrong, "Godkin and Chinese Labor," *AJES*, 21 (1962), 91–102; G. F. Seward, *Chinese Immigration in Its Social and Economic Aspects* (New York, 1881).

a friendly nation and an assault on the American tradition of free immigration. But his sympathy with the bill's intent was clear: "Our experience in dealing with weaker races—the Negroes and Indians, for example—is not encouraging." A revised treaty in 1880 gave the United States the right to "regulate, limit or suspend" the entry of Chinese laborers. And two years later an Exclusion Act—the first such in American history—forbade Chinese coolie immigration for ten years.[57]

The rise and fall of an expanded conception of American nationality also affected the status of women in American society. The women's rights movement had its origins in the prewar decades, along with antislavery and other social reforms. And as the Civil War opened new realms of achievement and aspiration to blacks, so did it invigorate the quest for female political and social equality. This was not a uniquely American cause. John Stuart Mill's powerful tract The Subjection of Women appeared in 1869, and John Bright proposed a women's suffrage bill to Parliament in 1870.

Some found a special consonance in the Negro suffrage and women's suffrage movements. The American Equal Rights Association formally linked the two causes in May 1866. As Indiana suffragists put it, "one class in society cannot properly represent the interests of another and . . . to secure justice to all, all must have a voice in making and enforcing our laws." A number of Republican senators supported women's suffrage legislation, and the Republican platforms of 1872 and 1876 spoke encouragingly, if vaguely, of "respectful consideration" for the "honest demands of this class of citizens for additional rights, privileges, and immunities." In 1879 Congress extended to women the right to practice before the federal courts.[58]

More concrete gains came on the state and local level. Substan-

57. HW, 14 (1870), 258; "California," AC (1871, 1876); Barnard, Hayes, 448. See also Roy T. Wortman, "Denver's Anti-Chinese Riot, 1880," ColM, 42 (1965), 275–291.

58. Eleanor Flexner, Century of Struggle: The Woman's Rights Movement in the United States (Cambridge, 1959), ch. 10; William L. O'Neill, Everyone Was Brave: The Rise and Fall of Feminism in America (Chicago, 1969), 14–29; "Indiana," AC (1869); Hans L. Trefousse, The Radical Republicans (New York, 1969), 23–27; Porter and Johnson, Platforms, 47, 54.

tial advances were made in "school suffrage"—the right to vote and run for school boards. Seven women were elected to the Boston School Committee in 1874 after the state Supreme Court upheld their right to be candidates. The Iowa, Kansas, and Minnesota legislatures were among those passing resolutions in favor of women's suffrage. And the Wyoming and Utah territories in 1870 became the first sizable political units to extend the vote to women.[59]

But as in the case of Negro civil rights, scattered successes were overwhelmed by more powerful countervailing attitudes. The call for women's civil and political equality stirred feelings comparable in their intensity to those evoked by attempts to alter the subordinate position of blacks. The minister Horace Bushnell spoke for many when he called female suffrage a "Reform Against Nature."

The Utah and Wyoming successes were isolated and unique: the product of a Mormon need to protect and justify polygamy in the one state, the product of a public relations gambit and a series of political miscalculations in the other. Otherwise, voters and legislatures overwhelmingly defeated attempts to add women to the polity. Kansas held the first referendum on female suffrage in 1867: the cause fared even worse than Negro suffrage. Referenda in Michigan (1874) and Colorado (1877) had similar results. Indeed, New Jersey in 1874 specifically restricted its suffrage to males, a provision that had not been in its statutes before. Attempts to permit taxpaying women to vote on municipal affairs were defeated in New York (1873), Rhode Island (1877), and Massachusetts (1878). When Susan B. Anthony and some of her associates sought to vote in Rochester in the 1872 election, they were successfully prosecuted under the Enforcement Act of 1870—a statute designed to protect black voters in the South—on the ground that they had interfered with the conduct of a general election. What was more, the judge directed the jury to come to a guilty verdict.[60]

59. D. H. Pingree, "Right of Women to Vote for School Officers," *CLJ*, 36 (1893), 154–156; Martha Strickland, "The Common Law and Statutory Right of Woman to Office," *ALR*, 17 (1883), 670–683. See also Ira V. Brown, "The Women's Rights Movement in Pennsylvania, 1848–1873," *PH*, 32 (1965), 153–165.

60. Bushnell, *Women's Suffrage; the Reform Against Nature* (New York, 1869); on Utah and Wyoming, Alan P. Grimes, *The Puritan Ethic and*

The courts severely constrained other rights of women. When Mrs. Myra Bradwell sought admission to the Illinois bar, the state supreme court rejected her application. The United States Supreme Court upheld that decision in 1873 on broad grounds of public policy. Justice Samuel Miller denied that the right to practice law was one of the privileges or immunities of national citizenship protected by the Fourteenth Amendment. His colleague Bradley went further, sweepingly objecting to the propriety of women practicing law. Bradley observed that "the natural and proper timidity and delicacy which belongs to the female sex evidently unfits it for many of the occupations of civil life," and that "the paramount destiny and mission of woman are to fulfill the noble and benign offices of wife and mother." Therefore it was "within the province of the legislature to ordain what offices, positions, and callings shall be filled and discharged by men, and shall receive the benefit of those energies and responsibilities, and that decision and firmness which are presumed to predominate in the sterner sex." In Minor v. Happersett (1875) Waite spoke for a unanimous court in declaring that citizenship was "membership of a nation, and nothing more," and did not include the right of female suffrage.[61]

Just as black political activity suffered from the worsening racial climate of the seventies, so did the women's rights movement bend before the chill wind of failure. Susan B. Anthony and Elizabeth Cady Stanton turned on other disadvantaged groups as impediments to their cause. Anthony blamed the movement's defeats on a misguided elite and on the "vast mass of ignorant, uneducated, degraded population in this country," and Stanton inveighed against the enfranchisement of "Africans, Chinese, and all the ignorant foreigners the moment they touch our shores." The American Equal Rights Association divided in 1869 over the Fifteenth Amendment and the future course of the movement.

Woman Suffrage (New York, 1967), 28, 47, 51; *AC*, states and years cited; on Anthony trial, John D. Lawson, ed., *American State Trials* (St. Louis, 1919), III, 54–69, and "Can a Judge Direct a Verdict of Guilty?" *ALJ*, 10 (1874), 33–35. See also Susan F. Cooper, "Female Suffrage," *HM*, 40 (1870), 438–446, 594–600.

61. Bradwell v. State, 16 Wall. 130, 141–142 (1873); Minor v. Happersett, 21 Wall. 162, 166 (1875). See also Ellen A. Martin, "Admission of Women to the Bar," *CLT*, 1 (1886), 76–92, and, for a critique of the Minor decision, "Woman Suffrage in its Legal Aspects," *CLJ*, 3 (1876), 51–54.

One offshoot, the National Woman Suffrage Association, headed by Anthony and Stanton, opposed the amendment because it provided only for Negro suffrage, and committed itself to work on the national level for a broad spectrum of political, social, and economic rights. The American Woman Suffrage Association, led by Lucy Stone, devoted itself to state and local pressure for the vote alone.[62]

A distinct and pervasive pattern emerges from this review of postwar northern social policy and action. In areas of concern as varied as public health, charity, and crime; the regulation of social behavior, education, and religion; and the civil status of blacks, Indians, Chinese, and women, the same sequence may be observed. First, in the wake of the war, there was an outburst of rhetoric and action designed to implement the war-born ideal of a unified, more egalitarian nation. And then there followed the resurgence—and usually the triumph—of countering nineteenth-century American values: laissez-faire, individualism, assumptions of racial and sexual inferiority.

62. Anthony quoted in Flexner, *Century of Struggle*, 144, Stanton in Grimes, *Puritan Ethic*, 87–88. See also James M. McPherson, "Abolitionists, Woman Suffrage, and the Negro, 1865–1869," *MAm*, 47 (1965), 40–47; Robert E. Riegel, "The Split of the Feminist Movement in 1869," *MVHR*, 49 (1962), 485–495.

The Political Economy
of Postwar America

THE CIVIL WAR left its mark on economic as well as social policymaking. Postwar northern economic policy had two distinctive features: a new readiness to call on government to assist economic development; and a perception of the economy (like the society at large) as a national fusion of harmonious, compatible interests.

But as in other areas of postwar public life, these assumptions were quickly overborne by opposing social realities. The respectability of laissez-faire economic theory, and a pervasive American individualism and localism, worked against any sustained state economic policy. And the underlying clash of interests—sectional, occupational, class, ideological—always present in American life was sharpened by the depression of the 1870s and the growth of American industrialism. By the mid-seventies the postwar hope that an active state might shape a more harmonious economic system was as chimerical as the hope that it might assure a more beneficent and egalitarian social order.

The Active State and the Harmony of Interests

The most influential pre-Civil War critic of laissez-faire was the Philadelphia economist Henry C. Carey, who vigorously championed a protective tariff and a "National school" of political economy. A high tariff, he argued, assured national prosperity and "harmony" among "the various portions of society." The *sauve qui peut* British system of Malthus and Ricardo led only to social conflict and lower class despair. A critic of the time decried Carey's "more than German readiness to refer to the co-ordinating power of the state, as a specific for social or economic discords." But that readiness had a special appeal to the generation that fought and won the Civil War.[1]

Philadelphia Republican Congressman William D. Kelley was Carey's leading postwar disciple. Kelley espoused a protective tariff (protective both of industry and wage scales), a mildly inflationary paper currency to stimulate economic growth, a federal eight-hour work law, and government-supported development of the Northwest. He rejected the "iron laws" of wages and labor prevalent in conventional economic thought: "The theory that labor ... is merely a raw material, and that that nation which pays least for it is wisest and best governed, is inadmissible in a democracy." Kelley derived his views from experience, not theory: "it became apparent to me, not only that Political Economy was not a science, but that it was impossible to frame a system of abstract economic propositions which would be universally applicable and beneficent." Fortunately, "the intimate relations of many ... students with the industries and people of the country render the scholasticisms of their teachers harmless."[2]

Kelley's perspective was hardly a disinterested one. Like Carey he spoke for Philadelphia manufacturers (and workers) who welcomed tariff protection and the debt-easing power of paper money. But his views were widely shared in postwar America. Horace Greeley's *Political Economy* (1871) attacked free trade, defended government subsidies for internal improvements, and endorsed labor unions. California insurance executive Caspar T. Hopkins

1. Carey, *The Harmony of Interests. Agricultural, Manufacturing and Commercial* (Philadelphia, 1872); Charles F. Dunbar, "Economic Science in America, 1776–1876," *NAR*, 122 (1876), 138. See also Arnold W. Green, *Henry C. Carey: Nineteenth Century Sociologist* (Philadelphia, 1951); Joseph Dorfman, *The Economic Mind in American Civilization* (New York, 1949), III, part I.

2. William D. Kelley, *Speeches, Addresses and Letters on Industrial and Financial Questions* (Philadelphia, 1872), v, xii, xx.

and *Alta California* editor John S. Hittell advocated similar policies.[3]

The most important postwar spokesman for a political economy of state intervention and harmonious interests was Francis A. Walker. The son of Amasa Walker, a leading prewar laissez-faire economist, the younger Walker fought in the war and emerged a brigadier general. He entered the federal bureaucracy in 1865, serving as David Ames Wells's assistant in the Bureau of Internal Revenue, and then as chief of the Bureau of Statistics, superintendent of the 1870 and 1880 censuses, and (briefly) as commissioner of Indian affairs. His wartime and postwar experience led him to challenge the reigning economic orthodoxy.

Walker like Kelley took issue with the prevailing theory that locked wages into an iron-bound relationship to national wealth. This he called "a complete justification for the existing order of things respecting wages." He argued that unions and strikes were appropriate devices for workers who sought to attain a greater share of the wealth generated by their labor, especially as technological change increased productivity. Walker thought it proper, too, for the state to guarantee laborers freedom of movement, an education, and decent working conditions. With typical postwar optimism he looked forward to a national future in which entrepreneurs and workingmen shared an ever higher level of national prosperity.[4]

This outlook—in part a continuation of prewar Whig-Republican ideas, in part a product of the special experience of the war—found fertile soil in the boom years after 1865. The economy of the late sixties and early seventies was dominated by "a rise of prices, great prosperity, large profits, high wages, and strikes for higher;

3. Greeley, *Political Economy* (Boston, 1871), 345; Charles A. Barker, *Henry George* (New York, 1955), 128–131. See also T. E. Cliffe Leslie, "Political Economy in the United States," *FRev*, 34 (1880), 493–498.

4. Walker quoted in Dorfman, *Economic Mind*, III, 104; Walker, "The Wage-Fund Theory," *NAR*, 120 (1875), 84–119. See also James P. Munroe, *A Life of Francis Amasa Walker* (New York, 1923); Bernard Newton, *The Economics of Francis Amasa Walker* (New York, 1968); Sidney Fine, *Laissez Faire and the General-Welfare State* (Ann Arbor, 1956), 73–79. On prewar Republican economic thought see Eric Foner, *Free Soil, Free Labor, Free Men* (New York, 1970), 12–23, 168–176.

large importations, a railway mania, expanded credits, over-trading, over-building, and high living."[5] The postwar economic boom was sparked by government-supported railroad construction. Trackage more than doubled from 35,085 miles in 1865 to 74,096 miles in 1875. State aid to canal and railroad building had been common in the years after 1815; but corruption and extravagance led to its widespread prohibition before the Civil War. Now once again government fueled the expansion of the American transportation system.

Between 1862 and 1872 a hundred million acres of land from the public domain, and about the same number of dollars in federal bonds and loans, went to the support of railroad construction. The apex of this effort was the "great national enterprise" of the transcontinental lines. The pioneering Union and Central Pacific (chartered in 1862 and 1864), the Northern Pacific (1864), the Atlantic & Pacific (1866), and the Texas & Pacific (1871) sought and usually received federal aid on an unprecedented scale. The Union Pacific was a mixed enterprise, with a congressional charter and public as well as private directors. When in May 1869 the Union Pacific and the Central Pacific met at Promontory, Utah, the event unleashed a flood of rhetoric. It symbolized the reunified republic, it marked "a new chapter in American nationality, in American progress and in American power."[6]

The federally aided transcontinental lines were only the most conspicuous examples of a massive postwar railroad expansion. Counties, cities, towns, and villages throughout the North lavishly subsidized lesser projects. Between 1866 and 1873, twenty-nine state legislatures approved over eight hundred proposals to grant local aid to railroad companies. The three leaders—New York, Illinois, and Missouri—authorized over $70 million worth of aid.

5. Quoted in David A. Wells, *Recent Economic Changes* (New York, 1889), 5. See also J. B. Hodgskin, "The Financial Condition of the United States," *NAR*, 108 (1869), 517–541; S. Morton Peto, *Resources and Prospects of America* (New York, 1866), 365, 377.
6. Carter Goodrich, *Government Promotion of Canals and Railroads, 1800–1890* (New York, 1960), 177, 183; Lewis H. Haney, *A Congressional History of Railways in the United States* (Madison, 1910), II, 214–227; Robert W. Fogel, *The Union Pacific Railroad: A Case in Premature Enterprise* (Baltimore, 1960); Willard H. Smith, *Schuyler Colfax* (Indianapolis, 1952), 321.

State legislatures (most of them constitutionally prohibited from granting direct subsidies) cooperated by passing local aid bills. Illinois in 1869 gave tax advantages to local units that issued railroad bonds. The euphoria transcended party lines. Democratic Governor Henry Haight of California strongly supported local aid in 1870, and Republican John W. Geary of Pennsylvania declared in his 1867 inaugural: "all public works, among these a liberal and properly restricted general railroad system, . . . should receive the fostering care and most liberal aid of the government."[7]

Assistance most commonly took the form of stock subscriptions by municipalities, paid for through tax-secured bond issues. Company bonds also were underwritten, and at times local authorities made outright gifts to railroad developers. Promoters were quick to capitalize on this openhandedness. The New York & Oswego Railroad meandered over the upstate New York countryside in search of local aid, finally touching (in both senses of the word) some fifty communities with 250 labyrinthine miles of track. The line was finished in 1873, just in time for the financial crisis of that year, and promptly went into bankruptcy.

By 1873 about a thousand state court and twenty Supreme Court decisions upheld state and local railroad aid. Iowa's judiciary, which had attempted to block city railroad bonding during the Civil War and had been countermanded by the state Supreme Court, underwent a "radical change" in 1869 and thereafter freely approved local aid.[8]

Government contributed in other ways to the railroad boom. The Hoosac Tunnel, penetrating the Berkshires to give Boston a direct rail link to the West, was a languishing prewar state project that gained new support after 1865. "The Great Bore"—a label

7. Goodrich, *Government Promotion*, ch. 7; "Illinois," *AC* (1869); "California," *AC* (1870); Harry M. Tinckum, *John White Geary* (Philadelphia, 1940), 120.

8. Robert S. Hunt, *Law and Locomotives: The Impact of the Railroad on Wisconsin Law in the Nineteenth Century* (Madison, 1958), 85; on New York & Oswego, Goodrich, *Government Promotion*, 242; estimate of decisions in Olcott v. Supervisor, 16 Wall. 678 (1873); Horace G. Wood, *A Treatise on the Law of Railroads* (Boston, 1885), 264; Gelpcke v. Dubuque, 1 Wall. 175 (1864). See also Ethan P. Allen, "Gelpcke v. The City of Dubuque," *IJHP*, 28 (1930), 177–193; Charles Fairman, *Reconstruction and Reunion 1864–88, Part One* (New York, 1971), 918 ff.

earned both by its five mile length and the interminable public controversy that it generated—was completed in 1872.

Another venture of the time was the Cincinnati Southern Railroad, a wholly public enterprise. Ohio's constitution forbade either state or local aid to railroad companies. But Cincinnati had a compelling need to obtain a direct rail route to the upper South (and ultimately to New Orleans), lest it lose out to its great commercial competitor Louisville. The city's voters in 1868 overwhelmingly approved a proposal that Cincinnati build its own line. The municipality floated some $18 million worth of construction loans over the ensuing decade and built a road that was run by city-appointed trustees. In 1872 Ohio's Boesel Law authorized all minor civil divisions to build, lease, or operate their own railroads. Before the state Supreme Court found the law unconstitutional a year later, about ninety local governments voted bonds for the construction of such lines.[9]

Contemporaries were increasingly concerned over the financial shakiness and political corruption that attended railroad subsidization. But there was more than jobbery and profiteering to the postwar railroad boom. The spreading web of trackage was a highly visible expression of a profound American desire to master space and distance—a desire fed by the postwar commitment to active government and a unified nation.

While railroads made the largest and most successful demands on government for aid, other interests turned to the state as well. Commercial and transportation conventions seeking government support flourished after the war. A number of such gatherings in 1869 called on the federal government to build canals across Michigan and Florida and to link the Mississippi and the Great Lakes so that ocean-going vessels might ply directly between the continental heartland and Europe, South America, and Asia.

Congress failed to respond to the more grandiose of these schemes. But it did vote substantial postwar rivers and harbors aid: a yearly average of $3,987,500 from 1866 to 1875, as compared to $370,100 from 1851 to 1860. And it assisted in the construction of

9. On Hoosac Tunnel, Edward C. Kirkland, *Men, Cities and Transportation* (Cambridge, 1948), I, 387–432, 454–455; J. H. Hollander, *The Cincinnati Southern Railway* (Baltimore, 1894).

telegraph lines and the establishment of steamship mail routes to Europe and the Far East. President Grant in 1871 asked Congress to set up a federal telegraph network operated by the Post Office Department, and Congressman James A. Garfield believed that the United States "must ultimately take control of the telegraph, or at least must have telegraph lines of its own."

States and municipalities also explored new economic roles. California in 1863 created a pioneering Board of Harbor Commissioners to own and operate a share of the city's port facilities. The Pennsylvania legislature of 1870 seriously considered assuming control of the state's telegraph system. Ben Butler observed of Massachusetts in 1871: "our whole state government has gone into commission." He estimated that in the preceding decade over thirty new state boards and commissions had been created.[10]

A new era in state data collection began in 1869 when Massachusetts created the first Bureau of Labor Statistics. Carroll Wright became the bureau's director in 1873, and made the gathering of information on the condition of workers a form of "practical sociology," designed to reveal social conditions that called for reform.

A number of states quickly followed Massachusetts's lead. At the same time, federal and state governments cooperated to establish agricultural experiment stations designed to increase the productivity of the nation's farmers. There was even an occasional glimmer of concern for the future of the country's natural resources. The 1867 Wisconsin legislature set up a commission to determine "whether the destruction of the forests of this state, now going on so rapidly, is likely to prove as disastrous to the future inhabitants . . . as is claimed by many."[11]

10. "Commercial Conventions," AC (1869); HS, 455; Grant in MP, IX, 4104; Garfield, Diaries, March 29, 1872, LC; Gerald D. Nash, State Government and Economic Development: A History of Administrative Policies in California, 1849–1933 (Berkeley, 1964), 114; "Pennsylvania," AC (1870); Butler, "Address at Springfield, Aug. 24, 1871," NYPL. See also John W. Joyce, "Early Oregon Public Utility Regulation, 1843–1899," CRev, 15 (1933–1934), 85–95; Gerald D. Nash, "Government and Business: A Case Study of State Regulation of Corporate Securities, 1850–1933," BHR, 38 (1964), 141–162.

11. James Leiby, Carroll Wright and Labor Reform: The Origin of Labor Statistics (Cambridge, 1960), ch. 3; on experiment stations, A. Hunter Dupree, Science in the Federal Government (Cambridge, 1957), 169; Robert

Postwar economic policy was marked not only by more active government, but also by the assumption that there was an underlying harmony to the economic interests of the American people. Again, this was not a new idea, nor was it unique to the postwar years. But in the wake of a war that affirmed the strength of American nationalism and the ideal of social unity, that belief now had special appeal.

The assumption of harmonious economic interests underlay the most important postwar labor and agrarian organizations. Large numbers of American workingmen responded to the organizational lessons and the hope of social betterment that were part of the legacy of the Civil War. Major advances in unionization occurred between 1862 and 1875: more so than at any time since the Jacksonian years. The National Labor Union, the first national organization of workers, began in 1866 as a coalition of established trade unions. But it soon reached out to include unskilled as well as skilled workers, blacks as well as whites, antimonopoly associations, land and labor leagues, and the Marxist International Workingmen's Association. Charles Sumner, Wendell Phillips, and Horace Greeley were members of the NLU, and at its peak in the late sixties it claimed a membership of between 200,000 and 400,000.[12]

The primary cause of the politically-minded NLU, and indeed of postwar organized labor in general, was the "all-absorbing subject of Eight Hours." Legislation enforcing a maximum number of hours in each workday was an issue well before the Civil War; but it peaked in appeal after 1865. Support was widespread and intense. In 1872 60,000 New York City workingmen marched to demonstrate their fealty to the cause. A shorter working day promised not only eased working conditions but also the leisure necessary for education and self-improvement. "Before this movement stops," said Wendell Phillips, "every child born in America must have an

N. Manley, "A Note on Government and Agriculture: A Nineteenth Century Nebraska View," NH, 45 (1964), 237–252; James W. Hurst, Law and Economic Growth: The Legal History of the Lumber Industry in Wisconsin, 1866–1915 (Cambridge, 1964), 446–447.

12. Gerald N. Grob, Workers and Utopia: A Study of Ideological Conflict in the American Labor Movement 1864–1900 (Evanston, 1961), 11–33; David Montgomery, Beyond Equality: Labor and the Radical Republicans, 1862–1872 (New York, 1967), 176 ff.

equal chance in life." Massachusetts governor Israel Washburn explained his support for a ten-hour bill for women and children in similar terms: "The assumption of our law is, that the highest intelligence of all is the highest goal of the entire people." The Greenback party argued in 1877 that shorter hours meant "more leisure for mental improvement and saving from premature decay and death." Congress in 1868 passed a bill fixing an eight-hour day for the federal government's manual workers. Andrew Johnson's administration held that a proportionate reduction in wages was consistent with the bill's intent; but President Grant ruled otherwise in 1869.[13]

There were other instances of heightened activity by and for labor in the postwar years. Small but active labor reform parties appeared in Massachusetts and other states. The 1872 Pennsylvania legislature repealed that state's Conspiracy Act, which impeded the organization of striking anthracite miners. A number of states passed laws regulating the hours and conditions of factory work. The first case involving a state law that limited the working hours of women and children came before the Massachusetts Supreme Judicial Court in 1876. The court readily concluded that the act was an appropriate application of the commonwealth's police power to protect public health.

Postwar publicists and intellectuals showed a·new concern for the problems of labor. *Nation* editor E. L. Godkin (who later displayed a strong antilabor bias) dwelt on the community of interest that united labor and capital. He and others called for profit-sharing plans and the arbitration of disputes to modify a divisive and class-breeding wage system. Leisure, education, land ownership, profit-sharing, arbitration: these were the themes of a public discourse that assumed the inherent harmony of worker and employer.[14]

13. Montgomery, *Beyond Equality*, 177; Norman J Ware, *The Industrial Worker 1840–1860* (Boston, 1924), chs. 8–9; Wendell Phillips, *Speeches, Lectures, and Letters*, 2d ser. (Boston, 1891), 539; "Massachusetts," *AC* (1874); Charles E. Persons, Mabel Parton, and Mabelle Moses, *Labor Laws and their Enforcement with Special Reference to Massachusetts* (New York, 1911), 95; John R. Commons, *History of Labour in the United States* (New York, 1921), II, chs. 3–4.

14. "Pennsylvania," *AC* (1872); Commonwealth v. Hamilton Manufacturing Company, 120 Mass. 383 (1876); E. L. Godkin, "Co-Operation," *NAR*, 106 (1868), 150–175; Samuel Eliot, "Relief of Labor," *JSS*, 4 (1871), 133–149.

Oliver H. Kelley, a clerk in the newly established Bureau of Agriculture, founded the National Grange of the Patrons of Husbandry in 1867. "Everything is progressing. Why not the farmers?" was his justification. The Grange combined a fraternal function—it was modeled on the Masons—with the goal of protecting its members "against the numerous combinations by which their interests are injuriously affected." Its conception of eligible membership was as broad as that of the NLU. Besides farmers, the Grange included grain dealers and commission men, an urban, YMCA-like Pandowdy Club, and even a workingmen's affiliate, the Sovereigns of Industry. By 1874, the organization claimed 450,000 family memberships in over 20,000 local chapters, primarily in the Midwest and the South.

Many Granges were active in the movement for railroad regulation during the seventies. But the Patrons of Husbandry hardly were a society of the poor and the dispossessed. Henry George thought that the Grange attracted "a class which . . . is the one least likely to accept radical ideas. It is warmly supported by men who hold five, twenty, fifty thousand acres of land." Just as organized labor drew on the higher ranks of skilled workingmen, so did the Grange consist of landed farmers rather than sharecroppers, tenants, or farm laborers. It is not surprising that the Grange, like its labor union counterparts, operated on the assumption that postwar America was a nation of harmoniously related producers, not of divided classes.[15]

The Regulatory Impulse

The impulse to regulate the economy was as potent a force in the postwar polity as the impulse to aid its development. The one did not necessarily exclude or conflict with the other; and both gained greater legitimacy from the new acceptability of active government.

15. Oliver H. Kelley, *Origin and Progress of the Order of the Patrons of Husbandry* (Philadelphia, 1875), 25, 128; "The Patrons of Husbandry," *AC* (1873); Stephe Smith, *Grains for the Grangers* (Philadelphia, 1874), 39 ff; Dennis S. Nordin, "A Revisionist Interpretation of the Patrons of Husbandry, 1867–1900," *Hist,* 32 (1970), 630–643; Solon J. Buck, *The Granger Movement* (Cambridge, 1913), ch. 2; Charles A. Barker, *Henry George* (New York, 1955), 262.

Postwar cities and states added substantially to an already developing body of licensing acts designed to control entry into and the conduct of medicine, dentistry, and pharmacy. An 1870 Wisconsin statute, for example, sought "to protect the people from empiricism in the practice of medicine." New trade associations such as the National Board of Trade (1868) and the American Bankers Association (1875) called on the federal government to meet their special needs. The Board of Trade asked for standardized weights and measures and uniform debt collection by the federal courts. Bankers wanted a national statute to replace state laws that limited interest rates and exempted personal property from attachment for debt. Similar pressure from manufacturers led Congress in 1870 to enact a national trade mark law.[16]

Bankruptcy had special importance in the volatile business world of the nineteenth century. National bankruptcy laws were passed in 1800 and 1841, but "that cankering jealousy of the general government with which some of the states are so deeply infected" and the conflicting interests of debtors and creditors led to their quick repeal. The business depression of the late 1850s, and then the commercial upset caused by the war, spurred demands for a new statute. Roscoe Conkling argued in 1863 for a uniform bankruptcy law on the ground that "now more than ever, it is to the public interest that all the energies of the country should be free." The bill that finally emerged in 1867 established a uniform system of bankruptcy proceedings, brought corporations within its rubric, and extended the bankruptcy jurisdiction of the federal courts. It was hailed as "the first [bankruptcy] bill constructed as a permanent piece of legislation and with a view to the interest of the Nation and of National commerce and not merely to the interest of individual debtors and creditors."[17]

16. George F. H. Markee, "Legislation in Relation to Pharmacy," *JSS*, 5 (1873), 122–135; "Wisconsin," *AC* (1870); on Board of Trade, George R. Woolfolk, *The Cotton Regency: The Northern Merchants and Reconstruction 1865–1880* (New York 1958), 23; 16 *SL* 198 (July 8, 1870). See also Stanley C. Hollander, "Nineteenth Century Anti-Drummer Legislation in the United States," *BHR*, 38 (1964), 479–500.

17. "On a National Bankruptcy Law," *AmJ*, 1 (Jan.-April 1829), 49; Charles Warren, *Bankruptcy in United States History* (Cambridge, 1935), 101, 109. See also Woolfolk, *Cotton Regency*, 40–41, and J. F. B., "Expediency of a Bankrupt Law," *ALReg*, ns, 4 (1864), 449–460.

Well before the Civil War the corporation had become an important device for accumulating capital and organizing enterprise. Corporate chartering (with the exception of the Bank of the United States) was the province of state legislatures, not Congress. But the congressional charters given to the Union Pacific and Central Pacific Railroads opened up promising prospects of federal incorporation. Democrats feared that "the dominant party means to commit Congress to a general incorporating policy—the granting of charters to railroads, banks, manufacturing companies, and so on."[18]

Most corporate enterprise of the time, small-scaled and geographically limited, was content with the weak system of state regulation that then prevailed. But a few businesses—railroads, express companies, most notably insurance—already were national in scope, and in the postwar years began to look to federal supervision as an attractive alternative to state surveillance.

The desire was especially strong in the insurance business, which because of its quasi-public nature had to deal with an unusually elaborate system of state regulation. Civil War financier Jay Cooke obtained a congressional charter for his National Life Insurance Company by locating it in the District of Columbia. Major northeastern insurance firms lobbied for a system of federal regulation, more uniform (and more pliable) than the varied controls of the states. The *Commercial and Financial Chronicle* called this "a fresh illustration of the prevailing mania for surrendering individual control into the hands of the general government."[19]

The Supreme Court was aware of the need to foster economic development that transcended state lines. In 1876 it struck down a Missouri law restricting the entry of Texas and Mexican cattle, even though the state's police power over public health was at

18. James W. Hurst, *The Legitimacy of the Business Corporation in the Law of the United States* (Charlottesville, 1970); Allan Nevins and Milton H. Thomas, eds., *The Diary of George Templeton Strong* (New York, 1952), IV, 287. See also William C. Kessler, "Incorporation in New England, 1800–1875," *JEH*, 8 1948), 43–62; George H. Evans, Jr., *Business Incorporations in the United States 1800–1943* (New York, 1948); Russell H. Curtis, "National Corporations," *ALR*, 21 (1887), 258–269.

19. Howard J. Graham, *Everyman's Constitution* (Madison, 1968), 83–85, 382 ff; Henrietta M. Larson, *Jay Cooke* (Cambridge, 1936), 239–242; *CFC*, 1 (1865), 708–709. See also "Foreign Corporations," *CLJ*, 2 (1875), 623–624.

issue. During the seventies the Court began to use the Constitution's commerce clause to void state laws that interfered with out-of-state salesmen or imposed burdens on interstate railroad traffic. As Justice Bradley put it, "the needs of the country require that corporations . . . should be able to transact business in different states." Companies responded by seeking to shift their litigation from state to federal courts, assuming with some justification that they would get a more sympathetic hearing there. The groundwork was being laid for the weakening of state authority over foreign (out-of-state) corporations that reached its peak at the turn of the century.[20]

In general, however, the postwar polity tended to sustain rather than limit corporation regulation by the states. A federal insurance law never got beyond congressional committee hearings. And the Supreme Court—in part because Congress had chosen not to regulate the insurance business—upheld a Virginia statute that restricted the activities of out-of-state insurance company salesmen. Justice Stephen Field's Paul v. Virginia opinion for a unanimous Court argued that insurance was not an article in interstate commerce, and that corporations were not citizens entitled to protection under the Constitution's privileges and immunities clause: "The corporation being the mere creation of local law, can have no legal existence beyond the limits of the sovereignty where created."[21]

John Marshall's Dartmouth College decision of 1819, which gave corporate charters the sanctity of contracts, came under public attack after the Civil War for shielding corporations from state supervision. Postwar judges frequently stressed the inherent limits of corporate status: "corporations, like natural persons, are subject

20. Welton v. Missouri, 91 U.S. 282 (1876); Hollander, "Anti-Drummer Legislation"; John N. Pomeroy, "Inter-State Commerce," SLR, ns, 4 (1878), 357–403; Felix Frankfurter, The Commerce Clause under Marshall, Taney and Waite (Chapel Hill, 1937), 74–114; Bradley in Doyle v. Continental Insurance Company, 94 U.S. 535 (1876); Gerard C. Henderson, The Position of Foreign Corporations in American Constitutional Law (Cambridge, 1918), 118–122, ch. 10; John F. Dillon, Removal of Causes from State to Federal Courts (St. Louis, 1876).

21. Paul v. Virginia, 8 Wall. 168 (1869); Stanley I. Kutler, Judicial Power and Reconstruction Politics (Chicago, 1968), 133–135; Fairman, Reconstruction and Reunion, 1396–1402; Graham, Everyman's Constitution, 367–437. See also Samuel T. Spear, "The Citizenship of Corporations," ALJ, 16 (1877), 344–347.

to remedial legislation and amenable to general laws." Nor were they uncritical of the excesses of the new industrial and financial capitalism: "the dollar has too much to say in the affairs of the Republic" (Waite); "a people disposed for freedom will not tolerate ... oppression at the hands of private corporations or powerful citizens" (Bradley); "the new breed of speculative capitalists engage in no commerce, no trade, no manufactures, no agriculture. They *produce nothing*" (Miller).[22]

The readiness of the Supreme Court to uphold state economic legislation appeared most dramatically in its Slaughterhouse decision of 1873. That landmark case in American constitutional history is commonly discussed in terms of the evolution of the due process and privileges and immunities clauses of the Fourteenth Amendment. But the decision is revealing also for the light it casts on the acceptance of legislative activism in the postwar years.

Louisiana's Republican legislature in 1869 chartered the Crescent City Live Stock Handling and Slaughterhouse Company and gave it a monopoly grip on the city's meat slaughtering business. Ostensibly this was an attempt to reform the chaotic and unsanitary meat preparation industry. But in fact much more was at stake. Groups of entrepreneurs and politicians were fiercely competing for control of the lucrative flow of Texas cattle to New Orleans and the distribution of processed meat elsewhere. One of these, consisting primarily of former Unionist Whigs, obtained the Crescent City monopoly. Ex-Confederate Democrats were conspicuous among their competitors.[23]

The excluded butchers and their supporters brought suit against the Crescent City company on the ground (among others) that its charter violated the Fourteenth Amendment protection of citizens'

22. On criticisms of Dartmouth College see "The Dartmouth College Case," *ALR*, 8 (1873–1874), 189–239, John M. Shirley, *The Dartmouth College Causes and the Supreme Court of the United States* (St. Louis, 1879), and Thomas M. Cooley, *Treatise on the Constitutional Limitations which Rest upon the Legislative Power of the States*, 2d ed. (Boston, 1871), 335n; *ALReg*, ns, 15 (1876), 176; C. Peter Magrath, *Morrison R. Waite: The Triumph of Character* (New York, 1963), 207–210; "Outline of my views on the subject of the Granger Cases," Bradley Mss, NJHS; Charles Fairman, *Mr. Justice Miller and the Supreme Court 1862–1890* (Cambridge, 1939), 67, 300.

23. Mitchell Franklin, "The Foundations and Meaning of the Slaughterhouse Cases," *TLR*, 18 (1943), 1–88.

privileges and immunities from harm by the state. John A. Campbell, who had left the Supreme Court to join the Confederacy in 1861, argued that this was only one instance of a general pattern of Radical Reconstruction misrule: "prodigal expenditures and jobs innumerable form only a portion of the mischiefs of a government destitute of any sense of moral responsibility." Opposing counsel Matt Carpenter, a Republican senator from Wisconsin, defended the Crescent City charter as an acceptable product of legislative activism: "the legislature is the sole and exclusive judge of whether a statute is reasonable for the benefit of the people."

Justice Miller's majority opinion was a notable instance of the postwar Court's readiness to let state legislatures act. The regulatory power, he argued, was paramount, even if it led to monopoly: "Upon it depends the security of social existence in a thickly populated community, the enjoyment of private and social life, and the beneficial use of property." To apply the Fourteenth Amendment in the present case would "constitute this Court a perpetual censor upon all legislation of the States on the civil rights of their own citizens," and thus impinge on licensing acts, liquor regulation, hours of labor and child labor laws, and the like.[24]

In this sense the Court joined the other sectors of the postwar polity in affirming the principle that government might act concretely, positively, indeed aggressively in the realm of economic policy.

Just as the railroads were the chief recipients of the postwar impulse to subsidize economic growth, so were they the primary objects of the collateral impulse to regulate the economy. As the railroad network thickened, and the lines turned to rate discrimination and rate-fixing to enhance their profits, the polity increasingly was called upon not to contribute to the development of the roads, but to check their awesome power. Garfield quoted Godkin of the *Nation* in 1873: "The locomotive is coming in contact with

24. Slaughter-House Cases, 16 Wall. 36 (1873); Campbell in 83 U.S. 398, Carpenter in 83 U.S. 399. See also Fairman, *Reconstruction and Reunion*, 1324–1363; Graham, *Everyman's Constitution*, ch. 7; William L. Royall, "The Fourteenth Amendment: The Slaughter-House Cases," *SLR*, ns, 4 (1878), 558–584.

the framework of our institutions. In this country of simple government, the most powerful centralizing force which civilization has yet produced must, within the next score years, assume its relations to that political machinery which is to control and regulate it."[25]

The idea of federal railroad regulation was a plausible one, given the strengthened nationalism of the postwar years. (Asked if he thought that Washington had the capacity to regulate the roads, a westerner replied: "Sir, you will never make me doubt that a government which could put down that mighty Rebellion can regulate the details of a few tariffs of some railroad corporation!") Isaac F. Redfield, author of the leading contemporary treatise on railroad law, was an early advocate of congressional railroad regulation under the Constitution's commerce power. Observing in 1874 that "all business, and almost existence itself, is at the mercy of railway transportation," he saw "no hope of relief from any imaginable source but in the national prerogatives."[26]

When Congress considered railroad regulation after the Civil War, pressure to do so came from farmers and commercial interests in the West and the South who objected to high freight rates. An 1874 bill proposed by Iowa Republican Congressman George W. McCrary sought to put a ceiling on the charges levied by monopolistic roads. But other exponents of federal regulation—eastern farmers, New York merchants—had very different concerns. The farmers feared that their western competitors would benefit from low through rates, and New York merchants wanted some check against discriminatory rate schedules favoring other eastern ports. Texas Democrat John H. Reagan, who had close ties with eastern merchant and shipping interests, was the leading champion of antidiscrimination legislation in the seventies. Further to complicate matters, the railroads themselves had varying views on federal regulation. Some lines saw in it a means of escaping from varied state restrictions; others preferred state to federal supervision; still

25. "Railroads in the United States," *AC* (1875); Garfield, *The Future of the Republic, Its Dangers and Its Hopes* (Cleveland, 1873), 20.

26. Westerner quoted in Charles F. Adams, Jr., "The Granger Movement," *NAR*, 120 (1875), 408; Redfield, "The Regulation of Interstate Traffic on Railways by Congress," *ALReg*, ns, 13 (1874), 10.

others—probably most—opposed regulation of any sort.[27]

Given these complexities of interest, and the weakening condition of the national government in the seventies, it is not surprising that railroad regulation developed first in the states. Massachusetts led the way by establishing a Board of Railroad Commissioners in 1869. Charles Francis Adams, Jr., was its first chairman, and in the postwar years emerged as the most important eastern advocate of state railroad supervision.

Adams's service as a Civil War officer schooled him in the possibilities of government power. He was influenced too by the fashionable social scientism of the time. He later recalled that when he read Mill's essay on Comte in November 1865, "I emerged from the theological stage in which I had been nurtured, and passed into the scientific." Concluding that railroads were "the most developing force and largest field of the day," Adams self-consciously embarked on a career as a railroad specialist. It eventually led this brother of Henry Adams to the chairmanship of the Union Pacific's government board of directors, and to the presidency of that line in 1884.[28]

Adams advocated state railroad regulation "in view of the great and growing incompetence so manifest in the national Congress." His solution to the wasteful and disorderly character of the railroad business was a commission of experts: "Whatever is attempted, let it be attempted knowingly and systematically; in obedience to some natural law." He proposed that Massachusetts gain control of the major rail route from Boston to the West and make its rates a competitive measuring rod for other, private lines: "we do not want to destroy competition by State ownership, but we want to get back to it through mixed ownership."

Regulation by experts precluded supervision by the legislature. Adams feared that "coercive legislation" would "by the imposition of traffic acts and regulations for the convenience or accommodation of the public, do everything but absolutely annihilate the essential franchises of railroad corporations." His Railroad Com-

27. Lee Benson, *Merchants, Farmers, and Railroads: Railroad Regulation and New York Politics 1850–1887* (Cambridge, 1955); Gabriel Kolko, *Railroads and Regulation 1877–1916* (Princeton, 1965), ch. 1.

28. *Charles Francis Adams, 1835–1915: An Autobiography* (Boston, 1916), 179, 170.

mission, not surprisingly, was a profoundly conservative instrument. Its major action was to break a Boston & Maine engineers' strike in 1877—and to do it so forcefully that New England had no further major railroad labor troubles for the rest of the century.[29]

Many midwestern advocates of regulation wanted a very different sort of railroad commission: one that would enforce a rate structure set by the legislature. The 1870 Illinois constitution required the legislature "from time to time" to "pass laws establishing maximum rates of charges for the transportation of passengers and freight." That body responded in 1871 by setting maximum freight and grain storage elevator rates, forbidding rate discrimination, and creating a railroad commission with supervisory and enforcement powers. Similar laws were adopted in Minnesota, Wisconsin, and Iowa. Because Grange members often were prominent advocates of rate regulation, these acts came to be known as the Granger laws.

But the rate regulation movement involved far more than an uprising of exploited farmers against voracious railroads. Attitudes toward the lines were highly ambivalent. Many of those who wanted controls also were inclined "to discountenance any action on this subject calculated to retard the progress of railroad enterprises, or work injustice to those invaluable auxiliaries to commerce and civilization." Some farmers wanted lower rates. Others wanted antidiscrimination rules that would *prevent* their competitors from getting lower rates. Still others, who wished to attract railroads to their area or wanted to keep the financially shaky lines that serviced them, opposed any regulation at all. Shippers and middlemen in river towns such as Dubuque and Saint Paul or lake ports such as Chicago sought regulation to prevent the railroads from charging lower rates for the through traffic that bypassed them.

While farmers generally wanted rate authority to rest in the state legislatures, shippers, merchants, and manufacturers preferred independent commissions. And as the seventies progressed they got their way. At the same time the major railroads challenged the

29. Adams, "The Government and the Railroad Corporations," NAR, 112 (1871), 35; Edward C. Kirkland, Charles Francis Adams, Jr., 1835–1915: The Patrician at Bay (Cambridge, 1965), 39, 46; Adams, "Legislative Control over Railway Charters," ALR, 1, (1866–1867), 473. See also Dorfman, Economic Mind, III, 24–36.

Granger laws in the courts and, more successfully, watered them down (or made them unworkable) in the legislatures. The combined force of intricately clashing interests, corporate power, and general hostility to active government reduced state railroad regulation to insignificance.[30]

But before the decade ended the Supreme Court in Munn v. Illinois (1877) once more showed its readiness to uphold the regulatory power of the legislature. Chief Justice Waite's majority opinion, which sustained an 1871 Illinois law setting maximum rates for grain storage, was steeped in the judicial assumptions of the postwar years. He took a broad view of the state police power, and upheld legislative action even though it limited property rights. His decision has been called "a brief in behalf of judicial deference to legislative decisions."

Waite applied a doctrine enunciated by Chief Justice Matthew Hale in England two hundred years before: that when private property was "affected with a public interest" it fell subject to public accountability and control. State courts in the early nineteenth century used the public interest standard to uphold the eminent domain power to take land for railroad and other purposes. Postwar courts did the same when they approved local taxing and borrowing to provide railroad aid. Now Waite extended the public interest standard to rate regulation as well.[31]

30. Buck, *Granger Movement*, chs. 4–5; Anti-Monopoly convention quoted in "Iowa," *AC* (1874). See also Harold D. Woodman, "Chicago Businessmen and the 'Granger' Laws," *AH*, 36 (1962), 16–24; Ward M. McAfee, "Local Interests and Railroad Regulation in California During the Granger Decade," *PHR*, 37 (1968), 51–66; Roy V. Scott, "Grangerism in Champaign County, Illinois, 1873–1877," *MAm*, 43 (1961), 139–163; George H. Miller, *Railroads and the Granger Laws* (Madison, 1971); Charles N. Glaab, *Kansas City and the Railroads: Community Policy in the Growth of a Regional Metropolis* (Madison, 1962), 175 ff.

31. Munn v. Illinois, 94 U.S. 113 (1877); Magrath, *Waite*, 188. See also Charles Fairman, "The So-Called Granger Cases, Lord Hale, and Justice Bradley," *StLR*, 5 (1953), 587–679; Harry W. Scheiber, "The Road to *Munn*: Eminent Domain and the Concept of Public Purpose in the State Courts," *PAH*, 5 (1971), 329–402. James K. Edsall, "The Granger Cases and the Police Power," *ABA Reports*, 10 (1887), 288–316, argues that Waite's decision was the "antithesis" of the Dartmouth College case in that it restored the principle of government control over private corporations.

Yet the Munn case also provided an outlet for views that militated against government supervision. Justice Field's dissenting opinion attacked the Illinois rate law as "nothing less than a bold assertion of absolute power by the State to control, at its discretion, the property and business of the citizen, and fix the compensation he shall receive." Privately he complained: "I think the doctrine announced by the majority practically destroys the guaranties of the Constitution intended for the protection of the rights of private property." Waite himself conceded that "under some circumstances" legislation might be held to violate the Fourteenth Amendment: a portent of the conservative jurisprudence of later years.[32]

The Limits of Government

The political and economic atmosphere of postwar America changed in the 1870s, and with it the relationship of government to the economy. Just as the postwar ideal of social unity ran afoul of the realities of racial antipathy and group difference, so did the vision of an active state fostering an economy of harmonious elements succumb to the prevailing belief in laissez-faire economics and to powerful class, sectional, and individual clashes of interest.

An observer predicted in 1871: "from this time forward, it will be incumbent upon Congress to devote its time and thought chiefly to the material interests of the nation." Certainly the economy of the seventies posed new and difficult problems. Widespread unemployment, bankruptcy, and labor unrest followed the panic of 1873, but did not impede economic growth. One measure (using an 1899 productivity index of 100) is that output, which had gone from 13 in 1860 to 23 in 1870, continued to rise to 39 in 1880. A third more wage earners were in manufacturing in 1879 than a dec-

---

32. Field in Munn v. Illinois, 94 U.S. 148, to David A. Wells, June 29, 1874, Wells Mss, NYPL; Magrath, *Waite*, 207–210. See also Charles Warren, *The Supreme Court in United States History* (Boston, 1923), III, 303–311, for contemporary reactions.

ade before; farm productivity spiraled upward. An increasingly mechanized agriculture supplying large urban and international markets; an expanding industrial plant dependent on ever more elaborate systems of transportation, marketing, and finance; growing problems of unemployment, falling crop prices, and maldistribution of wealth: this was the shape of the economy in the seventies.[33]

It was a new and puzzling economic order. The most consequential attempt of the time to explain it, Henry George's *Progress and Poverty* (1879), perceptively focused on the paradox of want and depression in the midst of technological progress and material abundance. But George's stress on the rent that derived from land ownership as the central source of inequality ignored the complexities of industrial capitalism. And for all the boldness of his core reform—that through taxation the possession of land be vested in the community at large—his ultimate social vision was the Jeffersonian one of a small-unit, decentralized economy.[34]

Most educated men of the time believed that natural laws controlled the market, the flow of money, and the cost of labor. New intellectual developments—social Darwinism, the rise of a statistical approach to economics—did not upset these assumptions. Simon Newcomb, an astronomer at the Naval Observatory in Washington and a pioneer in the application of mathematics to economic theory, warned that if government intervened too much in "the peculiar and limited field of political economy, nothing but harm will result." Legal tender, the protective tariff, laws limiting interest rates were instances of such improper meddling. "In the long run," Newcomb concluded, "each individual is a better judge of what is the most advantageous employment to his labor or his capital than any man or set of men can be." He was echoed by the government economist and statistician David Ames Wells, who warned against legislation that sought "the distribution of wealth by direct or indirect compulsion, or . . . diminishing the incentives for personal accumulation." William Graham Sumner, the great

33. Hamilton A. Hill, "The Relations of the Business Men of the United States to the National Legislation," *JSS*, 3 (1871), 151; Edwin Frichey, *Production in the United States 1860–1914* (Cambridge, 1947), 127. See also O. V. Wells, "The Depression of 1873–79," *AH*, 11 (1937), 237–249.

34. Barker, *George*, ch. 10.

academic proponent of laissez-faire in the late nineteenth century, already was telling his students at Yale: "You need not think it necessary to have Washington exercise a political providence over the country. God has done that a great deal better by the laws of political economy."[35]

The change in tone of Francis A. Walker's writings is a revealing measure of the degree to which the conventional economic thought of the nineteenth century overwhelmed the deviant views that followed the Civil War. Walker's postwar speculation as to the capacity of government and men to shape the economy was quickly subordinated to more conventional beliefs. He criticized "the weakening and distracting of the economical sense of the country, by the debasement and perversion of the national currency," and approved of those economic conditions that would "starve out the superfluous members, the poorest fruit" in the retail trades, "driving these to other more directly productive branches of industry."

Hostility to the active state went hand in hand with belief in a self-regulating economy. Politicians of the seventies were as much inclined that way as intellectuals and publicists. New York Republican leader Roscoe Conkling expressed a common attitude: "Legislation and administration will never create wealth, or pay debts or taxes. Statesmanship may do much, but all it can do is to clear the way of impediments and dangers, and leave every class and every individual free and safe in the exertions and pursuits of life . . . Wealth can never be conjured out of the crucible of politics." James A. Garfield, who once believed that the government should operate the telegraph system, had second thoughts: to do so would be unwise, since it would increase government centralization and create an additional source of political corruption. Republican Senator Timothy Howe of Wisconsin had no use for attempts to conserve natural resources: "If a full-grown man with unimpaired intellect really thinks he needs to cut down and cut up a pine tree, and is willing to pay a fair price for it to the owner of the tree, why

35. Newcomb, "The Method and Province of Political Economy," *NAR*, 121 (1875), 269; Wells, "Influence of the Production and Distribution of Wealth on Social Development," in his *Practical Economics* (New York, 1885), 248; Sumner quoted in Dorfman, *Economic Mind*, III, 67. See also Fine, *Laissez Faire*, ch. 3; Charles F. Dunbar, "Economic Science in America, 1776–1876," *NAR*, 122 (1876), 124–154.

should he not have that privilege? What right have we to say that he shall not have it?"[36]

This state of mind reinforced the tendency to draw back from or dismantle government intervention in the economy. The Supreme Court in 1879 found the 1870 Trade Mark Act to be unconstitutional. The 1867 Bankruptcy Act also fell victim to the pressure for federal disengagement. Its opponents concentrated on the high legal and receivership fees that came with a national system of bankruptcy, and on the fact that it exposed businessmen to the dangers of involuntary bankruptcy: a serious problem after the 1873 panic. Maine Democrats attacked the law for unduly interfering in private affairs. It was amended in 1874 to make involuntary bankruptcy more difficult, but state legislatures and business interests called for outright repeal. Though many merchants and boards of trade continued to support the 1867 law, Congress in 1878 overwhelmingly repealed it, thus leaving the bankruptcy process to the varied authorities of the states.[37]

By the end of the seventies, general incorporation acts—which began to appear before the Civil War—had superseded individual corporation chartering in almost every state. Special interests sometimes fostered this change. In New Jersey, for example, the Pennsylvania Railroad supported general incorporation as a means of closing the door to special (and potentially more favorable) charters to new railroad lines. But the major thrust behind the general incorporation movement was the desire to rob the corporation charter of its privileged character. General incorporation did this by making chartering an almost purely administrative process, accessible to all who could meet a few undemanding requirements. New Jersey's comptroller of the treasury said of special chartering acts: "if the state is governed too much, as the world is said to be, this is one of the appliances by which the thing is done, the unnecessary multiplication of the laws." Special charters implied that the legislature had a specific regulatory authority. Near-mechani-

36. Walker, "Some Results of the Census," *JSS*, 5 (1873), 95; Fine, *Laissez Faire*, 75; Conkling, "The Issues of the Day" (1876), NYPL; Garfield, Diaries, April 22, 23, 1872; on Howe, Hurst, *Law and Economic Growth*, 439.
37. *Trade-Mark Cases*, 100 U.S. 72 (1879); Warren, *Bankruptcy*, 123; John Lowell, "A United States Bankruptcy Statute," *IR*, 9 (1880), 697–703.

cal general incorporation implied an authority so vague and diffuse as to be all but meaningless.[38]

A policy that democratized incorporation, yet weakened the authority of government to check corporate abuses, nicely exemplified the ambiguities of political economy in the 1870s. Republicans no less than Democrats warned of corporate abuses. The Connecticut Republican platform of 1873 declared that it was the duty of the state "to be vigilant in the protection of the rights and interests of the people, against the encroachments of powerful corporations," and Garfield cautioned that corporations constituted an "Industrial Feudalism" that had be be contained. But a profound and not readily resolved tension existed between the fear of industrialism and corporate growth and the fear of government power strong enough to cope with the new economy.[39]

The railroads were the great beneficiaries of postwar government aid; and they bore the brunt of the reaction against such aid in the 1870s. By the middle of the decade the roads were staggering beneath the weight of their breakneck postwar expansion. Fierce competition in the East and Midwest forced rates and earnings down. The overcapitalized lines, with high fixed costs, suffered also from the price deflation of the seventies. Widespread bankruptcy, reorganization, consolidation, rate discrimination, and price-fixing pools were among the consequences of these conditions. All had the effect of increasing antirailroad sentiment.

There was ample ground by the seventies for dissatisfaction with government's relationship to the railroads. That great venture in mixed enterprise the Union Pacific became a major source of grievance. The UP's troubles stemmed in large part from the fact that it was a "premature enterprise": its cost far outreached its earning capacity. There also were difficulties inherent in the federal role in the railroad's capitalization and direction. Congressmen bitterly

38. Harold W. Stoke, "Economic Influences upon the Corporation Laws of New Jersey," *JPE*, 38 (1930), 565; John W. Cadman, Jr., *The Corporation in New Jersey: Business and Politics 1791–1875* (Cambridge, 1949), 162n. See also George J. Kuehnl, *The Wisconsin Business Corporation* (Madison, 1959), 213–214; Evans, *Business Incorporations*, 3, 11.

39. "Connecticut," *AC* (1873); Garfield, *Future of the Republic*, 31. See also F. B. Thurber, "The Influence of Steam and Electricity," *IR*, 2 (1875), 623–635.

protested the UP's inability (or disinclination) to meet its fiscal obligations to the government. But not until 1878 did the Supreme Court sustain the right of Congress to require that the UP and other transcontinental lines establish sinking funds to meet those debts. The directors and commissioners who were supposed to represent the public interest too often acquiesced in the company's policies. The Credit Mobilier scandal of 1872, in which stock in the construction company that built the UP was distributed to a number of highly placed politicians, epitomized the problems afflicting the venture: "What was labelled corruption was a result rather than a cause of the defects in the government, a mere symptom of a more pervasive flaw." The Pacific Railroad Commission finally concluded: "The sovereign should not be mated with the subject."[40]

Railroad land grants were another fertile source of controversy. Altogether too much of this subsidy remained in undeveloped limbo, or passed into the hands of speculators: "The chief beneficiaries, of late, have been neither the government, the railroad companies, nor the settlers, but the capitalists and middle-men." The House unanimously resolved in 1870 that "the policy of granting subsidies in public lands to railroads and other corporations ought to be discontinued." The very principle of such aid now came under attack: "These grants . . . have been made on the theory that government is an organized benevolence, and not merely a compact for the negative function of repelling a public enemy or repressing disorders." During the late seventies and early eighties Congress recovered over 28 million acres because of the railroads' failure to live up to the terms of their grants.[41]

Much of the public domain turned over to the states, and to individuals through the Homestead Act, also failed to serve its original purpose. A good deal of acreage was held off the market in hope of a future rise in value. Tenantry was on the increase (by 1880, one in five Nebraska settlers did not own the land he worked). An estimated 8 million acres in Illinois and 12 million acres in Iowa were held by speculators in 1866. The Morrill Land

40. Fogel, *Union Pacific;* Wallace D. Farnham, " 'The Weakened Spring of Government': A Study in Nineteenth-Century American History," *AHR,* 68 (1963), 677.

41. R. T. Colburn, "United States Land Grants," *IR,* 3 (1876), 363; Haney, *Congressional History of Railways,* II, 20–21.

Grant College Act acreage moved with distressing ease into the hands of jobbers. One such, Gleason F. Lewis of Cleveland, acquired scrip from a number of northern and southern states for some 5 million acres of Morrill Act lands.[42]

The consequences of state and local railroad aid were no less distressing. The New York educator-politician Andrew D. White's somber warning to Michigan jurist Thomas M. Cooley in 1867 came to be a widespread view: "So you [in Michigan] are at town-bonding. I don't know how you regard it, but I . . . am one of five in this body [the New York legislature] who have voted steadily against the whole batch of bonding bills last year and exemption bills this year, which last follow the first as sharks follow plague stricken ships." A substantially completed railroad network, debt-burdened towns and counties, and the hard times of the seventies squelched the postwar enthusiasm for subsidies. Governors John White Geary of Pennsylvania and John T. Hoffman of New York vetoed numbers of railroad aid bills as early as 1869; Henry H. Haight of California, under fire in 1871 for approving too many local subsidies, now condemned such aid. Most state legislatures in the 1870s limited or flatly prohibited local subsidies. The municipally owned Cincinnati Southern was leased to a private company in 1877.[43]

The judiciary added its weight to the backlash against government subsidization. Its entering wedge was the distinction between public and private enterprise. Deciding just what constituted a public purpose bore "a far closer resemblance to the deduction of a politician than the application of a legal principle by a judge." It was a pair of policy-minded jurists, John F. Dillon and Thomas M. Cooley, who led the assault on railroad and other aid.

Dillon, who served on the Iowa Supreme Court and the Eighth Federal Circuit, condemned subsidies as "a coercive contribution in favor of private railway corporations" which violated "the general spirit of the Constitution as to the sacredness of private prop-

42. William J. Stewart, "Speculation and Nebraska's Public Domain, 1863–1872," *NH*, 45 (1964), 265–272; Paul W. Gates, *Agriculture and the Civil War* (New York, 1965), 275–276, 288; on Lewis, Gates, "Western Opposition to the Agricultural College Act," *IMH*, 37 (1941), 132–133.
43. White to Cooley, March 2, 1967, Cooley Mss, MichHS; Taylor v. Commissioners of Ross County, 230 Ohio St. 22 (1873).

erty." Railroads were "not organized for the purpose of developing the material prosperity of the State, but solely to make money for their stockholders." Cooley, a justice of the Michigan Supreme Court, objected to railroad subsidization on similar grounds, arguing that "a large portion of the most urgent needs of society are relegated exclusively to the law of demand and supply."[44]

While this argument was not generally accepted with regard to railroad aid, it did serve to block other forms of subsidization. In Loan Association v. Topeka (1875) the Supreme Court in effect adopted the Dillon-Cooley view to void a Kansas law authorizing city aid for a prefabricated bridge factory. Justice Miller's majority opinion grudgingly conceded that railroads fell within the range of the public purpose rule. But he acidly observed: "Of the disastrous consequences which have followed its recognition by the courts and which were predicted when it was first established there can be no doubt." The Topeka attempt at government aid violated those limits "which grow out of the essential nature of all free governments," those "reservations of individual rights, without which the social compact could not exist."[45]

The Dimensions of Disharmony

As laissez-faire beliefs and conflicting interests reduced the role of government in the postwar economy, so did the economic depression and labor unrest of the seventies—culminating in the great railroad strikes of 1877—weaken the postwar stress on the harmony of capital and labor. In this sense John Hay's *The Breadwinners* (1883), a novel animated by a near-hysterical fear af "labor agitators," was a tract of its time comparable in its social anxiety

44. *ALReg*, ns, 15 (1876), 402; Dillon in Hanson v. Vernon, 27 Iowa 28, 45, 53 (1869); Cooley in People v. Salem, 20 Mich. 452, 484 (1870). See also Dillon, *Treatise on the Law of Municipal Corporations* (Chicago, 1872), 225 ff, 580 ff; William H. Burroughs, *A Treatise on the Law of Taxation as Imposed by the States and their Municipalities, or Other Subdivisions, and as Exercised by the Government of the United States* (New York, 1877).

45. Loan Association v. Topeka, 20 Wall. 655, 662, 663 (1875); Fairman, *Reconstruction and Reunion*, 1101–1112.

to the increasingly common Negrophobic discussions of race relations in the South.[46]

In 1872 New York City workingmen had marched by the thousands in support of eight-hour legislation. Two years later, in the wake of the panic of 1873, they took to the streets in a desperate appeal for jobs. Initially there was some response. Grant called for expanded public works in his December 1874 message to Congress, and cities such as New York, Boston, Philadelphia, and Indianapolis undertook large-scale public relief. But the strongest advocates of a vigorous government response to the depression of the seventies—labor leaders, antimonopolists, currency reformers, socialists—were marginal men, often rent by factionalism. By 1870 the National Labor Union was in the hands of splinter groups and had lost what little political influence it may once have had.[47]

Respectable public opinion frowned on public works and public welfare. The Democratic *New York World* could only suggest that the rich modify their consumption habits: "Possibly not so large a bill at the florist, a few nights reserved from the opera, a simpler form of entertainment, but a larger bill to the seamstress, no curtailment of washing lists." The *Journal of Social Science* complained that New York City's public relief interfered with the natural laws of the economy: "The whole settlement of the labor question was postponed by the overgenerous charity of the city." James A. Garfield, who was chairman of the House Appropriations Committee, said of Grant's proposal for large-scale public works: "We had somewhat of a struggle to keep him from drifting into that foolish notion that it was necessary to make large appropriations on public works to give employment to laborers." He and Treasury Secretary Bristow finally convinced the President that "it is no part of the business of government to find employment for people." In short, the polity was ideologically unable to cope with the distress created by the depression of the seventies. An 1874 resolution of the New Jersey legislature nicely summed up that

46. Montgomery, *Beyond Equality*, chs. 9–10. See also Henry A. James, *Communism in America* (New York, 1879).

47. Leah H. Feder, *Unemployment Relief in Periods of Depression* (New York, 1936), 37–70; Samuel Rezneck, "Distress, Relief, and Discontent in the United States during the Depression of 1873–78," *JPE*, 58 (1950), 494–512; Herbert Gutman, "The Failure of the Movement by the Unemployed for Public Works in 1873," *PSQ*, 80 (1965), 254–276.

incapacity: "Recognizing in labor the true basis of a nation's wealth and prosperity, and recognizing its rights to obtain full and equitable remuneration, we extend to our fellow-citizens now out of employment our sincere sympathies."[48]

But just as the white South overcame its bias against the active state when it came to enforce its view of race relations, so did state and federal government in the North act forcefully to contain labor unrest. Pennsylvania, New Jersey, and Missouri followed Massachusetts's lead in making it an offense for strikers to commit acts endangering commercial interests. Severe antitramp laws were widely enacted in the late seventies. State militia and (after some hesitation) federal troops were summoned to deal with the violence that accompanied the railroad strikes of 1877. Pennsylvania alone spent $700,000 to suppress disorders in the state.[49]

A study of the relationship between labor and postwar Radical Republicanism concludes that "class conflict . . . was the submerged shoal on which Radical dreams foundered." But the group consciousness of leading publicists and intellectuals in the seventies was as much social and cultural as it was economic. Corporations, speculators, the freedmen, and the Irish no less than "labor agitators" were among those elements that threatened a stable American society. When E. L. Godkin decried the role of "classes in politics," he meant not only labor but Negroes and the Irish as well. The reformist minister Lyman Atwater linked strikes— "conspiracies against the laws of God, the rights of man, and the welfare of society"—to the emancipation of "ignorant and improvident blacks" and the importation of the "dregs" of Europe as elements of a widespread American social disorder. The desire for a more secure social order had the ironic effect of reinforcing the "scientific" laws of laissez-faire liberalism: "Legislation cannot alter the laws of nature, or man, or political economics." The scientist Simon Newcomb spoke for many when he decried workingmen's efforts to better themselves through strikes, unions, and legislation: "the laboring classes can have their condition im-

48. *New York World*, Jan. 30, 1874; Robert T. Davis, "Pauperism in the City of New York," *JSS*, 6 (1874), 77; Mary L. Hinsdale, ed., *Garfield-Hinsdale Letters: Correspondence between James Abram Garfield and Burke Aaron Hinsdale* (Ann Arbor, 1949), 300; "New Jersey," *AC* (1874).
49. Grob, *Workers and Utopia*, 28–30; *AC* (1877–1878), states cited; Robert V. Bruce, *1877: Year of Violence* (Indianapolis, 1959).

proved, not by a general increase of wages, but only by a general increase in the effectiveness of their labor."[50]

The full impact of these views came in the 1880s and the 1890s, when the tensions engendered by rapid industrialization took a commanding place in American public life. But the experience of the 1870s gave fair warning that the postwar themes of social harmony and the active state faced powerful counterforces of interest and ideology.

The clash of interests that eroded the ideal of economic harmony may be seen in the economic issues that most directly entered into postwar politics: the currency and the tariff. The Civil War dramatically increased the volume of money, as over $400 million worth of greenbacks and other notes were added to the currency. Similarly productive of political controversy was a price level that rose during the war and with equal rapidity fell thereafter. Other fiscal legacies of the war—a greatly expanded tax system, a national debt which grew from under $65 million in 1860 to $2.5 billion in 1865—generated complex and persistent clashes of interest that the polity was called upon to resolve.

The postwar politics of money was enmeshed in the general political division of the time. Ohio Democrats, many of them wartime Copperheads, proposed that government bonds be redeemable in depreciated greenbacks. Charles Sumner was among those who condemned the proposal as an affront to national honor and the Union cause: "Every greenback," he said, "is red with the blood of fellow-citizens." The postwar Congress overwhelmingly pledged itself to the full and unqualified repayment of the debt.

Hugh McCulloch, Andrew Johnson's secretary of the treasury, adopted monetary policies that reflected the Conservative Unionism of the administration. This Democrat and former Indiana state banker condemned the "horrible immorality" of inflation and dwelt on the need to "return to the constitutional currency": the gold standard, with no greenbacks or other paper notes. The *Commercial and Financial Chronicle* also linked a contractionist position to Conservative political ideology: "Weary . . . of a constant

---

50. Montgomery, *Beyond Equality*, x, 335–336; Godkin, "The Labor Crisis," *NAR*, 105 (1867), 177–213; Atwater, "The Labor Question in its Economic and Christian Aspects," *PR*, ns, 1 (1872), 485; Newcomb, "The Labor Question," *NAR*, 111 (1870), 129.

procession of dearly bought experiences, do we now turn to the great leaders in political economy for wisdom and guidance . . . If we are determined . . . to try the merits of governmental interference and centralization, nothing will give us so much sound instruction on the subject as a little practical experience."[51]

In December 1865 McCulloch called for the immediate resumption of specie payments. At first Congress overwhelmingly endorsed this policy, and McCulloch aggressively used surplus federal revenue to retire note issues. But a potent Republican opposition to currency contraction took form in 1865 and 1866, an opposition that included eastern manufacturers and western bankers and merchants. Thaddeus Stevens, William D. Kelley, James G. Blaine, John A. Logan, Oliver P. Morton, and John Sherman spoke out against McCulloch's policies. In February 1868 Congress suspended the retirement of greenbacks. The issue had become part of the larger struggle between Johnson and congressional Republicans.

An anticontractionist policy was pursued by George S. Boutwell, Grant's secretary of the treasury. A founder of the Massachusetts Republican party, wartime commissioner of internal revenue, a member of the Joint Congressional Committee on Reconstruction, and one of the managers of Johnson's impeachment, Boutwell was an emblematic postwar Republican. He engaged in counterseasonal bond buying and other devices designed to adjust the volume of money to the economy's needs. Between 1867 and 1874, national bank notes increased by $40 million, greenbacks in circulation by almost $30 million.

Henry Adams complained that Boutwell "had all the theorists of Europe and America to choose from, but he did not listen to their teachings . . . He believed in common schools, but not in political science; in ledgers and cash-books, but not in Adam Smith or Mill." Boutwell, in short, was closer to the postwar political economy of William Kelley or Francis Walker than to the textbook precepts of his time.

Boutwell's position could not long stand up against the conventional financial wisdom. The resumption of specie payments on

51. David Donald, *Charles Sumner and the Rights of Man* (New York, 1970), 346; McCulloch quoted in Walter T. K. Nugent, *Money and American Society, 1865–1880* (New York, 1968), 93, and Robert P. Sharkey, *Money, Class, and Party* (Baltimore, 1959), 61; *CFC*, 1 (1865), 1–2.

greenbacks and other paper notes, like civil service reform or the end of Reconstruction, became an article of faith for most respectable, educated Americans in the 1870s. As *Harper's Weekly* put it: "If we finally take the road to specie payments, justice, prosperity, integrity, safety, and honor will result to our whole country." Those who believed in the morality of specie resumption were joined by holders of the great wartime debt and by others who stood to gain from a hard, deflationary currency.[52]

But falling prices, the maldistribution of credit, and the costs of agricultural and industrial expansion created an offsetting interest in easy credit and easy money. Labor reformers, antimonopoly groups, and the Greenback party touted an unsecured paper currency as a panacea for debt-pressed farmers, laborers, and small businessmen, and were no less convinced of the morality of paper money and the immorality of gold.

Further to confuse the matter, bimetallism emerged in the seventies as an issue with a life of its own. Silver was an accepted part of the nation's currency base until the Coinage Act of 1873 demonetized it. That bill was the work primarily of a group of experts—Director of the Mint Henry R. Linderman, Senate Finance Committee Chairman John Sherman, Treasury Secretary Boutwell—who feared that the imminent decline in the price of silver, brought on by new mines in the West, would make it a dangerously inflationary force.

By 1876 a substantial bimetallist interest was in full cry against the "Crime of '73." Western silver interests and inflation-minded farmers were part of this coalition. So also were currency contractionists such as Francis A. Walker and William Graham Sumner, who wanted to add silver to gold as a prop against an unsecured paper currency. Railroad lobbyist and publicist Henry Varnum Poor believed that both gold and silver "by the very instincts and passions of the human soul, are natural mediums of exchange."[53]

52. Adams, "The Session," *NAR*, 111 (1870), 36; Gamaliel Bradford, "The Treasury Reports," *NAR*, 110 (1870), 209–223; *HW*, 14 (1870), 66. See also Sharkey, *Money*, ch. 3, and Nugent, *Money*, parts I–IV.

53. On the monetary politics of the 1870s, see Irwin Unger, *The Greenback Era: A Social and Political History of American Finance 1865–1879* (Princeton, 1974), Allen Weinstein, *Prelude to Populism: Origins of the Silver Issue, 1867–1878* (New Haven, 1970), and Nugent, *Money*, part V; Poor, "The Currency and Finances of the United States," *NAR*, 118 (1874), 98.

The range and intensity of these interests made monetary policy the most important economic concern of the national government in the seventies. The economist Francis Bowen observed in 1877: "During the last eight years, the United States have been trying experiments in the management of the currency, in Banking, Finance, and Taxation, on a larger scale than the world had ever witnessed." But the scope of this response by no means guaranteed consistency of policy: indeed, quite the reverse. "The politics of resumption," economist Milton Friedman has observed, "are confused and contradictory." Three times in ten years the House of Representatives passed inflationary—or anti-inflationary—bills, and then quickly reversed itself. Garfield wryly noted in 1874 that one of his congressional colleagues, David B. Mellish of New York, had died in a lunatic asylum: "He devoted himself almost exclusively to the study of the currency, became fully entangled with the theories of the subject and became insane." The theories that unhinged Congressman Mellish were so arcane in part because of the scale and complexity of the interests that focused on the money question.[54]

The political leadership of the seventies sought to hack a path of compromise through this morass. The Resumption Act of 1875 authorized gold payments on greenbacks and other paper notes in 1879. But it also included a free banking provision which in theory gave currency-starved areas of the country the opportunity of expanding their money supply. "The bill . . . was at heart political in origin": an attempt to heal party divisions over fiscal matters in time for the 1876 election.

As the depression of the seventies continued, hostility to the resumption of specie payments grew. And bimetallists called for the remonetization of silver. Once again congressional leaders— this time of both parties—engineered a politic settlement. The Bland-Allison Act of 1878 sought to satisfy two major fiscal interests. The desire for silver remonetization was appeased by making the silver dollar legal tender and requiring the Treasury to buy

54. Francis Bowen, *American Political Economy: Including Strictures on the Management of the Currency and the Finances since 1861* (New York, 1877), iii; Milton Friedman and Anna J. Schwartz, *A Monetary History of the United States 1867–1960* (Princeton, 1963), 49–50; Garfield cited in Weinstein, *Prelude to Populism*, 244.

at least $2 million worth of the metal each month. At the same time a $4 million limit on monthly purchases assured specie resumptionists that bimetallism would not have inflationary consequences.

President Rutherford B. Hayes vetoed the bill. He had come to accept the view that silver monetization no less than unsecured paper was an immoral depreciation of the currency. But his veto was readily overriden by a Congress anxious to compromise on an issue that cut across party and other lines. Resumption began—with little fuss—on January 1, 1879.[55]

While the Bland-Allison Act quieted the currency controversy for a decade, it erupted again with even greater vigor when the free silver movement took fire in the 1890s. The money issue was too symptomatic an expression of the strains and anxieties generated by rapid economic change to be suppressed for long.

The same might be said of the tariff. Substantial interests had stakes in the scale and extent of protection. Eastern merchants opposed a protectionism that endangered foreign trade. And southern and western agrarian prosperity depended as much on access to overseas markets as on the state of domestic credit and the currency. Protectionist interests were comparably diverse, ranging from wool growers and copper miners to most of the still small-scale, newly developing industrial sector. (The net trade balance of goods and services rested consistently in the United States's disfavor during the postwar decade.)

As in the past, Democrats found low tariff doctrine a convenient expression of their laissez-faire, anticentralist ideology. Free trade appealed as well to the classical liberalism of men such as E. L. Godkin and David A. Wells. The varying strands of low tariff sentiment came together in the American Free Trade League, established in 1865.

But as a spur to American industry, a safeguard of workingmen's wages, and a worthwhile instrument of the active state, tariff protection was supported by most postwar Republicans. Garfield thought that it could be "sustained by large-minded men, for national reasons." A critic of high tariffs condemned postwar protec-

55. On Resumption Act, Unger, *Greenback Era*, 255. See also Friedman and Schwartz, *Monetary History*, 44–50.

tionism as "a part of the deplorable and general attempt . . . to make Congress do for the individual what it was his business to do for himself. Men seemed to believe that their fortunes depended on legislation."[56]

Tariff legislation in practice consisted not of general statements of public policy but the precise accommodation of particular interests. John L. Hayes's National Association of Wool Manufacturers, the most potent trade association of the time, secured the Wool and Woollens Act of 1867. The Copper Act of 1869 served the needs of the Lake Superior area copper mines. Leading railroads engaged the publicist Henry Varnum Poor to lobby—successfully—against the American Iron and Steel Association's quest for a higher rate on English steel rails.

When Congress passed broader tariff legislation, its purposes were as much political as economic. In 1870, an election year, it reduced the duties on widely used consumer items such as tea, sugar, coffee, molasses, and spices. In the presidential campaign year of 1872 rates were reduced generally by 10 percent, and the tea and coffee duties were eliminated. As Senator John Sherman explained: "It is better for the protected industries of the country that this slight reduction of duties should be made rather than to invite a contest which will endanger the whole system." In 1875, when economic conditions had worsened and no election loomed, the 1872 cuts were restored—with little political fuss.[57]

The tariff still lacked the saliency and the symbolic weight of the currency as a political issue. But in the late nineteenth century, when America's industrial capacity and her involvement in the economy of the Western world substantially grew, the tariff joined the currency as a major expression of the clash of interests generated by an increasingly complex and inharmonious economic order.

56. *HS*, 530; on Free Trade League, *NAR*, 108 (1869), 57–78; Garfield in U.S., *CR*, 45th Cong., 2d sess., House (June 4, 1878), Appendix, 292; Ida Tarbell, *The Tariff in Our Times* (New York, 1911), 51. See also Edward Stanwood, *American Tariff Controversies in the Nineteenth Century* (Boston, 1903), II, ch. 14; George E. Hunsberger, "The Development of Tariff Policy in the Republican Party," Ph.D. diss., University of Virginia, 1934.

57. F. W. Taussig, *The Tariff History of the United States*, 5th ed. (New York, 1903), 171 ff; Alfred D. Chandler, Jr., *Henry Varnum Poor* (Cambridge, 1956), 238–240; Sherman quoted in Tarbell, *Tariff*, 76.

CHAPTER 6

The Southern Experience

THE PUBLIC LIFE of the postwar South was compacted and mercurial: an initial reluctance to accept the implications of emancipation and military defeat; a brief interlude of Republican state government fostered by congressional Reconstruction; and then, in the 1870s, "Redemption"—the restoration of white Democratic rule.

Normally this sequence of events is viewed as peculiar to the South—the special experience of a region wracked by wartime defeat and charged with racial tension after the end of slavery. Certainly the condition of the postwar South dramatically differed from that of the bustling, confident, victorious North. The cost of civil war in the former Confederacy was measured not only in lives and treasure lost, but also (for the region's whites) by the trauma of defeat. History, as Toynbee put it, had "happened" to the people of the South on a scale previously unknown to Americans.

Yet for all this, the public life of the postwar South went forward in close cadence with that of the nation at large. Slavery had led the antebellum South to a cultural and economic separatism that culminated in secession. Emancipation and military defeat forcibly restored the South to the national polity. Southern Reconstruction and "Redemption" emerge not as events unique to that region, but rather as part of the shared experience of the postwar American polity. In the South as elsewhere, new forces and ideas surfaced in the wake of the war; and in the South—as elsewhere—older and deeper values in the American civic culture then reasserted themselves.

The Quest for Order

Scores of observers descended on the South in the wake of Appomattox. They varied in their reading of the prevailing popular mood. Some found a general acquiescence in the war's result; some found an intransigent sullenness. But one fact of postwar southern life was beyond dispute: the human, physical and institutional destruction wrought by the conflict.[1]

The more than a quarter of a million southern war dead was an especially chilling statistic when set against the population base. In Alabama, 29 percent of the 122,000 men who bore arms died. One-third of Florida's 15,000 soldiers failed to return. An estimated 23 percent of South Carolina's white male population of arms-bearing age was killed or wounded.

There was an even darker story of demographic devastation wrought by disease, want, and migration. Contemporaries dwelt especially on the fate of the black population. Wisconsin Senator James Doolittle reported from Louisiana in 1866: "All here concur in saying that at least 25 per cent of the negro population is gone"; thousands of freedmen were expected to starve during the coming winter. An 1866 Mississippi census concluded that in fifty of the state's sixty counties there had been an absolute decrease from 1860 of 14,210 whites and 52,318 blacks. The federal census of 1870 estimated that the American Negro population increased by 22.07 percent btween 1850 and 1860; the comparable figure for the next decade was 9.21 percent.[2]

1. Accounts of travel in the postwar South include Sidney Andrews, *The South since the War: As Shown by Fourteen Weeks of Travel and Observation in Georgia and the Carolinas* (Boston, 1866); James S. Pike, *The Prostrate State* (New York, 1874) Whitelaw Reid, *After the War: A Southern Tour, May 1, 1865 to May 1, 1866* (New York, 1866); John T. Trowbridge, *The South* (Hartford, 1866); John R. Dennett's *Nation* articles, collected in *The South As It Is 1865–1866* (New York, 1965); and Robert Somers, *The Southern States since the War 1870–1871* (London and New York, 1871).
2. *AC* (1865–1866), passim; Francis B. Simkins and Robert H. Woody, *South Carolina during Reconstruction* (Chapel Hill, 1932), 12; Doolittle

Hard data in fact was spotty and suspect. And to exaggerate the number of Negroes who died during and after the war suited the purposes of those who thought that they were unready for freedom. But it is clear that a great human tragedy had occurred.

The mass movement of freed Negroes added to the social chaos. It was estimated that the black population of Texas doubled between 1860 and 1865; but with the coming of peace thousands moved eastward into Louisiana. Large numbers of former slaves flocked to southern towns after emancipation. An 1866 Alabama census found that Mobile's black population had increased by 25 percent over 1860; in Montgomery the figure was 23 percent.

Vast numbers of whites as well as blacks were made destitute by the war. About 35,000 people in the counties around Atlanta relied on the federal government for food; a similar number of dependents existed in Georgia's northern counties. Alabama in 1865 gave state aid to 140,000 people.

The destruction wrought by war and the sudden act of emancipation had catastrophic effects on southern property values. Provisional Governor Isaac Murphy summed up the state of affairs in Arkansas (which was relatively untouched by fighting) in May 1865: "The desolations of war in our state are beyond description." South Carolina's property valuation of $400 million in 1860 shrank to $50 million in 1865. The state ranked third in the nation in per capita wealth in 1860; ten years later it was fortieth. Much of this decline, of course, represented the end of slavery. But the loss was nonetheless keen for southern white elites. And the drain of the war on the region's wealth was real enough.[3]

A corresponding sense of loss attached to the southern polity. (For some, that sense was total: Virginia secessionist leader Edmund Ruffin and Florida Confederate Governor John Milton re-

---

to Mary Doolittle, Nov. 11, 1866, Doolittle Mss, WSHS. See also E. Merton Coulter, *The South during Reconstruction 1865–1877* (Baton Rouge, 1947), 55; "United States," *AC* (1865). Vernon L. Wharton, *The Negro in Mississippi 1865–1890* (Chapel Hill, 1947), 53–54, questions the accuracy of the 1866 Mississippi census figures. See also Francis A. Walker, "Statistics of the Colored Race in the United States," *AStA Publications*, ns, 2 (1890–91), 91–106. Walker estimated that the black population declined from 14.1 percent to 13.1 percent of the total between 1860 and 1880.

3. Howard A. White, *The Freedmen's Bureau in Louisiana* (Baton Rouge, 1970), 116; Wharton, *Negro in Mississippi*, 107; *AC*, states and years cited.

sponded to defeat by committing suicide.) The collapse of the Confederacy threw large areas of the South into a political state of nature. Florida's provisional governor declared: "the State, though in the Union, is without a civil government." Public meetings in North Carolina called for the restoration of civil law. As late as 1866 it was the judgment of a legislative committee that no corporations existed as legal entities in that state.

The first business of southern men of affairs was to restore the forms of public authority. Andrew Johnson as military governor of Tennessee in early 1864 took it upon himself to appoint constables and justices of the peace on the ground that "there must be something done . . . for the purpose of bringing back order." Texas's provisional governor Andrew J. Hamilton announced that since there were "no civil officers in the State" he would appoint the key district and county officials. His Alabama counterpart, Lewis E. Parsons, set down the first task of his defeated people: "to lay anew the foundations of government." By proclamation he reaffirmed the legitimacy of the local officials upon whom civic order depended.[4]

Courts and legislatures, too, devoted themselves to preserving what they could of the existing southern polity. By the summer of 1866 all of the state court systems were operating again. Mississippi's legislature in late 1865 ratified the legal actions of the Confederate period. The governor of Texas declared laws passed after secession to be void, but authorized district courts to proceed with pending civil and criminal actions (while forbidding final judgments in debt cases).[5]

Constitutional conventions were a prime device in the quest for legitimacy and continuity. Between 1863 and 1866 every secessionist state replaced its Confederate charter with a new one. The very machinery by which the drafting conventions were formed preserved the existing order: incumbent sheriffs, probate judges,

4. "Florida," *AC* (1865), "North Carolina," *AC* (1866), "Tennessee," *AC* (1864), "Texas," *AC* (1865), "Alabama," *AC* (1865).

5. Erwin C. Surrency, "Legal Effects of the Civil War," *AJLH*, 5 (1961), 145–165; Kenneth E. St. Clair, "Judicial Machinery in North Carolina in 1865," *NCHR*, 30 (1953), 415–439; Henry R. Goetchins, "Litigation during the Reconstruction Period," *GaBA Reports*, 14 (1897), 66–107; Charles Fairman, *Reconstruction and Reunion 1864–88, Part One* (New York, 1971), ch. 15.

county clerks, coroners, and justices of the peace supervised the election of delegates.

The president of the October 1865 North Carolina convention told the assemblage: "Fellow-citizens, we are going home." It was in this spirit—not the establishment of a new order but the resumption of the old one—that the conventions did their work. Georgia's delegates ratified the wartime acts of guardians and trustees. Alabama's gathering reconfirmed the state's antebellum civil and criminal statutes and declared that all Confederate laws were in force unless they conflicted with federal law. The convention legitimated decrees handed down in wartime courts of record, judicial sales of property, and private contracts. This was necessary "to prevent a flood of litigation, uncertainty as to rights and property, and consequent derangement and trouble in every department of business."[6]

Southern reluctance to turn from the past also took more controversial forms. Northern public opinion was far from wrong when it concluded that the South's leaders were determined not to let the verdict of the battlefield carry over to courthouse or state house.

It is true that a number of prominent southerners counseled acceptance of defeat and acquiescence in the demands of the victorious North. But the mainstream of postwar southern public policy followed a quite different course. The Georgia, South Carolina, Florida, and Mississippi legislatures tried to avoid repudiation of their wartime Confederate state debts. Mississippi, North Carolina, and Georgia (as well as the Union states of Delaware and Kentucky) refused to ratify the Thirteenth Amendment.

Most southern states failed to satisfy even Andrew Johnson's mild terms of submission. The Virginia legislature convened on December 4, 1865, and on the following day passed a bill that in effect refused to accept the existence of West Virginia as a separate state. North Carolina's legislature engaged in actions which, said Johnson, "greatly damaged the prospects of the State in the restoration of its government." Prominent Confederates were elected in

6. Coulter, *South during Reconstruction*, 35–36; for new constitutions, see Francis N. Thorpe, comp., *The Federal and State Constitutions, Colonial Charters, and Other Organic Laws* (Washington, 1909); states cited, *AC* (1865–1866); "Alabama," *AC* (1865).

embarrassing profusion to state offices, constitutional conventions, even to Congress. Johnson warned (unavailingly) that "it would be exceedingly impolitic for ... [Confederate Vice President] A. H. Stephens's name to be used in connection with the [Georgia] Senatorial election ... He stands charged with treason and no disposition has been made of his case ... There seems in many of the elections something like defiance, which is out of place at this time."[7]

Southern intransigence blossomed in 1866 when the exigencies of national politics led the President to encourage it. Following his lead, every southern legislature but those of Tennessee and West Virginia rejected the Fourteenth Amendment—although the governors of Virginia, Louisiana, and Alabama were ready to acquiesce. A number of states created Committees on Federal Relations, as though the primacy of the central government was still a point at issue. The Arkansas legislature instructed state officers to behave as if the First Reconstruction Act had not been passed, and if pressed to engage in "passive resistance."

Johnson fostered this attitude, but he did not create it. Postwar southern rhetoric reflected a frame of mind for which the war had not ended, never would end; for which passionate allegiance to the past was a psychological (and perhaps a political) necessity. Mississippi Governor Benjamin G. Humphreys' characterization of the Fourteenth Amendment was typical:

> such an insulting outrage and denial of the equal rights of so many of our worthiest citizens who have shed glory and lustre upon our section and our race, both in the forum and the field, such a gross usurpation of the rights of the State, and such a centralization of power in the Federal Government, that I presume a mere reading of it will cause its rejection by you.[8]

Unabashed white supremacy smoothly fitted into postwar southern political life. A critic of the 1865 South Carolina constitution

---

7. Michael Perman, *Reunion Without Compromise: The South and Reconstruction 1865–1868* (Cambridge, Eng., 1973); Johnson quoted in James F. Rhodes, *History of the United States to the Compromise of 1850* (New York, 1904), V, 540.

8. Paige E. Mulhollen, "The Arkansas General Assembly of 1866 and Its Effect on Reconstruction," *ArkHR*, 20 (1961), 340–343; Joseph B. James, "Southern Reactions to the Proposal of the 14th Amendment," *JSH*, 22 (1956), 477–497; Mississippi," *AC* (1866).

—hardly a radical document—warned: "The appropriations to support free schools for the education of negro children, for the support of old negroes in the poor houses, . . . together with a standing army of negro soldiers, will be crushing and utterly ruinous to the State." The 1865 Louisiana Democratic platform flatly declared: "there can in no event nor under any circumstances be any equality between the white and other Races."

The provisional governors, for all their relative sensitivity to northern attitudes, were adamant on the issue of Negro civil rights. William Marvin of Florida did not think that holding public office or sitting on juries were "essential rights of freedom." As for blacks voting: "It is better, a thousand times better, that we should remain out of the Union." Robert M. Patton of Alabama warned: "it must be understood that, politically and socially, ours is a white man's government. In the future, as in the past, the State affairs of Alabama must be guided and controlled by the superior intelligence of the white man."[9]

These beliefs were translated into law on a massive scale. The Black Codes passed between October 1865 and March 1866 sought to define the status of the freedmen in the southern states. They varied in their severity: those of Mississippi, Alabama, South Carolina, and Florida were the most repressive. But they had a common spirit.

The codes did provide a floor of rights: the end of slavery, some access to the courts. But they set very severe limits on the economic, social, legal, and political status of the freedmen. The Florida code commissioners thought that the lack of legal marriage was "the only inherent evil of the institution of slavery as it existed in the Southern states." The prevailing model was the legal condition of the antebellum "free" Negro in the North as well as in the South: a twilight zone between freedom and servility. (Alabama simply reenacted its vicious prewar criminal code for free Negroes.) The codes set up elaborate systems of bound apprenticeship, labor restrictions, vagrancy laws, limits on property ownership and craft employment. They prescribed white supervision over almost every aspect of black lives. Control rested not in state but in local

9. *Respectful Remonstrance on Behalf of the White People of South Carolina against the Constitution of the late Convention of that State* (Columbia, S.C., 1868); "Louisiana," "Florida," "Alabama," *AC* (1865).

authorities. In Florida, enforcement lay in county criminal courts where no presentment, indictment, or written pleading was required. The bald declaration of Edmund Rhett of South Carolina —"the general interest both of the white man and of the negroes requires that he should be kept as near to the condition of slavery as possible, and as far from the condition of the white man as is practicable"—sums up the purpose of the Black Codes.[10]

The Thrust of Change

The first, instinctive response of the defeated South was to preserve its past. But powerful internal as well as external forces quickly eroded this adherence to the old order. Home-grown stimuli to change rapidly emerged. The war's transforming impact came first in the Union slave states—Maryland, Tennessee, Missouri—and in Louisiana, where federal authority was restored at an early stage of the conflict.

The non-Confederate portion of Louisiana had two parties by 1863: a Free State organization based in New Orleans and a Conservative party rooted in the planter country outside. They represented an old division obscured by the enforced unity of the pro-slavery and secession movements. Michael Hahn, the successful Free State party candidate for governor in 1864, was born in Bavaria, had the support of New Orleans workingmen and immigrants, and was a longtime opponent of slavery (but no supporter of Negro rights). His was a style of politics with numerous northern Democratic counterparts.

Hahn and his party dominated the 1864 state constitutional convention. The resulting charter made New Orleans the state capital; based legislative seats on the number of eligible voters

10. Texts of Black Codes in Edward McPherson, *The Political History of the United States of America during the Period of Reconstruction* (Washington, 1871), 29–44, and U.S., 39th Cong., 1st sess., House, Exec. Doc. 118, Rept. no. 30; Theodore B. Wilson, *The Black Codes of the South* (University, Ala., 1965); Rhett quoted in Joel Williamson, *After Slavery: The Negro in South Carolina during Reconstruction* (Chapel Hill, 1965), 74. See also John M. Mecklin, "The Black Codes," *SAQ*, 16 (1917), 248–259; Gilbert T. Stephenson, *Race Distinctions in American Law* (New York, 1910), 35–66; John B. Myers, "The Freedman and the Law in Post-Bellum Alabama, 1865–1867," *AlaR*, 23 (1970), 56–69.

rather than total population (thus strengthening the city as against the plantation parishes); called for free universal education, a progressive income tax, a nine-hour working day, and a minimum wage of two dollars a day on public works projects; ended slavery; and authorized the legislature, if it so desired, to vote taxes for Negro education and to permit Negro voting. Even by northern standards this was an advanced document, as Lincoln recognized when he gave it his cautious approval. It had much in common with the Radical Reconstruction constitutions to come—to the extent that the convention's costs (some $360,000, including $10,000 for liquor and $156,000 for printing) displayed the extravagance of political and social *arrivistes*.[11]

Maryland remained a Union state during the war. But with its relatively large free Negro population, its ethnic and religious diversity, and its large port city of Baltimore it closely resembled Louisiana. Not surprisingly, Maryland's politics had much in common with the other state. The dominant wartime Union party quickly divided into two factions, Montgomery Blair's Conditional Unionists (composed primarily of War Democrats and Conservative Republicans) and Henry Winter Davis's more Radical Unconditional Unionists. The two combined to write a new state constitution in 1864 and produced a document that closely resembled the Louisiana charter of the same year. It ended slavery; increased Baltimore's representation in the legislature; and prescribed a uniform, tax-supported system of common schools.[12]

The Tennessee and Missouri constitutions of 1865 reflected similar political conditions. William G. Brownlow, a picaresque east Tennessee editor and politician, was the state's Unionist leader. Like Hahn he was antislavery and "a National man," and as Tennessee's postwar governor vigorously fought ex-Confederates and the Klan.

Missouri's Unionists, like those of Maryland, divided after 1863

11. Roger W. Shugg, *Origins of Class Struggle in Louisiana: A Social History of White Farmers and Laborers during Slavery and After, 1840–1875* (University, La., 1939); "Louisiana," *AC* (1864–1865); Joe G. Taylor, *Louisiana Reconstructed, 1863–1877* (Baton Rouge, 1974), ch. 2.

12. William S. Myers, *The Self-Reconstruction of Maryland, 1864–1867* (Baltimore, 1909); Jean H. Baker, *The Politics of Continuity: Maryland Political Parties from 1858 to 1870* (Baltimore, 1973); Richard O. Curry, ed., *Radicalism, Racism, and Party Realignment: The Border States during Reconstruction* (Baltimore, 1969), 146–187.

into proemancipation (Claybank) and antiemancipation (Snow-flake) factions. By 1865 the Claybanks had control and convened a constitutional convention. The resulting document ended slavery; provided for free schools; and gave blacks the right to testify in court, write contracts, and not be "hindered in acquiring educa-tion, or be subjected to any other restraints or disqualifications, in regard to any personal rights, than such as are laid upon others." A motion to eliminate race restrictions in elections lost by a single vote. The prime mover here was Charles D. Drake, who shared with Brownlow a passionate antislavery unionism that reflected the special emotions of wartime border state politics. Unlike the others, Drake was to take a Radical Republican position in the postwar years.[13]

Even in the core Confederate states, political change occurred before congressional Reconstruction. South Carolina traditionally had the most oligarchical southern state government. But provi-sional Governor Benjamin F. Perry hoped that the 1865 constitu-tion would "conform to the great changes which have taken place in the State, and be more in accordance with republican principles of equality and representation." The document made the governor a popularly elected officer, substituted ballot for voice voting in the election of assemblymen, and equalized the prewar system of county representation in the legislature. This was not a unique occurrence. Arkansas's post-Confederate constitution of 1864 con-ceded that "all men, when they form a social compact, are equal"; Florida's 1865 document declared that "all freemen . . . have cer-tain inherent and indefeasible rights."[14]

Southern state governments occasionally acted in ways less ret-rograde than the Black Codes. A number of stay laws sought to ease the burden of debt payment. Aid to refugees gave legislatures new experience in providing for the general welfare. And a few leaders called for the South to adapt to the new state of affairs.

---

13. E. Merton Coulter, *William G. Brownlow* (Chapel Hill, 1937); Thomas B. Alexander, *Political Reconstruction in Tennessee* (Nashville, 1950); Curry, ed., *Radicalism*, 37–79; William E. Parrish, *Missouri under Radical Rule* (Columbia, 1965); David D. March, "Charles D. Drake and the Constitutional Convention of 1865," *MoHR*, 47 (1953), 110–124; Curry, ed., *Radicalism*, 1–36.

14. "South Carolina," *AC* (1865); Thorpe, comp., *Constitutions*, 289, 685.

Among those ready to accept limited black suffrage were Confederacy Vice President Alexander H. Stephens, Postmaster General John H. Reagan, Secretary of the Navy Stephen Mallory, and General Robert E. Lee, as well as postwar governors Francis H. Pierpont of Virginia, Benjamin F. Perry and James L. Orr of South Carolina, James M. Wells of Louisiana, and Joseph E. Brown of Georgia.[15]

More important sources of change were two other facts of postwar southern political life: the Union army and a southern Republicanism based on a coalition of the freedmen and a minority of whites.

Some thirty-five generals and thousands of federal troops had substantial public responsibilities between 1865 and 1877. The army's power began with the fact of occupation. Provost marshals often had broad-ranging civil jurisdiction, and Congressional Reconstruction in 1867 largely increased the scope of military authority. The First Reconstruction Act divided the South into five military districts; each in turn was minutely subdivided. General John M. Schofield, for example, partitioned the Virginia Military district into fifty-five subdistricts organized into groups of seven, each with a military commander.

The army made its presence felt in a variety of ways. Generals at times voided the election of local candidates whose loyalty was suspect or removed officials hostile to federal policy. General Daniel E. Sickles in 1867 dismissed the governor and lieutenant governor of North Carolina; John Pope of the Georgia-Alabama-Florida district removed mayors and other city officials in Mobile, Alabama, and Augusta, Georgia. Pope also took a hand in the selection of school commissioners, tax collectors, assessors, justices of the peace, sheriffs, judges, county commissioners, constables, and circuit court clerks. His successor, George G. Meade, removed the officials of Columbus, Georgia when they failed to arrest the murderers of a delegate to the state's 1868 constitutional convention. Philip H. Sheridan did the same in New Orleans after the massacre of July 1866.

At first military commanders helped planters maintain a stable

15. J. H. Thomas, "Homestead and Exemption Laws of the Southern States," *ALReg*, ns, 10 (1871), 1–17, 137–150; Rhodes, *History*, V, 605; John H. Reagan, *Memoirs* (New York, 1906), 286–298.

black labor force. Ugly stories drifted North of army officers using coercion—even torture—to force the freedmen to sign labor contracts. But as northern opinion changed, so did the role of the military. In January 1866, Major General Alfred H. Terry ordered Virginia magistrates not to enforce the Black Code's vagrancy laws. Combinations of employers, he charged, sought to push wages down and force Negroes to work. General James B. Steedman of Georgia warned: "The time when one man can reap the fruits of another's labor is forever past in the United States, and no person in Georgia will be allowed to do any act tending to restore the old order of things." Although he was a Conservative Unionist when Johnson sent him in 1865 to be military governor of North and South Carolina, Daniel Sickles voided the Black Codes of those states, saw to it that a special session of the legislature guaranteed Negro civil rights, ordered that taxpayers regardless of color appear on jury lists, and forbade discrimination on public carriers. In 1867 Johnson removed Sickles, Sheridan, and Pope from their district commands.[16]

Military men staffed the Bureau of Refugees, Freedmen, and Abandoned Lands, the primary civil instrument of the federal government in the defeated South. Its head was General Oliver O. Howard, a passionate abolitionist and self-proclaimed Christian humanitarian. The Freedmen's Bureau, he contended, had as its duty "the exercise of benevolent functions hitherto always contended against by our leading statesmen."[17]

In practice Howard's bureau was far from the instrument of higher purpose that he conceived it to be. And Howard himself too readily succumbed to the pressures of white southerners and the Johnson administration. Nevertheless, the bureau handed out some 20 million rations (about a quarter of them to white refugees), gave medical aid to almost a million people, and (often with the assist-

16. James E. Sefton, *The United States Army and Reconstruction 1865–1877* (Baton Rouge, 1967), passim; "Georgia," *AC* (1865); James R. Merrill III, "North Carolina and the Administration of Brevet Major-General Sickles," *NCHR*, 42 (1965), 291–305.
17. Howard quoted in John H. and La Wanda Cox, "General O. O. Howard and the 'Misrepresented Bureau,'" *JSH*, 19 (1953), 454–455; John A. Carpenter, *Sword and Olive Branch: Oliver Otis Howard* (Pittsburgh, 1964).

ance of the freedmen themselves) built schoolhouses serving half a million children.[18]

There were severe limits to the impact of the military on the postwar South. For one thing, the size of the occupying forces rapidly shrank. Over 200,000 troops were in the South in June 1865, only 18,000 by October 1866, and 11,000 by October 1869. The Freedmen's Bureau had a staff of about a thousand at the end of 1868; a year later only 158 were left. Nor were most officers comfortable with their quasi-political roles. As William T. Sherman put it in 1874: "we find North and South united against the doctrine of military compulsion, even to secure what we all aim at, the protection of the weak." And the great majority shared the prevalent antiblack attitude of the time: few had any commitment to the protection and encouragement of Negro civil equality. But the army did serve as a check on white behavior. Without its presence southern Republicanism could not have had even its brief moment in the sun.[19]

In every ex-Confederate state a new Republican party—biracial in makeup, nationally rather than sectionally oriented—constituted a presence as unsettling to traditional southern life as the Union army or the Freedmen's Bureau. Many white southern Republicans were onetime Whigs, as in Mississippi, where about 9,000 of them—15 percent of the white electorate—clustered in the traditionally Whig Delta counties. They called themselves Conservative Unionists or Conservative Republicans and tried to fit their old nationalistic Whiggery into the postwar Republican mold. James L. Alcorn, one of the richest of the antebellum Mississippi

18. William S. McFeely, *Yankee Stepfather: General O. O. Howard and the Freedmen* (New Haven, 1968) stresses the limited, conservative character of the work of Howard and the Bureau. See also George R. Bentley, *A History of the Freedmen's Bureau* (Philadelphia, 1955); Martin Abbott, *The Freedmen's Bureau in South Carolina, 1865–1872* (Chapel Hill, 1968); Howard A. White, *The Freedmen's Bureau in Louisiana* (Baton Rouge, 1970); Claude Elliot, "The Freedmen's Bureau in Texas," *SHQ,* 56 (1952), 1–24; Joe M. Richardson, "An Evaluation of the Freedmen's Bureau in Florida," *FlaHQ,* 41 (1963), 223–238.

19. On troops and personnel, Sefton, *Army and Reconstruction,* 50, Bentley, *Freedmen's Bureau,* 136; Sherman quoted in Sefton, *Army and Reconstruction,* 246.

planters, became the state's first Republican governor in 1870. He recognized, at least in his rhetoric, that social as well as political change was a necessary consequence of Confederate defeat:

> The Northern Democracy has overthrown the Southern Oligarchy! . . . Entering in our duty in acceptance of that result, we must go forward to make the overthrow of the old system that had reigned among us a practical reality, by insuring all the blessings of free government for the masses of the people . . . The reconstruction to which I go forward is a reconstruction which will make rich and poor equal *in fact* before the law. I move on with it, guiding a harnessed revolution over the ruins of the oligarchy.

Another wealthy planter, Thomas J. Robertson of South Carolina, called in 1867 for a Union Republican platform "broad enough to accommodate the human race." Men of similar stamp were the lawyer and large slaveholder Alexander H. White of Alabama, anxious for postwar southern economic development; Colonel A. S. Colyar, president of the Tennessee Coal, Iron and Railroad Company and a Confederate congressman; and Kentucky Unionists John M. Harlan and Benjamin H. Bristow. While most white Republican leaders were prewar Whigs, political ambition led an occasional figure such as Joseph E. Brown, the antebellum head of the Georgia Democratic party, to a brief flirtation with Republicanism.[20]

White southern Republicanism rested on more than oldtime Whiggery and political opportunism. The great majority of its voters came from relatively remote and infertile parts of the South —eastern Tennessee, western North Carolina, northwestern Arkansas, north central Georgia—where traditional antiplanter sentiment found a new voice in postwar Republicanism. But whatever their origins, and for all their rhetoric of change, white southern

20. Warren A. Ellem, "Who Were The Mississippi Scalawags?" *JSH*, 38 (1972), 217–240; Alcorn quoted in "Mississippi," *AC* (1870); Robertson quoted in "South Carolina," *AC* (1867); Derrell C. Roberts, *Joseph E. Brown and the Politics of Reconstruction* (University, Ala., 1973). See also William C. Harris, "A Reconsideration of the Mississippi Scalawag," *JMissH*, 32 (1970), 3–42; David H. Donald, "The Scalawag in Mississippi Reconstruction," *JSH*, 10 (1944), 447–460, who concludes that Mississippi's white Republicans for the most part were ex-Whigs; and Allen W. Trelease, "Who Were the Scalawags?" *JSH*, 29 (1963), 445–468, who thinks that they tended to be former Jacksonian Democrats.

Republicans found it exceedingly difficult to come to terms with black emancipation. They sought Negro votes, of course, but offered little in return. Most of their leaders joined the dominant Democrats in the 1870s.[21]

Southern Republicanism's radical tone—such as it was—came primarily from two other sources. One of these was the so-called carpetbaggers. The stock carpetbagger was the venal northerner come to batten on the prostrate south. And it is true that numbers of Union troops settled in the region: some 5,000 to 10,000 in Louisiana alone, about half of them in New Orleans. But many who bore the carpetbagger label in fact came to the South before the war, and by the time of Reconstruction were outlanders only in origin.

Whenever they arrived, more than greed and ambition were tucked into their carpetbags. A number had been educated in seedbeds of abolitionism. Senator Joseph C. Abbott of North Carolina and Governor Daniel Chamberlain of South Carolina attended Phillips Andover Academy in Massachusetts, John R. French of North Carolina and Joseph W. Clift of Georgia went to Phillips Exeter in New Hampshire. Charles W. Buckley, Alabama's superintendent of education and a congressman, went to Beloit College in Wisconsin and to Union Theological Seminary; Congressman D. Frank Whittemore of South Carolina attended Amherst. Stephen W. Dorsey, senator from Arkansas and later the Republican boss of New Mexico, was an examplar of the carpetbagger politician and entrepreneur; but he also was a native of Oberlin, Ohio, an antislavery center.[22]

Finally, the freedmen themselves influenced the character of southern Republicanism. A number of black leaders were forceful and influential men. P. B. S. Pinchback and Oscar J. Dunn of Loui-

21. Alexander, "Whiggery and Reconstruction in Tennessee," *JSH*, 16 (1950), 291–305, and "Persistent Whiggery in the Democratic South, 1860–1877," *JSH*, 27 (1961), 305–329; John V. Mering, "Persistent Whiggery in the Confederate South: A Reconsideration," *SAQ*, 69 (1970), 124–143; Otto H. Olsen, "Reconsidering the Scalawags," *CWH*, 12 (1966), 304–320.

22. Ella Lonn, *Reconstruction in Lousiana after 1868* (New York, 1918), 12n; Richard N. Current, "Carpetbaggers Reconsidered," in *A Festschrift for Frederick B. Artz* (Durham, N.C., 1964), 139–157; biographical data from *DAB*. See Otto H. Olsen, *Carpetbagger's Crusade: The Life of Albion Winegar Tourgée* (Baltimore, 1965), and Jonathan Daniels, *Prince of Carpetbaggers* [General Milton Littlefield] (Philadelphia, 1958).

siana, and Jonathan Wright and Robert B. Elliott of South Carolina, are examples. And the fact that the freedmen constituted the bulk of the southern Republican electorate constantly weighed against the Whiggish conservatism of many white Republican leaders.[23]

Composed of these disparate elements, buttressed by national Reconstruction legislation and the presence of the military, southern Republicanism entered into its brief and tenuous time of power. Prominent northern Republicans came down to cement interregional party ties (sometimes with riot the consequence, as when William D. Kelley of Pennsylvania addressed a Mobile rally in May 1867). Senator Henry Wilson of Massachusetts told a crowd of 5,000 blacks in Charleston: "The creed of equal rights, equal privileges and equal opportunities for all men in America is hereafter to be the practical policy of the Republic."[24]

Republicanism first gained a foothold in the postwar South through the large-scale disfranchisement of unregenerate white voters. Rigid franchise laws in Louisiana and the border states limited the vote to loyal whites. Tennessee's law of April 3, 1865 barred active Confederate leaders from politics for fifteen years; an eligible voter had to be "publicly known to have entertained loyal sentiments from the outbreak of the rebellion of 1861." On this basis the vote of twenty-nine counties was disregarded in the 1865 election, reducing the state total from 61,783 to 39,509. Yet except for high-ranking officials of the Confederate years, most southern whites quickly regained the franchise. Perhaps 100,000 potential white voters failed to cast a ballot in 1867 referenda on the Radical Reconstruction state constitutions; but a large proportion of these boycotted the elections.[25]

23. Richard Bardolph, *The Negro Vanguard* (New York, 1959), 80 ff; John Hope Franklin, *Reconstruction: After the Civil War* (Chicago, 1961). See also David C. Rankin, "The Origins of Black Leadership in New Orleans During Reconstruction," *JSH*, 40 (1974), 417–440.

24. Sarah W. Wiggins, "The 'Pig Iron' Kelley Riot in Mobile, May 14, 1867," *AlaR*, 23 (1970), 45–55; Simkins and Woody, *South Carolina*, 81. On northern ties, Jack B. Scroggs, "Southern Reconstruction: A Radical View," *JSH*, 24 (1958), 407–429.

25. "Tennessee," *AC* (1865); William A. Russ, Jr., "Registration and Disfranchisement under Radical Reconstruction," *MVHR*, 21 (1934–1935), 163–180, "Radical Disfranchisement in Georgia, 1867–1871," *GaHQ*, 19 (1935), 175–209, "Disfranchisement in Virginia under Radical Reconstruction," *THGM*, 17 (1935), 25–41; Eugene G. Feestman, "Radical Disfran-

Southern Republicanism relied on more than northern support and white disfranchisement. Political clubs helped reach a largely illiterate black electorate. Highly ritualistic organizations, laden with a secrecy that was a necessary protection from hostile whites as well as an emotive device, became an important part of southern Republicanism. The most substantial of these was the Union League, which developed a far broader popular base than its northern counterpart. In the fall of 1867 the Georgia Union League was active in 117 of the state's 132 counties. It had 300 black councils with a membership of 53,000, and 253 white councils with 27,830 participants. Other Republican organizations were the Lincoln Brotherhood and the Loyal League (whose ritual included a set of special arm movements accompanied by the intoning of the four L's: Liberty, Lincoln, Loyal, League).

A party often subject to the violent hostility of southern whites depended heavily on what protection the federal government could offer and (in Arkansas, South Carolina, Tennessee, and Texas) on the presence of black militia companies. These conditions strengthened the hand of the party's Radical wing in 1867 and 1868. And under the shield of congressional Reconstruction, the former Confederate states had a few years of governance that in part reflected Republican principles.[26]

Republicans in Power

The public life of the South underwent dramatic change during its time of Republican rule. The most formal expression of the new state of affairs was a set of Radical constitutions. In 1867 and 1868 almost every southern state received a new charter written by Republican-dominated conventions. The major purpose of these constitutions was to sustain the political power of the tenuous new

chisement in Arkansas, 1867–68," *ArkHQ*, 12 (1953), 126–168. Only 1,630 Mississippi whites were disqualified for the 1870 election under the Fourteenth Amendment: Harris, "Mississippi Scalawag," 25.

26. Olive H. Shadgett, *The Republican Party in Georgia from Reconstruction through 1900* (Athens, Ga., 1964), 2–3; on Loyal League, Simkins and Woody, *South Carolina*, 77, and Roberta F. Cason, "The Loyal League in Georgia," *GaHQ*, 20 (1936), 125–153; Otis A. Singletary, *Negro Militia and Reconstruction* (Austin, 1957).

Republican organizations. The chief means to that end was Negro suffrage, often linked to restrictions on white voting through test oath and disqualification provisions. But given the ideological milieu from which these charters emerged, it is not surprising that they embodied broader Radical ideals as well. The "fundamental theme" of the South Carolina constitution was "a raceless and classless democracy." Arkansas's document committed the state to "the political and civil equality of all men."[27]

Strong state government (including a powerful governor) was a common goal. Southern Republicans correctly viewed local autonomy as a major threat to their authority. The chief executive of the state often was given the power to appoint state, local, and county officials, including supreme court and circuit judges, clerks of election, and justices of the peace. At the same time, attempts were made in Virginia, North and South Carolina, and West Virginia to reorganize local government along the lines of the northern township system. South Carolina Radicals created school districts and townships on the New England model, and in a burst of democratic zeal made clerks, constables, highway commissioners, and overseers of the poor elected rather than appointed officials.[28]

The new constitutions often were accompanied by attempts at root-and-branch legal reform. Major revisions of state codes and judicial systems occurred in Louisiana, Arkansas, Alabama, Mississippi, and West Virginia. North Carolina carpetbagger Albion W. Tourgée induced his state's 1868 constitutional convention to adopt the Field Code of civil procedure already accepted by New York and Ohio. The Georgia courts in the Radical years tended to move from common law to equity in their treatment of relief and stay laws, Confederate contracts, and the status of the freedmen.[29]

27. Jack B. Scroggs, "Carpetbagger Constitutional Reform in the South Atlantic States, 1867–1868," *JSH*, 27 (1961), 475–493; Francis B. Simkins, "Race Legislation in South Carolina," *SAQ*, 20 (1921), 68–69.

28. On South Carolina, George E. Howard, *An Introduction to the Local Constitutional History of the United States* (Baltimore, 1889), I, 230. See also Eugene Cypert, "Constitutional Convention of 1868," *ArkHA Publications*, 4 (1917), 7–56; Jerrell H. Shofner, "The Constitution of 1868," *FlaHQ*, 41 (1963), 356–374.

29. *AC* (1867–1868), states cited; Olsen, *Tourgée*, 98–99; note 5, above. See also James R. Norvell, "The Reconstruction Courts of Texas, 1867–1873," *SHQ*, 62 (1958), 141–163.

Free and universal common schools were a central tenet of the Republican creed of government. While the reality was far from the ideal, the Radical constitutions and the governments that followed gave much of the South its first semblance of a public school system. Kentucky Republican Benjamin Bristow declared in 1871: *"I would take the rich man's property to educate his poor neighbor's child. I would tax the white man's property to educate the black man's child, and vice versa. In a word, I would tax all the property of the State to educate all the children of the State,"* Superintendents of education T. A. Parker, John Montheith, and James H. Robinson transformed Missouri's school system. The state had 4,840 schools with 169,270 students in 1867 and 7,547 schools with 280,473 students in 1870. William T. Harris, St. Louis superintendent of schools from 1868 to 1870 and a figure of national importance in educational reform, held that the schools were an agency to lessen caste distinctions.

Similar impulses were evident in the deep South. South Carolina's 1868 constitution declared: "All the public schools, colleges, and universities of this State supported by the public funds shall be free, and open to all the children and youths of the State, without regard to race or color." A debate ensued—tragicomically at odds with the realities of postwar South Carolina society—over whether to follow the Prussian or the Massachusetts system of compulsory education. The Massachusetts model won out. Acts in 1870 and 1871 established a system of free common schools. Textbooks would be free for those students who could not afford them; township meetings would select school trustees; teachers' associations were to be encouraged. Charleston's school superintendent, the New England journalist and Lyceum organizer James Redpath, devoted himself to Negro education. He believed that the Civil War was "the result of the enslavement of the poor blacks and the ignorance of the poor whites. By educating everybody we will take care to prevent a war of races."[30]

30. Ross A. Webb, *Benjamin Helms Bristow* (Lexington, Ky., 1969), 87; Parrish, *Missouri*, 120–125; Simkins and Woody, *South Carolina*, 441. See also Daniel J. Whitener, "Public Education in North Carolina during Reconstruction, 1865–1876," in Fletcher M. Green, ed., *Essays in Southern History* (Chapel Hill, 1949), 67–90; Richard P. Fuke, "The Baltimore Association for The Moral and Educational Improvement of the Colored People 1864–1870," *MdHM*, 66 (1971), 369–404.

New Orleans attempted something still bolder: integrated public education. An 1869 Louisiana law prescribed universal free schooling "without distinction of race, color, or previous condition," and in the early 1870s New Orleans superintendent Thomas W. Conway opened the schools to children of both races. Florida in 1869 allowed but did not require segregated schools; and state superintendent Charles Beecher (brother of the famous minister Henry Ward Beecher) sought to make the Freedmen's Bureau schools so attractive that whites as well as blacks would send their children to them. A visitor to Charleston in 1872 commented wonderingly on the phenomenon of "idle, ragged Negroes, who, with no visible means of support, . . . send an astonishing multitude to school." From another perspective, an upcountry South Carolina farmer complained in 1870: "Every little negro in the county is now going to school and the public pays for it."

White children, too, shared in this educational upsurge. The proportion of school age whites enrolled in South Carolina rose from 12 percent in 1869 to 50 percent in 1875; for blacks, the rise was from 8 percent to 41 percent. Forty-eight percent of Mississippi's white children and 45 percent of her black children were enrolled in 1876. Negro teachers in that year supposedly earned an average of $39.55 a month; the white average of $43 was only slightly higher.[31]

Other areas of social policy also were affected by the change in southern governance. The South, in a limited way, shared in the national postwar reform effort. A scattering of laws bettered the legal status of women and sought to improve prison, insane asylum, and almshouse conditions. But these causes, beset by difficulties in the North, fared even more poorly in the postwar South. The Georgia Board of Health tried to enforce compulsory public health regulations, but local opposition led to the end of that experiment —and, indeed, ended the Board of Health. A study of postwar social legislation in Florida suggests that men in public life, regard-

---

31. Louis R. Harlan, "Desegregation in New Orleans Public Schools during Reconstruction," *AHR*, 67 (1962), 663–675; Joe M. Richardson, *The Negro in the Reconstruction of Florida, 1865–1877* (Tallahassee, 1965), 108–116; Simkins and Woody, *South Carolina*, 316; Williamson, *After Slavery*, 148ff, farmer quoted at 155; educational data from *AC*, states and years cited.

less of party, were readier to support such acts than was the public at large. That readiness was hardly disinterested: South Carolina's State Orphan Asylum, created in 1869, quickly became a plaything of the politicians, who siphoned off its funds for their own use.[32]

One of the more important consequences of the Civil War was the rise in the expectations of the lower orders of American society. Southern Negroes in the postwar years had a sense of possibility that would not recur for a century. Emancipation and Reconstruction cleared the way for a wide range of devices to develop and marshal black public opinion. Churches and schools served this function, as did Negro newspapers in cities such as New Orleans. So, too, did the machinery of southern Republicanism: the picnics and meetings of the Union League and similar political organizations; the celebration of holidays such as Emancipation Day (January 1st) and the Fourth of July. Conventions and mass meetings often gave voice to the aspirations of a largely illiterate people.

Southern Republicanism opened the doors of political opportunity to Negro organizers and officeholders. Hundreds were delegates to Radical constitutional conventions and served in state legislatures; fourteen were congressmen; two were senators. Blacks played important party roles in Virginia, Georgia, South Carolina, and Louisiana. Many of these leaders had "advantages": they were educated, or light-skinned, or had lived in the North. But there were also indigenous, self-made spokesmen such as Samuel J. Lee, a South Carolina farmer and sawmill worker who prepared himself to enter the bar and served as speaker of the state legislature.[33]

Caution at first characterized the public declarations of the freedmen. A South Carolina Negro convention in November 1865,

32. On Georgia Board of Health, Ernest S. Griffith, *The Modern Development of City Government* (London, 1927), II, 97; Derrell Roberts, "Social Legislation in Florida," *FlaHQ*, 43 (1965), 359; Newton B. Jones, "The State Orphan Asylum of South Carolina: An Episode in Reconstruction," *FS*, 14 (1966), 24–37.

33. W. E. B. Du Bois, "Reconstruction and Its Benefits," *AHR*, 15 (1910), 781–799; Bardolph, *Negro Vanguard*, 83–98; Franklin, *Reconstruction*, 86–91. See also Samuel D. Smith, "The Negro in the United States Senate," in Green, ed., *Essays*, 49–66; E. Merton Coulter, "Henry M. Turner, Georgia Negro Preacher-Politician during the Reconstruction Era," *GaHQ*, 48 (1964), 371–410; Charles Vincent, "Negro Leadership and Programs in the Louisiana Constitutional Convention of 1868," *LaH*, 10 (1969), 339–352.

called "to deliberate upon our intellectual, moral, industrial, civil, and political condition," asked

> for no special privileges, or peculiar favors. We ask only for even-handed justice—for the removal of such positive obstructions and disabilities as past and recent legislation has thrown in our way and heaped upon us . . . We simply ask that we shall be recognized as men; that there be no obstructions placed in our way; that the same laws which govern white men shall govern black men; . . . that, in short, we be dealt with as others are—in equity and justice.

Five hundred blacks gathered at a "practical, moderate" Mobile, Alabama meeting in August 1865 to affirm their readiness to return to work for their former masters. A Baltimore convention at the end of the year appealed for aid in the rebuilding of seven churches burned by a white mob, asked for more schools, and extolled the virtues of hard work and land ownership.

But expectations soon increased. Martin Delany of South Carolina declared that "black men must have black leaders." Macon, Georgia postmaster Henry M. Turner told a mass meeting: "All bloods are one. The difference of race is nothing." Black political spokesmen became more assertive: Georgia's 1868 constitutional convention expelled Negro delegate Aaron A. Bradley for "gross insults" and for advocating "extreme" measures. A white delegate at the 1867 Mississippi convention moved that "colored" be put next to the appropriate names on the delegate list; James Lynch proposed that the color of each delegate's hair also be noted; and the matter was dropped. At South Carolina's convention, Governor Orr offered a resolution prohibiting intermarriage. A black delegate proposed life imprisonment for a white man cohabiting with a black woman; the amended resolution passed by a large majority. It may be assumed that the intentions of the white and the black Republicans who voted for this measure were very different.[34]

Possibility bred possibility. As a January 1866 petition of Negro property owners in Washington put it: "Experience . . . teaches that debasement is most humane which is most complete. The possession of only a partial liberty makes us more keenly sensible of the injustice of withholding those other rights which belong to a

---

34. "South Carolina," "Alabama," "Maryland," *AC* (1865); Delany and Turner in Williamson, *After Slavery*, 358, 253; "Georgia," *AC* (1868); Mississippi," "South Carolina," *AC* (1867).

perfect manhood." Black conventions in Mobile, Alabama called for military courts and commissions to try violators of the Civil Rights Act, and insisted on the right of blacks to serve on juries, ride in public conveyances, and use places of public amusement. A Baltimore gathering attacked the exclusion of Negroes from workshops and apprenticeships, and called for access to teaching and militia companies and for integrated accommodations on steamships and railroads. Attempts—sometimes successful—to break the color line on streetcars occurred in New Orleans, Louisville, and other southern cities. Equal accommodations acts were passed in South Carolina, Mississippi, Georgia, Louisiana, Arkansas, and Florida. A Nashville convention in 1874 raised money to assist a black imprisoned for marrying a white woman.[35]

Most black public demands dwelt on political and social equality. But economic needs won increasing attention. "Forty acres and a mule" from the federal government was a widespread expectation immediately after the war. These hopes were reinforced by occasional land distributions under the Freedmen's Bureau, by the wartime Sea Islands experiment of turning over cotton plantations to the former slaves, and by the Southern Homestead Act of 1866. South Carolina Republicans distributed some unused land to freedmen; a Land Commission in 1868 bought about 45,000 acres for resale in small parcels.[36]

But the enormous pressures against land distribution made these

35. James H. Whyte, *The Uncivil War: Washington during the Reconstruction* (New York, 1958), 50; "Alabama," *AC* (1867); "Maryland," *AC* (1869); Roger A. Fischer, "A Pioneer Protest: The New Orleans Street Car Controversy of 1867," *JNH*, 53 (1968), 219–233; Marjorie M. Norris, "An Early Instance of Nonviolence: The Louisville Demonstrations of 1870–1871," *JSH*, 32 (1966), 487–504; on equal accommodations acts, states cited, *AC* (1870–1874); "Tennessee," *AC* (1874). See also Paul C. Palmer, "Miscegenation as an Issue in the Arkansas Constitutional Convention of 1868," *ArkHQ*, 24 (1965), 99–119; Peter Kolchin, *First Freedom: The Responses of Alabama's Blacks to Emancipation and Reconstruction* (Westport, Conn., 1972).

36. James S. Allen, "The Struggle for Land during the Reconstruction Period," *SS*, 1 (1937), 378–401; Paul W. Gates, "Federal Land Policy in the South, 1866–1868," *JSH*, 6 (1940), 303–330; La Wanda Cox, "The Promise of Land for the Freedmen," *MVHR*, 45 (1958), 413–440; Willie Lee Rose, *Rehearsal for Reconstruction: The Port Royal Experiment* (New York, 1967); "South Carolina," *AC* (1868). See also Carol K. R. Bleser, *The Promised Land: The History of the South Carolina Land Commission, 1869–1890* (Columbia, S.C., 1969).

isolated developments. As it became clear that the future of the great majority of southern blacks lay in working white men's land, state labor conventions in South Carolina (1869) and Alabama (1873) called for district agents to oversee a uniform system of written contracts, for priority to wage suits on court calendars, and for a nine-hour work day. A black-dominated Richmond Republican convention in 1867 declared: "we recognize the great fact that the interests of the laboring classes of the State are identical, and that, without regard to color, we desire to elevate them to their true position; . . . the attainment of the greatest amount of happiness and prosperity to the greatest number, is our warmest desire."[37]

Southern Republicanism often has been treated as the advance agent of a northern capitalism seeking to batten on a fallen foe. Certainly the postwar South lured northern enterprise. Tom Scott of the Pennsylvania Railroad was deeply involved in the development of the Texas & Pacific line; the Pennsylvania and the Baltimore & Ohio jousted for control of Virginia's rail system. The Southern Railroad and Securities Company, a combine of northern and English investors, bought up a number of southeastern roads in the early seventies. Postwar state bond issues often included complex arrangements with Wall Street and foreign investors. The United States Mutual Protection Company was one of a number of northern land companies seeking to obtain and operate southern plantations.[38]

Republicans were not alone in the effort to reap advantage in postwar southern economic life. The Mutual Protection Company included supporters of Andrew Johnson as well as Republicans. Nor were southern Conservatives and Democrats reluctant to participate in entrepreneurial schemes. Pre- and post-Republican state governments in Georgia, Texas, Alabama, and Arkansas shared in the general postwar enthusiasm for subsidized railroad construction. The historian Horace Mann Bond has given us a vivid picture

37. "South Carolina," *AC* (1869); "Alabama," *AC* (1873); "Virginia," *AC* (1867).

38. John F. Stover, *The Railroads of the South 1865–1900* (Chapel Hill, 1955), 118n–119n, 65, 67; Coulter, *South during Reconstruction*, 204–205, 243–244.

of the complex mix of politics and entrepreneurship at play in postwar Alabama. State Republican leaders had close ties to the Nashville & Chattanooga Railroad, as well as to New York and Pennsylvania financiers; the Democrats backed opposing railroad interests, who were linked to the Louisville & Nashville line.[39]

In Virginia, too, railroad entrepreneurship and politics were intimately related. William Mahone, engineer and Confederate war hero, played a pivotal role in the state's postwar railroad consolidation. He sought through his Atlantic, Mississippi and Ohio Railroad Company to dominate the flow of traffic in the Southeast from the Ohio and Mississippi Rivers to the Atlantic seacoast. Mahone's fortunes were tied at first to the Virginia Republican party. His ambitions were fiercely resisted by the Baltimore & Ohio, which worked through the opposing Conservative party.

Corruption and fraud were endemic in the relationship between enterprise and politics in the postwar South. But these evils knew no party lines. When New Orleans Conservatives dwelt on the venality of the state's Republican legislature in 1870, Governor Henry C. Warmoth responded with some home truths: "You charge the legislature with passing corruptly many bills looking to the personal aggrandizement of individuals and corporations. Let me suggest to you that those individuals and corporations are your very best people." He pointed to the fact that a banking bill twice defeated in the legislature now was being lobbied through to passage. "Who are doing it? Your bank presidents. The best people of the city of New Orleans are crowding the lobbies of the legislature, continually whispering into these men's ears bribes to pass this measure.[40]

But the Republican interlude in the South did have distinctive economic consequences. When Virginia Republicans came to power in 1870, a friend of Mahone's wrote to him: "Now for the

39. Carter Goodrich, "Public Aid to Railroads in the Reconstruction South," *PSQ*, 71 (1956), 407–442; Horace M. Bond, "Social and Economic Forces in Alabama Reconstruction," *JNH*, 23 (1938), 290–348. See also Leonard Curry, *Rail Routes South: Louisville's fight for the Southern Market, 1865–1872* (Lexington, Ky., 1969).

40. Nelson M. Blake, *William Mahone of Virginia: Soldier and Political Insurgent* (Richmond, 1935); Warmoth in "Louisiana," *AC* (1870); Shugg, *Class Struggle*, 226. See also Clyde L. Ball, "The Public Career of Colonel A. S. Colyar, 1870–1877," *TennHQ*, 12 (1953), 23–47, 106–128, 213–238.

new regime in the *Old* Dominion. Effete politicians of obsolete ideas must give place to wide-awake men thoroughly imbued with the progressive spirit of the time." The Republican governments of Texas and South Carolina offered tax exemptions and other state aid for industrial development. As the governor of the latter state put it, "In a progressive age, legislation must do its part." Brownlow of Tennessee considered a rising state debt to be an essential factor in the growth of economic productivity. Republican governments were eager for congressional aid for major internal improvements: a ship canal across Florida, a water transportation system linking the Mississippi to the Atlantic.[41]

Most of all, the Republican regimes devoted themselves to heavy state borrowing and spending for railroad development, comparable to the flood of postwar northern county and local railroad aid. (Except for Virginia, postwar southern state constitutions differed from their northern counterparts in permitting state railroad subsidies.) This policy was far from unpopular. A Mississippi Democratic newspaper declared in 1871: "we can stand a pretty big 'steal' if we get railroads." Arkansas voters in 1868, called on to judge the state's Republican aid program, voted five to one "For Railroads."[42]

But for all their concordance with felt southern needs, the Republicans' economic policies were no better able than their governmental or social policies to give their party a firm foothold in the South. And in the early and mid-seventies the southern polity underwent yet another abrupt and widespread convulsion.

The Democratic Restoration

Southern Republicanism was a transitory political phenomenon. A biracial politics based on Republican precepts posed too great a challenge to the prevailing mores of the region. And in most south-

41. Blake, *Mahone*, 110; Simkins and Woody, *South Carolina*, 103; Coulter, *Brownlow*, 374–379. See also W. C. Nunn, *Texas Under the Carpetbaggers* (Austin, 1962), 34–37, 153 ff.

42. "Mississippi," *AC* (1871); on Arkansas, Goodrich, "Public Aid," 215. See also George H. Thompson, "Reconstruction and the Loss of State Credit," *ArkHQ*, 28 (1969), 293–308; Margaret L. Fitzsimmons, "Missouri Railroads during the Civil War and Reconstruction," *MoHR*, 35 (1941), 188–206.

ern states, blacks were not sufficiently numerous to provide a viable political base.

A revealing measure of this weakness was the decline of northern Republican support for the southern branch of the party. The Freedmen's Bureau rapidly faded after it helped to secure southern Republican votes in the 1868 election. Federal protection of Negro voting steadily diminished during the mid and late seventies. There were two hundred civil rights prosecutions in 1875, and only twenty-five in 1878. In 1877 Attorney General Charles Devens assured Senator John T. Morgan of Alabama, who wanted pending civil rights indictments dismissed: "The U.S. Attorneys will be instructed to prosecute only important cases, where the guilt is clear and the evidence overwhelming, and in such prosecutions to act without bias in favor of or against any political party."[43]

The erosion of national support went hand in hand with the internal weakness of southern Republicanism. Members of the party were demoralized by the social hostility that surrounded them. Factional infighting over patronage further weakened the party structure, as did continuing tension between its white and black members. White Republican leaders were interested primarily in patronage and in keeping ex-Confederates from voting or holding office. Some black spokesmen had more expansive political goals. A white delegate to the 1867 Alabama constitutional convention argued that the "great object" of disfranchisement was "to keep the State out of the control of disloyal men." But a black delegate had a different political ideal: "I have no desire to take away any of the rights of the white man; all I want is equal rights in the court-house and equal rights when I go to vote."[44]

White-black differences grew as the situation of southern Republicans worsened. White leaders sought to escape the onus of being identified with a biracial social policy. Brownlow of Tennessee opposed a national civil rights bill, and Warmoth of Louisiana was increasingly hostile to black civil equality. Warmoth refused to sign the state's civil rights acts of 1868 and 1870, or to enforce the

43. Everette Swinney, "Enforcing the Fifteenth Amendment, 1870–1877," *JSH*, 28 (1962), 202–218; Devons to Morgan, April 1877, Executive and Congressional Letterbooks, Department of Justice, NA.

44. "Alabama," *AC* (1867). See also Elizabeth S. Nathans, *Losing the Peace: Georgia Republicans and Reconstruction* (Baton Rouge, 1968).

prohibition of segregated schools. Many Louisiana blacks may have voted Democratic in the 1876 election because of the failure of the state Republican party to respond to their needs. By the end of the decade Republican tickets had disappeared from a number of southern states. North Carolina Republicans glumly concluded in 1878 that it might be best to disband the state party.[45]

As Republican power slackened, a resurgent Democracy took over. That restoration was achieved through a variety of means, violence not the least of them. More so than at any other time in the history of the United States, terrorism and murder became a frequent adjunct of the political process.

A number of Republican leaders—usually black, sometimes white—met violent ends. The toll included a state senator, a member of the Republican state central committee, three members of the general assembly, and a delegate to the 1868 constitutional convention, all in South Carolina; state senators in North Carolina (1870) and Florida (1876); a multitude of lesser officers such as a sheriff and clerk in Arkansas (1873); six white Republicans in Louisiana (1874); and black militia officers in Mississippi (1874). In Brownsville, Louisiana, a Negro leader was seized, his limbs were slowly broken, and then he was burned to death. A black Republican in Florida was tortured to reveal the strategy of the local Union League.

Mass violence for political ends—the New Orleans and Memphis massacres of 1866, the Vicksburg riot of 1874, the Hamburg, South Carolina killings of 1876—won considerable attention in the northern press. But these were only the tip of an iceberg of terror. Before the election of 1868 hundreds of blacks supposedly were killed in Louisiana's St. Landry, Bossier, and Caddo parishes. The word "bulldoze" took on a political connotation in these years, apparently deriving from the custom of using a bullwhip to keep blacks from the polls.[46]

45. Coulter, Brownlow, 389; Althea D. Pitre, "The Collapse of the Warmoth Regime, 1870–72," LaH, 6 (1965), 161–187; T. B. Tunnell, Jr., "The Negro, the Republican Party, and the Election of 1876 in Louisiana," LaH, 7 (1966), 101–116; "North Carolina," AC (1878).

46. On South Carolina, Scroggs, "Southern Reconstruction," 419; AC, states and years cited; on Louisiana black leader, H. Oscar Lestage, Jr., "The White League in Louisiana and Its Participation in Reconstruction Riots," LaHQ, 18 (1935), 681; Ralph L. Peek, "Lawlessness in Florida, 1868–1869,"

"Regulators" and "night-riders"—bands violently enforcing their own standard of civil order—had long been a feature of southern life. The presence of large numbers of former Confederate soldiers and the inflamed passions of Reconstruction stimulated the reappearance of such groups in the postwar South. Armed groups roamed Alamance county in North Carolina and the South Carolina upcountry, areas that had seen such "Regulator" activity in the eighteenth century.

The Ku Klux Klan was the instrument of organized terror that attracted the greatest attention, although during its heyday from 1867 to 1871 it was active in only a quarter of the South's counties. The Klan sought to keep the freedmen in their social and economic place, but its major function was to suppress black (and white) Republican political activity. It played an important role in a number of southern states during the 1868 election, terrorizing thousands and throwing Georgia and Louisiana to the Democrats. Nine Louisiana parishes with 11,604 registered Republicans cast 19 votes for Grant; in seven parishes, with 7,253 Republican registrations, no Grant votes at all were recorded. Similar precipitous declines occurred in a number of Tennessee and Georgia counties.[47]

The ultimate consequence of this violence and intimidation was the restoration of white Democratic rule in the South. The Democratic party led a shadow-life in the region during the immediate postwar years, masquerading under other names: Conservative, Constitutional Union, Conservative Union. Even in the Union border state of Missouri, the party had its difficulties. In disarray at the end of the war, it gradually reorganized on the local level. By the end of 1868 there was a formal Democratic party structure in

FlaHQ, 40 (1961), 166; on Louisiana parishes, U.S., CR, 46th Cong., 2d sess. (June 14, 1880), 4525; on "bulldoze," Mitford M. Mathews, ed., A Dictionary of Americanisms on Historical Principles (Chicago, 1951), 215.
47. Allen W. Trelease, White Terror: The Ku Klux Conspiracy and Southern Reconstruction (New York, 1971), 64, 185, et passim; Thomas B. Alexander, "Kukluxism in Tennessee, 1865–1869," TennHQ, 8 (1949), 195–219; Herbert Shapiro, "The Ku Klux Klan during Reconstruction: The South Carolina Episode," JNH, 49 (1964), 34–55; on Louisiana votes, U.S., CR, 46th Cong., 2d sess. (June 14, 1880), 4525; on Georgia, Shadgett, Republican Party, 14. See also Edward C. Williamson, "The Alabama Election of 1874," AlaR, 17 (1964), 210–218; Joe Gray Taylor, "New Orleans and Reconstruction," LaH, 9 (1968), 189–208.

almost seventy Missouri counties. But caution continued to be the watchword: in 1870 Missouri's Democrats adopted a "possum policy" of avoiding a convention or a state ticket. Virginia's Conservative party convention of 1871 offered no platform, only a plan for county organization.[48]

The more general pattern was the steady—and in many places rapid—resurgence of the prewar Democracy. Mississippi's Constitutional Unionists assumed the old party name as early as 1868, Tennessee's Conservative Unionists did so in 1870, Georgia's Conservatives in 1872. Democrats dominated almost all southern legislatures and congressional delegations by 1874.

The southern Democracy restored itself in part through its identification with the national party. The Alabama Conservative convention of 1867 copied the platform of Pennsylvania's Conservative Unionists; and interregional political alliances were quickly restored or newly created in the immediate postwar years. Ceremonial occasions such as the Philadelphia "arm-in-arm" convention of 1866 or the dedication of a statue of Thomas Hart Benton in Missouri contributed to a sense of Democratic party continuity, reaching back over secession and the Civil War, that had a powerful appeal to a postwar southern leadership hungry for restoration.

The postwar southern Democracy rested as well on assumptions about government and society that were shared by northern Democrats and accorded with the views of the majority of southern whites. The most powerful of these was white supremacy. Alabama's State Conservative Committee designated January 30, 1868 a day of fasting and prayer to deliver the people of the state "from the horrors of negro domination." Mississippi Democrats in 1868 condemned the black members of the state's Radical constitutional convention as "destitute alike of the moral and intellectual qualifications required of electors in all civilized communities." North Carolina Conservatives passed white supremacy resolutions in the same year, declaring: "We recognize the radical distinctions of color, blood, physical form, and peculiarities of intellect, between the white and negro races."[49]

48. On party names, C. Vann Woodward, *Origins of the New South 1877–1913* (Baton Rouge, 1951), 3; Parrish, *Missouri*, 238; "Virginia," *AC* (1871).

49. *AC*, states and years cited.

A variety of other devices assisted the party's return to power. Economy, retrenchment, and reform—political tenets with national appeal in the early 1870s—were recurrent themes in the southern Democratic assault on Republican state regimes. Taxpayers' Unions in Texas and South Carolina dwelt highmindedly on the need for honest and frugal government, while other men in other guises did more ugly work. As a South Carolina aphorism of the time had it, "Old men in the Tax Unions and young men in the Rifle Clubs."

The Liberal Republican movement of 1872 served as a conduit for many white southern Republicans on their way to the Democratic party. Grant observed with some accuracy: "I regard the [Missouri Liberal Republican] movement . . . as similar to the Tennessee and Virginia movement, intended to carry a portion of the Republican party over to the Democracy." Coalitions of the two parties uniformly ended in the strengthening of the Democrats and the disappearance of the Liberal Republicans.[50]

While white supremacist, Negrophobic sentiments predominated in the postwar southern Democracy, they coexisted with recurrent efforts to secure the support of black voters. From the retrospect of the early 1900s, when the exclusion of blacks from southern politics was all but total, it may well have seemed that that end was foreordained. But in the wake of the war, Democrats frequently toyed with the possibility (or accepted the necessity) of a biracial politics.

A number of former Confederate leaders—Wade Hampton of South Carolina was the most conspicuous—thought that black voters would be docile, manipulable supporters of a resurgent Democracy. Hampton dwelt on the virtues of Democratic political regularity in an address to a black meeting in Columbia, South Carolina in March 1867. An 1868 convention of Democratic clubs recognized that blacks were "an integral part of the body politic," and numerous state platforms echoed the view of Arkansas's Democrats in 1871 that "the equality of all men before the law" was one of "the *accomplished facts of the war*." The anti-Republican, New Orleans-based Reform party of Louisiana pro-

50. Simkins and Woody, *South Carolina*, 184; Grant quoted in Norma L. Peterson, *Freedom and Franchise: The Political Career of B. Gratz Brown* (Columbia, Mo., 1965), 186.

posed a broad-gauged program of racial unification in 1873. A number of substantial citizens endorsed the Fifteenth Amendment, Negro officeholding, and the integration of schools and other public facilities. The *New Orleans Times*, speaking for the city's business community, lent its support; and a biracial Committee of One Hundred (of the sort that often figured in genteel northern urban reform) was formed. Virginia's Conservatives, the state's dominant party during the 1870s, adopted policies that put them somewhere between southern Republicanism and the unregenerate Democracy. They endorsed black suffrage and civil rights (but not social equality), a strong public school system, national patriotism, and accommodation to federal supremacy.[51]

Amicable gestures toward blacks continued even after the Democratic restoration. Wade Hampton said of his 1876 election to the South Carolina governorship: "I regard myself as having been elected by the colored people." Louisiana Democrats made a strong appeal for Negro votes in 1876 and enrolled thousands of blacks in Democratic political clubs. Mississippi Democrats in 1876 pledged themselves to "free schools, free suffrage, equal rights." A resolution of the state's 1877 legislature thanked its black members for their "uniform courtesy, and manly dignified devotion to public duty," piously congratulating the voters "upon the selection of representatives so worthy from that race and upon the arrival of that happy epoch where race prejudice and bitterness of feeling exists in our borders no longer." Florida's Democratic governor proclaimed in 1877: "our colored fellow-citizens may finally rest assured that their rights . . . will be fully sustained."[52]

It may be that these declarations are evidence that many white southerners were genuinely ambivalent in their response to emancipation and Reconstruction, that in the postwar years an alternative to institutionalized racism was possible. But the flight in the

51. Hampton N. Jarrell, *Wade Hampton and the Negro: The Road Not Taken* (Columbia, S.C., 1949), 19; "South Carolina," *AC* (1868), "Arkansas," *AC* (1871); T. Harry Williams, "The Louisiana Unification Movement of 1873," *JSH*, 11 (1945), 349–369; Jack P. Maddex, Jr., *The Virginia Conservatives 1867–1879: A Study in Reconstruction Politics* (Chapel Hill, 1970), 54 ff; Robert R. Jones, "James L. Kemper and the Virginia Redeemers Face the Race Question: A Reconsideration," *JSH*, 37 (1972), 393–414.

52. Jarrell, *Wade Hampton*, 61; states cited, *AC* (1876–1877); on Louisiana, Tunnell, "Election of 1876," 112.

1870s and after from the social, political, and governmental innovations of the postwar years was a national and not just a southern phenomenon. Given prevailing attitudes—both popular and elite —toward race relations and the role of government, it is difficult to imagine that southern Republicanism could have been followed by anything other than the Democratic restoration.

Democrats in Power

Substantial changes in the structure of southern government followed on the Democrats' return to political power during the early and mid-seventies. It was common to reverse, to ignore, even to deny the reality of the Republican interlude. Texas courts refused to accept the Republican state supreme court's decisions as precedents. Louisiana's capital was moved in 1877 from tainted New Orleans to Baton Rouge. Legislatures repealed Republican militia, election, and education laws wholesale.

Gerrymandering ensured the dissolution of Republican voting strength. Tennessee in 1870 created a Knoxville congressional district that ran like a battering ram from the North Carolina border into the middle of the state. Missouri redistricting in 1880 produced congressional seats varying in population from 20,000 to 50,000. One of these was two miles wide and thirty miles long, crossing the sinuous Missouri River three times.

A variety of devices restricted the Negro vote. Delaware in 1872 assessed county taxes (a voting prerequisite) six months before the election; New Castle county tax collectors skipped large numbers of blacks and thus deprived them of the ballot. A number of states disfranchised those (often blacks) who were convicted of petty larceny. At the end of the decade Virginia, Kentucky, and Missouri adopted a "living-voice" method of voting in place of paper ballots: a technique that eased the path of intimidation.[53]

The Democratic return to power frequently led to the modifica-

53. Norvell, "Reconstruction Courts of Texas"; *AC*, states and years cited. On the effacement of the records of Republican rule see William E. B. Du Bois, *Black Reconstruction* (New York, 1935), 721. Only Tennessee adopted the poll tax as a vote-restricting device at this time. Frank B. Williams, "The Poll Tax as a Suffrage Requirement in the South, 1870–1901," *JSH*, 18 (1952), 469.

tion or replacement of state constitutions. Governor Coke of Texas bluntly announced in 1874: "The causes which one year ago rendered it imprudent to call together a constitutional convention have ceased to exist . . . We no longer fear Federal interference." Previous constitutional declarations that all men were created equal now gave way to more equivocal statements: "all men are created equally free and independent" (Arkansas, Alabama); "all men are equal before the law" (Florida). Often the new documents made segregated schools obligatory when no such requirement existed before.

The theoretical commitment of the "redeemers" to local government was strong. Theirs was the spirit of the 1872 Missouri Liberal Republican convention: "local self-government, with impartial suffrage, will guard the rights of all citizens more securely than any centralized authority." Like their northern counterparts, the new or revised southern constitutions of the 1870s frequently limited special or local lawmaking and other forms of legislative activity.

The presence of black-dominated counties and townships posed a problem. A common solution was to vest considerable power over county and local officials in the safely white-dominated state legislatures. Thus North Carolina in 1877 required that the three justices of the peace for each township be chosen by the legislature; they in turn selected the county commissioners. Townships, frequently created during the Reconstruction years, disappeared entirely in South Carolina, West Virginia, Virginia, and Missouri.[54]

But the Reconstruction past could not be expunged completely. Mississippi, South Carolina, and Georgia lived with their (modified) Republican constitutions until the turn of the century. The abolition of slavery; token political and legal equality; at least the principle of universal public education: these remained.

Democratic redeemers frequently assaulted the fiscal misdeeds of their predecessors: corrupt and wasteful borrowing, railroad subsidization, and indebtedness. Undeniably those abuses occurred, and left a heavy legacy of fiscal obligation and oppressive taxation. According to one estimate, by 1874 over 2,900 pieces of Charleston

54. "Texas," *AC* (1874); constitutions in Thorpe, ed., *Federal and State Constitutions*; "Missouri," *AC* (1872); on townships, Herman G. James, *Local Government in the United States* (New York, 1921), 112.

real estate and 343,971 acres of South Carolina land had been for-feited for nonpayment of taxes. A Mississippi taxpayers' convention in 1875 claimed that the tax rate on land multiplied fourteen times between 1869 and 1874. The new regimes adopted a variety of devices for altering the pattern and scale of state expenditure. Limits on state and local spending and debt were common. Tax rates were slashed by a third in Missouri (1876); state budgets were drastically reduced, to the detriment of education and other public services.[55]

Redemptionist governments struggled with the servicing of state and local debt—a national problem in the seventies, but compounded in the South by the poverty of the region. In extended negotiations with bondholders, the states sought to refund or scale down their existing obligations. Every state but Kentucky and Texas engaged in at least some outright repudiation. State and county courts allied with the legislatures of Arkansas and Missouri to block the tax collections required to service municipal bonds. Bitter struggles over the legality of these actions ensued between state authorities and the federal courts, with the latter ultimately victorious.

A special air of desperation prevailed in debt-laden southern cities. When a federal court ordered the Montgomery, Alabama City Council to levy a tax to pay bond obligations, most of the council resigned rather than obey—and were then found to be in contempt of court. A number of communities went into bankruptcy—Nashville was in the hands of a receiver as early as 1869—or were dissolved as municipal corporations and then reconstituted in an attempt to escape the burden of debt. Thus Memphis's charter was repealed in 1879 and the city was reorganized as a group of "taxing districts"; Mobile was rechartered as the "Port of Mobile," the City of Selma as "Selma." But while the United States Supreme Court conceded the right of a state legislature to dissolve and then reconstitute a municipal corporation, it did not allow these "new" municipalities to escape the debts incurred by their predecessors.[56]

55. *AC*, states and years cited. For discussions of southern economic policy in the 1870s see Coulter, *South During Reconstruction*, ch. 9, and Woodward, *New South*, ch. 5; Allen J. Going, *Bourbon Democracy in Alabama 1874–1900* (University, Ala., 1951), 80, 84.

56. William A. Scott, *The Repudiation of State Debts* (New York, 1893), 276; Reginald C. McGrane, *Foreign Bondholders and American State Debts*

The post-Reconstruction South was not of one mind on the handling of indebtedness. The popular desire for outright repudiation of heavy state and local debts constantly clashed with the concern of many substantial Democrats for fiscal soundness and unimpaired credit. Democrats in Virginia, South Carolina, Tennessee, and elsewhere divided into debt and antidebt factions during the late seventies. Generally, white (and black) farmers favored repudiationist policies; planters, businessmen, and city interests worried about their communities' future credit standing.

But more subtle considerations often modified these alignments. The pressure for repudiation at the 1875 Alabama constitutional convention came not only from poorer hill county whites but also from Black Belt planters who had been excluded from the major railroad bond syndicates in the state. And whites in the heavily black counties of Virginia, fearful of biracial politics, supported the antirepudiation (and lily white) Funders against the repudiationist Readjusters.[57]

In other areas of public policy, too, the line between Republican reconstructionists and Democratic redeemers was obscured by particularities of self-interest. The reaction against postwar spending was a national phenomenon and cut across party lines. As early as 1869, Texas's Republican constitution limited the state aid that could be extended to private enterprise, and Republican governor Edmund J. Davis vetoed a number of railroad aid bills in 1870.

Nor were the Democrats more reluctant than the Republicans to stimulate entrepreneurship and industrial development in the region. A Direct-Trade Union was organized in Georgia in 1874 to encourage closer commercial relations between southern ports and Europe and to agitate for an Atlantic and Great Western Canal that would connect the state to the Mississippi River. Florida Democrats amended the state constitution in 1874 to permit tax exemp-

(New York, 1935), 282 ff; on municipal bonds, Fairman, *Reconstruction and Reunion*, 1069–1101; Parrish, *Missouri*, 209; on cities, John F. Dillon, *Commentaries on the Law of Municipal Corporations*, 4th ed., (Boston, 1890), I, 251–252; Lucius S. Merriam, "The Appointment of a Receiver for the City of Nashville in 1869," *ALR*, 25 (1891), 393–399; Harshman v. Bates, 92 U.S. 569 (1876); Douglass v. Pike County, 101 U.S. 677 (1879).

57. Maddex, *Virginia Conservatives*, chs. 15–16; Allen W. Moger, *Virginia: Bourbonism to Byrd 1870–1925* (Charlottesville, 1968), chs. 1, 2; Bond, "Alabama Reconstruction"; Going, *Bourbon Democracy*, chs. 4–5.

tions to new textile mills, sugar refineries, and other industries.

The Democratic restoration frequently led to transfers of economic control rather than to changes in economic policy. State-owned railroad stock was sold off to those interests that had the greatest political influence. Thus the Alabama and Chattanooga Railroad went in 1876 for a modest $310,000 to a representative of Daniel N. Stanton—who had originally organized the road when the Republicans were in control. The 1878 South Carolina legislature repealed all charters previously given to river mining companies—and then incorporated fifteen new firms. When in 1874 the Louisville and Nashville Railroad went into bankruptcy, a sympathetic Alabama Democratic administration accepted a settlement whose terms were set by an L&N attorney.[58]

Southern Democrats, supported by their northern counterparts, criticized the Southern Homestead Act of 1868 for slowing the region's economic development. A Wilkes County, Georgia grand jury argued in 1875 that the act had led to "stagnation of the mercantile and agricultural interests of the country." The law had been designed to make land available to the freedmen. But the often unproductive character of the available land, the costs of clearing and obtaining a fair title, and white hostility limited black homesteads to 4,000 by 1870. The act was repealed in 1875; and in the late seventies and early eighties large blocs of state-controlled public land in Florida, Louisiana, and Mississippi were thrown open to lumber and land companies.[59]

Similar qualities typified post-Reconstruction southern social policy. Here too there was a strong reaction against the tendencies of postwar Republicanism. But it was a reaction tempered by the fact that restoration in the literal sense of the word was not to be: the antebellum South was gone.

The regulation of social behavior, increasingly important in the northern states, had southern analogues. Lotteries were prohibited in Arkansas (1875) and Georgia (1877); duelists were more severely punished and excluded from officeholding; public executions were

58. Goodrich, "Public Aid"; Nunn, *Texas*, 100; *AC*, states and years cited; Thompson, "Reconstruction and Loss of State Credit."
59. "Georgia," *AC* (1875); Warren Hoffnagle, "The Southern Homestead Act: Its Origins and Operation," *Hist*, 32 (1970), 612–629.

forbidden in Alabama (1878) and Kentucky (1880); legislatures frequently taxed and more closely regulated the sale of liquor.

Licensing of professions and occupations and a heightened concern over public health—characteristic features of the postwar northern polity—often appeared in the South as well during the seventies. Typical was South Carolina's 1875 act "to regulate the practice of dentistry, and protect the people against empiricism in relation thereto." A number of states created boards of pharmacy, of medical examiners, and of health. But there was a distinct small-government, economizing bias to the Democratic redemption. A North Carolina referendum of 1880 made it optional, not obligatory, for the state to provide aid for the poor or the handicapped. The sixteen deep South and border states gave aid to 22,845 paupers in 1870; to 17,614 in 1880.[60]

Education, that sensitive repository of social values, bore the brunt of the Democratic restoration. Here both racism and a belief in thrifty and decentralized government found ample room for expression. The border states, less influenced by Republican Reconstruction, led the way. Public schools closed in some parts of Maryland in 1871 for lack of financial support. In 1872 only a third of Tennessee's counties levied school taxes; 28 percent of the state's children attended school. When the head of the Delaware normal school criticized the state's educational system, an angry legislature revoked the school's charter.

The Democratic return to power often was accompanied by an assault on state support for education. A Mississippi taxpayers' convention in 1875 called for free education only in common schools and for a reduction of the education tax. Everywhere the active state superintendents and the nominally centralized school systems of the Republican years gave way to inertia and decentralization in theory as well as in fact.

These policies had substantial popular support. Missouri voters in 1878 by better than eight to one rejected a constitutional amendment that would have provided a one dollar poll tax for the school fund. In 1878 West Virginia's legislature expanded the system of normal schools; but public disapproval forced a cut in appropria-

60. AC, states and years cited; S.C. Acts 1875, no. 683; on paupers, U.S., Bureau of the Census, Compendium of the Ninth Census (Washington, 1872), 531, Compendium of the Tenth Census (Washington, 1883), 1675.

tions in the following year. The debt burdens and hard times of the seventies left their mark: Virginia's school attendance in 1879 was half that of the year before, as the lack of funds forced some local boards to keep their schools closed.

Hostility to Negro education was widespread and overt. Superintendents of education in North and South Carolina, Georgia, and Virginia questioned the educability of black children. State laws in the seventies firmly prescribed segregated schools. Mississippi's 1878 education act specified that white and black students were not to be taught in schoolhouses closer than two and a half miles from one another; Kentucky set limits of one mile in rural areas and six hundred feet in cities and towns.

Separate tax bases in some states limited the resources available for Negro education to the scanty funds that blacks themselves could raise. (Even these may not have been fully used for their intended purpose: county sheriffs did the collecting in Kentucky.) Kentucky in 1879 allocated a minute $1.60 a year for the education of each white child—and 52¢ for each black student. Delaware offered no public education at all to Negro children until 1875. Then a property tax of 30¢ per $100 was levied on blacks, the revenue to be expended by the Delaware Association for the Moral Improvement and Education of Colored People. By 1878 there were forty-six Negro schools in the state, each subsisting on $6 to $10 a month from the Association and what supplementary aid the black community could provide.

But however stunted, Negro common school education steadily spread. A total of 134,671 black children were enrolled in 1870; 789,319 in 1880. Maryland in 1873 appropriated $50,000 for the establishment of Negro schools, and the state's Democrats committed themselves in 1876 to the creation of a common school fund "without respect to race or color." The Louisiana legislature in 1877 pledged itself to "secure the education of the children of white and colored citizens equally," as did the Arkansas legislature in 1874. In education as in other areas of the South's social structure, the postwar polity left a mark not readily effaced.[61]

The South by 1880 still did not have the highly articulated sys-

61. On education, AC, states and years cited; Woodward, Origins, 61–63; John Hope Franklin, "Jim Crow Goes to School: The Genesis of Legal Segregation in Southern Schools," SAQ, 58 (1959), 225–235. See also Going, Bourbon Democracy, chs. 10, 12.

tem of legal segregation of the races that existed by the early twentieth century. But the commitment of the resurgent Democracy to black subordination was strong and unequivocal. Again, the border states were especially quick to write prejudice into law. An 1876 Maryland statute excluded Negroes from admission to the state bar. Tennessee and Louisiana passed pioneering acts limiting the access of blacks to railroad accommodations.

A revealing measure of the worsening situation of southern Negroes was the Exodus of 1879. Many thousands (estimates range from 15,000 to 60,000) left for Kansas, Indiana, and other states, with the encouragement of a black leadership that saw little promise in the region.[62]

Perhaps the most horrendous consequence of the Democratic restoration was the expansion of the convict lease system. The policy of leasing prisoners to private contractors began during the provisional and military governments of the postwar years, and the Radical governments continued the practice on a small scale. But under the "redemption" regimes the system became a substantial and permanent means of state economizing, personal profit-making, and social control. In 1876 three Georgia companies contracted to lease the state's convicts for twenty years, in return for a $25,000 annual payment. Mississippi in 1876 leased its prisoners to James S. Hamilton, who subleased them to planters, railroad companies, and levee contractors. Tennessee's convicts went *en bloc* to Colonel A. S. Colyar's Tennessee Coal and Iron Company for $101,000 a year.

The system was linked to criminal statutes and enforcement policies that doubled or tripled the number of black convicts during the seventies. In sum it provided thousands of Negroes to do work for which free labor would have been difficult or impossible to obtain; gave lucrative revenues to cabals of politicians and entrepreneurs; and furnished one of the authentic horror stories of American history. Death rates were ferociously high; labor camp conditions were brutal and degrading; convict leasing, corruptly

62. *AC*, states and years cited; S. J. Folmsbee, "The Origin of the First 'Jim Crow' Law," *JSH*, 15 (1949), 235–247; "Exodus of the Colored People," *AC* (1879); "The Senate Report on the Exodus of 1879," *JNH*, 4 (1919), 57–92; Coulter, *South During Reconstruction*, 100–101. See also Barry A. Crouch and L. J. Schultz, "Crisis in Color: Racial Separation in Texas During Reconstruction," *CWH*, 16 (1970), 37–49.

made and corruptly maintained, was stubbornly resistant to reform or eradication.[63]

For all its special tone and setting, the public experience of the postwar South did not differ fundamentally from that of the nation at large. True, the fact of defeat made possible a more dramatic application of the war-born legacies of active government and civil equality than was the case in the North. And there was a distinctive—indeed, a tragic—quality to the reimposition in the 1870s of policies that embodied the racism, localism, and hostility to government of the dominant white culture. Nevertheless, in a larger view southern Reconstruction and redemption is best seen as a sectional manifestation of an experience common to the postwar polity.

63. Fletcher M. Green, "Some Aspects of the Convict Lease System in the Southern States," in Green, ed., *Essays in Southern History*, 112–123; Woodward, *Origins*, 212–215; Mark T. Carleton, *Politics and Punishment: The History of the Louisiana State Penal System* (Baton Rouge, 1971), 13–22.

CHAPTER 7

The Triumph of
Organizational Politics

IN THE CENTENNIAL year of 1876, the Yale social
scientist William Graham Sumner reviewed the past century of
American political life. Politics in the wake of the Civil War, he
concluded, had been dominated by "national pride and consciousness of power." But complex public issues could not "be decided by
reference to a general political dogma, or a moral principle, or a
text of Scripture." There was a growing need for better trained
leaders. Yet "intelligent men" shunned politics. By default (yet of
necessity) the boss and the machine filled the gap.[1]

Party leaders and political organizations hardly were unknown
in what Sumner called the "golden age" of the 1860s. Nevertheless,
during the 1870s the character of American politics sharply
changed. The passionate, ideologically charged political ambiance
of the Reconstruction years gave way to a politics that rested on
the perpetuation of party organization rather than the fostering of
public policy. In this sense party politics no less than the policies
of government retreated from the purposeful activism of the immediate postwar years. The triumph of organizational politics is
the final measure of the postwar polity's rejection of the legacy of
the Civil War.

1. William G. Sumner, "Politics in America, 1776–1876," *NAR*, 122
(1876), 79.

238

The Culture of Party Politics

There was a striking contrast in the 1870s between the apparent decline of the active state and the scale of the governmental and political processes. The federal bureaucracy grew from 51,000 employees in 1871 to 100,000 in 1881. Local officeholding flourished as well. Pennsylvania county officials in the seventies included inspectors of flour, lumber, domestic spirits, sole and harness leather, banks, petroleum, illuminating gas, and pickled fish; auctioneers, slaters of weights, measurers, railroad policemen, county marshals, quarantine masters; and a multitude of other placeholders. It was estimated that one in twelve household heads in New York City had a public position. An opponent of efforts to prohibit civil servants from participating in politics pointed out that there were more than 140,000 federal, state, and local officeholders in New York—about one out of eight voters. With some cause, he argued: "The exclusion of public servants from political action would disfranchise a great body of our fellow-citizens."[2]

The overblown public buildings that rose across the land in the 1870s, like the swollen ranks of public employees, were testimony not to the active state but to the growing strength of organizational politics. Indiana's grandiose new capitol, for example, was completed in 1877 after seven years' work. A Board of Commissioners, composed of the governor and—appropriate in a state whose politics were in delicate equipoise—representatives from each of the major parties, oversaw its construction. The building cost almost $5,000,000. Rich frescoes and a Venetian supreme court chamber "rather too gorgeous for a Court of Justice" were among its features. New York's ornate capitol was finished in 1879, with even finer court chambers. City halls—notably those of Philadelphia and San Francisco—rose in comparable splendor.

Spectacular corruption attended the construction of these buildings. The foundation stones of the new Iowa capitol split and cost the state $50,000 to replace; the names of the culpable building

2. *HS*, 710; Erwin S. Bradley, *The Triumph of Militant Republicanism: A Study of Pennsylvania and Presidential Politics 1860–1872* (Philadelphia, 1964), 278; David D. Field, "Corruption in Politics," *IR*, 4 (1877), 85, "New York," *AC* (1877). See also Duncan C. McMillan, *The Elective Franchise in the United States* (New York, 1878), 50; Matthew P. Breen, *Thirty Years of New York Politics Up-to-Date* (New York, 1899), 236.

commissioners were removed from the cornerstone. Favored contractors shared with politicos the profits from grossly inflated charges. The New York County Court House—"The House that Tweed Built"—cost more than four times as much as Britain's Houses of Parliament. Over $13,000,000 went into its construction from 1869 to 1871, and the building never was completed.[3]

As massive in their way were the frequent party meetings and conventions. An American explained this feature of his country's political life to an English audience: "It is a land of conventions and assemblies, where it is the most natural thing in the world for people to get together in meetings, where almost every event is the occasion for speechmaking, and where oratory has a very perceptible influence in acquiring public authority." Conventions reflected the character of the parties that staged them. A British visitor "was told the Democratic conventions were marked by comparative turbulence and irregularity," were "more boisterous and peremptory" than their Republican counterparts.

Whatever the reality of insider control, elaborate systems of delegate selection and hugely attended gatherings (18,000 at the 1880 Republican national convention in Chicago, for example) fostered a sense of popular participation. New York City's parties in 1880 required 72 primary elections and 111 convention nominations to make up their tickets. Members of that city's Republican Associations—about one in four party voters—could participate in delegate selection, providing they agreed to abide by some forty-two pages of regulations and signed a pledge to "recognize the authority of the association." New Jersey Republicans proposed in 1872 that there be a delegate to the state convention for every two hundred party votes cast in the preceding election, and that every ward and township have at least one representative. The 1,000 delegates to the 1877 New Jersey Democratic convention were not an uncommonly large attendance.[4]

3. "Indiana," AC (1877), and John Leng, America in 1876. Pencillings During a Tour in the Centennial Year (Dundee, Scotland, 1877), 87–88; on Iowa statehouse, Edward Younger, John A. Kasson (Iowa City, 1955), 244; Alexander B. Callow, Jr., The Tweed Ring (New York, 1966), 197–206.

4. George M. Towle, American Society (London, 1870), I, 84 ff; George J. Holyoake, Among the Americans (Chicago, 1881), 52; on New York primaries, F. W. Whitridge, "A Brake on the Machine," IR, 8 (1880), 242–

The electoral process was of comparable scale and density. The sheer number of elections could be overpowering. An Iowa politician complained, "We work through one campaign, take a bath and start in on the next." But there was good reason for this "exasperation of political excitement, ... prolonged electioneering turmoil." Much was at stake: "So many offices depend upon the result of the elections that electioneering is made a business, and politics are reduced to a trade." The range of interests that made claims on the parties intensified the pressure. A Michigan Supreme Court justice running for re-election in 1871 commented feelingly on the bewildering variety of blocs with which he had to deal:

> I had not thought of the Homeopaths, but the other Elements of discord I have had brought too closely to be overlooked. The Railroad vote on a single issue would amount to nothing; but when the Democrats hang together—as they will—it makes a large defection ... The Prohibition movement in this light is important, for a vote for Williams who has always been very Radical is as much against me as one for Hughes, and some who would not vote for a Democrat will vote for Williams. The colored vote ... will be against me ... There is a quarrel among them which arises as I am informed somewhat out of my nomination ... There is a special grievance arising out of the Tax title question which will not appear openly ... It is impossible to know just what wires are working.[5]

These conditions put a premium on the organized, professional conduct of elections. A visitor to Republican headquarters at Indianapolis in 1876 was impressed by the "very systematic" work going on there and by the fact that "the ... printed matter preparing for distribution was, like everything American, on a monstrous scale." The paraphernalia of a political campaign—leaflets and pamphlets (more than 13,000,000 by the Republicans alone in 1872), flags and banners, buttons and kerchiefs, suitably inscribed novelties (playing cards, cloth collars, clay pipes)—poured forth in abundance at election time.

252, Junius [Dorman B. Eaton], *The Independent Movement in New York as an Element in the Next Elections and a Problem in Party Government* (New York, 1880), 83, 86, 94; "New Jersey," AC (1872, 1877).

5. Leland Sage, *William Boyd Allison: A Study in Practical Politics* (Iowa City, 1956), 59; Leng, *America in 1876*, 324; James V. Campbell to Thomas M. Cooley, March 22, 1871, Cooley Mss, Mich HS.

This effort bore fruit in voter turnout. Despite the relative lack of major national issues, balloting—and straight ticket voting—in the 1870s and 1880s was at or near the highest level in American history. The electorate voted with passion as well as in numbers. Great campaign parades, the excitement of national contests (the disfranchised wife of Chief Justice Morrison Waite wrote yearningly on election day, 1876, "I should want to vote all day"); elaborate rites of victory and defeat—all testified to the compelling quality of the electoral process.[6]

Ballots before the 1890s were prepared by the parties themselves and were cast in public. Long, distinctive "slip tickets" encouraged straight party voting and were readily identifiable when the voter deposited them in the ballot box. Large-scale payments to voters were commonplace in tightly contested states such as Indiana. The going rate for imported voters in a Pennsylvania Congressional election was $30 plus room and board. Electoral totals could be fabricated: it was estimated that 25,000 fraudulent Democratic votes were recorded in the 1868 New York Democratic tally. The 1872 Philadelphia returns may have been manipulated so that gamblers could make good on their wagers that the Republican candidate would win by more than 20,000 votes. Boss William Marcy Tweed of Tammany Hall authoritatively interpreted one New York canvass: "The ballots made no result. The counters made the result."[7]

Election laws multiplied rapidly in the 1870s. By the end of the decade they filled 150 pages of New York's statutes. But party interests ran roughshod over regulation. Postwar registration acts were designed primarily to limit urban immigrant Democratic voters; when New York's Democrats regained power in 1868, they abolished registration in New York City. Redistricting too, then as always, served the interest of the party in power. After New Jersey Republicans finished gerrymandering the state's legislative

6. Leng, *America in 1876*, 85; *The Republic* (1873), 81; artifacts in Political History Collection, Smithsonian Institution; Walter D. Burnham, "The Changing Shape of the American Political Universe," *APSR*, 59 (1965), 7–28; C. Peter Magrath, *Morrison R. Waite* (New York, 1963), 137.

7. Bryce, *American Commonwealth*, 3d ed. (New York, 1895), II, 143; Bradley, *Triumph*, 297, 413; John C. Davenport, *The Election and Naturalization Frauds in New York City 1860–1870* (New York, 1894), 222; on Tweed, New York State Senate, *Report of the Special Committee*, Doc. no. 52 (Albany, 1869), 133–134.

districts in 1871, not even a Democratic majority of more than 15,000 votes took the state Assembly out of Republican hands.

This massive, complex political system entailed heavy costs— costs that could be met only by illicit means. The basic forms of corruption—officeholder and contractor kickbacks, contributions from individuals and companies—already were established facts of American political life. Indeed, the growing strength of organizational politics may have lessened individual freebooting: "The weakness of party organization is the opportunity of corruption." It was estimated that from 1834 to 1861 an average of $2.58 was stolen from every $1,000 in federal expenditures; from 1861 to 1876 the rate was 96¢ per $1,000. But of course the latter figure was based on a greatly expanded federal budget. And state defalcations were numerous in the 1870s: in the Radical (and post-Reconstruction) South and among state treasurers (Minnesota, 1873; New Jersey, 1875), land commissioners (Michigan, 1871), and school trustees (Nebraska, 1871; Kansas, 1875) in the North.[8]

Large and growing sums of money were needed to fuel increasingly expensive party machinery. The banker Jay Cooke contributed $1,000 to the Pennsylvania Republican effort in 1864—and $30,000 in 1872. The Tweed Ring's exactions from New York— estimates range from 45 to 200 million dollars—handsomely rewarded its leaders; but it also paid for a massive, expensive political organization. As Tweed grandly explained, "the money . . . was distributed around in every way, to everybody, and paid for everything, and was scattered throughout the community."

Besides contractor kickbacks, systematic assessments from government employees provided substantial sums. In 1878 the secretary of the Republican Congressional Campaign Committee raised over $100,000 by asking all federal officeholders who made more than $1,000 a year to contribute at least 1 percent of their salaries. Twelve separate assessment letters went from the New York Republican Committee to federal employees during the 1880 campaign.[9]

8. "New Jersey," AC (1871); Henry J. Ford, The Rise and Growth of American Politics (New York, 1898), 322; U.S., CR, 44th Cong., 1st sess., House (July 29, 1876), 4967–4968; AC, states and years cited.

9. On Cooke, Bradley, Triumph, 205, 411; Callow, Tweed, 196; Dorothy G. Fowler, The Cabinet Politician: The Postmaster General 1829–1909 (New York, 1943), 170; Thomas C. Reeves, "Chester A. Arthur and Campaign Assessments in the Election of 1880," Hist, 31 (1969), 573–582.

"Legislative bribery, and its satellite, lobbying, have become the most grievous political evil of the country," the *Galaxy* complained in 1876. The corrupt congressman or state legislator was a stock figure in the political fiction and reformist nonfiction of the day. A Harrisburg newspaper in 1869 estimated that only 22 of 133 Pennsylvania legislators were honest men. Election to the United States Senate was especially costly. The 1872 contest in the Kansas legislature between Samuel C. Pomeroy and John J. Ingalls was notable for its open and spectacular bribery. Alexander Caldwell, another Kansas senator, supposedly paid out $60,000—twice his salary for a six-year term—to get his seat.

The phrase Black Horse Cavalry entered American political language in the late 1860s when an organized group of New York state legislators threatened to pass harmful bills unless they were bought off by the Erie Railroad. Dean Richmond, New York Democratic leader and president of the New York Central, was reported to have spent $157,000 within the legislature and $48,000 outside it to obtain a bill raising the ceiling on passenger fares. Governor Reuben Fenton, who had supported this legislation, thereupon threatened to veto it. Richmond is supposed to have offered a year's fare receipts—about $1,500,000—to get the bill signed. Elevation to the United States Senate did not lessen Fenton's reputation for acquisitiveness. A colleague considered him to be "the most expensive man" in that not uncostly body.

Sam Ward, a colorful, expansive political fixer, was the King of the Lobby in postwar Washington. Hundreds of others plied that trade in and about the nation's statehouses. They offered lavish entertainment as well as bribes during legislative sessions. One of them took eighty rooms in a Topeka hotel during the 1867 meeting of the Kansas legislature, conducting what was allusively called The Soup House and the Bread Riot. So frequent—and disreputable—were lobbying contracts that the Supreme Court in the 1870s held them to be against public policy and hence legally unenforceable.[10]

10. *Galaxy*, 2 (1867), 687–688; Bradley, *Triumph*, 330; "Kansas," *AC* (1872–1873); Hudson C. Tanner, *"The Lobby," and Public Men from Thurlow Weed's Time* (Albany, 1888), 42–45 ff; Lately Thomas, *Sam Ward, "King of the Lobby"* (Boston, 1965); "Kansas," *AC* (1872); "Lobbying Contracts," *CLJ*, 38 (1894), 123–126; Trist v. Child, 21 Wall. 441 (1874).

Gilded Age corruption is a familiar theme in American political history. The dreary litany of wrongdoing includes the Credit Mobilier affair, in which a number of prominent men, including Vice President Schuyler Colfax and Congressmen Blaine and Garfield, accepted stock in the Union Pacific's construction company; the Belknap scandal, in which the secretary of war took some $25,000 in bribes from an Indian post trader; and the Whiskey Ring, an elaborate system of collusion between revenue agents and whiskey distillers to avoid the federal excise tax on alcohol. In the late 1870s and early 1880s, western mail delivery franchises—lucrative Star Routes—were given to favored rings of contractors.

This surge of scandal is usually linked to the slackened morality of post-Civil War American life, or to a burgeoning capitalism that contaminated the political system. But there was another dimension to corruption in government. These scandals touched on activities—the Pacific Railroad, Indian policy, excise taxes, the postal service—that were part of the postwar expansion of the national government. The polity had neither the theoretical nor the organizational means to handle this growth effectively. Bribery and kickbacks were a form of accommodation, a way of getting things done.

The corruption of these years may also be counted part of the cost of sustaining an increasingly expensive Republican party organization. The central figure in the Whiskey Ring was General John A. McDonald, an old army associate of Grant who in 1870 was appointed superintendent of internal revenue for the St. Louis District. The money—some of the money—paid over by distillers went to aid the party cause in midwestern municipal, state, and congressional campaigns and in the presidential election of 1872. This was an expensive and dangerous mode of fund-raising. The members of the Whiskey Ring substantially enriched themselves, and their exposure generated much publicity harmful to the party. But the rising costs of organizational politics had to be met.[11]

The style and tone as well as the structure of postwar party politics reflected the shift from an ideological to an organizational base.

11. William B. Hesseltine, *Ulysses S. Grant, Politician* (New York, 1935); Allan Nevins, *Hamilton Fish: The Inner History of the Grant Administration* (New York, 1936); John McDonald, *Secrets of the Great*

The vocabulary of political life—boss, machine, ring, lobby, campaign—reflected the primacy of organizational concerns. Political oratory and debate remained flamboyant, but became less substantive. The utterances of Webster, Calhoun, Douglas, Lincoln, or Sumner had been as notable for their substance as for their style. Now political rhetoric evoked admiration not for its (often vapid) content but for its sound and sentiment, as in the cases of Blaine's eulogy of the assassinated President Garfield, Robert G. Ingersoll's "Plumed Knight" nomination speech for Blaine in 1876, or the oratorical clashes between Blaine and Conkling. James Russell Lowell lamented the decline of senatorial oratory:

> Is this debating club, where boys dispute,
> And wrangle o'er their stolen fruit
> The Senate, erstwhile cloister of the few,
> Where Clay once flashed and Webster's cloudy brow
> Brooded those bolts of thought that all the horizon knew?

A revealing development in political symbolism was the cartoonist Thomas Nast's invention in the 1870s of the Tammany tiger, the Republican elephant, and the Democratic donkey. Nast's fierce, rapacious Tammany tiger of 1871 properly belonged to the passionate ideological politics of the Reconstruction years. But the animals that he chose to embody the major parties—undramatic, without distinct symbolic meaning—reflected the less substantive politics that was taking form in the seventies.[12]

Finally, one may trace the rise of organizational politics in the style of its practitioners. Politicos in the 1870s appeared to be members of a distinct occupational group: "Short tenures, innumerable

---

Whiskey Ring (St. Louis, 1880); H. V. Boynton, "The Whiskey Ring," *NAR*, 123 (1876), 280–327; Lucius E. Guese, "St. Louis and the Great Whiskey Ring," *MoHR*, 36 (1942), 160–183; J. Martin Klotsche, "The Star Route Cases," *MVHR*, 22 (1935), 407–418. See also Eric L. McKitrick, "The Study of Corruption," *PSQ*, 72 (1957), 502–514; James D. Norris and Arthur H. Shaffer, eds., *Politics and Patronage in the Gilded Age: The Correspondence of James A. Garfield and Charles E. Henry* (Madison, 1970).

12. H. L. Mencken, *The American Language: Supplement One* (New York, 1945), 280; Maximilian Schele De Vere, *Americanisms: The English of the New World* (New York, 1872), 249–294; Lowell, "An Ode for the Fourth of July, 1876," *Poems* (Boston, 1890), IV, 96; Morton Keller, *The Art and Politics of Thomas Nast* (New York, 1968); William Murrell, "Rise and Fall of Cartoon Symbols," *AS*, (1935), 306–315.

appointments and elections have developed those who hold and who seek office into a class." More than a common social function brought politicians together. Republican National Committee Secretary Stephen J. Dorsey and Democratic National Committee Chairman William H. Barnum were officers in the same business enterprise, the Bull-Domingo Company. Family ties and oldtime friendships eased the way of congressional amnesty for ex-Confederate leaders. Marriages frequently occurred between politicians' families. Michigan Senator Zachariah Chandler's daughter married Maine Senator Eugene Hale; New York Republican leader Roscoe Conkling wed the daughter of New York Democratic leader Horatio Seymour (and, in bipartisan spirit, carried on a liaison with Kate Chase Sprague, daughter of the Chief Justice and wife of Rhode Island Republican Senator William Sprague); antiorganization Pennsylvania Republican Wayne MacVeagh married the daughter of state boss Simon Cameron; Iowa Senator William Allison married the adopted daughter of his predecessor (and party rival) James W. Grimes; Simon Cameron's son Don married Ohio Senator John Sherman's niece (who thereupon carried on a love affair with Henry Adams).[13]

A rough-hewn masculinity was another bond tying together the politicians of the Gilded Age. During a debate over whether or not to bar whiskey from the Senate, James A. McDougall of California is supposed to have declared: "I believe in women, wine, whiskey, and war." Ben Butler's coarseness—he said of his 1876 quest for a Congressional seat: "I have no hesitation in speaking about it. I am not a maiden, but more like a widow, for I know what I want and I am not afraid to ask for it"—was shared by many of his colleagues. A contemporary described Zach Chandler of Michigan as a "vulgar, ignorant man . . . profane in conversation and often times filthy and obscene . . . [indulging in] constant, nasty talk about women." James A. Garfield was capable of crude, vivid imagery: "It would be an exceedingly awkward thing to go to bed alone with your political doctrine, trusting and believing in it,

13. Whitridge, "Brake on the Machine," 242; on Dorsey and Barnum, Harry J. Sievers, *Benjamin Harrison* (Chicago, 1952), 180n; Jonathan T. Dorris, *Pardon and Amnesty under Lincoln and Johnson* (Chapel Hill, 1953), 365; *DAB*, passim.

thinking it is true, and wake up in the morning and find it a corpse in your arms."[14]

Reformers frequently were the objects of comments that questioned not only their political capacity but their masculinity. They were "political flirts"; the editor of *Harper's Weekly* was "calico Curtis." Roscoe Conkling lashed out at "the man-milliners, the dilettanti and carpet-knights of politics . . . they forget that parties are not built up by deportment, or by ladies' magazines, or gush." His great enemy Blaine shared Conkling's contempt for those who opposed professional politics and politicians: "upstarts, conceited, foolish, vain, without knowledge of measures, ignorant of men, . . . noisy but not numerous, pharisaical but not practical, ambitious but not wise, pretentious but not powerful."[15]

But there was more to these men than brute force. Many were able and dedicated practitioners of a complex, exacting trade. Conkling declared in an 1876 campaign speech: "We are told the Republican party is a machine. Yes. A government is a machine; the common-school system of the State of New York is a machine; a political party is a machine. Every organization which binds men together for a common cause is a machine." His rival, New York Democratic leader Samuel J. Tilden, was no less committed to organizational politics. A party, he said, was "a living being, having all the organs of eyes, ears, and feelings." Tilden's biographer said of him: "From boyhood to death, the . . . Party . . . took the place of wife, children and church." And Conkling once observed: "If any Church is worth belonging to, it is worth belonging to not a little . . . That is as true in politics as in religion.[16]

The politicos could not escape the tension between the often

14. On McDougall, William N. Stewart, *Reminiscence* (New York, 1908), 211; Hans W. Trefousse, *The South Called Him Beast: Ben Butler* (New York, 1957), 232; Mary K. George, *Zachariah Chandler: A Political Biography* (East Lansing, 1969), 171; *Speech of Hon. James A. Garfield, at Cleveland, Ohio, Oct. 11, 1879*, NYPL.

15. Gordon Milne, *George W. Curtis and the Genteel Tradition* (Bloomington, 1956), 180; Alfred R. Conkling, *The Life and Letters of Roscoe Conkling* (New York, 1889), 538 ff; David S. Muzzey, *James G. Blaine: A Political Idol of Other Days* (New York, 1934), 180–181. See also Richard Hofstadter, *Anti-Intellectualism in American Life* (New York, 1963), 189–191.

16. Conkling, *Life and Letters*, 510; Earle D. Ross, "Samuel J. Tilden and the Revival of the Democratic Party," *SAQ*, 19 (1920), 53; Alexander C. Flick, *Samuel Jones Tilden* (New York, 1939), 532; Conkling, *Life and Letters*, 62.

brutal realities of organizational politics and the surface gentility of nineteenth century middle class mores. Hungrily ambitious politicians were expected to disclaim any lust for office. Blaine responded to a flood of letters calling on him to run for the presidency by telling his secretary: "I will not touch them. Get such help as you want and answer them yourself." In the midst of his preconvention maneuvering in 1876 he collapsed; as he regained consciousness he murmured "church . . . mother." Conkling's arrogant public demeanor—"his grandiloquent swell, his majestic, supereminent, overpowering turkey-gobbler strut," in Blaine's scorching words—coexisted with such private traits as a strong aversion to handshaking or backslapping, an obsessive insistence on neatness and order, and the use of mauve ink in his correspondence.

These intensely matter-of-fact party leaders appear to have been strongly superstitious. A number of them shared the widespread mid-nineteenth century belief in spiritualism. Chief Justice Edward G. Ryan of the Wisconsin Supreme Court told a friend that, like Ulysses Grant, "I think that there is an impropriety in publishing the likeness of the living." Garfield wrote in his diary of an evening with Blaine and other congressional leaders that was devoted to the telling of ghost stories—not only for titillation, but as evidence of the interposition of the supernatural in everday affairs. These men, often from humble rural or small town origins, were charged with running an enormously complex political system, with governing a nation fresh from a traumatic civil war and in the throes of massive economic and social change. They bridged preindustrial and industrial America; and their behavior and beliefs reflected that fact.[17]

Ideology and Organization

Complex ethnic, religious, and cultural factors determined the political affiliations of most Americans from the very beginnings of the party system. While the Civil War broadened the appeal of the Republican party in the North and the Midwest, and Reconstruc-

17. Thomas H. Sherman, *Twenty Years with James G. Blaine* (New York, 1928), 61, 63; on spiritualism, Garfield, Diaries, May 25, 1872, LC, Carl Schurz, *Reminiscences* (New York, 1908), III, 154 ff; Ryan to P. M. Reed, May 28, 1880, Ryan Mss, WSHS; Garfield, Diaries, April 30, 1872.

tion created a substantial (if temporary) southern black Republican vote and led many prewar southern Whigs to become postwar Democrats, the basic political alignments of the late 1850s persisted after the war.

The Republicans drew their core strength from demographic and cultural groupings that stretched in a great band from New England and the Northeast to the upper Midwest and the Pacific. Membership in the more pietistic branches of Protestantism correlated most highly with Republican party identification. The Democrats, too, had distinctive sociocultural sources. White southerners, inhabitants of the lower Midwest and the Southwest from southern origins, adherents of the more liturgical Protestant persuasions, Catholics everywhere: these were the groups that subscribed to the Democracy. In sample areas of Illinois and Indiana during the 1870s, the pietist-liturgical religious correlation with party identification was the most salient one for every occupational group but high-status businessmen and low-status farm tenants and laborers.[18]

Because each of the parties recruited from so wide a range of social sources, they tended to be evenly balanced. The Civil War and its aftermath upset that equilibrium, but by the 1870s it was well on its way to being restored. In the presidential contest of 1880 the Republicans won 48.32 percent of the popular vote, the Democrats 48.21 percent. The Congress elected in that year had 147 Republicans and 135 Democrats in the House, and 37 of each party in the Senate. Scientist Simon Newcomb noted: "one of the curious phenomena of the present time is the tendency to a balance between the two parties—a tendency which seems to be rather on the increase." Henry Adams would later observe that though "no real principle divides us, ... some queer mechanical

18. On demographic patterns, Cuthbert Mills, "The Philosophy of the Presidential Election," *IR*, 9 (1880), 431–437; Paul Kleppner, *The Cross of Culture: A Social Analysis of Midwestern Politics 1850–1900* (New York, 1970); Richard Jensen, "The Religious and Occupational Roots of Party Identification: Illinois and Indiana in the 1870s," *CWH*, 16 (1970), 325–343. See also Thomas A. Flinn, "Continuity and Change in Ohio Politics," *JP*, 24 (1962), 521–544; William G. Carleton, "Why Was the Democratic Party in Indiana a Radical Party, 1865–1890?" *IMH*, 42 (1946), 207–228; Herman J. Deutsch, "Yankee-Teuton Rivalry in Wisconsin Politics of the Seventies," *WMH*, 14 (1931), 262–282, 403–418.

balance holds the two parties even," and concluded that "in democratic politics, parties tend to an equilibrium." But the very fact
of the party system's collapse in the 1850s indicates that this was
not always the case; and the Civil War showed that demonic
forces could be unleashed when politics failed.[19]

The process by which American politics moved from the irreconcilable passions of the early 1860s to the equilibrium of 1880
may be observed in the interplay of ideology and organization.
The rhetorical and ideological fervor of the 1860s did not abruptly
stop. Republicans still considered theirs to be "the party of progress," the Democrats "a *negative* party" unconcerned with "education, temperance, moral reform, or the elevation of the artisan
and laborer." As party spokesman Robert G. Ingersoll put it, Republicanism "has in it the elements of growth. It is full of hope. It
anticipates. The Democratic party remembers." The journalist
Charles Nordhoff thought that Republicans were "men who desire
change," Democrats "men who cling to that which is." "Which
party," asked *Harper's Weekly* editor George W. Curtis, "depends
upon the ignorance and prejudice of the voters? Which is
strongest in the slums of great cities, and in rural parts of
the Union where there are fewest schools?" The Republicans were
the proper custodians of the nation's wellbeing—and of its vested
interests. A party document delicately observed: "It is vain to expect wise or beneficial legislation in behalf of great interests at the
hands of men [that is, Democrats] towards whom those who control these interests do not stand in the close relationship of
constituency."[20]

Republican spokesmen often warned that the Democratic party
was the advance agent of an unregenerate South—thereby "waving

19. Simon Newcomb, "Our Political Dangers," *NAR*, 130 (1880), 262;
Ernest Samuels, *Henry Adams: The Middle Years* (Cambridge, 1965), 271.

20. Stephen M. Allen, *Origin and Early Progress of the Republican
Party in the United States* (Boston, 1879), v; Allen, *The Old and New
Republican Parties* (Boston, 1880), ii; Ingersoll in *Washington Sunday
Post*, Nov. 14, 1880; Charles Nordhoff, *Politics for Young Americans* (New
York, 1876), 34; *HW*, 19 (1875), 554; *The Commercial Aspects of the Pres-
ent Political Contest*, 1880 Republican Campaign Documents, no. 36,
NYPL, 6–7. See also John Hay, *The Balance Sheet of the Two Parties*
(Cleveland, 1880).

the bloody shirt," in the phrase of the time. A supporter told Republican presidential candidate Rutherford B. Hayes in 1876: "A bloody-shirt campaign, with money and Indiana is safe; a financial [campaign stressing debt and currency issues] and no money, and we are beaten." The theme served well as an emotional counter to the ceaseless process of party diffusion. And it gave newly arrived Republicans (such as John A. Logan of Illinois, who joined the party in 1864) a needed sense of continuity and commitment. A link with the stirring, if recent, past was forged when an 1880 audience was reminded that "the parties which confronted each other *then*, confront each other now, much aged in purpose, in temper, and in character."[21]

The Democrats, too, dwelt on themes that sustained a sense of party cohesion and continuity. Negrophobia served this purpose. But a more frequent mode of Democratic identification was states' rights and limited government: Retrenchment and Reform. The theme appealed to the Irish, who linked the active state to prohibition and other unwanted policies; to white southerners; to the parochial and tradition-minded everywhere.

By the same token Republicans were identified with "a system of political usurpation and official corruption now foreshadowing the coming empire." New York Democrat Clarkson Potter distinguished between the two parties:

> One for having the government power do much; the other for having them do little; one for having the exercise of government centralized, the other for having it localized. One, the party which would hold up the weak, aid the feeble, and protect the needy; the other, a party insisting that, beyond preserving order and administering justice, government should interfere with the action of its citizens as little as possible; and that while the general government should prescribe those regulations which affect the whole people, local affairs should be left to the people of the localities.

The 1874 Minnesota Democratic state platform spoke of "Home rule to limit and localize most zealously the few powers entrusted to public servants." Senator James Beck of Kentucky was more blunt: "there is that contemptible word *Nation*—a word which no

---

21. "Indiana," *AC* (1876); Jay A. Hubbell, *The Overshadowing Issue: The True Inwardness of the 'Solid South'* [1880; NYPL].

good Democrat uses, when he can find any other, and when forced to use it, utters in disgust. This is no nation. We are free and independent States."[22]

More productively, Democrats sought to link their emphasis on local and limited government to the antimonopoly rhetoric of their party's Jacksonian past. They attacked "paternal control, with its tariffs, and monopolies, and sumptuary laws, and government oversight, which leaves the citizen no individual action or judgment." New York Democratic attorney David Dudley Field found it "quite natural" that Republicans whose theory of government "does not forbid its use for any purpose they deem useful, should seek its intervention in such schemes as require great power or capital. Not one dollar should Congress or any State legislature hereafter grant to any road, canal, or other enterprise owned by any corporation or individual." The party's ultimate appeal was to "old simplicity and purity and frugality"; to those who believed that "the curse of our time is too much legislation, too much patronage, too much interference with natural laws."[23]

But both parties sought to modify or soften their ideological identities in the 1870s, as the issues of the Civil War and Reconstruction faded. Republican state platforms began to respond to the strong popular sentiment against centralized government: "the States should be left to regulate their own internal affairs without interference" (Connecticut, 1874); "While we believe that the national Government is entirely independent of the States, when acting in its own proper circle, we also believe that the State Governments are entirely independent of the national when acting within their own proper circles" (Indiana, 1876); "the powers of the General government having been stretched to an unhealthy extent, to meet the crisis of civil war and reconstruction, [they] should now be restored to their normal action" (Kansas, 1874).

22. William O. Bateman, *Political and Constitutional History of the United States* (St. Louis, 1876); Potter, *The Danger and Duty of the Democracy* (New York, 1876; NYPL), 3–4; "Minnesota," *AC* (1874); Beck in *New York Tribune*, Aug. 13, 1875. See also Orrin Skinner, *The Issues of American Politics* (Philadelphia, 1873); Montgomery Blair, "The Republican Party as It Was and Is," *NAR*, 131 (1880), 422–430; David D. Field, "Centralization in the Federal Government," *NAR*, 132 (1881), 407–426.

23. *Remarks of Hon. Clarkson N. Potter... at Tammany Hall, July 4, 1871* [NYPL]; Field, "Corruption in Politics," 82–83.

Democrats had even more reason to escape from the ideological issues of the 1860s. Minnesota Democrats in 1869 announced their "desire to act independently of mere forms and theories which have lost their substance, to consign settled questions to the past and to appeal to the people of Minnesota upon the living issues of the present and future which concern the material interests of every citizen of the state." Tweed lieutenant Peter B. Sweeny thought that "we ought to get rid of the negro question. It hurts more than the negro vote could injure us ... [It] introduces a moral issue—a sentiment of justice—and presents the captivating cry of universal suffrage, which carries away many votes, especially among the Germans, and prevents the legitimate political questions of the country from having their just weight before the people." Sweeny trusted Tammany's ability to win black votes: "Our boys understand how to get them." Bitter Kentucky Republicans reported on Democratic tactics in Louisville's 1870 municipal election: "The sight was glorious grand to see them cajoling elbowing etc. the negroes. Color was forgotten ... in a few years the democrats will all be swearing that they are the best friends the colored people ever had."[24]

The need for a new tone was especially keen in Ohio, where Democrats were heavily burdened by their wartime Copperheadism. The 1870 Montgomery County Democratic convention proposed a "New Departure," the work primarily of antiwar Democrat Clement Vallandigham. While duly committing itself to "anti-centralization," the convention platform went on to "accept the material and legitimate results of the war ... including the three ... amendments *de facto* to the Constitution ... and acquiesce in the same as no longer issues before the country." A number of state Democratic platforms echoed these sentiments, and in theory at least the rigid Democratic resistance to Reconstruction came to an end.

Party ideologues opposed this development. Francis P. Blair of Missouri warned that "it meant acquiescence in all the usurpa-

24. Albert V. House, "Republicans and Democrats Search for New Identities," *RP*, 31 (1969), 466–476; platforms in *AC*, states and years cited; Peter B. Sweeny, "The Democratic Policy," *New York Herald*, Nov. 20, 1869; W. A. Meriwether to Benjamin H. Bristow, Nov. 11, 1870, Edgar Needham to Bristow, Nov. 15, 1870, Bristow Mss, LC.

tions of the Radical party since it has come into power," and Gideon Welles stubbornly declared: "I do not take 'departure' with Valandigham, Pendleton & Co. There is no necessity for unwise and unprincipled committals to usurpations and fraud, in order to beat the radicals." He attributed the change to a swarm of Democratic presidential hopefuls, "all relying on petty party management and not on honest principle." But New York Congressman S. S. Cox more accurately perceived the character of the new political atmosphere: "I think it does not become any one belonging to so mosaic a party to be anxious about Democratic consistency."[25]

These shifts of tone were accompanied by substantial changes in party leadership. In state after state men who placed greater weight on organization than on ideology came into or retained power. Pioneer Republican George W. Julian of Indiana morosely concluded in 1878 that his party's new chieftains "were not only in favor of perpetuating the organization, but they treated it as an institution."

In part the change was generational. New men replaced the Republican party's founders: "henceforth the young, vigorous, live men must rule." Such was the case in New York, where Roscoe Conkling defeated Reuben Fenton in an 1871 contest for a seat in the United States Senate; in Illinois, where John A. Logan in 1871 defeated Lyman Trumbull; and in Maine, where in 1868 James G. Blaine took control of the state party from supporters of the recently deceased William P. Fessenden. In Iowa the pioneering Republican leaders James W. Grimes and James Harlan gave way to William B. Allison and railroad magnate Grenville Dodge. Lesser figures, too—George Robeson in New Jersey, William E. Chandler in New Hampshire, Elisha Keyes in Wisconsin—came into their own around 1870.[26]

25. "Ohio," AC (1870 ff); Speech of Hon. Francis P. Blair . . . before the Missouri Legislature, . . . January 9, 1872 [NYPL], 4; Gideon Welles to James R. Doolittle, June 10, 1871, Doolittle Mss, WSHS; Welles to Montgomery Blair, June 27, 1870, Blair Family Mss, LC; Grant or Greeley? Speech of S. S. Cox . . . on the Issues of the Presidential Campaign of 1872 [NYPL].
26. George W. Julian, "The Death-Struggle of the Republican Party," NAR, 126 (1878), 267; Donald B. Chidsey, The Gentleman from New York: A Life of Roscoe Conkling (New Haven, 1935), 114; on Maine,

But when Pennsylvania's Simon Cameron returned to power in 1867 by defeating wartime governor Andrew Curtin for a Senate seat, when Zachariah Chandler fended off the challenge of another wartime chief executive, Austin Blair, in Michigan, or when Oliver Morton did the same with George Julian of Indiana in 1870, the contest was not so much between political generations as between political styles. And victory went to the stronger, more skillful organization men. A number of those who lost out in these struggles—Fenton, Curtin, Trumbull, Julian, Blair—bolted to the Liberal Republicans in 1872.[27]

Federal patronage was of prime importance to the Republican state organizations of the seventies. One of the attractions of the Senate was that it gave state leaders access to the jobs and money dispensed by the federal government. The New York and Detroit customs houses were important political instruments. They employed thousands of staffers who in fact worked for the party. More important still was the nation's postal system. James N. Tyner, who became postmaster general on the eve of the 1876 election, was "appointed not to see that the mails were carried, but to see that Indiana was carried." Wisconsin Republican leader Elisha Keyes, who spent twenty-one years as postmaster of Madison, declared that "Post Offices should be filled by men who are competent to run the Party machine in their vicinity." Blaine pressed for the appoinment of a special postal agent on the ground that he was "the best political worker in New England."[28]

Charles A. Jellison, *Fessenden of Maine* (Syracuse, 1962), 251, 255; on Iowa, Sage, *Allison*; on New Jersey, Herrmann K. Platt, ed., *Charles Perrin Smith New Jersey Reminiscences 1828–1882* (New Brunswick, 1965), 181–192; on New Hampshire, Leon B. Richardson, *William E. Chandler* (New York, 1940); on Wisconsin, David P. Thelen, "The Boss and the Upstart: Keyes and LaFollette, 1880–1884," *WMH*, 47 (1963–1964), 103–115.

27. On Pennsylvania, Bradley, *Triumph*, Frank B. Evans, *Pennsylvania Politics, 1872–1877: A Study in Political Leadership* (Harrisburg, 1966), Erwin S. Bradley, *Simon Cameron* (Philadelphia, 1966), Brooks M. Kelley, "Simon Cameron and the Senatorial Nomination of 1867," *PMHB*, 87 (1963), 375–392; Harriette M. Dilla, *The Politics of Michigan 1865–1878* (New York, 1912). For similar developments in the territories see Howard R. Lamar, "Political Patterns in New Mexico and Utah Territories, 1850–1900," *UHQ*, 29 (1960), 360–387.

28. Fowler, *Cabinet Politician*, 146–147, 156–157.

The situation of the Democrats, shut off from federal patronage, was more difficult. The national organization of a party out of power and in principle dedicated to localism inevitably was weak. August Belmont, Rothschilds' American representative, was the unlikely (and ineffective) caretaker chairman of the Democratic National Committee from 1860 to 1872. Postwar Democratic reconstitution went on at the state and local levels: and here the party's experience closely paralleled that of the Republicans. In New Jersey "a masterful coterie of party managers" made the state an important Democratic stronghold. Samuel Randall of Pennsylvania and Samuel J. Tilden of New York emerged as strong state leaders.[29]

The most spectacular postwar Democratic organization-builder was William Marcy Tweed of Tammany Hall. In many respects Tweed and his followers relied on established techniques of city politics. An 1866 investigation of New York City's government— several years before the Tweed Ring reached its apogee—revealed "in how many ways, and under what a variety of names and pretexts, immature and greedy men steal from that fruitful and ill-fenced orchard, the city treasury." The City Council chamber was "furnished with preposterous magnificence"; the tax rate during the past thirty-six years had gone from $2.50 to $40 per inhabitant; corrupt voting and the sale of franchises were common before the Civil War.

But the scale of the Tweed Ring's corruption, and its reliance on a powerful immigrant-based machine, made it something new in American politics. The Ring's substantial aid to the Catholic church and parochial schools and large-scale distribution of food and fuel to the poor were as disturbing as its massive stealing. Tweed's associate Peter Sweeny conveyed something of the intensity and scale of the Ring's work: "To do what we did in bringing out our vote, getting it registered and then polled, required

29. Irving Katz, *August Belmont: A Political Biography* (New York, 1968), 91n, 125; William E. Sackett, *Modern Battles of Trenton* (New York, 1914), II, 13; Albert V. House, "Men, Morals, and Manipulation in the Pennsylvania Democracy of 1875," *PH*, 23 (1956), 248–266; Earl D. Ross, "Samuel J. Tilden and the Revival of the Democratic Party," *SAQ*, 19 (1920), 43–54. See also Horace S. Merrill, *Bourbon Democracy of the Middle West 1865–1896* (Baton Rouge, 1953), chs. 1–7.

constant and very great as well as expensive labor. At our great ratification meeting [in 1869] we had 50,000 live Democrats in procession. This was no small work to accomplish." Tammany's power, he concluded, lay not so much in its political ideology as in "the completeness of its organization and the thoroughness of its discipline . . . The organization works with the precision of a well-regulated machine."[30]

If Tweed was the archetypal Democratic city boss, Tilden was the party's most prominent state and then national leader during the seventies. Although he stood firmly in the ideological tradition of the mid-century Democratic party—Montgomery Blair described him as *"par excellence* the representative man of the old square toed . . . states rights-economical democracy"–Tilden's real strength lay in his organizational talents. He maintained a correspondence with two or three friends in each of New York's hundreds of election districts; he believed that "the Divine Being has impressed upon everything order, method and law."

During the 1876–1877 electoral dispute, when his claim to the presidency—and it was a good one—was at stake, Tilden maintained an Olympian (or a neurotic) calm. He busied himself for one critical month during the crisis by compiling a history of past electoral counts. When the issue finally was resolved against him, he looked forward to private life "with the consciousness that I shall receive from posterity the credit of having been elected to the highest position in the gift of the people without any of the cares and responsibilities of the office." The retreat from the purposive, ideological politics of the Civil War could not have been more complete.[31]

30. James Parton, "The Government of the City of New York," *NAR,* 103 (1866), 415; John W. Pratt, "Boss Tweed's Public Welfare Program," *NYHS Quarterly,* 45 (1961), 396–411; Sweeny, "Democratic Policy," *New York Herald,* Nov. 20, 1869.
31. William E. Smith, *The Francis Preston Blair Family in Politics* (New York, 1933), II, 472; Robert Kelley, "The Thought and Character of Samuel J. Tilden: The Democrat as Inheritor," *Hist,* 26 (1964), 187, and *The Transatlantic Persuasion: The Liberal-Democratic Mind in the Age of Gladstone* (New York, 1969), ch. 7; Allan Nevins, *Abram S. Hewitt with Some Account of Peter Cooper* (New York, 1935), 344, 388. See also Mark D. Hirsch, "Samuel J. Tilden: The Story of a Lost Opportunity," *AHR,* 56 (1951), 788–802.

The Drama of National Politics

Major political developments—the Grant administration, the elections of 1872 and 1876, Hayes's presidency, and finally the election and assassination of Garfield—reveal the profound change wrought in American public life during the 1870s by the shift from ideological to organizational politics.

Grant entered the presidency in 1869 on the crest of a wave of approval. Matthew Arnold said of the taciturn war hero: "I prefer him to Lincoln . . . I hardly know anyone so *selbst-ständig*, so broad and strong-sighted, as well as firm-charactered, that [the Americans] . . . have had." The *Atlantic Monthly* summed up "The Intellectual Character of President Grant" in 1869: "Clearness of judgment, knowledge of character, sagacity and tact in dealing with men, broad views of affairs, prompt intelligence in unexpected and pressing emergencies, ability to control numerous and vast and complicated interests . . . —if these are not the intellectual components of a character fit to govern a great nation at a critical period, then all history is at fault." Charles Francis Adams found Grant "a very extraordinary man . . . of the most exquisite tact and judgment." No one, thought James Russell Lowell, "ever had a better chance to be a great magistrate."[32]

Then came the Grant presidency. Henry Adams later summed up the attitude of a disillusioned generation: "Grant's administration is to me the dividing line between what we hoped, and what we have got." What had happened? The usual explanation is that Grant's political innocence and simpleminded respect for wealth made him the dupe of the politicos and speculators who surrounded him. His critics' disillusionment was in part the product of their exaggerated hopes. The Civil War generation insisted on finding hidden depths in Grant, as they did (with more reason) in Lincoln. A profound humanity and wisdom was read into his re-

32. Matthew Arnold, *General Grant with a Rejoinder by Mark Twain*, ed. John Y. Simon (Carbondale, Ill., 1966), 3; "The Intellectual Character of President Grant," *AM*, 23 (1869), 635; Adams quoted in Ernest Samuels, *The Young Henry Adams* (Cambridge, 1948), 171; Lowell to Leslie Stephen, Nov. 25, 1868, in Charles E. Norton, ed., *Letters of James Russell Lowell* (London, 1894), II, 8.

mark "Let us have peace," when in fact its context was quite prosaic: "Peace, and universal prosperity, its sequence, with economy of administration, will lighten the burden of taxation, while it constantly reduces the national debt. Let us have peace."

But it is by no means clear that the character of Grant's administration was beyond his comprehension—or his control. He brought to the White House a conception of leadership and a coterie of men drawn from his wartime experience. He planned to govern through a staff of former army associates and a cabinet of friends and prominent respectables. As he put it, "I am not a representative of a political party, though a party voted for me." Henry Adams observed of Grant's initial cabinet selections that only Postmaster General J. A. J. Creswell was "distinctly a representative rather of the Republican party than of the Republican sentiment of the country."[33]

Grant's expectations quickly clashed with the realities of party politics. Even Tweed lieutenant Sweeny took the new chief executive to task for acting "as owner, instead of trustee, of his party ... The Republican party was built up by its political leaders, and they should have been allowed to administer the estate which they had secured." Pressure from party leaders who convincingly showed that the appointment was illegal led Grant to drop New York merchant A. T. Stewart, his first choice for secretary of the treasury ("I wanted the Treasury conducted on strict business principles") and instead appoint party regular George S. Boutwell. Similarly, he accepted New York City Republican leader Tom Murphy rather than merchant Moses Grinnell as the politically important collector of the New York Customs House.[34]

According to his close friend Adam Badeau, Grant at first was "shy" in the Presidency. "He did not like the atmosphere; he was not at home in it." Grant himself admitted in 1871: "I always feel unhappy when the time comes to commence the job of writing a message, and miserable until it is completed. I believe I am lazy and don't get credit for it. The fact is circumstances have thrown me into an occupation uncongenial to me."

33. Adams to Charles F. Adams, Jr., Nov. 10, 1911, in Newton Arvin, ed., *The Selected Letters of Henry Adams* (New York, 1951), 266; "peace" statement in "United States," *AC* (1868); Hesseltine, *Grant*, 141; Adams, "Civil Service Reform," *NAR*, 109 (1869), 444.

34. Sweeny, "Democratic Policy"; Hesseltine, *Grant*, 140, 212.

Yet Grant spent more time in office than any chief executive between Andrew Jackson and Grover Cleveland and was the first President actively to seek a third term. In part his was a personal adjustment. He made the presidency acceptable—indeed, pleasurable—by shirking much of the responsibility that attached to it. He neglected his correspondence and spent long periods in restless visits to his Long Branch, New Jersey summer home and to the houses of wealthy friends. Secretary of State Hamilton Fish noted "how little the affairs of Government trouble the President." Garfield acidly observed that Grant "has done much to show with how little personal attention the Government can be run."[35]

But his adaptation was political as well. Grant's goals were "economy, retrenchment, faithful collection of the revenue, and payment of the public debt." Nothing if not reality-oriented, he quickly saw that good relations with his party's regulars was a necessity. As his old army associates fell away (usually in disgrace), Grant found his new companions among the politicos— Zach Chandler, Simon Cameron, Oliver Morton, even his wartime enemy Ben Butler. Their rough-hewn *personae*, and their roles as captains of political machines, fighters in political wars, made them compatible associates. Grant's passing annoyance that Morton "would have a candidate for every place that might be vacant" was a minor irritation when set against basic affinities of style and outlook. Attorney General E. Rockwood Hoar warned Grant of "the danger of losing his original and strong friends by giving too much confidence to another class." But it was precisely this implied social distinction that led Grant to prefer politicians to respectables—and, finally, to acede to their demands that Hoar leave the cabinet.[36]

Grant found the ideology of wartime and postwar Republicanism increasingly congenial. Although he shared the general unconcern for the social and economic wellbeing of the freedmen, he had an active interest in the maintenance of southern Republicanism through black voting. And in messages to Congress he fostered

35. Adam Badeau, *Grant in Peace* (Hartford, 1887), 15; Grant quoted in Evans, *Pennsylvania Politics*, 25; Hamilton Fish, Diaries, Sept. 16, 1873, LC; James A. Garfield, Diaries, June 12, 1872.

36. Hesseltine, *Grant*, 139; Grant on Morton in Fish, Diaries, April 28, 1874; Nevins, *Fish*, 377.

such causes as federal aid to education and the taxation of church property. George Julian of Indiana feared that "thorough schooling of the President and his party in the use of power had familiarized them with military ideas and habits, and drawn them toward loose and indefensible opinions respecting the powers of the General and State Governments and the prerogatives of the Executive." But in fact the prevailing view (in the words of the journalist James S. Pike) was that an "administrative stage" had been reached where "striking schemes" and "sharp-edged radical policies" must give way to "wise, cautious, conservative measures." Far from seeking to formulate policy, Grant let the lead come from congressional Republicans.

The election of 1872 made clear the degree to which organizational necessity was blurring the ideological lines of the sixties. The Liberal Republican movement of that year in part was a revolt by Republican purists against the politicos' domination of the Grant administration. But the Democrats endorsed Horace Greeley, the Liberal Republican nominee, as their own candidate despite the fact that few men in the past generation had differed more profoundly from them on slavery, Negro civil rights, the tariff, and states' rights. An attempt by some Democrats to run a candidate more compatible with the party's principles had no success. Nor did Republican defections from Grant amount to much. Despite their reservations—"Grant was not fit to be nominated, Greeley was not fit to be elected," Garfield complained—almost all dissident Republicans returned to the fold for the 1872 election. Grant won with the largest popular (and electoral) margin of any candidate between 1828 and 1904.[37]

A still greater test of organizational politics came in the Hayes-Tilden controversy of 1876–1877. Both Republican candidate Rutherford B. Hayes and Democratic nominee Samuel J. Tilden were well-established party regulars; and there was no third party effort in 1876 comparable in scale to the 1872 Liberal Republican movement. But the struggle between embattled Republicans and

37. Julian, "Death-Struggle," 271; Robert F. Durden, *James S. Pike* (Durham, 1957), 183; Robert G. Caldwell, *James A. Garfield: Party Chieftain* (Indianapolis, 1931), 180. See also Charles F. Adams, Jr., "The 'Independents' in the Caucus," *NAR*, 123 (1876), 437–467.

rising Democrats in South Carolina, Louisiana, and Florida produced conflicting vote totals—and presidential electors—in those states. A single electoral vote from any of them (or a contested electoral vote in Oregon) would give Tilden the presidency. A grim, complex battle ensued over certification of the contested electoral votes. Democrats made threatening noises. A mass gathering of Kentucky county leaders declared that "an appeal to arms is the last desperate remedy of a free people in danger of being enslaved." Henry Watterson of the *Louisville Courier-Journal* proposed that 100,000 Democrats converge on Washington when the electoral votes were counted, to ensure that Tilden received his due. Secretary of State Hamilton Fish anxiously observed that "the language of the Democrats now was more desperate and threatening and violent than that of the Southern men on the election of Lincoln in 1860."

But very different political conditions now prevailed. The politics of organization had superseded the politics of ideology. Months of negotiation led to the creation of a Joint Electoral Commission, composed of congressmen, senators, and Supreme Court justices, which by a strict party division gave every contested electoral vote to Hayes. A saving number of Democratic congressmen accepted this resolution in return for pledges by Republican leaders to remove the remaining federal troops from South Carolina and Louisiana, to support congressional approval of Texas and Pacific Railroad bonds, and to back federal expenditures for Mississippi River levee improvements.[38]

This settlement has been called a triumph of reaction, an intersectional arrangement among leading politicians, investors, and entrepreneurs, with newspaper editors acting as middlemen. George W. Julian concluded that "the timidity of capital turned the tide" against the Democrats. Conservative ideologue Montgomery Blair told the Maryland legislature: "It . . . appears that the constitutional question . . . had no part whatever in determining the contest; but that it was in fact determined by a body of men elected by one party, but openly acting with their opponents,

38. "Kentucky," *AC* (1876); Joseph F. Wall, *Henry Watterson: Reconstructed Rebel* (New York, 1956), 144; Fish, Diaries, Nov. 14, 1876; C. Vann Woodward, *Reunion and Reaction: The Compromise of 1877 and the End of Reconstruction* (Boston, 1951).

in the interest of certain railroad corporations, at the decisive moment."

From this perspective the Compromise of 1877 nicely symbolized the shift from the issues of the Civil War and Reconstruction to the issues of economic expansion. But it was the product of a new political milieu as well: one in which understandings between like-thinking politicos took precedence over the passionate pursuit of principle.[39]

The electoral crisis of 1876–1877 displayed not only the adaptive powers of a politics of organization, but also the tensions with which it had to cope. Maintaining a united front within each party proved enormously taxing. Roscoe Conkling, for example, seemed at times to prefer Tilden to Hayes, and of course the Democrats' party unity finally cracked.

The closeness of the party balance nationally and in many states, and the constant jockeying for power within each party structure, made organizational stability a prized but elusive goal. The Wisconsin Republican machine of Elisha Keyes, solid and substantial in the early seventies, was a shambles by the end of the decade. Tweed's Tammany successor John Kelly waged vicious factional war against Tilden and ensured Republican victory in 1879 by running an independent campaign for the New York governorship. In the securely Democratic state of Delaware, Eli and Gove Saulsbury corrosively fought for their brother Willard's Senate seat. The tenure of an organization leader, often mean and brutish, frequently also was nasty and short.[40]

The *International Review* thought that Hayes had the opportunity "to break the bonds of that servitude to party which has cursed the country for nearly fifty years, and to remand party to its proper subordination." And soon after taking office the new President issued an executive order that no federal official "shall be required or permitted to take part in the management of political organizations, caucuses, conventions or election campaigns."

39. Julian, "The Abuse of the Ballot and its Remedy," *IR*, 8 (1880), 538; Blair in "Maryland," *AC* (1878). See also J. S. Black, "The Electoral Conspiracy," *NAR*, 125 (1877), 1–34, and T. W. Stoughton, "The 'Electoral Conspiracy' Bubble Exploded," *NAR*, 125 (1877), 193–234; Keith I. Polakoff, *The Politics of Inertia: The Election of 1876 and the End of Reconstruction* (Baton Rouge, 1973).
40. See notes 26–27 above; "Delaware," *AC* (1871).

But the dictates of political reality could not be ignored. Hayes by patronage and policy soon sought to develop a Republican organization loyal to himself. He removed a number of Grant-appointed officeholders from key patronage positions, including St. Louis Postmaster (and Missouri Republican boss) C. I. Fuller and Chester Arthur, head of the New York Customs House and Roscoe Conkling's right-hand man. Hayes's leading cabinet members—Secretary of State William M. Evarts, Secretary of the Interior Carl Schurz, Attorney General Charles Devens, Postmaster General David M. Key—had little influence with the congressional Republican leadership. Indeed, Key was a Democrat and all had supported Horace Greeley in 1872.

The reaction was quick and fierce. Patronage and party constancy were too important to be treated lightly. Conkling turned his considerable talent for invective against the chief executive. Simon Cameron of Pennsylvania resigned from the chairmanship of the Senate Foreign Relations Committee because Hayes failed to put his son Donald in the cabinet. Blaine was so angered by the appointment of a United States marshal in Maine that he did not see Hayes for two years.[41]

Policy differences widened the gulf. The President hoped to establish a Whiggish southern Republicanism, acceptable to better-off southern whites, that could work harmoniously with a similarly structured northern Republican party. Walt Whitman put a poet's gloss on Hayes's intentions: "Underneath, his objects are to compact and fraternize the States, encourage their materialistic and industrial development, soothe and expand their self-poise, and tie all and each with resistless double ties not only of interstate barter, but human comradeship."

But the Democrats swept the South in the 1878 elections. The number of Republican counties in the region dropped to 62 from an 1876 total of 125. Hayes conceded that his policy was "*a failure.*" By repudiating the postwar Republican attempt to create a southern party built on the votes of the freedmen, Hayes irrepa-

---

41. "The New Federal Administration," *IR,* 4 (1877), 311; executive order in Schurz, *Reminiscences,* 382; on Fuller, *Nation,* 27 (1878), 154; on Blaine, Garfield, Diaries, April 14, 1880. See also Harry Barnard, *Rutherford B. Hayes and His America* (Indianapolis, 1954) and John W. Burgess, *The Administration of President Hayes* (New York, 1916).

rably deepened his feud with the congressional Republican leadership and thus assured himself a one-term presidency.[42]

Party factionalism dominated American politics by the time of the election of 1880. In sharp contrast to previous presidential elections, intramural squabbles overshadowed issue differences between the parties. The Democrats settled on the pallid and unexceptionable Civil War general Winfield Scott Hancock of Pennsylvania, in a convention torn by factional disputes within the Indiana, New York, Ohio, and Pennsylvania delegations. Republican leaders from New York, Ohio, and Pennsylvania joined with the hollow southern state parties to put forward a willing Grant for a third term. Other ambitious politicos—Blaine, Garfield, and John Sherman of Ohio—blocked that effort. Out of the ensuing chaos dark horse James A. Garfield emerged as the party nominee.

Garfield like Hayes gave lip service to reform, antiorganization sentiments. But he too played the game the only way it could be played. During the campaign he concentrated on strategy rather than issues: "Nothing is wanting except an immediate and a liberal supply of money for campaign expenses to make Indiana certain. With a victory there, the rest is easy." With impressive precision he predicted a Republican Indiana plurality of 5,350 votes; the official margin was 6,642. The razor-close national result—Garfield had 9,457 more votes than Hancock out of 9,219,467 ballots cast—was the product not of a keen struggle over major issues, but rather of highly organized, closely balanced national parties bringing out their supporters.[43]

Garfield soon was caught up in factional conflict even more severe than that of the Hayes years. "Stalwarts" who had supported

42. Floyd Stovall, ed., *Walt Whitman Prose Works 1892*, I, *Specimen Days* (New York, 1963), 227; Stanley P. Hirshson, *Farewell to the Bloody Shirt: Northern Republicans and the Southern Negro, 1877–1893* (Bloomington, Ind., 1962), 48–49. See also Vincent P. DeSantis, *Republicans Face the Southern Question—The New Departure Years, 1877–1897* (Baltimore, 1959).

43. Albert V. House, "Internal Conflict in Key States in the Democratic Convention of 1880," *PH*, 27 (1960), 188–216; Frank B. Evans, "Wharton Barker and the Republican National Convention of 1880," *PH*, 27 (1960), 28–43; Sievers, *Harrison*, 176; Caldwell, *Garfield*, 304 ff. See also Herbert J. Clancy, *The Presidential Election of 1880* (Chicago, 1958).

Grant for a third term—among them Cameron of Pennsylvania, Chandler of Michigan, Logan of Illinois, Conkling of New York, and Morton of Indiana—wrangled over patronage with "Half-Breeds"—Blaine, John Sherman of Ohio, George Frisbie Hoar of Massachusetts—who accommodated to Garfield. Conkling's hostility was ensured when Garfield made his bitter rival Blaine secretary of state and a major dispenser of patronage.

In the long view of history, the noisy struggle between Stalwarts and Half-Breeds may appear to have all of the meaning—or, better, lack of meaning—of the conflicts between Byzantine Greens and Whites or Florentine Guelfs and Ghibellines. And yet it took the center of the American political stage for several years, and served as the excuse for the assassination of a President.

More than differences over patronage separated Stalwarts from Half-Breeds. The Stalwarts were the first generation of postwar Republican leaders. They created the organizational Republicanism that weathered the political storms of the seventies. They made Grant their leader because he embodied that central event in their lives, the Civil War. The labels that they adopted—Stalwarts, the Old Guard—and their readiness to speak of the Republicans (all of twenty-five years old in 1880) as the Grand Old Party, reflect their patriarchal attitude.

The Half-Breeds tended to be newer public men, ready to abandon a Negro-based southern Republicanism, to pay lip service to civil service reform, to respond to current issues rather than dwell on past principles. Pennsylvania Stalwart Simon Cameron contemptuously called the Half-Breeds "that new school of politicians who indulge in modish sentimentalism and cowardice calling them statesmanship, and go about sneering at obsolete courage and political conviction, calling them 'radicalism.' "[44]

On July 2, 1881—six weeks after the assassination of Czar Alexander II—a madman named Charles Guiteau shot Garfield, declaring: "I am a Stalwart and now Arthur is President." The proximate cause of his act was that he had failed to obtain an ap-

44. Caldwell, *Garfield*, 340; William G. Eidson, "Who Were the Stalwarts?" *MAm*, 52 (1970), 235–261; Bradley, *Cameron*, 379. See also Matthew Josephson, *The Politicos* (New York, 1938), 213–216; Richard E. Welch, Jr., *George Frisbie Hoar and the Half-Breed Republicans* (Cambridge, 1971), 90–91; Thomas C. Reeves, *Gentleman Boss: The Life of Chester Alan Arthur* (New York, 1975).

pointment from the new administration. As much as John Wilkes Booth's assassination of Lincoln, Guiteau's crime casts a revealing light on the political ambiance of its time. Booth's madness fed on the defeat of the South, on the intensely ideological character of the wartime polity. Guiteau's derangement fed on the factionalism of place-seeking politicians. The statements that Guiteau issued from his cell—"The President of the U.S. would never have been shot if it had not been for the political situation as it existed last May and June"; "The President's tragic death was a sad necessity but it will unite the Republican party and save the Republic"— were, in their distorted way, a measure of the degree to which factionalism and office-seeking had come to dominate the political system. Booth the avenger of the Lost Cause of southern independence to Guiteau the disappointed office-seeker: these were bench marks of the shift from a politics of ideology to a politics of organization.[45]

The Reformist Critique

James Russell Lowell, whose "Commemoration Ode" in 1865 reflected the euphoria of that moment, wrote a very different "Ode to the Fourth of July, 1876":

> Is this the country that we dreamed in youth
> Where wisdom and not numbers would have weight,
> Seed-field of simpler manners, braver truth,
> Where shame should cease to dominate
> In household, church, and state?
> Is this Atlantis?[46]

Lowell was not alone in his disillusionment. A distinctive literary genre—the political satire—commented on the rise of the boss and the machine. *The Gilded Age* (1873) by Mark Twain and Charles Dudley Warner, John W. De Forest's *Honest John Vane* and *Playing the Mischief* (both published in 1875), and Henry Adams's

45. Stewart Mitchell, "The Man Who Murdered Garfield," *MHS Proceedings*, 67 (1941–1944), 467–468; Charles E. Rosenberg, *The Trial of the Assassin Guiteau: Psychiatry and Law in the Gilded Age* (Chicago, 1968), 5, 214. See also "Guiteau's Trial," *AC* (1881).

46. Lowell, "Ode," *Poems*, IV, 96. See also James R. Lowell, "The World's Fair, 1876," *Nation*, 21 (1875), 82.

Democracy (1880) had a common theme: the grossness and corruption of the political system and, beyond that, the failure of democracy itself.

The Gilded Age: A Tale of To-Day was "a novel of reaction and despair," one which contrasted the venality of the present with a simpler and more honest past. Its central characters Colonel Beriah Sellers and Senator Abner Dilworthy (the latter modeled on Kansas Senator Samuel C. Pomeroy) represented the corrupt alliance of entrepreneurship and politics. Twain bitterly observed at the time: "This nation is not reflected in Charles Sumner, but in Henry Ward Beecher, Benjamin Butler, Whitelaw Reid, Wm. M. Tweed. *Politics* are not going to cure moral ulcers like these, nor the decaying body they fester upon."

De Forest's novels, too, dwelt on the interplay of politics and moneymaking. The protagonist of *Honest John Vane*, an innocent new congressman quickly turned spoilsman, is counseled by a more experienced colleague: "Don't go into the war memories and the nigger worshipping; all those sentimental dodges are played out ... Spend yourself on the tariff, the Treasury, the ways and means, internal improvements, subsidy bills, and relief bills ... Special legislation—or, as some people prefer to call it, finance—is the sum and substance of Congressional business in our day."

Henry Adams's *Democracy* also dealt with corruption in the nation's capital and was filled with the sense that popular government had failed. Mrs. Lightfoot Lee, the book's heroine (and Adams's alter ego), speculates: "suppose society destroys itself with universal suffrage, corruption, and communism." Adams later told his brother Brooks: "I bade politics good-bye when I published *Democracy*."[47]

The grossness and venality of Gilded Age politics was real enough. But the indictment leveled by postwar novelists, journalists, and intellectuals had personal and social sources as well. Some of them hoped to shape or at least to influence the postwar course of public affairs. The antislavery movement and the War for the Union had schooled them in the power of words and ideas. But the

47. Justin Kaplan, *Mr. Clemens and Mark Twain* (New York, 1966), 166, 158; De Forest, *Honest John Vane* (State College, Pa., 1960), Introduction, 84, 124; Adams, *Democracy and Esther* (Garden City, N.Y., 1961), 45; Ernest Samuels, *Henry Adams: The Middle Years* (Cambridge, 1958), 89.

growth of a politics of organization widened the gulf between those who commented on public life and those who lived it. And in this case distance lent disenchantment.

A measure of this change was the declining influence and growing disillusionment of the humorist David Ross Locke (creator of Petroleum V. Nasby) and the cartoonist Thomas Nast. Locke sourly told Mark Twain in the 1870s: "I've settled down upon the belief that there is but one thing in this world better than a dollar, and that's a dollar-and-a-half." Nast finally broke with the Republican party in 1884. But well before this his cartoons had lost their power. His and Locke's were pens suited to the passionate issues of the Civil War and Reconstruction years, not to the pallid organizational politics that followed.[48]

Personal financial or political setbacks fed this disaffection. Nast invested heavily in the brokerage firm of Grant & Ward, whose collapse so badly hurt Ulysses S. Grant. Mark Twain himself had much of the desire, and the inability, to get rich quick that he bestowed on his great comic figure Colonel Sellers. Adams, De Forest, and *Harper's Weekly* editor George W. Curtis had frustrated political ambitions. *Nation* editor E. L. Godkin's increasing mordancy in the 1870s stemmed in part from the knowledge that he did not have a voice in public affairs comparable to that of Horace Greeley in the antislavery years. Editor Whitelaw Reid of the *New York Tribune* was the most influential journalist of the seventies and the eighties because he combined the control of a leading Republican newspaper with the talents and career of an organizational party leader.[49]

Most intellectuals assumed that scientific laws governed politics, the economy, and society—laws that an educated elite was best able to interpret. But, as the scientist Simon Newcomb pointed out, governance lay in the hands of "men who are not only ignorant of social laws, but incapable of exact reasoning of any kind what-

48. James C. Austin, *Petroleum V. Nasby* (New York, 1965), 42; Keller, *Nast*, 279–284.

49. Milne, *Curtis*, 108, 150; E. L. Godkin, *Problems of Modern Democracy*, ed. Morton Keller (1896; Cambridge, 1966), xix–xxv; Royal Cortissoz, *The Life of Whitelaw Reid*, 2 vols. (New York, 1921); Bingham Duncan, *Whitelaw Reid* (Athens, Ga., 1975).

ever." *Harper's Weekly* dwelt on the need for an elite trained "in the laws which regulate human society" to rule, rather than those who had a "happy-go-lucky view of society, which laughs at political economy and sneers at intelligence and thought and common-sense as . . . impracticable."[50]

Given "the alienation of the educated class from politics," its only recourse was to try to shape "that sovereign Public Opinion." The evils afflicting the political system were legion: the Reconstruction regimes of the South, the immigrant-based Democratic city machines, the state party organizations, venal legislators and a patronage-ridden bureaucracy. But each was part of a corrupt and corrupting whole. Ralph Waldo Emerson bitingly observed in 1876: "The country is governed in bar-rooms and in the mind of bar-rooms. The low can best win the low, and each aspirant for power vies with his rival which can stoop lowest." Henry Adams deplored "the debauching effect of the system upon parties, public men, and the morals of the State." Government was reduced to "plundering the people in order to support party organizations." Never before had the parties been so powerful—"our parties manufacture our politics"—and never had they been so void of larger purpose: "No man can name any well-defined question on which they are divided. Their paradise is power, and it furnishes the sole basis and inspiration of their contention."[51]

Most critics of this stripe linked political corruption to active, centralized government, to the "great system which pervades all parts of the Union alike—the system of corrupt consolidation." *Politics for Young Americans* (1876), a primer by journalist Charles

50. Simon Newcomb, "Abstract Science in America, 1776–1876," *NAR*, 122 (1876), 122; *HW*, 14 (1870), 72. See also George M. Fredrickson, *The Inner Civil War* (New York, 1965), ch. 13, and Richard Hofstadter, *Social Darwinism in American Thought 1860–1915* (Philadelphia, 1945), chs. 1–2.

51. Jeremiah L. Diman, *The Alienation of the Educated Class from Politics* (Providence, 1876), 23; *The Works of Ralph Waldo Emerson* (Boston, 1878), XI, 402; Adams, "The Session," *NAR*, 108 (1869), 616, 618; Charles Reemelin, *A Critical Review of American Politics* (Cincinnati, 1881), xxii; George W. Julian, "The Abuse of the Ballot and Its Remedy," *IR*, 8 (1880), 543. See also George W. Curtis, *The Public Duty of Educated Men* (New York, 1877) and Ezra C. Seaman, *The American System of Government* (New York, 1870), dedicated to members of the bar and the press "as the most effective classes of persons to aid in enlightening and forming public opinion" and to offer reforms "to arrest the downward course of our political system."

Nordhoff that went through a number of editions, argued that the post office, highways, even education should be given over to private enterprise. In this sense the critics of a politics of organization, no less than the politicos themselves, contributed to the erosion of the postwar commitment to strong and purposeful government.[52]

Reformers continually searched for ways to check the power of party and of politicians. Proportional representation, open primaries, a hierarchy of electors choosing government officials were among the schemes proposed. Some sought to make government more honest or efficient; others to strip it of power. But in general the intent was to give special weight to elites. As one defender of a property qualification for voting frankly put it: "What God has made unequal, cannot be made equal by human laws and regulations."[53]

By far the most important proposal was to depoliticize the civil service. This was the touchstone of postwar reform, a panacea that in retrospect seems almost giddily inadequate to its purpose. But civil service reform had strong attractions. It promised "to elevate the class of men in the more important places of public life"; to give education and "intelligence" their due place in the political order; to counter what Lowell called "the mischievous notion . . . that, because in this country any man may aspire to any place, any man is therefore fit for any place." Written examinations and permanency in office held out the prospect of entry to a class of people—the reformers' class—otherwise denied access to government. The British civil service system was the model for prominent advocates such as the New York lawyer Dorman B. Eaton and Rhode Island Congressman William A. Jenckes: there education and social status had due recognition.[54]

52. Robert W. Dale, *Impressions of America* (New York, 1878), 52; Nordhoff, *Politics for Young Americans*, 15, 22.

53. Josiah Riley and W. S. Rosecrans, *Popular Government. A New and Simple Plan for Making Ours Effectively a Government 'Of the People, for the People'* (San Francisco, 1878); Charles C. P. Clark, *The Commonwealth Reconstructed* (New York, 1878), 13, 117–118; Brooks Adams, "The Platform of the New Party," *NAR*, 119 (1874), 33–60; Seaman, *American System*, 128. See also Francis Parkman, "The Failure of Universal Suffrage," *NAR*, 127 (1878), 1–20, answered by George W. Julian, "Suffrage a Birthright," *IR*, 6 (1878), 2–20.

54. Lowell, "Look Before and After," 266; Dorman B. Eaton, *The Experiment of Civil Service Reform in the United States* (n.p., 1875); Henry

Civil service reform had another attraction, the promise of efficiency and expertise: "If the reign of demagogues is ever to cease and intelligence to regain her sway, it will be through science." One advocate found a parallel with public health reform: "That aims to do for the physical health of the people something quite analagous to what reform in the civil service aims to do for their political health." Business, too, offered a promising model. Some wished "to apply to the civil service, completely and thoroughly, the plain principles of common business administration." Above all, civil service reform might lead to economy in government and thus to reduced debt and taxes. "The perilous questions of fundamental policy have been determined," said George W. Curtis, who served as a civil service commissioner under Grant from 1871 to 1873, "and the paramount interests of the country are now those of administration. Honesty and efficiency of administration of the settled national policy will now be the chief demand of every party."[55]

Civil service reform could be many things to many men. Ben Butler observed that it "is always popular with the 'outs' and never with the 'ins' unless with those who have a strong expectation of soon going out." Congress passed a limited civil service act in 1871, and Grant established the first Civil Service Commission under its provisions.

But opposition from the politicos forced the repeal in 1875 even of this halting effort. A critic argued that competitive written examinations would be "practically limiting entry to the graduates of colleges." Attorney General George H. Williams observed that "it is not always true that persons having the best scholarly attain-

---

W. Bellows, *Civil Service Reform* (New York, 1877); Henry B. Adams, "Civil Service Reform," *NAR*, 109 (1869), 443–475; "The History and Literature of Civil Service Reform," *PR*, 42 (1870), 1–21; Ari Hoogenboom, *Outlawing the Spoils: A History of the Civil Service Reform Movement 1865–1883* (Urbana, 1961). On elitism, Albert Stickney, *A True Republic* (New York, 1879); Alexander H. Bullock, *Intellectual Leadership in American History* (Worcester, 1875); Theodore D. Woolsey, *The Relations of Honor to Political Life* (New Haven, 1875).

55. Arthur Sedgwick in *NAR*, 113 (1871), 198; George L. Prentiss, *Our National Bane; or, the Dry-Rot in American Politics* (New York, 1877), 75; Jacob D. Cox, "The Civil Service Reform," *NAR*, 112 (1871), 97; Edward Cary, *George William Curtis* (Boston, 1894), 227.

ments make the best clerks." And a civil service system raised more basic issues:

> The fact is that the business of politics, including party management, has become both an art and a science of great complexity and difficulty, requiring, for its understanding and management, high capacity, reinforced by the training of a life. It requires a special class set apart to its study—a political priesthood ... The politician in a democratic country is the ripe fruit of its civilization. If the politician is of a low type, it is because the people want such.

This "political priesthood" expected to be rewarded for its efforts. "It takes *labor* and *money* to successfully work any Political Party," an Illinois Republican reminded Grant. "If there is to be no reward, or hope of reward for *services* rendered and *money* expended—by appointment to some official position, do you ... suppose, that this necessary *labor* and *money* will come to the Party?" It was "our much-abused politicians," after all, who engineered the settlement of the electoral controversy of 1876–1877. "The extreme plan of civil service reform, so alien to our institutions, is the teaching of *doctrinaires* in politics—men outside of practical politics, who sneer at parties and partisan work, and proclaim their independence."[56]

But politicians in the 1870s were no more inclined than reformers to regard government as an instrument of social change. Ohio Senator John Sherman celebrated "the strong conservative power in a government by the people, where the majority must always be independent farmers, mechanics, and working men who have respect for law, religion, and order." And Indiana Republican leader Oliver Morton unfavorably contrasted the "restlessness and the spirit of change" of the upper class to the middle class "balance-wheel in our political machine." The real point of contention between reformers and regulars was political control. The advocates of civil service reform—publicists, intellectuals, mid-

56. Butler quoted in Hoogenboom, *Spoils*, ix; William M. Dickson, "The New Political Machine," *NAR*, 134 (1882), 42–43; Williams to George S. Boutwell, May 13, 1875, Executive and Congressional Letterbooks, Department of Justice, NA; Dickson, "Political Machine," 46; Illinois Republican quoted in Fowler, *Cabinet Politician*, 149; Dickson, "Political Machine," 51. See also Albion W. Tourgée, "Reform *versus* Reformation," *NAR*, 132 (1881), 305–319.

dling business and professional men—were in effect a distinct interest group, contesting with another bloc—the professional, organizational politicians—for government power.

The clash between reformers and politicos involved more fundamental issues still. The politicians, in however faulty and corrupt a manner, subscribed to the democratic tradition. Morton, for example, criticized the electoral college for its unrepresentativeness. The reformers, however elevated their motives and informed their critique, were less comfortable with the principle of popular government. The Russian novelist Ivan Turgenev eloquently argued the case against elitist reform:

> In my opinion, he who is weary of democracy because it creates disorder, is very much in the state of one who is about to commit suicide. He is tired of the variety of life and longs for the monotony of death. For as long as we are created individuals, and not uniform repetitions of one and the same type, life will be motley, varied, and even disorderly. And in this infinite collision of interests and ideas lies our chief promise of progress. To me the great charm of American institutions has always been in the fact that they offer the widest scope for individual development, the very thing which despotism does not and cannot do.[57]

The Politics of Dissent

The great majority of American voters found political representation in the Republican and Democratic parties. But the size and complexity of American society, and the dissatisfaction generated by rapid change, created groups for whom the style and content of the major parties did not suffice.

As in the past, such persons turned to third party movements. This was a phenomenon as old as democratic party politics itself. Anti-Masons, prohibitionists, nativists, antislavery advocates had formed separate political organizations in the pre-Civil War decades. The Republicans themselves began as an extra-party move-

57. *Speech Delivered by Hon. John Sherman . . . at Mansfield, Ohio, . . . Aug. 17, 1877* (Washington, 1877); Morton, "The American Constitution," *NAR*, 156 (1877), 343–345; Hjalmar H. Boyeson, "A Visit to Tourguénoff," *Galaxy*, 17 (1874), 459–460.

ment. The experience of the 1860s supported the view that parties were ephemeral things, rising and falling with the causes that gave them meaning. Many feared—or hoped—that with the removal of what Grant's vice president, Schuyler Colfax, called "the strong cohesive power of the Reconstruction issues," the major postwar parties would not survive. George Templeton Strong found in 1873 "a prevalent feeling that a new party is wanted . . . New political combinations are almost certainly forming." Garfield in 1871 saw "many ugly signs of disintegration in our party." A year later he was convinced that "the dissolution of parties is near at hand."[58]

That expectation was encouraged by the rapid growth of the Liberal Republican movement in the early 1870s. But Liberal Republicanism never became a grass-roots popular party. It served rather as a mode of expression for certain groups of political influentials. These included wartime supporters of the Union Republican coalition who at heart were Democrats; journalists and reformers; and founders of the Republican party distressed by the postwar course of political events. "The whole movement," said one observer, "had the questionable aspect of proceeding downward from the leaders, instead of upward from the masses."

Liberal Republicanism attracted a galaxy of journalists. A "Quadrilateral" consisting of Samuel Bowles of the *Springfield Republican*, Murat Halstead of the *Cincinnati Commercial*, Horace White of the *Chicago Tribune*, and Henry Watterson of the *Louisville Courier-Journal* had a major role at the party's 1872 Cincinnati convention. A contemporary observed that "it was less a theory of politics than a theory of journalism which constituted the motive power" of the Liberal Republican movement. But that theory of journalism came close to being a theory of politics. A third party resting on issues rather than organization was the response of these editors to the postwar decline of the politics of ideology.[59]

58. Willard H. Smith, *Schuyler Colfax* (Indianapolis, 1952), 325; Allan Nevins and Milton H. Thomas, eds., *The Diary of George Templeton Strong* (New York, 1952), IV, 485; Mary L. Hinsdale, ed., *Garfield-Hinsdale Letters* (Ann Arbor, 1949), 172; Harry J. Brown and Frederick D. Williams, eds., *The Diary of James A. Garfield* (East Lansing, 1967), II, 61.
59. "The Political Campaign of 1872," *NAR*, 115 (1872), 406; Everett Chamberlin, *The Struggle of '72. The Issues and Candidates of the Present Political Campaign* (Chicago, 1872), 310. See also John G. Sproat, *"The Best Men": Liberal Reformers in the Gilded Age* (New York, 1968), 75–83; Lena C. Logan, "Henry Watterson and the Liberal Convention of 1872," *IMH*, 40 (1944), 330.

Horace Greeley's *New York Tribune* had been the great voice of antislavery Republicanism in the 1850s and 1860s. Now that influence was fading; but Greeley's desire to be a force in public affairs remained. He ran unsuccessfully for a New York congressional seat against the Democrat S. S. Cox in 1870. By 1872 he was ripe for the Liberal Republican revolt. It was profoundly fitting that the dean of American journalism during the Civil War era should be the presidential candidate of a movement designed in part to restore issues to a central place in the political process.

A number of politicians also found themselves in limbo by the early 1870s. In state after state, Liberal Republican organizations emerged from the welter of factionalism that came with the breakup of the wartime Union Republican coalition. Charles Sumner and Nathaniel Banks of Massachusetts, Lyman Trumbull, John Palmer, and Gustav Körner of Illinois, Jacob Cox and Stanley Matthews of Ohio, George Julian of Indiana, James Harlan of Iowa, Austin Blair of Michigan, Andrew Curtin of Pennsylvania, Carl Schurz and B. Gratz Brown of Missouri: all of these men saw their political power slip away to a new breed of organizational Republicans. Inevitably, Sumner, "the great civic leader" of the Civil War and the chief spokesman of postwar ideological Republicanism, broke with Grant, "the great representative of the military forces that subdued the revolution" and the leader of the organizational Republican party of the 1870s.[60]

The fact that Liberal Republicanism served a variety of political needs gave it substantial initial strength. But it guaranteed also a disastrous eclecticism of issues and organizational chaos. Liberal Republican state platforms dwelt on government reform, tariff reduction, and the end of Radical Reconstruction. But these were

---

60. Glyndon G. Van Deusen, *Horace Greeley* (Philadelphia, 1953), chs. 24–25; on Sumner and Grant, Chamberlin, *Struggle of '72*, 284; George F. Hoar, "Charles Sumner," *NAR*, 126 (1878), 1–26. See also David Donald, *Charles Sumner and the Rights of Man* (New York, 1970), 516 ff, 551–555; Richard A. Gerber, "The Liberal Republicans of 1872 in Historiographical Perspective," *JAH*, 62 (1975), 40–73; Earle D. Ross, *The Liberal Republican Movement* (New York, 1919); Patrick W. Riddleberger, "The Break in the Radical Ranks: Liberals vs. Stalwarts in the Election of 1872," *JNH*, 44 (1959), 136–157; Thomas S. Barclay, *The Liberal Republican Movement in Missouri 1865–1871* (Columbia, Mo., 1926); Mildred Throne, "The Liberal Republican Party in Iowa, 1872," *IJH*, 53 (1955), 121–152; Bentley B. Gilbert, "Some Aspects of Ohio's Part in the Liberal Republican Movement," *HPSO Bulletin*, 13 (1955), 191–202.

not necessarily compatible positions. Anti-Grant Republicans such as Sumner could not be expected to subscribe to the Missouri Liberal Republicans' attack on "unconstitutional laws to cure Ku-Klux disorders, irreligion, or intemperance," or accept their view that "local self-government, with impartial suffrage, will guard the rights of all citizens more securely than any centralized authority." A movement including Radical Republicans unhappy over the retreat from the great causes of the Civil War and Reconstruction and border state Unionists making their way back to the Democrats was bound to run into ideological difficulties.

These contradictions, and the anomaly of a new party many of whose members were at war with party organization per se, made a shambles of the 1872 Liberal Republican convention. The candidate of the reformist Liberal Republicans was Charles Francis Adams, Jr., whose political ambitions may be judged by his preconvention observation to David Ames Wells: "If I am to be negotiated for and have assurances given that I am honest, you will be so kind as to draw me out of that crowd. . . . I never had a moment's belief that when it came to the point, any one so entirely isolated as I am from all political association of any kind could be made acceptable as a candidate for public office."[61]

This crusade against machine politics put on a parodic display of factional fights, bolts by the disgruntled, and control by insiders. The eventual selection of Greeley satisfied the need for a candidate of issues and ideas. But the contrast of Greeley's past views on the tariff and Reconstruction with the Liberal Republican position, plus the fact that he turned out to be an inept and eccentric campaigner, showed how disfunctional that approach to politics was in the 1870s. "The movement was a revolution but the revolt has revolted," Garfield observed. "Was there ever so strange a freak in the history of politics!" Godkin of the *Nation*, Bowles of the *Springfield Republican*, Charles A. Dana of the *Sun* scurried back to Grant and the Republicans. Blaine said of Greeley: "He called out a larger proportion of those who intended to vote against him than any candidate had ever before succeeded in doing."

Liberal Republicanism quickly disintegrated after the 1872 fiasco. Charles Francis Adams in 1873 wanted "to show the country . . .

61. "Missouri," *AC* (1872); Adams to Wells, April 18, 1872, Wells Mss, NYPL.

that we yet live" by holding a meeting at which "every man of the stripe who ruined us at Cincinnati must be rigidly excluded." There was a scattering of state Independent and Reform parties in the mid-seventies. But from now on specific social or economic issues, not an assault on organizational politics as such, would spur third party politics. What remained, finally, of Liberal Republicanism was a tradition: a genteel distaste for organization politics that would figure in American public life for generations to come.[62]

A variety of social and economic discontents led to other separate party movements in the seventies. Eccentric reformers such as Victoria Woodhull and George Francis Train played at running for President. In 1872 Mrs. Woodhull campaigned on an equal rights ticket, calling for civil rights for blacks and women and proposing a pastiche of labor and currency reforms. Robert G. Ingersoll, a lawyer who managed to be both a prominent Republican orator and an advocate of atheism, was ready in 1879 "to help organize a new political party based: *First*, upon the utter divorce of Church and State. *Second*, a divorce of Church and School. *Third*, the taxation of all private property. *Fourth*, the repeal of all laws abridging work for one day in the week . . . and of laws denying to any man any civil rights on account of his belief or unbelief."[63]

Efforts began in 1869 to form state Prohibition parties on the ground that "the distinctive political issues that have for years past interested the American parties are now comparatively unimportant, or fully settled." New Hampshire's prohibitionists declared: "Parties are valuable so far as they subserve valuable principles; and, when they cease to do that, they cease to have any claim upon the name of true principle." A national Prohibition

62. Garfield, Diaries, April 27, 1872; James G. Blaine, *Twenty Years of Congress* (Norwich, Conn., 1886), II, 534; Adams to Wells, Nov. 13, Dec. 1, 1873, Wells Mss, NYPL. See also Matthew T. Downey, "Horace Greeley and the Politicians: The Liberal Republican Convention in 1872," *JAH*, 53 (1967), 727–750.

63. Victoria Woodhull, *The Origin, Tendencies and Principles of Government; or, A Review of the Rise and Fall of Nations* (New York, 1871); George F. Train, *The Man of Destiny. Presidential Campaign, 1872. The Most Remarkable Book of Speeches in the World* (n.p., [1872]), NYPL; Eva I. Wakefield, ed., *The Letters of Robert G. Ingersoll* (New York, 1951), 163.

party candidate ran for the presidency from 1872 on. But prohibitionists constantly agonized over whether to break cleanly with the Republicans or to remain a pressure group within the party. Even in the banner dry state of Maine they decided in 1871 to make no separate nominations, defining themselves as "rather of a moral and socialistic character than political."[64]

Economic discontent fed a recurring politics of protest in the seventies. In one sense the political movements that appeared under such labels as Anti-Monopoly, Labor Reform, Greenback, National, and Greenback Labor belonged to a tradition stretching from the Workingmen's parties of the 1830s to the Populists of the 1890s and beyond. More significant, however, were the links that bound these third parties to the political situation of their own time. They persisted in the hope "that party lines are weakening and fading out," and that a politics of issues and programs might be revived. But the weight of the organizational politics of the postwar years proved to be too great. Unfailingly these protest movements were repelled by or coopted into the major parties.

Anti-Monopoly parties, primarily seeking rate regulation to counter the growing economic power of the railroads, cropped up in eleven states (most of them in the Midwest) during the mid-seventies. Like their Independent, Reform, and Prohibition counterparts, the Anti-Monopolists sought to fill the void left by the rise of a politics of organization. But in fact the Anti-Monopoly parties appear to have been primarily the carriers of old Democratic party rhetoric, appealing to midwesterners so inclined: "we are in favor of a strict construction of our constitution by the Supreme and other courts, and are opposed to the exercise of all doubtful powers by judicial or other officers." Democratic leader John P. Irish was active in the formation of Iowa's Anti-Monopoly party, and made sure that it was committed to states' rights and free trade.[65]

The Labor Reform parties that appeared in the Northeast during the early 1870s had ties to Radical Republicanism. Abolitionist Wen-

64. "United States," *AC* (1869); "New Hampshire," *AC* (1870); "Maine," *AC* (1871). See also "Massachusetts," *AC* (1870).

65. Stephe Smith, *Grains for the Grangers* [Philadelphia, 1874], 20; Solon J. Buck, *The Granger Movement* (Cambridge, 1913), ch. 3; "Iowa," *AC* (1873); Mildred Throne, "The Anti-Monopoly Party in Iowa, 1873–1874," *IJH*, 52 (1954), 289–326. See also Fred E. Haynes, *Third Party Movements since the Civil War with Special Reference to Iowa* (Iowa City, 1916).

dell Phillips ran for governor of Massachusetts on a Labor Reform ticket in 1870, as did Ben Butler in 1872. Butler conducted what respectables considered a campaign "of the lowest possible order," with Phillips standing behind him "like an American Rousseau." There was a scattering of other, more or less radical political efforts. Workingmen's and Socialist party candidates ran for state and local offices in Indiana, Illinois, Wisconsin, and New York. Denis Kearney's Workingman's party was a potent force in San Francisco and California politics at the end of the seventies. These splinter groups put some pressure on the major parties to take heed of issues such as railroad rate regulation and labor conditions. But they attracted no more than a few thousand voters and led brief and inconsequential lives.[66]

Third party economic protest peaked in the Greenback movement of the late 1870s. Under a variety of labels—Greenback, Greenback Labor, National—this effort to secure an expanded paper currency won over a million votes in 1878, electing fourteen congressmen and a number of lesser officials. One observer interviewed thirty-four Pennsylvania, New York, and New Jersey rank-and-file Greenbackers. He found them to be honest, upstanding, native-born Protestants. More than half had been school teachers at some time in their lives. They favored a protective tariff, feared Chinese immigration, and were aware of and resented the opposition of the college-educated and professionals to their cause. More than half of them believed that the spirit world inspired their movement—that the National party was aided by "the superior spheres." Mediums and "trance-speakers" were influential Greenback orators, as were women, who had their own National Clubs.

These qualities help explain why Greenbackism was more a movement than a party. Internal policy disputes plagued the Greenbackers. In Michigan, for example, a National faction calling for nonconvertible low-interest bonds to expand the money supply

66. David Montgomery, *Beyond Equality: Labor and the Radical Republicans 1865–1872* (New York, 1967), 186–196; on Butler and Rousseau, "The Butler Canvass," *NAR*, 114 (1872), 149, 152; "Warrington," "General Butler's Campaign in Massachusetts," *AM*, 28 (1871), 742–750; *AC* (1877–1878), passim; Bessie L. Pierce, *A History of Chicago* (New York, 1957), III, 353 ff; on Kearney, Charles A. Barker, *Henry George* (New York, 1955), 256–259. See also William P. Mallam, "Butlerism in Massachusetts," *NEQ*, 33 (1960), 186–206.

clashed with a Greenback faction opposed to any interest-bearing notes. Northern Greenbackers differed over tariff policy. More serious was their inability to develop a party *persona*. They remained a composite of ex-Democrats and ex-Republicans, hopelessly at odds with one another. Conservative Democrat "Brick" Pomeroy helped organize large numbers of Greenback clubs, and the Indiana Nationals displayed their Democratic origins by calling for "simple, plain, and economical government; as few laws as possible, and they rigidly enforced; as few officials as possible, and they held to a close accountability." But Iowa Greenback leader James B. Weaver, the party's 1880 presidential candidate, had an essentially Republican outlook. "Every good Greenbacker," he declared, "spells the word 'Nation' with the biggest kind of an N."[67]

The major parties readily exploited or absorbed the Greenback movement. Indiana Republicans subsidized the state Greenback party on the assumption that it would draw crucial Democratic votes in that tightly contested state. In Kansas the Greenback cause appealed primarily to Republican farmers; and there the Democrats offered their support. Every one of the successful Greenback congressional candidates in 1878 ran on a coalition ticket. And if absorption failed, other weapons lay at hand. Interracial Greenback Labor alliances in the South were charged with threatening white supremacy. Zach Chandler of Michigan linked Greenbackers to "the vicious socialistic and communistic organizations and their advocates throughout the land." The politicos had numerous ways of preserving their two-party hegemony.[68]

Despite the economic and social turbulence of the 1870s, there was no serious challenge to the highly organized, professionally

67. Sample interviewed in [Jonathan B. Harrison], "The Nationals, Their Origin and Their Aims," *AM*, 42 (1878), 521–530; "The Constituency of the Nationals," *Nation*, 27 (1878), 221–222; Clyde O. Ruggles, "The Economic Basis of the Greenback Movement in Iowa and Wisconsin," *MVHA Proceedings*, 6 (1912–1913), 142–165; Dilla, *Politics of Michigan*, 219; Richard M. Doolen, "The National Greenback Party in Michigan Politics, 1876–88," *MH*, 47 (1963), 161–183; "Indiana," *AC* (1878); on Weaver, Haynes, *Third Party Movements*, 3–4.

68. On Indiana, Barnard, *Hayes*, 300–301; "Kansas," *AC* (1876, 1878); Herbert G. Gutman, "Black Coal Miners and the Greenback-Labor Party in Redeemer Alabama, 1878–1879," *LH*, 10 (1969), 506–535; Chandler quoted in "Michigan," *AC* (1878). See also Reginald C. McGrane, "Ohio and the Greenback Movement," *MVHR*, 11 (1924), 526–542.

run major parties. Only in the critiques of disaffected publicists and reformers, and in peripatetic attempts at third party politics, did dissent find expression. The fevered ideological politics of the Civil War and Reconstruction was gone. It had been succeeded by a politics of organization; by parties that relied on general socio-cultural rather than specific ideological appeals. In this sense, the evolution of American parties and politics during the 1870s closely paralleled—indeed, was part of—the larger experience of the post-war polity. A politics of organization was better suited than a politics of ideology to the demands of a society so strongly committed to localism, so hostile to large and purposeful public policies.

PART TWO

The Industrial Polity 1880-1900

THE AMERICAN POLITY took on a new tone and texture in the late nineteenth century. The issues that dominated the Civil War and postwar years—the relationship of the states to the national government, the status of the freedmen—declined in importance. Instead, the polity dealt more and more directly with the economic and social effects of industrialism. Structurally, too, the process of public policymaking changed. Congress and the executive became less significant instruments of governance than state legislatures, the courts, and the major political parties.

But for all these transformations, important continuities linked the postwar and industrial polities. Public life in the years immediately after the Civil War was dominated by the conflict between the impulse to foster an active state and a broader national citizenship on the one hand, and deeply rooted countervalues of localism, racism, and suspicion of government on the other. A similar tension between new conditions and old values characterized the polity's confrontation with industrialism in the late nineteenth century.

American historical writing has been strongly committed to the proposition that during this period the United States evolved from a collection of isolated, individualistic "island communities" to an increasingly homogeneous and organized, "metropolitan" nation. As one of the leading proponents of this view puts it: "human relationships of ethnicity, religion, and race, of the small community, of primary group ties gave way to the secondary relationships of specialized, widely organized, cosmopolitan, technical society."[1]

No one would deny that these were among the evident effects of industrialism. But in a larger view, the coming of the factory had more varied, more ambiguous consequences. Preindustrial values had a longer, continually reinforced existence than is allowed by those who dwell on the transforming effects of industrialism. The immigrants brought with them traditions of localism, hostility to government, and self-help that buttressed already widespread American attitudes. An Irish or Italian or Bohemian peasant was no less suspicious of the state than a Vermont Yankee or a Georgia redneck. The pervasive geographic mobility of the time—catching up both natives and newcomers—reinforced those views. "All migration," observed the British economist Alfred Marshall, "tends to foster isolated action and individualistic aims: separated from old associates, each one is apt to care mainly for his own interests."[2]

In this sense, industrialism was a source of social continuity as well as a force for change. Native Americans no less than immigrants, town and country dwellers alike, were caught up in a similar ambivalence of thought and action. Their desire to retain old ways and their desire to adapt to a new physical, economic, and social landscape were inextricably intertwined.

Late nineteenth century American politics, government, and law reflected this uncertainty of social purpose. The polity was called on to achieve a variety of ends. It was expected to serve the values of democracy and individual freedom—and at the same time respond to the desire for greater social control over a tumultuous, rapidly changing society. It was supposed to meet the demands

1. Samuel P. Hays, "The New Organizational Society," in Jerry Israel, ed., *Building the Organizational Society: Essays on Associational Activities in Modern America* (New York, 1972), 13. See also Hays, *The Response to Industrialism 1885–1914* (Chicago, 1957); Robert Wiebe, *The Search for Order, 1877–1920* (New York, 1967); Louis Galambos, "The Emerging Organizational Synthesis in Modern American History," BHR, 44 (1970), 279–290; and John A. Garraty, *The New Commonwealth, 1877–1890* (New York, 1968).

2. Alfred Marshall, *Industry and Trade: A Study of Industrial Techniques and Business Organization: and of their Influences on the Conditions of Various Classes and Nations,* 3d ed. (London, 1920), 149. See also Herbert G. Gutman, "Work, Culture, and Society in Industrializing America, 1815–1919," AHR, 78 (1973), 531–588.

of varied, often conflicting economic interests—but also to provide the regulatory and amelioratory services that an industrial order required. The public life of late nineteenth century America was dominated by the resulting tension between the new political, legal, and governmental needs of an industrializing society, and the persistence (indeed, often the strengthening) of social values and expectations as old as the polity itself.

CHAPTER 8

Governance in an Industrial Age

AMERICAN LIFE CHANGED as rapidly in the late nineteenth century as at any time in the nation's history. Massive industrialization and agricultural expansion, a rising tide of new immigration and enormous internal mobility, cities changing in character as rapidly as they increased in size and number: these were measures of a profound transformation in the texture of society.

In all of this push and frenzy, American government seemed to pose a dramatic contrast. This was a time when, in the phrase of the Russian political sociologist Moisei Ostrogorski, the springs of government were weakened everywhere. But in fact late nineteenth century American governance was not so much stagnant as it was held in suspension between old and new social values. American political thought, the presidency, Congress, the federal bureaucracy, and state and local government felt the effects of industrialization and its social consequences. But in each case, traditional values and established modes of governance checked the forces of change.

The Old State and the New

The Civil War and Reconstruction, it was widely assumed in the 1870s, put the finishing touches on the structure of American government. Ohio Congressman Jacob D. Cox announced in 1873 that

289

the "internal organization of the nation and the physical character of the people" now were fixed. Charles Nordhoff's widely read *Politics for Young Americans* typified this view: "*Stability of laws, stability in industry and business, stability of character and of purpose in the individual, are all of far greater importance than the most brilliant experiments in government.*" Mainstream political theory continued to be dominated by the abstract nationalism that flourished in the wake of the war. Writers still dwelt on "the oneness of the national being," on "the intense longing which the nation feels for an expression of its nationality."[1]

But a variety of spokesmen insisted that new social realities required new approaches to governance. Intellectuals and publicists such as James Russell Lowell, Charles Eliot Norton, Henry Adams, E. L. Godkin, George W. Curtis, and Richard Watson Gilder, and magazines such as the *North American Review*, the *Atlantic Monthly*, the *Nation, Harper's Weekly*, the *Forum*, and the *Century* led a sustained assault on ignorant voters, corrupt politicians, and corrupting private interests. Defining themselves as the "educated classes," speaking as they thought for the "honest, intelligent, industrious population of all grades," these genteel reformers dwelt on the dangers posed by a mass electorate, spoilsman government, and most of all the party machines: "we are governed by an oligarchy of professional politicians, or at best by two oligarchies holding power alternately."[2]

1. Jacob D. Cox, *Our Country's New Era* (n.p., 1873; NYPL), 24; Charles Nordhoff, *Politics for Young Americans* (1875; rev. ed., New York, 1886), 148–149; William W. Crane and Bernard Moses, *Politics: An Introduction to the Study of Comparative Constitutional Law* (New York, 1884), 23; "The Political Situation," *NPR*, 1 (1886), 75. See also John W. Burgess, "The American Commonwealth," *PSQ*, 1 (1886), 9–35; Philemon Bliss, *Of Sovereignty* (Boston, 1885); John C. Hurd, *The Union-State: A Letter to Our States-Rights Friend* (New York, 1890); Denton J. Snider, *The State, Especially the American State, Psychologically Treated* (St. Louis, 1902); Charles E. Merriam, *American Political Ideas: Studies in the Development of American Political Thought 1865–1917* (New York, 1923).

2. John G. Sproat, *"The Best Men": Liberal Reformers in the Gilded Age* (New York, 1968); Leonard W. Bacon, *The Defeat of Party Despotism by the Reenfranchisement of the Individual Citizen* (Boston, 1886), 5. See also John Tomsich, *A Genteel Endeavor: American Culture and Politics in the Gilded Age* (Stanford, 1971); John G. Clark, "Reform Currents in Polite Monthly Magazines, 1880–1900," *MAm*, 47 (1965), 3–23; Charles Reemelin, *A Critical Review of American Politics* (Cincinnati, 1881); Albert Stickney, *The Political Problem* (New York, 1890).

These critics laid bare some of the grosser realities of late nineteenth century American public life. But they were also projecting onto the polity their personal anxieties and frustrations, their sense of displacement by new men and new values. Through their writings and organizations they sought to exert the influence on public affairs that the dominance of the professional politicians denied them. They spoke of "The public duty of educated men." Curtis of *Harper's Weekly* almost wistfully asserted: "The duty of an editor, who would be both honest and independent, is not unlike that of a great public officer."

An unhopeful estimate of the future of American democracy readily went with this point of view. James Russell Lowell wondered whether "equality ... may not ... prove dangerous when interpreted and applied politically by millions of newcomers alien to our traditions ... We have great and thus far well-warranted faith in the digestive and assimilative powers of our system; but may not these be overtaxed?" The journalist-politician Carl Schurz observed in 1892 that "there is a school of pessimists growing up among us who, whenever anything goes wrong, are ready to declare democratic government a failure and to despair of the Republic."[3]

E. L. Godkin of the *Nation* was the most unrelenting critic of late nineteenth century American public life. He exemplified the mix of analytic insight and frustrated personal ambition that so often fueled the genteel reformers. Godkin came to the United States in the 1850s, an Irish Protestant in flight from a caste-bound English society to the freedom and opportunity of the New World. At the end of the century—and of his life—he returned to England because he found there an ordered, stratified society infinitely preferable to the raw, discomfiting America of immigrants and bosses and plutocrats.

Henry Adams underwent a similar internal exile into the realms of history and philosophical pessimism. This grandson and great-grandson of Presidents had hoped to be a political power in his own

3. Curtis, *The Public Duty of Educated Men* (Albany, 1878); Gordon Milne, *George W. Curtis and the Genteel Tradition* (Bloomington, Ind., 1956), 162; Lowell, "The Place of the Independent in Politics," *Literary and Political Addresses* in *Writings* (Riverside Edition) (Boston, 1890), VI, 275; Schurz in Frederic Bancroft, ed., *Speeches, Correspondence and Political Papers of Carl Schurz* (New York, 1913), V, 88.

right. But the American mission in Guatemala City was the only government post ever offered to him, and he came to regard politics as "the single uncompensated disappointment of life." Asked what ailed Adams, Oliver Wendell Holmes replied that he wanted public office "handed to him on a silver platter."[4]

Genteel reformers proposed a variety of devices designed to limit the power of politicos and of popular majorities. These included civil service reform most of all, proportional representation, and restrictions on the nomination and election of officeholders. But the reformers had varied and conflicting political models: the British system of government, the early Republic, the business corporation. And their influence was lessened by their ambivalent attitude toward democracy itself. Critics effectively scored them for their distrust of popular rule; for their Anglophilia; for their failure to recognize that "the United States is first a political and second a business organization," and that by being closely linked to politics, government was more likely to be responsive to the popular will. For all the acuity of their critique, the genteel reformers were impelled more by the desire to restore an imagined golden past than by the desire to shape a new American polity.[5]

There were other perspectives from which to argue that changing conditions demanded fresh approaches to governance. One of these was a left critique of industrial capitalism: sometimes from a Marxian socialist viewpoint, more often in the native American traditions of antimonopoly and equal rights. It appeared in the writings of Henry George, Laurence Gronlund, Edward Bellamy, and Henry Demarest Lloyd; in the minute radical movements of the time; and in the polemical literature of the Granger and antimonopoly movements of the 1870s, the Knights of Labor in the 1880s, and the agrarian and labor protests of the 1890s. But most

4. E. L. Godkin, *Problems of Modern Democracy*, ed. Morton Keller (1896; Cambridge, 1966), Introduction; Ernest Samuels, *Henry Adams: The Middle Years* (Cambridge, 1958), 158, *Henry Adams: The Major Phase* (Cambridge, 1964), 193.

5. John F. Baker, *The Federal Constitution: An Essay* (New York, 1887), 79, 82; James M. Ashley, *The Impending Political Epoch* (n.p., 1891); Richard H. Dana, "Points in American Politics," *NAR*, 124 (1877), 1–30; Herbert Tuttle, "The Despotism of Party," *AM*, 54 (1883), 374–384; for criticisms, Jesse S. Clarkson, "The Politician and the Pharisee," *NAR*, 152 (1891), 613, General John Pope, "Common-Sense and Civil-Service Reform," *NAR*, 149 (1889), 265–277.

critics of the left sought a larger share in the existing system; only a few espoused a socialist alternative.[6]

There emerged, too, a skeptical, ironic mode of political analysis distinct alike from the genteel and the radical perspectives. Henry Adams had something of this quality, although by age and social disposition he was linked to the genteel critics. William Graham Sumner was closer to the mark. He expected little from reform: "We must reject the method of political progress which consists in forming an ideal and then trying to devise means for realizing it." But he was acutely aware of the impact of industrialism and social change on American life. He warned that "when the old fashioned theories of state interference are applied to the new democratic state, they turn out to be simply a device for setting separate interests in a struggle against each other." The consequence was likely to be rule either by the mobocracy or by the plutocracy. In either case, Sumner's "forgotten man"—the middle class American—would be the loser.[7]

John Jay Chapman struck a different note around the turn of the century. This passionate man of letters—in a fit of remorse after besting a rival suitor, he burnt his hand off—had a romantic's distaste for the politics of the ordinary. The novelist Owen Wister called him a "belated abolitionist." At the same time Chapman had acute insight into the sources and character of politics in the industrial age. He fastened on commerce as the central force in American public life: "Misgovernment in the United States is an incident in the history of commerce. It is part of the triumph of industrial progress." He perceived that "the change of motive power behind the party organizations—from principles to money —was silently effected during the thirty years which followed the [Civil] war. Like all organic change, it was unconscious." He had little use for party politics: the 1896 McKinley-Bryan election was

6. Sidney Fine, *Laissez Faire and the General-Welfare State* (Ann Arbor, 1956), 253–264; Charles N. R. McCoy, "American Political Philosophy after 1865," *Thought*, 21 (1946), 249–271; Howard H. Quint, *The Forging of American Socialism* (Indianapolis, 1953); Chester M. Destler, *American Radicalism, 1865–1901* (1946; Chicago, 1966).

7. William G. Sumner, "The Theory and Practice of Elections," *Collected Essays in Political and Social Science* (New York, 1885), 102, "State Interference," *NAR*, 145 (1887), 116, "The Absurd Attempt to Make the World Over," *Forum*, 17 (1894), 92–102, "The Forgotten Man," in Albert G. Keller and Maurice R. Davie, eds., *Essays of William Graham Sumner* (New Haven, 1934), I, 466–496.

a contest "between organized capital and organized waste." Reform of the traditional sort Chapman dismissed as "a sort of guerilla warfare." But he foresaw the rise of a new generation that would find in political innovation a challenge of the sort that a mature business system no longer provided. His ironic, urbane analyses appeared in his iconoclastic journal *Political Nursery* (1897–1901) and in his book *Causes and Consequences* (1898). In many respects he was a precursor of those twentieth century skeptics Randolph Bourne and H. L. Mencken.[8]

Finally, the late nineteenth century saw the rise of a new "political science": a view of politics and government that stressed their historical and social context and the capacity of trained intelligence to shape their character. Anglo-American political theorists were caught up in the belief that the principles of a science of government were as discoverable as those of a science of nature, or law, or society. Walter Bagehot's *Physics and Politics* (1873) appeared two years after Darwin's *Descent of Man*. Sheldon Amos, another British analyst, wrote *The Science of Politics* (1883) after a two-year investigation of governments around the world, in conscious emulation of Darwin's voyage on the *Beagle*. Amos announced: "The scientific method, in politics as elsewhere, is slowly and surely getting the better of the empiric."

The paradigm of evolution soon affected American political analysis. An 1889 review of American history textbooks observed that older works "made the United States an isolated community, built upon the false bottom of the Constitution, and under the control of the dominant political party." More recent texts stressed "the development of society, the meaning of civil polity, and, above all, the evolution of political institutions." This newer approach gave "some notion of the organic growth of the nation, its inheritance from other times and peoples, and the conflicting forces which have been involved in the historical development."[9]

Woodrow Wilson's *The State* (1889) traced the origins of govern-

8. Richard B. Hovey, *John Jay Chapman: An American Mind* (New York, 1959); Chapman, *Causes and Consequences* (New York, 1898), 3, 5, 124, "The Capture of Government by Commercialism," *AM*, 81 (1898), 145.

9. Amos, *The Science of Politics* (London, 1883), 20; "Recent American History," *AM*, 63 (1889), 118.

ment to the family rather than to an ahistorical social contract. John W. Burgess's *Political Science and Constitutional Law* (1890) was strongly influenced by German idealism and post-Civil War nationalism, but it also offered a new, comparative historical analysis of American and European government. A. Lawrence Lowell did the same with the legislative behavior of Congress and Parliament, and Henry Jones Ford's *The Rise and Growth of American Politics* (1898) pioneered in the realistic examination of the party system.[10]

Implicit in this approach was an assault on nineteenth century laissez-faire. Lester Ward's *Dynamic Sociology* (1883) linked a science of society to increased government direction and supervision. Political analysts dwelt increasingly on the need of the state to live by the same precepts of organization and efficiency that were taking hold in the industrial economy. Henry C. Adams, holder of the first Ph.D. in economics from Johns Hopkins and director of statistics for the Interstate Commerce Commission, observed: "Organization is the most potent fact in the industrial history of the nineteenth century, and it must either be used for the good of society, or society must bear the ills which it brings." In his influential essay "Relation of the State to Industrial Action" (1887), Adams argued for active government in an industrial age.

The sociologist Charles Horton Cooley at the turn of the century nicely delineated the altered perspective that separated him from the generation of his father, jurist Thomas M. Cooley. He noted that advances in communication and technology not only increased the complexity of society, but made it possible for social change itself to become "in some degree a matter of knowledge and choice." Westel W. Willoughby's *The Nature of the State* (1896) argued in a similar vein that the mores and economic interests of the people were as much the government's responsibility as its traditional obligations to protect property, preserve order, and conduct foreign relations. These men shared a common belief that

10. Wilson, *The State* (Boston, 1889); Burgess, *Political Science and Comparative Constitutional Law* (Boston, 1890); Lowell, "The Influence of Party upon Legislation in England and America," *AHA Annual Report*, 1 (1901), 319–542; Ford, *The Rise and Growth of American Politics* (New York, 1898). See also David J. Rothman, *Politics and Power: The United States Senate, 1869–1901* (Cambridge, 1966), ch. 8; Anson P. Morse, "The Natural History of Party," *YR*, 2 (1893), 74–93.

the state was "rapidly becoming, if it is not already, the central factor of social evolution."[11]

Just as the views of the genteel reformers had a social as well as an intellectual context, so too did the perceptions of the new political and social scientists. Located as they were in professional academic disciplines, they naturally stressed the importance of systematic, scientific analysis. A complex "national system" of government took trained experts to describe and, by implication, to run. The United States, said Woodrow Wilson in 1889, faced "chiefly problems of organization and leadership." He concluded that "the size of modern democracy necessitates the exercise of persuasive power by dominant minds." And of course Wilson ultimately deviated from the normal political impotence of academicians to the extent of achieving the presidency.[12]

Public administration was the means by which scientific government would be attained. Wilson was a pioneer in its development. He argued that "the field of administration is a field of business. It is removed from the hurry and strife of politics; it at most points stands apart even from the debatable ground of constitutional study." Like the genteel reformers Wilson wanted a "technically schooled civil service." But his purposes differed from theirs. He sought not economy and government restraint so much as a bureaucracy that could respond positively to the problems of a complex industrial society. And his administrators were to have a symbiotic rather than an adversary relationship to party politics and politicians. Other political analysts of the time—Henry Jones Ford, A. Lawrence Lowell, Frank J. Goodnow—joined Wilson in dwelling on the need for strong, responsible party government.

11. Ward, *Dynamic Sociology*, 2 vols. (New York, 1883); Adams, "An Interpretation of the Social Movements of Our Time," *PCSU*, ser. B, no. 2 (May 15, 1895), 14, "Relation of the State to Industrial Action," *AEA Publications*, 1 (1887), 465–549; Cooley, "The Process of Social Change," *PSQ*, 12 (1897), 72–73; Willoughby, *The Nature of the State* (New York, 1896); Munroe Smith, "Introduction: The Domain of Political Science," *PSQ*, 1 (1886), 8. See also Herman Belz, "The Constitution in the Gilded Age: The Beginnings of Constitutional Realism in American Scholarship," *AJLH*, 13 (1969), 110–125.

12. Woodrow Wilson, *The State and Federal Governments of the United States* (Boston, 1889), iii, "Character of Democracy in the United States," *AM*, 64 (1889), 585–588. See also Albert Stickney, *Democratic Government* (New York, 1885), 166, which speaks of an age of organization having arrived after the previous stages of founding and consolidation.

The writings of Goodnow—especially his *Comparative Administrative Law* (1893) and *Politics and Administration* (1900)—and of University of Chicago law professor Ernst Freund did much to establish the new field of administrative law. Goodnow distinguished between constitutional law, which dealt with the anatomy of government, and administrative law, which dealt with its physiology. While parties and politicians were charged with the task of articulating the popular will, it was the function of administrative law to execute public policy.[13]

By the turn of the century, American political analysis embraced numerous modes of perception: genteel reform, socialism, skepticism, functional analysis. But for all this, it was a limited, bloodless body of writing, detached from concrete policy, from specific governmental purposes. The work of political scientists such as Wilson and Goodnow had an abstract, exhortatory quality that was reminiscent of the post-Civil War analysts and their unprogrammatic celebrations of American nationalism. There did not yet exist the conceptual framework, or the body of public opinion, that could give meaning to the concept of the active state.

President and Congress

New views of government had little evident effect on the office of the presidency. It remained small in scale and limited in power, caught up more in the vicissitudes of party politics and patronage than in the formulation and conduct of public policy. Late nineteenth century Presidents had little say over the estimates, appropriations, expenditures, and policies of government bureaus and departments. These agencies were much more responsive to the House Appropriations Committee and other organs of Congress than to the White House. Chester Arthur was said to have "done

13. Wilson, "The Study of Administration," *PSQ,* 2 (1887), 209–210, 216; Austin Ranney, *The Doctrine of Responsible Party Government* (Urbana, 1954); Goodnow, *Comparative Administrative Law* (New York, 1893), *Politics and Administration: A Study in Government* (New York, 1900); Ernst Freund, "The Law of the Administration in America," *PSQ,* 9 (1894), 403–425; Oscar Kraines, *The World and Ideas of Ernst Freund* (University, Ala., 1974).

well . . . by not doing anything bad." Grover Cleveland engaged George F. Parker, a newspaper reporter, to serve as his press aide during the 1892 campaign, but nothing like the modern presidential press secretary emerged from that experiment. In 1901 the President's staff consisted of a secretary, two assistant secretaries, two executive clerks, four lesser clerks or telegraphers, and a few doorkeepers and messengers.[14]

✓ Patronage was the chief responsibility of late nineteenth century Presidents. James A. Garfield complained to James G. Blaine after he entered the White House in 1881: "All these years I have been dealing with ideas, and here I am dealing only with persons. I have heretofore been treating of the fundamental principles of government, and here I am considering all day whether A or B should be appointed to this or that office." Despite the rise of civil service classification in the decades after Garfield's assassination, chief executives continued to be besieged by office-seekers and immersed in the business of patronage. Executive orders between 1883 and 1901 dealt almost exclusively with the extension of the civil service list—usually to protect existing jobholders as one administration gave way to another.[15]

Toward the end of the century, signs of a more forceful and assertive presidential style began to appear. Grover Cleveland's adversary relationship to a Republican Senate encouraged him to stress the independent, policymaking character of his position: "It should be remembered," he said, "that the office of President is essentially executive in its nature." He came to believe that his most important duty was to assert the "entire independence" of the executive from the legislative branch. Cleveland's major weapon (besides patronage) was the veto. During his first term (1885–1889)

14. James Bryce, The American Commonwealth (1888; 3d ed., New York, 1893), I, 54, 65; on Arthur, Frank G. Carpenter, Carp's Washington (New York, 1960), 30; Gordon A. Moon II, "George F. Parker, A 'Near Miss' as First White House Press Chief," JQ, 41 (1964), 183–190; Leonard D. White, The Republican Era: 1869–1901 (New York, 1958), 101–105.

15. Thomas H. Sherman, Twenty Years with James G. Blaine (New York, 1928), 78, and Robert G. Caldwell, James A. Garfield, Party Chieftain (Indianapolis, 1931), 340; Allan Nevins, Grover Cleveland: A Study in Courage (New York, 1932), 235, 515–516; Harry J. Sievers, Benjamin Harrison: Hoosier President (Indianapolis, 1968), 39–41, 73; Margaret Leech, In the Days of McKinley (New York, 1959), 133–135; on executive orders, White, Republican Era, 97.

he turned back three times as many bills as all of his predecessors combined.

But this was a distinctly negative use of presidential power. It stemmed from party conflict between President and Congress rather than from broader policy considerations. (Cleveland's vetoes of pension and spending bills often had a strongly partisan tinge.) Less visible but in the long run more significant was the gradual growth of systematic executive administration. A longtime White House secretary said that up to the late 1870s "hardly a scrap of paper was kept here to show what a President did or why he did it. Now we keep a record of everything." At the end of the century, William McKinley's secretary George B. Cortelyou brought new standards of efficiency to the office. The rise of a more intensely ideological politics in the 1890s, culminating in the Bryan-McKinley election of 1896, and the increase of executive power during the Spanish-American War, set the stage for the transformation of presidential leadership in the early twentieth century under Theodore Roosevelt and Woodrow Wilson.[16]

Wilson thought in 1879 that there "could be no more despotic authority wielded under the forms of free government than our national Congress now exercises," and in 1885 he called "Congressional Government" the "predominant and controlling force, the centre and source of all motive and of all regulative power." A variety of sources contributed to that authority: the presence of state and local party leaders as senators and representatives; congressional control over budgetary and fiscal policy; the weakness of the President and the lack of a strong, independent bureaucracy; the growing centralization of congressional leadership and the institutionalization of congressional procedure.[17]

16. Cleveland quoted in White, *Republican Era*, 25; Edward C. Mason, *The Veto Power: Its Origin, Development and Function in the Government of the United States* (Boston, 1890), 128; on Cleveland vetoes, White, *Republican Era*, 39; on White House records, Carpenter, *Carp's Washington*, 298; Leech, *McKinley*, 471; Woodrow Wilson, *Constitutional Government in the United States* (New York, 1908), 59. See also John D. Long, "Use and Abuse of the Veto Power," *Forum*, 4 (1887–1888), 253–267.

17. Wilson, "Cabinet Government in the United States," *IR*, 7 (1879), 163, *Congressional Government* (1885; New York, 1956), 31. See also White, *Republican Era*, 46 ff.

This is not to say that Congress was a streamlined, efficient instrument of government. The late nineteenth century legislature was a clubby and often casual institution. Admirers festooned the members' desks with flowers when the second session of the 47th Congress got under way on December 4, 1882. Fruit and tobacco stands did business in the House wing of the Capitol until Speaker Thomas B. Reed abolished them in the 1890s. The Hole in the Wall —a bar discreetly tucked into a corner of the Capitol—dispensed liquor until 1903. Congressmen came and went in large numbers (though the percentage of first-term members was declining), and they brought with them the mores of the small town, rural, or working class city districts that most represented. Bryce found them to be much more homogeneous than the members of European assemblies; the prevalent type was the shrewd, second-rate lawyer.[18]

Beneath its easy ways, the late nineteenth century Congress was an institution in flux. A polysyllabic political scientist calls this a time when universalistic and automated replaced particularistic and discretionary decisionmaking. Congress in the early and mid-nineteenth century was primarily a deliberative and legislative body. By the end of the century its role as a forum for debate was much reduced; its lawmaking was under tighter control by the congressional leadership; and through its committees it had a large administrative role in the federal government.

One reason for this change was the increasing scale and complexity of American life itself. Garfield thought that the work of Congress in 1877 was ten times heavier and more complicated than it had been forty years before. Twelve annual appropriations bills occupied two-thirds of each session, when a generation earlier they had been dealt with in a week. The business that came before Congress inexorably grew: 37,409 public and private bills were introduced from 1871 to 1881; 73,857 from 1881 to 1891; 81,060 from 1891 to 1901. The *Congressional Globe* of 1839–1840 had 1,405 pages; the *Congressional Record* of 1889–1890 was 11,568 pages long. The sheer weight and diversity of interests made tariff scheduling an increasingly complicated and technical process. The Rivers

18. Bryce, *American Commonwealth*, I, 304, 309; Carpenter, *Carp's Washington*, 10 ff, 14; Robert Luce, *Legislative Assemblies* (Boston, 1924), 641; Bryce, *American Commonwealth*, I, 147–148.

and Harbors appropriations bill of 1888 took care of individual congressmen's interests in traditional pork barrel fashion; but its drafters also had to take into account detailed surveys and estimates submitted by local engineers, the chief of army engineers, and the secretary of war. By the end of the century permanent expenditures were allocated through 185 separate acts, including 13 major annual appropriations bills.[19]

While the scale of congressional work expanded, so too did the likelihood of changes in party domination in one or another House or in the presidency—and the unlikelihood that one party would control both the legislative and executive branches. Congress and the presidency were Republican from 1861 to 1875 and again from 1897 to 1909. But only during the 47th (1881–1883), 51st (1889–1891), and 53d (1893–1895) Congresses were both branches of government under single party control.

These conditions fostered a gradual but steady regularizing of congressional procedure. By 1890 all bills and committee reports were referred to the clerk of the House, thus saving an estimated three to five hours of Congress's time a week. The *Congressional Record* came to be far more than a transcript of proceedings. Members were able to edit their remarks, insert [Laughter] and [Applause] as they chose, and add speeches and other materials that in fact had never been presented on the floor.[20]

The business of the House came increasingly under the control of the leading committees and the speaker. The power of the Committee on Rules grew substantially in the 1880s. Democratic Speaker of the House John G. Carlisle (1883–1889) and his Republican successor Thomas B. Reed (1889–1891, 1895–1899) adopted the practice of making themselves and the chairmen of the Committees on Appropriations and Ways and Means a majority of the Rules Committee—in effect, "a masterful steering committee"

19. Nelson W. Polsby, "The Institutionalization of the House of Representatives," *APSR*, 62 (1968), 144–168; Garfield cited in Robert Luce, *Legislative Procedure* (Boston, 1922), 477; *HS*, 690; on *Globe* and *Record*, Luce, *Legislative Procedure*, 265; Albert B. Hart, "Biography of a Rivers and Harbors Bill," *AHA Papers*, 3 (1888), 180–196; on expenditures, Rollo Ogden, "The Rationale of Congressional Extravagance," *YR*, 6 (1897–1898), 37, 49.

20. *HS*, 791; Luce, *Legislative Procedure*, 65; Neil MacNeil, *Forge of Democracy: The House of Representatives* (New York, 1963), 58.

which resolved procedural problems and controlled the course of legislation. The speaker could do much to block enactment. In 1887 a congressman paraded in front of Carlisle for three hours, vainly seeking to be recognized so that he might introduce a measure. Finally in frustration he tore his bill to pieces. The Blair Act for federal aid to education passed the Senate three times in the 1880s, but never came before the House because Speaker Carlisle —"the premier"—refused to permit it.[21]

"Czar Reed" forcefully moved to make the House a more efficient body in 1890. He was one of those men whose gifts of intellect and character refute the adage that in the late nineteenth century the most talented Americans went into business, not politics. Reed's influence rested on a formidable intelligence (he was a highly cultivated man, an omnivorous reader who owned a notable private library), a mastery of House affairs, and a biting, ironic wit that was reminiscent of Thaddeus Stevens. He resembled Stevens, too, in his dedication to black voting and civil rights, and in his principled opposition to turn-of-the-century American imperialism.

It was Reed who defined a statesman as "a successful politician who is dead." When some of his constituents wanted him to secure condemned army cannon for a Civil War soldiers' monument he impatiently replied, "I am not in the old junk business." Powerful enough to be a prominent contender for the 1896 Republican presidential nomination—but too acerb to stand a real chance of getting it—he realistically assessed his chances: "They might do worse and they probably will." In his style and principles Reed was a throwback to the Civil War–Reconstruction period. But his chief legacy was structural not ideological: a Congress more tightly controlled by its leadership.

21. On Rules Committee, Luce, *Legislative Procedure*, 479–480, and Hannis Taylor, "The National House of Representatives: Its Growing Inefficiency as a Legislative Body," *AM*, 65 (1890), 766–773; on Carlisle, Herbert B. Fuller, *The Speakers of the House* (Boston, 1909), 211, Luce, *Legislative Procedure*, 457. See also George B. Galloway, *History of the House of Representatives* (New York, 1961); Congressional Quarterly, *Guide to the Congress of the United States* (Washington, 1971), 39–41; Bryce, *American Commonwealth*, I, chs. 13–15; Henry L. Nelson, "The Speaker's Power," *AM*, 64 (1889), 64–73.

Reed struck out at the "disappearing quorum," where members sat mute during attendance roll calls, thus blocking the quorum necessary to conduct the business of the House. He counted them whether they signified their presence or not and faced down the protests of the Democratic opposition. The Supreme Court in 1891 upheld this and other "Reed rules." Charles F. Crisp, his Democratic successor as speaker in 1891, ended this procedure; but Reed turned the disappearing quorum device on him and forced the reinstatement of the new rule. A no-filibustering rule passed under Reed in 1891 was repealed by the Democrats in 1893. When the Republicans regained control in 1895 it was permanently reinstated.

In 1907 House parliamentarian Asher B. Hinds published an eight-volume work, *Precedents of the House of Representatives*, that included 7,346 procedural technicalities: a monument to the belief that the rules of the House had developed to the point where codification was in order. Speaker and committee domination of congressional procedure would frequently come under challenge in the twentieth century. But the transformation that occurred in the late nineteenth century would not be substantially modified.[22]

A comparable change occurred in the Senate. Woodrow Wilson in the mid-eighties called that body "a small, select, and leisurely House of Representatives." But only a few years later James Bryce was struck by the Senate's "modern, severe, and practical" character. A forceful leadership imposed controls on Senate proceedings paralleling those that Reed and others wrought in the House. William B. Allison of Iowa, chairman of the Committee on Appropriations from 1881 to 1908, Finance Committee Chairman Nelson W. Aldrich of Rhode Island, and influential figures such as Orville H. Platt of Connecticut, Mark Hanna of Ohio, John C. Spooner of Wisconsin, and the Democrat Arthur P. Gorman of Maryland brought a previously unknown degree of party and procedural discipline to the Senate. From the mid-1880s on the Republican Steering Committee, through its control of the all-

22. William A. Robinson, *Thomas B. Reed, Parliamentarian* (New York, 1930), 14, 138, 140, 147, 100, 327; Luce, *Legislative Procedure*, 39, 287 ff; *United States v. Ballin*, 144 U.S. 1 (1891); Hinds, *Hinds' Precedents of the House of Representatives*, 8 vols. (Washington, 1907–1908).

important committee assignments, took over the scheduling of legislative business.[23]

The committee system was of key importance to the late nineteenth century Congress. In the House, said Wilson, "committee work is everything and discussion nothing but 'telling it to the country.'" Indeed, said Bryce, that body was "not so much a legislative assembly as a huge panel from which committees are selected." The leading congressmen and senators chaired the most important standing committees: Appropriations, Rules, and Ways and Means in the House; Appropriations and Finance in the Senate. Connecticut Senator Orville Platt observed in 1895: "I should care nothing for being President *pro tempore* [of the Senate], but I should care very much for a place on the Finance Committee."

But while overall authority tended to flow into a few hands, the work of the committees was more and more decentralized—a result of the growing workload that descended on Congress. The House Committee on Rivers and Harbors, created in 1883, took over from the Committee on Commerce the politically sensitive task of drafting the annual internal improvements appropriations acts. A few years later supply bills totaling about half of all government expenditure were moved from Appropriations to Consular and Diplomatic Service, Army, Naval Affairs, Post Offices and Post Roads, and Indian Affairs. The proximate cause of the change was the desire to reduce Democratic Speaker Samuel J. Randall's control over expenditures through the Appropriations Committee. But it reflected too the need to have more informed committee oversight of allocations.[24]

A number of new committees added in the 1880s and 1890s also testified to the growing complexity of late nineteenth century American governance. Education and Labor were divided into separate committees in 1883 and Rivers and Harbors was estab-

23. Wilson, *Congressional Government*, 145; Bryce, *American Commonwealth*, I, 118; Rothman, *Politics and Power*, ch. 2. See also George H. Haynes, *The Senate of the United States: Its History and Practice*, 2 vols. (Boston, 1938).

24. Wilson, *Congressional Government*, 145; Bryce, *American Commonwealth*, I, 159; Louis A. Coolidge, *An Old-Fashioned Senator: Orville H. Platt* (New York, 1910), 540; Bryce, *American Commonwealth*, I, 177; on Randall, Thomas B. Reed, "Appropriations for the Nation," *NAR*, 154 (1892), 319–328.

lished; Merchant Marine and Fisheries were added in 1887; Expenditure in the Department of Agriculture in 1889; Immigration and Naturalization, Civil Service, and Alcoholic and Liquor Traffic in 1893; Insular Affairs in 1899; Census and Industrial Arts and Expositions in 1901. By 1892 there were forty-four standing committees in the Senate and fifty in the House, passing on all general and special legislation and appropriations bills and subjecting much of the federal bureaucracy to close and continuing scrutiny.[25]

Important changes in the character of congressional membership went hand in hand with these developments. For one thing, the average length of congressional tenure steadily increased. Fifty-eight percent of the 44th Congress (1875–1877) consisted of first-term members; the range in the 1880s was 30 to 40 percent; in the 1890s, 20 to 30 percent. Fifty-three percent of the 42nd Congress (1871–1873) was reelected; 63 percent of the 50th Congress (1887–1889). Senators tended to be older and more experienced. Their average age in 1860 was fifty; in 1900, fifty-seven. The seniority rule for committee chairmanships became the norm during these years. In the 47th Congress (1881–1883) it was followed in two cases and ignored in thirty-seven; by the time of the 57th Congress (1901–1903) it applied to forty-nine of fifty-seven committee heads.

One estimate is that the proportion of senators with business backgrounds rose from 27 percent in 1860 to 34 percent in 1900; another, for the same group, is 27 percent in the 1870s, 28 percent in the 1880s, and 24 percent in the 1890s. In any case, the solid majority of senators (as of other federal and state legislators) were lawyers—73 percent in the 1870s, 68 percent in the 1880s, 57 percent in the 1890s—who thus shared important modes of thought and expression.[26]

25. Committee list in Galloway, *House,* 66–67; Bryce, *American Commonwealth,* I, 156. See also Lauros G. McConachie, *Congressional Committees* (New York, 1898); "History of the United States House of Representatives," U.S., 89th Cong., 1st sess., House, Doc. no. 250.

26. On tenure, Polsby, "Institutionalization," 146, and Luce, *Legislative Assemblies,* 365; on age, Ari Hoogenboom, "Industrialization and Political Leadership: A Case Study of the United States Senate," in Frederick C. Jaher, ed., *The Age of Industrialism in America* (New York, 1968), 50; on seniority, Nelson W. Polsby and others, "The Growth of the Seniority System in the U.S. House of Representatives," *APSR,* 63 (1969), 792; on backgrounds, Hoogenboom, "Political Leadership," 53–56, and Rothman, *Politics and Power,* ch. 4.

Another sign of institutional stability was the treatment of contested elections. These were more and more frequent. Seventy-one seats were contested from 1789 to 1839; 278 from 1839 to 1889; 88 in the 1890s alone. It became necessary in 1895 to divide the House Elections Committee into three separate units. The resolution of contested elections traditionally followed party lines; Reed caustically remarked that "the House never divides on strictly partisan issues except when it is acting judicially." But the tendency was to be increasingly protective of the claims of incumbents. From 1895 to 1897 there were ten decisions for the Republican majority and twenty-five for the Democratic minority: incumbency was more important than party. Reed, among others, called for the judiciary to decide contested elections.[27]

Finally, an outburst of important legislation—the Interstate Commerce Act of 1887, Omnibus Statehood bill of 1889, Sherman Antitrust Act, McKinley Tariff, Sherman Silver Purchase Act, and Dependent Pension Act of 1890—marked the rise of party discipline and institutional efficiency. So too—in a negative way—did the ability of the congressional leadership to restrict the number of bills enacted into law. Twenty-two percent of the acts proposed in the 1860s were passed; 10 percent in the 1870s and 1880s; 7 percent in the 1890s.[28]

It is instructive to compare the late nineteenth century Congress to Parliament. Debate still was central to parliamentary procedure. Commons membership was more stable: the fact that one-third of the 1885 Parliament had not sat in 1880 attracted wide attention. Parliamentary committees were fewer and more broadly charged; most statutes were drafted by specialists in the Treasury. It seemed to James Bryce that the legislative competence of Congress was

27. Reed quoted in Luce, *Legislative Assemblies*, 202–205. See also C. H. Rammelkamp, "Contested Congressional Elections," *PSQ*, 20 (1905), 421–442; Chester H. Rowell, *A Historical and Legal Digest of all the Contested Election Cases in the House of Representatives of the United States* (Washington, 1901), U.S., 56th Cong., 2d sess., House, Doc. no. 510; Thomas B. Reed, "Contested Elections," *NAR*, 151 (1890), 112–120; Hinds, *Precedents*, I–II, chs. 21–40.

28. Wilson, *Congressional Government*, 79–80; Rothman, *Politics and Power*, ch. 3; *HS*, 690. See also Thomas A. Bailey, "Party Irregularity in the Senate of the United States, 1869–1901," *SPSQ*, 11 (1930–1931), 355–376.

"incomparably smaller" than that of Parliament. Most American public and private laws, he observed, were passed by state legislatures. Critics of Congress looked admiringly at what they imagined to be the more elevated tone of parliamentary debate, at the expert draftsmanship of public acts, and at the practice of treating private or local bills more like petitions to a court than as pieces of legislation to be lobbied through.

These differences underlined the fact that Congress, for all its internal rationalization, still was strongly affected by the intense political localism of nineteenth century America. Bryce was struck by its relative weakness when compared to European legislatures: "Congress does not guide and illuminate its constituents. It is amorphous, and has little initiative." The reason, he thought, was that Americans had little need or desire for national leadership: "People are contented if things go on fairly well as they are."[29]

The Federal Branch

The federal bureaucracy also had to respond to changing conditions in American life, while remaining under the sway of old assumptions as to the role of government. Patterns of revenue and expenditure reflected this tension. The national government's Civil War period income peaked at $558 million in 1866. Then it declined to a low of $257 million in 1878; after that it gradually rose again to $567 million in 1900. As in the past, customs duties accounted for the major share of federal revenue: 56 percent in 1880, 57 percent in 1890, 41 percent in 1900. (In free-trade Great Britain, the comparable figures were 26 percent in 1880, 21 percent in 1890, and 18 percent in 1900.) Excise taxes, which constituted about 30 percent of British national revenue through the late nineteenth century, provided an increasing share of United States government income: 34 percent in 1880, 35 percent in 1890, 43 percent in 1900. Levies on whiskey and tobacco made up most of this total, not only

29. Bryce, *American Commonwealth*, I, 136; Simon Sterne, "The Prevention of Defective and Slipshod Legislation," *ABA Reports*, 7 (1884), 275–301; for comparisons see *NAR*, 158 (1894), 257–269, 159 (1894), 225–311, 161 (1895), 740–765, 162 (1896), 14–20; Bryce, *American Commonwealth*, I, 304, 309. See also Simon Sterne, *The English Methods of Legislation Compared with the American* (Philadelphia, 1879).

because they were widely consumed commodities, but also because their morally questionable character made them especially vulnerable to taxation.[30]

Other sources of revenue were more problematical. Death, property, and income taxes made up 20 percent of British government income in 1880, 29 percent in 1900. But in America these were nominal or nonexistent. An income tax was the most obvious alternative to customs and excise duties, but it encountered fierce resistance. The Civil War income tax was abolished in the early 1870s, to almost universal acclaim. A number of proposals to reinstate the tax soon came before Congress, primarily from midwestern and southern Democrats seeking an alternative source of revenue that would weaken the case for a high tariff. Pressure for an income tax came to a head in the early 1890s. For years, tariff duties had produced an annual revenue surplus; public opinion was increasingly disturbed by what seemed to be growing inequities of wealth and taxation; and hard times began in 1893. Congress in 1894 passed an income tax provision as part of a tariff bill designed to reduce customs duties. Proponents of the tax dwelt on its greater fairness, and occasionally on its utility as a means of securing a more equitable distribution of wealth. But the prevailing assumption was that its revenue would replace existing levies (particularly customs duties) rather than serve as the basis for an expansion of government services.[31]

The tax itself—a 2 percent levy on (self-declared) incomes over $4,000—hardly was confiscatory. Nevertheless, it stoked the already active social fears of the comfortable and the conservative. These anxieties found voice in the Supreme Court's Pollack v. Farmers' Loan and Trust decision (1895), which held the tax to be unconstitutional. Justice Stephen J. Field wrote in his concurring opinion: "The present assault on capital is but the beginning. It will be but the stepping-stone to others, larger and more sweeping, till our political contests will become a war of the poor against the rich; a war constantly growing in intensity and bitterness." Justice

30. Data and percentage computations from HS, 711–713, BHS, 393–394.
31. Sidney Ratner, American Taxation (New York, 1942), 148 ff; Edwin R. A. Seligman, "The Income Tax," PSQ, 9 (1894), 610–648; George Tunnell, "The Legislative History of the Second Income-Tax Law," JPE, 3 (1895), 311–337; Charles F. Dunbar, "The New Income Tax," QJE, 9 (1894), 26–46. See also Elmer Ellis, "Public Opinion and the Income Tax, 1860–1900," MVHR, 27 (1940), 227–235.

John M. Harlan, one of the dissenters, observed that Field "has often acted like a mad man during the whole of this contest about the income tax."

The national government continued to come under pressure to extract levies from the growing pools of wealth created by a changing economy. Spanish-American War taxes on boards of trade and other exchanges, on stock sales, and on inheritances were upheld by the Supreme Court. But federal revenue in the early twentieth century did not keep pace with economic growth, and not until the Sixteenth Amendment (1913) legitimized the income tax and the United States entered the First World War did its size and character substantially change.[32]

Expenditure, too, was caught up in the conflict between old values and new needs. Late nineteenth century government spending grew sharply: from a prewar average of $60 million a year in the 1850s to $270 million annually in the 1870s and over $400 million in the 1890s. Federal expenditure between 1885 and 1898 increased relative to prices and population; from 1878 to 1908 it rose by 400 percent, while the population rose 84 percent.

In part these outlays met the continuing costs of the Civil War. Veterans' expenditures and debt servicing together accounted for 57 percent of federal spending in 1880, 45 percent in 1890, and 35 percent in 1900. The net effect was an expenditure pattern not unlike that of Great Britain. Federal spending for purposes other than the military, veterans, and the debt averaged about 30 percent of the budget in the late nineteenth century; comparable British expenditures were about 35 percent of that country's total.[33]

But important national differences lay below the surface. The

32. Field in Pollock v. Farmers' Loan and Trust Company, 157 U.S. 429, 607 (1895); David G. Farrelly, "Harlan's Dissent in the Pollock Case," SCLR, 24 (1951), 179; Nicol v. Ames, 173 U.S. 509 (1899); Thomas v. U.S., 192 U.S. 363 (1904); Knowlton v. Moore, 178 U.S. 41 (1900). See also William H. Dunbar, "The Constitutionality of the United States Inheritance Tax," QJE, 15 (1901), 292–298; Loren P. Beth, The Development of the American Constitution 1877–1917 (New York, 1971), 157–159.

33. Data and percentage computations from HS, 718; M. Slade Kendrick, A Century and a Half of Federal Expenditures (New York, 1955), 8; Henry J. Ford, The Cost of our National Government: A Study in Political Pathology (New York, 1910); BHS, 396–397. British defense and social expenditure sharply rose from 1870 to 1890: Henry Roseveare, The Treasury: The Evolution of a British Institution (New York, 1969), 188.

major fiscal problem facing the federal government, as James Bryce noted, was not raising but spending its revenue. Rising national wealth and the protective tariff produced a surplus every year from 1866 to 1893. The annual average during the 1880s was $100 million. The need to protect the tariff by spending off the surplus and the use of federal funds to help finance a costly system of party politics, rather than any new view of the purposes of government, were the prime determinants of late nineteenth century federal expenditure.[34]

The central role of party politics and patronage may be seen in the most costly government agencies of the time, the Post Office Department and the Bureau of Pensions. The Post Office employed 56,421 people—56 percent of the federal workforce—in 1881; 95,449 (61 percent) in 1891; 136,192 (57 percent) in 1901. In part this growth was a response to the rising postal needs of the nation: 3.7 billion pieces of mail were handled in 1886, 7.1 billion in 1900. Special delivery service began in 1885, rural free delivery and parcel post came to be widespread in the 1890s. But the needs of an elaborate and expensive party system also were served. Postmasterships were patronage appointments, and post offices—there were 42,989 of them in 1880, 62,401 in 1890, 76,688 in 1900—were "centres of political activity." In many rural areas there was one fourth class postmaster for every hundred voters. Republican politician James Tyner thought that the Post Office was second only to the Treasury in political importance: "It is the keeper of Administration politics," with its scores of thousands of appointees "scattered everywhere, the walking representatives of the dominant party constantly within the gaze of the people."

When administrations changed, so did this army of party workers. Some 40,000 postmasters were replaced during Grover Cleveland's first term by "Headsman" Adlai E. Stevenson, the first assistant postmaster general. But the frequent turnovers in national party control also fostered the inclusion of Post Office jobs in the civil service classified list. Each outgoing administration sought thereby to protect some of its placeholders. And as the volume of mail increased, adequate mail service came to have greater political importance than the department's patronage function. An 1891

34. Bryce, *American Commonwealth*, I, 182; *HS*, 712, 710.

reorganization made patronage appointments the concern not of the first but the fourth assistant postmaster general, and small post offices were steadily merged into larger—and hence more business-like, less purely political—units. A number of smaller postmaster-ships came under civil service rules in 1895.[35]

The Bureau of Pensions was the most uncompromisingly politi-cal branch of the late nineteenth century federal bureaucracy. Veterans' pensions consumed 21 percent of the federal budget in 1880, 34 percent in 1890, 27 percent in 1900. They were granted not by an administrative agency but by special acts of Congress. In the 49th Congress (1885–1887), 40 percent of the legislation in the House and 55 percent in the Senate consisted of special pension acts. It was customary for Friday evening to be "pension night" during congressional sessions. More than a third of the northern and border state congressmen were Union army veterans; and the Grand Army of the Republic, the leading veterans' organization, steadily grew in membership—from 60,678 in 1880 to 269,689 in 1885 and 427,981 in 1890—and political influence.

The Pension Act of 1890 made almost every northern Civil War veteran and his dependents eligible. By 1900, 753,000 veterans (75 percent of the total) and 241,000 dependents were receiving pen-sions. The Pension Office in 1891 had 6,241 employees. Com-missioner Green B. Raum, typical of the party stalwarts who supervised the system, called it "the largest executive bureau in the world." An extensive infrastructure of pension and claim agents, pension attorneys (an estimated 60,000 by 1898), medical boards, and 4,000 examining surgeons served this first large-scale federal welfare system. Attorney George E. Lemon, who edited the GAR newspaper, represented over 8,000 pension claimants for fees totaling about $100,000.

As in the case of the Post Office, the intensely political character of the Pension Bureau lessened at the turn of the century. The extravagance of the Pension commissioners—one of them was

35. HS, 496–497; Dorothy G. Fowler, The Cabinet Politician: The Post-masters General 1829–1909 (New York, 1943), 192, 204; Tyner quoted in Edward Younger, John A. Kasson (Iowa City, 1955), 282; on Stevenson, Joseph L. Bristow, Fraud and Politics at the Turn of the Century (New York, 1952), 42. See also John R. Procter, "The Emancipation of the Post Office," AM, 77 (1896), 95–97.

James Tanner, a legless veteran, GAR leader, and Washington lobbyist who roundly proclaimed "God save the surplus"—made the bureau as much a liability as an asset to the Republican cause. When the hard times of the 1890s produced annual federal deficits rather than surpluses, the importance of pension expenditures as a prop to the tariff declined. And of course the inexorable facts of the mortality table began to take their toll. In 1897 President McKinley found it prudent to appoint a commissioner who made the bureau a less political—and more efficient—government agency.[36]

The structure of the federal bureaucracy changed little in the late nineteenth century. A handful of new units came into existence between 1880 and 1900: some specialized bureaus in the Department of Agriculture; the Bureau of Labor (1884); and the Civil Service (1883) and Interstate Commerce (1887) Commissions. Set against the transformation of American economic and social life that went on during these decades, this was a minimal response.

Alterations in the conduct of government business also were minor and gradual. A budget for the executive branch came into use in 1882; the 1890 Census pioneered in the use of Hollerith machines to sort and tabulate data, thereby speeding computation and making possible a wider range of statistical correlations. From 1887 to 1889 the Senate's Cockrell Committee conducted the first substantial congressional inquiry into the administration of the federal bureaucracy. The committee was created in response to a flood of complaints over delays in the Pension, Land, and Post Offices: symptoms of the discordance between a static bureaucracy and a growing society. But ex-Confederate Francis M. Cockrell, a senator from Missouri, hardly was one to spark the modernization of the federal government. His committee's report dwelt on the need for more efficient work procedures, the adoption of better

36. *HS*, 741; Raum quoted in White, *Republican Era*, 211. See also Donald L. McMurry, "The Political Significance of the Pension Question, 1885–1897," *MVHR*, 9 (1922–1923), 19–36, "The Bureau of Pensions during the Administration of President Harrison," *MVHR*, 13 (1926–1927), 343–364; William Barlow, "U.S. Commissioner of Pensions Green B. Raum of Illinois," *ISHS Journal*, 60 (1967), 293–312; Mary R. Dearing, *Veterans in Politics: The Story of the G.A.R.* (Baton Rouge, 1952).

bookkeeping methods, and greater economy. Another Senate inquiry in 1893, headed by Missouri Democrat Alexander M. Dockery, again contented itself with palliative proposals for better accounting and bookkeeping.[37]

The major change in federal personnel policy during these years was the growth in the number of positions under civil service rules following the passage of the Pendleton Act of 1883: 13,789 in 1884; 30,626 in 1890; 94,893 in 1900. And the appearance of more technically demanding divisions of government increased the number of skilled civil servants such as Carroll Wright of the Bureau of Labor, the scientists who served in the various divisions of the Department of Agriculture, Edward Moseley, the first secretary of the Interstate Commerce Commission, and the economist Henry C. Adams, who was the commission's chief statistician.[38]

But this still was far from being the professional civil service bureaucracy of Wilhelmine Germany or Victorian England. The growing number of federal positions under civil service rules was the product not so much of a rising bureaucratic *esprit* as of frequent changes of national party control—in 1885, 1889, 1893, 1897—that led outgoing administrations to give some of their officeholders the protection of civil service status. And the social character of government in the United States sharply differed from its European counterparts. For all their surface similarities, the civil service reform movements in England and America had very different targets. The Northcote-Trevelyan Report of 1854, which opened the British civil service to entry through competitive examination, was an assault on the corruption and inefficiency of a gentry-dominated system of patronage. American civil service reform aimed at the excesses of democracy, not aristocracy. It sought to get rid of uneducated placeholders with party connec-

37. "Administrative Procedures in Government Agencies," U.S., 77th Cong., 1st sess., Senate, Doc. no. 8 (Washington, 1941), 9; Carpenter, *Carp's Washington*, 123–124; on Hollerith, Daniel J. Boorstin, *The Americans: The National Experience* (New York, 1973), 172, and William R. Merriam, "The Census of 1900," *NAR*, 170 (1900), 99–108; Oscar Kraines, "The Cockrell Committee 1887–1889: The First Comprehensive Congressional Investigation into Administration," *WPQ*, 4 (1951), 583–609; White, *Republican Era*, 87–90.

38. *HS*, 710; White, *Republican Era*, chs. 14–16; Carl R. Fish, *The Civil Service and the Patronage* (New York, 1905), ch. 9.

tions. If English civil service reform seemed to succeed, this was because it coincided with the growing political power of that country's middle class. Its American counterpart had less impact on the character of government because it went against the grain of popular distrust of apolitical bureaucratic experts and the growing power of the party machines.[39]

In theory, the social and economic changes of the late nineteenth century should have had their greatest impact on the Departments of Agriculture and Labor (both raised to that status in 1889), the Interior Department, and the Department of the Treasury. But the ambivalent attitude toward government that was so pervasive in American life kept these from becoming important instruments of an active national state.

By the end of the century the Department of Agriculture had a number of new, specialized divisions: Forestry (1880), Animal Husbandry (1884), Entomology (1885), Pomology (1886), Ornithology and Mammalogy (1887), the Office of Experiment Stations (1887), the Weather Bureau (1890), Plant Industry (1901). A series of strong secretaries of agriculture from 1889 to 1913—Jeremiah Rusk, J. Sterling Morton, James Wilson—made the department a powerful force in the federal bureaucracy. And an agricultural establishment consisting of the department, land grant colleges, and agricultural experiment stations took form during those years.

But bureaucratic incompetence, internal rivalries, and a research and development emphasis on exotic rather than staple products limited the department's influence on late nineteenth century American agriculture. It ignored the increasingly important problems of crop prices, land ownership, tenantry, and farm laborers. The modes of agricultural production, and the lives of the people who worked the farms, were not substantially affected by this agency of government.[40]

39. Jenifer Hart, "The Genesis of the Northcote-Trevelyan Report," in Gillian Sutherland, ed., *Studies in the Growth of Nineteenth-Century Government* (London, 1972), 63–81; Ari Hoogenboom, *Outlawing the Spoils: A History of the Civil Service Reform Movement 1865–1883* (Urbana, 1961).

40. On Agriculture bureaus, Lloyd M. Short, *The Development of National Administrative Organization in the United States* (Baltimore, 1923), 381–386; White, *Republican Era*, 232–256; E. D. Ross, "The United States

Labor, a branch of the Interior Department from 1884 until it became a (noncabinet) department in its own right in 1888, remained little more than a data-collecting office. There was strong and persistent opposition to the idea that workers should be recognized as a distinct interest group. Congress in 1903 ignored the wishes of most labor unions and merged the Labor Department into a new cabinet Department of Commerce and Labor: an implementation of the view that no profound conflict of interest separated labor from business.

Interior continued to be the government's "Great Miscellany," in 1900 a grab-bag of more than twenty agencies, including Indian Affairs, Education, the Pension Office, the Land Office, the Census, the Geological Survey, and the Commissioner of Railroads. A familiar bureaucratic pattern prevailed in the department: stagnation, inefficiency, occasional corruption, an inability to cope with rising levels of work. The Land Office in 1883 reported a three-year backlog of 600,000 claims not acted upon. By the late 1880s some improvement had occurred. But there were still 275,000 claims pending and 39,554 unresolved cases before the Land Office's Board of Review.

At a time when British imperial administration reached the peak of its power, the grasp of the Interior Department—and of the federal government—over its territories was slack indeed. The Harrison Act of 1886 did set limits on territorial indebtedness, and some constraints were placed on territorial courts and legislatures. But aside from a strong campaign against polygamy in Utah and Idaho, and of course the Indian reservation policy, federal administration of the territories was minimal. Policy was colored by the assumption that these lands (save Alaska) soon would be coequal states of the Union. In 1889 and 1890, when the Republicans held the presidency and both Houses of Congress for the first time since 1883, Washington, Montana, North and South Dakota, Idaho, and Wyoming were admitted into the Union. Democratic Arizona and New Mexico had to wait for a more favorable political climate, which came when the Democrats gained control of the House in 1910.

Department of Agriculture during the Commissionership: A Study in Politics, Administration, and Technology, 1862–1889," AH, 20 (1946), 129–143.

An important change in territorial policy occurred at the turn of the century, when the noncontiguous territories of Puerto Rico and the Philippines came under American control. A system of territorial administration took form in the early twentieth century designed to deal with large, settled populations not thought of as future members of an American state: one among many indicators of a change in the character of the American polity after 1900.[41]

A number of the most consequential affairs of the federal government—banking, taxation, currency, customs, immigration— were under the wing of the Treasury. Its personnel increased from 4,000 in 1873 to almost 25,000 by the end of the century. Like the Land Office the Treasury piled up huge backlogs of unprocessed paper, and pressure mounted for greater efficiency. Double entry replaced single entry bookkeeping in Treasury accounts in 1894. And the customs houses in New York and elsewhere, traditional centers of political jobholders, came substantially under the civil service merit and tenure system by the end of the century. The need for more efficient processing of American international trade made the change desirable; and the declining political importance of customs house rings made it possible. The customs houses underwent changes similar to those that occurred in the postal and pension services.

But for all the intrinsic importance of its business, the American Treasury did not match the power of its British counterpart. Unlike the latter, it did not control the budget estimates of other government agencies, or check on their administration. The influence of the British Treasury stemmed in part from the need to keep tight controls on national spending in order to fend off pressure for a revenue-producing tariff. The situation was quite the reverse in the late nineteenth century United States. There the need to dispose of surplus federal revenue in order to preserve the

41. On Labor, Short, *Development*, 397–405; on Interior, White, *Republican Era*, 175–195, 201–202; William M. Neil, "The American Territorial System since the Civil War: A Summary Analysis," *IMH*, 60 (1964), 219–240; Earl S. Pomeroy, *The Territories and the United States, 1861–1890: Studies in Colonial Administration* (Philadelphia, 1947); Jack E. Eblen, *The First and Second United States Empires: Governors and Territorial Government, 1784–1912* (Pittsburgh, 1968); Frederick L. Paxson, "The Admission of the 'Omnibus' States, 1889–90," *WSHS Proceedings* (1911), 77–96.

protective tariff system fostered slack accounting and oversight. Then too, the British Treasury had traditions of elitism and continuity of personnel that no American government department could hope to match.[42]

Although the State, War, and Navy Departments moved into a palatial new building around 1880, they remained weak, thinly staffed, relatively inconsequential agencies of government until the last years of the nineteenth century. Again, the contrast with their British counterparts, who were charged with the responsibilities of empire, was dramatic. The major activity of the War Department was to tame and police the Indians of the West. The Spanish-American War in 1898 suddenly and vastly expanded the department's functions, and revealed the dry rot that had accumulated over the years. An investigation led to the departure of Secretary of War Russell A. Alger in 1899. Elihu Root took over and began a process of reorganization, including the creation of an army general staff, that belongs in time and spirit to the administrative history of the twentieth century.[43]

The late nineteenth century Navy Department showed more vigor. American commercial interests made heavier demands on its services, and naval technology was more costly and innovative than that of the army. William E. Chandler, the Republican secretary of the navy from 1881 to 1885, and his Democratic successor William C. Whitney (1885–1889) had much in common. Both were well-connected party politicians; both were responsive to a changing naval technology and to the political and economic benefits that accrued from contracts for armor plate, naval cannon, and warships. Benjamin F. Tracy, secretary of the navy from 1889 to 1893, established a Board of Construction to coordinate the work of the department's various bureaus and began to build the fleet that performed with such spectacular success in the Spanish-American War.[44]

---

42. White, *Republican Era*, 110–133; Roseveare, *Treasury*, chs. 6–7; Maurice Wright, *Treasury Control of the Civil Service* (Oxford, 1969), 329–330.

43. White, *Republican Era*, 134–153; Edward Ranson, "The Investigation of the War Department, 1898–1899," *Hist*, 34 (1971), 78–99; Richard E. Leopold, *Elihu Root and the Conservative Tradition* (Boston, 1954), ch. 2.

44. White, *Republican Era*, 154–174; Leon B. Richardson, *William E.*

Between Hamilton Fish's reorganization of the Department of State in 1870 and Elihu Root's reorganization in 1909, there was little change in the foreign affairs branch of the government. A knowledgeable politician summed up the prerequisites for a secretary of state in 1888:

> Any man well up in social etiquette, with capacity to employ diplomatic language (which means high sounding language full of polite expressions), with enough judgment to consult the President and Secretary of the Treasury about any commercial questions that may arise, and with an ample fortune to furnish terrapin and champaign [sic] at diplomatic dinners, will answer our purposes. That Department is the dress parade part of the Government.

American foreign affairs sharply increased in scale and complexity around the turn of the century. But the structure of the department did not change accordingly. When Root became secretary of state in 1905, he complained that "he was like a man trying to conduct the business of a large metropolitan law-firm in the office of a village squire." It is sufficient commentary that Second Assistant Secretary of State Alvey A. Adee all but ran the operations of the department through the late nineteenth century.[45]

A number of factors worked against the modernization of American government. These included the established traditions of laissez-faire and localism; the pressure to distribute a persisting revenue surplus quickly and to partisan political advantage; the bias against rule by elites; above all, the lack of any broad conception as to what the central government might *do*, save collect taxes, provide patronage, guard the coasts, fight Indians, and preserve order. It is revealing that while a substantial historical literature has explored the intellectual origins, structure, and functions of public administration in Victorian Britain, no comparable body of American historical writing exists.[46]

Chandler (New York, 1940), chs. 14–15; Mark D. Hirsch, *William C. Whitney* (New York, 1948), ch. 11; John K. Mahon, "Benjamin Franklin Tracy, Secretary of the Navy, 1889–1903," NYHQ, 44 (1960), 179–202.

45. James Tyner quoted in Younger, *Kasson*, 281; Short, *Development*, 225 ff, 230.

46. Gillian Sutherland, "Recent Trends in Administrative History," VS, 13 (1970), 408–411, and Roy M. MacLeod, "Statesmen Undisguised," AHR, 78 (1973), 1386–1405, review the literature.

The States

Late nineteenth century state no less than federal authority felt the tension between established views of governance and the demands of a changing society. The depression of the 1870s put a stop to the state activism of the post-Civil War years. Old traditions of localism, individualism, and hostility to government reasserted themselves. The economist Henry C. Adams observed in 1887: "The corporations rose upon the ruins of the States as centers of industrial administration."[47]

But beneath its surface desuetude, state government was beginning to respond to the new conditions of American life. A growing body of social and economic legislation and the beginnings of new fiscal and taxation policies laid the groundwork for the notable expansion of state government that occurred in the early twentieth century.

The American habit of state constitution writing and amending continued unabated in the late nineteenth century. There were twenty-eight constitutional conventions in seventeen states during the decade from 1877 to 1887. Between 1874 and 1902, the ten Confederate states of the South replaced their Reconstruction charters; and the six western states admitted in 1889 and 1890 (plus Utah in 1896 and Oklahoma in 1907) entered with new constitutions. Substantial revisions of existing documents occurred in New Hampshire (1876, 1889, 1903) and New York (1894).[48]

The general tendency of this constitutional creation and revision was to crimp the lawmaking power of state legislatures. The "keynote" of Oklahoma's constitution was "distrust in the legislature." An observer noted in 1897: "the passionate desire of an American democracy to control and limit public government, at the present day, is in strong contrast with the deferential and implicit confidence which the common people reposed in their representatives, those especially of their legislatures, a century ago."

47. Henry C. Adams, *Public Debts: An Essay in the Science of Finance* (New York, 1887), 393.

48. Henry Hitchcock, *American State Constitutions: A Study of their Growth* (New York, 1887), 14; James Q. Dealey, *American State Constitutions* (Philadelphia, 1907), 89. See also Bryce, *American Commonwealth*, I, 427 ff.

Shorter legislative sessions (usually sixty days or less) that met biennially rather than annually; the enumeration of dozens of categories in which legislatures were prohibited from passing special or local acts; proscriptive, codelike constitutions (the Louisiana document of 1908 had 45,000 words); a strengthened executive veto power (by the early 1900s, only North Carolina and Rhode Island denied that privilege to their governors); a larger role for the courts: these were among the ways in which the legislatures were contained.[49]

Hostility to active government appeared also in the frequent defeat of proposed constitutional ·revisions. Six revised charters were rejected by popular vote between 1877 and 1887. A new Rhode Island constitution failed in 1898 and 1899, a new Connecticut charter in 1902 and 1907. An 1891 proposal for a constitutional convention in Pennsylvania lost by a popular margin of 2½ to 1; a similar proposition narrowly lost in Kansas in 1892. Oregon's governor saw no need for constitutional revision in 1886: "We have a safe conservative Constitution now, and the necessary changes, if any, can be made by the slower and better way—that of legislative suggestion." But amendments also met with frequent opposition. Between 1880 and 1897, 486 amendments to the 1879 California constitution were introduced; 35 were passed by the legislature and submitted to popular referenda; 17 were adopted.[50]

We know relatively little about the structure and makeup of state legislatures in this period. The Massachusetts legislature was

49. John B. Sanborn, "The Oklahoma Constitution," *ALR*, 42 1908), 368; James Schouler, *Constitutional Studies, State and Federal* (New York, 1897), 209–210; on legislative sessions, *ABA Reports*, 13 (1890), 213; Charles C. Binney, *Restrictions upon Local and Special Legislation in State Constitutions* (Philadelphia, 1904), 130 ff. See also E. Benjamin Andrews, *The History of the Last Quarter-Century in the United States* (New York, 1896), II, 146–148; A. O. Wright, *American Constitutions* (Madison, 1888), 161 ff; Horace Davis, *American Constitutions* (San Francisco, 1884), 79–82, for tables on state executive, legislative, and judicial terms and powers.

50. Hitchcock, *Constitutions*, 14; Dealey, *Constitutions*, 13; "Pennsylvania," *AC* (1891); "Kansas," *AC* (1892); "Oregon," *AC* (1886); Samuel E. Moffett, "The Constitutional Referendum in California," *PSQ*, 13 (1898), 13. See Edward McPherson, *Hand-Book of Politics* (1872–1894; New York, 1972), passim, for the texts of a number of these amendments.

dominated by farmers and lawyers. In 1891, 20 percent of the Assembly and 3 percent of the Senate was foreign-born, as compared to about 29 percent of the Commonwealth's population. Membership turned over at a very high rate. Only four participants in the 1896 Massachusetts legislature were there in 1889, and none had served throughout that period. Reelections of Connecticut legislators declined from 26 percent in 1820 to 10 percent in 1870 and 2.8 percent in 1897. The tendency of voters and party organizations was to regard a term in the legislature as a perquisite to be as widely shared as possible. While the influence of legislative lobbies was pervasive, and corruption was common, party discipline was slack. State legislation—the bulk of it local and particular —did not often encourage divisions along party lines. As Bryce said of the legislatures: "The spirit of localism ... completely rules them."[51]

Despite these restraints, late nineteenth century state legislatures passed an increasing number of laws that touched on important areas of American social and economic life. A review of Massachusetts legislation from 1878 to 1888 concluded: "The state is continually extending its sphere of action and shows no sign of a change in its policy." One measure of the scale and significance of this legislation was the growing number of publications that annually surveyed it. These included a number of state bar association journals and the annual address of the president of the American Bar Association; the *Quarterly Journal of Economics* and the *Economic Review*; and from 1890 on, the New York State Library's comprehensive *Index to Legislation*.

In 1901 the state legislatures passed 13,854 laws, 5,318 of them general and the remainder private or local bills. Enacted laws were only a small proportion of those that were introduced. The 1881 California legislature passed 50 of the 800 bills that came

51. F. H. Howland, "Nativity and Occupation of Members of the Massachusetts Legislature," *ASA Publications*, ns, 4 (1894–1895), 15–19; on turnover, Francis C. Lowell, "Legislative Shortcomings," *AM*, 79 (1897), 367, Clarence Deming, "Town Rule in Connecticut," *PSQ*, 4 (1889), 426; on party discipline, Lowell, "Shortcomings," 367, Robert Luce, *Legislative Procedure* (Boston, 1922), 492–493, Lowell, "Influence of Party"; Bryce, *American Commonwealth*, I, 544.

before it. In Alabama the figure was 350 of 1,456; 1,003 of the 2,992 acts proposed in the 1896 New York legislature became law.[52]

American Bar Association president Moorfield Storey characterized the state legislation of 1896 as "the refinement of civilization" rather than an effort to deal with "fundamental questions of government." He concluded that in the American states "the essential principles are settled; the general scheme is complete." And indeed, in their number and specificity state statutes (like the state constitutions of the time) had a distinctly administrative quality.

But the needs of an increasingly complex society required something more than administration by statute. In some states—New York, Ohio, Michigan, and Massachusetts among them—there was a tendency to centralize the administration of education, public health, charity and corrections, and taxation and local finance. State auditors had growing authority in tax matters. Secretaries of state took over corporation chartering after the passage of general incorporation acts; land commissioners had more to say in land title issues; the courts assumed an ever larger supervisory role. Massachusetts led in the development of more active state government. In 1885 it created a state civil service commission, and within a year almost 6,000 of the commonwealth's employees were on the classified list. For the most part, however, late nineteenth century administration (such as it was) remained in the hands of county and local authorities. The traditional decentralized structure of American government proved to have enormous staying power.[53]

Fiscal policy on the state as on the national level was profoundly influenced by the needs of party politics. The parties counted on government revenue and expenditure to sustain their increasingly

52. Raymond L. Bridgman, *Ten Years of Massachusetts* (Boston, 1888), 6–7; 1901 estimate in James Q. Dealey, *Our State Constitutions* (Philadelphia, 1907), 52; "California," *AC* (1881); "Alabama," *AC* (1881); "New York," *AC* (1896). See also F. J. Stimson, *American Statute Law* (Boston, 1886); Bryce, *American Commonwealth*, I, 545.

53. Storey, "Address of the President," *ABA Reports*, 19 (1896), 180; Goodnow, *Politics and Administration*, 122–123, 126; Bryce, *American Commonwealth*, I, 460; John A. Fairlie, *The Centralization of Administration in New York State* (New York, 1898); Robert H. Whitten, *Public*

expensive machines. And the traditional demands of pork barrel and patronage were supplemented now by the growing public (and hence political) call for expanded public services to meet the needs of an urban-industrial society. But against these spurs to increased getting and spending must be set a general public hostility to taxation and expenditure.

The result was a hodgepodge of extravagance and parsimony that came under increasing attack toward the end of the century. Criticism dwelt on the unsystematic and irrational way in which taxes were levied and collected and on the waste and corruption that so often went with government expenditure. In particular, holders of real property became more and more restive under a property tax that heavily weighed on them.

That tax was by far the most important source of state revenue, producing about 65 percent of the commonwealths' tax receipts in the late 1880s. But while the tax rate remained stable—averaging 72¢ per $100 of the estimated true value of property in 1880, and 74¢ per $100 in 1900—the character (and concealability) of property itself changed. Bonds, stocks, bank and vault deposits, mortgages, and notes gained in value as against more visible assets such as buildings, crops, animals, and personal possessions.

The consequence was a sharp growth in evasion and inequity. Those whose property was readily assessable—farmers, home-owners, storekeepers—paid an undue proportion of state revenues. In Pennsylvania and Massachusetts, railroad, bank, and insurance taxes provided substantial state income. But in general the less visible forms of property massively evaded taxation. One estimate is that about 75 percent of the true value of realty was assessed; when all other forms of property are added, the figure drops to 40 percent.[54]

Administration in Massachusetts: The Relation of Central to Local Authority (New York, 1898); Samuel P. Orth, *The Centralization of Administration in Ohio* (New York, 1903); on limits, Ernest S. Griffith, *The Modern Development of City Government in the United Kingdom and the United States* (Oxford, 1927), I, 91n.

54. Clifton K. Yearley, *The Money Machines: The Breakdown and Reform of Governmental and Party Finance in the North, 1860–1920* (Albany, 1970); Carl C. Plehn, "Revenue Systems of the State and Local Governments," in U.S., Department of Commerce and Labor, Special Reports of the Census, *Wealth, Debt, and Taxation* (Washington, 1907), 850, 829, 845. See also Bryce, *American Commonwealth*, I, 512 ff.

Evasion reached levels that would have done credit to a French peasant village. A "desolating wave of poverty" swept over Ohio at assessment time. About one-third as much personal as real property appeared on the assessors' books, when the true order of value probably was the reverse. Nebraska's governor estimated in 1888 that property was assessed at a tenth of its real value. Some states and cities, if their assessments were to be believed, were in economic decline. New York's personal property was valued at $452 million in 1871 and $411 million in 1893. California's figures were $220 million in 1872, $174 million in 1880, and $164 million in 1887. New York City in 1875 had more than a million people, but only 8,900 admitted to owning taxable goods; personal property was assessed at $118,602 in 1863 and $346,611 in 1888. It appeared that Kansas's Rawlins County had no silver plate or jewelry in 1898. The residents of Stevens County had only $20 in cash; Haskell County could claim only three gold and five silver watches, and no piano.[55]

Despite this evasion, taxes were assessed and collected through a complex and highly structured system. Assessors were appointed or elected at the township or county level. County boards of review or equalization and state boards of assessment set or adjusted tax rates. State tax commissioners and boards of equalization were charged to ensure equitable taxation. State corporation taxes, light and spotty as they were, had thirteen different bases of valuation by 1890, including the cost or value of corporate property, the par or market value of corporate stock, and company earnings. License and occupation taxes produced in sum only about $750,000 in the late 1880s. But they too were highly diverse—and specific—in character. Thus Tennessee in 1893 levied a "privilege tax" on dozens of specific occupations, ranging from artists and architects to feather renovators and tombstone dealers.

Corporate interests frequently avoided paying their due share of taxes—or, occasionally, paid more than their portion. An 1880

---

55. On Ohio, Yearley, Money Machines, 46; "Nebraska," AC (1888); on New York and California, Frederic C. Howe, "Some Possible Reforms in State and Local Taxation," ALR, 33 (1899), 700, Edwin R. A. Seligman, "The General Property Tax," PSQ, 5 (1890), 28; on New York City, Yearley, Money Machines, 42–43; Seligman, "General Property Tax," 28; "Kansas," AC (1898).

New York tax on life insurance companies was repealed in 1887, thereby taking an estimated $1,000,000 a year from the state treasury. Arkansas railroads in 1883 almost completely avoided taxation; New Jersey's lines were notorious for their underassessment and evasion. But in Kansas and Nebraska, railroad lands apparently were disproportionately taxed.[56]

The states turned to tax commissions (some forty of them in the post-Civil War years), boards of equalization, "back-tax commissioners" in a few southern states, and constant legislative tinkering in their efforts to make taxation more equitable and effective. Detailed, consolidated tax laws such as those of Indiana (1881) and Alabama (1882–1883) frequently were enacted. New York (1881) revised its laws to block evasion and define the taxable out-of-state property of domestic corporations. Illinois switched from quadrennial to annual real estate assessments; Indiana sought to close loopholes in property declarations and prohibit the common practice of transfering taxable bonds to a dummy purchaser on assessment day. In 1886 the governor of Illinois, noting a decline of $7,400,000 in property valuation from the preceding year, proposed a revenue code designed to relieve real estate and visible personal property and tap the growing hoard of "intangible and hidden wealth."[57]

But popular hostility to taxation and active government and the lack of effective administrative controls worked against these efforts. Ohio allowed counties and cities to engage "tax inquisitors" empowered to root out concealment (especially of stocks and bank deposits) for a percentage of the proceeds. Hamilton County (Cincinnati) hired Henry W. and C. E. Morgenthaler for this purpose in the early 1880s. But the brothers returned only $840,000 in a twelve-year period, and engaged in bribery and self-enrichment on a scale that made them and the inquisitor system objects of intense public hostility. There was a similar adverse reaction to 1898

56. Plehn, "Revenue Systems," 617 ff; Edwin R. A. Seligman, "The Taxation of Corporations," *PSQ*, 5 (1890), 467; *Acts of Tennessee*, 1893, ch. 89; *New York Laws* 1880, ch. 534, 1887, ch. 699–700; "Arkansas," *AC* (1883); Leslie E. Decker, *Railroads, Lands, and Politics: The Taxation of the Railroad Land Grants, 1864–1897* (Providence, 1964), 249.

57. Plehn, "Revenue Systems," 619; *Indiana Acts* 1881, ch. 96; *Alabama Laws* 1882–1883, no. 62; *New York Laws* 1881, ch. 361; *Laws of Illinois* 1881, pp. 132–136; "Illinois," *AC* (1886).

Virginia "landgrabber" acts designed to collect delinquent taxes by selling land. And always there was the pressure to economize by reducing government services and the taxes that supported them. Alabama's governor in 1882 recommended a lower tax rate; the governor of Maine in 1886 called for a 27 percent decrease in state taxation; New York's 1892 rate was the lowest since 1857.[58]

The conflict over state tax policy came to a head in the 1890s. An increasingly influential body of tax reformers argued for a system based on ability to pay, on the taxation of income more than of property, on progressive tax rates and equitable property assessment and valuation. Their cause was furthered by the economic depression of the nineties and a shrinkage of property values. An 1897 Georgia commission found that taxable values in 1896 were $51,000,000 less than they had been in 1891. Iowa's county auditors reported a heavy decline in taxable property during 1896. All but six of Kentucky's three hundred distilleries (an important revenue source) closed down for eighteen months in August 1896 because of market conditions.[59]

New forms of taxation came into use, and for the most part withstood the test of court review. There were exceptions: the Maryland Supreme Court quickly voided an 1892 law that allowed the town of Hyattsville to levy a single tax on unimproved land and end all other property levies; in 1899 the Pennsylvania Supreme Court found that state's inheritance tax unconstitutional. But the Michigan Supreme Court upheld a state mortgage tax, and in 1898 the United States Supreme Court did the same with an Illinois levy on inheritances. Between 1890 and 1900, eighteen states adopted inheritance taxes.[60]

Corporation levies produced less than a quarter of state income in 1887–1888, almost a third in 1902. In a series of cases stretching

58. E. A. Angell, "The Tax Inquisitor System in Ohio," YR, 5 (1896–1897), 350–373; T. N. Carver, "The Ohio Tax Inquisitor Law," AEA Studies, 3 (1898), 163–212; Yearley, Money Machines, 46–47; "Virginia," AC (1898), Christian v. Taylor, 96 Va. 503 (1898); AC, states and years cited.

59. Yearley, Money Machines, ch. 9; "Georgia," AC (1897); "Iowa," AC (1896); "Kentucky," AC (1896).

60. Wells v. Hyattsville, 77 Md. 125 (1893); Cope's Estate, 191 Pa. 34 (1899); Common Council v. Assessors, 91 Mich. 78 (1892); Magoun v. Illinois Trust and Savings Bank, 170 U.S. 283 (1898); Ratner, Taxation, 234 ff.

from the mid-seventies to the mid-nineties, the Supreme Court upheld a variety of state taxes on railroad, telegraph, express, and insurance companies. Justice Joseph Bradley, dissenting to one of these decisions in 1891, observed: "This court and some of the state courts have gone a great length in sustaining various forms of taxes upon corporations...I do not know that jealousy of corporate institutions could be carried much further...If the interstate commerce of the country is not, or will not be, handicapped by this course of decision, I do not understand the ordinary principles which govern human conduct." But his colleague David Brewer, normally accounted one of the more conservative members of the late nineteenth century Court, voiced the prevailing attitude toward corporate taxation:

> This is eminently a practical age;...courts must recognize things as they are and as possessing a value which is accorded to them in the markets of the world, and...no finespun theories about situs should interfere to enable these large corporations, whose business is carried on through so many states, to escape bearing in each State such burden of taxation as a fair distribution of the actual value of their property among those States requires.[61]

The conditions that determined state tax policy also affected the pattern of state expenditure. Here, too, the weight of traditional values and practices was substantial. Between a quarter and a third of all state funds went to support public schools in the late nineteenth century; 20–25 percent went for debt servicing; 15–20 percent for public welfare and protection; less than 10 percent for economic development. British local authorities made far smaller educational outlays—less than 10 percent of the total—but spent rapidly rising sums for other public services: 8 percent in 1880, 39 percent in 1890.

61. Seligman, "Taxation of Corporations," 269–308, 438–467, 636–675; State Railroad Tax Cases, 92 U.S. 575 (1875); Kentucky Railroad Tax Cases, 115 U.S. 321 (1885); Western Union Telegraph Company v. Massachusetts, 125 U.S. 533 (1888); Home Insurance Company v. New York, 134 U.S. 594 (1890); Bradley in Maine v. Grand Trunk Railway, 142 U.S. 217, 235 (1891), Brewer in Adams Express Company v. Ohio, 166 U.S. 185, 225 (1897). See also Howe, "Some Possible Reforms," 694–695, and George G. Tunnell, "The Taxation of Express, Telegraph, and Telephone Companies in Ohio," *JPE*, 5 (1897), 244–245.

While state expenditure fell into a few familiar categories, the pressures of diversity and localism created a structure of spending no less complex than the tax system. State funds were allocated under a number of special designations, such as the "strangulated counties fund" in Arkansas, the "revolving fund" in California, and the "literature fund" in New York. There were as many as forty-six such categories in a single state's budget during the late 1880s. Michigan had seventy-one separate units of expenditure in the 1870s, although most were closed out by the end of the decade.[62]

State spending did not keep pace with economic or population growth in the late nineteenth century. North Carolina's expenditures dropped from $387,048 in 1869 to $148,217 in 1881. Texas in 1879 inaugurated a pay-as-you-go policy that required reductions in school and other social expenditures: the state spent $5.1 million in 1881–1883 and $4.5 million in 1883–1885. This trend was not limited to the South. California's government expenditures and tax rate declined in the mid-1880s; Iowa's 1879–1881 expenditures were lower than at any time since 1869, although its population had increased by 50 percent. Ohio's financial outlays were static in the 1880s, despite rapid population and economic growth; Wisconsin spending on prisons and other state institutions totaled $797,830 in 1879–1880 and $788,109 in 1889–1890. Only in the 1890s did public service expenditures begin to rise: per capita state spending went from $1.22 in 1890 to $2.26 in 1903. But this compares with federal per capita figures of $4.61 in 1890 and $5.87 in 1903, and local government figures of $7.72 and $11.27. The states were a relatively minor source of expenditure.[63]

It is a revealing commentary on prevailing fiscal attitudes that the reduction of debt was a major category of state outlay in the

62. Percentages calculated from Edwin R. A. Seligman, "Finance Statistics of the American Commonwealths," *ASA Publications*, ns, 1 (1888–1889), table 4, U.S., Census Office, *Wealth, Debt, and Taxation*, 976–979, and *BHS*, 416–417; on state funds, Seligman, "Finance Statistics," 354–355.

63. "North Carolina," *AC* (1881); "Texas," *AC* (1885) and Edmund T. Miller, *A Financial History of Texas* (Austin, 1916), 198; "California," *AC* (1885); "Iowa," *AC* (1881); Ernest L. Bogart, *Financial History of Ohio* (Urbana, 1912), 106–107; Raymond W. Phelan, *Financial History of Wisconsin* (Madison, 1908), 468; on per capita spending, Breck P. McAllister, "Public Purpose in Taxation," *CalLR*, 18 (1930), 128n.

1870s and 1880s. State indebtedness declined by 26 percent in the eighties. Given the debt burden assumed during the Civil War period, and the secular price decline of the late nineteenth century, this was sound fiscal policy: debt payment was increasingly costly in real dollar values. It accorded, too, with the prevailing popular hostility to active government and the conventional economic wisdom of prudent money management. National and local authorities pursued a similar policy, with the result that public indebtedness per $100 of estimated wealth in the United States shrank from $10.64 in 1870 to $3.06 in 1890 and $2.85 in 1902.

The price of this policy was skimping on state support for education and other public services. Massachusetts—where the effects of industrialism and urbanization were most intensely felt—became the notable exception to the prevailing pattern of state debt reduction. Toward the end of the century, that commonwealth substantially increased its investment in local improvements and other forms of expenditure. By 1902, the Massachusetts state debt was $56.9 million, 31 percent of the national total.[64]

In a number of southern and western states, the management of debt became an important political issue, pitting those who saw quick and full payment as a way of sustaining the state's credit against those who regarded it as a windfall for speculators. Tennessee Democrats in 1881 divided into "state-credit" and "low-tax" factions. Virginia politics around 1880 was dominated by the clash between debt-paying Funders and debt-evading Readjusters. County and township railroad bonding, loans, and stock purchases led to similar controversies in the Midwest, and the Missouri, Kansas, and Iowa courts upheld state legislative attempts to scale down or repudiate the more questionable (and onerous) of these obligations.

Between 1870 and 1896 the United States Supreme Court heard more than 350 railroad bonding cases. The problem, as treatise writer John F. Dillon observed, was "full of difficulties." The sanctity of contract and the inviolability of debt dictated full payment. Yet all too often these obligations had been fraudulently incurred. Nevertheless, the Supreme and other federal courts "set a

64. Yearley, *Money Machines*, 15; U.S., Census Office, *Wealth, Debt, and Taxation*, 131–132; on Massacusetts, B. U. Ratchford, *American State Debts* (Durham, 1941), 256.

face of flint against repudiation." In decisions such as Cass County v. Johnston (1877) and Poindexter v. Greenhow (1885) the Court held state and local governments to full accountability for their debts. Justice Samuel Miller bitterly called this a "farce whose result is invariably the same, namely to give more to those who have already, and to take away from those who have little, the little that they have." It was also another demonstration of the tough-fibered value system that impeded government's adaptation to changing economic and social conditions.[65]

Locality and City

By 1900 there were more than 10,000 incorporated units—townships, towns, boroughs, villages, counties, cities—in the United States. But despite the social and economic transformation of the late nineteenth century, change in the governance of minor civil divisions was glacially slow.

In part this was due to the great number and variety of local units. It was difficult for new approaches to spread across so dense and heterogeneous a landscape. County government was all-powerful in the South, but a hollow shell in New England (though by the end of the century the New England towns appeared to be losing some of their authority to the counties). County supervisors prevailed in New York, Michigan, Illinois, Wisconsin, and Nebraska; boards of county commissioners were the norm in Pennsylvania, Ohio, Indiana, Kansas, and Missouri. Town trustees flourished in Indiana, Missouri, and Kansas; town chairmen in Wisconsin.[66]

Those changes that did occur in local government were gradual and subtle. The numerous local officials—court officers in par-

65. "Tennessee," AC (1881); John F. Dillon, Commentaries on the Law of Municipal Corporations, 4th ed. (Boston, 1890), 642; on municipal bonding cases, Charles Fairman, Reconstruction and Reunion 1864–88, Part One (New York, 1971), 918 ff; Cass County v. Johnston, 95 U.S. 360 (1877); Poindexter v. Greenhow, 114 U.S. 270 (1885); Miller quoted in Fairman, Reconstruction, 937.

66. John A. Fairlie, Local Government in Counties, Towns and Villages (New York, 1906); Goodnow, Comparative Administrative Law, I, 178 ff. See also Bryce, American Commonwealth, I, 589 ff.

ticular, supervisors, assessors, collectors, constables, highway commissioners, overseers of the poor, justices of the peace—tended increasingly to be elected rather than appointed. State supervision (though not operation) of local finance and education grew, as did the consolidation of county administration. But this was a slow and spotty process. In comparison to Europe, local autonomy remained strong. There were no counterparts to the powerful, centrally-appointed prefects of the 40,000 or so French communes. Nor was there the central administrative control of health, education, and local government that developed in Victorian Britain.[67]

Reform efforts in Indiana reveal something of the hoary character of local government. The state's governor in 1886 wanted to separate the offices of township trustee, treasurer, and clerk: there was too great a possibility of fraud when one person held all of those posts. Not until 1891 did the legislature end the fee system for county officials and create a salary scale. An 1899 law altered Indiana county and township government. It provided for a three-member advisory board in each township and seven-member county councils charged to set tax levies and make appropriations. But the aim was to reduce costs, not to secure more effective local administration. This desire for economy was pervasive: new Massachusetts towns such as Belmont and Wellesley appeared in the late nineteenth century because their inhabitants hoped thereby to avoid rising taxes.[68]

Local public finance was handled through a system of great complexity—charged to serve fiscal policies of great frugality. A rural county in late nineteenth century Wisconsin labored under a "fantastic labyrinth of intergovernmental finance." The county had elaborate commitments to raise money for and make payments to the state and to its townships; the other levels of government had similar obligations. Not surprisingly, the various jurisdictions frequently overlapped or clashed. Railroad lands in Kansas and

67. Herman G. James, *Local Government in the United States* (New York, 1928), 112; George E. Howard, *An Introduction to the Local Constitutional History of the United States* (Baltimore, 1889), I; Theodore Zeldin, *France 1848–1940: Ambition, Love, and Politics* (Oxford, 1974), 522, 530 ff; Goodnow, *Comparative Administrative Law*, I, 241, 258.

68. "Indiana," *AC* (1886); *Indiana Acts* 1891, ch. 194, 1899 ch. 154; Eugene E. Oakes, *Studies in Massachusetts Town Finance* (Cambridge, 1937), 218–220.

Nebraska were subject to real estate, personalty, corporate, and property levies handled by five separate tax jurisdictions: state, county, township, precinct, and school district.[69]

As on the state level, the major source (about 80 percent) of local revenue was the general property tax. Poll and license levies provided lesser amounts. (Great Britain's local authorities had a more varied revenue structure. About 40 percent of their income came from taxes, 25 percent from loans. By the end of the century, another 20–25 percent derived in equal portion from government grants and receipts from publicly owned utilities.) American local revenue, like government itself, was fixed in established ways.

Local like state debt was sharply reduced in the 1870s. But rising demands on government for education and other services put a stop to that decline. The per capita debt of counties and minor civil divisions remained stable or rose slightly between 1880 and the end of the century. The states in 1902 spent $1.2 billion; the counties $166 million; the minor civil divisions $1.6 billion. This was still a highly decentralized polity.[70]

It was in the late nineteenth century city that the tension between old values and new realities was most keenly felt. Cities came to be seen—with good reason—as distinct social entities. Their growing size and complexity seemed to require forms of governance suited to their special character. But what, precisely, was the proper way to run these places, so full of the promise— and the menace—of modern industrial life? Was the municipal corporation to be freed from its legal position as "a creature of the state, made for specific purposes, to exercise, within a limited sphere, the powers of the state"? Or was it a mistake to foster self-government in these hotbeds of the foreign-born, the working class, the poor? Should cities be run by venal politicians (who

69. Merle Curti, *The Making of an American Community: A Case Study of Democracy in a Frontier Democracy* (Stanford, 1959), 270, 268–281; Plehn, "Revenue Systems," 617 ff; Decker, *Railroads, Lands, and Politics*, chs. 7–10.

70. U.S., Census Office, *Wealth, Debt, and Taxation*, Part II; *BHS*, 414, 422; A. T. Peacock and J. Wiseman, *The Growth of Public Expenditure in the United Kingdom* (Princeton, 1961), 39; on debt, U.S., Census Office, *Wealth, Debt, and Taxation*, 133, 395 ff; John A. Kasson, "Municipal Reform," *NAR*, 137 (1883), 218–230.

nevertheless had broad popular support), or by the well-off and the educated (who often were remote from the people)?

Given the rapid growth of American cities, their diverse and transient populations, and the deep divisions of opinion as to the proper way to govern them, it is not surprising that many agreed with James Bryce that urban government was "the one conspicuous failure" of late nineteenth century American democracy. The cities of the United States frequently were compared—for the worse —with European municipalities. The general belief was that European cities better handled the problems of urban growth. Much was made of their freedom from national or provincial interference, their ancient traditions of urban autonomy. City streets, for example, were municipal property in the Old World. In the United States they were under state control, and state legislatures often gave away valuable franchises to transit companies. European cities in general could do what they wished unless specifically forbidden by the central legislature. American cities could not act unless their state legislatures specifically authorized them to do so.

Laws such as England's Municipal Corporations Act of 1882, Public Health Act of 1875, and County Council Act of 1887, and the French Commune Act of 1884, underscored the scope, and the limits, of European urban autonomy. English and French municipalities had greater power to act than their American counterparts. But they also remained under closer administrative control by the national government.[71]

Major political and social contrasts between the cities of the Old World and the New contributed to the differences in their governance. The British Liberal leader and onetime mayor of Birmingham John Chamberlain compared his city to Boston in 1892. He noted the greater honesty and efficiency of administration in the English city (which had a civil service): the costs of government were five times higher in Boston than in Birmingham. But wages were higher in the American city, and its suffrage was more extensive. And American cities had an ethnic and cultural diversity

71. William M. Ivins, "Municipal Government," *PSQ*, 2 (1887), 295; Bryce, *American Commonwealth*, I, 637; Frank P. Crandon, "Misgovernment of Great Cities," *PSM*, 30 (1886–1887), 296–310, 520–529; Griffith, *Modern Development*, I, 16–17; Goodnow, *Comparative Administrative Law*, I, 241–245, 285–292.

—with attendant problems of politics and government—that was unknown in Europe. The net immigration to London each year in the 1870s was less than 11,000, and only 6 percent of the city's population was foreign born in 1881. In 1870, 44 percent of New York City's people had been born abroad.[72]

American cities, like other minor civil divisions, widely differed in their forms of governance. Political scientist Frank Goodnow concluded that "we really have no system of city government." City councils, popular in the early nineteenth century, and boards (of police, finance, and the like) dating from the mid-century decades coexisted with the strong mayors that became more common in the late nineteenth century. Brooklyn's mayor was given unprecedented powers in 1882; Quincy, Massachusetts added further to the authority of its city executive in the late eighties. But the mayors of Philadelphia and San Francisco remained figureheads. Cleveland had a strong mayor around 1900; municipal authority in Cincinnati, in the same state, rested primarily with the City Council and the Board of Aldermen. The government of Providence in the late 1880s was "strictly local" (that is, rooted in the wards and precincts). But in New Haven under the charter of 1881 a Board of Commissioners with equal representation from the two major parties ran things: "The actual governing force of the town is . . . an oligarchy in the bosom of a slumbering democracy."

As with states and counties, the structure of city government often reflected the main lines of westward migration, so that adaptations of the municipal structure of New York City or Philadelphia often could be found elsewhere. Ethnicity and religion also mattered. Cities such as Cincinnati and Philadelphia, with large numbers of native-born Protestants, had Republican political machines.

72. John Chamberlain, "Municipal Institutions in America and England," Forum, 14 (1892), 267–281; on London immigration, Frank J. Goodnow, City Government in the United States (New York, 1904), 5n; Adna F. Weber, The Growth of Cities in the Nineteenth Century (1899; Ithaca, 1967), 264; Kate H. Claghorn, "The Foreign Immigration in New York City," U.S. Industrial Commission, Reports (Washington, 1901), XV, 464 ff. See also Albert Shaw, "Municipal Government in Great Britain," PSQ, 4 (1889), 197–229, and Seth Low's defense of American city government, "An American View of Municipal Government in the United States," in Bryce, American Commonwealth, I, 650 ff.

Irish Catholic-dominated New York and Boston had Democratic ones. In a more subtle but nonetheless real way, cities could be differentiated by the style and values of their elites. It was said at the time that the prime test of social acceptability in Boston was "How much do you know?" in New York, "How much are you worth?" in Philadelphia, "Who was your grandfather?"[73]

But for all these distinctions, certain facts of public life were common to late nineteenth century American cities. Regardless of the form of government, the real locus of power was the party machine. And everywhere, cities had to cope with their peculiar status as municipal corporations in a federal system of government.

As nineteenth century cities grew in size and importance, their subjection to state legislative authority increased: "The position of the city has been changed from that of an organization for the satisfaction of local needs to that of a well-organized agent of state government." The Pennsylvania legislature appointed a committee to direct the construction of Philadelphia's City Hall. The New York and other legislatures granted streetcar franchises without compensation to the cities involved; there were frequent state restrictions on urban debt, taxation, police, and the like. Between 1884 and 1889 the New York legislature enacted 1,284 statutes affecting thirty cities; 390 of them dealt with New York City. This legislative authority became a major issue in the late nineteenth century: "the history of American city government since 1870 came to be largely involved in a struggle for emancipation from central control."[74]

73. Goodnow, *City Government*, 154, 67, 65; on Quincy, Charles F. Adams, "Municipal Government: Lessons from the Experience of Quincy, Massachusetts," *Forum*, 14 (1892), 282–292; George G. Wilson, *Town and City Government in Providence* (Providence, 1889), 77; Charles H. Levermore, *The Town and City Government of New Haven* (Baltimore, 1886), 69; W. Glazier, *Peculiarities of American Cities* (Philadelphia, 1886), 397–398.

74. Goodnow, *City Government*, 40–41, 55; on Philadelphia, Frank J. Goodnow, *Municipal Home Rule: A Study in Administration* (New York, 1895), 25–29; Frank J. Goodnow, "The Legislature and the Streets," *ALR*, 26 (1892), 520–539; on New York laws, Goodnow, *Municipal Home Rule*, 23; Griffith, *Modern Development*, I, 23. See also Jon C. Teaford, "City versus State: The Struggle for Legal Ascendancy," *AJLH*, 17 (1973), 51–65; Howard L. McBain, "The Doctrine of an Inherent Right of Local Self-Government," *ColLR*, 16 (1916), 190–216, 299–322—denying that such a right exists.

But for all this power over city affairs, constitutional limits on special or local legislation made it difficult for state legislatures to deal with the growing body of urban needs. One response was to classify cities according to population size, thus making it possible to pass laws tailored to particular urban problems. Ohio's legislature passed more than 1,200 acts dealing with city matters between 1876 and 1892. It circumvented the state constitutional ban on local statutes by devices such as an 1877 law authorizing improvements by any city "of the second class in this state, which, by the last federal census, had a population of twelve thousand six hundred and fifty two"; or an 1885 act authorizing "any city of the second grade of the first class . . . to issue bonds . . . to provide means to construct and rebuild a bridge on Walworth Run, on Pearl street, in the city of Cleveland." The Ohio Supreme Court sought to put a stop to this practice in the early nineties.[75]

The state courts were as important as the legislature in defining the range and limits of urban governance. Municipal corporation law became a major area of judicial decisionmaking in the late nineteenth century. John F. Dillon's massive treatise, *The Law of Municipal Corporations*, appeared in 1872 and went through five editions by 1911. The sheer bulk of its case law and the complexity of its analysis was evidence of the degree to which the problems of the city had come to figure in the business of the courts.

Judges distinguished between the public character of the municipal corporation (over which the legislature's authority was absolute) and its private or proprietary character (in which the city could enjoy the powers and be subject to the constraints of a private corporation). Within the tests of reasonableness and due process municipalities could destroy or remove nuisances, regulate telephone charges, force telephone and telegraph wires underground, and supervise what went on in the streets. The net effect was to enhance the city's control over its affairs. By the early twentieth century, the old rule of strict construction of municipal powers was beginning to break down.[76]

75. Delos F. Wilcox, *Municipal Government in Michigan and Ohio: A Study in the Relation of City and Commonwealth* (New York, 1896), 78–79; *Ohio Laws* 1877, p. 174, 1885, p. 114; State v. Smith, 48 Ohio 211 (1890). See also Milo R. Maltbie, "Home Rule in Ohio," *MA*, 6 (1902), 234–244.

76. Dillon, *Municipal Corporations*, 107 ff; Howard L. McBain, *American City Progress and the Law* (New York, 1918), 1. See also John B. Uhle,

A more direct assault on legislative control was the movement for home rule, enabling cities to frame their own charters. Missouri was the first state to allow this, and St. Louis wrote a pioneering home rule charter in 1875. California (1879), Washington (1889), and Minnesota (1896) followed. But whether they were the product of the city or the legislature, urban charters had much in common. They tended to be codelike documents: by the early 1900s the New York City charter had more than 400,000 words and was devoted to "bureaucracy pure and simple."

There is a shadow-play quality to the sober, extended disquisitions on the structure of urban government that so frequently appeared in the late nineteenth century. Several factors materially reduced the significance of state or home rule, or the formal allocation of authority among mayors, aldermen, councils, and boards. One of these was the prevalence of boss-led machines, which normally controlled the machinery of government whatever its form. In addition, there flourished an "unofficial government of cities," composed of quasi-public charitable and welfare organizations, libraries, and the like. Finally, the sheer scale of class, ethnic, and religious diversity meant that the character of urban government was less important than the clash of social and economic interests.[77]

It was in this context that municipal reform—and that unhardy perennial the municipal reformer—emerged on the late nineteenth century urban scene. Reformers usually called for home rule—and in doing so, as in New York during the 1870s, they often found themselves in awkward alliance with the city machine. But on the question of who should rule at home, the reformers' struggle with the politicos was grim and persistent. Philadelphia's Committee of

"Summary Condemnation of Nuisances by Municipal Authorities," *ALReg*, ns, 30 (1891), 157–189; Henry C. McDougal, "Power of Municipal Corporations to Regulate Telephone Charges, Control Streets, and Force Overhead Wires into Conduits," *ALR*, 30 (1896), 381–397; H. M. Wiltse, "The Proper Relations of the State to its Municipal Corporations," *TennBA Proceedings*, 5th (1886), 159–176; J. R. Berryman, "Constitutional Restrictions upon Legislation Concerning Villages, Towns, Cities, and Counties," *ALR*, 22 (1888), 403–418.

77. John A. Fairlie, *Municipal Administration* (New York, 1901), 92 ff; Harvey N. Shephard, "The Mayor and the City," *AM*, 74 (1894), 85–94; on New York charter, Albert Shaw, "The Municipal Problem and Greater New York," *AM*, 79 (1897), 733–748, McBain, *American City Progress*, 3; Everett P. Wheeler, "The Unofficial Government of Cities," *AM*, 85 (1900), 370–376.

100 in the early 1880s supposedly established "the great principle
... that partisan politics should have no place in municipal affairs." But the continuing dominance of the city's seamy Republican machine belied that optimism. A San Francisco Committee of
22 secured a new city charter in 1880—which was rejected in a city
election by a vote of 19,000 to 4,000.

Reformers sought separate city elections, the direct nomination
of candidates, and the regulation of primaries. They supported independent or fusion candidates for mayor (as in New York in 1894,
1897, and 1901). A National Municipal League composed of local
reform groups appeared in the mid-nineties. But by the end of the
century it was clear that the party organizations had more successfully adapted to the political realities of America's immigrant-
industrial cities.[78]

The impact of the municipal reform movement was limited by
its narrow social base. Its proposals frequently stemmed from the
assumption that the propertied and the educated should have a
greater voice in city affairs. (Editor-reformer Albert Shaw wanted
an appointed board of wealthy citizens to have the final say in New
York budgetary and administrative policy.) Many reformers believed that "a city is a corporation; ... as a city it has nothing
whatever to do with general political interests; ... party political
names and duties are utterly out of place there ... Under our
theory that a city is a political body, a crowd of illiterate peasants
freshly raked in from Irish bogs, or Bohemian mines, or Italian
robber nests, may exercise virtual control."

The municipal reform movement gradually adopted a broader
view of urban problems. By the end of the century advocates of the
taxation (or municipal ownership) of public utilities, and of tenement, vice, and public health reform, increasingly influenced the
terms of the debate over the governance of America's cities.[79]

78. George Vickers, *The Fall of Bossism* (Philadelphia, 1883), I, ix—
significantly, no volume II appeared; "California," *AC* (1880); Clifford
W. Patton, *The Battle for Municipal Reform: Mobilization and Attack,
1875 to 1900* (Washington, 1940).

79. Shaw, "Municipal Problem"; White, "Government of American
Cities," 368. See also Simon Sterne, "Administration of American Cities,"
in John J. Lalor, ed., *Cyclopaedia of Political Science, Political Economy,
and of the Political History of the United States* (Chicago, 1882), I, 463;
David P. Thelen, *The New Citizenship: Origins of Progressivism in Wisconsin, 1885–1900* (Columbia, Mo., 1972), chs. 7–9.

The possibilities (and the limits) of change in late nineteenth century urban government may be observed in three important policy areas: annexation, finance, and public utilities.

Cities such as Philadelphia, Chicago, and Boston frequently engaged in the large-scale annexation of adjoining areas during the nineteenth century. Many of their neighbors welcomed the opportunity of sharing in the heady prospect of urban growth. The final major consolidation of the period came in 1898, when Greater New York was created out of Manhattan (the original city), the city of Brooklyn, portions of adjoining Westchester and Nassau Counties (which became the boroughs of the Bronx and Queens), and Staten Island. The lure of governmental efficiencies of scale was a compelling one: the creation of the London County Council in 1888 and the London Government Act of 1899 had similar motives. But at the same time the widening social and economic gulf between the cities and their environs fed a growing popular hostility to annexation. Brookline voted not to join Boston in 1883; and an 1896 attempt to create a Greater Boston failed.[80]

Finance became an increasingly important issue as urban government grew more costly and the party machines refined their methods of using city revenues for their own purposes. Municipal reformers dwelt on the need for economy and tighter budgetary controls. They were not alone in this. Limits on the capacity of cities to incur debt were enthusiastically endorsed by state legislatures and in popular referenda. New York voters in 1884 passed one such proposal by a margin of 109,761 to 1,758. Pennsylvania enacted a pay-as-you-go law in 1879 which specified that after the Philadelphia City Council set the tax rate and calculated the yield, appropriations could not go beyond that figure.[81]

City tax and expenditure rates varied widely, in part a function of differing degrees of state aid, in part a product of each city's history and population makeup. So too did per capita debt. In 1880

80. Sam B. Warner, Jr., *The Private City: Philadelphia in Three Periods of Its Growth* (Philadelphia, 1968), 152–155, *Streetcar Suburbs: The Process of Growth in Boston 1870–1900* (Cambridge, 1962), 163; Bessie L. Pierce, *A History of Chicago* (New York, 1940, 1957), II, 306n, III, 334; Griffith, *Modern Development*, I, 201–202.

81. William M. Ivins, "Municipal Finance," HM, 69 (1884), 779–787; "New York," AC (1884); Edward P. Allinson and Boies Penrose, *The City Government of Philadelphia* (Baltimore, 1887), 58.

it ranged from lows of $19.62 in Detroit and $18.69 in Milwaukee to $127.45 in Jersey City and $135.58 in Memphis. The economizing and debt reduction that went on in the states during the 1880s occurred in most cities as well. Urban per capita indebtedness sharply declined between 1880 and 1890. But the pressure of population growth and the demand for new services led to rising expenditures and rising debt levels after 1890.[82]

The most striking instance of the adaptation of city government to changing urban needs—and of the constraints limiting that adaptation—occurred in the realm of public utilities. Municipally owned utilities rapidly developed in nineteenth century British and Continental cities. But there was strong and persisting resistance to them in the United States. The courts were hostile to many municipally owned activities, as were the legislatures. By 1888 only about a dozen states allowed municipalities to own gas works, and all electric and streetcar companies were privately owned. A review of Pennsylvania municipal ownership in 1898 concluded: "the powers of municipalities in this state to erect their own plants . . . are much more limited than is popularly supposed."[83]

Instead, the public utilities corporation emerged as a distinctively American solution to the problem of meeting the needs of modern cities. At first the courts tended to treat these quasi-public companies as they did private corporations in general. They held that exclusive public utilities franchises were contracts rather than applications of the police power of the state. But by the end of the century there was growing judicial recognition of the fact that these companies had a public role that set them apart from the ordinary private corporation.

82. Debt data from U.S., Census Office, *Wealth, Debt, and Taxation,* 452 ff. See also J. Rogers Hollingsworth and Ellen J. Hollingsworth, "Expenditures in American Cities," in William O. Aydelotte and others, eds., *The Dimensions of Quantitative Research in American History* (Princeton, 1972), 347–383; John R. Commons, "Taxation in Chicago and Philadelphia," *JPE,* 3 (1895), 434–460; Charles C. Williamson, *The Finances of Cleveland* (n.p., 1907), 123; Charles P. Huse, *The Financial History of Boston* (Cambridge, 1916), 178–179, 225–226, 230 ff.

83. Griffith, *Modern Development,* I, 182–183; "The Relation of Modern Municipalities to *Quasi*-Public Works," *AEA Publications,* 2, no. 6 (1888), 73; William D. Crocker, "Limitations of Municipal Ownership in Pennsylvania," *ALReg,* ns, 37 (1898), 171. See also Jabez Fox, "Constitutional Checks upon Municipal Enterprise," *HLR,* 5 (1891–1892), 30–34.

The frequently (but not always) lucrative franchises secured by private interests and the importance of the services provided spurred demands for public ownership. Rapid transit was a particularly sensitive area. Its technology was changing rapidly—from the horse car to the cable car, the electric trolley, the elevated railway, and finally the subway—and such matters as fares and the extent and quality of service were questions of prime political and economic concern. Boards of Rapid Transit and joint ventures by the city and private interests to build the expensive new subways of New York and Boston were among the ways in which the needs of supervision and improvement were met.[84]

A Michigan law in 1899 empowered the Detroit Common Council to acquire and operate the city's street railways. The attorney general of the state, arguing against the act's constitutionality, held it to be "an entirely new departure in this country, in relation to the ownership and management of one of the most important interests in the business world." The court agreed that the law was invalid, on the ground that this would be an internal improvement of the sort that the state constitution forbade the legislature —and by implication its creature the municipal corporation—from undertaking.

Privately owned utilities corporations controlled the provision of city services into the twentieth century. In 1902, 18 million incandescent bulbs were lit by the current provided by electric utilities companies, 1.5 million by public power. Wisconsin and New York created state public service commissions in 1907 to regulate these enterprises, and in the next few years most states followed their lead.[85]

84. Henry A. Williams, "The Validity of Contracts and Franchises Held by Quasi-Public Municipal Corporations," ALR, 26 (1892), 677–679; Harold F. Kumm, "The Legal Relations of City and State with Reference to Public Utility Regulation," MinnLR, 6 (1921–1922), 54; Harry J. Carman, The Street Surface Railway Franchise of New York City (New York, 1919); Charles W. Cheape III, "The Evolution of Urban Public Transit Policy, 1880–1910: A Study of Three Cities," Ph.D. diss., Brandeis University, 1976.

85. Attorney General v. Pingree, 120 Mich. 550, 553 (1899); electric bulb data in Carman F. Randolph, "Municipal Ownership of Public Utilities," YLJ, 22 (1913), 366; on commissions, Kumm, "Legal Relations," 36–37. See also Thomas W. Brown, "The Detroit Street Railway Decision," ALR, 33 (1899), 853–868.

In every area of city government—administration, taxation, public services—established structures and modes of procedure felt the pressure of socioeconomic change. There were observable consequences. The municipal corporation gradually reduced its dependence on the state. There was growing administrative centralization, and pressure for more efficient, businesslike government. Public utilities provided a widening range of municipal services. But clashing ethnic, religious, and class interests, corrupt and particularistic political machines, widespread hostility to active (and expensive) government, and the continued subjection of the city to state legislative control made efficient urban government an elusive goal. In short, both the institutional framework and the social realities of the late nineteenth century American city limited the extent of its response to industrialism. In this sense, what happened —and did not happen—to urban governance reflected the experience of late nineteenth century American government at large.[86]

86. L. S. Rowe, "The Political Consequences of City Growth," *YR*, 9 (1900), 20–32.

CHAPTER 9

The Province
of the Law

THE LEGAL SYSTEM—that densely woven fabric of
lawyers and judges, cases and decisions—was a distinct and important part of the late nineteenth century American polity. Indeed, the relative influence of lawyers and courts on the character
of public policy notably expanded during the years of America's
industrialization.

The growth of the economy and the increasing variety and complexity of the social system produced a steadily rising number of
conflicts that called for resolution by the polity. But neither the
party system, nor the state or national legislatures, nor a still primitive structure of public administration could respond to these problems in a precise and highly articulated way. The result was a void
in governance that often was filled by the pervasive and authoritative structure of the courts.

The Function of the Law

On the surface, English and American common law had many
similarities. Leaders of the bench and bar frequently dwelt on the
"developed and perfected shape" of Anglo-American law, "the best
system of enlightened and practical justice that the world has ever
seen." Sir Henry Maine's *Ancient Law* (1861), which celebrated the
triumph of contract over status in the common law, had a great
vogue in the United States as well as Great Britain. An English

work on *The Science of Law* (1874) set down principles that had a transatlantic appeal: "It is the characteristic end of law, as an instrument of Government, to maintain the identity, the coherence, and the vitality of all the groups of which the State is composed, and to ascertain and regulate the workings of the several groups to one another, and to the State as a corporate whole."[1]

But in fact American common law had been diverging from its English counterpart at least since the time of the Revolution and continued to do so in the late nineteenth century. This was true not only of doctrinal niceties but also of the legal system as an instrument of public policy. A. V. Dicey's seminal work on the relation of law to public opinion in nineteenth century England (1905) made it clear that parliamentary acts and official boards and commissions determined policy more than did judicial decisions. By the end of the nineteenth century American courts had much greater influence in numerous areas of public concern.[2]

One measure of this authority was an increasingly elaborate apparatus of journals and treatises, legal theory, and legal professionalism. Before the Civil War, law journals generally confined themselves to case reporting and articles on specific points of law. But in 1866 the *American Law Review* appeared, offering commentary on public and constitutional questions from a legal standpoint. Among its early editors were the abolitionist Moorfield Storey, Arthur G. Sedgwick, who wrote the *Nation's* legal and constitutional articles, and Oliver Wendell Holmes, Jr. The *American Law Review* spoke to and for an audience increasingly distrustful of the political and legislative processes, increasingly

1. John F. Dillon, *Our Law: Its Essential Nature and Ethical Foundations and Relations* (Iowa City, 1893); Sheldon Amos, *The Science of Law* (New York, 1874), vii. See also Dillon, *The Laws and Jurisprudence of England and America* (Boston, 1895), "American Institutions and Laws," *ABA Reports*, 7 (1884), 203–239.
2. A. V. Dicey, *Lectures on the Relation between Law and Public Opinion in England during the Nineteenth Century* (London, 1905). See also Brian Abel-Smith and Robert Stevens, *Lawyers and the Courts: A Sociological Study of the English Legal System 1750–1965* (Cambridge, Eng., 1967), 88, 112–115, 122n; Morton Horwitz, "The Emergence of an Instrumental Conception of American Law, 1780–1820," *PAH*, 5 (1971), 287–326; Lawrence M. Friedman, *A History of American Law* (New York, 1973); J. Willard Hurst, *Law and the Conditions of Freedom in the Nineteenth Century United States* (1956; Madison, 1964).

disposed to favor the judicial resolution of public issues.[3]

More influential still were the treatises of the time. A flood of specialized texts appeared in the late nineteenth century: guidebooks to the legal problems of an increasingly complex society. Roscoe Pound has called this an "organizing, systematizing" period, when treatises and digests sought to rationalize the decisions of scores of state jurisdictions: "Writers assumed to find a rule for everywhere in a common-law decision anywhere."[4]

There appeared, too, work of another order: treatises that provided a rationale for the supremacy of the judicial over the legislative and executive branches of government. The most influential of these books was Michigan Supreme Court Justice Thomas M. Cooley's *Treatise on the Constitutional Limitations which Rest upon the Legislative Power of the States* (1868). Cooley wrote *Constitutional Limitations* at the height of the legislative activism of the postwar years. He did not flatly advocate judicial supremacy, warning that judges should not "run a race of opinions upon points of rights, reason, and expediency with the law-making power." But his Jacksonian intellectual origins made him sensitive to "unbridled authority by any one man or body of men, whether sitting as a legislature or as a court." He thought it the duty of the judiciary to intervene when legislation threatened the "personal, civil, and political" rights of the individual.[5]

Cooley's strong, sinewy text was a useful tool for lawyers and judges seeking to check active legislatures. It became the best-selling American law book of its time. Judges cited the work in decisions which, when added to the footnotes of later editions,

3. Dillon, *Laws and Jurisprudence*, 266n; Charles Fairman, *Reunion and Reconstruction: 1864–1888, Part I* (New York, 1971), 563, on *American Law Review*. Other important law journals founded in this period were the *Albany Law Journal* (1870) and the *Central Law Journal* (1874).

4. Francis R. Aumann, *The Changing American Legal System: Some Selected Phases* (Columbus, O., 1940), 206; Charles Warren, *A History of the American Bar* (Boston, 1911), 548 ff; Roscoe Pound, *The Formative Era of American Law* (Boston, 1938), 157.

5. Thomas M. Cooley, *Treatise on the Constitutional Limitations which Rest upon the Legislative Power of the States of the American Union* (1868; 2d ed., Boston, 1871), iv, 5, *The General Principles of Constitutional Law in the United States of America* (Boston, 1880), 248–249. See also Alan Jones, "Thomas M. Cooley, and 'Laissez-Faire Constitutionalism': A Reconsideration," *JAH*, 53 (1967), 751–771; Clyde E. Jacobs, *Law Writers and the Courts* (Berkeley and Los Angeles, 1954), 27–32.

strengthened its authority. *Constitutional Limitations* was influential, too, because it discussed broad issues of public policy—the constitutionality of legislation, the protection of personal liberty and property, the power of taxation—in a supposedly apolitical legal context. Boston attorney John C. Ropes called this book, which in fact deeply affected the course of American government in the late nineteenth century, "a purely legal work. No political objects lure the writer from the safer business of expounding the law."[6]

John F. Dillon's *Treatise on the Law of Municipal Corporations* (1872) did to the taxing and subsidizing powers of local government what Cooley's *Constitutional Limitatiōns* did to the legislative power of the states. Dillon, who in the course of his career would be editor of the *Central Law Journal*, chief justice of the Iowa Supreme Court, and a federal circuit court judge, shared Cooley's distaste for active government: "it has unfortunately become quite too common with us to confer upon our [municipal] corporations extraordinary powers . . . which are better left to exclusively private capital enterprise." But the principal effect of the widely influential writings of Iowa Judge Dillon, as of Michigan Judge Cooley, was to strengthen the case for more intensive judicial review of other units of government.[7]

For all its differences of style and content, Oliver Wendell Holmes's *The Common Law* (1881) had a generic relationship to the work of Cooley and Dillon. No less than the others, Holmes viewed the legal process as a prime instrument of public policymaking. His famous declaration—"The life of the law has not been logic: it has been experience. The felt necessities of the time, the prevalent moral and political theories, intuitions of public policy, avowed or unconscious, even the prejudices which judges share with their fellow-men, have had a good deal more to do than the syllogism in determining the rules by which men should be governed"—was hardly a call for judicial restraint. In Holmes's work appear many of the qualities that made the legal system so potent a force in the late nineteenth century American polity: vigor, self-confidence, erudition, authoritativeness. By examining the origins

6. Ropes in *ALR*, 3 (1868–1869), 344.
7. John F. Dillon, *Treatise on the Law of Municipal Corporations*, 2 vols. (Chicago, 1872), Preface; Jacobs, *Law Writers*, 111–112.

and the historical evolution of the common law, Holmes hoped to foster a more realistic and what he believed to be a scientific legal approach, with all of the implications of heightened authority that these qualities implied. The major topic of his work was the development of the law of contract—the most important legal instrument in the market economy of the nineteenth century.[8]

The continuing controversy over codification also tells us much about the character and function of late nineteenth century American law. The impulse to rationalize court decisions and legislative acts in a single code was an old and powerful one. In pre-Civil War America, codification also appealed to many because it promised to make the law less arcane, more accessible to the average citizen. New York attorney David Dudley Field took the lead during the 1850s in drafting codes of civil and criminal procedure, common law, and public law. He worked assiduously for decades to induce state legislatures and the legal profession to accept his codes. Field and other advocates of codification such as John F. Dillon's *Central Law Journal*, the *American Law Journal*, and New York corporation attorney Thomas G. Shearman hoped thereby to secure a systematic, ordered, efficient legal system. An 1876 survey of American law discerned a trend "towards *organic statute law* and towards the *systematizing* of law; in other words, towards *written constitutions and codification.*"[9]

But few jurisdictions adopted Field's codes. Late nineteenth century law and legislation was too much involved in a fast-changing society to be so contained. Chancellor James Kent's old warning— "The great objection to all kinds of codification, when it runs into detail, is that the rules are not malleable, they cannot accommodate to circumstances, they are imperative"—had fresh pertinence in late nineteenth century America. As one commentator of the time

8. Oliver Wendell Holmes, *The Common Law*, ed., Mark DeWolfe Howe (1881; Cambridge, 1963), 5.

9. Aumann, *American Legal System*, 208–214; George Martin, *Causes and Conflicts: The Centennial History of the Association of the Bar of the City of New York 1870–1970* (Boston, 1970), 143–154; Benjamin V. Abbott, *Judge and Jury: A Popular Explanation of Leading Topics in the Law of the Land* (New York, 1880), 188–193; G. T. Bispham, "Law in America 1776–1876," *NAR*, 122 (1876), 174. See also David D. Field, *Law Reform in the United States* (St. Louis, 1891).

put it: "where laws have become complex from the circumstance that the social relations which they regulate are intricate and varied, . . . no code or statute can compel simplicity in rules of civil conduct." The Field code of civil procedure adopted by New York vividly illustrated the point. It had 473 sections in 1876; more than 3,300 in 1880; ultimately it grew to be an unwieldy mass of some 50,000 procedural specifics.

James C. Carter, New York attorney and a founder of the New York City and American bar associations, led the opposition to the Field codes. He drew a sharp distinction between the "science of legislation" and the "science of jurisprudence." Legislation *made* "political regulations," while judges *discovered* "the rules of justice." Law was an inductive science through which the underlying values of the society were revealed and implemented. In this sense, "law is a department of sociology." It was the task of the legislature to formalize the discoveries of the courts, not to codify and thus rigidify that process of revelation.[10]

Codification of the rules of civil procedure would spread rapidly in the twentieth century. But it is not difficult to see why Carter's objections to the codification of substantive law won the support of most legal spokesmen of the time. They readily agreed that the law had a life and character of its own, that it was, in truth, a distinct sector of the polity. And in practice, late nineteenth century law burst the bounds of legislative definition that Field's codes sought to impose. The prevailing attitude of judges and lawyers appeared in Supreme Court Justice Joseph Bradley's observation that "the law is a science of principles, by which civil society is regulated and held together"; or in the text for beginning law students that announced: "The *law* is the presiding element of our social existence."[11]

10. Kent quoted in "Codification," *AC* (1865); Bispham, "Law in America," 190; J. Willard Hurst, *The Growth of American Law: The Law Makers* (Boston, 1950), 76; James C. Carter, "The Provinces of the Written and the Unwritten Law," *ALR*, 24 (1890), 4, "The Ideal and the Actual in the Law," ibid., 769–770. See also Emory Washburn, "Jurisprudence as an Element of Social Science," *JSS*, 3 (1873), 114–126, and Irving B. Richman, "Law and Political Fact in the United States," *AM*, 64 (1889), 205–219.

11. Bradley in William D. Lewis, ed., *Great American Lawyers* (Philadelphia, 1909), VI, 402; Thomas W. Powell, *Analysis of American Law*, 2d ed. (Philadelphia, 1878), 21.

The Legal Profession

From the early days of the Republic, lawyers occupied an exceptionally important place in American society. Foreign observers frequently commented on this fact. Hector St. John de Crèvecoeur noted in the 1780s: "Lawyer or merchant are the fairest titles our towns afford." Fifty years later Alexis de Tocqueville concluded that "lawyers form the highest class and the most cultivated circle of society."[12]

This primacy appears to have eroded somewhat during the middle of the nineteenth century, in part because of the growing importance of businessmen, in part because of the character of the national crisis during those years. The ideologue, the publicist, the politician, and the soldier took center stage in the determination of public policy. The *American Law Review* observed in 1871 that Tocqueville "could not forecast the influences which in the last quarter of a century have so enormously increased the control of mere politicians; did not see that they would master the art of association more thoroughly than any other class in the community." James Bryce, the leading English observer of post-Civil War America, also took note of this development: "The function of a class of men who devote themselves to politics solely (some of whom, of course, were originally lawyers) has done a good deal to jostle the legitimate lawyers out of political life."[13]

But while professional politicians controlled the party system, lawyers became increasingly influential in other areas of late nineteenth century American society. The British historian Edward A. Freeman recognized in 1880 that American attorneys occupied a distinctly more prominent place than their British counterparts. He observed that legal-commercial terms such as "endorse," "balance," and "real estate" were much more widely used in American than in English popular speech. Another foreign commentator noted that American lawyers were "not so much masters of a rec-

---

12. J. Hector St. John de Crèvecoeur, *Letters from an American Farmer* (1782; New York, 1957), 36; Alexis de Tocqueville, *Democracy in America* (1835–1840; New York, 1945), I, 285–286.

13. "The Bar Association of the City of New York," *ALR*, 5 (1870–1871), 444; James Bryce, "The Legal Profession in America," *MacM*, 25 (1871–1872), 213.

ondite craft, but rather practical men, versed in a particular and very practical part of daily life."[14]

Attorneys played an especially active role in the development of corporate capitalism. One observer thought that their "chief office ... is to supervise, direct, and promote the great business interests of the country." The most prestigious and remunerative legal work came to be advising corporate clients rather than courtroom argument: "Litigation has declined, and counsel work has become the leading feature of practice. The chief forum of the lawyer has been transferred from the court house to the office." Bryce noted that American attorneys were "practically just as much businessmen as lawyers," and an 1883 discussion of legal practice observed: "Oratory has passed away. Thorough preparation and a statement bristling with points like an auditor's report has taken its place."[15]

The rhetoric of legal conservatism blossomed as lawyers and judges came to regard themselves the chief engineers of the new business economy. One spokesman termed the legal system "the conservative power which has ... reconciled diverse and conflicting interests and held the safeguards of life and property secure amid this surging sea of popular suffrage." John F. Dillon worried over the danger posed by "Karl Mark" and other socialist theorists, and dwelt on "the magic of property." Lawyers, it was said, "ought to constitute a conservative class." Law school graduates were reminded that "the Bar is the natural enemy of anarchy and despotism."[16]

14. Edward A. Freeman, *Some Impressions of the United States* (London, 1883), 69–70, 90 ff; "The English and the American Bar," *ILT*, 6 (1872), 20.

15. Charles C. Bonney, "The Relation of the Legal Profession to the Active Business of the Country," *CLN*, 1 (1868), 3; "The Decline of Litigation," *AL*, 1 (1893), 5; Bryce in Charles N. Gregory, "American Lawyers and their Making," *ALR*, 31 (1897), 189; John M. Shirley, "The Future of our Profession," *ALR*, 17 (1883), 669. See also Hurst, *Growth*, 347–353; Theron G. Strong, *Landmarks of a Lawyer's Lifetime* (New York, 1914), ch. 17.

16. J. H. Benton, Jr., *Influence of the Bar in our State and Federal Government* (Boston, 1894) 11; John F. Dillon, "Property—Its Rights and Duties in Our Legal and Social Systems," *ALR*, 29 (1895), 165–166; Charles A. Kent, *Closing Address Delivered to the Senior Class, Law Department of the University of Michigan* (Ann Arbor, 1874), 12; Thomas Durfee [Chief Justice, Rhode Island Supreme Court], *Oration Delivered at the Dedication of the Providence County Court-House* (Providence, 1879), 34.

Along with social and economic conservatism—hardly new to the legal profession—a sense of the law's social importance appears to have become increasingly explicit in the late nineteenth century. Oliver Wendell Holmes, Jr., the most powerful legal mind of his time, reflected this. Seriously wounded three times in an eighteen-month stretch of Civil War combat duty, Holmes emerged from his ordeal an exceptionally tough-minded man. His contempt for politics and government was withering: "I loathe the thick-fingered clowns we call the people—especially as the beasts are represented at political centers—vulgar, selfish, and base." Washington was "absolutely loathsome"; the city "stinks of meanness." But he had a passionate commitment to the law as a social instrument: "I venerate the law, and especially our system of law, as one of the vastest products of the human mind." As a legal scholar and then from 1882 to 1902 as a member of Massachusetts's Supreme Judicial Court, Holmes found a means of influencing American life that was relatively divorced from politics and popular clamor. He "retreated into participation; he withdrew into public responsibilities."[17]

Men of the law assured one another that they were well advised to avoid the seamy life of public office. The Vermont judge and treatise writer Isaac F. Redfield argued in 1871 that "a lawyer in the legislature is no more in the profession than a merchant, a banker, or a mechanic." Wisconsin's Chief Justice Edward A. Ryan comforted a friend who had failed to win the governorship: "I think . . . that it is a sore damage to a successful lawyer to be taken from his profession by any political office . . . Your position and prospects in the profession are quite too high to be sacrificed for the really paltry office of Governor."[18]

Lawyers displayed a growing concern for the character and standards of their profession. New York attorney David Dudley Field

---

See also Norbert Brockman, "Laissez Faire Theory in the Early American Bar Association," *NDL*, 39 (1964), 269–285.

17. Mark De Wolfe Howe, *Justice Oliver Wendell Holmes: The Shaping Years, 1841–1870* (Cambridge, 1957), 140; Yosal Rogat, "The Judge as Spectator," in "Mr. Justice Holmes: Some Modern Views," *UCLR*, 31 (1964), 243.

18. Isaac F. Redfield, "The Responsibilities and Duties of the Legal Profession," *ALReg*, ns, 10 (1871), 547; Ryan to James G. Jenkins, Nov. 9, 1879, Ryan Mss, WSHS.

and *Springfield Republican* editor Samuel Bowles engaged in a revealing and widely noted exchange in 1871. Bowles attacked Field for representing the shady railroad speculators Jim Fisk and Jay Gould. Field responded that his professional duty obligated him to do so. What began as a political controversy—Field was close to Tammany, Bowles was a Republican—attracted attention because it raised an important question of professional ethics. Needless to say, the general view of the New York bar was that Field had the better of the argument.[19]

The postwar expansion of bar associations testified to a growing legal professionalism. The Association of the Bar of the City of New York appeared in 1870. The egregious behavior of Tweed-controlled judges was the immediate cause of its founding. A number of prominent attorneys were concerned over the threat that machine politics posed to the legal process. Samuel J. Tilden, who was a leading railroad lawyer as well as a Democratic party leader, warned: "it is impossible for New York to remain the centre of commerce and capital for this continent, unless it has an independent Bar and an honest judiciary." Beyond this special need was the more general desire of lawyers to define and defend their professional character. As one of the founders of the New York City Bar Association put it: "I think I can express the idea of this association, and the purpose for which it is to be formed, by saying that we shall aim to make ourselves once more a *profession*."[20]

A similar intent lay behind the creation of the American Bar Association in 1878. The ABA showed some concern for the character of legislation and the purity of politics. But its primary emphasis was on legal education and standards of admission to the bar. It sought to make lawyers more professional and the law more systematic and scientific: in short, to attune the legal process to the complex needs of an industrializing society. A rival national federation of state and local bar associations, the National Bar Associa-

19. Field-Bowles correspondence in *The Lawyer and His Clients* (Springfield, 1871); Albert Stickney, "Lawyer and Client," *NAR*, 112 (1871), 392–421.
20. Tilden quoted in Martin, *Causes and Conflicts*, 38; James Emmott quoted in Alfred Z. Reed, *Training for the Public Profession of the Law* (New York, 1921), 207n; "Bar Association of City of New York," 443–455; Hurst, *Growth*, 286–287.

tion, was established in 1888, but failed in a few years in part because it did not match the ABA's stress on professional standards.[21]

To foster the attributes of professionalism, new standards of legal accreditation and education were necessary. New Hampshire created the first state board of bar examiners in 1878. The ABA lobbied for a New York law that gave the state Court of Appeals control over admission to the bar. Massachusetts's Supreme Judicial and Superior courts assumed a similar authority in 1876.

The casual legal apprenticeship of the past gave way to more formal educational prerequisites. By 1895, twenty-four states required from one to four years' study (or a college degree) before a candidate could take the bar examination. The growing belief that law could be taught only by "strictly scientific methods," that "interpretation and administration of . . . law often involve consideration of science, in its more exact as well as in its broader and more general forms," spurred the development of formal legal education.[22]

Christopher C. Langdell, dean of the Harvard Law School from 1870 to 1895, was the most influential exponent of this view. Convinced that "law is a science" and that "all the available materials of that science are contained in printed books," he created a form of legal instruction tailored to that belief. Langdell's case method, which by the turn of the century dominated American legal education, placed great weight on leading decisions—and, by implication, on the judges who wrote them. It schooled students in a national rather than varied state common law, and in this sense fitted them to deal with the social and economic conditions of an increasingly nationalized society.[23]

21. Edson R. Sunderland, *History of the American Bar Association and Its Work* (n.p., 1953), 3–13; Norbert Brockman, "The National Bar Association, 1888–1893: The Failure of Early Bar Federation," *AJLH*, 10 (1966), 122–127.

22. On requirements, Hurst, *Growth*, 277, Ralph Stone, "Admission to the Bar in the United States," *AL*, 3 (1895), 158–160; "Legal Education and the Present State of the Literature of the Law,"*ALRec*, 3 (1874–1875), 38, 44; Emory Washburn, "Testimony of Experts," *ALR*, 1 (1866), 45.

23. Arthur H. Sutherland, *The Law at Harvard* (Cambridge, 1967), 174–175; Robert Stevens, "Two Cheers for 1870: The American Law School," *PAH*, 5 (1971), 424–441.

The Judicial System

The social importance of the late nineteenth century American legal system may be gauged by the range and scale of judicial activity. The primary role of the courts was to decide on the vast number of disputes between private parties that came before them. In addition they played an increasingly important part in the determination of public policy—a part that had a substantial (if implicit) administrative as well as judicial character.

The courts interpreted general incorporation laws; controlled bankrupt railroads through their equity power of receivership; constantly passed on state taxation and regulation of corporations; decided on railroad and industrial accident compensation; interpreted public health statutes; granted divorces, changed names, approved of adoptions; passed on the conduct of elections: in short, had a large and active hand in the governance of a rapidly changing society. As one contemporary put it: "The judiciary alone can hold the conflict of selfish interests, which is an essential element of the growth of society, within the just limitations of the fundamental law."[24]

An elaborate court structure—federal, state, and local; original and appellate—tended to this business. The federal system alone included special judicial commissions, the Court of Claims, about sixty district and nine circuit courts, nine circuit courts of appeal after 1891, and the Supreme Court. California had a state supreme court, twenty district courts, fifty-three county courts, and numerous probate courts, justices' courts (in which justices of the peace conducted proceedings in rural areas), and municipal courts. Arkansas, Georgia, and Texas had separate tribunals for felonies and misdemeanors. New York City's judicial system included the Superior Court, the Court of Common Pleas, the Marine Court, the Court of Oyer and Terminer, the Court of General Sessions, and numerous magistrates' courts. By the turn of the century, the work

24. Simeon E. Baldwin, *The American Judiciary* (New York, 1905), 22 ff; Benton, *Influence of the Bar*, 19. For a modern discussion of "political jurisprudence," see Martin Shapiro, *Law and Politics in the Supreme Court* (New York , 1964), 6 ff. James Bryce in *The American Commonwealth*, 3d ed. (New York, 1893), I, 239 ff, argues against the view "that America is the country in which the province of the judiciary has been most widely extended." See also Friedman, *American Law*, 323–339.

of the nation's appellate courts alone amounted to about 25,000 cases (reported in some four hundred volumes) each year. New York's Court of Appeals handed down between five hundred and seven hundred decisions a year; the Illinois Supreme Court from seven hundred to nine hundred.[25]

The lack of printed reports and the great magnitude of their business make it difficult to say much about the character of the lower courts' decisionmaking. But it is clear that they bore the brunt of the growing recourse to the law that came with the economic transformation of the late nineteenth century. New Hampshire's county circuit courts—trial courts of general jurisdiction— had 4,400 continued cases in 1876; another 6,000 were added in the following year. Ohio's courts of first instance in 1873 handed down over 15,000 civil judgments, involving monetary transfers of more than $8,500,000. One Wisconsin trial court, serving a rural county of about 15,000 people, disposed of 236 criminal and 1,981 civil suits—almost 80 percent of the latter involving economic matters —during the 1875–1884 decade. In December 1903 there were over 5,100 cases on the dockets of Kansas City's courts. About 60 percent of these were liability claims against companies.[26]

The jurisdiction of the federal courts expanded greatly in this time of increasing economic nationalism. The Judiciary Act of March 1875 "amplified the Federal judicial power almost to the full limits of the Constitution." Numerous causes of action were removed from the state to the federal courts: admiralty, bankruptcy, and corporation law were among the areas affected. The United States Court of Claims passed on more than $80,000,000 worth of

25. Hurst, *Growth*, 122–123; on California, "Legal Institutions and Procedure in the United States," *SJ*, 20 (1876), 256, 276–277; Thomas G. Shearman, "The Judiciary of New York City," *NAR*, 105 (1867), 149–176; "Criminal Jurisdiction in the United States," *AC* (1882); F.W.S., "Our Judiciary System," *NJLJ*, 12 (1889), 24–28. See also John Rumm, "Statistics Relative to the Judiciary of the Various States," *BAT Proceedings*, 13th (1894), 49–66; Russell M. Ross, "The Iowa Judicial System," *IJH*, 54 (1956), 97–116; Baldwin, *American Judiciary*, 125 ff, 261; on Illinois courts, Hiram T. Gilbert, *The Municipal Court of Chicago* (Chicago, 1928), ch. 1; John D. W. Guice, *The Rocky Mountain Bench: The Territorial Supreme Courts of Colorado, Montana, and Wyoming, 1861–1890* (New Haven, 1972).

26. "New Hampshire," *AC* (1876–1877); "Ohio," *AC* (1873); Francis W. Laurent, *The Business of a Trial Court* (Madison, 1959), 43, 116, 161; on Kansas City, Baldwin, *American Judiciary*, 371.

private claims on the government between 1867 and 1880, and made awards totaling about $20,000,000. The growth of federal jurisdiction led in 1872 to the first treatise on Supreme Court practice and to revised rules of federal practice, and in 1874 to the first comprehensive digest of federal decisions.[27]

A flood of cases engulfed the federal courts in the post-Civil War decades: "the small tide of litigation that formerly flowed in Federal channels has swollen into a mighty stream." In 1880, 38,194 cases were pending before the federal district and circuit courts. The Supreme Court's docket averaged 240 cases per term in the 1862–1866 period; 855 from 1878 to 1882, 1,124 from 1886 to 1890. The *American Law Review* ascribed this development to "the steady growth of our population, the creation of new states, the ever-varying experiments of constitution-makers and legislators, the more intimate business association between the citizens of different states, and the mass of litigation which of necessity has grown out of the general disturbance of established relations caused by the war." The bulk of the postwar increase came from diversity of citizenship cases (that is, litigation between residents of different states); patent, copyright, and trade mark litigation; and criminal cases (the attorney general complained in 1872: "The criminal business has so accumulated as to make it nearly impossible for a court to hear any civil cases"). In later years, litigation generated by a corporate economy took an ever larger place in federal dockets.[28]

A variety of reforms sought to lessen the burden of work that fell on late nineteenth century American courts. The need was clear enough: a special ABA committee reported in 1885 that law

27. John F. Dillon, *Removal of Causes from State to Federal Courts* (St. Louis, 1876), Preface; William M. Wiecek, "The Reconstruction of Federal Judicial Power, 1863–1875," *AJLH*, 13 (1969), 333–359; Stanley Kutler, *Judicial Power and Reconstruction Politics* (Chicago, 1968), chs. 4, 8; Harvey D. Goulder, "Evolution of the Admiralty Law in America," *AL*, 5 (1897), 314–318; William A. Richardson, "History, Jurisdiction, and Practice of the Court of Claims of the United States," *SLR*, ns, 7 (1882), 781–811; [James Schouler], "Government Claims," *ALR*, 1 (1866–1867), 653–667; Philip Phillips, *The Statutory Jurisdiction and Practice of the Supreme Court of the United States* (Washington, 1872); Benjamin V. Abbott, ed., *United States Digest* (Boston, 1874).

28. Dillon, *Removal of Causes*, Preface; Felix Frankfurter and James M. Landis, *The Business of the Supreme Court: A Study of the Federal Judicial*

suits took from one and a half to six years to be decided. Changes did not come easily. Democrats often resisted attempts to expand the federal judiciary, particularly when appointments were to be made by Republican Presidents. But the growing weight on the federal court system finally led to the passage of the Circuit Courts of Appeals Act of 1891. This law created nine new circuit courts of appeals standing between the Supreme Court and the existing Federal district and circuit courts. In addition, it gave the Supreme Court the right of discretionary review. The impact of the 1891 law was immediate: the high court heard 623 cases in the 1890 term, 383 in 1891, 290 in 1892.[29]

A number of states created special bodies to assist their over-burdened tribunals. New York's Commission of Appeals, established in 1870 with a five-year tenure, disposed of about 1,000 cases. Indiana in 1891 established a special appellate court for six years to relieve the Supreme Court docket of misdemeanors, landlord–tenant cases, and estate litigation. Nebraska in 1895 set up a State Board of Irrigation with judicial powers: this body handled about 1,000 claims thus removed from the regular courts. New Hampshire in 1878 passed a referee law that removed petty controversies from normal court proceedings, and in Massachusetts jurisdiction over divorce and other matters was transferred from the Supreme Judicial Court to the superior courts.[30]

The burden of litigation led also to efforts to do something about the elaborate and often stultifying rules of nineteenth century legal procedure. The distinction between law and equity declined in the United States as it did in Great Britain. Attorney General Benjamin H. Brewster in 1883 dwelt on the need to simplify criminal pleadings, establish a uniform system of challenges, and free criminal trials from "the technical objections and numberless dilatory mo-

---

System (New York, 1928), 60–69; *ALR*, 9 (1874–1875), 349; Willard L. King, *Melville Weston Fuller* (New York, 1950), 148–149; Attorney General George H. Williams to James A. Garfield, Feb. 4, 1875, Executive and Congressional Letterbooks, Dept. of Justice, NA.

29. *ABA Reports* (1885), 325; Henry Hart and Herbert Wechsler, *The Federal Courts and the Federal System* (Brooklyn, 1953), 44–47; Frankfurter and Landis, *Supreme Court*, 56–112; Hurst, *Growth*, 118–119.

30. Hurst, *Growth*, 101, 105; "New York," *AC* (1870–1875); "Indiana," *AC* (1891); "Nebraska," *AC* (1900); "New Hampshire," *AC* (1878). See also "California," *AC* (1890).

tions" that so often afflicted them. A number of attempts were made to abolish or circumvent the process of grand jury indictment. Samples of reported cases in the early 1890s revealed that about half the grounds for appeal considered by higher courts were questions of procedure rather than substantive issues. Pleadings, forms of action, the proper joinder of parties, testimony, examination of witnesses, the form and scope of judgment: these were as likely as the substance of a lower court decision to be the cause of an appeal.

But the inherent conservatism of the judicial system limited structural change. Representatives of Indiana's county bar associations met in 1870. They were concerned over the fact that direct appeals could be made from common pleas, district, and circuit courts to the state supreme court. The resulting flood of appeals reflected "the diversity of so many different minds thus engaged in the administration of a somewhat complicated judicial system." But they could agree only on the less than sweeping reform of increasing Supreme Court's membership from four to five.[31]

The Activist Courts

The role of the late nineteenth century courts was defined not only by the scale of the litigation that came before them but also by their relationship to the polity at large—that is, by their capacity (and inclination) to act as an independent, policymaking branch of government.

As before and after, political, party, and patronage considerations often determined the selection of judges. In the early 1890s, Senator David B. Hill of New York, the state's Democratic leader, blocked two of Grover Cleveland's nominees to the Supreme Court. About two-thirds of the states elected their supreme and superior court judges, thus enmeshing them in politics—as

31. U.S., Dept. of Justice, Report of the Attorney General (Washington, 1883), 23; on grand juries, "Wisconsin," AC (1869), "Indiana," AC (1875), "Iowa," AC (1878), ALReg, ns, 14 (1875), 433–439; on case samples, "Proceedings of the Section on Legal Education," ABA Transactions (1894), "A Reproach to Legal Practice," AL, 2 (1894), 412–413; "Indiana," AC (1870). See also J. Newton Fiero, "Report of Commission on Uniform System of Legal Procedure," ALJ, 54 (1896), 198–206.

Thomas M. Cooley discovered in 1885 when, in part because he was thought to have too close an identification with railroad interests, he lost a bid for reelection to the Michigan Supreme Court. When the Democrats came to power in New Hampshire in 1874, they reorganized the state Supreme Court into the Court of Judicature, and replaced the incumbent judges. The Republicans regained control in 1876, and restored the former Court and its members. Politicos also made heavy, if largely unrecorded, demands on sitting judges, as the subservience of New York Supreme Court Justices George G. Barnard and Albert Cardozo to the dictates of Tammany's Boss Tweed dramatically demonstrated.[32]

But the judiciary and its defenders strenuously—and, it would seem, with increasing success—resisted the incursion of party politics into the judicial process. Bar associations and civic reformers spoke out against the popular election of judges. Minnesota Republicans in 1875, "believing it a duty to elevate the choice of judges above whatever is debasing in party contests," made no formal nomination for chief justice of the state supreme court. The two Colorado parties agreed in 1877 to let the bar select a nonpartisan candidate for the state's high bench. After a sharply contested judicial election in 1879, Wisconsin's parties did the same.[33]

In substance as well as form, the relationship of the courts to the political branch gradually changed. The intensity of the party struggle, and the growing density of election laws, gave the judiciary an increasingly important role in determining election controversies. George W. McCrary's pioneering *Treatise on the American Law of Elections* (1875) was dedicated to Supreme Court

32. Frank G. Cook, "Politics and the Judiciary," *AM*, 83 (1899), 743–749; Harold M. Helfman, "The Contested Confirmation of Stanley Matthews to the United States Supreme Court," *HPSO Bulletin*, 8 (1950), 155–170; "Popular Elections—Defeat of Judge Cooley," *ALRec*, 13 (1884–1885), 762–764; on New Hampshire, John P. Reid, *Chief Justice: The Judicial World of Charles Doe* (Cambridge, 1967), 314; Hurst, *Growth*, 142–145. See also James Bryce, "American Judges," *MacM*, 25 (1871–1872), 422–432.

33. Dorman B. Eaton, *Shall Judges be Elected? or the Experiment of an Elective Judiciary* (New York, [1873]); "An Elective Judiciary," *ALR*, 8 (1873–1874), 1–12; "Minnesota," *AC* (1875); "Colorado," *AC* (1877); "Wisconsin," *AC* (1879), John B. Winslow, *The Story of a Great Court* (Chicago, 1912), 369–375.

Justice Samuel Miller and sought "to introduce the principle that an election . . . should be treated as a judicial question." State and federal courts frequently passed on the eligibility of candidates, the propriety of election practices, and the legality of primary and registration laws and ballot counts. A court injunction blocked the swearing in of Kentucky's governor-elect after a contested election in 1900. The North Carolina Supreme Court in 1891 decided that a railroad was likely to suffer irreparable harm from the results of a special municipal election, and forbade the contest from being held. During the 1890s courts in more than twenty states reviewed reapportionment acts, and (as in Indiana, New Jersey, and Michigan) they were not reluctant to strike down redistricting when it failed to meet what they judged to be constitutional standards.[34]

In several New England states, Florida, Colorado, and South Dakota, the governor or the legislature could ask the state supreme court to provide opinions on the constitutionality of statutes before they were legally tested or even enacted. At times the courts were reluctant to perform this function. But several state legislatures held that they were obligated to do so: testimony to the utility of the courts' adjudicating function. It is suggestive, too, that House Speaker Thomas B. Reed and New York Democratic boss David B. Hill wanted the courts to settle contested elections.[35]

Another measure of the increasingly important role of the late nineteenth century courts was the use of writs and other devices that enhanced the judiciary's quasi-administrative powers. The

34. George W. McCrary, *A Treatise on the American Law of Elections* (Chicago, 1875), Preface; "Decisions of Political Questions by the Judicial Courts," *ALR*, 18 (1884), 1040–1042; "Crimes against the Elective Franchise," *CLM*, 2 (1881), 449–467; "Legal Question in the Kentucky Election Case," *ALR*, 34 (1900), 257–261; Murfreesboro Railroad Co. v. Commissioners, 108 N.C. 56 (1891); Hurst, *Growth*, 43; John M. Palmer, "The Courts and Political Questions," *NLR*, 1 (1893), 113–124. See also D. H. Pingrey, "The Right of the Federal Courts to Punish Offenders against the Ballot Box," *ALReg*, ns, 29 (1890), 337–375; Cooley, *Constitutional Limitations*, ch. 17; "Elections," *AEEL*, X, 552–859.

35. Hugo A. Dubuque, "The Duty of Judges as Constitutional Advisers," *ALR*, 24 (1890), 369–398; Thomas B. Reed, "Contested Elections," *NAR*, 151 (1890), 112–120; Robert Luce, *Legislative Assemblies* (Boston, 1924), 200.

number of government authorities to whom a writ of certiorari (that is, of a court's capacity and readiness to review an official action or a lower court decision) might issue, substantially increased during these years. The New York Court of Appeals appears to have been particularly active in extending its certiorari power beyond the traditional scope of the writ. The justices on that bench turned it into a device for shielding private property rights from what they held to be administrative abuse. Similar use was made of the writ of mandamus. And complaints appeared in the early 1880s that federal district judges were using their habeas corpus power as a means of reviewing the decisions of state courts.[36]

The most consequential of these developments was the expansion of the courts' injunction power. An injunction—which could compel a party to perform or (more usually) stop performing an act—was a judicial remedy that was flexible, precise, and above all swift. "Of life and business, in the present age, and especially in this country, *rapidity* is now the most striking feature," an 1874 treatise on *The Law of Injunctions* pointed out. A notable instance of this form of judicial intervention occurred during the late 1880s, when federal district judges, who had taken a number of railroad lines into receivership, began to issue the first labor injunctions against railroad unions.

Critics charged that labor injunctions enabled judges to impose criminal sanctions on union leaders without affording them their right to a jury trial. In other ways, too, the power of juries was reduced by late nineteenth century judicial interpretation. The Massachusetts Supreme Judicial Court held in 1860 that a directed verdict was necessary when the evidence at hand was held to be insufficient for a jury decision. Laws limiting the scope of judges' charges to juries began to be modified in the sixties. The role of judicial interrogation in jury selection was strengthened. In 1895

---

36. Frank J. Goodnow, "The Writ of Certiorari," *PSQ*, 6 (1891), 493–536; Harold Weintraub, "Mandamus and Certiorari in New York from the Revolution to 1880: A Chapter in Legal History," *FLR*, 32 (1964), 747; Seymour D. Thompson, "Abuses of the Writ of Habeas Corpus," *ABA Reports*, 6 (1883), 243–267. See also Ernst Freund, "American Administrative Law," *PSQ*, 9 (1894), 417; Frank J. Goodnow, "The Executive and the Courts," *PSQ*, 1 (1886), 539, 559; Hurst, *Growth*, 93, 103, 399.

the Supreme Court reaffirmed that juries in federal criminal cases could not pass on questions of law, but only of fact.[37]

Judicial review of legislation was the most conspicuous form of legal activism. The Supreme Court found only two federal laws unconstitutional before 1864, ten between 1864 and 1875, eleven from 1875 to 1898. Of 217 state laws struck down by the Court from its beginnings to 1910, 48 were voided in the peak decade of the 1880s. State courts also reviewed—and rejected—increasing numbers of legislative acts. The Supreme Judicial Court of Massachusetts considered 62 laws down to 1860 and found 10 of them unconstitutional; it struck down 17 of 103 reviewed between 1860 and 1880, 14 of 55 from 1880 to 1893. The Virginia Supreme Court found against one in three of the statutes that came before it during the late nineteenth century; Ohio's court held 15 state laws to be unconstitutional in the 1880s, 42 in the 1890s.[38]

A debate as old as the Constitution heated up once again: what were the proper limits of judicial review? A defender of the courts argued that "the law of judicial decision is not only absolutely necessary in every free and progressive society, but ... contributes far more to the full and free development of such society than what may be termed ... the law of statute or legislative enactment." Judge John F. Dillon engaged in some special pleading for his branch of government: "It is the high and delicate office of the judiciary department to elaborate the rough outlines of our daily

37. Francis Hilliard, *The Law of Injunctions* (Philadelphia, 1874), iii; Richard C. McMurtrie, "Equity Jurisdiction Applied to Crimes and Misdemeanors," *ALReg*, ns, 31 (1892), 1–17; T.M.C., "Some New Aspects of the Right of Trial by Jury," *ALReg*, ns, 16 (1877), 705–721; "The Changing Role of the Jury in the Nineteenth Century," *YLJ*, 74 (1964–1965), 170–192; Commonwealth v. Merrill, 80 Mass. 415 (1860); Sparf and Hansen v. U.S., 156 U.S. 51 (1895). See also William H. Dunbar, "Government by Injunction," *LQR*, 13 (1897), 347 ff.

38. Benjamin F. Wright, *The Growth of American Constitutional Law* (New York, 1942), 86; on Massachusetts, "Unconstitutional Legislation," *ALR*, 28 (1894), 245–246; Margaret V. Nelson, *A Study of Judicial Review in Virginia 1789–1928* (New York, 1947); Ohio figures compiled from Joseph H. Hixson, "The Judicial Veto in Ohio," M.A. thesis, Ohio State University, 1922. Edward S. Corwin, "The Extension of Judicial Review in New York, 1783–1905," *MLR*, 15 (1917), 281–313, found that the percentage of legislative acts declared unconstitutional in the state declined during the 1870s and 1880s.

experience and litigation into the enduring products of law and justice, and to place on record for our instruction and guidance the reasons of the Judges for every step in this wondrous, this ceaseless, this beneficent progress."[39]

But others shared the fears of the Michigan law professor who criticized the judicial tendency "to set aside legislative enactments because in conflict with unwritten principles of constitutional law. If this claim becomes established, . . . there will be . . . a most material change in the source of our laws, and a great increase in the powers of the judiciary." Populists and others unhappy with the courts' social and economic policies were not the only ones who accused them of assuming powers and responsibilities that properly belonged to the legislatures. The *American Law Review,* originally an advocate of judicial activism, turned under editor Seymour D. Thompson (1883–1904) into the leading professional critic of aggressive judicial review. Philadelphia lawyer George Wharton Pepper warned in 1898: "Our constitutional law is fast taking on the aspect of the legislative will . . . Our courts must . . . curb their newly developed tendency to fetter governmental action by constitutional restraints." A more passionate critic charged that "sovereign legislation has shrunk to the dimension of corporate by-laws and . . . the legislatures of States that were once called sovereign lie helpless at the feet of the Federal judiciary."[40]

The character of the debate over judicial review is revealing. Defenders of the courts and of the legislatures alike assumed that the other branch of government was increasingly active, and each was right. If the courts struck down larger numbers of laws, there was far more legislation to be reviewed. In this sense legislatures and courts were responding, each in their own way, to new demands imposed by the changing conditions of American life.

39. David A. Wells, "The Theory and Practice of Local Taxation in the United States," *AM,* 33 (1874), 68; Dillon, *Municipal Corporations* (4th ed., 1890), vii. See also Charles Warren, *The Supreme Court in United States History* (Boston, 1923), III, 411.

40. Kent, *Closing Address,* 11; Alan F. Westin, "The Supreme Court, the Populist Movement and the Campaign of 1896," *JP,* 15 (1953), 3–41; Arnold M. Paul, *Conservative Crisis and the Rule of Law* (Ithaca, 1960), 43–44; Pepper quoted in W. U. Hensel, "The Legislation of 1897 as an Illustration of the Decadence of the Legislative Branch of our State Government," *PBA Reports,* 4 (1898), 110–111; *ALR,* 27 (1893), 75.

The growing authority of the late nineteenth century courts was fostered by a number of strong-minded state and federal judges. Among them were Charles Andrews, Charles J. Folger, and Rufus W. Peckham of the strategically located New York Court of Appeals; Thomas M. Cooley, James W. Campbell, Isaac P. Christiancy, and Benjamin F. Graves, the "big four" of the Michigan Supreme Court; George Sharswood, a strict constructionist Pennsylvania Supreme Court justice from 1868 to 1882; Mercer Beasley, New Jersey's chief justice from 1864 to 1890 ("To review his work on the bench would be to outline the development of law in New Jersey for a generation"); Edward G. Ryan of the Wisconsin Supreme Court, the epitome of judicial self-importance ("the bench symbolizes on earth the throne of divine justice . . . Law in its highest sense is the will of God"); George W. Stone of Alabama, who wrote almost 2,000 opinions between 1876 and 1894; and Oliver Wendell Holmes, who prepared some 1,300 opinions during his twenty-year tenure (1882–1902) on Massachusetts's Supreme Judicial Court.[41]

The major state courts—New York, Massachusetts, Michigan—usually took the lead in the evolution of late nineteenth century American common law. But it was possible for a skillful and imaginative judge in a relatively minor jurisdiction to make a noticeable imprint on the law of the time. Such was the case with Charles Doe of New Hampshire. Doe was a member of the state supreme court from 1859 to 1896, and chief justice for the last twenty years of his long tenure. Like Holmes of Massachusetts and Ryan of Wisconsin, he had a majestic contempt for the political process. He once told New Hampshire Republican boss William Chandler: "The whole business of politics is to me unutterably distasteful, and I shall always be grateful to you or anyone who does anything to keep me out of it." Nevertheless—according to Chandler—Doe was "the uncontrolled and mighty ruler and governor of New Hampshire; superior to the executive and legislative branches of the government." His judicial style—"utter

41. *DAB*, passim; on Ryan, Stone, and Sharswood see Lewis, ed., *Great American Lawyers*, VI, passim; Alan Jones, "Thomas M. Cooley and the Michigan Supreme Court: 1865–1885," *AJLH*, 10 (1966), 97–121; Hurst, *Growth*, 122–146. See also Irving Browne, "The New York Court of Appeals," *GB*, 2 (1890), 277–291, 321–341.

disregard for precedent and the remarkable search for abstract justice"—enabled Doe to make major contributions to the law of railroad regulation and to the modification of civil procedure—what he called "new-modelling the forms."[42]

Ultimately it was the Supreme Court of the United States that set the tone for a judicial generation. The late nineteenth century Court dealt increasingly with litigation produced by a burgeoning industrial capitalism; and in doing so it exemplified the judicial activism of the time.

Morrison R. Waite, who succeeded Chase as chief justice in 1874 and served until 1888, was a strong, unabashed Republican partisan. He acidly commented on Lyman Trumbull's 1872 bolt to the Liberal Republicans: "When a man gets to 'lying around loose' as he has done, it don't do to bet on him"; and he excoriated President Rutherford B. Hayes's flirtation with southern Democrats: "I hope he will learn by and by that he must be either the one thing or the other in politics." But Waite's career as chief justice was notable chiefly for his dedication to strengthening the position of the Supreme Court as *primus inter pares* among the branches of government. He once observed that Senators Henry B. Anthony of Rhode Island and George F. Edmunds of Vermont were "innocent fools . . . do they yet know that they only formulate a mass of stuff printed as the Statutes of the U.S. but that nine fellows, sitting in black gowns made the '*Laws*' of the U.S."[43]

The other important additions to the Court in the 1870s—William Strong and Joseph Bradley (1870), John Marshall Harlan (1877)—also had Republican political backgrounds, which appeared in their support of national over state power and in Harlan's civil rights opinions. But for the most part they did not perpetuate the ideological divisions that characterized the postwar Court. Samuel Miller, the justice who was closest to the Republican spirit of the 1860s, was less influential from the mid-seventies until his departure in 1890. He often clashed with Bradley, and in the 1880s devoted himself to the relatively noncontroversial task of improving the federal court system.[44]

42. Reid, *Chief Justice*, 85, 96, 201, 265.

43. C. Peter Magrath, *Morrison R. Waite: The Triumph of Character* (New York, 1963), 84, 112, 137.

44. Charles Fairman, *Mr. Justice Miller and the Supreme Court 1862–1890* (Cambridge, 1939), 373–374, ch. 17; Magrath, *Waite*, 217.

Stephen Field, the doyen of conservatism on the postwar Court, gained new supporters in the 1880s and the 1890s. Grover Cleveland sent Lucius Q. C. Lamar, an ex-Confederate officer and Mississippi Democratic senator, to the Court in 1888. In the same year Illinois Democrat Melville W. Fuller replaced Waite as chief justice, to serve in that capacity until 1910. Louisiana Catholic Democrat Edward D. White joined the Court in 1894; Rufus W. Peckham of New York, who was close to state Democratic boss David Hill and subscribed to the "old time Democratic ideas" of strict construction and limited government, was appointed in 1895. David J. Brewer of Kansas, the most important Republican appointee of the late nineteenth century (1889), was a nephew of Field and shared many of his uncle's views. "The paternal theory of government is to me odious," he once declared.[45]

The Court did not seriously challenge legislative activism until the late 1880s. Before then almost all of the state social and economic legislation passed under the police power was allowed to stand. It seemed to one observer as late as 1889 that the Court "has . . . given the benefit of the doubt to the State, rather than to the individual; to the people, rather than to the person."[46]

One of the truisms of American constitutional history is that during the late 1880s and the 1890s the judiciary became markedly more hostile to legislation that in its view threatened corporate interests. The *American Law Review* charged in 1894: "it has come to be the fashion . . . for courts to overturn acts of the State legislatures upon mere economical theories and upon mere casuistical grounds."

The evidence to support this view is familiar and impressive. It includes the use of the liberty of contract doctrine and the due process and equal protection clauses of the Fourteenth Amendment to void state laws that regulated working conditions, taxed rail-

45. King, *Fuller*; on Peckham, Sen. William Lindsay to Daniel S. Lamont, Feb. 1, 1894, Peckham Mss, LC; Brewer in Budd v. New York, 143 U.S. 517, 551 (1891).

46. A. H. Wintersteen, "The Sovereign State," *ALReg*, ns, 28 (1889), 139. See also Walter D. Coles, "Politics and the Supreme Court of the United States," *ALR*, 27 (1893), 182–223; Hollis R. Bailey, "A New Nation," *HLR*, 9 (1895), 309–323; Fred. Perry Powers, "Recent Centralizing Tendencies in the Supreme Court," *PSQ*, 15 (1890), 389–410; Warren, *Supreme Court*, III, chs. 35–36.

roads, or controlled their rates. The culmination came in that unholy trinity of Supreme Court decisions in the mid-nineties: *In re Debs*, which sustained a federal injunction against striking railroad workers; *U.S. v. E. C. Knight*, which severely (if briefly) limited the scope of the Sherman Antitrust Act; and *Pollack v. Farmers' Loan and Trust*, which struck down the 1894 federal income tax. These have been called "related aspects of a massive judicial entry into the socioeconomic scene, ... a conservative-oriented revolution."[47]

It was true that "the notion seems to be thoroughly fixed in the minds of some judges that there are certain natural rights of property which are beyond the control of the legislature." But the performance of the late nineteenth century courts had deeper sources as well. Judges shared the widespread fear of the time that American society was being wrenched out of recognition by industrialism and its consequences. Justice Stephen Field defended judicial activism on this ground:

> As population and wealth increase—as the inequalities in the conditions of men become more and more marked and disturbing—as the enormous aggregation of wealth possessed by some corporations excites uneasiness lest their power should become dominating in the legislation of the country ... —as population in some quarters presses upon the means of subsistence, and angry menaces against order find vent in loud denunciations—it becomes more and more the imperative duty of the court to enforce with a firm hand every guarantee of the constitution.

This was something more than subservience to vested interests. Field adhered to old American values of private right and individual freedom that led him to be as ill at ease with corporate power as he was with legislative activism. Brewer, too, strongly opposed monopolies, and accepted state police power regulation that placed some restraints on acquisitive capitalism. Much the same could be said of Thomas M. Cooley. And John F. Dillon, who held that "private property is rightful, beneficial and necessary to the public

47. *ALR*, 28 (1894), 306; Paul, *Conservative Crisis*, 2. See also Arthur S. Miller, *The Supreme Court and American Capitalism* (New York, 1968), 18 ff; John R. Dos Passos, "The United States Supreme Court and the Commercial Era," *YLJ*, 17 (1908), 573–584; John R. Commons, *The Legal Foundations of Capitalism* (New York, 1924).

welfare, and that all attempts to pillage and destroy it . . . are as baneful as they are illegal," insisted "with equal eagerness upon the proposition that such property is under many important duties toward the State and society, which the owners generally fail to appreciate."[48]

The instrument of court review most commonly identified with the conservative judicialism of the late nineteenth century was the use of the due process and equal protection clauses of the Fourteenth Amendment to strike down state taxation and regulation of corporations. The idea that corporations were legal "persons," entitled to safeguards originally designed to protect the freedmen, only gradually emerged. Even Justices Field and Bradley, who pioneered in the application of Fourteenth Amendment due process to property rights, did not have large corporations in mind. The amendment was designed, Field said in 1884, "to secure to every one the right to pursue his happiness unrestrained, except by just, equal, and impartial laws." Bradley shared this view: "I hold that the liberty of pursuit—the right to follow any of the ordinary callings of life—is one of the privileges of a citizen of the United States . . . Monopolies are the bane of our body politic at the present day. In the eager pursuit of gain they are sought in every direction."[49]

The Supreme Court in fact was slow to use the amendment to protect *any* rights, civil or property. Forty-six Fourteenth Amendment cases came before the Court from 1872 to 1886. Corporations were parties in twelve of these actions, Negroes in eight; forty decisions went for the state, six for the plaintiff pleading the amend-

48. T. V. Brown, "Due Process of Law," *ALR*, 32 (1898), 25; Stephen Field, "The Centenary of the Supreme Court of the United States," *ALR*, 24 (1890), 366–367; Robert Goedecke, "Justice Field and Inherent Rights," *RP*, 27 (1965), 198–207; Robert E. Garner, "Justice Brewer and Substantive Due Process: A Conservative Court Revisited," *VLR*, 18 (1965), 615–641; Jones, "Cooley, and 'Laissez-Faire Constitutionalism' "; Dillon in *NYSBA Proceedings*, 18 (1895), 36. See also Charles W. McCurdy, "Justice Field and the Jurisprudence of Government-Business Relations: Some Parameters of Laissez-Faire Constitutionalism, 1863–1897," *JAH*, 61 (1975), 970–1005.

49. Field and Bradley in Butchers' Union Slaughter-House Co. v. Crescent City Co., 111 U.S. 746, 759, 764 (1884). See also Howard J. Graham, *Everyman's Constitution* (Madison, 1968), chs. 9, 13; John P. Roche, "Entrepreneurial Liberty and the Fourteenth Amendment," *LH*, 4 (1963), 1–31.

ment. Justices Miller and Field, who sharply differed on many issues, had a shared reluctance to apply Fourteenth Amendment due process. In 1878, when scarcely more than a dozen such cases had come before the Court, Miller thought it overused. He wanted the amendment's meaning to emerge through a "gradual process of judicial inclusion and exclusion." Field warned in 1886: "This court is not a harbor where refuge can be found from every act of ill-advised and oppressive State legislation." Not surprisingly, an 1886 review of railroad law concluded that the application of Fourteenth Amendment due process "has been determined to be untenable." Brewer in 1891 thought that instead of making the amendment "a national guarantee against future state invasion of private rights, . . . judicial decisions have shorn it of strength."[50]

From the late 1880s on, there occurred what has been called a judicial revolution in the use of Fourteenth Amendment due process. Between 1887 and 1910, the Supreme Court handed down 558 decisions based primarily on the Fourteenth Amendment. But this was far from being a wholesale assault on the regulatory powers of the states. Of the 243 pre-1901 Fourteenth Amendment decisions, 93 percent upheld the state law at issue. (Of the 315 decisions from 1901 to 1910, 76 percent went for the state.) Substantial majorities of the late nineteenth and early twentieth century Supreme Court decisions that invoked the Constitution's contract and commerce clauses—83 percent of the 1873–1912 contract cases, 74 percent of the commerce cases—also upheld the constitutionality of state laws. At least in quantitative terms, the late nineteenth century Supreme Court was restrained in its review of state legislation.[51]

What all of this suggests is that the rise of judicial activism in the late nineteenth century had as much to do with the structural relationship of the courts to other sectors of the polity as with the

50. Charles W. Collins, *The Fourteenth Amendment and the States* (Boston, 1912), 183; Miller in Davidson v. New Orleans, 96 U.S. 97, 104 (1877); Field in Missouri Pacific Railroad Co. v. Humes, 115 U.S. 512, 520–521 (1885); John W. Smith, "State Regulation of Railway Corporations as to Rates," *CLJ*, 23 (1886), 106; David J. Brewer, *Protection to Private Property from Public Attack* (New Haven, 1891).

51. Collins, *Fourteenth Amendment*, 183; Charles Warren, "The Progressiveness of the United States Supreme Court," *ColLR*, 13 (1913), 294–

social and economic predilections of the judges. The growing professionalism of the law and the increasing activism of the judges filled a void in governance. But the men of the law had varied goals and varying ways to attain them. An old concern for private rights and individual freedom coexisted with the desire to foster the development of a national economy. The quest for social stability in a time of rapid change might lead either to support for or constraints on legislative and administrative activism. The legal system, no less than the other sectors of the late nineteenth century polity, was caught up in the tension between the desire to preserve an endangered American past and the need to come to terms with the tumultuous present.

313, and "A Bulwark to the State Police Power—The United States Supreme Court," ibid., 667–695. See also Felix Frankfurter, Mr. Justice Holmes and the Supreme Court (Cambridge, 1939), Appendix I, for data on Fourteenth Amendment cases; Edward S. Corwin, "The Supreme Court and the Fourteenth Amendment," MLR, 7 (1908–1909), 643–672; Robert E. Cushman, "The Social and Economic Development of the 14th Amendment," MLR, 20 (1922), 737–767.

The Political Economy of Industrialism

THE CENTRAL FACT of late nineteenth century American economic life was the growth of industrial and agricultural productivity. The value added by industrial production (in 1879 prices) increased from $2.0 billion in 1879 to $6.3 billion in 1899; the increase in agriculture was from $2.6 to $3.9 billion. The gross national product (measured in 1947 dollars) averaged $16.4 billion ($370 per capita) a year during the 1869–1879 decade, and rose to $65.8 billion ($800 per capita) from 1899 to 1908. By another measure (using an 1899 index of 100), American industrial production ✓ went from 39 in 1880 to 103 in 1900.[1]

By the end of the century, large corporations, complex production and distribution processes, and a national domestic market for consumer goods—in effect, the economy of the twentieth century—had come into being. An economist has observed that "the structure of relative prices in 1890 was more typical of 1960 than of 1820," which is to say that the watershed dividing the early from the modern American economy had been crossed.

Late nineteenth century agriculture closely resembled the industrial sector in its mechanization, its increasingly complex mar-

---

1. On value added, *HS*, 139; on GNP, Seymour Harris, ed., *American Economic History* (New York, 1961), 70; Edwin Frickey, *Production in the United States 1860–1914* (Cambridge, 1947), 127. See also Lance E. Davis and others, *American Economic Growth* (New York, 1972), ch. 2; Jeffrey G. Williamson, *Late Nineteenth-Century American Development: A General Equilibrium History* (Cambridge, Eng., 1974), part III.

keting system, and a productivity that drove down unit costs and prices. Its important differences were the persistence of small production units, a relatively greater dependence on overseas markets, and varying regional characteristics.[2]

This was growth fueled neither by territorial expansion nor by massive government aid. One estimate is that the state was responsible for less than 5 percent of capital formation in the period. The primary sources of capital were reinvestment, lower labor costs per unit of production, and the accumulation of investment capital through intermediaries such as banks, insurance companies, and securities markets. And it was growth without inflation. A long-term downward movement of prices—some 25 to 30 percent between the early 1870s and the late 1890s—resulted from technology-assisted productivity increases and the expansion of the labor force through massive immigration as well as natural population increase. But while this was a powerfully productive economy, it was also an erratic one. Speculative panics, business failures, and substantial unemployment frequently occurred, most notably from 1873 to 1878, from 1882 to 1885, and from 1893 to 1897.[3]

The new economy had an enormous impact on late nineteenth century public policy. But it was an impact constantly tempered by diverse and clashing economic interests, regional and local resistance to economic consolidation, and ambivalent attitudes toward the active state and, indeed, toward economic modernization itself.

2. Alfred D. Chandler, Jr., "The Beginnings of 'Big Business' in American Industry," *BHR*, 33 (1959), 1–31; Harvey S. Perloff and others, *Regions, Resources, and Economic Growth* (Baltimore, 1960), part III; Dorothy S. Brady, "Relative Prices in the Nineteenth Century," *JEH*, 24 (1964), 195; on agriculture, Fred A. Shannon, *The Farmer's Last Frontier: Agriculture, 1860–1897* (New York, 1961). See also National Bureau of Economic Research, *Trends in the American Economy in the Nineteenth Century* (Princeton, 1960).

3. On government, Simon Kuznets, *Capital in the American Economy: Its Formation and Financing* (Princeton, 1961), 406. See also Lance E. Davis and John Lengler, "The Government in the American Economy, 1815–1902: A Quantitative Study," *JEH*, 26 (1966), 514–522; Henry W. Broude, "The Role of the State in American Economic Development 1820–1890," in Hugh G. J. Aitken, ed., *The State and Economic Growth* (New York, 1959), 4–25.

The New Political Economy

The consequences of economic change were as central a concern of thoughtful Americans in the late nineteenth century as slavery and the character of the Union had been in the mid-century decades. Commentators dwelt on the magnitude, wealth, power, and unlimited future of industrial America—and as often on the slums, the immigrants, the social disorder and class conflict that came with the new economy.

The content of the federal census gave fair warning of these social effects. The census of 1880 included, for the first time, data on wealth, debt, and taxation; on strikes; and on the social statistics of cities. The 1890 census reported on farm and home mortgages, home ownership, and the distribution of wealth; on crime, pauperism, and benevolence; and on education. It reported too the end of the frontier as a continuous line of settlement, and revealed that for the first time more net value had been added to the national product by manufacturing than by agriculture. From the census of 1900 came studies of employers and wages, of working women and child labor.

The appearance of data on the distribution of wealth in the United States led to considerable discussion of its meaning. According to the 1890 census, less than half of American families owned their own homes. Ninety-one percent of the nation's families owned 29 percent of the national wealth, while 9 percent controlled the remaining 71 percent. The 1900 Report of the United States Industrial Commission concluded that between 60 percent and 88 percent of the American people could be classified as poor or very poor.

The New York corporation lawyer (and follower of Henry George) Thomas G. Shearman believed that the maldistribution of wealth in the United States was greater than in England and was getting worse. But statistician Carroll Wright thought that the percentage of the population in the lowest class category was declining. Edward Everett Hale probably represented prevailing opinion when he portrayed an American population with few that were very rich or very poor, and with widespread property ownership. Nevertheless, the new economy evoked fresh concern over the distribution of wealth and property.[4]

Analysts embarked also on broad inquiries into the character of the economic transformation of their time. David Ames Wells's *Recent Economic Changes* (1889) perceptively discussed the new realities of improved transportation and communication, rising consumption, production and (he thought) overproduction. During the 1890s Simon N. Patten began to explore economic abundance as a condition new to human experience. And Thorstein Veblen (whose *Theory of the Leisure Class* appeared in 1899) commented with subtle irony on the consequences of industrial and finance capitalism.[5]

But prescribing remedies for the social evils of the new economy —maldistribution of wealth, corporate power, industrial and agricultural depression, urban blight—proved to be as difficult for late nineteenth century economic analysts as applying the new nationalism in a programmatic way had been for post-Civil War political theorists.

One response was a genre of popular economic diagnosis that began with Henry George's *Progress and Poverty* in 1879, and continued to the end of the century with Laurence Gronlund's *The Cooperative Commonwealth* (1884), Edward Bellamy's *Looking Backward* (1888), and Henry Demarest Lloyd's *Wealth Against Commonwealth* (1894). More or less socialist models of social and economic reform were common to the works that came after *Progress and Poverty*, though with distinctive American modifications. Gronlund's book was the first popular introduction of

4. George K. Holmes, "The Concentration of Wealth," *PSQ*, 8 (1893), 589–600; Charles B. Spahr, *An Essay on the Present Distribution of Wealth in the United States*, 2nd ed. (New York, 1896); C. K. Yearley, *The Money Machines* (Albany, 1970), 27; Thomas G. Shearman, "The Owners of the United States," *Forum*, 8 (1889), 262–273; Carroll D. Wright, "Are the Rich Growing Richer and the Poor Poorer?" *AM*, 80 (1897), 300–309; Edward E. Hale, *What Is the American People?* (Boston, 1885), 8–16. See also Lee Soltow, "Evidence on Income Inequality in the United States, 1866–1965," *JEH*, 29 (1969), 279–286, which concludes that the proportionate income share of the rich did not increase in the late nineteenth century.

5. David A. Wells, *Recent Economic Changes and their Effect on the Production and Distribution of Wealth and the Well-Being of Society* (New York, 1889); Simon N. Patten, *The New Basis of Civilization*, ed. Daniel M. Fox (1907; Cambridge, 1968). See also Joseph Dorfman, *The Economic Mind in American Civilization* (New York, 1949), III, ch. 5.

Marxian socialism to American readers. But his cooperative commonwealth was a national not an international one, and after using "the foreign word, Solidarity" in the first edition of the work, he dropped it in his 1890 revision. Bellamy's Looking Backward, the most popular of these books, has been called "an exposition of the ethics of solidarity derived in large part from its author's mystical interpretation of the Civil War." The journals through which Bellamy sought to transform his ideas into a political movement— The Nationalist, The New Nation—suggest that his postcapitalist Utopia was based on national rather than class cohesion.

These assaults on monopoly, privilege, and exploitation, accompanied by proposals for social reconstruction through harmony and cooperation, tell us much about the American response to the coming of industrialism. Their popular appeal stemmed in part from their stress on the restoration of community by substituting a cooperative for a competitive model of social and economic behavior. They were attractive, too, because they mixed "moral earnestness and religious feeling." Bellamy's Looking Backward has been called "a religious fable." They spoke to a generation likely to respond to prescriptions for change that rested on familiar precepts of national unity and Christian morality.[6]

The work of more formal, academic economists had much in common with these popular analyses. The founders of the American Economic Association in 1885 were strongly influenced by German economic thought of the time, which placed considerable stress on the active, regulatory state, and they were concerned far more than their laissez-faire predecessors with the social problems that stemmed from industrialism. Nevertheless, leading scholars such as Richard T. Ely, John Bates Clark, and Simon Patten spoke of "the solidarity of society," "brotherhood," and "the Social Commonwealth." They stressed Christian morality and the restoration of community, as did George and Bellamy.[7]

6. Laurence Gronlund, The Cooperative Commonwealth, ed. Stow Persons (1884; Cambridge, 1965), xiii; Edward Bellamy, Looking Backward 2000–1887, ed. John L. Thomas (1888; Cambridge, 1967), 2, 41. See also Thomas, "Utopia for an Urban Age: Henry George, Henry Demarest Lloyd, Edward Bellamy," PAH, 6 (1972), 135–166; Sidney Fine, Laissez Faire and the General-Welfare State (Ann Arbor, 1956), ch. 7; R. Jackson Wilson, In Quest of Community: Social Philosophy in the United States, 1860–1920 (New York, 1968).

7. John R. Everett, Religion in Economics: A Study of J. B. Clark, R. T.

The problem of facing the realities of the new economy with social values that were rooted in a preindustrial society was not unique to the economic analysts of the time. It recurred in a variety of forms as the late nineteenth century American polity responded to the unsettling consequences of rapid economic change.

Tariff and Currency

Despite the sweeping economic transformation of the late nineteenth century, the major economic policy concerns of Congress and the political parties were old and familiar ones: the tariff and the currency. Indeed, in these years the two issues reached the peak of their importance and came to serve as repositories for a wide range of popular wants and fears.

As political issues, the tariff and the currency had two distinct components. On one level they were defined by the jousting of specific economic interests, whose positions reflected facts of economic life such as the flow of credit and capital, the state of foreign and domestic markets, and the relative costs of raw materials and finished products.

But tariff and currency policy also bore a heavy symbolic meaning. Protection and free trade, the gold standard and free silver were important ideological, even psychological rallying points in the politics of the late nineteenth century. They were evocative expressions of the anxieties of a people swept up in massive economic change.

The availability of markets abroad and the protection of markets at home had obvious importance in an economy whose industrial and agricultural productivity were rapidly expanding. But a wide gap separated the reality and the rhetoric of the tariff issue in the late nineteenth century. It is doubtful whether the ups and downs of tariff policy had major consequences for the economy. Both exports and imports remained well under 7 percent of the gross national product; comparable figures for Great Britain ranged from

Ely, S. N. Patten (New York, 1946). See also Dorfman, Economic Mind, III, part II; Fine, Laissez Faire, ch. 7.

20 to 40 percent. No less an authority than Andrew Carnegie found the impact of the tariff on the iron and steel industry to be "trifling." The statistician Carroll Wright was all for setting the tariff on a "scientific basis," but admitted that its effect on manufacturing was "unclear." It is a mark of the confusion attending the subject that the economic sophistication displayed in the major congressional tariff debate of 1894 was markedly inferior to that of 1824, seventy years before.[8]

Certainly there were interest groups for whom tariff rates were important. Louisiana beet growers, Pennsylvania iron and steel manufacturers, West Virginia coal miners, Ohio and Texas wool growers, hemp and flax farmers feared foreign competition. New York City importers, iron manufacturers dependent upon imported ore, railroads seeking lower prices for steel rails, Chicago meat packers after a reduction in salt duties, farmers and cattlemen with large overseas markets had similarly solid stakes in rate reductions.

As a result, the major tariff bills of the period were patchwork quilts of hundreds of adjustments for special interests. What was said of the 1883 tariff applied as well to its successors: "Its general character cannot be easily described; in truth, it can hardly be said to have any general character." Republicans in the presidential election of 1880 derided Democratic candidate Winfield S. Hancock for declaring that the tariff was a local issue. But that was a coldly accurate statement—as Hancock's Republican opponent James A. Garfield had recognized some years before: "It is . . . manifest that the [tariff] question has assumed a local rather than a national aspect." Low tariff Republicans and high tariff Democrats were not uncommon in Congress during the early eighties.[9]

8. *HS*, 537–538; *BHS*, 283–284, 367; Carnegie quoted in Edward C. Kirkland, *Industry Comes of Age: Business, Labor, and Public Policy 1860–1897* (New York, 1961), 189; Carroll D. Wright, "The Scientific Basis of Tariff Legislation," *JSS*, 19 (1884), 11; Richard C. Edwards, "Economic Sophistication in Nineteenth Century Congressional Tariff Debates," *JEH*, 30 (1970), 802–838. See also G. R. Hawke, "The United States Tariff and Industrial Protection in the Late Nineteenth Century," *JEH*, 28 (1975), 84–99; Bennett P. Baack and Edward J. Ray, "Tariff Policy and Comparative Advantage in the Iron and Steel Industry," *EEH*, 11 (1973), 3–24.

9. F. W. Taussig, *The Tariff History of the United States*, 8th rev. ed. (New York, 1930), 249; Robert G. Caldwell, *James A. Garfield* (Indianapolis, 1931), 196. See also Edward Stanwood, *Tariff Controversies in the Nineteenth Century* (Boston, 1903), vol. II; Ida M. Tarbell, *The Tariff in Our Times* (New York, 1911).

However, the issue became an increasingly important measure of party difference. One measure of this change was the choice of low tariff advocate John Carlisle over protectionist Samuel Randall to be Democratic speaker of the house in 1883. Another was President Grover Cleveland's December 1887 message to Congress, which was devoted solely to the need for tariff reduction. The message "crystallized tariff sentiment in both parties." Thereafter national politics frequently pivoted on the clash between Republican protectionism and Democratic reductionism.

Enormous stores of rhetorical ammunition were expended in congressional tariff debates. The House endured 151 speeches when it considered the abortive Democratic Mills tariff of 1888. But while this and the Wilson tariff of 1894 were advertised as fulfillments of Democratic pledges to reduce rates, and the McKinley bill of 1890 and the Dingley tariff of 1897 (with greater reason) as triumphs of Republican protectionism, the nuts and bolts of tariffmaking remained firmly in the hands of spokesmen for special interests. The Senate added more than six hundred amendments to the 1894 bill, over eight hundred to the 1897 measure.[10]

A recurrent theme in tariff discussions was the need to protect and enhance American markets abroad. Until the last years of the century, this was of much greater concern to agricultural than to industrial producers. Democrats argued that lower rates on incoming finished products would smooth the way for the overseas sale of American fibers and foodstuffs. Republicans such as James G. Blaine stressed reciprocity treaties and granting the President the authority to adjust rates downward through special arrangements with other countries. But reciprocity and flexible ratemaking foundered on the shoals of special interests. Tariff policy remained a mix of general party positions in principle and the highly detailed accommodation of particular needs in practice.[11]

The importance of the tariff issue rested in great part on this very duality. The frequency and specificity of rate revision gave

10. Tarbell, *Tariff*, 154; Clarence L. Miller, *The States of the Old Northwest and the Tariff, 1865–1888* (Emporia, Kan., 1929). See also Taussig, *Tariff History*, on legislative details.

11. Tom E. Terrill, *The Tariff, Politics, and American Foreign Policy, 1874–1901* (Westport, Conn., 1973).

politicians the opportunity of making recurrent calls on the support of interest groups concerned with particular schedules. Beyond this, the polar party tariff positions—Republican protectionism, Democratic free trade—appealed to large sectors of the body politic.

The very term "protection" offered the prospect of security in an unstable, rapidly changing economy, "the maintenance of the *status quo* during the period of transition." It promised to shield American industry, agriculture, and wage scales from cheap products and sweated labor overseas. Simon N. Patten, who pioneered in the formulation of an economic analysis of abundance rather than scarcity, was the most distinguished academic advocate of protection. He argued that a high tariff (along with internal improvements) would foster a vigorous national life. From its origins as "a temporary expedient to gain specific ends," tariff protection had evolved into "a consistent endeavor to keep society dynamic and progressive."[12]

High tariffs accorded, too, with the traditional Republican stress on the active state: "protection, in the broadest sense of the term, is not only the sole function of government, but the primal object sought in establishing its authority." Tariff defenders argued that "the nation has the intelligence and the authority to effect a coordinate development of its industries by law," that protection was "essential to the life of the nation, for the production upon which depend vitality and strength, and for the wages and comforts and elevation of the citizens, upon which rest national sanity and growth, and the conditions of greatness and splendor." This was rhetoric reminiscent of the Civil War–Reconstruction era, applied now to the problems of a new economy.[13]

12. David Rothman, *Politics and Power: The United States Senate 1869–1901* (Cambridge, 1966), ch. 7; Stanwood, *Tariff Controversies*, II, 256; Patten, *The Economic Basis of Protection* (Philadelphia, 1890), 7–8 et passim.

13. David H. Mason, "Protection in the United States," in John J. Lalor, ed., *Cyclopaedia of Political Science, Political Economy, and of the Political History of the United States* (New York, 1884, 1890), III, 423; Robert E. Thompson, "Benefits of the Tariff System," *NAR*, 139 (1884), 391; Ellis Roberts, "Moral Aspects of the Tariff," *NPR*, 3 (1887), 331. See also William E. Gladstone and James G. Blaine, "A Duel: Free Trade or Protection," *NAR*, 150 (1890), 1–54; for "tariff reform" (that is, protection) in England, Benjamin H. Brown, *The Tariff Reform Movement in Great Britain 1881–1895* (New York, 1943).

Free trade doctrine found a comparably congenial home in the Democratic party. John Q. Mills of Texas, William L. Wilson of West Virginia, and James B. Beck of Kentucky made tariff reduction the central expression of their Jeffersonian, small-government political faith. Because free trade held out the prospect of the United States becoming a major competitor of the British in world markets, the creed was attractive to Irish Democrats as well.[14]

In addition, a number of publicists, intellectuals, professionals, and small businessmen found in the cause of tariff reduction a means of conveying their concern over the rise of large industries and the supremacy of professional politicians. These tariff reformers attacked protection as evidence of the politicos' subservience to corporate interests and their readiness to ignore the natural laws of political economy in order to woo the electorate.

The most vocal of these antitariff spokesmen was the economist David Ames Wells. Free trade, he said, exemplified the "economic axiom . . . that that government is best which governs least." *Nation* editor E. L. Godkin warned that protection eroded the freedom of the individual and encouraged labor to expect something for nothing: "If the protectionist policy is persisted in, the process of assimilating American society to that of Europe must go on." William Graham Sumner, the leading academic proponent of laissez-faire, dismissed protection as "an arrant piece of economic quackery" which hindered growth by blocking the free flow of trade. The economist Francis A. Walker agreed. Protectionists, he charged, would "substitute aims proposed by the State for those which would otherwise be sought by its citizens upon their own individual initiative." The tariff debate thus caught up in familiar and evocative terms many of the concerns generated by the economic transformation of the time.[15]

The politics of money underwent a strikingly similar development. Currency like tariff policy was important because of its close connection with the shock effects of the new economy,

14. Festus P. Summers, *William L. Wilson and Tariff Reform* (New Brunswick, 1953), 94; Geoffrey Blodgett, *The Gentle Reformers: Massachusetts Democrats in the Cleveland Era* (Cambridge, 1966), ch. 4.

15. Wells, "Free Trade," in Lalor, ed., *Cyclopaedia*, II, 289; Godkin, "Some Political and Social Aspects of the Tariff," NPR, 3 (1887), 176;

and because the gold standard and free silver had a symbolic importance camparable to protection and free trade.

The resumption of specie payments for greenbacks, combined with Treasury silver purchases to sustain a bimetallic currency, was the bipartisan solution of the Bland-Allison Act of 1878 to post-Civil War fiscal problems. Resumption did not have the deflationary consequence that its opponents predicted. By 1884 the money supply had risen to 50 percent more than its 1879 low point. The basic reason was that the balance of trade had shifted to the favor of the United States—a tribute to the rising productivity of American industry and agriculture. In consequence the overseas pull on American gold eased off.

But this did not eliminate the grounds for dispute over fiscal policy. Serious problems persisted: sectional disparities in access to money and credit; the credit strains (particularly for farmers) engendered by falling prices and high production costs; the impact of changes in the international flow of credit and gold; the uncertain state of the gold-silver ratio and indeed of bimetallism itself. Many of these were transnational problems beyond the control of American public policy. But they bred a discontent that inevitably had political consequences.

The most pressing fiscal problem of the 1880s was the large revenue surplus generated by rising tariff receipts. Republicans sought to spend off this surplus in order to maintain the protective tariff system. One way of doing so was to retire the outstanding national debt as quickly as possible. The gross public debt declined from $2,755,764,000 in 1866 to a low of $961,432,000 in 1893. From 1886 to 1890 alone, a third of a billion dollars was applied to this purpose, with constricting effects on the circulation of bank-note currency. Another outlet for surplus revenue was the veterans' pension system. Pension Bureau expenditures rose from a post-Civil War low of $27,100,000 in 1878 to an 1893 peak of $159,400,000—42 percent of the federal budget—in apparent defiance of the mortality tables. Rivers and harbors public works

---

Sumner, *Protectionism, the Issue that Teaches that Waste Makes Wealth* (New York, 1887), vi; Walker, "Protection and Protectionists," *QJE*, 4 (1889–1890), 250. See also Fred B. Joyner, *David Ames Wells: Champion of Free Trade* (Cedar Rapids, Ia., 1939), and Tom E. Terrill, "David A. Wells, the Tariff, and the Democracy, 1877–1894," *JAH*, 56 (1969), 540–555.

spending also rose, from $8,100,000 in 1880 to a high of $20,800,000 in 1898.

The tangled web of credit, prices, bullion, and currency stock that enmeshed the late nineteenth century American economy was the greatest source of political contention. Farmers in particular suffered from a tightening price and credit bind. Foreign competition and their own productivity led to a steady decline in the prices that wheat and cotton growers received for their crops. But fixed costs for land, machinery, and credit imposed a growing fiscal burden. In addition, the declining value of silver compared to gold and the European countries' abandonment of a bimetallic currency threatened the monetary compromise of 1878.

From this mix of problems two political movements emerged. Silver miners pressed for the maintenance of a fixed gold-silver ratio through large-scale Treasury silver purchases. Agrarians demanded a more inflationary money policy. These causes came together in the late eighties, with explosive political consequences.

The first legislative achievement of this new political force was the Sherman Silver Purchase Act of 1890, which obligated the Treasury to make monthly silver purchases sufficient to absorb the country's entire output of the metal. The new currency issuing from these purchases was supposed to satisfy agrarian inflationist sentiment. But falling American crop prices, high imports, and heavy sales of American securities by British investors created a massive drain on the gold supply of the United States. President Grover Cleveland's response—a series of government bond issues designed to lure gold back to America—had two adverse effects. It put a new strain on the domestic money supply, and it strengthened the political appeal of the view that identified gold with deflation and silver with inflation.

The politics of money grew more intense when a financial panic and industrial depression came in 1893, and Congress repealed the Sherman Silver Purchase Act in 1894. This step was designed to stanch the flow of gold from the Treasury. The growing imbalance in value between gold and silver led to a steady conversion of Treasury notes into gold and weakened the international credit of the United States. Bitter sectional divisions—the East and Midwest against the West and South—marked the debate over repeal. By 1896, economic depression and the government's contractionist fiscal policy had made the free coinage of silver at a 16 to 1 value ratio to gold the great panacea of discontented agrarians.[16]

It is not surprising that this was the case. Even more than the tariff, the politics of gold and silver had a resonance that made it an important expression of the economic anxieties of the late nineteenth century. As a contemporary put it, "certain peculiar romantic, sentimental or otherwise irrational, ideas connected with the product of the precious metals" had wide popularity.

Western and southern agrarians came to see free silver as an economic cure-all. Silver was the people's money, gold the money of plutocracy and exploitation. These stark and satisfying beliefs were nurtured by tracts such as William H. Harvey's *Coin's Financial School* (1894), which sold about a million copies. Free silver (helped by the money of the silver miners) became the ideological core of the Populist party. With the rise of the Democrat William Jennings Bryan the faith found its great political prophet.[17]

A comparable moral weight and social meaning came to rest on the adoption of the gold standard. Business and financial interests concerned over the state of American credit in a gold-standard world economy; middle class Americans fearful lest free silver erode the value of their pensions, life insurance policies, and other fixed sources of income; economists such as J. Laurence Laughlin who identified the gold standard with the natural laws of economics and with prosperity, stability, civilization itself: these made gold the measure of fiscal soundness and public morality.[18]

It was through the tariff and currency issues that the political

16. The foregoing discussion is based on Alexander D. Noyes, *Forty Years of American Finance*, 2d ed. (New York, 1909), Milton Friedman and Anna J. Schwartz, *A Monetary History of the United States, 1867–1960* (Princeton, 1963), ch. 3, and Paul Studenski and Herman E. Krooss, *Financial History of the United States*, 2d ed. (New York, 1963), chs. 19, 20; *HS*, 721, 741, 455.

17. Francis A. Walker, "The Free Coinage of Silver," *JPE*, 1 (1892–1893), 164; William H. Harvey, *Coin's Financial School*, ed. Richard Hofstadter (1894; Cambridge, 1963).

18. J. Laurence Laughlin, *The History of Bimetallism in the United States* (New York, 1886) and *Facts about Money* (Chicago, 1895), a critique of *Coin's Financial School*; Fine, *Laissez Faire*, 67–71, 106–107; J. Rogers Hollingsworth, *The Whirligig of Politics: The Democracy of Cleveland and Bryan* (Chicago, 1963), 69–72.

system began to grapple with the economic problems of an industrial society. Their very familiarity as political issues, and the strong emotional content that inhered in protection and free trade, free silver and hard money, added to their political saliency. But the impact of economic change reached far beyond the tariff and the currency. Land and labor issues also made heavy new demands on the industrial polity—demands that often involved state legislatures and the courts more than national party politics and legislation.

Land

When Henry George made land use and value the heart of his analysis in *Progress and Poverty*, he reflected the prevailing American scale of economic priorities. For all the rush of industrialism, the land and its products kept a commanding place in the economy. There still were more farm than nonfarm manual workers in 1900, and the value added by agriculture was about three-quarters of that added by manufacturing.

Nineteenth century Americans valued land for its rapid and untrammeled use, and government land policy served that purpose. It was designed to smooth the path of acquisition, and then to let the free play of the market take over. (In Wisconsin it was only a misdemeanor to trespass on state-owned mineral lands, but a felony to do so on private or leased public land.) As Republican congressional leader Thomas B. Reed put it: "I tell you each can take care of itself, each generation is sufficient unto itself."[19]

But the closing of the frontier, growing disparities of wealth and power, and most of all the complexity of the economic system required more than way-clearing from land policy. Increasingly the late nineteenth century polity was called on to arbitrate, supervise, even to restrict land allocation and use.

The 1880 census was the first to provide data on farm tenancy, mortgages, and the size of landholdings. From then on there was much worried commentary on the decline of the family-owned and operated farm. The great majority of blacks and growing numbers of southern whites fell into the distinctive tenant-

19. *HS*, 74, 139; James A. Lake, *Law and Mineral Wealth: The Legal Profile of the Wisconsin Mining Industry* (Madison, 1962), 64 ff; Reed quoted in Tarbell, *Tariff*, 125.

sharecropping-crop lien system that took form after the Civil War. About half of the region's farms were tenant-run by 1890. And in areas like the Yazoo Mississippi Delta or the timber lands of Florida and the Carolinas, large-scale operations with gangs of convict or hired labor steadily expanded. Farm tenantry was on the rise as well in the East, the Midwest, and the Prairie states. Over 25 percent of the farms in the North Central region and 20 percent of those in the North Atlantic states were tenant-operated by 1890. The depression-ridden nineties saw an increase in the number of tenants and farm laborers that was not matched until the 1920s.[20]

Farm mortgaging rapidly grew outside of the South. During the 1880s mortgage indebtedness increased by 71 percent, two and a half times as fast as agricultural wealth. About half of the mortgages incurred in Indiana between 1878 and 1880 were foreclosed ten years later. In 1890 mortgages were carried by 41 percent of the farms in New York, 49 percent in Michigan, 33 percent in Indiana; by 1896, the figures were 60 percent in Kansas, 55 percent in Nebraska, 47 percent in Iowa. It is true that most mortgage debt was incurred for purposes of expansion and represented durable property. And there is some question as to whether the rates charged were exorbitant. The lenders' risks were high (especially in the Great Plains); at the same time, competition among lending agencies exerted a downward pressure on interest rates. Nevertheless, the specter of mortgage debt was a matter of wide concern, and added to the general fear that the core American socioeconomic unit—the family farm—was in danger.[21]

20. Theodore Saloutos, "Southern Agriculture and the Problems of Adjustment: 1865–1877," *AH*, 30 (1956), 58–76; Robert L. Brandfon, *Cotton Kingdom of the New South: A History of the Yazoo Mississippi Delta from Reconstruction to the Twentieth Century* (Cambridge, 1967); George K. Holmes, "Tenancy in the United States," *QJE*, 10 (1895), 34–53; Edward W. Bemis, "The Discontent of the Farmer," *JPE*, 1 (1893), 193–213; Thomas P. Gill, "Landlordism in America," *NAR*, 142 (1886), 52–67; John D. Black and P. H. Allen, "The Growth of Farm Tenancy in the United States," *QJE*, 51 (1937), 412. See also La Wanda C. Cox, "Tenancy in the United States, 1865–1900: A Consideration of the Agricultural Ladder Hypothesis," *AH*, 18 (1944), 97–105, and "The American Agricultural Wage Earner, 1865–1900: The Emergence of a Modern Labor Problem," *AH*, 22 (1949), 95–114.

21. C. P. Emerick, "Agricultural Discontent in the United States," *PSQ*, 11 (1896), 601–602; D. M. Fredericksen, "Mortgage Banking in America," *JPE*, 2 (1894), 203–234; J. P. Dunn, Jr., "The Mortgage Evil," *PSQ*, 5 (1890),

Given the prevailing political and economic beliefs of the time, there was little that the polity could do about southern tenantry or midwestern and Plains mortgaging. The major interaction between public policy and agricultural reality came with the disposition of the public lands in the trans-Mississippi West—that sweep of two-thirds of the nation embracing the Great Plains, the Rockies and Sierras and the high plateaus between, and the Pacific coast.

Distance and aridity led to new forms of land use in this area. Bonanza farming—large-scale, highly organized wheat growing that relied on farm machinery and hired labor—spread through the Red River Valley of Minnesota and the Dakotas and the Central Valley of California. The special techniques of dry farming developed on the western prairies and the arid Great Plains. Cattle raising of necessity took the form of large herds grazing over vast areas. Big operators inexorably drove out lesser ones. A similar sequence occurred in the remote mining areas of the mountains and in the timber lands of the Northwest.[22]

The public land policies of the time, rooted in the agricultural experience of the East and the Midwest, were of little use in the face of these new realities. The Homestead Act of 1862 was designed to encourage family settlement; but only 3.5 percent of the territory west of the Mississippi was settled under the act. Eighty-four out of every one hundred new farms in the late nineteenth century came not from homesteading but from the subdivision of older private holdings or by purchase from railroads and other landholders.

Policymakers were aware of these new problems. John Wesley Powell's *Report on the Lands of the Arid Region of the United States* (1878) powerfully made the point that the area between the Rockies and the Sierras could not be settled and farmed in the traditional American way. A Public Land Commission, created in 1879, was charged to codify the land laws and recommend ways of disposing of the remaining public domain that took account of varying conditions. But here as elsewhere, old values and assump-

---

65–83; Allan Bogue, *Money at Interest: The Farm Mortgage on the Middle Border* (Ithaca, 1955).

22. Walter P. Webb, *The Great Plains* (Boston, 1931); Shannon, *Farmer's Last Frontier* (New York, 1945); Ray A. Billington, *Westward Expansion: A History of the American Frontier* (New York, 1949); Paul W. Gates, *History of Public Land Law Development* (Washington, 1968).

tions maintained a stubborn hold. The Desert Land Act of 1877 and the Timber and Stone Act of 1878 applied the traditional homestead principle to the lands of the West. In practice they allowed cattlemen, lumbermen, and miners to gain control of vast tracts through fraudulent claims and dummy purchasers.

The inadequacy of "an incongruous land system" was evident in the development of New Mexico Territory. In 1885 George W. Julian, a founder of the Indiana Republican party and now an ardent spokesman for land reform, was appointed surveyor general of the territory to "break up the [land] rings in New Mexico." Julian arrived, looked over the situation, and recommended the invalidation of claims to 1,600,000 acres of public lands. He estimated that 90 percent of the land claims in the territory were fraudulent. But powerful local opponents led by politician-entrepreneur Stephen W. Dorsey successfully resisted, arguing that the arid climate made the 160-acre homestead farm unfeasible.[23]

The fate of the transcontinental railroad land grants showed how complex were the factors affecting trans-Mississippi land policy, and how limited were the government's instruments of administration. The western railroads received over 180,000,000 acres—more than twice the total of Homestead grants—from the federal and state governments. But it is not clear that the lines reaped enormous gains from these grants. A study concludes that they increased the unaided rate of return of the Central Pacific and the Union Pacific by about 9 percent: less than the costs of construction.[24]

One reason for this limited benefit was the slowness with which the railroads took full possession of their grants and sold them off

23. Fred A. Shannon, "The Homestead Act and the Labor Surplus," AHR, 41 (1936), 637–651; Paul W. Gates, "The Homestead Law in an Incongruous Land System," AHR, 41 (1936), 652–681; Roy M. Robbins, Our Landed Heritage (Princeton, 1942), 289–290, 302; R. Hal Williams, "George W. Julian and Land Reform in New Mexico, 1885–1889," AH, 41 (1967), 73. See also Powell, Report on the Lands of the Arid Region of the United States, ed. Wallace Stegner (1878; Cambridge, 1962).

24. L. J. Mercer, "Land Grants to American Railroads, Social Cost or Social Benefit," BHR, 43 (1969), 134–151; Stanley L. Engerman, "Some Economic Issues Relating to Railroad Subsidies and the Evaluation of Land Grants," JEH, 32 (1972), 443–463; Robert Fogel and Jack L. Rutner, "The Efficiency Effects of Federal Land Policy, 1850–1900," in William Aydelotte and others, Dimensions of Quantitative Research in History (Princeton,

to settlers. By 1890, only about one-third of the lands had been conveyed. And between 1877 and 1887 Congress recovered over 28,000,000 acres in undeveloped, forfeited grants. Some lines delayed perfecting their titles in order to avoid state and local taxation or to wait for a rise in land values. But this policy slowed the agricultural settlement upon which land values and railroad revenues alike depended. Major roads such as the Union Pacific, the Central Pacific, and the Kansas Pacific generally favored rapid surveying and patenting of their lands and lost little by forfeiture.

The federal government itself was of two minds as to the desirability of rapid surveying and patenting. There was much pressure from the West to do so. But delaying final transfer was the best way to assure that the railroads would pay the surveying costs, and kept open the possibility of the forfeiture of untransferred lands if it appeared that the railroads were unable to meet their bond and loan obligations to the government. Thus the transfer of Kansas Pacific lands was suspended from 1868 to 1874; Northern Pacific land patenting was halted from 1874 to 1882. Kansas Congressman John A. Anderson pressed for the state taxation of unpatented lands to speed their transfer. But George W. Cassidy of Nevada and William S. Holman of Indiana opposed taxation because they feared that it would interfere with forfeiture legislation and that the railroads would buy up the lands cheaply at tax sales.

A final source of confusion was the fact that the sheer scale of land transfer overwhelmed the administrative capacity of the General Land Office. An economy move in 1875 reduced its staff by 25 percent to 145 clerks, fewer than in 1855. Although that number increased by two and a half times in the next decade, the acreage of land to be processed rose five times. Not surprisingly, the Land Office was noted for its slowness, inefficiency, and (to a lesser extent) corruption. A farm journal ironically saluted a retiring Land Office law officer in 1885 for furnishing "valuable precedents on all sides of nearly every question of importance."[25]

1972), 390–418. See also Robert S. Henry, "The Railroad Land Grant Legend in American History Texts" and the responses evoked by that pro-railroad argument, collected in Vernon Carstensen, ed., The Public Lands: Studies in the History of the Public Domain (Madison, 1963), 121–179; Heywood Fleisig, "The Union Pacific Railroad and the Railroad Land Grant Controversy," EEH, 11 (1973–1974), 155–172.

25. Leslie E. Decker, Railroads, Lands, and Politics: The Taxation of the Railroad Land Grants, 1864–1897 (Providence, 1964), 68–69, 40, 54;

Pressure mounted on government to take account of the disparity between principle and practice in the development of the public domain. One consequence was the appearance of laws forbidding alien landholding. The amount of land owned by foreigners was exaggerated. But the case of William Scully, a British citizen who held title to more than 134,000 acres of Kansas and Nebraska land, was real enough. Congress stoked the fires by publishing a list of alien landholders, in which titled Englishmen were conspicuous. A federal law in 1887 forbade aliens from buying territorial lands, and a number of states passed similar acts. But even here, conflicting interests were at play. The desire of mining companies to retain access to foreign capital led to the repeal of Colorado's restrictive law in 1891.

The years around 1890 saw the culmination of efforts to create a public land policy that took account of new conditions. Congressional acts in 1887 and 1890 required railroads to forfeit unearned or unused lands. The General Land Revision Act of 1891 was "the first fundamental break with the underlying philosophy of our land system—the desire to dispose of the lands and hasten their settlement." It repealed or limited previous laws that had led to corruption or to the growth of large landholdings and authorized the President to set aside timber lands as national parks. But the conditions that shaped the late nineteenth century disposition of the public domain could not be so easily changed by legislative fiat. The courts blocked any major surrender of railroad lands under the forfeiture laws. A 1903 commission looking into the state of the land laws found that corporate acquisition of timber and mineral lands continued unchecked.[26]

Changing conditions affected areas of land law and policy other than the opening of the public domain. A striking instance was the appearance of new forms of riparian law in the mining areas of the far West. Pacific coast courts in the 1860s accepted the right of miners to divert and use river waters under the "prior appropriation" rule, and to maintain those privileges against later down-

Paul W. Gates, *Fifty Million Acres: Conflicts over Kansas Land Policy, 1854–1890* (New York, 1966), ch. 8; Harold H. Dunham, "Some Crucial Years of the General Land Office, 1875–1890," *AH*, 11 (1937), 119.

26. Roger V. Clements, "British Investment and American Legislative Restriction in the Trans-Mississippi West, 1880–1900," *MVHR*, 42 (1955),

stream users. This significant modification of riparian law was affirmed by Congress in its Mining Act of 1866.

As agricultural settlements spread, opposition grew to the prior appropriation doctrine. The diversion and pollution of river waters by the miners made farmland irrigation "practically impossible." California's Wright law of 1887 created a new government entity, the public irrigation district, which by claiming these waters for public use could override the prior appropriation rule. The courts accepted these districts and in the 1890s began to hand down injunctions against the miners' contamination and diversion of upstream waters.[27]

Mining and gas and oil drilling raised comparable problems concerning subsurface property rights. An 1872 congressional law added the right of "extralateral pursuit"—following mineral veins even if they went under land owned by others—to the traditional common law entitlement to deposits under one's own property. Gas and oil deposits posed a similar problem, and the courts came up with a similar solution. The Pennsylvania Supreme Court in 1889 devised the "rule of capture." Analogizing gas and oil to a wild animal—a *ferae naturae*—that moved from one property to another, the court ruled that what was "captured" by a well belonged to the driller regardless of its effect on the pool under adjacent land.[28]

Important changes occurred also in the law of eminent domain: the power of the state to take property for public use. The earlier American conception of eminent domain was an expansive one. Railroads and mills were given wide latitude to take land and use

207–228; Harold H. Dunham, *Government Handout: A Study in the Administration of the Public Lands 1875–1891* (New York, 1941), 332–333; on Scully, Gates, *Fifty Million Acres*, 286; David M. Ellis, "The Forfeiture of Railroad Land Grants, 1867–1894," MVHR, 33 (1946), 27–60; on 1891 Act, Gates, "Homestead Law," 681; Robbins, *Our Landed Heritage*, 296–297, 313–314.

27. John N. Pomeroy, "Riparian Rights—West Coast Doctrine," WCR, vols. 1–3 (1884); Joseph Ellison, "The Mineral Land Question in California, 1848–1866," SHQ, 30 (1926), 34–55; "California," AC (1888, 1892). See also Gordon M. Bakken, "Contract Law in the Rockies, 1850–1912," AJLH, 17 (1974), 33–51; Fallbrook Irrigation District v. Bradley, 164 U.S. 112 (1896); Gordon R. Miller, "Shaping California Water Law, 1781 to 1928," SCQ, 55 (1973), 9–42.

28. "Mining Law," AC (1888); Westmoreland v. De Witt, 130 Pa. St. 235 (1889); Davis and others, *American Economic Growth*, 111–112.

water on the ground that the public benefited from the growth of enterprise. The resulting impairments, damages, and annoyances generally were accepted—and compensation denied—as necessary costs of social progress.

But from the middle of the century on, the courts more narrowly defined the public use concept. They limited it to direct use by public authorities and excluded private use which had a public benefit. At the same time, the injury or destruction of adjacent property was more and more frequently defined as a "taking," and thus subject to recovery for damages. One observer concluded: "The meaning of the word 'property' seems to be undergoing a modification."

The Supreme Court's Head v. Amoskeag decision (1885) was a milestone in the restriction of eminent domain. The Court upheld a New Hampshire law that required mill and factory owners to pay damages if they flooded others' lands. Its ground for doing so was that the state's police power prevailed here over the right of eminent domain. Similarly, the Massachusetts Supreme Judicial Court in 1888 allowed Fall River to increase its use of the water in Watuppa Pond without compensating adversely affected mill owners. Critics called the decision "a wide departure from the spirit which has in the past led the Commonwealth of Massachusetts to foster its manufacturing industries by every means in its power." And indeed the Watuppa Pond case was part of a gradual limitation of property rights brought on by the economic changes of the late nineteenth century.[29]

While the courts frequently handed down judgments on abutments, prior use, nuisance, and other causes of action stemming from land use, there was little urban land policy as such. New York, Washington, and Boston placed some limits on building heights, but there was no general city zoning ordinance until New York adopted one in 1916.[30]

29. Arthur Lenhoff, "Development of the Concept of Eminent Domain," *ColLR*, 42 (1942), 596–638; Philip Nichols, Jr., "The Meaning of Public Use in the Law of Eminent Domain," *BULR*, 20 (1940), 615–641; A. G. Sedgwick, "Constitutional Protection of Property Rights," *NAR*, 135 (1882), 257; Head v. Amoskeag, 113 U.S. 9 (1885); Samuel D. Warren, Jr., and Louis D. Brandeis, "The Watuppa Pond Cases," *HLR*, 2 (1888–1889), 211.

30. John Delafons, *Land-Use Controls in the United States*, 2d ed. (Cambridge, 1969), 19–20; Corwin W. Johnson, "Constitutional Law and Community Planning," *LCP*, 20 (1955), 199–217.

Urban land transfer was of greater concern than land use in the late nineteenth century. The sheer bulk of transactions in the growing cities was enormous. Suffolk County (Boston) recorded its land transfers from 1650 to 1800 in 193 volumes. By 1890, these records filled almost 2,000 six-hunded-page books. The time and cost of title searches grew accordingly. The problem was heightened by the large number of officials—judges, clerks of court, county clerks, notary publics, justices of the peace—who were authorized to certify land conveyances: a state of affairs that made fraud and forgery easy.

New institutions rose to provide greater order and safety for land transfer. The first title insurance company appeared in Philadelphia in 1876; Illinois instituted title guaranty in 1887; the Chicago Real Estate Board was created in 1883, the New York Board in 1885. New York's Block Indexing Act of 1889 was designed to simplify real estate conveyancing in New York City.

A Real Estate Congress held at the 1893 Chicago World's Fair focused attention on the Torrens title registry system. Already in use in Australia and parts of Canada, the Torrens system allowed title to pass by entry of the land transfer in an official register. The deed was to be regarded only as a personal contract. Title was authenticated by a certificate of registry (subject to court review). The goal was to make land transfer as straightforward a transaction as the conveyance of stock. Illinois, Massachusetts, and California were among the states that adopted the Torrens system in the 1890s. But the scale and complexity of the interests involved in land transfer worked against the acceptance of a quasi-official title registry system, and the rise of title insurance companies ended the Torrens movement. Inertial forces worked against any substantial change in private no less than public land policy.[31]

The changing economic and social order of the late nineteenth century led not only to a growing (if limited) apparatus of rules

31. On Boston, Charles F. Libby, "Land Transfer Reform," *ALR*, 28 (1894), 199; Thomas M. Cooley, "The Recording Laws of the United States," *ABA Reports*, 4 (1881), 199–221; Pearl J. Davis, *Real Estate in American History* (Washington, 1958), 35–51; New York *Laws*, 1889, ch. 349. On Torrens system, John T. Hassam, "Land Transfer Reform," *HLR*, 4 (1890–1891), 271–279, Dwight H. Olmstead, "Land Transfer Reform," *ABA Reports*, 13 (1890), 265–289.

and regulations concerning land use, but also to some erosion of the prevailing assumption that the land and its products had value only insofar as they might be immediately exploited. In one sense, the conservationist outlook was as old as pantheism. In another, it was the product of a time when nature changed from a challenge and an inexhaustible source of wealth to a threatened, potentially scarce commodity.

The impulse to shield the land from man's spoliation took a variety of forms. As early as 1879, a Colorado law sought to protect the countryside from rampant advertising: in Clear Creek County, it appeared, "every available rock was already plastered and printed over." This was not a uniquely American problem. A British National Society for Checking the Abuses of Public Advertising sought a restraining act from Parliament during the 1890s which would "mark the turning-point in the contest between the forces which make for restfulness and order . . . and the forces which make for vexatious confusion."[32]

The depletion of fish and game, timber, and other resources evoked increasing concern in the late nineteenth century. State game laws were expanded and strengthened (as in Massachusetts in 1870), State Forestry Associations were created (as in Minnesota and Washington in 1896), and halting attempts were made to stem the waste of oil and gas. The earliest federal conservation laws appeared in this period. Grant's creation of Yellowstone National Park on March 1, 1872, was the world's first instance of large-scale preservation of wilderness. The Lacey Act of 1900 prohibited the interstate shipment of birds and game that had been killed in contravention of state law. And the Refuse Act of 1899 made it unlawful to throw waste into federal waters. (The law remained a dead letter until the 1960s, when it became an important legal instrument in the new assault on pollution.)[33]

It is in the late nineteenth century, too, that two distinctive

32. "Colorado," AC (1879); Richardson Evans, "Advertising as a Trespass on the Public," NC, 37 (1895), 978–979. See also Ernst Freund, The Police Power (Chicago, 1904), 165–166.

33. "Laws for the Preservation of Birds and Game in the United States of America," LT, 53 (1872), 98–99; Roderick Nash, "The American Invention of National Parks," AQ, 22 (1970), 726–735; Diane D. Eames, "The Refuse Act of 1899: Its Scope and Role in Control of Water Pollution," CalLR, 58 (1970), 1444–1473.

schools of conservationist thought—one esthetic and preservationist, the other scientific and use-oriented—emerged. John Muir, the champion of wilderness preservation in the western national parks, spoke for the first view. His great achievement was the Yosemite Act of 1890 (secured with the help of the tourist-conscious Southern Pacific Railroad). Gifford Pinchot, a pioneering professional forester, won a victory for the scientific maintenance of natural resources with the passage of the Forest Management Act of 1897. He became chief of the Agriculture Department's Division of Forestry in 1898.

The two faces of conservation—the scientific development of natural resources and wilderness preservation—reflected the conflict between public policy as an instrument of change and public policy as an instrument to *prevent* change that infused the late nineteenth century polity. It was especially appropriate that the land—the primal American economic asset—should be a major battleground for that clash of values.[34]

Labor

A rising level of labor-capital conflict came with the industrial growth of the late nineteenth century. Major strikes swept over large portions of the railroad system in 1877, 1886, and 1894, the anthracite coal mines in 1887–1888, and the bituminous fields in 1897. The bitter Homestead strike of 1892 occurred at the newest and largest plant of the burgeoning steel industry. There were 477 reported work stoppages in 1881, 1,897 in 1890, 1,839 in 1900. Pennsylvania in 1894 had 52 major strikes, twice as many as in 1892. Thirty-two were in the bituminous fields, 9 in iron and steel; others involved carpet weavers, chinaware makers, cloakmakers; none was successful. Omaha labor disturbances in 1881 brought out four companies of infantry. Illinois quarrymen in 1886, driving away scab replacements, were fired on by sheriffs' forces and several were killed or wounded.

34. Roderick Nash, *Wilderness and the American Mind* (New Haven, 1967), chs. 7–8; Samuel P. Hays, *Conservation and the Gospel of Efficiency: The Progressive Conservation Movement 1890–1920* (Cambridge, 1959).

The frequency and violence of late nineteenth century labor unrest deeply disturbed contemporary observers. Few shared the remove of William Graham Sumner, who theorized that strikes were the means by which the relationship between capital and labor was defined and a new social harmony attained: "Industrial war is, in fact, an incident of liberty." Nor did many take note of the fact that most of the major strikes occurred in response to wage reductions. This was a workforce as likely to react against worsening conditions as to seek substantial changes in the industrial order.[35]

As unsettling as the strikes themselves was the belief that they reflected the rising power of organized labor. But unionization in fact did not keep pace with the rise of the industrial workforce. In 1870 it was 9.1 percent unionized; in 1900, 8.4 percent—and the 868,000 union members of that year were almost double the total of 457,000 in 1897. A canvass of 4,650 Michigan workers in 1896 revealed that fewer than 9 percent belonged to unions, while three times as many were members of fraternal societies. Indeed, what success unions attained in the late nineteenth century stemmed in great part from their ability to tap the fraternal instinct. Less than 7 percent of the strikes in 1881 involved the issue of unionization itself; by the turn of the century a quarter to a third did so.[36]

The first national organization of workingmen in the post-Civil War years, the National Labor Union, was more concerned with broad national policy than with bread-and-butter issues. It dwelt on such causes as the need for an expanded paper currency, an eight-hour workday, the exclusion of the Chinese, and the creation of a national Department of Labor. The Knights of Labor in the 1870s and 1880s also stressed monetary reform, the eight-hour day, cooperative schemes, and state and local political influence. Yet the Knights were unaffected by the spread of socialist ideology that

35. On work stoppages, *HS*, 99; "Pennsylvania," *AC* (1894); "Nebraska," *AC* (1881); "Illinois," *AC* (1886); William G. Sumner, "Do We Want Industrial Peace?" *Forum*, 8 (1889), 410; J. E. George, "The Coal Miners' Strike of 1897," *QJE*, 12 (1898), 186–208; "Strikes," *AC* (1887). Carroll Wright thought that the great majority of strikes in the 1881–1886 period were called for wage increases and reductions in hours worked. Wright, "Compulsory Arbitration an Impossible Remedy," *Forum*, 15 (1893), 328.

36. *HS*, 98; Lloyd Ulman, *The Rise of the National Trade Union*, 2d ed. (Cambridge, 1966), 19; "Michigan," *AC* (1890); *HS*, 99.

occurred in the British and continental European labor movements of this period. It is true that their 1878 declaration of principles warned: "The alarming development and aggressiveness of great capitalists and corporations, unless checked, will inevitably lead to the pauperization and hopeless degradation of the toiling masses." But their greater commitment was to the belief that workers, along with farmers and capitalists, were members of a broad producing class. The Knights accepted entrepreneurs and employers, excluding only those in occupations that they deemed beyond the pale: bankers, saloonkeepers, lawyers, and doctors. This Noble Order of the Knights of Labor, full of ritual and secrecy—enough to cause poor relations with the Catholic church—was more like a branch of the Masons (whose ceremony the Knights copied) than a branch of the International.

The reform unionism and the centralized organization of the NLU and the Knights worked against their survival. The ethnic and geographical spread of the labor force, American localism and laissez-faire, and the hostility of corporate employers saw to that. The contrast with Britain is pronounced. There a culturally homogeneous workforce and old corporative traditions of social organization produced an increasingly centralized, political, socialist labor movement: quite the reverse of the American experience.[37]

The labor organizations that best survived the storms of American industrialization were the craft brotherhoods, which often had a distinctive ethnic cast. A number of these trade unions came together in the American Federation of Labor from 1886 on. The Federation's leader, Samuel Gompers, was well aware of the class

37. See in general Norman J. Ware, *The Labor Movement in the United States 1860–1890* (New York, 1929), Gerald Grob, "Reform Unionism: The NLU," *JEH*, 14 (1954), 126–142 and *Workers and Utopia: A Study of Ideological Conflict in the American Labor Movement, 1865–1900* (Evanston, 1961), John H. M. Laslett, *Labor and the Left: A Study of Socialist and Radical Influences in the American Labor Movement, 1881–1924* (New York, 1970), and Irwin Yellowitz, *The Position of the Worker in Industrial Society, 1865–1896* (Englewood Cliffs, N.J., 1969); Francis A. Walker, "The Knights of Labor," *NPR*, 6 (1881), 196–209; Carroll D. Wright, "An Historical Sketch of the Knights of Labor," *QJE*, 1 (1886–1887), 137–168; on British labor, Eric J. Hobsbawm, *Laboring Men: Studies in the History of Labour* (New York, 1964), Asa Briggs and John Saville, eds., *Essays in Labour History, 1882–1923* (London, 1971), Henry Pelling, *The Origins of the Labour Party, 1880–1900* (London, 1954).

interests of workingmen. But he took account of American conditions. As he explained in 1896, "he was a trade unionist in America and England, but he would be a socialist in Germany and in Russia a nihilist." While by no means opposed to a labor presence in politics, Gompers expected little from a government controlled by labor's class enemies. He relied instead on collective bargaining and the strike.[38]

This is not to say that organized labor was without political influence in the late nineteenth century. There were intermittent state labor parties and city labor tickets: in Chicago (1877, 1882, 1886, 1893) and most notably in New York City, where in 1886 Henry George ran a strong campaign for mayor. Over three hundred unionists sought state and local offices in 1894, most of them on Populist tickets.

More important was the ability of unions to influence the major parties and state and national legislation. The Window Glass Workers secured the passage of a congressional act prohibiting the importation of contract labor in 1885, and organized labor in California and elsewhere worked to restrict Chinese immigration. Equally successful were campaigns for state laws limiting or prohibiting contract labor, controlling methods of wage payment, and establishing some minimal regulation of working conditions. As these suggest, the legislative goals of organized labor were protective and preservative, not innovative. The Knights of Industry, the overtly political branch of the Knights of Labor, called in 1892 for the imposition of higher tariffs on foreign goods; restrictions on the flow of cheap labor from abroad; and the prohibition of prison, contract, and child labor. The economist Richard T. Ely observed in 1887 that in many respects labor organizations were "conservative forces."[39]

The late nineteenth century polity was far from being unremittingly hostile to the interests and desires of American workingmen. Both the success ethic—the belief that opportunity should

38. Philip Taft, The AFL in the Time of Gompers (New York, 1957), 133; Gerald N. Grob, "Origins of the Political Philosophy of the A.F. of L., 1886–1896," RP, 23 (1960), 496–518. See also Stuart B. Kaufman, Samuel Gompers and the Origins of the American Federation of Labor, 1848–1896 (Westport, Conn., 1973).

39. Edward B. Mittelman, "Chicago Labor in Politics 1877–96," JPE, 28 (1920), 402–427; Ware, Labor Movement, 362–365; Charlotte Erickson,

be open to all—and the producer ethic—the assumption that workers and employers shared common interests—weighed against class-conscious, antilabor public policy. And the widespread acceptance of the view that the state bore some minimal responsibility for the safety and well-being of its citizens fueled efforts to soften the impact of industrialism.

When embattled workers faced large, impersonal corporations, as in the 1877 railroad strikes in Pittsburgh, Baltimore, and Cincinnati, or in the Homestead strike of 1892, they won substantial public support. Of necessity there was much prolabor sentiment during strikes in factory towns and smaller cities. Shopkeepers, editors, and politicians found it to their interest to side with textile workers against absentee corporate employers during a series of strikes in Paterson, New Jersey in the late 1870s. Similar conditions prevailed during the 1887–1888 anthracite strike in Pennsylvania communities, where company stores threatened local merchants. The surest sources of support for corporate employers were nonlocal authorities: the courts, state governors, the state militia.[40]

Even in this time of breakneck industrialization and laissez-faire political ideology, government paid increasing attention to the conditions of labor. The Massachusetts Bureau of Labor Statistics under Carroll Wright gathered and published data on the wages and living standards of industrial workers. A number of other industrial states created such bureaus in the 1880s. The Senate Com-

---

American Industry and the European Immigrant 1860–1885 (Cambridge, 1957), 152–166; Grob, Workers and Utopia, 79 ff; "Knights of Industry," AC (1892); Richard T. Ely, "Labor Organization," Forum, 3 (1887), 56. See also Sidney Fine, "The Eight Hour Day Movement in the United States, 1888–1891," MVHR, 40 (1953), 441–462.

40. Robert V. Bruce, 1877: Year of Violence (Indianapolis, 1959); Herbert Gutman, "Class, Status, and Community Power in Nineteenth-Century American Industrial Cities—Paterson, New Jersey: A Case Study," in Frederick C. Jaher, ed., The Age of Industrialism in America (New York, 1968), 263–287; Harold W. Aurand, "The Anthracite Strike of 1887–1888," PH, 35 (1968), 168–185; Ronald M. Gephart, "Politicians, Soldiers and Strikes: The Reorganization of the Nebraska Militia and the Omaha Strike of 1882," NH, 46 (1965), 89–120. See also Gutman, "The Worker's Search for Power: Labor in the Gilded Age," in H. Wayne Morgan, ed., The Gilded Age: A Reappraisal (Syracuse, 1963), 38–68; Philip E. Mackey, "Law and Order, 1877: Philadelphia's Response to the Railroad Riots," PMHB, 96 (1972), 183–202.

mittee upon the Relations between Labor and Capital (1883) heard abundant and vivid testimony from working people and labor leaders on factory and living conditions. As a result, Congress in 1884 created a national Bureau of Labor (directed by Wright), whose reports dwelt on the harmful consequences of overproduction and underconsumption. The massive report of the United States Industrial Commission (1900–1901) was a landmark inquiry into the character and consequences of "this new and strange industrialism" that had come to the United States.[41]

A growing number of state laws were designed to alleviate some of the more visible and least conscionable inequities of the industrial order. By the mid-nineties this legislation was exceeded in quantity only by liquor regulation laws: a category with which labor legislation had some affinity as state intervention to preserve basic social values.[42]

Statutes prohibited wage payments in scrip, required weekly paydays, forbade wage forfeits because the worker damaged his tools or materials, regulated working hours (especially for women and children), and banned Yellow Dog contracts that prevented workers from joining unions. Such acts were far from universal; enforcement was minimal; and they varied widely: laws regulating the hours of child and female labor ranged from a fifty-six-hour weekly maximum in New Jersey to fifty-eight in Massachusetts, sixty in New York and Pennsylvania, and up to seventy-two hours in the South. But the character of these laws tells us something about the goals of labor policy in the late nineteenth century. Their primary concern was with practices whose manifest injustice de-

41. James Leiby, *Carroll Wright and Labor Reform: The Origins of Labor Statistics* (Cambridge, 1960); Richmond Mayo-Smith, "The National Bureau of Labor, and Industrial Depressions," *PSQ*, 1 (1886), 437–448; "U.S. Congress," *AC* (1884); S. N. D. North, "The Industrial Commission," *NAR*, 168 (1899), 710.

42. Richard T. Ely and L. S. Merriam, "Report on Social Legislation in the United States for 1889 and 1890," *ER*, 1 (1891), 237–238; William B. Shaw, "Social and Economic Legislation of the States in 1890," *QJE*, 5 (1891), 385–396; F. J. Stimson, "Recent Economic and Social Legislation in the United States," *YR*, 5 (1896–1897), 251–257, and 6 (1897–1898), 184–195; New York State Library Bulletin, *Index to Legislation* (Albany, 1890 ff). Stimson categorized this as legislation "in the interest of morality, of order, or the laboring masses" (*YR*, 5 (1896–1897), 252).

graded the contractual relationship between employer and employee. They sought not to change that relationship, but to check the abuses that threatened it.[43]

That preservative impulse fostered an effort to create a system of arbitration for labor-capital disputes. Proponents of this "middle class panacea" included conservatives such as President Grover Cleveland and jurist Thomas M. Cooley, the reformer-economist Richard T. Ely, and the socialist Henry Demarest Lloyd. Beginning with Maryland in 1878, almost every industrial state passed laws creating machinery for collective bargaining and arbitration. Several states strengthened the hand of labor negotiators by restricting settlement benefits to those workers who had agreed to be so represented.

At first the arbitration movement stressed voluntary use and compliance. But as the number and intensity of strikes grew in the 1880s, attempts were made to give state boards of arbitration greater power to intervene and to make their decisions stick. Grover Cleveland proposed federal arbitration machinery in his special message to Congress of April 1886, which dealt with the railroad strikes of that year. He evenhandedly condemned the "grasping and heedless exactions of employers" and "those who, under the pretext of an advocacy of the claims of labor, wantonly attack the rights of capital and . . . sow seeds of violence and discontent." Cleveland called for a three-man government commission to provide voluntary arbitration. His proposal got nowhere, but the Erdman Act of 1898, which established arbitration machinery for railroad labor disputes, marked the beginning of a federal role in collective bargaining.

For all its appeal, government-sponsored arbitration played almost no part in late nineteenth century labor relations. Unions generally opposed it as a threat to their ability to bargain collectively. Probusiness conservatives resisted what they took to be government paternalism. And there was the additional stumbling block of a common law that made little provision for arbitration as a means of settling contract disputes. As one critic of arbitration

43. Frederic C. Woodward, "Statutory Limitations of Freedom of Contract between Employer and Employé," *ALR*, 29 (1895), 236–265; North, "Industrial Commission," 711.

machinery put it, "these boards must follow the existing, settled rules of law, and thus be wholly useless; or they must adopt socialism as the system of jurisprudence they are to administer." The tenets of an individualistic society and the weakness of the state outweighed the appeal of arbitration as an instrument for maintaining social harmony.[44]

The most frequent contact between the worker and the polity came when victims of industrial accidents or their dependents sought compensation from the courts. By one estimate, about 45,000 appellate decisions reviewed railroad and industrial negligence and liability cases between 1875 and 1905. Not until the Federal Railroad Employers' Liability Act of 1906 and the state workmen's compensation laws of the following decade did accident compensation begin to move from the purview of the courts to an administrative insurance system.

Compensation through the judicial process was limited by the character of liability law, which weighed heavily against the employee (the servant, in the revealing terminology of the common law). The employer (or master) bore no liability for his employees' accidents unless he was directly responsible. The fellow-servant doctrine, laid down by Massachusetts Justice Lemuel Shaw in 1842, exempted the master from liability for accidents due to the negligence of his servant's co-workers. Subsidiary doctrines—contributory negligence, assumption of risk—further limited employer liability. The net effect was that the employee assumed all the risks ordinarily associated with his work, plus *"all other open and visible risks, whether usually incident to the business or not."*[45]

By the late nineteenth century these doctrines were solidly entrenched in American law and had powerful backing from cor-

44. William E. Akin, "Arbitration and Labor Conflict: The Middle Class Panacea, 1886–1900," *Hist*, 29 (1967), 565–583; Herbert Schreiber, "The Majority Preference Provisions in Early State Labor Arbitration Statutes— 1880–1890," *AJLH*, 15 (1971), 186–198; Edward Cummings, "Industrial Arbitration in the United States," *QJE*, 9 (1895), 353–371; Cleveland in *MP*, 4979–4982; G. C. Clemens, "Industrial Arbitration," *KLJ*, 3 (1886), 117.

45. Richard A. Posner, "A Theory of Negligence," *JLS*, 1 (1972), 34; Leonard W. Levy, *The Law of the Commonwealth and Chief Justice Shaw* (Cambridge, 1957), ch. 10; Wex S. Malone, "The Formative Era of Contributory Negligence," *ILR*, 41 (1946), 151–182; Horace G. Wood, *A Treatise on the Law of Railroads* (Boston, 1885), III, 1454 (his italics).

porate interests. When the 1875 Wisconsin legislature sought to modify the fellow-servant doctrine, railroad companies attacked the resulting law as "class legislation" and it was repealed in 1880. More important was the pervasive nineteenth century belief that each participant in the play of the market was a free agent: "that a party who voluntarily and intelligently exposes himself to certain risks, such risks being the incidents to a lawful business, cannot recover if he is hurt by the exposure." The concept of employer liability was "in direct antagonism with that broader doctrine that every person shall be held to answer for his own wrongs; therefore it is regarded with much jealousy by the courts, and is circumscribed into as narrow limits as is consistent with the true interests of society.[46]

The effect, and to a considerable degree the intent, of these rules was that workers bore the cost of accidents. But as the havoc wrought by technology increased—by the 1890s, railroads alone were killing 6,000 to 7,000 and injuring 30,000 to 45,000 people each year; a third of the killed and three-quarters of the injured were employees—pressure grew to modify the stringent law of liability.

A number of states copied some or all of the British Employers' Liability Acts of 1880 and 1887, which increased employer liability for on-the-job accidents. The courts, too, began to modify the fellow-servant and allied doctrines. In 1875 the Rhode Island Supreme Court held that an employer was liable for injuries suffered by an employee who had been ordered to perform a dangerous task. A commentator conceded that those "who ... look first for symmetry, and then for justice" in the law would disapprove of this decision. But he could not deny its propriety. The Wisconsin Supreme Court used procedural rules—presumption, constructive knowledge, burden of proof, instructions to trial courts—to require that crucial issues of fact in injury cases be submitted to juries. A number of southern and western courts developed the superior servant rule, which held that the fellow-servant doctrine did not apply if the blame for the injury lay with an employee of a higher

46. Robert S. Hunt, *Law and Locomotives: The Impact of the Railroad on Wisconsin Law in the Nineteenth Century* (Madison, 1958), 148; Francis Wharton, "Master's Liability to Servant," *SLR*, 3 (1877), 750; Horace G. Wood, *A Treatise on the Law of Master and Servant* (Albany, 1877), 534.

grade than the victim: a principle that the United States Supreme Court adopted for a few years and then dropped.[47]

By 1895 the Connecticut Supreme Court detected a "tendency in nearly all jurisdictions to limit rather than enlarge" the fellow-servant doctrine. But not all of the old rules were overturned. An 1897 survey concluded: "In this country the rule that, when the knowledge of the servant has been found, the court will infer assumption of risks, as a matter of law, is still virtually unshaken." It seemed to many that liability law had fallen into "a state of inextricable confusion." Decisions were "hopelessly irreconcilable, . . . a veritable chaos of conflicting precedents." This disarray stemmed from the fact that the old liability rules were not applicable to a mature industrial society, yet were only gradually and irregularly modified. A conservative jurist such as John F. Dillon might find traditional liability doctrine a "plain, sound, safe and practicable" standard. But courts confronting the reality of railroad and industrial accidents could not be so complacent. In 1892 the influential Massachusetts Supreme Judicial Court adopted the "just and reasonable" English doctrine that abridged the voluntary assumption of risk by an employee working under dangerous conditions.[48]

By their number and character, liability decisions in effect were a judicial system of accident insurance compensation. A study of the appellate court decisions in this period found that juries decided for the injured plaintiff at a 10 to 1 rate; that the damages

47. *HS*, 437; "Law of Railroad Accidents," *AC* (1886); William M. McKinney, "Statutory Changes in the Doctrine of Co-Service in the United States," *LQR*, 6 (1890), 189–203; on Rhode Island case, Isaac F. Redfield note, *ALReg*, ns, 14 (1875), 665–667; *ibid.*, 15 (1876), 140–145; on Wisconsin, Hunt, *Law and Locomotives*, 153, 159–160; on superior servant rule, McKinney, "Statutory Changes," 189; Ross v. Milwaukee & St. Paul Railroad, 112 U.S. 377 (1884); Baltimore & Ohio Railroad v. Baugh, 149 U.S. 368 (1893). See also "The Fellow-Servant Rule," *ALR*, 31 (1897), 269.

48. Connecticut court cited in Lawrence M. Friedman and Jack Ladinsky, "Social Change and the Law of Industrial Accidents," *ColLR*, 67 (1967), 59; C. B. Labatt, "The Relation between Assumption of Risks and Contributory Negligence," *ALR*, 31 (1897), 684, 667; Speed Mosby, "The Fellow-Servant Doctrine," *ALR*, 30 (1896), 840–846; John F. Dillon, American Law Concerning Employer's Liability," *ALR*, 24 (1890), 189; Mahoney v. Dore, 155 Mass. 513 (1892). See also N. M. Thygeson, "Why Are the Decisions under the Fellow-Servant Doctrine So Vacillating and Contradictory?" *ALR*, 31 (1897), 93–98.

awarded were equivalent to what might have been expected from a formal accident compensation system; and that the probability of these awards increased the value of safety measures. But surely this was compensation and regulation at a remove. The facts on which the courts acted were provided by the parties, not by independent investigation. This was a spotty, adversary system which left from 70 to 90 percent of industrial accidents uncompensated and had no measurable impact on the rate of railroad accidents.[49]

The constraints that worked against adequate compensation for railroad and industrial accident victims were part of a more general legislative and judicial insensitivity to the needs of labor. This state of affairs is customarily blamed on the proemployer bias of judges and legislators and on the prevailing belief in self-help and laissez-faire. But its broader source was a fear of social disorder that led to restraints on labor as well as to reform of working conditions: that, indeed, made both restraints and reform related parts of the polity's response to the new conditions of American life.

State legislatures enacted a growing number of antiunion statutes. An 1885 Alabama law banning boycotts and picketing that blocked strikebreakers was frankly titled "An Act to protect and encourage industry within the State." Typical of the new legislative mood was a Rhode Island act of 1895 which imposed penalties on strikers who obstructed the passage of streetcars. In the wake of the Chicago Haymarket explosion of 1886, when a bomb killed seven policemen and a group of anarcho-communists was charged with the deed, Illinois passed the first state criminal syndicalism law.

The most potent antilabor policies stemmed from the judiciary. The legal position of organized labor had improved during the midcentury decades. Massachusetts Justice Lemuel Shaw's Commonwealth v. Hunt decision in 1842 gave new legitimacy to unions and

49. Posner, "Theory of Negligence," passim; Friedman and Ladinsky, "Social Change," 60–61. George W. Alger, "The Courts and Factory Legislation," *ASR*, 6 (1900–1901), 406n, examined the accident liability cases that came before the New York Court of Appeals from 1891 to 1898 (126–156 NY), and found twenty-eight reversals of thirty cases where the juries awarded substantial damages to the plaintiff.

strikes by ending the identification of a striking union with a criminal conspiracy and by sanctioning the closed shop. Shaw's rationale—"the belief that benefits to the public might accrue from the contest between unions and employers"—harmonized well with the libertarian, confident tone of mid-nineteenth century American life. A survey of labor law in the mid-1870s concluded that the rights of unions to exist and to strike generally were upheld by the courts.[50]

But as labor-management conflict increased in the late nineteenth century, the courts raised new obstacles to strikes and boycotts. They did so primarily on the basis of their equity power to take bankrupt railroad lines into receivership. In the wake of the 1877 railroad strikes, several federal judges declared the action of the workers to be in contempt of court and issued special warrants empowering United States marshals to intercede in these labor disputes.[51]

The precedent thus set was pursued with even greater rigor after the railroad strikes of 1885–1886. Between 1886 and 1888 federal judges issued writs of assistance and bench warrants and held contempt proceedings. Again, they did so on the basis of their receivership jurisdiction over bankrupt roads. And in these years state and federal benches began to use what became the most fearsome restraining instrument of all: the labor injunction.

Union boycotts of struck companies were the first major targets of court injunctions in labor disputes. Boycotting was widely regarded as beyond the pale of acceptable weapons in labor-capital conflict. The term itself dated from the early 1880s: it derived from the actions taken by the Irish Land League against one Captain Boycott, an estate manager. This connotation of lawlessness persisted when the boycott became an instrument in American labor disputes. The courts enjoined boycotts on a variety of grounds: as a continuing trespass or a public nuisance or a conspiracy in restraint

50. "Alabama," *AC* (1885); "Rhode Island," *AC* (1895); "Illinois," *AC* (1887); Levy, *Shaw*, 204–205; Walter Howe, "The Legal Relations of Capital and Labor," *NYSBA Reports*, 1 (1876), 101–138.

51. Gerald G. Eggert, *Railroad Labor Disputes: The Beginnings of Federal Strike Policy* (Ann Arbor, 1967); Elwin W. Sigmund, "Railroad Strikers in Court: Unreported Contempt Cases in Illinois in 1877," *ISHS Journal*, 49 (1956), 190–209; Bruce, *1877*, 287–289, 308; *CLJ*, 5 (1877), 97–98.

of trade, or because the conduct of a business in itself was a form of property and hence entitled to protection.[52]

The use of the injunction in labor disputes expanded substantially in the nineties. Several federal judges (including a future President, William Howard Taft) handed down injunctions against boycotts and other union activities during the 1893 railroad strikes. As one of them put it: "It is idle to talk of a peaceable strike. None such ever occurred . . . All combinations to interfere with perfect freedom in the proper management and control of one's lawful business, to dictate the terms upon which such business shall be conducted, by means of threats . . . are within the condemnation of the law." Over the dissents of Oliver Wendell Holmes the Massachusetts Supreme Judicial Court pioneered in state court antistrike injunctions. Especially notable was the decision in Vogelahn v. Guntner (1896), which upheld an injunction leveled against a two-man picket line.[53]

The Supreme Court put its imprimatur on the labor injunction in the Debs case of 1895. A federal court ordered Eugene Debs's American Railway Union not to interfere with the passage of the mails during the Pullman strike of 1893. Justice David J. Brewer's majority opinion upheld the injunction on broad grounds: "The strong arm of the National Government may be put forth to brush away all obstructions to the freedom of interstate commerce or the transportation of the mails . . . the army of the Nation, and all its militia, are at the service of the Nation to compel obedience to its laws." In the early twentieth century the Supreme Court went a

52. E. P. Cheyney, "Decisions of the Courts in Conspiracy and Boycott Cases," *PSQ*, 4 (1889), 261–278; "Boycotting in the United States," *CLJ*, 21 (1885), 326; John H. Wigmore, "The Boycott and Kindred Practices as Ground for Damages," *ALR*, 21 (1887), 509–532; Clifford Brigham, "Strikes and Boycotts as Indictable Conspiracies at Common Law," *ALR*, 21 (1887), 41–69; Seymour D. Thompson, "Injunctions against Boycotting," *ALR*, 33 (1899), 815–888, and 34 (1900), 161–185. See also Felix Frankfurter and Nathan Greene, *The Labor Injunction* (New York, 1930); Arnold M. Paul, *Conservative Crisis and the Rule of Law* (Ithaca, 1960), ch. 6.

53. "Federal Injunctions against Boycotts," *ALR*, 27 (1893), 405–410; Aldace F. Walker, "Recent Labor Rulings by Federal Courts," *Forum*, 15 (1893), 311–322; Judge Jenkins in Farmers' Loan and Trust v. Northern Pacific, 60 Fed. 803, 821 (1894); Sherry v. Perkins, 147 Mass. 212 (1888); Vogelahn v. Guntner, 167 Mass. 97 (1896). See also Herbert B. Shoemaker, "Federal Power to Regulate Interstate Commerce and the Police Powers of the States," *ALR*, 29 (1895), 59–72.

step further, upholding antiboycott injunctions on the basis of the Sherman Antitrust Act's prohibition of conspiracies in restraint of trade.[54]

The late nineteenth century courts struck also at the growing body of state laws regulating the terms and conditions of labor. The most notable of these decisions was In re Jacobs (1885), when the New York Court of Appeals annulled a law banning the manufacture of cigars in tenements. Attorney William M. Evarts, representing the manufacturers, spoke of tobacco's aroma as a healthful form of fumigation, and expanded on the "beneficent influence" of a family working together in its quarters. The Massachusetts Supreme Judicial Court, striking down a law that forbade the fining of workingmen for damage done to their tools or materials, relied on the sanctity of contract and on the protection in "acquiring, possessing and protecting property" accorded by the state's Declaration of Rights.[55]

But the extent of this antilabor decisionmaking often has been exaggerated. An 1897 review of 1,639 state labor laws enacted during the preceding twenty years found that only 114 of them— 7 percent—had been held unconstitutional. (More disturbing was the fact that laws had been voided in twenty-three out of forty-three areas of labor legislation.) The police power of the states to regulate working conditions continued to be a powerful and widely accepted legal doctrine. Critics of labor injunctions had a strong array of arguments. They held that when the courts ordered workers to return to their jobs this was in effect enforcing a form of slavery; and that when judges issued injunctions in their equity capacity, they were imposing criminal sanctions without a jury trial or other common law safeguards. Equity was being transformed, charged one critic, from the protection of private rights

54. In re Debs, 158 U.S. 564, 582 (1895); Loewe v. Lawlor, 208 U.S. 274 (1908). See also Donald L. McMurry, "The Legal Ancestry of the Pullman Strike Injunctions," ILRR, 14 (1961), 235–256.

55. C. B. Labatt, "State Regulation of the Contract of Employment," ALR, 27 (1893), 857–875; In re Jacobs, 98 N.Y. 98 (1885); Commonwealth v. Perry, 155 Mass. 117, 121 (1891); James Bryce, The American Commonwealth (New York, 1893), I, 439. For other cases see Woodward, "Statutory Limitations"; Paul, Conservative Crisis, 15–18; Loren P. Beth, The Development of the American Constitution 1877–1917 (New York, 1971), 219–222.

to "the perversion of public rights, or the punishment of private wrongs.[56]

The activism of the courts in labor matters was blamed on "the dry rot which has attacked our state executives and our state legislatures, which renders them unable to perform in anything like an efficient manner their proper functions." But precisely because so much was expected of the courts, they could not act indefinitely in a sensitive area like labor relations without taking account of public opinion or economic and social realities. By the late 1890s, the influential New York and Massachusetts courts were increasingly inclined to uphold state laws affecting the conditions of labor. In Holden v. Hardy (1898) the United States Supreme Court sustained a Utah eight-hour law for miners. The courts, in sum, were no more single-minded in their response to a new, industrial America than were the other sectors of the polity.[57]

56. F. J. Stimson, "Democracy and the Laboring Man," *AM*, 80 (1897), 606; W. A. Coutts, "State Regulation of the Payment of Wages," *MLJ*, 4 (1895), 217–223; T.M.C., "Some New Aspects of the Right of Trial by Jury," *ALReg*, ns, 16 (1877), 705–721. See also Charles C. Allen, "Injunction and Organized Labor," *ALR*, 28 (1894), 828–859.

57. William D. Lewis, "Strikes and Courts of Equity," *ALReg*, ns, 37 (1898), 11–12; "Comment," *YR*, 7 (1898–1899), 5–7; Frederic J. Stimson, "The True Attitude of Courts and Legislatures upon Labor Questions," *GB*, 10 (1898), 103–107; Holden v. Hardy, 169 U.S. 366 (1898); Florence Kelley, "The United States Supreme Court and the Utah Eight-Hours' Law," *ASR*, 4 (1898–1899), 21–34.

CHAPTER 11

The Structure
of Economic Regulation

IT IS CUSTOMARY to assume that the high noon of laissez-faire came in the latter half of the nineteenth century. Certainly the conventional economic thought of the time, the weakness of government as a supervisory force, and self-seeking entrepreneurs and corporations worked against an effective system of economic regulation. But the rise of an industrial economy produced conflicts of interest that led to increasing demands on the state.

The polity's response was equivocal. One element consisted of attempts to shield existing interests from the consequences of economic change. But there was as well growing pressure for government regulation designed to foster a new, national economy. Judges and legislators had a shared commitment to laissez-faire and the free play of the market. Yet a changing economic order increasingly required exceptions, adjustments, accommodations. The consequence was a gradually thickening system of government supervision, but one that rested on traditional conceptions of public power and was constantly circumscribed by an ingrained hostility to the active state.

The Regulation of a National Economy

The police power—the right (and duty) of the American commonwealths to protect the health, morals, and safety of their citizens

—was the rationale for most state economic regulation. Contemporary observers thought that the application of that power was extensive indeed. The president of the American Bar Association estimated in 1897 that more than 90 percent of state legislation rested on the police power. Christopher Tiedeman's influential 1886 treatise, *Limitations of the Police Power in the United States* (which like Cooley's *Constitutional Limitations* was as much a plea for what should be as a description of what was), complained: "The State is called on to protect the weak against the shrewdness of the stronger, to determine what wages a workman shall receive for his labor, and how many hours daily he shall labor. Many trades and occupations are being prohibited because some are damaged incidentally by their prosecution." Another critic condemned the growth of "the *police* theory of political economy." Oliver Wendell Holmes caustically said of the police power: "We suppose this phrase was invented to cover certain acts of the legislature which are seen to be unconstitutional, but which are believed to be necessary." If by later standards the economic regulation of the time was a pitifully inadequate response to the problems posed by an industrial economy, to a number of contemporaries it was a disturbing extension of the active state.[1]

Much of this regulatory growth was a near-automatic response to the evolution of the American economy. State supervision of public service activities, for example, was established practice. Now a flood of new gas, electric, street railway, telephone, and water companies joined older enterprises such as banking, insurance, and railroads as fit subjects for regulation. New technology of necessity led to new constraints. An 1884 New York law required all electric, telephone, and telegraph lines in cities with half

1. Ernst Freund, *The Police Power* (Chicago, 1904); James M. Woolworth, "Address of the President," *ABA Reports*, 20 (1897), 239; Christopher G. Tiedeman, *A Treatise on the Limitations of the Police Power in the United States* (St. Louis, 1886), vi; Francis Wharton, "Political Economy and Criminal Law," *CLM*, 3 (1882), 1; Holmes in *ALR*, 6 (1871–1872), 140–142. See also Lewis Hochheimer, "The Police Power," *CLJ*, 44 (1897), 158–162; D. H. Pingrey, "The Power of the Sovereignty to Regulate the Conduct of Citizens toward Each Other," *CLM*, 13 (1891), 695–718; Alfred Orendorff, "Public Policy, and the Police Power of the State," *CLN*, 14 (1882), 256–257; "Acts which the Legislature may and may not Declare Criminal," 78 *AmStR* 235–274; Alfred Russell, *The Police Power of the State* (Chicago, 1900).

a million people or more to be placed underground. An 1891 Indiana statute set standards for the strength of pipes used to carry natural gas. Hundreds of similar acts dotted the statute books of the period: testimony to the regulatory response elicited by the fact of economic change.[2]

Laws governing entry into and the conduct of occupations also made up an important and growing category of police power regulation. The egalitarian impulse of the 1830s and 1840s had led to the repeal of many older restrictions of this sort. But organized groups ranging from craft unions and employers' associations to professionals, tradesmen, and skilled workers sought protective legislation in the late nineteenth century. For the most part, trades and professions were allowed to define their own terms of entry and performance: a form of "law making by private groups" that became widespread in the twentieth century.[3]

The practice of medicine, an occupation with manifest public consequences, was particularly subject to licensing and other forms of regulation. Certification as a prerequisite for medical practice steadily spread. The Supreme Court in 1888 held that the authority to do so lay comfortably within the states' police power. State Boards of Health and local medical societies successfully restricted practice by doctors whom they deemed unqualified. Thus in 1893 the Iowa Supreme Court rejected an attempt by the Eclectic Medical College of Des Moines to have its graduates certified under the state medical practices act.

But medical science still was unformed and immature in the

2. Charles K. Burdick, "The Origin of the Peculiar Duties of Public Service Companies," *ColLR*, 11 (1911), 514–531, 616–638, 743–764; Allen R. Foote and Charles E. Everett, *Economic Legislation of All the States: The Law of Incorporated Companies Operating under Municipal Franchises*, 2 vols. (Cincinnati, 1892), which sought "to place the organization, management, and control of public industrial corporations upon a true economic basis"; "New York," *AC* (1884); "Indiana," *AC* (1891). See also M. F. Tyler, "The Legal History of the Telephone," *JSS*, 18 (1883), 163–177; Walter S. Allen, "The State and the Lighting Corporations," *AAPSS Annals*, 2 (1892), 131–139.

3. Louis L. Jaffe, "Law Making by Private Groups," *HLR*, 51 (1937), 201–253; Lawrence M. Friedman, "Freedom of Contract and Occupational Licensing 1890–1910: A Legal and Social Study," *CalLR*, 53 (1965), 487–534; William L. Hodge, "Municipal Ordinances for the Regulation of Occupations by Means of Licenses," *ALR*, 25 (1891), 595–609. See also Tiedeman, *Police Power*, 271–289.

late nineteenth century, and the regulatory system reflected that fact. Michigan in 1899 established a Board of Regulation for medical practice that included one physiomedic, two homeopathic, and five allopathic practitioners. A South Carolina law of 1900 allowed homeopathic physicians to have their own examining board, and an osteopath successfully petitioned the Kentucky Court of Appeals in 1900 to grant an injunction restraining the state Board of Health from interfering with his practice.[4]

The licensing and certification of occupations posed in an acute form the tension between the desire to preserve a society of free competitors and the desire to secure protection from the rigors of a market economy. When state courts approved the licensing of barbers and blacksmiths, but not of horseshoers, it was evident that the principles governing certification were—to put it charitably—elusive ones. Occupational groups mounted considerable political pressure in their quest for control over entry and practice. They faced a strong countertradition of popular hostility to expertise and privileged status. A Milwaukee plumber in 1898 petitioned the city's Superior Court to void the state licensing law. He argued successfully that its test of expertise in house draining and plumbing ventilation was not a reasonable requirement for entry into the trade. But by the turn of the century, the general trend was clear: legislatures and courts acceded to the push of organized occupations for greater control over admission to their ranks.[5]

The police power was implemented with special vigor when public health and morals appeared to be at stake. A case in point was the regulation of the liquor business. The Supreme Court upheld the right of the states to forbid the manufacture and sale of alcohol and refused to accept the due process clause of the Fourteenth Amendment as a defense against state liquor legislation. In a federal circuit court decision, Justice David J. Brewer held that Kansas's 1885 prohibition act applied to those who had invested in the liquor business before its passage: "No man can build a Chinese wall around legislation by the assurance of capital in enterprises to increase crime and pauperism." The New York Court of

4. Dent v. West Virginia, 129 U.S. 114 (1888); "Iowa," AC (1893); "Michigan," AC (1899); "South Carolina," AC (1900); "Kentucky," AC (1900). See also Charles Z. Lincoln, "Law and Doctors in New York," ALJ, 41 (1890), 45–48, 64–68; ALReg, ns, 32 (1893), 22–27; Richard H. Shryock, Medical Licensing in America, 1650–1965 (Baltimore, 1967), 51 ff.

5. Friedman, "Freedom of Contract," 502, 521–523.

Appeals, upholding a law that allowed saloonkeepers to be sued for injuries stemming from the intoxication of their customers, declared: "That a statute impairs the value of property does not make it unconstitutional."[6]

More dramatic still was the extensive regulation—indeed, the near-crippling—of the oleomargarine industry. Margarine, an artificial substitute for butter derived from animal or vegetable fats, was invented in 1869 and went into American production in 1874. Its cheapness and resistance to spoilage made it a fearsome threat to dairy farmers, who called on their state legislatures for protection. New York passed a law restricting margarine in 1877, and by 1886 twenty-two states either heavily taxed the product or required unattractive coloring or labeling. In 1886 a federal law— "protection run mad," said an outraged critic—required that the product be called "oleo" (rather than "butterine" or other enticing names) and subjected it to a high license and manufacturing tax.

The courts generally sustained the antimargarine laws. New Jersey's Supreme Court upheld legislation whose "object was to secure to dairy men and to the public at large a fuller and fairer enjoyment of their property, by excluding from the market a commodity prepared with a view to deceive those purchasing it." In Powell v. Pennsylvania (1888), the United States Supreme Court approved a Pennsylvania antioleo statute on the ground that the state's police power over public health was sufficient justification. In his dissent Justice Stephen Field argued that new, cheap, wholesome foods were socially desirable. But the Court responded rather to the plea of counsel for the Commonwealth: "In a complex social system the tendency necessarily must be towards affirmative exercise of governmental powers."[7]

The imputation of unwholesomeness that helped to justify anti-

6. Bartemeyer v. Iowa, 18 Wall. 129 (1874); Mugler v. Kansas, 123 U.S. 123 (1887); Brewer quoted in James M. Mason, "The Walruff Case," *KLJ*, 3 (1886), 37; Berthoff v. O'Reilly, 74 N.Y. 509, 521 (1878). See also H. Campbell Black, "The Police Power and Public Health," *ALR*, 25 (1891), 170–184.

7. J. H. van Stuyvenberg, ed., *Margarine: An Economic and Scientific History 1869–1969* (Liverpool, 1969); Henry C. Bannard, "The Oleomargarine Law: A Study of Congressional Politics," *PSQ*, 2 (1887), 546; State v. Newton, 50 *N.J.L.R.* 534 (1888); Powell v. Pennsylvania, 127 U.S. 678 (1888); counsel quoted in Wintersteen, "The Sovereign State," *ALReg*, ns, 28 (1889), 129–139. See also R. Alton Lee, *A History of Regulatory Taxation* (Lexington, Ky., 1973), ch. 2; McCray v. U.S., 195 U.S. 27 (1904).

margarine laws was part of a growing concern over the purity of food and drugs. A California legislative committee in 1881 spoke of the dangers of adulterated products in language that foreshadowed the pure food and drug movement of the early twentieth century: "Our children are poisoned by dyestuffs used upon their dresses and their stockings. The candy they eat is poisoned. The papers which we put upon our walls are poisoned. The artificial flowers our wives and daughters employ are poisoned." State laws similar to Illinois's 1881 statute penalizing the sale of adulterated food, drink, and medicine multiplied during the late nineteenth century. British pure food and drug acts from 1875 on frequently served as a model for American legislation.

But vested interests, public indifference, varied state standards, and inadequate inspection worked against effective regulation. An 1884 attempt in Congress to establish a Bureau of Animal Industry was blocked on the ground that it was unconstitutional and would create an unwanted new bureaucracy. When Nebraska created a State Food Commission in 1899, a packing company sought an injunction restraining the commission from interfering with its business. Beyond this, state controls could not cope with an increasingly national system of food distribution. The 1899 Virginia legislature feared that because of more rigorous food laws in other commonwealths the state had become a dumping ground for adulterated food and feeds and for oleo (which was sold in the state as "Virginia butter").

The Federal Meat Inspection and Pure Food and Drug laws of 1906 marked the entry of the national government into this realm of regulation. But they came only after an aroused public opinion conjoined with commercial self-interest: some of the larger food and meat companies wanted federal standards that would weigh heavily on their smaller competitors.[8]

The pull between the commitment to the free play of the market and the need to deal with the distasteful consequences of that free-

8. "California," *AC* (1881); "Illinois," *AC* (1881); "Adulteration of Food," *AC* (1884); "Congress," *AC* (1884); U.S., *CR*, 48th Cong., 1st sess., House (Feb. 5, 1884), 899–906; "Nebraska," *AC* (1899); "Virginia," *AC* (1899); W. E. Mason, "Food Adulteration," *NAR*, 170 (1900), 548–552; Gabriel Kolko, *The Triumph of Conservatism* (Glencoe, Ill., 1963), 108–110.

dom arose as well in the area of commodities speculation. Southern and midwestern Boards of Trade—in New Orleans, St. Louis, Minneapolis, Kansas City, and especially Chicago—became markets in agricultural futures soon after their establishment during the mid-nineteenth century. The commodity futures market offered farmers and middlemen a means of hedging against price fluctuations and had a long-term leveling effect on commodities prices. But it also played a purely speculative role. By the end of the century, the sum total of commodity futures traded was seven times the size of the actual crops involved. Speculation in the price of staples such as wheat was morally distasteful to many Americans. And the possibility that speculators might corner the future supply of a commodity posed a threat to the public interest.

Another source of concern was the spread of "bucket shops": small establishments in which, under the pretense of buying and selling commodities, patrons gambled on the hour-by-hour fluctuation of commodity futures at the Chicago Board of Trade and other exchanges. These shady enterprises depended on direct telegraph communication with the Boards of Trade. The Chicago Board took the lead in opposing the bucket shops: in part because they besmirched futures trading (they were, after all, sleazy but uncomfortably close replicas of the commodities exchanges themselves); and in part because they interfered with the ability of the Board of Trade accurately to register the market price of crops. An 1887 Illinois law (upheld by the state supreme court) banned bucket shops. But the Chicago board failed to restrict the reporting of its futures quotations. The Illinois court in 1889 unanimously held that these were in the public domain.

Commodity futures trading came under constant assault in the late nineteenth century. The Illinois legislature and the state supreme court agreed in the 1870s that a commodity futures contract was legitimate only if it included the actual delivery of the produce involved. The California constitution of 1879 flatly forbade futures contracts, and a number of western states passed antifutures laws in the 1880s. Futures trading was a major object of Populist criticism in the nineties; and grain and hog merchants (as well as Charles A. Pillsbury, the nation's leading flour miller) complained that it placed control over crop prices in the hands of a few men in the Chicago Board of Trade. In 1892 Congress considered (but failed to pass) bills that put a prohibitive tax on grain and cotton sales where the seller did not own the commodities offered.

But for all this antifutures sentiment, the process was too essential a part of the national—indeed, international—market system to be abolished. Legal concepts such as intended delivery and the command order made delivery a possible but not necessarily an actual part of every futures transaction. The Illinois Supreme Court decided that these devices satisfied the statutory delivery requirement; and the Chicago Board of Trade continued to act as the great futures market for American agricultural commodities. Under public pressure, the board itself began to reform its procedures around the turn of the century. In 1905 the United States Supreme Court decided that by self-regulation the board was meeting its public responsibilities.[9]

The felt need to put some contraints on the economy left its mark even on that most sacrosanct of nineteenth century market devices, the contract. This "basically negative, passive and untechnical" instrument was peculiarly suited to the small-unit economic development of the early and mid-nineteenth centuries. But while the judicial doctrine of liberty of contract reached its peak at the end of the nineteenth century, a countering view was taking hold. If a contract was at odds with "the wants, interests, or prevailing sentiment of the people ... or is repugnant to the morals of the times, it is void." In a variety of ways, late nineteenth century courts and legislatures contained freedom of contract. They forbade the waiver of homestead exemptions, granted stays of execution, voided contracts that limited the time in which a suit might be brought, prohibited agreements not to go to court,

9. Jonathan Lurie, "Private Associations, Internal Regulation, and Progressivism: The Chicago Board of Trade as a Case Study," *AJLH*, 16 (1972), 215–238, "Commodities Exchanges, Agrarian 'Political Power,' and the Antioption Battle 1890–1894," *AH*, 48 (1974), 114–125; Cedric B. Cowing, *Populists, Plungers, and Progressives: A Social History of Stock and Commodity Speculation, 1890–1936* (Princeton, 1965), ch. 1; "Comment," *YR*, 1 (1892–1893), 116–120. See also Tiedeman, *Police Power*, 262–271; Carl Parker, "Government Regulation of Speculation," *AAPSS Annals*, 38 (1911), 126–154.

and voided contracts in restraint of trade or in which employees were paid in other than lawful money.[10]

The subtle process by which the sanctity of contract was modified to take account of changing economic realities may be seen in the case of one of the most widely used contract forms, the life insurance policy. Traditionally, the rule of warranty governed these contracts: that is, any false declaration by the insured voided the policy. This was the product of a time when small underwriters needed protection from large mercantile policyholders. But by the late nineteenth century, millions of people were buying life and industrial insurance from national companies. Strict application of the warranty rule would have wreaked havoc with these policyholders' equities; indeed, would have crippled the life insurance business itself. By holding that contested contract declarations were only stipulations, and not full warranties; by new interpretations of the legal doctrines of waiver and estoppel; and ("an American innovation in the law of insurance") by liberally admitting parol (verbal) waivers as evidence, the turn-of-the-century courts substantially reduced the importance of the warranty rule in life insurance law. State legislatures, too, enacted a growing body of laws designed to protect the interests of policyholders.[11]

These attempts to deal with a complex economy frequently involved objects of direct and manifest public concern: medicine, liquor, foodstuffs, commodity futures, life insurance policies. This was the work of a polity with no strong traditions of bureaucratic control, with no articulated theory of the active state. The police

10. Lawrence M. Friedman, *Contract Law in America: A Social and Economic Case Study* (Madison, 1965), 23; Elisha Greenhood, *The Doctrine of Public Policy in the Law of Contracts* (Chicago, 1886), 1; Roscoe Pound, "Liberty of Contract," *YLJ*, 18 (1909), 454–487; D. H. Pingrey, "Limiting the Right to Contract," *CLJ*, 34 (1892), 91–96; H. Campbell Black, "Legislation Impairing the Obligations of Contracts," *ALReg*, ns, 25 (1886), 81–97. A Liberty and Property Defense League in England also was concerned over the rise of legislation interfering with contract obligations: "Statutes Interfering with the Obligations of Contracts," *ALR*, 28 (1894), 110–111. See also Grant Gilmore, *The Death of Contract* (Columbus, 1974).

11. Morton Keller, "The Judicial System and the Law of Life Insurance, 1888–1910," *BHR*, 35 (1961), 317–335. See also Spencer L. Kimball, *Insurance and Public Policy* (Madison, 1960).

power concept provided a useful but limited rationale for the task of developing a regulatory structure in response to the tremendous economic changes of the late nineteenth century.

The insufficiency of the police power became more and more apparent as the century neared its end. In part this was due to the opposition of those ideologically committed to an unregulated market economy, or particular interests who opposed state regulation for their own ends. But a more important source of strain was the imbalance between state regulation and an increasingly national economy.

Conflict grew between the states' police power and the interstate commerce power of the federal government. By 1899, the Supreme Court had found twenty-nine state laws unconstitutional because they conflicted with the commerce clause of the Constitution. In Leisy v. Hardin (1890) the Court voided an Iowa law that blocked the entry of bottled liquor into the state, on the ground that the movement of an "original package" (in this case, the liquor bottle) was protected by the national interstate commerce power. A critic called the decision "the most crushing blow against the rights of the States which has ever been dealt by that tribunal." An aroused Congress quickly passed the Wilson Act, which held liquor subject to state law regardless of its packaging. The Court upheld the statute on the ground "that the common interest did not require entire freedom in the traffic in ardent spirits." But it continued to apply the original package doctrine against state laws restricting the entry of items such as oleomargarine and cigarettes. And in Champion v. Ames (1903) the Court upheld a national antilottery law, thus opening the prospect that the commerce power might justify broad federal regulation for public purposes, a national counterpart to the police power of the states.[12]

12. Leisy v. Hardin, 135 U.S. 100 (1890); "The 'Original Package' Case," *ALR*, 24 (1890), 474; Charles Warren, *The Supreme Court in United States History* (Boston, 1922), II, 731–732; Champion v. Ames, 188 U.S. 321 (1903). See also Charles C. Bonner, "The Relation of the Police Power of the States to the Commerce Power of the Nation," *ALR*, 25 (1891), 159–169; Charles A. Culberson, "The Supreme Court and Interstate Commerce," *ALR*, 24 (1891), 26–63; William R. Howland, "The Police Power and Inter-State Commerce," *HLR*, 4 (1890–1891), 221–233; A. H. Wintersteen, "The Commerce Clause and the State," *ALReg*, ns, 28 (1889), 733–747.

The emergence of a complex national economy led also to growing demands for a commercial law transcending state boundaries. But this was difficult, given the facts of governmental federalism and the great range and diversity of economic interests. The influential jurist John F. Dillon argued that "state lines for commercial and social purposes have almost disappeared"; but for legislative and legal purposes they most certainly had not. The variety of state laws regarding usury, bankruptcy, debt collection, the execution of deeds and wills, and negotiable instruments obstructed the transactions of an interstate economy. Attempts to codify the law within each state only reinforced this diversity: "In Europe, the purpose of codification is to obtain common national law; in this country the effect of state codification is to destroy our national common law."[13]

These conditions spurred a movement to create uniform commercial laws. A bill standardizing the laws governing bills of exchange and other commercial paper came before Congress in 1884. Its model was the 1882 British Bills of Exchange Act, and the American Bankers Association had much to do with its drafting. But this was too sweeping an assertion of federal authority, and it failed to pass. The real impetus came from the states themselves. Between 1890 and 1896 over half of them appointed commissioners on uniform state laws. From 1891 on conferences of the state commissioners working with the American Bar Association sought to draft acceptable statutes. A Uniform Negotiable Securities Law was devised in 1896, a Uniform Warehouse Receipts Act and a Uniform Sales Act in 1906. By 1898 a General Act Relating to Negotiable Instruments had won unanimous approval from the House of Representatives and was adopted by New York, Massachusetts, and a number of other states. Congress's Harter Act of 1892 restated the law of bills of lading in order to right imbalances that had developed in the relations among carriers, shippers, and underwriters.[14]

13. Dillon quoted in S. P. Wheeler, "The Necessity for Uniform Laws Governing Commercial Paper in the United States," *BLJ*, 13 (1896), 694; Munroe Smith, "State Statute and Common Law," *PSQ*, 2 (1887), 161.

14. Nathaniel A. Prentiss, "Unification of the Law," *ALR*, 16 (1882), 307–317; " 'The Bills of Exchange Act, 1884,' " *ALR*, 18 (1884), 863–870; William L. Snyder, "The Problem of Uniform Legislation in the United

Patents, trade marks, copyright, and bankruptcy were comparably important subjects of commercial law in the late nineteenth century, and they too were affected by the economic changes of the time. The purpose of patenting was to stimulate creativity by assuring inventors the fruits of their work. But the system came under increasing pressure in the late nineteenth century. As the number of patents grew—from 13,417 granted in 1880 to 26,398 in 1900—the Patent Office adopted stricter rules of acceptability. Complaints mounted that wealthy or corporate claimants were likely to triumph over lone inventors. Another source of strain was the rise of complex and costly struggles between corporations over valuable basic patents. Prolonged litigation over key telephone patents was finally decided in 1887 by a closely divided Supreme Court in favor of the American Telephone and Telegraph Company. A conflict of comparable magnitude over electrical patents embroiled General Electric and Westinghouse in the 1890s. A patent system designed to deal with individual inventors appeared to be less and less functional. But by the end of the century no legislative or administrative solution was in sight.[15]

Trade mark law, too, felt the impact of a new business economy. The Supreme Court in 1879 found the Federal Trade Mark Act of 1870 to be unconstitutional, on the ground that a trade mark was neither writing nor property and hence was not entitled to the protection of the law. But the commercial value of exclusive brand names was obvious, and the decision annulled reciprocal trade mark treaties with other nations. Congress quickly reenacted the

States," *ABA Reports*, 15 (1892), 287–311; "State Commissions to Promote Uniformity of Legislation," *ALR*, 27 (1893), 414–415; James W. Hurst, *The Growth of American Law: The Law Makers* (Boston, 1950), 71–72; Everett P. Wheeler, "The Harter Act: Recent Legislation in the United States Respecting Bills of Lading," *ALR*, 33 (1899), 801–826. See also Henry C. Tompkins, "The Necessity for Uniformity in the Laws Governing Commercial Paper," *ABA Reports*, 13 (1890), 247–263; Leonard A. Jones, "Uniformity of Laws through National and Interstate Codification," *VSBA Reports*, 7 (1894), 157–180.

15. *HS*, 607; John M. Perkins, "Shall the Patent Laws be Repealed?" *ALJ*, 34 (1886), 188–190; "Patents," *AC* (1883); John B. Uhle, "The Law Relating to Telephones," *ALReg*, ns, 28 (1889), 65–81; The Telephone Cases, 126 U.S. 1 (1888); Harold C. Passer, *The Electrical Manufacturers 1875–1900* (Cambridge, 1953), ch. 20. See also "Patents in England and America," *LT*, 48 (1870), 309; Bruce V. Bugbee, *Genesis of American Patent and Copyright Law* (Washington, 1967).

law in 1881 under its commerce power, and the Court accepted this reformulation.[16]

The traditional American view of copyright was lax and limited. A federal district court in 1853 refused to take action against an unauthorized German translation of *Uncle Tom's Cabin,* arguing that by the act of publication the book's author had voluntarily relinquished her control over abridgments, translations, and the like. The United States refused to subscribe to international copyright agreements, thus allowing large-scale transatlantic literary piracy to flourish.

But conditions changed in the late nineteenth century. Copyright registrations increased from 19,311 in 1880 to 95,573 in 1900, and both authors and publishers sought greater protection of their interests. In 1870 the national copyright law was amended to give authors the right to control translations and dramatizations of their work. Writers and publishers lobbied for American participation in international copyright agreements. Success came with the passage of an international copyright law in 1891 and a new American copyright code in 1909.[17]

Finally, the growing tension between state regulation and a national economic system restoked the demand for a federal bankruptcy law. The post-Civil War national bankruptcy act of 1867 had been repealed in 1879. Business interests immediately called for a new law. As the president of the National Board of Trade put it: "We are a homogeneous people." State bankruptcy laws favored their own creditors and varied in their terms of discharge from debt. A national law, it was argued, would encourage interstate business and keep prices down by increasing the likelihood that obligations would be met. A new federal bankruptcy statute was passed in 1898. But its provisions favored voluntary over involuntary bankruptcy, and the American Bar Association, the

16. Trade Mark Cases, 100 U.S. 82 (1879); "The Federal Trade-Mark Statutes," *ALJ,* 19 (1879), 5–9; Hugh Weightman, "Trade-Marks," *ALReg,* ns, 20 (1881), 304–316.

17. Benjamin Kaplan, *An Unhurried View of Copyright* (New York, 1967); Richard R. Bowker, *Copyright: Its History and Its Law* (Boston, 1912), ch. 4; Stowe v. Thomas, 23 Fed. Cas. 201 [E.D. Pa.] (1853); James O. Pierce, "Anomalies in the Law of Copyright," *SLR,* ns, 5 (1879), 420–436; *HS,* 606; Aubert J. Clark, *The Movement for International Copyright in Nineteenth Century America* (Washington, 1960).

National Association of Manufacturers, the Commercial Law League of America, the United States Chamber of Commerce, and the boards of trade sought amendments designed to bring the bankruptcy process into closer accord with the conditions and the interests of a national, corporate economy.[18]

These instances of regulation attracted relatively little public attention. Often local or technical in nature, they fitted smoothly into the normal course of economic life. Nor did the instrumentalities of this regulation—the police power of the states, the oversight of the courts, an occasional federal commercial statute—dramatically depart from established modes of public policy and practice.

But the emergence of an integrated railroad network and the rise of large, consolidated corporations led to new federal laws that broke with the regulatory past. The 1887 Interstate Commerce Act (which created the Interstate Commerce Commission) and the 1890 Sherman Antitrust Act were prototypes for the structure of supervision that came into being in the twentieth century. At the same time they reflected the ambivalence of attitude toward freedom and control, toward preserving the past and fostering change, that pervaded the political economy of the late nineteenth century United States.

Railroads

Unique in their size and capital, their interstate range of activity, and their economic importance, railroads made heavy calls on the attention of the late nineteenth century American polity. The railroad lobby was a potent force in Washington and the state

18. Charles Warren, *Bankruptcy in United States History* (Cambridge, 1935), 127 ff; quotation from Samuel Wagner, "The Advantages of a National Bankrupt Law," *ABA Reports*, 4 (1881), 233; S. Whitney Dunscomb, Jr., *Bankruptcy: A Study in Comparative Legislation* (New York, 1893), 152. See also "Bankrupt Law," *CLJ*, 23 (1886), 25–26; H. Teichmueller, "A Uniform System of Bankruptcy," *ALR*, 26 (1892), 231–238; Edwin S. Mack, "Bankruptcy Legislation," *ALR*, 28 (1894), 1–8; Dunscomb, "The Federal Bankruptcy Law," *PSQ*, 13 (1898), 606–616; William H. Hotchkiss, "Bankruptcy Laws, Past and Present," *NAR*, 167 (1898), 580–591, "Two Years of the Federal Bankruptcy Law," *NAR*, 172 (1901), 573–583; George C. Holt, "Merits and Defects of the Bankrupt Law," *JSS*, 40 (1902), 96–109.

capitals. Few businessmen so conspicuously engaged in political manipulation as did the railroad magnates: Jay Gould, Jim Fisk, and Daniel Drew of the Erie; Franklin B. Gowan of the Reading; Charles E. Perkins of the Chicago, Burlington & Quincy; Leland Stanford and Collis P. Huntington of the Central and Southern Pacific; Milton H. Smith of the Louisville & Nashville. But the more profoundly the railroads worked their way into the heart of the American economy, the more insistent was the call for government supervision. The most important American enterprise of the time became the object of the first substantial attempt at federal regulation.[19]

Direct government subsidies for railroad construction—bonds, loans, land grants—all but ended in the 1870s. Company earnings and private investment paid for the massive expansion of the railroad system (from 93,000 miles of track in 1880 to almost 260,000 miles in 1900) that went on for the rest of the century. At the same time, the focus of railroad policy shifted from stimulation to containment. Large-scale bankruptcy, swindles, and defaulting during the depression years of the 1870s fed a movement to reduce or prohibit local subsidies. An 1879 Minnesota constitutional amendment restricting such aid to 5 percent of a locality's assessed valuation was adopted by a popular vote of 55,143 to 1,702. Counties and towns that invested heavily in the coming of the railroad now sought to avoid the tax levies that their obligations compelled them to impose. But the federal courts held communities in Missouri and Kansas to strict accountability, even for clearly fraudulent railroad bond issues. The states' courts, governors, and legislatures fiercely but in the end unsuccessfully opposed these judgments. Nothing so clearly illustrates the changing relationship of railroads to the polity as does this shift from eager competition for railroad development to desperate efforts to escape the ensuing legacy of debt.[20]

Railroad rates were a no less fruitful source of controversy. State commissions and legislatures in the 1870s sought to forbid rate

19. Thomas C. Cochran, *Railroad Leaders, 1845–1890: The Business Mind in Action* (Cambridge, 1953), ch. 14; Harry P. Robison, "A Railway Party in Politics," *NAR*, 156 (1893), 552–560.

20. "Railway Service of the United States," *AC* (1884); "Minnesota," *AC* (1879); Charles Fairman, *Reconstruction and Reunion, 1864–88, Part One* (New York, 1971), ch. 18.

discrimination and prevent exorbitant charges. But prorailroad court decisions, compliant state railroad commissions, and railroad lobbying that secured the modification or repeal of regulatory laws made a mockery of state supervision.

This is not to say that the railroads thrived in some laissez-faire Elysium. Competition and a falling price level put great pressure on the rate structures of lines burdened with heavy capital and operating costs. Rate wars beset the trunk lines that connected the agrarian West to the seaports of the East. The roads sought to solve their problems by rate pooling agreements. But these had no standing in law; and between 1874 and 1898 the trunk line pool went through four major and numerous minor reorganizations, as rate agreements constantly broke down. Some railroad leaders began to look to the federal government to provide a rate stability that they could not secure for themselves.[21]

The railroads' search for a stable rate structure was hardly the only, or even the major, source of pressure for government supervision. Antirailroad sentiment was part of the stock in trade of late nineteenth century politicians, in the East as well as in the agrarian South and West. The governor of Pennsylvania complained in 1892 that railroad consolidation eliminated competition "which had previously existed . . . to the advantage of the people." The chief executive of railroad-dominated New Jersey charged that the lines paid far less than their due share of taxes. When a New Hampshire line petitioned in 1897 to extend its right of way through a wooded valley, the legislature refused on the ground that the removal of a large number of trees would not be in the public interest.[22]

The courts, too, were far from being consistent champions of railroad interests. The tendency after the Munn v. Illinois decision of 1877 was "towards a liberal exercise of the police power of the

21. Paul W. MacAvoy, *The Economic Effects of Regulation: The Trunk-Line Railroad Cartels and the Interstate Commerce Commission before 1900* (Cambridge, 1965); William S. Ellis, "State Railroad Commissions," *ALReg*, ns, 32 (1893), 632–639, 709–721; Gideon D. Bantz, "Legislative Power to Regulate Railroad Franchises," *CLJ*, 12 (1881), 194–199; Charles C. Savage, "State Legislation Affecting Railroad Traffic," *ALReg*, ns, 23 (1884), 81–93.

22. "Pennsylvania," *AC* (1892); "New Jersey," *AC* (1884, 1892); "New Hampshire," *AC* (1897). See also James F. Hudson, *The Railways and the Republic* (New York, 1886).

State over these corporations in all matters where it might be exercised over natural persons." A count of the Supreme Court's railroad decisions during the 1884 to 1888 terms found that forty-nine cases went against the lines, forty-eight for them; in the 1892 to 1896 terms, the totals were ninety-six against, forty-eight in favor.

But from the mid-1880s on, the federal courts were increasingly concerned lest state regulation and taxation interfere with the flow of commerce. The Supreme Court in 1886 struck down an Illinois attempt to regulate freight rates on the ground that the statute disrupted interstate commerce, a holding that led directly to Congress's creation of the Interstate Commerce Commission. The Court went further in Chicago, Milwaukee & St. Paul v. Minnesota (1890), which in effect overturned the Munn decision by asserting that the reasonableness of rate regulation was a judicial and not a legislative matter. The implicit policy view appeared to be that ratemaking should rest in the hands of the managers of interstate railroad lines—and be subject to the review of federal courts rather than particularistic state courts and legislatures. An uncomfortable observer thought that "long tables of railway statistics, with the accompanying analyses, look strangely out of place in a volume of United States Reports": testimony to the new, quasi-administrative role assumed by the Court.[23]

The most significant judicial oversight of the railroads came through federal court receivership of bankrupt lines. This bold extension of judicial authority had as its primary intent not a change in the character of the railroads' management and financial structures, but rather their perpetuation under the umbrella of the courts.

Heavy indebtedness and hard times swept a number of lines into deep financial trouble during the 1870s. By 1874, 25 percent of the

---

23. Horace G. Wood, *A Treatise on the Law of Railroads,* 3 vols. (Boston, 1885), 1706; "Record of the Supreme Court of the United States in Railway Cases," *ALR,* 32 (1898), 897–899; Wabash, St. Louis & Pacific Ry. Co. v. Illinois, 118 U.S. 557 (1886); Chicago, Milwaukee & St. Paul Ry. Co. v. Minnesota, 134 U.S. 418 (1890); Arthur T. Hadley, "Legal Theories of Price Regulation," *YR,* 1 (1892–1893), 56–67; Max West, "The Fourteenth Amendment in the Light of Recent Decisions," *YR,* 8 (1890), 391. See also Ward M. McAfee, "A Constitutional History of Railroad Rate Regulation in California, 1879–1911," *PHR,* 37 (1968), 265–280.

bonded railroad debt was in default. Under traditional bankruptcy procedure, these troubled roads would have been placed under trustees. Thus "regalvanized," they would operate under their former managers, the trusteeships serving to block foreclosure.

But complaints grew that this system led to favoritism among bond and mortgage holders and other creditors. And the repeal in 1878 of the federal bankruptcy law subjected insolvent lines to the varying bankruptcy statutes of the states. Federal district judges in their capacity as chancellors in equity began to accept receivership petitions from railroads in difficulty and to appoint receivers of the lines. Chief Justice Waite in 1879 authorized receivers to pay for labor, improvements, and newly incurred debts over the claims of mortgage bondholders. In 1881, the Supreme Court held that the primary responsibility of a railroad receiver was not to wind up the business, but to continue it (even at the cost of assuming a substantial new burden of debt). "The new and changed condition of things which is presented by the insolvency of such a corporation as a railroad company," said the Court, "has rendered necessary the exercise of large and modified control over its property by the courts."[24]

Because the receiver was neither the agent of the railroad company nor of its creditors, but was an officer of the court, a number of advantages accrued. The lines were not liable for injuries resulting from the receivers' negligence. Receivers had no personal liability for the debts of their roads. And obligations incurred in the operation of receiver-run lines took precedence over existing mortgage debt. Receivers' certificates became an important new form of railroad obligation, allowing bankrupt lines to raise the funds necessary for their maintenance and improvement.[25]

Between 1884 and 1896 over four hundred lines went into receivership. In 1893 about one-sixth of the nation's railroad mile-

24. John F. Crowell, "Railway Receiverships in the United States," YR, 7 (1898–1899), 319–330; Fosdick v. Schall, 99 U.S. 235 (1879); Barton v. Barbour, 104 U.S. 126, 134–135 (1881). See also Warren, Supreme Court, II, 361; Albro Martin, "Railroads and the Equity Receivership: An Essay on Institutional Change," JEH, 34 (1974), 685–709.

25. George W. McCrary, "Of the Enforcement of Debts Contracted and Liabilities Incurred by Receivers of Railroads," ALR, 17 (1883), 833–848; Robert L. Fowler, "Some Federal Decisions Affecting Railway Securities," ALR, 24 (1890), 428–441.

age was run by court-appointed receivers. The governor of Colorado reported in 1895: "With one principal exception, all the railroads of this State are now in the hands of the courts, and are being managed by receivers." A Vermont railroad was run by court-appointed receivers for twenty-seven years.

Railroad receivership constituted "an enormous increase in the work of these Courts and the assumption of new duties and new responsibilities, . . . requiring the control of railroads to be taken from the hands of State commissions and State officials and placed in the custody and direction of the judicial branch of the National government." But this hardly marked the beginning of a new era in government supervision or in the conduct of the railroad business. Receivers almost always were drawn from the existing management. Their commissions were high enough to elicit adverse comment. And federal judges issued the first labor injunctions in the late 1880s against railroad unions on strike against "their" roads. The courts used the receivership power to protect the existing railroad system from the threats of heavy indebtedness and labor unrest.[26]

The scale and complexity of the interests affected by the railroads; the necessarily limited character of state regulation; the increasing assumption of regulatory oversight by the federal courts; the competitive problems of the major roads themselves: all fed a movement for national supervision that culminated in the passage of the Interstate Commerce Act of 1887.

In its early stages the call for federal regulation was primarily eastern, and came from interests with specific grievances. These included New York merchants and farmers suffering from trunk line rate schedules that favored other eastern ports or western farmers, and independent oil producers and refiners (and the Reading Railroad) unhappy over rebate arrangements between the Standard Oil Company and the Pennsylvania Railroad. But the national scale of railroad problems, and the growing tendency of

26. Crowell, "Railway Receiverships," 321; "Colorado," *AC* (1895); on Vermont, Seymour D. Thompson, "The Court Management of Railroads," *ALR*, 27 (1893), 483–484; quote from Barton v. Barbour, 104 U.S. 134–135 (1881); D. H. Chamberlain, "New-Fashioned Receiverships," *HLR*, 10 (1896), 139–149.

the courts to intercede in rate regulation, broadened the base of support for a federal statute. One proposal in 1880 called for a Tribunal of Transportation, staffed by experts who would settle rate and discrimination disputes. Hundreds of petitions for federal regulation poured into Congress during the early 1880s; more than 150 bills were introduced; both national party platforms endorsed federal regulation in 1884. As major shippers of raw materials, foodstuffs, and manufactured products improved their bargaining position with the railroads, presidents A. B. Stickney of the St. Paul and A. J. Cassatt of the Pennsylvania called for regulation to prevent rebates and other forms of favored treatment. They were joined in this by smaller manufacturers, who feared the capacity of large companies to win rate advantages from the roads.[27]

But most railroad presidents were hostile to or skeptical of government regulation. (Told that it would not be difficult to defeat the Interstate Commerce Act, Jay Gould supposedly replied: "Let it go, or we will get a worse dose next season.") Nor was it clear to what degree a federal commission would be under the control of the railroads—or of which railroads—or of the shippers—or would serve a more general public interest. The entry of the national government into the realm of railroad regulation was a leap in the dark.[28]

The Interstate Commerce Act of 1887 defined and laid down the

27. Robert P. Harlow, "The Propriety of Regulating Commercial Intercourse," NYSBA Reports, 4 (1880), 207–240; Edwin E. Sparks, National Development 1877–1885 (New York, 1907), 65; Robert E. Cushman, The Independent Regulatory Commissions (New York, 1941), 41; Chester M. Destler, "The Opposition of American Businessmen to Social Control during the 'Gilded Age,'" MVHR, 79 (1953), 666; Edward A. Purcell, Jr., "Ideas and Interests: Businessmen and the Interstate Commerce Act," JAH, 54 (1967), 561–578. See also David Wagner, "The Power of the State and National Governments to Regulate and Control Railroads," SLR, ns, 7 (1881), 377–399; Gerald D. Nash, "Origins of the Interstate Commerce Act of 1887," PH, 24 (1957), 181–190.

28. On Gould, John R. Dos Passos, "The United States Supreme Court and the Commercial Era," YLJ, 17 (1908), 579. Gabriel Kolko's Railroads and Regulation, 1877–1916 (Princeton, 1965) argues that the large railroads were the prime movers behind the Interstate Commerce Act; he is supported by Robert B. Carson, "Railroads and Regulation Revisited: A Note on Problems of Historiography and Ideology," Hist, 34 (1972), 437–446. For rebuttals, see Purcell, "Ideas and Interests," Robert W. Harbeson, "Railroads and Regulation, 1877–1916: Conspiracy or Public Interest?" JEH, 27 (1967), 230–242, and Albro Martin, "The Troubled Subject of Rail-

penalties for rate discrimination, and created an Interstate Commerce Commission with the power to investigate and prosecute violators. The first federal regulatory agency, it was a milestone in the late nineteenth century effort to impose some restraints on an industrial economy of frightening scale and power.

But the primary purpose of the act was negative: to block pooling and other cartel arrangements, not to secure a stable railroad rate structure. The ICC's performance showed how difficult it was to establish a bureaucratic mode of regulation in the late nineteenth century American polity. Comparison with Great Britain is instructive. In that country a strikingly similar coalition of agricultural, mining, and manufacturing interests and antirailroad public opinion led to the passage of the Railway and Land Traffic Act of 1888 and the Railway and Canal Traffic Act of 1894 (which included an independent Railway and Canal Commission). The path of administrative supervision of the British railway system was smoothed by the fact that for decades the Board of Trade had been charged with regulatory oversight of the British lines.[29]

The prevailing form of American supervision was judicial, and the ICC conformed to that model. Its first chairman, Thomas M. Cooley, was a judge and treatise writer steeped in the assumptions and procedures of the judicial process. He announced: "The Commissioners realize that they are a new court, . . . and that they are to lay the foundations of a new body of American law." He set out to create a common law of railroad regulation. But this is not to say that Cooley was a catspaw of the railroads. Judicial-like supremacy and not service to the lines was his goal. He believed that he and his fellow commissioners "ought to make ourselves felt more by the railroads: be masters of the situation: be the authority in railroad matters."

During the first ten years of its existence, the ICC handed down rulings on more than eight hundred rate controversies. But the size, complexity, and intensely competitive character of the railroad

---

road Regulation in the Gilded Age—A Reappraisal," *JAH*, 61 (1974), 339–371.

29. Martin, "Troubled Subject," 343; Philip Williams, "Public Opinion and the Railway Rate Question in 1886," *EHR*, 67 (1952), 37–73; Henry Parris, *Government and the Railways in Nineteenth-Century Britain* (London, 1965).

business, and the lack of a supervisory function or infrastructure, limited the commission's impact. Railroads, shippers, and (increasingly) the railroad unions engaged in an ever more elaborate *pas de trois* of competing interests. And the courts continued to assert their ultimate authority to subject rate decisions to the rule of reasonableness. The major effect of the ICC was to bring about greater uniformity in railroad accounting and the classification of operating costs, and to secure greater public access to information on the conduct of the railroad business.[30]

Neither state nor federal supervision resolved the conflicts raised by the interplay of railroads, shippers, labor, and the public. Demands rose in the 1890s for government ownership and operation of the lines, or at least for more rigorous supervision by a national Department of Transportation. But as Cooley observed, this was beyond the capacity of the late nineteenth century American polity: "The perpetuity of free institutions in this country requires that the political machine called the United States Government be kept from being overloaded beyond its strength. The more cumbrous it is the greater is the power of intrigue and corruption under it."

Nor did a solution come in the twentieth century. The Elkins Act of 1903, the Hepburn Act of 1906, the Mann-Elkins Act of 1910, and the Transportation Act of 1920 attested to the continuing effort to make federal railroad regulation more effective. The increasingly parlous state of American railroads in the twentieth century was a monument of sorts to that effort's failure.[31]

30. Allan Jones, "Thomas M. Cooley and the ICC: Continuity and Change in the Doctrine of Equal Rights," *PSQ*, 81 (1966), 613; Cooley, Diaries, April 26, 1888, MichHS; Henry C. Adams, "A Decade of Federal Railway Regulation," *AM*, 81 (1898), 433–443.

31. "The State Ownership of Railroads," *ALR*, 28 (1894), 608–611; Arthur T. Hadley, "Railroad Problems of the Immediate Future," *AM*, 67 (1891), 386–393; Henry J. Fletcher, "A National Transportation Department," *AM*, 76 (1895), 119–126; Cooley to J. R. Burns, April 30, 1886, Cooley Mss, MichHS; Albro Martin, *Enterprise Denied: Origins of the Decline of American Railroads, 1897–1917* (New York, 1971); Stanley P. Caine, *The Myth of a Progressive Reform: Railroad Regulation in Wisconsin 1903–1910* (Madison, 1970); K. Austin Kerr, *American Railroad Politics 1914–1920* (Pittsburgh, 1968). See also Samuel P. Huntington, "The Marasmus of the ICC: The Commission, the Railroads, and the Public Interest," *YLJ*, 61 (1952), 467–509.

Corporation, Trust, and Antitrust

The business corporation was an increasingly common form of economic organization in the late nineteenth century. State general incorporation acts, widespread by the 1880s, made the act of incorporation little more than an administrative formality for small as well as large enterprises. There was scant regulation of corporate management and investment, in part because incorporation was so widespread, in part because few corporations sold stock to the public. (Less than a dozen industrial companies were listed on the New York Stock Exchange in 1886; only sixteen mining and manufacturing issues were actively traded in 1894.) While the British courts were hostile to stock dividends based on "fictitious increase," American tribunals generally permitted this means of enhancing a corporation's attraction to investors.[32]

Competition among the states added to the prevailing disregard of corporations' internal affairs. West Virginia, Delaware, and New Jersey became "snug harbors" not only for large companies doing an interstate business but for marginal "tramp" and "piratical" corporations as well. The already permissive New Jersey law was further liberalized in 1899, so that "the conduct and condition of [a corporation's] . . . business are treated as private and not public affairs." The 1903 Massachusetts legislature, under the charge to "consider and determine whether the corporation laws of other states or countries are not more favorable than those of this Commonwealth," passed a revised corporation act based on the "modern . . . theory . . . that an ordinary business corporation should be allowed to do anything that an individual may do."[33]

The impact of corporations on the society at large was another

32. James W. Hurst, *The Legitimacy of the Business Corporation in the Law of the United States 1780–1970* (Charlottesville, 1970); Donald Dewey, *Monopoly in Economics and Law* (Chicago, 1959); on corporate stocks, Hurst, *Legitimacy,* 86, Dewey, *Monopoly,* 55; M. Dwight Collier, "Stock Dividends and their Restraint," *ABA Reports,* 7 (1884), 257–274. See also J. L. High, "Of the Jurisdiction of Equity to Enjoin Corporate Elections," *SLR,* ns, 3 (1877), 211–226.

33. "West Virginia Corporations," *ALR,* 27 (1893), 105–109; "The Naturalization of Tramp Corporations," *ALR,* 27 (1893), 252–255; Edward Q. Keasbey, "New Jersey and the Great Corporations," *HLR,* 13 (1899), 210–211; E. Merrick Dodd, "Statutory Developments in Business Corporation Law, 1886–1936," *HLR,* 50 (1936), 33–36.

story. Most courts narrowly interpreted the powers granted by corporate charters and held them subject to modification by state legislatures. Corporations were liable for the nonmalicious acts of their employees—"a rule not of logic but of public safety; that the public know the corporation only through its ministerial agents and servants; that the corporation touches the public only at the hands of these agents and servants." A commentator in 1884 worried over "The Rise and Probable Decline of Corporations in America"; another in 1887 concluded that "the present tendency of legislation is not, to say the least, favorable to corporations." But these fears—to say the least—proved to be unfounded. The utility of the corporate form ensured its continued widespread use, and the increasing power of large, national corporations enabled them to burst the bounds of state regulation.[34]

A revealing example was the fate of the *ultra vires* rule that a corporation could not go beyond the powers specifically delegated to it by its charter. Through the early and mid-nineteenth century the rule was rigorously applied by the courts. An 1879 discussion of *ultra vires* concluded: "The revolution is now complete. Instead, as under the common law, of [corporations] being permitted to act as individuals may . . . it is now imperative to refer to their charter . . . to know whether or not a given contract would be lawful." But if this was revolution, counterrevolution soon followed. *Ultra vires* began to succumb to the pressures "imposed by the necessity for untrammeled development of our vast industrial activities." It was argued that general incorporation acts contained "no implied prohibition of, nor is public policy violated by, corporate acts simply *ultra vires*." The courts were increasingly liberal in their reading of the powers that resided in corporate charters: "The field of corporate action in respect to the exercise of incidental powers is an expanding one. As industrial conditions change, business methods must change with them, and acts become permissible which at an earlier period would not have been considered to be

34. Seymour D. Thompson, "Liability of Corporations for Exemplary Damages," *CLJ*, 41 (1895), 312; Andrew Allison, "The Rise and Probable Decline of Private Corporations in America," *ABA Reports*, 7 (1884), 241–256; William D. Wells, "The Dartmouth College Case and Private Corporations," *ALRec*, 15 (1887), 590. See also "Changes in Corporation Law in Various States," *NJLJ*, 17 (1894), 69–77, 102–106; Edward C. Moore, Jr., "Corporate Taxation," *ALR*, 18 (1884), 749–777.

within corporate power." At the same time, the courts continued to frown on corporations pleading *ultra vires* to escape their contractual obligations: "the defense of *ultra vires* is very generally regarded by the courts as an ungracious and odious one." By the end of the century the doctrine appeared to be "in a state of hopeless and inextricable confusion."[35]

The legal status of foreign (out-of-state) corporations also changed. The Supreme Court's Paul v. Virginia decision of 1869 appeared to give the states the power to tax or even to exclude foreign corporations. National citizenship, it seemed to one commentator, "does not, in any manner, apply to corporations; partly, because they can have no *personal rights* anywhere, but only *property rights*; and partly, because they exist only in the jurisdiction which gave them their charters."

But this view rapidly faded. The Ohio Supreme Court took the lead in developing the doctrine that in the absence of prohibitory legislation its corporations had an implicit right to do business anywhere they chose. Pennsylvania chartered a corporation—the New York and California Vineyard Company—that was authorized *only* to operate in other states. In Barron v. Burnside (1887) the Supreme Court for the first time decided that state regulation of foreign corporations could be of doubtful constitutionality. Thereafter the courts rapidly strengthened the legal status of corporations outside of their chartering states. By the early twentieth century the "liberal theory" of foreign corporations was the prevailing one. A milestone in that development was Allgeyer v. Louisiana (1896), which voided a Louisiana attempt to keep its citizens from doing business with a New York life insurance company.[36]

35. Frederick L. Cline, "The Doctrine of Ultra Vires in the Law of Corporations," *SLR*, ns, 5 (1879), 402; Frederick H. Cooke, "Should the *Ultra Vires* Doctrine be Applied to Business Corporations?" *ALR*, 28 (1894), 227; J. C. Harper, "The Doctrine of Ultra Vires: Under What Circumstances and in Whose Favor It Is Applicable," *CLJ*, 12 (1881), 386–390; "Ultra Vires," *AEEL*, XXIX, 47, 45; Seymour D. Thompson, "The Doctrine of Ultra Vires in Relation to Private Corporations," *ALR*, 28 (1894), 376. See also "The Plea of Ultra Vires," *ALR*, 24 (1890), 508–509; Miller in Salt Lake City v. Hollister, 118 U.S. 256, 260 (1892); Howard A. Street, *A Treatise on the Doctrine of Ultra Vires* (London, 1930), 1.

36. "Inter-State Citizenship," *ILM*, 1 (1883), 336, 337, 340; Barron v. Burnside, 121 U.S. 186 (1887); Allgeyer v. Louisiana, 165 U.S. 578 (1896); Gerard C. Henderson, *The Position of Foreign Corporations in American Constitutional Law* (Cambridge, 1918), ch. 8.

Until the early 1880s "the rule that corporations were *not* to be regarded as constitutional 'persons' theoretically was the law of the land." But as early as 1871 a congressional act codifying the procedure for drafting and enacting legislation specified: "the word 'person' may extend and be applied to bodies politic and corporate." And the judiciary offered a broad array of constitutional protections to corporations, most notably the due process, privileges and immunities, and equal protection clauses of the Fourteenth Amendment. By the turn of the century corporations had much of the legal standing that attached to national citizenship.[37]

While the polity thus accommodated itself to the rise of corporations doing an interstate business, it responded in a far more critical way to the fact that large corporations had the power to crush competition, fix prices, and control the marketing of their goods. Monopolies and combinations in restraint of trade long had been objects of judicial and legislative disapprobation. Big business gave a frightening new meaning to these old threats to a free market economy.

The first danger signal was the appearance of railroad trunk line pooling and numerous price and production-fixing agreements in industries such as oil and salt during the 1870s. Pooling, however, had no legal or legislative sanction to give it force, and state courts frequently invalidated attempts to control prices or production. While cartel agreements of this sort were upheld by English courts by the end of the century, American courts and legislatures found them too direct a challenge to old common law *caveats* against conspiracies in restraint of trade.

But the large, consolidated corporations themselves posed more difficult regulatory problems. Railroads took the lead in the process whereby a number of small firms combined into a larger one. Standard Oil pioneered in the industrial sector. At the turn of the century an outburst of consolidation in effect created the modern American corporate structure. Between 1898 and 1902 there were

37. Howard Jay Graham, *Everyman's Constitution* (Madison, 1968), 382; Samuel T. Spear, "The Citizenship of Corporations," *ALJ*, 16 (1877), 344–347; 41st Cong., 3d sess., ch. 71 (Feb. 25, 1871).

2,653 recorded mergers, involving more than $6.3 billion in capitalization.[38]

Corporate consolidation had to override the constraints built into the existing system of state chartering. The trust was the first legal instrument devised to evade these limitations. John D. Rockefeller's attorney Samuel C. T. Dodd created the first corporate trust agreement between 1879 and 1882. The stock of Standard Oil and a number of other oil companies was turned over to a Rockefeller-dominated board of trustees, who issued trust certificates in return. The arrangement allowed Standard Oil to circumvent its Ohio charter, which forbade it from holding the stock of other companies or owning property outside the state.

The venerable instrument of the trust had been turned into "a perfectly new device in the law." Its precise legal standing was unclear: "The Standard Oil has grown to be a more powerful— corporation, shall we call it? or what? for this is one of our questions—than any other below the national government itself." But there was no doubt as to the usefulness of this ambiguity: "The only effect of such a consolidation [of corporations from different states] is the creation of a community of interest. Their powers, rights and duties remain distinct as before. There is a union of interest and property, but not of personal or legal identity."[39]

It could be argued that trusts led to economies of scale and consequent price reductions. They were defended too on the ground that they were a natural result of competition: "The right of association is the child of freedom of trade. It is too late to banish it." In any event, the actual number of trusts created during the 1880s was small: about ten in all. The value of the trust was further diminished by the fact that West Virginia, Delaware, and New Jersey amended their corporation laws to allow one company to hold the stock of another. And after 1890 another device, the holding company (a corporation, not a trust, created for the specific

38. Dewey, *Monopoly*, chs. 9–10; Frank J. Goodnow, "Trade Combinations at Common Law," *PSQ*, 12 (1897), 212–245; on consolidation, Dewey, *Monopoly*, 55, Hurst, *Legitimacy*, 84.

39. On Dodd, Daniel J. Boorstin, *The Americans: The Democratic Experience* (New York, 1973), 416–419; Charles B. Elliott, "The Consolidation of Corporations Existing under the Laws of Different States," *CLJ*, 17 (1883), 383; F. J. Stimson, "Trusts," *HLR*, 1 (1887), 133–134.

purpose of holding the stock and thus controlling the management of other companies), served as the major legal instrument of corporate consolidation.[40]

Nevertheless, the trust in the generic sense of a "huge, irrepressible, indeterminate" corporation became an object of growing public concern. By 1890 about ten states had passed antitrust laws, and six state supreme courts had found trust agreements illegal as monopolies, conspiracies in restraint of trade, or against public policy. An influential antitrust coalition, including the traditional antimonopoly sentiment in American public opinion, smaller competitors smarting from corporate consolidation, and economists and lawyers with a belief in government regulation, called for a federal antitrust statute.[41]

The Sherman Act of 1890, passed by bipartisan coalitions in both Houses of Congress (the Senate vote was 52 to 1), relied on the commerce power to outlaw "every contract, combination in the form of trust or otherwise, or conspiracy, in restraint of trade or commerce." In the vagueness of its formulation, and its dependence on the courts rather than an administrative agency to define and enforce its provisions, the Sherman Act reflected the still-undeveloped state of federal regulation. But in other ways it was a sophisticated statute. By stressing the old common law concept of conspiracy in restraint of trade, its framers avoided the risk of having the law declared unconstitutional, and made it clear that the purpose of the act was to check manifestly illegal combinations, not to fix an unrealistic standard of small-unit competition on the economy.[42]

40. Theodore W. Dwight, "The Legality of Trusts," PSQ, 3 (1888), 631; Jeremiah W. Jenks, "Capitalistic Monopolies and their Relation to the State," PSQ, 9 (1894), 486–509, "The Michigan Salt Association," PSQ, 3 (1888), 78–98; George Gunton, "The Economic and Social Aspects of Trusts," PSQ, 3 (1888), 385–408; James C. Bonbright and Gardiner C. Means, The Holding Company (New York, 1932), 55–65; Boorstin, Americans, 419.

41. Stimson, "Trusts," 143; Hans B. Thorelli, The Federal Antitrust Policy: Origination of an American Tradition (Baltimore, 1955), chs. 2–3; on state cases, John D. Lewis, ed., American Railroad and Corporation Reports (Chicago, 1895), I, 620–639; Sanford D. Gordon, "Attitudes towards Trusts Prior to the Sherman Act," SEJ, 30 (1960), 156–167; William Letwin, Law and Economic Policy in America (New York, 1965), ch. 3.

42. Letwin, Law and Economic Policy; Thorelli, Antitrust, ch. 4; Wil-

Even so, enforcement was full of difficulty. The Justice Department of the 1890s lacked the manpower, the financial resources, and the inclination to prosecute vigorously under the Sherman Act. The courts, too, severely limited its utility. They argued that a firm could come to dominate a sector of the economy without doing anything illegal and developed a distinction between reasonable and unreasonable restraint of trade, between legitimate business practices and "illegal commercial piracy."

The Supreme Court dealt a heavy blow to the antitrust law with its decision in U.S. v. E. C. Knight (1895). It held that the Sherman Act did not apply to the American Sugar Refining Company, even though that firm controlled more than 90 percent of the nation's sugar refining capacity. The reason: sugar refining was a manufacturing process and hence did not come under the regulation of interstate commerce that justified the act.

The Knight decision was a suspect and inconclusive attempt to narrow the scope of the Sherman Act. Attorney General Richard Olney—to put it gently—was unforceful in his presentation of the government's case. The *American Law Review* bitterly called the decision "the most deplorable one that has been rendered in favor of incorporated power and greed . . . since the Dartmouth College case." When private parties brought suit against corporate trade and price cartels, the Supreme Court was not reluctant to rely on the Sherman Act in voiding them. Under the reasonableness rule, the judiciary continued to act in effect as a regulatory agency, deciding cases on grounds that were more administrative than constitutional.[43]

By the turn of the century, the problem of corporate regulation was "rapidly assuming phases which seem beyond the scope of

---

liam Letwin, "Congress and the Sherman Antitrust Law: 1887–1890," *UCLR*, 23 (1955), 221–258. See also J. D. Forrest, "Anti-Monopoly Legislation in the United States," *AJS*, 1 (1895–1896), 411–425.

43. Thorelli, *Antitrust*, ch. 7; Letwin, *Law and Economic Policy*, ch. 5; William H. Tuttle, "Legitimate Competition," *CLJ*, 43 (1896), 302–306; U.S. v. E. C. Knight Co., 156 U.S. 1 (1895); Alfred S. Eichner, *The Emergence of Oligopoly: Sugar Refining as a Case Study* (Baltimore, 1969); "Combinations in Restraint of Interstate Commerce," *ALR*, 29 (1895), 306; U.S. v. Trans-Missouri Freight Association, 166 U.S. 290 (1897); U.S. v. Joint-Traffic Association, 171 U.S. 505 (1898); Addystone Pipe and Steel Co. v. U.S., 175 U.S. 211 (1899); Thorelli, *Antitrust*, 477 ff.

courts of justice." The "state of warfare between producers and consumers" required political rather than judicial solutions.[44] But the ongoing conflict between those who spoke for old and new enterprise, for management and labor, for manufacturers and marketers, for particular interests and the larger public good, assured that there would be a continuing ambivalence in the polity's response to corporate capitalism. Perhaps this, as much as particular regulatory tools and concepts, was the major legacy of the late nineteenth century political economy to the century that followed.

44. Lionel Norman, "Legal Restraints on Modern Industrial Combinations and Monopolies in the United States," *ALR*, 33 (1899), 502–503.

CHAPTER 12

The Shock of Social Change: The Definition of Status

LATE NINETEENTH CENTURY American social policy displayed the same ambiguities as did economic policy. Just as the polity sought to subject the new economy to checks and controls, so was it under pressure to regulate numerous areas of social status and behavior: citizenship, race, the family, education, crime, poverty, public mores, private rights. But as economic regulation was hobbled by conflicting purposes (to preserve or restore the past, to adapt to the present) and by the weakness of government, so did American social diversity and the values of liberty and individualism pose obstacles to the imposition of social controls.

Were Americans freer in 1850 than they were in 1900? In some ways, yes; in others, no. Of necessity, the answer must be an uncertain one. That in itself is testimony to the diversity of purposes that shaped late nineteenth century social policymaking.

Nationality

Caspar T. Hopkins's *Manual of American Ideas* provides a revealing measure of the late nineteenth century drift from the post-Civil War ideal of the unity and equality of the American people. When it first appeared in 1873, this civics text assured its readers that "it is not the *pedigree* but the *thoughts* of the man that make him an American." But by 1887 revision was necessary: "in deference to the present uncertainty, the Lecture in former issues of this work on the 'Universal brotherhood of man,' has been omitted from the present edition. For the design of this work limits it to the exposition only of those ideas which are universally accepted."

Such skepticism did not go unchallenged. The belief persisted that the nation's strength lay in its ability to absorb diverse peoples. An 1887 discussion of "The Future America" held that "this formation of a single race of men out of all races, can only be regarded as a colossal scheme of nature to infiltrate new life into humanity, and produce an enduring and higher type of man and language." The economist Richmond Mayo-Smith, who was a staunch critic of the new immigration, nevertheless believed: "it is not in unity of blood, but in unity of institutions and social habits and ideals that we are to seek that which we call humanity." Former President Rutherford B. Hayes interested himself in a variety of reform causes, strong in the faith that differences among people stemmed from individual character, not group characteristics. Andrew Carnegie's *Triumphant Democracy* (1886) regarded the nation's past, present, and future alike with satisfaction. When *Harper's Weekly* editor George W. Curtis asked the book's author: "what had become of the shadows?" Carnegie replied: "Triumphant Democracy was written at high noon, when the blazing sun overhead casts no shadow."[1]

But less complacent views gained currency as the century approached its end. American optimism always coexisted with the anxieties bred by an unsettled society, and these fears took on new and heightened forms in the late nineteenth century. The factory, the city, the immigrant threatened to transform the American scene. "Is our civilization perishable?" a writer asked in 1884. He answered with a litany of dangers that included the aversion of the upper class to marriage; the effects of steam power, the printing

1. Hopkins, *A Manual of American Ideas*, 3d ed. (San Francisco, 1887), 19, 21; William H. Ballou, "The Future America," *NAR*, 145 (1887), 290; Mayo-Smith, "Assimilation of Nationalities in the United States," *PSQ*, 9 (1894), 670; David P. Thelen, "Rutherford B. Hayes and the Reform Tradition in the Gilded Age," *AQ*, 22 (1970), 150–165; Andrew Carnegie, *Triumphant Democracy*, rev. ed. (New York, 1893), v; John E. Higgins, "Andrew Carnegie, Author," *PMHB*, 88 (1964), 445. See also C. W. Eliot, *The Working of the American Democracy* (Cambridge, 1888); J. L. M. Curry, *Causes of the Power and Prosperity of the United States* (Ann Arbor, 1889); George C. Eggleston, "The American Idea," *NPR*, 4 (1887), 317–327.

press, and electricity; the conflict between capital and labor; and even the threat of a catastrophe descending from outer space. A rich literature of social cataclysm, ranging from the popular dystopias of Ignatius Donnelly and Jack London to the cultivated pessimism of Henry and Brooks Adams, appeared in the last years of the century. *Our Country* (1886), the widely read work of the missionary-publicist Josiah Strong, was filled with a sense of dread in the midst of success. Like Carnegie, he celebrated American wealth and power. But he dwelt also on a wide range of social dangers: immigration, Romanism, religion and the public schools, Mormonism, intemperance, socialism, wealth, the city. The very eclecticism of these concerns contributed to their cumulative impact on social policy.[2]

The character of American nationality and citizenship was an obvious focal point for many anxieties. "*Where* is the American people, and who and what are they," asked a South Carolina lawyer in 1890. No longer was there an "American people, pure and simple." The nation now included large numbers of newer European immigrants, blacks, and Orientals, and "we cannot persist in calling all of these Americans."

Belief in a fixed and limited nationality expressed itself in commemorations of the American past. The South avidly went about the business of glorifying its Lost (white) Cause. New England, too, had a special past to preserve. Hundreds of Village Improvement Societies in the 1870s sought to encase the New England town in amber. New Hampshire's governor explained the celebration of his state's Old Home Week in 1900: "the loss and decay in some of the agricultural sections of New Hampshire were brought closely home to me, and ... the idea of Old Home Week occurred to me as a possible help in restoring lost people and conditions." More than a hundred towns joined this effort to recapture the past. On a national scale, hereditary organizations such as the

2. J. A. Jameson, "Is Our Civilization Perishable?" *NAR*, 138 (1884), 205–215; Frederick C. Jaher, *Doubters and Dissenters: Cataclysmic Thought in America, 1885–1918* (Glencoe, Ill., 1964); Josiah Strong, *Our Country*, ed. Jurgen Herbst (1886; Cambridge, 1963); Dorothea R. Muller, "Josiah Strong and American Nationalism: A Re-evaluation," *JAH*, 53 (1966), 487–503. See also "Certain Dangerous Tendencies in American Life," *AM*, 42 (1878), 385–402.

Daughters of the American Revolution gave ancestry-conscious Americans the opportunity to make public display of their special claim to social distinction.[3]

But however satisfying, celebration of the past did not eliminate the need to face the unsettling present. One way to do so was to limit the civic participation—and the civil rights—of various segments of the population.

Women were the largest group to have a special status in American politics, law, and legislation. Legal barriers to female equality continued to diminish during the late nineteenth century, as they had for decades before, but within distinct limits. When state and federal courts held that women could not practice law, legislation usually removed that disability. However, in 1894 the Supreme Court reaffirmed that a state's refusal to allow a female attorney to practice did not violate her constitutional rights.

Women participated more freely in those areas of public life where, it was agreed, they had a special stake. Between 1875 and 1890, seventeen states permitted women to vote in school board elections and three allowed propertied women to vote on tax and bond referenda. But opposition to women's suffrage remained strong. Between 1870 and 1910, suffrage advocates conducted 480 campaigns in thirty-three states to get the issue on the ballot, and seventeen state referenda (all but three west of the Mississippi) were held. Only two were successful: Colorado in 1893, Idaho in 1896. More typical were the 1884 defeats in Nebraska and Oregon by margins of two or three to one. Even though a Massachusetts suffrage referendum in 1895 allowed the participation of women eligible to vote in school board elections, the turnout was small

3. A. M. Lee, "Popular Government, and Constitutional Limitation to Suffrage," SCBA Transactions, 6th (1890), 95–96; on Village Improvement Societies, John B. Jackson, American Space: The Centennial Years 1865–1876 (New York, 1972), 37, 102–103; "New Hampshire," AC (1900); Wallace E. Davies, Patriotism on Parade (Cambridge, 1955). See also Arthur M. Schlesinger, The Rise of the City 1878–1898 (New York, 1933), 410–411; Paul C. Nagel, This Sacred Trust: American Nationality 1798–1898 (New York, 1971), ch. 5; Putnam P. Bishop, American Patriotism (New York, 1887); Albion W. Tourgée, "The Renaissance of Nationalism," NAR, 144 (1887), 1–11.

and the proposal was overwhelmingly defeated. Not until after the First World War did the national women's suffrage movement succeed, and then only when many were convinced that it would enhance social stability by increasing the relative voting strength of native white Protestants.[4]

Immigrants also faced growing constraints. The Chinese, the most exotic newcomers to nineteenth century America, were the objects of a variety of social and economic fears. They were charged with having a special affinity for drugs, dirt, and prostitution; with offering low-paid competition to other American labor; with threatening to divide American society "into an opulent class on the one hand, and, upon the other hand, a class of propertyless laborers."

The consequence of these concerns was persistent pressure for an end to further Chinese immigration and restrictions on those already in the United States. Organized labor agitated for Chinese exclusion, and anti-Chinese riots in the West testified to the intensity of popular feeling. A California referendum of the 1870s by a vote of 150,000 to 900 endorsed the total exclusion of the Chinese. That state's 1879 constitution excluded all resident Chinese from the suffrage and forbade their employment on public works. Ensuing laws penalized corporations who hired Chinese labor, empowered municipalities to remove them from city limits, and prohibited "aliens incapable of becoming electors" from obtaining occupational or even fishing licenses. The Ninth Circuit Court of Appeals, headed by Supreme Court Justice Stephen Field, struck down most of this legislation. It too blatantly violated the Fourteenth Amendment. But Field himself had no special concern for Chinese civil equality: "Our institutions," he said, "have made no impression on them during the more than thirty years they have

4. *In re* Lockwood, 154 U.S. 116 (1894); D. H. Pingrey, "Right of Women to Vote for School Officers," *CLJ*, 36 (1893), 155–156; James A. Webb, "A Legal View of Women's Suffrage in America," *ALR*, 31 (1897), 404–409; Francis Minor, "Women's Political Status," *Forum*, 9 (1890), 150–158; Eleanor Flexner, *A Century of Struggle* (Cambridge, 1959), 174–176; James J. Kenneally, "Woman Suffrage and the Massachusetts 'Referendum' of 1895," *Hist*, 30 (1968), 617–633; Alan P. Grimes, *The Puritan Ethic and Woman Suffrage* (New York, 1967), ch. 6. On the more restricted political status of British women see "The Legal Disqualification of Women from Election to School Boards," *LMR*, 4th ser., 23 (1897–1898), 99–106.

been in the country . . . They do not and will not assimilate with our people."[5]

While President Chester Arthur vetoed the first version of the Chinese Exclusion Act of 1882, he welcomed a renewed effort to meet "the expectations of the people." When Congress reduced the exclusion period from twenty to ten years, he signed the revised bill. Lax enforcement and the continuing demand for cheap Chinese labor undercut the 1882 act. But supplementary laws in 1884 and 1888 tightened controls on immigration and on those Chinese already in the country. The Supreme Court in 1887 refused to accord resident Chinese the protection of the Civil Rights and Enforcement Acts. In 1889 the Court upheld Chinese immigration restriction. Field confessed to "a well-founded apprehension—from the experience of years—that a limitation to the immigration of certain classes from China was essential to the peace of the community on the Pacific Coast, and possibly to the preservation of our civilization there."[6]

In 1892 Congress overwhelmingly agreed to renew Chinese exclusion for another decade. The bill required the registration of resident Chinese laborers, with an affidavit by one or more white witnesses that the registrant had entered the country legally. No bail was permitted during expulsion proceedings. There were a few dissents: "Let us treat Chinese as we would English; and, above all, let us respect the rights of men." But California Congressman John W. Geary, who sponsored the extension, voiced the prevailing attitude: "There is not room in this country for the establishment of . . . races that are not willing to submit to the authority of our American laws."[7]

The Supreme Court in 1893 found the 1892 act constitutional

5. John H. Durst, "The Exclusion of the Chinese," NAR, 139 (1884), 270; Alexander Saxton, The Indispensable Enemy: Labor and the Anti-Chinese Movement in California (Berkeley and Los Angeles, 1970); "California," AC (1879, 1880); on Ninth Circuit, Howard J. Graham, Everyman's Constitution (Madison, 1968), 144–150; Field in Chen Heong v. U.S., 112 U.S. 536, 567 (1884). See also D. H. Pingrey, "A Legal View of Racial Discrimination," ALReg, ns, 30 (1891), 98–104; Elmer C. Sandmyer, The Anti-Chinese Movement in California (Urbana, 1939).

6. MP, X, 4699; J. Thomas Scharf, "The Farce of the Chinese Exclusion Laws," NAR, 166 (1898), 85–97; Baldwin v. Franks, 120 U.S. 678 (1887); Chae Chan Ping v. U.S. (Chinese Exclusion Case), 130 U.S. 581, 594 (1889).

7. M. J. Farrelly, "The United States Chinese Exclusion Act," ALR, 28 (1894), 734–753; John R. Young, "The Chinese Question Again," NAR,

on the grounds that a sovereign nation had the power to exclude or expel foreigners and that since an expulsion proceeding was not a criminal trial it did not require the niceties of due process. Justice David Brewer, one of the dissenters, did not think that the government had the power "of determining whether whole classes in our midst shall, for no crime but that of their race and birthplace, be driven from our territory." Field, too, could accept exclusion but not deportation. He warned that naturalized citizens might be the next victims. An American Bar Association commission criticized "the very extreme doctrine of the court," and in 1898 the tribunal conceded that a child born of Chinese parents within the United States automatically became an American citizen—although its parents were denied that status. These policies had visible consequences. There were about 101,000 Chinese in the United States in 1880; 104,000 in 1890; about 85,000 in 1900. And in 1902 Chinese immigration was suspended indefinitely.[8]

Japanese immigration, which increased sharply around the turn of the century, also felt the force of restrictionist sentiment. Legal scholar John H. Wigmore tried to distinguish between the two groups: "it appears that, in the scientific use of language and in the light of modern anthropology, the term 'white' may properly be applied to the ethnical composition of the Japanese race." But a Massachusetts federal district court held that the Japanese like the Chinese were not eligible to become citizens on the ground that the naturalization laws limted citizenship to white and African immigrants. The Gentleman's Agreement of 1907–1908, coming in the wake of West coast riots and agitation similar to those directed against the Chinese several decades before, severely limited the entry of unskilled Japanese laborers.[9]

The massive late nineteenth century immigration from southern and eastern Europe evoked responses that differed more in degree than in kind from the sentiment against Orientals. A growing body

154 (1892), 596–602; quotes from "Should the Chinese be Excluded?" NAR, 157 (1893), 58, 67.

8. Brewer and Field in Fong Yue Ting v. U.S., 149 U.S. 698, 737–738, 754–761 (1893); "The American Bar Association and the Chinese Exclusion Case," ALR, 28 (1894), 289–293; U.S. v. Wong Kim Ark, 169 U.S. 649 (1898); HS, 9.

9. John H. Wigmore, "American Naturalization and the Japanese," ALR, 28 (1894), 827; In re Saito, 62 Fed. 126 (C.C.D. Mass. 1894).

of literature discussed the harmful impact of the new immigration on the "social environment." Henry Cabot Lodge linked southern lynching and uncontrolled immigration as symptoms of a general national malaise, and glumly listed the unpalatable results of free access to the United States: the Irish labor terrorist Molly Maguires of the 1870s, the German anarchists of the Haymarket affair, the Italian Mafia of the 1890s. Economist Francis A. Walker, who had welcomed the rapid growth of the American population after the Civil War, now feared that American wages and living standards lured the mudsills of other countries, and called for a means test as a requirement for entry into the United States. An 1892 discussion of "The Immigration Problem in America" by Britain's *Westminster Review* concluded: "The era of the encouragement of immigration has passed, and . . . the time for repression is at hand."[10]

Supervision of the immigrant flow, once casual and localized, now moved into the hands of the federal government. In 1882 the secretary of the treasury was given authority over state immigration agencies; in 1891 Congress ended state regulation and created a federal superintendent of immigration. The pressure of organized labor combined with the more general fear of undesirable immigration to produce laws excluding convicts and paupers in 1882 and contract labor in 1885.

Few objected to supervision by the national government, or to the exclusion of manifestly undesirable categories of immigrants. But a general exclusionist policy (the Chinese aside) was another matter. The traditional policy of the open gate and the continuing need for labor were powerful props to free immigration. In 1897 Congress enacted a literacy test requirement for newcomers—a restrictionist device that appealed to those who equated illiteracy with a lower class threat to American society. Grover Cleveland successfully vetoed the bill, arguing that it was safer to admit 100,000 unlettered but hardworking immigrants than one revolutionary: "Violence and disorder do not migrate with illiterate laborers. They are rather the victims of the educated agitator."

10. Henry C. Lodge, "Lynch Law and Unrestricted Immigration," *NAR*, 152 (1891), 602–612; Francis A. Walker, "Immigration," *YR*, 1 (1892–1893), 125–145; "The Immigration Problem in America," *WR*, 138 (1892), 70.

Nevertheless, the future course of immigration policy was clear. Scientific and popular racism, the belief that immigration was a prime cause of social ills, labor's fear of job competition: all were well-established themes in American public discourse by the turn of the century. William E. Chandler, chairman of the Senate Committee on Immigration, called for the temporary suspension of all immigration in 1893, until new laws excluding "degraded immigrants" from southern and eastern Europe were devised. This, he said, was a step essential to protect domestic labor and maintain "a high order of American civilization." Continued mass immigration in the early twentieth century and the xenophobic backwash of the First World War finally led in the 1920s to restriction based on national origin quotas that favored old north European over new southern and eastern European immigrant sources.[11]

Even by 1900, American naturalization laws had become stricter than those of most other countries. State and federal statutes limited the employment of aliens on public works projects and restricted or prohibited alien land ownership. The denaturalization of foreign-born citizens, in the past a rare occurrence, became more common in the 1890s. And with the acquisition of Puerto Rico and the Philippines in 1900, a whole new category of quasi-citizenship was added to American law. The political and other citizenship rights of residents in the new territories were limited on the ground that they were an "abnormally incorporated people." Supreme Court Justice John Harlan argued (as he had for blacks, Indians, and the Chinese) that the full rights of American citizenship should be granted. But his was a lone and unheeded voice.[12]

11. John Higham, *Strangers in the Land* (New Brunswick, 1955), 35–130; *MP*, XIII, 6191; William E. Chandler, "Shall Immigration be Suspended?" *NAR*, 156 (1893), 8. See also Henry C. Hansbrough, "Why Immigration Should Not be Suspended," *NAR*, 156 (1893), 220–227; John P. Altgeld, "The Immigrant's Answer," *Forum*, 8 (1890), 684–696.

12. George Lawyer, "Aliens and Citizenship," *CLJ*, 40 (1895), 106–110; John P. Roche, "Pre-Statutory Denaturalization," *CLQ*, 35 (1949), 133 ff; H. Sidney Everett, "Immigration and Naturalization," *AM*, 75 (1895), 345–353; DeLima v. Bidwell (Insular Cases), 182 U.S. 1 (1901); Don v. U.S., 195 U.S. 138 (1904); Dudley O. McGooney, "American Citizenship," *ColLR*, 11 (1911), 342. See also Prentiss Webster, "Citizenship by Naturalization in the United States," *ALR*, 24 (1890), 616–628; Frederick Van Dyne, *Citizenship of the United States* (Rochester, 1904).

Race

Nowhere did the constriction of the rights of American citizenship go further, or have more baleful consequences, than with the status of Negroes. Old assumptions of black racial inferiority were reinforced now by scientific racism and the anxieties that stemmed from rapid social change. The British observer James Bryce saw three major related American social problems in 1891: labor unrest, immigration, and race relations. A Negrophobic tract related its special bias to broader national developments: "Some of the wisest men of our country are persuaded that our free institutions are in great peril from sundry causes, and they are sounding notes of alarm." Editors such as E. L. Godkin of the *Nation*, George W. Curtis of *Harper's Weekly*, and Henry Bowen of the *Independent* moved from antislavery in the 1860s to a racism in the 1880s that was part of their more general distaste for the course and character of American life. Richard P. Hallowell, one of the few oldtime abolitionists whose faith in racial equality did not falter, cuttingly observed in 1890 that the genteel reformer, with his "learned disquisitions upon ethnology, which . . . invariably brings him to the conclusion that it is both wise and legitimate for the strong to oppose the weak," constituted "perhaps the most dangerous political class in our community."[13]

But just as immigration restriction was not easily translated into public policy, so too did legal discrimination based upon race encounter obstacles. The post-Civil War commitment to equal national citizenship continued to have a place in the rhetoric (and occasionally the votes) of Republican politicians. After the Supreme Court all but invalidated the 1875 Civil Rights Act in 1883, a number of northern states passed civil rights laws which in theory guaranteed equal access to public establishments. Several

13. James Bryce, "Thoughts on the Negro Problem," *NAR*, 153 (1891), 641–660; H. S. Fulkerson, *The Negro: As He Was; As He Is; As He Will Be* (Vicksburg, Miss., 1887), 3; Richard P. Hallowell, *The Southern Question: Past and Present* (Boston, 1890), 25–26. See also George M. Frederickson, *The Black Image in the White Mind: The Debate on Afro-American Character and Destiny, 1817–1914* (New York, 1917), chs. 7–8; James M. McPherson, "The Antislavery Legacy: From Reconstruction to the NAACP," in Barton J. Bernstein, ed., *Towards a New Past: Dissenting Essays in American History* (New York, 1969), 126–157.

states forbade racial discrimination in life and industrial insurance policies.

Late nineteenth century northern courts generally upheld state laws forbidding discrimination in theaters, restaurants, barber shops, and skating rinks. (The degree to which those laws were enforced is another matter.) Occasionally a judge rested his decision on broader principles than the state's police power: "Both justice and the public interest concur in a policy which shall elevate [Negroes] . . . as individuals and relieve them from oppression or degrading discrimination, and . . . give them a fair chance in the struggle of life, weighted, as they are at best, with so many disadvantages"; "[discrimination] is not the true theory of either the Divine or human law to be put in practice in a republican form of government."[14]

The strongest defense of racial equality came from blacks themselves. Frederick Douglass was the most eloquent and insightful Negro spokesman of the 1880s. His "Address to the People of the United States," delivered to the 1883 Louisville Convention of Colored Men, eloquently condemned the discrimination and poverty that kept blacks from enjoying the fruit of their legal freedom. Similar gatherings through the 1880s reiterated these themes, often with force and passion, but to little effect. In *The Nation's Problem* (1889) Douglass acutely observed that the situation of American blacks was the worst since the time of slavery and would further decay. He warned against black nationalism as a response: "a nation within a union is an anomaly." But by the turn of the century conditions were such that Booker T. Washington's defensive separatism had become the predominant black strategy. A Negro intellectual speculated on what the shift revealed about the changing character of late nineteenth century American life:

> Douglass [who died in 1895] lived in the day of moral giants; Washington in the era of merchant princes. The contemporaries of Douglass emphasized the rights of man; those of

14. Valeria W. Weaver, "The Failure of Civil Rights 1875–1883 and Its Repercussions," *JNH*, 54 (1969), 368–382; Leslie H. Fishel, Jr., "The Genesis of the First Wisconsin Civil Rights Act," *WMH*, 49 (1966), 324–333; Andrews, J., in People v. King, 110 N.Y. 418, 426 (1888); Morse, J., in Ferguson v. Gies, 82 Mich. 358, 367 (1890). See also Gilbert T. Stephenson, *Race Distinctions in American Law* (New York, 1910), 120 ff.

Washington his productive capacity. The age of Douglass acknowledged the sanction of the Golden Rule; that of Washington worships the Rule of Gold. The equality of men was constantly dinned into Douglass' ears; Washington hears nothing but the inferiority of the Negro and the dominance of the Saxon. Douglass could hardly receive a hearing today; Washington would have been hooted off the stage a generation ago.[15]

A final line of defense lay in the fact that many conservative southern whites agreed that blacks had legitimate (if limited) political rights. Bishop Atticus G. Haygood, the president of Emory College, predicted in 1881 that the Negro "will never be re-enslaved; he will never be disfranchised." David M. Key, a Confederate general who served as Rutherford B. Hayes's postmaster general, reviewed the "civil and political status of the Negro" in 1885. While endorsing segregation and white superiority, he believed that "the right of the colored man to vote and have his vote counted rests upon the same fundamental doctrine as the jury right." But these were thin reeds on which to rest the hope of improving the status of blacks. By the turn of the century majority white opinion, the social views of intellectuals, publicists, and other influentials, and public policy had created an imposing structure of segregation and discrimination in American life.[16]

A 1910 survey of race distinctions in American law observed that "law is crystallized custom. Race distinctions now recognized by law were habitually practiced long before they crystallized into custom." But it can be argued that there were real alternatives to the rise of legalized Jim Crow in the Reconstruction period, and that the situation of blacks worsened later—especially in the troubled 1890s. Beyond the special history of Negro-white relations, what happened to the legal and political status of blacks in

15. Philip S. Foner, *The Life and Writings of Frederick Douglass* (New York, 1955), IV, 373–392; Frederick Douglass, *The Nation's Problem* (Washington, 1889), 14; anonymous statement in *Boston Transcript*, Sept. 18, 1903. See also August Meier, *Negro Thought in America 1880–1915* (Ann Arbor, 1963).

16. Atticus G. Haygood, *Our Brother in Black: His Freedom and His Future* (New York, 1881), 81; David M. Key "Civil and Political Status of the Negro," *BAT* Proceedings, 4th (1885), 141. See also C. Vann Woodward, *Origins of the New South 1877–1913* (Baton Rouge, 1957), 103–105, and Paul Gaston, *The New South Creed* (New York, 1970), ch. 4.

the late nineteenth century was part of a more general constriction of American nationality and citizenship.[17]

Separation was the chief goal of late nineteenth century race policy. Between 1881 and 1907, every southern state but Missouri segregated its railroads and streetcars. Blacks vigorously opposed such laws as the Arkansas Separate Coach Act of 1891 and a Kentucky bill in 1892, but to no avail. Segregated transportation facilities were unequal in purpose as well as practice. The president of the Texas Bar Association frankly urged that the state's separate car law allow whites to use a "colored car" when it suited their convenience: "If this cannot be legally done as the law is now written, it should be speedily amended so that it can be executed in harmony with its obvious purpose and intent."[18]

Judges usually raised no objections to this legislation, though at times the federal courts found for black plaintiffs when conditions were grossly unequal. A 1906 treatise concluded that while the exclusion of blacks from public accommodations on overt racial grounds was "too broadly stated as a common-law proposition," objectionable persons might be excluded under the state police power. Even without statutory authority, courts upheld separate accommodations in public transportation, hotels and restaurants, and theaters unless a state civil rights act specifically forbade segregation.

The courts were more than ready to sustain laws forbidding racial intermarriage. A Georgia federal circuit court judge summed up the prevailing view in 1890: "In this country, the home life of the people, their decency and their morality, are the bases of that vast social structure of liberty, and obedience to law, which excites the patriotic pride of our countrymen and the admiration of the world." Laws forbidding racial intermarriage preserved that structure, and "the creatures who defy them should be condemned by

17. Stephenson, *Race Distinctions*, 5; C. Vann Woodward, *The Strange Career of Jim Crow* (New York, 1955); Charles E. Wynes, *Race Relations in Virginia 1870–1902* (Charlottesville, 1961); Germaine A. Reed, "Race Legislation in Louisiana, 1864–1920," *LaH*, 6 (1965), 379–392.

18. Sarah M. Lemmon, "Transportation Segregation in the Federal Courts Since 1865," *JNH*, 38 (1953), 174–195; John W. Graves, "The Arkansas Separate Coach Law of 1891," *JW*, 7 (1968), 531–541; "Kentucky," *AC* (1892); "The Texas Bar Association," *ALR*, 26 (1892), 268–269.

all." By the early twentieth century, twenty-six states—including the nonsouthern commonwealths of Indiana, Nebraska, Oregon and California—forbade such unions.[19]

Schooling was hardly less sensitive an issue, and here too the polity lent its support to segregation. Despite scattered attempts at integrated education during Reconstruction, there never was a serious alternative to separate schools in the postslavery South. By the end of the century this was true of most border and many northern states as well. Kentucky in 1884 forbade blacks from voting for the trustees of white schools and required separate attendance, a separate institute for black teachers, and separate teachers' associations. But there were limits: the courts struck down Kentucky and North Carolina attempts to create distinct taxes and school funds for the two races.

As long as state law did not explicitly forbid segregated schools, northern courts allowed them. In the phrase of the time, equality of rights did not necessarily require identity of rights. New York's Court of Appeals observed that there was a natural distinction between the races; that legislation could not enforce racial amity; and that laws reflecting these differences were not discriminatory. A treatise summed up the legal status of segregated schools at the turn of the century: "Separate education may be justified like the prohibition of intermarriage, by the specific bearing of race upon the subject: there is sufficient ground for maintaining that in view of the different mental characteristics of the two races separate schools can produce better results, or that separation is desirable in the interest of discipline. The distinction of race in this matter is analogous to the distinction of sex."[20]

This is not to say that segregation was everywhere the rule by

19. See, e.g., Gray v. Cincinnati Southern, 11 Fed. 683 (C.C.S.D. Ohio 1882) and The Sue, 22 Fed. 843 (D.C.D. Md. 1885); Joseph H. Beale, Jr., *The Law of Innkeepers and Hotels Including other Public Houses, Theaters, Sleeping Cars* (Boston, 1906), 64; State v. Tutty, 41 Fed. 753, 762 (C.C.S.D. Ga. 1890); Stephenson, *Race Distinctions*, 80, 89–90; Pingrey, *Legal View*, 95–98. For a rare contemporary criticism of intermarriage laws see Christopher G. Tiedeman, *A Treatise on the Limitations of Police Power in the United States* (St. Louis, 1886), 536–537.

20. "Kentucky," AC (1884); Dawson v. Lee, 83 Kent. 49 (1884); Puitt v. Commissioners, 94 N.C. 709 (1884); King v. Gallagher, 93 N.Y. 438, 450 (1883); Ernst Freund, *The Police Power: Public Policy and Constitutional Rights* (Chicago, 1904), 718. See also Stephenson, *Race Distinctions*, 154 ff.

1900. New Jersey, California, and Illinois laws specifically forbade segregated schools, or took the power to create them from local boards. And in these states the courts struck down segregation attempts. Black parents in northern cities struggled with some success to improve their children's educational opportunities. They took the lead in a movement to end segregated schools in New York, and (with Governor Theodore Roosevelt's help) in 1900 an equal access law was passed. But this was a policy at odds with the prevailing conventional wisdom. The Illinois Supreme Court, upholding a state antisegregation law in 1899, felt compelled to add: "It may be that the wisest of both races believe that the best interests of each would be promoted by voluntary segregation in the public schools."[21]

The racial segregation of American institutions peaked in the early twentieth century. But its legislative and legal underpinnings were fully developed by 1900. At the end of the century it was possible to see the evolution of the law of race relations as a

> progress *from* an inhuman and unenlightened attitude *through* an oversentimental attempt to correct this (1867–1870), ... *to* a poised and temperate level of common-sense, in which the courts most usually declare that in any community where the relations between the races are of such a character that a compulsory herding of them together is likely to result in breaches of the peace or discomfort, in such circumstances it is wise and proper that they should have equally good but separate accommodations.

Of course, what went unsaid was that separate almost never meant equal; that behind the facade of sensible accommodation ("there is no discrimination as long as there is equality of opportunity, and this equality may often be attained only by a difference of methods ") was a grim reality of discrimination and repression.[22]

The climactic Supreme Court pronouncement on segregated in-

21. Pierce v. Trustees, 46 N.J.L. 76 (1884); Wysinger v. Crookshank, 82 Cal. 588 (1890); People v. Board, 101 Ill. 308 (1882); Robert H. Bremner, ed., *Children and Youth in America: A Documentary History* (Cambridge, 1970), II, 1299–1301; Timothy L. Smith, "Native Blacks and Foreign Whites: Varying Responses to Educational Opportunity in America, 1880–1950," *PAH*, 6 (1972), 309–335; People v. Mayor, 179 Ill. 615 (1899).

22. Owen Wister in *ALReg*, ns, 32 (1893), 756; Stephenson, *Race Distinctions*, 3. See also E. Irving Smith, "The Legal Aspect of the Southern Question," *HLR*, 2 (1888–1889), 358–376.

stitutions was Plessy v. Ferguson (1896). By a seven to one margin, the Court upheld an 1890 Louisiana separate accommodation law. The decision stressed the familiar test of the statute's reasonableness under the state police power. But it went on to make a broader social statement, which put the Supreme Court's imprimatur on the decades-long flight from the egalitarianism of the Civil War era: "Legislation is powerless to eradicate racial instincts or to abolish distinctions based upon physical differences, and the attempt to do so can only result in accentuating the difficulties of the present situation . . . If one race be inferior to the other socially, the Constitution of the United States cannot put them on the same plane." What is evident here is not only the Court's acceptance of an overtly racist social policy, but also the desire—visible everywhere in the late nineteenth century American polity—to avoid social conflict and preserve public order.

Justice John Marshall Harlan's Plessy dissent was an eloquent statement of the countertradition of racial equality. He predicted that one day the decision would be judged as "pernicious" as the Dred Scott case, that it would increase rather than alleviate racial tensions, that the Thirteenth and Fourteenth Amendments "removed the race line from our governmental systems" and consequently "the Constitution is color-blind." But even Harlan—the most forceful judicial opponent of legalized segregation—did not seriously question the racial inequality of blacks. He made a clear distinction between legal and social equality. And in 1899 he implicitly sustained the right of the states to segregate schools.[23]

Although voting was more securely protected by law than other black civil rights, it too eroded in the 1880s. One-party Democratic rule came to Virginia in 1883, and blacks were effectively disfranchised for the next decade. In the 1890s, agrarian-populist discontent and the consequent threat of new competition for black votes fed a rising demand for a racially purified ballot (and, it was assumed, greater social stability). The result was a movement to make black disfranchisement both legal and complete. Mississippi

23. Plessy v. Ferguson, 163 U.S. 537, 551–552, 559 (1896); Barton J. Bernstein, "*Plessy v. Ferguson*: Conservative Sociological Jurisprudence," *JNH*, 48 (1963), 196–205; Cumming v. Board, 175 U.S. 528 (1899). See also Richard A. Maidment, "Plessy v. Ferguson Re-examined," *JAS*, 7 (1973), 125–132.

led the way in its 1890 constitutional convention by levying a two-dollar poll tax on voters and restricting voter registration to those who could read and "understand" a prescribed section of the state constitution. Other southern states followed suit. Louisiana's 1898 constitution added another device: the "grandfather clause," which ingeniously limited the ballot to those whose grandfathers could vote in 1867, before the state's blacks were enfranchised. Even more important were numerous statutes regulating voter qualification, registration, and balloting.[24]

There was little attempt to conceal the purpose behind these changes. The governor of South Carolina warned in 1895: "Constitution or no constitution, law or no law, court or no court, the intelligent men of South Carolina intend to govern her." And Alabama's governor proudly proclaimed in 1899: "White supremacy is as complete and all-pervading as it is possible to be. There is not a negro in all the Commonwealth holding an office under the present Constitution, not a justice of the peace, not a Constable nor a single member of the General Assembly."

The 1898 election in North Carolina reveals something of the popular attitudes that undergirded black disfranchisement. A substantial biracial politics existed in that state during the nineties. North Carolina Populists appealed to Negro voters, and about a thousand blacks held state and local offices. White Democrats reacted with passion. A mass meeting in the eastern part of the state declared: "We have contemplated no violence, but we are determined to use all proper means to free ourselves of this negro domination, which is paralyzing our business, and which hangs like a dark cloud over our homes. . . . we affirm that North Carolina shall not be negroized. It is, of all the States of the Union, peculiarly the home of the Anglo-Saxon, and the Anglo-Saxon shall govern it." The Democrats did indeed win in 1898—with the aid of violence and terror. The editor of the *Wilmington Record* and a number of other Negro political leaders were expelled from the state, the con-

24. J. Morgan Kousser, *The Shaping of Southern Politics: Suffrage Restriction and the Establishment of the One-Party South, 1880–1910* (New Haven, 1974); Paul Lewinson, *Race, Class, and Party* (New York, 1932), ch. 5; Woodward, *Origins*, 322–345; Wynes, *Race Relations in Virginia*, 23; William I. Hair, *Bourbonism and Agrarian Protest: Louisiana Politics, 1877–1900* (Baton Rouge, 1969), 114–116. See also Walter C. Hamm, "The Three Phases of Colored Suffrage," *NAR*, 168 (1899), 285–296.

stitution was changed in 1900 so as to disfranchise most black voters, and North Carolina settled down to half a century of racially pure politics.[25]

These developments met with national acquiescence. The last attempt to extend federal protection to southern black voters was the proposed Federal Elections Bill of 1890, quickly labeled the Force Bill by its opponents. This act, which provided for federal election supervision as in Reconstruction days, was an evanescent revival of a political ideology that had long lost what vitality it may once have had. Its leading congressional proponent, Massachusetts Representative Henry Cabot Lodge, already was closely identified with a racist-minded policy of immigration restriction: hardly testimony to his devotion to the old equal rights tradition. James Bryce's view that the election bill was an attempt "to overcome nature by force of law" was widely shared. Terence V. Powderly of the Knights of Labor conceded that blacks were "outrageously deprived of their rights in being driven from the polls by the Democrats." But he opposed the bill because he feared that federal election inspectors would be used as well to oversee—and overawe —immigrants voting in Northern cities. Ultimately, adamant Democratic opposition and Republican defections killed the act. A Democratic Congress in 1894 went further. It repealed all but seven of the forty-nine sections of the 1870–1871 Enforcement Acts, and federal protection of black voting remained a lost cause until the mid-twentieth century.[26]

The judiciary did not impede black disfranchisement. The Supreme Court in 1898 accepted the "understanding" clause of the 1890 Mississippi constitution and its enforcing statutes, arguing that "they do not on their face discriminate between the races," that "it has not been shown that their actual administration was evil, only that evil was possible under them." In 1903 the Court blocked the use of the Fifteenth Amendment to bring suit against Alabama state officers who kept blacks from voting. Oliver Wen-

25. "South Carolina," *AC* (1895); "Alabama," *AC* (1899); "North Carolina," *AC* (1898).

26. Lodge and Powderly in "The Federal Election Bill," *NAR*, 151 (1890), 257–273; Richard E. Welch, Jr., "The Federal Elections Bill of 1890: Postscripts and Prelude," *JAH*, 52 (1965), 511–526; Bryce, "Thoughts on the Negro Problem," 654; on Democratic repeal, Milton R. Konvitz, *A Century of Civil Rights* (New York, 1961), 66.

dell Holmes, speaking for the majority, argued that relief "from a great political wrong" must come from "the legislative and political department of the government of the United States."[27]

While the segregation of blacks was enforced by law as well as custom, a substantial assault was directed at Indian separatism. In 1891, when black disfranchisement was rapidly growing, United States Indian Commissioner Thomas J. Morgan declared: "The end at which we aim is that the American Indians shall become as speedily as possible Indian-Americans; that the savage shall become a citizen." White Mississippians, who sought to isolate blacks from the larger culture, at the same time welcomed the fact that Indians in their state were beginning to assume English surnames.

In great part the call for Indian assimilation stemmed from white economic self-interest. Western farmers, ranchers, and railroad men hungered for reservation lands. It was easy to rationalize that desire, as did the governor of Montana, by arguing that reservation life "necessarily isolates [the Indians] ... from civilizing influences," and to propose that "they should be brought into direct contact with the modes of life of the frontier farmer and stockgrower." Oklahoma Democrats in 1896 wanted Indian reservation land thrown open to white settlers; the state's Republicans wanted individual land sales to Indians first. But the smell of gain hung over both proposals, and their ultimate goal—the end of tribal separatism (and tribal lands)—was the same.[28]

The movement for Indian assimilation had other, less materialistic sources as well. The concentration of Indians on reservations after the Civil War led to abuses—the forced exodus of the Poncas and the Nez Percé in 1878–1879, the suppression of the Ute uprising in 1879—that had a strong impact on public opinion. A Nebraska federal district judge declared that the Poncas had the right to file for a writ of *habeas corpus* to stop their removal: "Indians

27. Williams v. Mississippi, 170 U.S. 213, 225 (1898); Holmes in Giles v. Harris, 189 U.S. 475, 488 (1903). See also James v. Bowman, 190 U.S. 127 (1903); Stephenson, *Race Distinctions*, 294–295.

28. Morgan quoted in Leonard D. White, *The Republican Era: 1869–1901* (New York, 1958), 185; "Mississippi," *AC* (1898); "Oklahoma," *AC* (1894, 1896); "Montana," *AC* (1884). See in general Loring B. Priest, *Uncle Sam's Stepchildren: The Reformation of United States Indian Policy, 1865–1887* (New Brunswick, 1942).

possess the inherent right of expatriation, as well as the more for-
tunate white race." Helen Hunt Jackson's *A Century of Dishonor*
(1881) and *Ramona* (1884), one a factual, the other a fictional rendering of the Indians' plight, fed popular sympathy. With slavery
gone and concern for black civil rights rapidly diminishing, here
was a new, comfortably remote, attractive cause.

The Indian Rights Association, organized in 1882, spoke out
against the government's reservation policy. Reformers called for
individual land ownership and for the integration of Indians into
the larger society: "the crisis will not be past until the law of the
white man is the law of the red man, and the Indian finally takes
his place as a citizen of the United States."[29]

The Indian reform movement had what Louis Hartz has called a
"superbly bourgeois" quality. Social and material improvement—
education, landholding, a nuclear family life—superseded (or gave
a new context to) traditional concern for the moral and religious
state of the Indians. The great legislative achievement of the
reformers was the Dawes Severalty Act of 1887, which enabled individual Indians to obtain homesteads and United States citizenship, and thus take on "the habits of civilized life." Senator Henry
L. Dawes of Massachusetts, who gave his name to the bill, expected it "to fit the Indian for civilization and absorb him into it."
There was much western support, too, for an act which promised
the rapid disintegration of the Indian reservations.

A number of Indian leaders opposed severalty, as did the National Indian Defense Association. Helen Hunt Jackson herself
warned against too speedy a process of assimilation. But even the
defenders of tribal life regarded it as a transitional stage of Indian
development, and Jackson was "largely concerned with questions
of occupancy and contract right" rather than with the preservation
of tribal culture.[30]

Inevitably the issue of Indian assimilation merged into the larger
question of the place of disparate groups in the nation. The ex-

29. Robert W. Mardock, *The Reformers and the American Indian* (Co-
lumbia, Mo., 1971), 197 ff; "Nebraska," *AC* (1879); Henry S. Pancoast,
The Indian before the Law (Philadelphia, 1884), 20.
30. Louis Hartz, *The Founding of New Societies* (New York, 1964), 97;
Henry L. Dawes, "Have We Failed with the Indian?" *AM*, 84 (1899), 281;
Mardock, *Reformers*, 213; Hartz, *Founding*, 97.

pectation that Indians would be absorbed into American society was eroded in the late nineteenth century by racist assumptions and by the reality of deep-seated and persistent cultural differences. One commentator glumly listed the "undesirable classes" pouring into the country—the Irish, Russian Jews, French Communards, German socialists, Russian nihilists—added the "unresolved" problems of the Chinese and the Negroes, and concluded: "it requires great faith in our robust virtues and the saving efficacy of republican institutions to believe that we can with safety absorb the Indians into our population, and make them partners in the political functions of government." While the ultimate solution must be "the destruction of the Indians as tribes, and their absorption into our civilization and citizenship," this was an end, not the means to an end.

Most antiassimilation sentiment rested on a belief in Indian racial and cultural unreadiness. The American Bar Association's Committee on the Legal Status of Indians warned: "It would not, of course, be expedient to naturalize at once all Indians, since that would necessarily involve . . . the right of suffrage, for which most of them are manifestly wholly unprepared and unfitted." Even Dawes warned that his act was being implemented too quickly. Secretary of the Interior Lucius Q. C. Lamar, a Mississippian, opposed assimilation on the basis of his experience with blacks: "The tribal system must be adhered to. It is the normal condition of the existence of this race . . . To take [the Indian] . . . out of it is to change his social conditions, his religious and hereditary impressions, before he is fitted for higher civilization. I am a conservative, and have been made so by a costly experience."[31]

As so frequently was the case in nineteenth century American group relations, the political and legal status of the Indians became a focal point of discussion. Although formal Indian treatymaking ended in 1871, the view persisted that the tribes "constitute alien nations, distinct political communities, with whom the United States negotiate." Congress and the courts "continued to recognize the Indian tribe as a distinct, quasi-sovereign people." It was argued that Indian-white relations should be viewed "in the light of that

31. G. M. Lambertson, "Indian Citizenship," *ALR*, 20 (1886), 189, 193; William B. Hornblower, "The Legal Status of the Indians," *ABA Reports*, 14 (1891), 275; Lamar quoted in Priest, *Uncle Sam's Stepchildren*, 104.

larger reason which constitutes the spirit of the law of nations." The consequence was a shadowy form of tribal nationality, and for individual Indians the status of "domestic subjects": a condition not unlike that of America's overseas subjects after 1900. Tribal Indians did not get general citizenship until 1924.[32]

The Supreme Court of the 1880s narrowly defined nontribal Indian civil rights. As in the case of blacks, the Court affirmed what popular opinion held to be the case. Elk v. Wilkins (1884)—coterminous with the Civil Rights Cases—said that Indians were not citizens within the meaning of the Fourteenth Amendment. An Indian who left his reservation and took up residence in Omaha could not vote, since he had not become a naturalized citizen. But since the reservations were within the territory of the United States, Indians presumably were not subject to naturalization procedures. How, then, could they become citizens? As it turned out, only by congressional acts granting citizenship to specific tribes or individuals. Justice Harlan's dissent in Elk v. Wilkins properly accused his colleagues of holding that "there is still in this country a despised and rejected class of citizens, with no nationality whatever."

Justice Stanley Matthews declared in Ex parte Crow Dog (1883) that the Federal courts had no jurisdiction over an offense committed within the Sioux reservation. Its inhabitants were a people "separated by race, by tradition, by the instincts of a free though savage life, from the authority and power which seeks to impose upon them the restraints of an external and unknown code." The implication that reservations were "distinct political communities, occupying land where our laws have in general no force and our courts no jurisdiction," raised fears of unchecked crime and disorder. Indian police and tribal courts were set up in a number of reservations. But these had uncertain status and were regarded as tools of the Department of the Interior.[33]

32. Pingrey, "Legal View of Racial Discrimination," 104; George F. Canfield, "The Legal Position of the Indian," ALR, 15 (1881), 24; Austin Abbott, "Indians and the Law," HLR, 2 (1888–1889), 167–179; Pancoast, Indian, 8.
33. Elk v. Wilkins, 112 U.S. 94, 122 (1884); Ex parte Crow Dog, 109 U.S. 556, 571 (1883); Canfield, "Legal Position," 23; William T. Hagan, Indian Police and Courts: Experiments in Acculturation and Control (New Haven, 1966), 110–111.

Congress in 1885 extended the jurisdiction of the federal territorial courts to cover crimes committed by reservation Indians, and the Supreme Court sustained the act. Justice Samuel Miller explained that despite the "anomalous" and "complex" relation of the tribes to the government, they *"are* the wards of the Nation . . . The power of the General Government over these remnants of a race once powerful, now weak and diminished in numbers, is necessary to their protection, as well as to the safety of those among whom they dwell."

But in many noncriminal areas of jurisdiction, the reservation Indians remained "a people without law." Their numbers were increasing; their lands were growing in value; they had numerous contacts with an often avaricious and exploitative white society. Important legal spokesmen sought a full-fledged court system for reservation Indians. The Curtis Act of 1898 ended the tribal courts and brought the reservations under the jurisdiction of the federal judicial system.[34]

Segregation and exclusion, it appears, were not the only goals of late nineteenth century American race policy. The primary thrust of Indian law legislation was to reduce separatism, not to strengthen it. Nevertheless, there was an underlying uniformity to the polity's treatment of blacks and Indians. In each case, the assumption of white racial and cultural superiority shaped public policy. Segregation and severalty each in its own way defined the relationship between a superior white society and its weaker, lesser members. Beyond this, policy was shaped by the felt need to shape race relations so that they might assure social peace. Techniques ranged from enforced segregation to enforced assimilation. But the ultimate social purpose was the same.

Parent and Child, Husband and Wife

In the fluid and individualistic society of the nineteenth century United States, family relations normally were viewed as the private concerns of the persons involved. Yet even here the anxieties at-

34. U.S. v. Kagama, 118 U.S. 375, 383–384 (1886); James B. Thayer, "A People without Law," *AM,* 68 (1891), 540–551, 676–687.

tending socioeconomic change left their mark. Courts and legislatures increasingly were called on to define the status of parents
and children, and of husbands and wives, in ways that served the
interests of society at large.

The traditional common law rule was that a parent exercised a
"natural guardianship" over the child—an obligation which
"springs from social law"—and in return was entitled to control
the child's actions and benefit from its service, subject to "the
bounds of reason and humanity." But this was hardly a contractual
relationship. Unless a statute required it, the parent's duty to support the child was only moral. Nor, unless the parent specifically
assumed the responsibility, was he or she liable for torts committed
by the child.

The parent-child relationship rested on a concept of servitude
and dependence, on a fixed status between unequal parties. Blackstone's *Commentaries* did not accord the child standing as a person
in the common law. As late as 1900, the California Supreme Court
held that a father's claim to his child's service was "strictly
a property right, for the loss of which—as in the case of servants
generally—an action could at common law be maintained."
Parents successfully sued for damages on the ground that the
seduction of a minor daughter led to a loss of her service. Indeed,
nineteenth century American judges appear to have been more
generous than their English counterparts in awarding damages to
a parent for the injury or loss of a child.[35]

But during the late nineteenth century, the courts circumscribed
parental authority. It came to be regarded as "a power in trust . . .
The authority to control the child is not the natural right of the
parents; it emanates from the State, and is an exercise of police
power." The Kansas Supreme Court held in 1881 that parental custody was not a property right and could be ended if it hurt the child.
The parent's obligation to support the child was gradually divorced
from the child's obligation of service to the parent. In the leading
case of Porter v. Powell (1890), the Iowa Supreme Court required

35. Charles A. Buchanan, "Parent and Child," *CLJ*, 15 (1882), 23–26;
Fletcher v. Illinois, 52 Ill. 395 (1869); Florence Kelley, "On Some Changes
in the Legal Status of the Child since Blackstone," *IR*, 13 (1882), 83–98; *In
re* Campbell, 130 Cal. 380 (1900). See also "The Value of Children," *CLJ*,
15 (1882), 286–288; James Schouler, *Law of the Domestic Relations* (Boston, 1905), part III.

a parent to pay for his child's medical care, even though the girl was seventeen years old and lived (and worked) away from home: "This obligation to support is not grounded on the duty of the child to serve, but rather upon the inability of the child to care for itself."

By the end of the century, every state held child support to be a moral obligation—and the great majority held it to be a legal duty—that did not depend on the child's service. This was a distinctively American development. In France "the reciprocal relations of parent and child are legally, and in reality, far more intimate than with us." A French father could appeal to the police if his child did not obey him, and a disobedient child could be imprisoned for up to a month if under sixteen, for six months if between sixteen and twenty-one years old.[36]

The status of illegitimate children, minimal under the common law, showed some improvement in the nineteenth century. Legislatures on both sides of the Atlantic modified the common law rule to give mothers as well as fathers custody rights over an illegitimate child. And a number of American statutes accorded such children a restricted capacity to inherit from their father's estate. The Connecticut Supreme Court held in 1875 that an illegitimate child might inherit from collateral as well as lineal relatives: "Do not reason and justice loudly demand that the disability should fall on the erring parent rather than on the innocent child?" But these gains were limited. The social and moral implications of illegitimacy were too unsettling to accord the child full rights.[37]

The status of adoption underwent a similar, though more dramatic, evolution. Massachusetts passed the first general adoption act in 1851. By the end of the 1870s, most states had such laws.

36. Freund, *Police Power*, 248; Tiedeman, *Limitations of Police Power*, 554; Chapsky v. Wood, 26 Kans. 650 (1881); Porter v. Powell, 79 Ia. 151, 158 (1890); Bremner, ed., *Children and Youth*, II, part two; "The Family Relation in France—Parent and Child," *ALJ*, 32 (1885), 244; Edmond Kelly, "The French Law of Marriage," *ALR*, 18 (1884), 933–960. See also *ALReg*, ns, 30 (1891), 20–55; Theodore Zeldin, *France, 1848–1940: Ambition, Love, and Politics* (Oxford, 1973), 361.

37. Ernst Freund, *Illegitimacy Laws of the United States* (Washington, 1919), 9–10, 29; Dickinson's Appeal from Probate, 42 Conn. 491, 508 (1875); Schouler, *Domestic Relations*, 271–276.

The scope and character of adoption varied widely. New York's 1873 law limited the process to minors; but other states at that time required new members of a household to have attained their majority. Statutes differed as to whether a parent could adopt his or her illegitimate child. Vermont, with fine moral nicety and a sharp eye for fraud, forbade the adoption of one's wife or mother.[38]

The pioneering Massachusetts act implied that an adopted child had the same rights of inheritance as a natural child. But this was to give too much standing to what was widely regarded as an artificial family relationship: "The permanent transfer of the natural rights of a parent was against the policy of the common law." New York barred adopted children from inheritance by descent, and the Massachusetts court in 1876 imposed a similar limitation. These restrictions stemmed from the fear that the testamentary purposes of grandparents and the vested property rights of blood relatives might be threatened by adoption.

The scope of adoption was limited, too, by the rise of a scientific hereditarianism that gave blood lines new importance. An 1875 treatise on adoption law observed: "considering ... the growing belief that many traits of mind are hereditary and almost ineradicable, it may be questioned whether the great laxity of the American rule [of adoption] is for the public benefit." The evolution of the law of adoption is a prime example of the tension between the extension of individual rights and the pressure for social order, a tension that was not resolved but, if anything, was heightened by the socioeconomic changes of the late nineteenth century.[39]

Outside of the family setting, too, the state extended its control over the life of the child. The care of homeless and ill-treated children, child labor and compulsory education laws, special judi-

38. "The Law of Adoption," *CLJ*, 3 (1876), 397–398; on New York, Philip J. Joachimsen, "The Statute to Legalize the Adoption of Minor Children," *ALJ*, 8 (1873), 357; on Vermont, William H. Whitmore, *The Law of Adoption in the United States, and Especially in Massachusetts* (Albany, 1876), 75.

39. Quotation from Ferguson v. Jones, 17 Ore. 204, 217 (1888); Sewall v. Roberts, 115 Mass. 262 (1874); Whitmore, *Law of Adoption*, 74. See also Leo A. Huard, "The Law of Adoption: Ancient and Modern," *VLR*, 9 (1956), 743–763; "The Law of Adoption," *ALR*, 9 (1874–1875), 74–84; Simon Obermyer, "The Effect of the Law of Adoption upon Rights of In-

cial procedures for juvenile offenders, concern over delinquents (in the literal sense of those who had failed to meet their social responsibilities): these activities stemmed from an awareness of what industrial society was doing to children and what these children might do to themselves and to society.

Most American states in the nineteenth century adhered to the common law rule that the minimum age of consent to sexual intercourse was ten; Delaware's, incredibly, was seven. From the late 1880s on, the age of consent outside of the South was raised to fourteen or more. The age of consent to marriage (fourteen for males and twelve for females in the common law) also was raised substantially in a number of commonwealths. Protection of the morals of the young took on added importance in an urban-industrial society. Early marriage no longer was as socially desirable or economically necessary as it had been in a sparsely populated, agrarian America.[40]

The New York Society for the Prevention of Cruelty to Children, the first organization of its kind in the world, was established in 1874. The public-spirited lawyer Elbridge Gerry headed the New York SPCC from 1879 to 1901. By the turn of the century about 250 towns and cities had such institutions. Gerry previously was legal adviser to the SPCC's parent organization, the Society for the Prevention of Cruelty to Animals, a line of descent that is eloquent testimony to the sentimentality spurring child reform.

The state took on a larger role in what came to be called "child saving." Child labor, a practice traditionally regarded as beneficial to the child (and in any event a concern of the parent), now began to be seen as a danger to both the child and the larger society—and a matter for the state, not the parent, to decide. By the end of the century, almost thirty states had some form of child labor regulation, which the courts rarely contested. Most of these laws had little effect; the demand for cheap labor and the income needs of working class families were too strong. But more potent statutes

---

heritance," *SLJ*, ns, 1 (1875), 70–85; "Adoption by One Person of the Children of Another," *AStR*, 39 (1894), 210–231; "Children by Adoption," *VaLR*, 1 (1895), 462–463.

40. Pivar, *Purity Crusade*, 104–105, 139–146; "The Shame of America—The Age of Consent Laws in the United States: A Symposium," *Arena*, 11 (1895), 192–215.

such as the Massachusetts labor laws of 1894 and child labor reformer Florence Kelley's Illinois eight-hour law of 1893 were preludes to the widespread movement of the early twentieth century.[41]

Compulsory education and the increasing curricular and disciplinary authority of teachers and school officials further limited a parent's authority over the life of the child. The California Supreme Court in 1900 argued that children had a basic right to education: "Hence it is the clear right and duty of the state . . . to control and limit, and under certain circumstances to terminate, the right of the father." An 1882 Massachusetts statute gave the state Board of Health, Lunacy, and Charity custody over (and the power to institutionalize) a wayward child under fourteen, if the cause of his delinquency was the "neglect, crime, drunkenness or other vice of his parents." An appalled observer of infant mortality rates in New York City called for a state commission "to enter the privacy of every family, to carefully investigate the manner in which the children are provided for, physically, morally and intellectually, and, in every case, where the requirements fall below a prescribed standard, to remove the children and place them under the control of the State."[42]

These policies did not develop unopposed. The Illinois Supreme Court in 1870 argued that a child's commitment to a reform school without trial was unconstitutional: "Can the State, as *parens patriae*, exceed the power of the natural parent, except in punishing crime? . . . The principle of the absorption of the child in, and its complete subjection to the despotism of, the State is wholly inadmissible in the modern civilized world." Another source of contention was the fact that many child-saving institutions were run by religious or other private groups. The propriety of public support for such establishments, though generally affirmed by the

41. Bremner, ed., *Children and Youth*, II, 117 ff, 601 ff; Freund, *Police Power*, 246 ff. See also Joseph M. Hawes, *Children in Urban Society: Juvenile Delinquency in Nineteenth-Century America* (New York, 1971); Anthony M. Platt, *The Child Savers: The Invention of Delinquency* (Chicago, 1969).

42. *In re* Campbell, 130 Cal. 380, 382 (1900); on Massachusetts law, David D. Field, "The Child and the State," *Forum*, 1 (1886), 106–109; J. Francis Tucker, "A Need of Reform in the Police Regulations Concerning Parent and Child," *ILJ*, 2 (1893), 234–236. See also E. C. Wines, *The State of Prisons and of Child-Saving Institutions in the Civilized World* (Cambridge, 1880); Bremner, ed., *Children and Youth*, II, 247 ff, 440 ff.

courts, was a matter of continuing controversy. So was the supervisory power of the state. In 1900 the New York Court of Appeals ruled that the SPCC was not subject to the authority of the state Board of Charity, a decision that substantially weakened the power of the state to regulate private charities.

There was some concern, too, over the way in which juvenile institutionalization was handled. An occasional critic argued that institutional correction had disastrous consequences for many inmates. Reformers at the end of the century sought to change the procedure which committed juveniles to reform schools. The prevailing legal view was that these were not penal institutions and that juvenile offenders did not require the legal safeguards extended to adults unless they were formally accused of a crime. But the pioneering Illinois Juvenile Court Act of 1899 created a special equity court to deal with minors.[43]

Indeed, the general trend was to enhance the authority of the state over the child. In 1882 the Illinois Supreme Court reversed its 1870 decision and authorized the commonwealth to commit young delinquents to industrial schools. "We live in an age of inquiry and innovation," observed the normally conservative Chief Justice Edward G. Ryan of the Wisconsin Supreme Court when he handed down a similar ruling in 1876. The philosophy of juvenile institutions—"the teaching of lower-class skills and middle-class values"—reflected the mix of Christian benevolence, moral reform, "scientific" human improvement, and protection of a threatened social order that so often characterized late nineteenth century social policy.[44]

Marriage had an ambiguous place in Anglo-American common law. Traditionally it was held to be a form of social status; a special social compact; an application of natural, moral, or religious law. But marriage also was a contract, entered into by competent parties,

43. People v. Turner, 55 Ill. 280, 283–284 (1870); State Board v. New York SPCC, 161 N.Y. 233 (1900); Bremner, ed., *Children and Youth*, II, 334–337; Ex parte Ah Keen, 51 Cal. 280 (1876); Platt, *Child Savers*, ch. 5; Hawes, *Children*, ch. 10.

44. Ex parte Ferrier, 103 Ill. 367 (1882); Milwaukee Industrial School v. Supervisors, 40 Wis. 328, 331 (1876); Henry S. Williams, "What Shall be Done with Delinquent Children?" *NAR*, 164 (1897), 404–414; quotation from Platt, *Child Savers*, 69.

with mutual promises of fealty the binding consideration. This second view in part was a Protestant alternative to the Catholic conception of marriage as a sacrament. And it accorded with the nineteenth century stress on contract. By 1889, eighteen states held marriage to be a civil contract; elsewhere it was defined as a status attained through the contract instrument.

Nineteenth century American law diverged from its European counterparts in treating marriage as a compact that was peculiarly the business of the two parties involved. One critic found this an undue "assertion of the rights of the individual at the expense of the rights of society." Other Western countries were more inclined to safeguard the interests of the families of the bride and groom, and to regulate the character of the marriage ceremony, on the assumption that larger social concerns were at stake.[45]

But the importance of marriage as a source of social stability led to increasing government supervision in the late nineteenth century United States. A higher age of consent, physical and mental health requirements, regulation of the marriage ceremony, and the outlawing of certain kinds of unions (between the races in the South and border states, polygamy in Utah and Idaho) testified to the growing belief that marriage was too vital a social institution to be left solely to the partners to that contract.

Calif.?

As marriage moved from status to contract in the nineteenth century, so too did the legal and economic position of married women. Anglo-American judicial decisions and legislative acts gradually modified the common law assumption that the legal identity and property rights of wives were surrendered to the husband: "that, in the eye of the common law, husband and wife are

45. Schouler, *Domestic Relations,* 15–43; Tiedeman, *Limitations of Police Power,* 528–529; Samuel W. Dike, "Statistics of Marriage and Divorce," *PSQ,* 4 (1889), 596; quotation from Frank G. Cook, "The Marriage Celebration in the United States," *AM,* 61 (1888), 528; Cook, "The Marriage Celebration in Europe," *AM,* 61 (1888), 245–261. See also Maynard v. Hill, 125 U.S. 190 (1888); Frederick C. Hicks, "Marriage and Divorce Provisions in the State Constitutions of the United States," *AAPSS Annals,* 26 (1905), 745–748; Frederic J. Stimson, *American Statute Law* (Boston, 1886), 664–682; Oliver E. Bodington, "A New Departure in French Marriage Law," *ALR,* 31 (1897), 28–32; George E. Howard, *A History of Matrimonial Institutions,* 3 vols. (Chicago, 1904); William P. Eversley, *The Law of the Domestic Relations,* 3d ed. (London, 1906), 2–5.

one person, and that one is the husband." The movement had particular appeal in the nineteenth century United States, a "new, poor, rapidly-growing country, the needs of which required that money should be tied up as little as possible." The ideal of the freely contracting wife, with full control over her property, accorded with prevailing standards of social justice and political economy. Commentators argued that "any subjection by law of the wife to the commands of the husband would be a deprivation of the wife's liberty without due process of law"; that "just as in political control the overmastering impulse of growth is in the direction of the *greatest possible freedom of the individual, consistent with social cohesion*, so in domestic control the irresistible movement is in the direction of the most perfect *legal equality of the married partners, consistent with family unity*."

By the end of the century, married women had broad legal capacity to contract, lend and borrow, transfer property, escape attachment for their husbands' debts, and maintain control over property that they brought to their marriage or acquired thereafter. This was an Anglo-American development: an English commentator concluded in 1897 that the "old doctrine of unity of person and possessions . . . is in great measure swept away."[46]

But there were revealing limits to the extension of married women's property rights. Here as elsewhere the nineteenth century impulse to greater individual freedom conflicted with the felt need—intensified by the pressures of industrialism—to preserve established social standards. Legislatures and courts sought to maintain "the family relations upon which . . . the healthy life of organized society depends." There was a persistent "recognition of the inherent incapacity of women, as a rule, to deal judiciously with their own property, or to act with even ordinary wisdom in

46. Schouler, *Domestic Relations*, 6; Charles C. Savage, "Some Points of Comparison between English and American Legislation, as to Married Women's Property," *ALReg*, ns, 22 (1883), 762; J. E. G. de Montmorency, "The Changing Status of a Married Woman," *LQR*, 13 (1897), 197; Anna G. Spencer, "The Legal Position of Married Women," *PSM*, 18 (1881), 652, 648. See also "The Historical Development of the Doctrine of the Separate Estate of Married Women in Equity," *ALRec*, 15 (1886), 1–19; Henry Hitchcock, "Modern Legislation Touching Marital Property Rights," *JSS*, 13 (1881), 12–35; Isidore Loeb, *The Legal Property Relations of Married Parties: A Study in Comparative Legislation* (New York, 1900); Zeldin, *France*, 356.

the making of contracts." The law continued to regard a wife "as not only under the created disability of womanhood, but under the added disability of the overshadowing influence of the stronger nature of her husband, and the further disability of a necessary seclusion with her family and its duties, making her incapable of guarding her property interests."

Law and legislation retained "a sort of guardianship over the power and property of married women." In many jurisdictions, wives could not make contracts with their husbands, be executors or administrators of estates, be guardians of their children, enter into contracts of suretyship, or convey property apart from their husbands. A number of states limited the wife's right to go into business for herself. The prevailing legal assumption was that if a wife committed a crime in her husband's presence, she did so under his coercion. A husband could recover damages from the co-respondent in a divorce proceeding, and in some states obtain a divorce on the ground of his spouse's "misconduct." A wife could not.[47]

These contraints stemmed not only from a belief in the inferior economic and social capacity of women, but also from a sense of the importance of marriage and the family as guarantors of social order: "Whatever tends to deteriorate the marriage relation and consequently the home, tends to deteriorate the whole machinery of life, whether social or political." The spread of antiabortion and antibirth control laws reflected that assumption. Though the frequency of abortion was "simply frightful," doctors could legally prescribe it only if the life of the mother was at stake.[48]

Divorce—the most direct threat to the sanctity of marriage and the family—became a matter of special concern. During the early and mid-nineteenth century, marriages were dissolved with in-

47. Savage, "Some Points of Comparison," 768; James F. Mister, "Law of Married Women," *ALR*, 20 (1886), 360 ff; Tiedeman, *Limitations of Police Power*, 544–546; Mary A. Greene, "Married Women's Property Acts in the United States and Needed Reforms Therein," *ALJ*, 48 (1893), 206–209.

48. Abba G. Woolson, *Women in American Society* (Boston, 1873), 82; Edward A. Belcher, "Criminal Abortion," *CLM*, 17 (1895), 141–150. See also C. Thomas Dienes, *Law, Politics, and Birth Control* (Urbana, 1972), chs. 1–2; David M. Kennedy, *Birth Control in America: The Career of Margaret Sanger* (New Haven, 1970), 36 ff.

creasing ease. By 1867, thirty-three of the thirty-seven states had substituted judicial for legislative divorce. Some jurisdictions were noted for the ease and frequency with which they granted divorces. These included Connecticut (where one in ten marriages was dissolved), Ohio, Kansas, Indiana (whose law listed seven grounds for separation, including "any other cause for which the court shall deem it proper that a divorce shall be granted"), and cities such as Chicago and San Francisco. Fargo, North Dakota had a reputation as a "divorce colony" in the 1890s. In 1896, divorce-seekers there spent $3,000 to $3,500 a month on hotels and $5,000 to $10,000 on attorneys' fees. In 1903 a new state residence law launched Nevada on its notable twentieth century career as the kingpin of the divorce industry. Marriage, thought one late nineteenth century commentator, had become *"a contract easily made and easily ended."*[49]

A strong countercurrent set in during the last decades of the nineteenth century. In 1886, Carroll Wright of the national Bureau of Labor published an unsettling report on American marriage and divorce. He estimated that in 1885 the United States granted more divorces than the rest of the Western world combined, and that from 1867 to 1886 a third of a million marriages had been dissolved. In fact the proportion of divorces to marriages changed little during these years. But pressure mounted to check what was widely regarded as a growing social evil. Rhode Island's governor warned in 1883: "Our statute practically limits the causes of divorce to the discretion of the court, and . . . instances are not rare of persons coming to the State and remaining the time required to obtain standing in our . . . courts." A Divorce Reform League actively lobbied for tighter laws—and in 1896 changed its name to the League for the Protection of the Family. Among its proposals was a constitutional amendment empowering Congress to pass national marriage and divorce laws. This got nowhere, but a number of states tightened their divorce statutes. It was estimated in 1887 that the statutory grounds for divorce had been reduced from over four

49. Boorstin, *Americans: The Democratic Experience*, 64 ff; "American Divorces," *CLN*, 12 (1880), 324; William L. O'Neill, *Divorce in the Progressive Era* (New Haven, 1967), ch. 1; on San Francisco, *ALR*, 14 (1880), 151; "North Dakota," *AC* (1896); Frederic J. Stimson, *The Ethics of Democracy* (New York, 1887), 66. See also "The Law of Marriage and Divorce in America and England," *LMR*, 19 (1865), 58–75; Zeldin, *France*, 291, 357 ff.

hundred to less than twenty. By the end of the century only Washington, Kentucky, and Rhode Island retained the "omnibus" provision that permitted the courts to grant divorces for any cause they deemed proper.[50]

Inevitably the issue of divorce merged into the larger late nineteenth century concern over the state of American society. A few feminist defenses of divorce as a necessary escape route from unhappy marriages were drowned out by the charge that it threatened social stability, that it was "a step in the general movement for greater social freedom which characterizes our modern age." One commentator argued that while marriage was a private matter, divorce had broad public significance: not least because it led to smaller native American families while immigrant families grew.[51]

Attempts to determine the causes of divorce turned into a litany of the sources of late nineteenth century American social anxiety: adultery, drunkenness, desertion and cruelty, crime, immigration, industrialism, urbanization, mobility, strikes and radicalism, the evolution of marriage from a divine to a civil institution, individual liberty, free love, the loosening of family and social ties. As one observer concluded: "Certain disintegrating tendencies in modern society are common to both Europe and America; but they exist in more marked forms here than elsewhere."[52]

50. Carroll D. Wright, *Marriage and Divorce in the United States, 1867 to 1886* (Washington, 1889); Paul H. Jacobson, *American Marriage and Divorce* (New York, 1959), 90; "Rhode Island," *AC* (1883); Pivar, *Purity Crusade*, 227–228; Samuel Maxwell, "National Divorce Legislation," *ALR*, 21 (1887), 675–678. See also E. J. Phelps, "Divorce in the United States," *Forum*, 8 (1889), 349–364; Samuel W. Dike, "Statistics of Divorce in the United States and Europe," *AStA Publications*, ns, 1 (1888–1889), 206–214; Frank G. Cook, "A Different Problem in Politics," *AM*, 63 (1889), 55–62; Edmund H. Bennett, "National Divorce Legislation," *Forum*, 2 (1887), 429–438.

51. Elizabeth C. Stanton, "The Need of Liberal Divorce Laws," *NAR*, 139 (1889), 234–245, "Are Homogeneous Divorce Laws in all the States Desirable?" *NAR*, 170 (1900), 405–409; "Divorce," *NAR*, 136 (1883), 316; Noah Davis, "Marriage and Divorce," *NAR*, 139 (1884), 30–41.

52. Walter F. Willcox, "A Study in Vital Statistics," *PSQ*, 8 (1893), 69–96; Rev. I. E. Dwinnell, "Easy Divorce: Its Causes and Evils," *NE*, 43 (1884), 48–66; E. James, "Divorce, Sociologically Considered," *NE*, 54 (1891), 395–402; quotation from Samuel W. Dike, "The Effect of Lax Divorce Legislation upon the Stability of American Institutions," *JSS*, 14 (1881), 163.

CHAPTER 13

The Shock of Social Change: The Control of Behavior

THE DEFINITION OF social status in the late nineteenth century was intimately linked to the control of social behavior. The degree to which public authority might regulate behavior was of prime concern in areas such as education, violence and crime, social welfare, public mores, and private rights. As with the determination of social status, there was no single, unilinear policy. Social and economic change gave new force to old concerns over the threat to public order posed by deviant or idiosyncratic behavior. At the same time it strengthened humanitarian and liberalizing tendencies in American life. The conflict between freedom and constraint of course predated industrialism; the coming of a new economic and social order heightened rather than resolved that tension.

The School

Of those institutions that late nineteenth century Americans relied on to regulate social behavior, none was more important than the school. But the social functions of education were defined in different ways by different people. Some Americans thought that an industrial society required major changes in the curriculum, centralized school administration, and teachers who practiced a profession rather than followed a calling. Others believed with equal conviction that local control and traditional ways were the

473

proper responses to social change; that the school was an adjunct to and not a replacement of the family, the home, the church. Disputes over curriculum and administration, attendance and expenditure, the conflicting rights of parents and the state, and the place of religion in education defined the relationship of the late nineteenth century polity to the school.[1]

About 70 percent of the five to seventeen age cohort was enrolled in school by 1900. Students averaged about 100 days' attendance a year; expenditure per pupil increased by 50 to 100 percent between 1880 and 1900. But these totals conceal wide regional and other disparities. The north Atlantic and western states spent up to four times as much per child as the south Atlantic region. In 1900 the average school year was less than 100 days in the Southeast, but about twice as long in New England. North Carolina teachers in 1900 had an average annual salary of $82.87; their Massachusetts counterparts received an average of $566.09. Massachusetts and New York more generously supported their school systems than did Illinois and Michigan, which in turn fared better than Pennsylvania, Ohio, and Indiana. All other regions spent much more than the South, where per capita wealth was less than half the national average.

Variations on the county, township, and school district levels also were substantial. Although state aid to education came from a variety of sources—taxes, fines, license fees—the states in sum provided only a quarter as much as did the minor civil divisions. Many poor districts kept their schools open only long enough to qualify for state aid. Although Pennsylvania and Georgia in 1898 passed laws adopting sliding levels of state support to fit local needs, the century ended with enormous fiscal disparities among local districts.[2]

1. Robert Wiebe, "The Social Functions of Public Education," *AQ*, 21 (1969), 147–164.
2. Data from David B. Tyack, "Education and Social Unrest, 1873–1878," *HER*, 31 (1961), 194–197; Robert H. Bremner, ed., *Children and Youth in America* (Cambridge, 1970), II, 1102; Lewis C. Solmon, "Estimates of the Costs of Schooling in 1880 and 1890," *EEH*, 7 (1970), Supplement, no. 4, p. 570, Albert Fishlow, "The American Common School Revival: Fact or Fancy?" in Henry Rosovsky, ed., *Industrialization in Two Systems: Essays in Honor of Alexander Gerschenkron* (New York, 1966), 40–67, U.S., Bureau of Education, *Report of the Commissioner of Education for the Year 1899–1900* (Washington, 1901), I, xii–xiii; "Pennsylvania," "Georgia," *AC* (1898).

Complex variables of ethnic makeup, economic well-being, and popular attitudes toward education lay behind these differences. Sex and race distinctions added to the range of educational quality and opportunity. Male teachers earned two to three times as much as women. In Wisconsin at the close of the century the salary contrast was five to one. At the same time the ratio of female to male teachers steadily increased, from 4:3 in 1880 to 5:2 in 1900. This was a reflection not only of the parsimony of school boards and the growth of alternative male careers, but perhaps also of an inclination to regard education as an instrument of social stability rather than a means of individual advancement.

Southern schooling suffered not only from poverty and popular indifference (if not hostility), but also from a pervasive racism. Negro public education, painfully instituted in the postwar years, did not disappear with the end of Reconstruction. By official accounts, 34.1 percent of black males and 33.5 percent of black females received some schooling in 1880. Delaware, the last state to adopt the principle of public education for blacks, finally made something more than token expenditures for this purpose in 1880 and 1881. North Carolina equally divided $4,000 between its black and white normal (teacher training) schools in 1881. Texas Democrats in 1882 gave lip service to "the fullest education of the masses, white and colored, in separate common schools."

But during the next two decades, hardening racial attitudes and educational economizing eroded the fragile system of black education in the South. By 1900, 29.4 percent of the region's black males and 32.8 percent of its black females—smaller percentages than twenty years before—were enrolled. White registration percentages dropped, too: indifference to schooling and parsimonious educational expenditures were a regional and not just a racial policy. Nevertheless, in every respect Negro education remained far inferior. Louisiana in 1884 reported a white student-teacher ratio of 35 to 1, a black ratio of 87½ to 1. By 1900, half as much money was expended per capita for the education of black as for white children. South Carolina's Negroes made up 61 percent of the population but got less than 23 percent of the state school fund. The differentials between white and black school terms and teacher salaries were comparably wide. And what little black schooling there was could be perceived as a racial threat. "I was driving along a country road to catch an early train," reported

Georgia's state education commissioner in 1897. "I passed a field where half a dozen white children were at work, and shortly after came across a party of negro children going to school. The whites in the field, the negroes at school! My heart bled for my race."[3]

Sex and race distinctions in late nineteenth century American education accorded with prevailing public attitudes, and rarely led to political controversy. But other areas of educational policy—school administration, curriculum content, compulsory school attendance, the place of religion in the schools—were fruitful sources of conflict.

Highly localized school systems, a characteristic feature of American public education, came under increasing attack in the 1880s. Administrative localism could be intense indeed. Vermont in 1884 had 2,550 public schools and 2,290 school districts; Illinois had 20,500 teachers and 78,000 district trustees and treasurers. State law gradually but steadily merged these mini-districts into larger, more economical, more efficient systems. The courts affirmed that education was the responsibility of the state, not the community: "school districts are but agents of the commonwealth." The one-room country school, the one-school district, and teaching as a casual occupation began to give way in the late nineteenth century.

Consolidation was a slow business, constantly checked by localism. But the potential for greater efficiency and economy was alluring. Iowa in 1900 created central township schools in several counties, with carriages bringing in students from the surrounding countryside. Enrollments rose; attendance was more regular; the quality of teaching improved; not least important, per pupil costs went down.

Similar tendencies were evident in the cities. Reformers, seeking to wrest control of the schools from local machine politicians, allied with professional educators to campaign for the replacement of ward and district school systems and their trustees by single, citywide boards of education. After a long campaign, New York City's schools were centralized in 1896.[4]

3. *HS*, 208; *AC*, states and years cited. See also Louis R. Harlan, *Separate and Unequal: Public School Campaigns and Racism in the Southern Seaboard States 1901–1915* (New York, 1958), 8–9, 12; Bremner, ed., *Children and Youth*, II, 1226.
4. "Vermont," *AC* (1884); William C. Webster, *Recent Centralizing*

The consolidating impulse affected the distribution of textbooks as well. A number of states adopted laws providing standard, free texts. The evolution of Kansas's textbook statutes was typical. In 1869 uniform texts were prescribed for each school district; in 1885, county uniformity was imposed; in 1897 a state textbook commission was given the power to compel the statewide use of standard texts.

A variety of interests opposed uniform textbooks. The city of Topeka challenged the 1897 Kansas law on the ground that it voided existing contracts with textbook suppliers. But the state supreme court upheld the statute. A major political battle erupted over Indiana's 1889 state textbook law. The existing textbook lobby—the "book trust"—led the opposition. Advocates of local control and Catholics also were involved. Indiana Democrats wanted school children to be able to buy texts at a discount price—which would allow parochial school pupils to participate. Republicans wanted free textbooks—limited to public school children. The state court resolved the controversy by holding that the legislature had the exclusive power to prescribe uniform texts and a standard course of study.[5]

Educational professionalism and specialization went hand in hand with administrative consolidation. By the end of the century teachers' institutes and normal schools, teacher certification, standard salary grades, state superintendents and boards of education, graded schools, specialized curricula, and compulsory attendance laws were common.

Tendencies in State Educational Administration (New York, 1897), 23 ff; Ford v. School District, 121 Pa. St. 543, 547 (1888); "Iowa," *AC* (1900); Diane Ravitch, *The Great School Wars: New York City, 1805–1973* (New York, 1974), chs. 11–14; David B. Tyack, "City Schools: Centralization of Control at the Turn of the Century," in Jerry Israel, ed., *Building the Organizational Society* (New York, 1972), 57–72. See also William H. Issel, "Modernization in Philadelphia Public School Reform, 1882–1905," *PMHB*, 44 (1970), 358–383; "Laws Relating to City School Boards," U.S., Bureau of Education, *Report of the Commissioner of Education for 1895–1896* (Washington, 1897), ch. 1; Michael B. Katz, "The Emergence of Bureaucracy in Urban Education: The Boston Case, 1850–1884," *NEQ*, 8 (1968), 155–188, 319–357; David B. Tyack, *The One Best System: A History of American Urban Education* (Cambridge, 1974).

5. "Kansas," *AC* (1869, 1885, 1897); on Topeka, State v. Board of Education, 59 Kans. 501 (1898); on Indiana, Jeremiah W. Jenks, "School-Book Legislation," *PSQ*, 6 (1891), 90–125; State v. Haworth, 122 Ind. 462 (1890).

Reliance on the school as a socializing agent spurred the adoption of forms of learning appropriate to the changing character of American life. Secondary schools grew in importance. Michigan Supreme Court Justice Thomas M. Cooley handed down an influential decision in 1874 that approved the collection of school taxes for high schools. Wisconsin established a free secondary school system in 1875. The 23,634 secondary school graduates in 1880 (2.5 percent of the nation's seventeen year olds) increased to 94,883 (6.4 percent of the age cohort) in 1900.[6]

A committee headed by Harvard President Charles W. Eliot proposed a standardized high school curriculum in 1893. When critics attacked its solidly academic emphasis, Eliot replied that democracy was fostered by a single curriculum that ignored class distinctions. Others wanted a more varied offering that distinguished between academic and manual or industrial training; one commentator expected the high school to reduce the "tyranny of insolvent wealth" while it "detects and exposes the fallacies of socialism." The same social complexity that encouraged the spread of high schools led to diverse expectations as to what they might accomplish.

The rapid growth of an industrial economy—and the hard times of the 1870s—stimulated interest in industrial and commercial education. State governors touted its virtues. Senator Justin Morrill thought that it would help workers to escape "the imported barbarous despotism reigning over our trade unions." The American Social Science Association called for the creation of "School-Shops," and Edward Everett Hale declared: "We wish the State to add this developing system to its system of schools, because the State can do it better than any private corporation."[7]

---

6. Charles R. Starring and James O. Knauss, *The Michigan Search for Educational Standards* (Lansing, 1969), ch. 7; Irwin Taylor, *Public School Law of the United States, as Administered by the Courts* (Topeka, 1892); on high schools, Edward A. Krug, *The Shaping of the American High School*, 2 vols. (New York, 1964, Madison, 1971); Bremner, ed., *Children and Youth*, II, 1387 ff; Stuart v. School District, 30 Mich. 69 (1874); HS, 207.

7. Eliot in Bremner, ed., *Children and Youth*, II, 1400–1407; J. E. Seaman, "High Schools and the State," ibid., 1387–1389; on industrial education, "Pennsylvania," "New Jersey," "New York," AC (1878); Morrill quoted in Merle Curti, *The Social Ideas of American Educators* (Paterson, N.J., 1959), 221; Hale in American Social Science Association, *Report on a Developing School, and School-Shops* (Boston, 1877), 15.

The "transformation of the school" through progressive education was a twentieth century movement. But it had important late nineteenth century sources. The educational reformer Francis Parker, who ran the schools of Quincy, Massachusetts in the 1870s, believed that abstract principles should be taught through concrete objects and examples, not by rote. Massachusetts was the source of much school innovation, in part because it was deeply rooted in the state's tradition, in part because there the sense of an older social order shattered by industry, cities, and immigrants was especially keen. Reformers persistently sought for ways in which old social values might be taught to a new, polyglot student population. Home and handicraft skills—sewing and cooking for girls, woodworking and gardening for boys—were taught to immigrant children in the mill towns and cities. Efforts were made to wean the immigrant young from their homes—and their families' ways —at an early age. The kindergarten was one such device. Its leading exponent, Elizabeth Foster Peabody, described it as "children in society—a commonwealth or republic of children—whose laws are all part and parcel of the Higher Law alone." The teaching of American history and civics, and ritual ceremonies such as reciting the pledge of allegiance to the flag, served a similar acculturating purpose.

But the cultural diversity that made these measures necessary also limited their effectiveness. The pull of the street, the home, the shop and factory were more compelling than the fabricated world of the school. The kindergarten program ended in Massachusetts at the turn of the century, a victim of the strain it imposed on school budgets, of immigrant parents refusing to send their children, and of educators squabbling over whether to stress formal or "play" learning.[8]

The strength of those forces that opposed educational expansion and centralization was evident in the failure of the late nineteenth century effort to secure federal aid for the schools. Advocates

8. Lawrence A. Cremin, *The Transformation of the School: Progressivism in American Education, 1876–1957* (New York, 1961); on Parker, Michael B. Katz, "The 'New Departure' in Quincy, 1873–1881: The Nature of Nineteenth Century Educational Reform," *NEQ*, 40 (1967), 3–30; Marvin Lazerson, *Origins of the Urban School: Public Education in Massachusetts, 1870–1915* (Cambridge, 1971), 38 ff.

argued that a large and rising rate of illiteracy, especially in the South, was a social danger that called for the intervention of the national government. Education was the device that would bring the South "in line with republican ideas and institutions." But the problem was a national one: *"In all portions of the Union, it is practically impossible for the leading classes to submit to the governing of great, wealthy cities and States by the lower class of voters."*

Senator Henry W. Blair of New Hampshire, the chief Republican advocate of federal aid to education, linked his cause to Protestant-American nationalism. He sought a constitutional amendment requiring each state to maintain a system of free public schools and to instruct the young "in virtue, morality, and the principles of the Christian religion." Discussing the "two great institutions in our society [that] undertake to control the education of the child"—public and parochial schools—he concluded: "One is freedom, the other slavery. The one not only permits, but insures the perpetuation of the Republic, the other destroys it."[9]

In the late eighties southern Democrats, many of whom had previously supported a federal aid bill (the 1882 South Carolina Democratic platform declared: "A National danger calls for National action and National aid"), joined Catholics and northern Democrats in opposition. Southern interest in education—especially Negro education—was declining; the issue had become a measure of party differentiation; it was feared that federal aid would create a centralized system of education and propagate "Anti-Christian and atheistic unbelief."

Three times in the 1880s the Senate passed a federal aid bill. But the House never voted on the measure, and in 1890 the Senate reversed itself, thus ending the possibility of national aid to education until the mid-twentieth century. The underlying tensions between Catholics and Protestants, between advocates of centralized government and supporters of states' rights and localism, between northerners who saw education as a prop to social stability and southerners who saw it as a threat, combined to put federal

9. Rev. A. D. Mayo, "National Aid to Education," *JSS*, 17 (1882), 10, 20–21; Blair in U.S., *CR*, 51st Cong., 1st sess. (Feb. 21, 1890), 1534 ff. See also "Education and Illiteracy," *AC* (1882); Bremner, ed., *Children and Youth*, II, 1260 ff.

aid beyond the capacity of the late nineteenth century polity.[10]

The family, too, was a force to be reckoned with by those who wished to reform or rationalize education. Consider the case of Annie Sheibley, a Nebraska high school student around 1890. Her father initially wanted her to study grammar. But he soon changed his mind on the ground that the subject was not taught "as he had been instructed when he went to school." He told his daughter to refuse to do her assigned work. The Nebraska Supreme Court upheld the Sheibleys: "who is to determine what studies she shall pursue in school: a teacher who has a mere temporary interest in her welfare, or her father, who may reasonably be supposed to be desirous of pursuing such a course as will best promote the happiness of his child?"

But this would not be the prevailing view. Education was too important to the public interest. "Under the influence of the social forces now at work," most courts held that parental responsibility for a child's education was a duty, not a right, and that teachers were not merely agents of the parent (a traditional view) but of the state as well.[11]

The conflict between those who regarded education as an instrument of social policy and those who regarded it as a matter of individual and family preference came to a head over compulsory education. One observer warned in the 1880s that required school attendance "will meet with a determined opposition from a large part of the population." For many families, child labor was economically necessary and socially desirable. Their numbers grew with industralization and the flood of new immigrants. En-

10. On South Carolina platform, Mayo, "National Aid," 21–22; "Education Bills before Congress," NPR, 2 (1886), 134; Allen Going, "The South and the Blair Education Bill," MVHR, 44 (1957), 267–290; Willard B. Gatewood, Jr., "North Carolina and Federal Aid to Education: Public Reaction to the Blair Bill, 1881–1890," NCHR, 40 (1963), 465–488; John W. Evans, "Catholics and the Blair Education Bill," CHR, 46 (1960), 294. See also Daniel W. Crofts, "The Black Response to the Blair Education Bill," JSH, 37 (1971), 41–65; "The Constitutionality of the Blair Educational Bill," ALR, 21 (1887), 457–459.

11. State v. School District, 31 Neb. 552, 554, 556 (1891); Christopher G. Tiedeman, A Treatise on the Limitations of Police Power (St. Louis, 1886), 563; William P. Borland, "The Law of Schoolmaster and Pupil as to Punishment," MLJ, 2 (1893), 201. See also Morrow v. Wood, 35 Wis. 59 (1874); Rulison v. Post, 79 Ill. 567 (1875).

forcement of compulsory attendance laws was spotty. New Jersey's 1885 act was a dead letter in the cities (in part because of a classroom shortage): in 1886 an estimated 38,000 children of school age were not enrolled.

Nevertheless, all but two nonsouthern states had compulsory attendance laws by the end of the century. Usually these were passed after a state had a high level of school enrollment—and a political constituency of educators and parents anxious to enforce attendance. In the South no such pressures existed, and only Kentucky had a compulsory attendance law by 1900.[12]

Compulsory education enacted into law the growing belief that schooling was socially necessary, that "the very safety of the State imperatively demands a certain securing of this great *essential* of good citizenship to every child." The Iowa Supreme Court declared in 1871: "As we all surrender to society some of our natural rights that we may enjoy its great advantages, so must the parent give up the society and service of his child for the incalculably greater benefit of the education which his offspring will receive from attendance at the public school." The Indiana Supreme Court came to a similar conclusion in 1901. That state's attendance law had come under attack as an invasion of "the natural right of man to govern and control his own children." But the court concluded that in the realm of education the parent must be "subordinate to the power of the State." Indiana distributed some $2,000,000 to its schools each year, and "no parent can be said to have the right to deprive his child of the advantages so provided."[13]

Because education was so important a socializing agent, who taught what in schools and colleges became a matter of public concern. Confederate and Union veterans' groups policed the textbook treatment of the Civil War. Defenders of free silver fared poorly in a number of eastern colleges during the 1890s. Brown

12. Tiedeman, *Limitations of Police Power*, 562; "New Jersey," *AC* (1886); William M. Landes and Lewis C. Solmon, "Compulsory Schooling Legislation: An Economic Analysis of Law and Social Change in the Nineteenth Century," *JEH*, 32 (1972), 54–89.

13. Webster, *Centralizing Tendencies*, 46–47; Burdick v. Babcock, 31 Ia. 562, 568 (1871); State v. Bailey, 157 Ind. 324, 326, 329–330 (1901); see also *In re* Campbell, 130 Cal. 380 (1900); Bremner, ed., *Children and Youth*, II, 1422–1428.

University President E. Benjamin Andrews was forced to resign because of his belief in bimetallism. Southern and western states at times dealt harshly with dissident faculty. The Board of Regents deposed the greater part of the Kansas Agricultural College faculty in 1897. The Texas legislature in that year called for an inquiry into rumors that the state university faculty included "those who are not in sympathy with the traditions of the South, . . . and circulate and teach political heresies in place of the system of political economy that is cherished by our people."[14]

A number of eastern and midwestern states around 1890 considered or passed laws requiring that the curricula of public and private schools be taught in English. The most controversial of these statutes were Wisconsin's Bennett Law and Illinois's Edwards Act of 1889. Catholics and German Lutherans reacted violently and made the acts prime political issues. Illinois Democrats condemned "a law which takes from the parent the right to educate his child according to the dictates of his conscience." Republicans countered that "since the success of universal suffrage and of popular government requires universal intelligence," school authorities must have the power to regulate the curriculum of private as well as public schools.

In St. Louis the issue took a somewhat different form: whether or not to end the compulsory teaching of German in the city's public schools. But everywhere the underlying social tensions that led to these actions were the same. And while the Republicans paid a grievous political price in the early 1890s for their support of compulsory education in English, the general trend of public opinion was in their favor. By the end of the century New York, Massachusetts, and Illinois required state certification that "competent" instruction was being offered in private schools and prescribed the teaching of English grammar and American history. Pennsylvania in 1905 obliged its children to go to schools where "the common English branches of learning" were taught.[15]

14. "Virginia," AC (1898); "Indiana," AC (1896); Mary R. Dearing, *Veterans in Politics: The Story of the G.A.R.* (Baton Rouge, 1952), ch. 11; Laurence R. Veysey, *The Emergence of the American University* (Chicago, 1965), 384 ff; "Kansas," "Texas," AC (1897).

15. John Bascom, "A New Policy for the Public Schools," *Forum*, 11 (1891), 59–66; William F. Vilas, "The 'Bennett Law' in Wisconsin," *Forum*, 12 (1891), 196–207; E. M. Winston, "The School Controversy in Illinois,"

The place of religion in the public schools was the educational issue that most often led to legal and political conflict. The courts frequently dealt with the thorny issue of school Bible reading. Most states allowed this without exegesis, and the courts approved so long as attendance or participation was voluntary. The Iowa Supreme Court went further, upholding a law that prohibited the exclusion of Bible reading from the schools: "Possibly the plaintiff is a propagandist, and regards himself charged with a mission to destroy the influence of the Bible . . . it is sufficient to say that the courts are charged with no such mission." But the Wisconsin court denied the constitutionality of school Bible readings. While conceding that "morality and good conduct may be inculcated in the common schools, and should be," it pointed to the diversity of the state's population and warned: "The connection of church and state corrupts religion, and makes the state despotic."[16]

Equally troublesome was the question of state aid to parochial schools. The National League for the Protection of American Institutions was one of many Protestant spokesmen opposing state aid. This was a frequent political issue in the early nineties, as tension heightened between urban Catholics and rural Protestants. New York's Blaine Amendment of 1894 (named after James G. Blaine, who in the 1870s sought a constitutional amendment forbidding federal aid to parochial schools) was one of a number of restrictions on state support to church-related schools imposed at the time. By the turn of the century, twenty-three states forbade public grants to religious schools. Pennsylvania's "religious garb" bill of 1895 prohibited nuns from teaching in public schools or public school teachers from wearing religious dress or insignia.[17]

---

ibid., 208–214; "Illinois," AC (1892); Jack Muraskin, "St. Louis Municipal Reform in the 1890's: A Study in Failure," Bulletin of the MoHS, 25 (1968), 44; Freund, Police Powers, 252–254; "Pennsylvania," AC (1895). See also Howard Weisz, "Irish-American Attitudes and the Americanization of the English-Language Parochial Schools," NYH, 53 (1972), 157–176.

16. Tiedeman, Limitations of Police Power, 161–162; Ernst Freund, The Police Power (Chicago, 1904), 492–493; Moore v. Monroe, 64 Ia. 367, 370 (1884); State v. District Board, 76 Wis. 177, 221 (1890). See also Cardinal Manning, "The Bible in the Public Schools," Forum, 7 (1889), 52–66.

17. Daniel F. Reilly, The School Controversy (1891–1893) (Washington, 1943), 33; on New York, Samuel T. McSeveney, The Politics of Depression: Political Behavior in the Northeast, 1893–1896 (New York, 1972), 70–80; Carl Zollmann, American Church Law (St. Paul, 1933), 78–79; "Pennsylvania," AC (1895).

Both Protestants and Catholics (with some reason) regarded the public schools as places where an essentially Protestant world view was taught. Some Catholic leaders—notably Archbishop John Ireland of St. Paul and Cardinal James Gibbons of Baltimore—favored compulsory public school attendance and welcomed the Americanization of Catholic children. But the dominant church view, especially as religious conflict intensified toward the end of the century, was that parochial education was the only answer to the "school problem" in America. In 1885 an attempt was made to block congressional confirmation of Zachariah Montgomery, a Catholic, as assistant attorney general because of his supposed hostility to public education.

Protestant-Catholic controversy over the schools was especially keen in Boston. Catholics in 1888 complained that a standard history textbook and a public school history teacher were virulently anti-Catholic. The school board voted to drop the text and censured the teacher. Protestants rose in indignation over these acts and launched a successful drive to get Protestant women to vote in the next school board election, when the candidate supporting the Catholic position was defeated.[18]

"The public-school failure" was a common theme in the late nineteenth century. The schools were criticized for their rigidity and "rote efficiency"—and for their lack of discipline; for the fact that they cost too much—and because too little was spent on education. The problem, as an acute observer put it in the late 1880s, was that the schools had no single, widely accepted social purpose. The old religious-moral aims were under challenge, new civic and social goals still were developing.

The late nineteenth century normally is viewed as a stagnant time in the history of American education: as a Sargasso Sea between the earlier development of the common school and the later rise of educational progressivism. But in fact these were years when profoundly opposed social values confronted one another over the

18. Robert D. Cross, *The Emergence of Liberal Catholicism in America* (Cambridge, 1958), 130 ff; Cross, "Origins of the Catholic Parochial Schools in America," *ABR*, 16 (1965), 194–209; Lois B. Merk, "Boston's Historic Public School Crisis," *NEQ*, 31 (1958), 172–199. See also Alvin W. Johnson and Frank H. Yost, *Separation of Church and State in the United States* (Minneapolis, 1948), ch. 3.

schools. The forces of social and economic change that spurred administrative centralization, increasing professionalism, and new educational goals also stimulated a heightened traditionalism, localism, and group autonomy. If there was not yet a clear-cut resolution of this conflict, it was because the opposing interests were in close and uneasy balance.[19]

Violence and Crime

Violence has etched a dark streak through American history. Whether or not in fact the United States has been more violence-prone than most other societies is debatable. The level of violence in the late nineteenth century may well have been no higher than in earlier times. But more so than before, it seemed to threaten the social fabric. The goals of social harmony and individual security had a special appeal to a people who had lived through the Civil War and now were caught up in an onrushing industrialization.

Violence had another face as well. Civil disturbances in late nineteenth century America often were essentially conservative responses to social change. The disruption of established economic relationships (such as employment or wage scales) and real or imagined threats to prevailing race relations or other social mores were the most frequent sources of strikes, riots, vigilantism, and lynching.[20]

Many of the major labor disputes of the late nineteenth century erupted over wage cuts or other alterations of existing conditions. Labor violence in the South frequently flared when blacks were brought in to replace white strikers, as in the New Orleans levee

19. Richard G. White, "The Public-School Failure," *NAR*, 131 (1880), 537–550, answered by John D. Philbrick, "The Success of the Free-School System," *NAR*, 132 (1881), 249–262; A Teacher [Thomas Davidson], "American Education," *WR*, 128 (1887), 414–426. See also Joseph M. Rice, *The Public School System of the United States* (New York, 1893); Rebecca H. Davis, "The Curse in Education," *NAR*, 168 (1899), 609–614; W. F. Edwards, "Civics and Education: Grave Evils in Our Public School System," *GM*, 16 (1899), 269–278; Cremin, *Transformation*, ch. 1; Ravitch, *Great School Wars*, 126 ff; Tyack, *One Best System*, part III.

20. See in general Hugh P. Graham and Ted R. Gurr, eds., *Violence in America* (New York, 1969) and Richard Hofstadter and Michael Wallace, eds., *American Violence: A Documentary History* (New York, 1971).

riots of 1894–1895 or the Alabama miners' strike of 1894. Usually it was the authorities, not the strikers, who were responsible for the greater loss of life. The Haymarket bomb explosion of 1886 had a profound impact on public opinion in part because its ideological context and the killing of seven policemen were so unusual.

Intergroup tensions were no less fertile a source of violence. The New York militia killed thirty-seven Irish Catholics who tried to disrupt an Orange Day march of Ulster Protestants in 1871. The Chinese were frequent victims of mob action, as in a wave of far West riots in 1885 and 1886. Eleven Italians were lynched in 1891 after being blamed for the murder of New Orleans's chief of police; five years later three Italians accused of homicide in that city met the same fate. Two Seminole Indians charged with murder were burned at the stake in Oklahoma in 1898.[21]

Extralegal social control through direct action was not limited to minorities. An 1884 protest against the lenient treatment of murderers in Cincinnati developed into a full-scale riot, which left in its wake a partially destroyed courthouse and about fifty dead. Vigilantism—an old American phenomenon—continued to flourish. There were at least 190 vigilante organizations between 1861 and 1890. The reasons that led groups of citizens to take the law into their own hands were as varied as American life itself: among them, horse thievery (anti-horse-thief associations, sometimes with state charters, flourished in the Great Plains); the persistence of toll turnpikes in Kentucky; the desire to control the price of flour or of tobacco.

Most vigilantism occurred in the more remote rural areas, where state or national authority was thin. Bald-Knobbers, "night-riding bands of regulators," terrorized the Ozarks in the mid-eighties, burning, whipping, and killing in a jihad against theft, drinking, gambling, and prostitution. White Caps in Kentucky and southern Indiana and Ohio engaged in similar attempts at social regulation. In 1897 South Carolina Regulators (the inheritors of a tradition—and a name—that reached back to the eighteenth century) burnt down a Mormon church and a theater. The governor of Ohio, reporting to the legislature on that state's White Cap activities,

21. "Louisiana," *AC* (1894–1895); "Alabama," *AC* (1894); Robert H. Marr, "The New Orleans Mafia Case," *ALR*, 25 (1891), 414–431; "Louisiana," *AC* (1896); "Oklahoma," *AC* (1898).

observed that respectable citizens were involved and that their victims had committed crimes that normally escaped the slow, expensive process of the law.[22]

A major category of violence in the late nineteenth century was by whites against blacks. After the end of southern Reconstruction, social reasons—accusations of rape, theft, or murder, challenges to white supremicist racial mores—became more important than political ones for terrorizing blacks. Between 1882 and 1903, over 3,300 lynchings were reported (clearly far below the actual total): 2,000 of the victims were Negroes.

The causes varied greatly, but always within the context of maintaining white supremacy. Four South Carolina whites beat three blacks to death in 1896 because they suspected that the victims stole a Bible from a church. (The assailants were tried and acquitted.) In 1899, a black worker killed the superintendent of construction at a Pennsylvania coke company; he was pursued into the mountains by a mob and killed there. The white citizens of an Alabama county filed a petition in 1897 for a special court session to try several blacks accused of rape. If the session were not held, they warned, the prisoners would be lynched. A special term of court was hurriedly convened, and a number of legal executions followed. Throughout the South and the border states, vigilante groups terrorized, beat, and in some cases killed blacks who lived in the wrong place, or in the wrong way.

Negroes were not always passive victims, especially as conditions worsened in the 1890s. Cases of arson and dynamiting by blacks were reported in Tennessee in 1894, and in Brooks County, Georgia in 1895. Blacks and police battled in the streets of Winchester, Kentucky in 1896; and in that year troops were called out to quell a supposed Negro uprising in Orangeburg County, South Carolina. Rumors of imminent mass action by blacks swept Little River County, Arkansas, and Jefferson County, Alabama in 1889.

While collective violence at times had the sanction of public authorities, there were frequent instances of official disapproval as well. Vigilante groups often were sternly suppressed. The Arkansas Bald-Knobbers were crushed by fines and imprisonment; the governors of Kentucky (1895) and Texas (1898) called on their

---

22. "Ohio," *AC* (1884); Graham and Gurr, eds., *Violence*, 63–65, 154; "Missouri," *AC* (1887); "South Carolina," *AC* (1897); "Ohio," *AC* (1888).

legislatures to take strong action against White Cappers in their states. Lynching, too, stirred considerable opposition. Seattle's Law and Order League sought to protect the city's Chinese from mob action in 1887. A number of states passed antilynching laws, and officials frequently condemned the practice as a threat to social order. Bar associations in the nineties coupled lynch mobs with strikes as a dangerous form of social disruption. In 1893 Governor Thomas G. Jones of Alabama called lynchings "flagrant insults to the dignity and sovereignty of the people as would be an attempt to disperse the legislature by force or overawe its highest court by violence"—a revealing glimpse of the deeper fears besetting those in authority during the 1890s. In 1899 a Hinds County, Mississippi judge charged a grand jury to take steps against lynching: "Surely the time has come to strike this representative of anarchy with the mailed fist of the law, before the law itself—yes our very civilization—goes down in wreck and ruin." The belief that violence was a cause of as well as a response to social disorder led to a variety of legislative controls. "Pistol bills" outlawing the sale of certain types of weapons were enacted in several cities during the early 1880s. Massachusetts in 1885 prohibited newspapers devoted to tales of crime and bloodshed.[23]

But these were objections to the lawlessness of vigilantism and lynching, not to the social attitudes responsible for them. The fear of anarchy—stoked by the Paris Commune of 1871, the 1877 railroad strike riots, the Haymarket affair of 1886, and the strikes of the nineties—was especially strong. Typical was the comment of an observer in 1895: "The history of the United States is approaching what seems to be a dangerous point . . . When the demagogues' call to arms is as rampant as it is to-day it behooves every state to preserve peace and liberty in all ways possible." State laws in the wake of the 1877 riots allowed legal action against communities for mob damage. The Illinois legislature in 1879 prohibited armed bodies from drilling or parading except with a special license; the United

23. Graham and Gurr, eds., *Violence*, 72; *AC*, states and years cited; "Law and Order League of the United States," *AC* (1887); William Aubrey, "Mob Law," *TBA Proceedings*, 16th (1897), 126–148; "Alabama," *AC* (1893); "Georgia," *AC* (1899); "Mississippi," *AC* (1899); on arms restrictions, "Arkansas," *AC* (1881), and Freund, *Police Power*, 90–91; "Massachusetts," *AC* (1885). See also George C. Holt, "Lynching and Mobs," *JSS*, 32 (1894), 67–81.

States Supreme Court upheld the statute. The Illinois anarchist law of 1887—passed in the wake of Haymarket—authorized the use of deputy sheriffs and the militia "to secure the peace and good order of society."

Armories rose in the cities from the 1870s on, and state militias got a new lease on life. The National Guard, based on the 1792 Militia Act obligating all men aged eighteen to forty-five to serve in the state militia, was a paper organization until the late seventies. Then in 1879 a National Guard Association was formed, and between 1881 and 1892 every state revised its military code to provide for an organized militia. By 1896 the Guard numbered 100,000 men, four times the size of the regular army. As a guardian of public order, this force was especially strong in the large industrial states. It fostered a mystique of fraternalism, manliness, duty, discipline, patriotism—and a commitment to the preservation of social order.[24]

The depression of the seventies produced a new figure on the American scene: the tramp, a jobless wanderer given mobility by the railroad. The vagabond, traditionally a romantic figure, now came to be viewed as a social threat. A number of states passed "tramp laws" that punished vagrants for failing to prove means of support or to seek employment, for suspicious appearance or a bad reputation, or for "criminal idleness."

Generally the courts upheld these tramp and vagrancy acts. The Ohio Supreme Court in 1881 approved a Cincinnati ordinance permitting the arrest and confinement of "known thieves," even though their "offense does not consist of particular acts, but in the mode of life, the habits and practices of the accused." Twenty years later the same tribunal decided that the Ohio tramp law was not in conflict with the Bill of Rights or the Fourteenth Amendment: "We are of opinion that the law in question is one calculated to secure the repose and peace of society . . . He who, being able to work, and not able otherwise to support himself, deliberately plans to exist by the labor of others, is an enemy to society and to the commonwealth."

24. Frank White, "Municipal Liability for Mob Damages," *NLR*, 4 (1895), 23; Presser v. Illinois, 116 U.S. 252 (1886); *Ill. Laws* 1887, 239–241; Martha Derthick, *The National Guard in Politics* (Cambridge, 1965), 16–22. See also Commonwealth v. Murphy, 166 Mass. 171 (1896); Charles N. Hall, *Patriotism and National Defense* (New York, 1885).

But there was a continuing strain of judicial uneasiness with this new criminal category. Occasionally a court, citing the Fourteenth Amendment, refused to uphold a state or municipal vagrancy law. The Appeals Court of the District of Columbia decided that an 1898 ordinance directed at "all suspicious persons" violated the Fourth and Eighth Amendments. And authorities at times were prevented from forcibly confining habitual drunkards: "A man may be said to have a natural right to drink intoxicating liquor as much as he pleases, provided that in doing so he does not do or threaten positive harm to others ... A man has the legal right to live a life of absolute idleness if he chooses, provided he does not, in so doing, violate some clear and well-defined duty of the state."[25]

The tension between personal freedom and social order, between the state as a threat to liberty and as a source of social protection, was as old as Western society itself. The weight of law and custom in the pre-Civil War United States had come to rest heavily in favor of the (white male) individual. Now in the late nineteenth century the pressures of economic and social change were shifting the balance toward those policies that promised to reduce the threat of social disorder—at the cost of greater state control. But that shift was accompanied by continuing doubt and uncertainty.

It seemed at the time that the nation's crime rate was rising. The attorney general estimated that the number of homicides increased from 4,000 in 1887 to 10,500 in 1899. Yet the available data for Boston suggests that the rate of serious crimes against the person—assault, homicide—declined from the 1830s on, while crimes against public order such as drunkenness rose. Whatever the facts, the prevailing view was that immigrants and factories and cities meant an increase in lawlessness.[26]

25. Paul T. Ringenbach, *Tramps and Reformers, 1873–1916: The Discovery of Unemployment in New York* (Westport, Conn., 1973), xiii–xiv; on tramp laws, Freund, *Police Power*, 97 ff; Morgan v. Nolte, 37 Ohio St. 23, 24, 26 (1881); State v. Hogan, 63 Ohio St. 202, 220, 211 (1900); Stoutenburgh v. Frazier, 16 App. D.C. 229 (1900); Tiedeman, *Limitations of Police Power*, 561, 563. See also "Vagrancy," *AStR* 38 (1894), 643–646; Samuel Leavitt, "The Tramps and the Law," *Forum*, 2 (1886–1887), 190–200; C. G. Tiedeman, "Police Control of Dangerous Classes, other than by Criminal Prosecutions," *ALR*, 19 (1885), 561–568.

26. "Is Crime Increasing?" *PSM*, 43 (1893), 399–405; Roger Lane, "Crime and Criminal Statistics in Nineteenth-Century Massachusetts," *JSocH*, 2

Crime became a major social concern. The Society for the Prevention of Crime, dedicated to removing "the causes and sources of crime by enforcement of the laws and arousing public opinion," was organized in New York City in 1877. But what *were* crime's causes? The range of determining factors was extensive indeed, according to one analysis: heredity, intemperance, ignorance, idleness, avarice and cupidity, personal ambition, the conflict between labor and capital, population increase, the influx of foreigners, the rise of the city. The *Chicago Tribune* attributed the great majority of homicides to quarrels generated by the tensions of American life. The Italian criminologist Cesare Lombroso speculated in 1897 on the reasons why murder was on the rise in the United States in contrast to Europe, where homicide appeared to decline as wealth, literacy, and population increased. His explanation: America's unique mix of "undercivilization" (as exemplified by the black population) and "overcivilization" (which brought with it drugs, alcohol, and the lure of material wealth).[27]

Expert analysis dwelt increasingly on the hereditary as well as the environmental causes of crime. But this did not lighten the moral responsibility of the individual for his acts, or the duty of the state to deal firmly with crime as a threat to the social order. Zebulon Brockway, the leading penologist of the time, warned: "Crime is contagious; it is a disease," and held that the state must prevent the procreation of criminal stock, or remedy it through treatment. A turn of the century treatise concluded: "The attitude of modern social science toward the graver crimes against person and property is that their commission is in most cases attributable to hereditary causes or social conditions which produce degeneracy and criminality. The attitude of the law is that the commission of each offense involves a distinct moral responsibility of the individual,

---

(1968), 156–163. On the unreliability of crime statistics, see Louis N. Robinson, "History and Organization of Criminal Statistics in the United States," Ph.D. diss., Cornell University, 1911.

27. On Society, "New York City," *AC* (1894); Sanford M. Green, *Crime: Its Nature, Causes, Treatment, and Prevention* (Philadelphia, 1889); "The American Murder Roll of 1892," *ALR*, 27 (1893), 415–417; Cesare Lombroso, "Why Homicide Has Increased in America," *NAR*, 165 (1897), 641–648, *NAR*, 166 (1898), 1–11. See also J. L. Pickard, "Why Crime Is Increasing," *NAR*, 140 (1885), 456–463; "Law and Order League of the United States," *AC* (1887).

which demands and justifies the infliction of punishment."

After the Civil War the common law M'Naghten rule, that an insanity defense in a criminal case lay in the demonstration that the accused was unable to distinguish right from wrong, came under attack. New Hampshire Chief Justice Charles Doe argued that the rule treated criminal responsibility as a question of law when properly it should be treated as a question of fact, with appropriate procedural safeguards. But this assault on the M'Naghten rule did not get very far. The belief in moral responsibility for crime was too strong. Indeed, one authority argued that the criminal insane should be punished when and if their sanity was restored, on the ground that protection of the public, not reformation of the criminal, was the major purpose of the penal system.[28]

"Scientific" criminology thus justified severe punishment, as did the stern moral code of the past. The *Journal of Social Science* proposed in 1882 that felons be permanently disfranchised. A minister defended the death penalty on grounds of social policy: "In the United States, amidst increasing perils from the socialism of ignorant masses, annually multiplying by millions; with all conflicting infidel speculations and political theories, from Nihilism to Mormonism, let loose, and sensual and intoxicating habits unrestrained; with the suffrage universal, and violent factions, and strifes for office, gain, and power universal also; with scientific dynamites of revenge inviting every disappointed villain's handling," it was essential to maintain the divine law against murder. Public policy reflected these attitudes. Maine in 1883 restored the death penalty; the Michigan legislature came within a single vote of doing so. Death sentences in Georgia and Alabama increased in the early 1880s. The governor of Kansas complained in 1882 that prisoners awaiting execution were too well treated.[29]

28. Brockway, "The State and the Criminal," *Forum*, 2 (1886–1887), 262–263; Freund, *Police Power*, 95; John P. Reid, *Chief Justice: The Judicial World of Charles Doe* (Cambridge, 1967), 115–118; Tiedeman, *Limitations of Police Power*, 113–114, 557–561. See also Henry Maudsley, "Law and Insanity," *PSM*, 5 (1874), 77–88; J. G. Lodge, "Law and Insanity," *SLR*, ns, 3 (1877), 447–468.

29. James F. Colby, "Disfranchisement for Crime," *JSS*, 17 (1882), 71–98; Rev. George B. Cheever in "The Death Penalty," *NAR*, 133 (1881), 541; "Maine," *AC* (1883); J. M. Buckley, "Capital Punishment," *Forum*, 3 (1887), 381–391; "Kansas," *AC* (1882).

There were frequent charges that the lax character of criminal law encouraged lawbreakers. A North Carolina Supreme Court judge argued that lynching, "evil that it is," also was "a protest of society against the utter inefficiency of the courts . . . to protect the public against murder. It is an evidence that society, under that first of laws, the right of self-preservation, is endeavoring to protect itself when the costly machinery of the courts has failed." Procedural subtleties, the time it took to obtain a conviction, the readiness of appellate courts to grant new trials: all came in for criticism. Roscoe Pound thought that the "hypertrophy" of criminal procedure "reached its high point about 1875" and "began to show signs of abating about 1890." Prominent New York attorney David Dudley Field complained to the American Bar Association that it was unconscionably difficult to convict a criminal in the United States, and sought to simplify procedure through a criminal code (adopted by New York and California). By 1900, thirteen states had abolished the unanimous jury requirement in criminal cases.[30]

The areas of conduct subject to penal sanctions grew in the mid- and late nineteenth century. They came to include a long list of social and economic crimes, ranging from the threat to subvert state government to the sale and use of alcohol or adulterated food and drugs, as well as more traditional criminal acts. Similarly, the trend in criminal law (one that became more pronounced in the early twentieth century) was to modify the rule that criminal statutes had to be strictly construed and that doubt always had to be resolved in favor of the accused. The decline of the doctrine of specific intent, the diminishing inclination to accept the defense of mistake in fact or law, and the growing use of presumption of guilt contributed to the stiffening of American criminal law. Perhaps because of the unsettled character of American society, United States criminal law rested heavily on the assumption that private wrongs had public consequences. In Britain, a felony action was supposed to come from the party injured by the crime. But in

30. "Lynching: How Far the Courts Are Responsible for its Prevalence," *ALR*, 33 (1899), 597; Roscoe Pound, *Criminal Justice in America* (New York, 1930), 165; on Field, *ABA Reports* (1889), 227 ff; on juries, *ALR*, 34 (1900), 248. See also I. C. Parker, "How to Arrest the Increase of Homicides in America," *NAR*, 162 (1896), 667–673; W. H. Whittaker, "Prosecution and Defense under the Present System," *ALRec*, 8 (1879–1880), 129–135; "Justice and Magistracy in the United States," *LT*, 50 (1871), 496.

America a criminal proceeding was instituted by a public prose-
cutor; the district attorney was an American invention.[31]

The harshest system of punishment was the convict lease system
of the South. By the early 1880s every southern state but South
Carolina, Texas, and Virginia leased its convicts to private contractors; 90 percent of this involuntary workforce was black. The
mortality rates of convict lessees, and of those in county
workcamps, were staggering. In 1881, 125 of Mississippi's 876 convicts died. The annual death rate was 10 to 15 percent through the
decade, and was twice as high for black as for white convicts. An
1888 investigation of conditions in Arkansas's Coal Hill convict
labor camp uncovered horrendous living conditions and instances
of torture that were all too common throughout the South. The
prisons themselves were little better. A Virginia inquiry in 1896
revealed that over 1,200 male convicts were crammed into 190 cells.
Conditions were if anything worse in the county jails, as an 1898
Alabama report made clear.

But the economic utility of convict leasing was a powerful
incentive. S. L. James & Company had a profitable monopoly of
the Louisiana lease system through the late nineteenth century.
Florida in 1891 leased all of its convicts to one contractor, who
subleased them to turpentine farms, phosphate mines, and plantations. Large numbers of South Carolina convicts were leased to the
state's phosphate mining companies; Mississippi in 1893 leased all
but 125 of its state penitentiary inmates to planters.

The horrors of the system led to sporadic attempts to reform or
eliminate it. The annual death rate of Alabama's convict laborers
supposedly dropped from 25 percent to 5 percent after stricter state
controls were imposed in 1883. Boards of Managers were created in
Alabama (1892) and Arkansas (1893) to supervise the treatment of
leased convict labor. The South Carolina Supreme Court decided

31. Livingston Hall, "The Substantive Law of Crimes—1887–1936,"
HLR, 50 (1937), 616–653; Thomas M. Cooley, *A Treatise on the Law of
Torts*, 2d ed. (Chicago, 1888), 101; Delmar Karlen, *Anglo-American Crim-
inal Justice* (New York, 1967), 19, 21. See also Samuel J. Barrows, *New
Legislation Concerning Crimes, Misdemeanors, and Penalties* (Washing-
ton, 1900). Less than three out of every thousand convicted felons in
turn-of-the-century New York County secured a reversal on appeal: Simeon
E. Baldwin, *The American Judiciary* (New York, 1905), 250.

in 1894 that chain gangs were unconstitutional. Laws under which "vagrants" could be sold to contractors for terms of years were voided (Kentucky, 1899) or repealed (Missouri, 1897). The 1890 Mississippi constitution and the Louisiana constitution of 1898 ended the convict leasing system in those states. But state and county chain gangs and work camps continued into the twentieth century, to remain the most notorious scandal in the American penal system.[32]

Prison reform in the North continued to elicit some interest, but less than in earlier times. As the number of convicts mounted, hopes for rehabilitation ebbed, and prison policy and practice focused on discipline and a placid inmate population. It says much about the prevailing value system that the major change in late nineteenth century northern prisons came through a union campaign against contract labor. A New York referendum in 1883 produced a 60 percent majority (and a 9 to 1 margin in New York City) against convicts producing manufactured goods. New York and Ohio passed laws forbidding the transportation of prison-made articles. When the courts voided these acts because they interfered with interstate commerce, Congress nearly enacted a law forbidding convict-made goods from being shipped across state lines. Several states (among them Illinois in 1886 and Minnesota in 1894) flatly forbade prison contract labor, and New York's Fassett bill of 1889 restricted convict work to rehabilitation purposes. Massachusetts in 1897 abolished prison-work contracts, and adopted a state-use system. Belief in the curative value of useful labor had little chance when it came into conflict with the late nineteenth century quest of economic groups for protection from "unfair" competition.[33]

For all their severity, American criminology and penology could not free themselves from the tension between the belief that the polity must check social disorder and the belief in individual rights

32. Blake McKelvey, *American Prisons: A Study in American Social History Prior to 1915* (Chicago, 1936), ch. 8; *AC*, states and years cited; Mark T. Carleton, *Politics and Punishment: The History of the Louisiana State Penal System* (Baton Rouge, 1971) Jane Zimmerman, "The Penal Reform Movement in the South during the Progressive Era, 1890–1917," *JSH*, 17 (1951), 462–492.

33. McKelvey, *American Prisons*, ch. 5; *AC*, states and years cited.

and the rehabilitation of criminals. A growing body of professionals —wardens, doctors, criminologists—had a stake in the belief that criminals could be reformed. The National Prison Association, revived in the early 1880s after a period of stagnation, represented their views. John Peter Altgeld, later a reform governor of Illinois, attacked the abuses of the state's prison system in *The Penal Machinery and Its Victims* (1884). Robert G. Ingersoll, a lawyer and Republican orator who thrilled large audiences with boldly atheistic public lectures, argued that severe punishment did not deter crime: "As long as children are raised in the tenement and gutter, the prisons will be full."[34]

There were intermittent attempts in the late nineteenth century to make criminal prosecution and punishment more humane. Over a dozen state legislatures in 1896 considered acts to set up public defenders who would be officers of the court. Iowa's governor urged in 1881 that new convicts be segregated from their more experienced fellows: "a much larger proportion of the younger class of criminals ... would become good citizens ... if it were not for the contaminating influence of older, vicious, and hardened convicts with whom they are compelled to work ... during their term of service." Minor reforms occasionally cropped up. Indiana (1892) allowed prisoners a free hour in their cells and provided a private box for their complaints. Connecticut (1898) divided prisoners into three grades according to their "antecedents, disposition, and prison conduct." The Elmira Penitentiary in New York, whose warden was Zebulon Brockway, attracted much attention for its innovations during the 1870s. But by the 1890s it was accused of being no less harsh than other American prisons.[35]

While prison conditions altered little in the late nineteenth century, important changes occurred in sentencing, probation, and parole. Laws permitting indeterminate sentences were adopted in a

34. David J. Rothman, *The Discovery of the Asylum: Social Order and Disorder in the New Republic* (Boston, 1971), chs. 3–4; McKelvey, *American Prisons*, ch. 4; Altgeld essay reprinted in his *Live Questions: Including Our Penal Machinery and Its Victims* (Chicago, 1890); Robert G. Ingersoll, "Crimes against Criminals," *ALR*, 24 (1890), 204.

35. Clara Foltz, "Public Defenders," *ALR*, 31 (1897), 393–403; "Iowa," *AC* (1881); "Indiana," *AC* (1892); "Connecticut," *AC* (1898); on Brockway, McKelvey, *American Prisons*, 108–115. See also Harold M. Helfman, "Party Politics and Michigan Prisons, 1883–5," *MH*, 33 (1949), 240–247.

number of states. Massachusetts's pioneering probation act passed in 1878. By 1898, twenty-five states had some sort of parole law. The Ohio, Illinois, and Indiana supreme courts upheld these acts, but flexible sentences and terms of imprisonment did not go unchallenged. Parole boards were held to be unconstitutional in several instances, on the grounds that they encroached on the executive's pardoning power and gave prison authorities an essentially judicial role.

The persisting ambivalence in criminal law appeared in an 1891 Michigan Supreme Court decision. An 1889 state law allowed a trial judge to levy indeterminate sentences, which would be reviewed and could be terminated by a Board of Prison Control. The court found the law to be unconstitutional, in part because it threatened to inundate the state with prematurely freed criminals and in part because those criminals would be subject to reincarceration by a Board with the "despotic" power to impose standards of behavior on them. The opinion was a revealing expression of the unresolved tension between the fear of social disorder and the commitment to individual liberty that so frequently surfaced in the public life of late nineteenth century America.[36]

That ambivalence emerged, too, in controversy over whipping as a form of punishment. Delaware won national attention for its frequent use of the whipping post. An 1882 Maryland law—approved by the state supreme court—permitted the use of the lash on those convicted of wife beating. A commission of the American Bar Association in 1886 recommended the reinstatement of whipping for this and other assaults on the weak and helpless, and for the use of weapons such as brass knuckles and blackjacks. But after extensive and heated debate the association defeated the proposal. Virginia repealed its whipping post law in 1882, and an attempt in Indiana to institute that form of punishment was defeated.

Capital punishment also engendered mixed emotions. Tennessee and Arkansas ended public executions in the 1880s. A New York commission in 1887, charged with finding the most humane

---

36. Albert J. Harno, "Some Significant Developments in Criminal Law and Procedure in the Last Century," *JCL*, 42 (1951), 440 ff; State *v.* Peters, 43 Ohio St. 629 (1885); George *v.* Illinois, 167 Ill. 447 (1897); Miller *v.* State, 149 Ind. 607 (1898); People *v.* Cummings, 88 Mich. 249 (1891). See also Freund, *Police Power*, 103–108.

method of inflicting the death penalty, settled on the electric chair. In 1889, final review of death sentences in the federal system was raised from the circuit courts to the Supreme Court. The Curtis Act of 1897 ended capital punishment under the federal code for all crimes but murder and rape. Before this, the United States Code had been one of the most sanguine in the world, specifying sixty offenses that were punishable by death.[37]

The English jurist Henry Maine observed of British criminal law in 1864: "All the old theories on the subject of punishment have more or less broken down. We are again at sea as to first principles."[38] The same could be said of the late nineteenth century United States. The old severity was under assault by a new humanitarianism, the old moral certitude by relativistic views of human behavior. At the same time, traditional approaches to crime were buttressed by a belief in its hereditary sources and by rising fears of social disorder. The resulting indeterminacy had its fullest effect on criminal law, penology, and criminology in the twentieth century. But even before 1900, new social conditions were intensifying the ambiguities inherent in modern society's treatment of criminals.

The Ills of Mankind

The ills of mankind—disease, insanity, poverty—posed problems for late nineteenth century Americans not unlike those raised by violence and crime. The very existence of these maladies implied an inability to cope that did not sit well with a people convinced of their omnipotence, and posed a threat to social order. But, as was the case with violence and crime, other values limited the capacity of the polity to take remedial action. Popular pressure for government economy and hostility to an active state, the persisting belief

37. "Delaware," "Maryland," AC (1882); Foote v. State, 59 Md. 264 (1882); ABA Reports (1886), 286–292; (1887), 55–78; "Virginia," AC (1882); "Indiana," AC (1881); "The Death Penalty in the United States," GB, 9 (1887), 129–131; David K. Watson, "Growth of Criminal Law of the United States," U.S., 57th Cong. 1st sess., House, Doc. no. 362. See also "Whipping Not a Cruel and Unusual Punishment," CLM, 4 (1883), 401–410; Lewis Hochheimer, "The Whipping-Post," PSM, 28 (1886), 830–834.
38. Maine quoted in Harno, "Significant Developments," 427.

that unfortunates were responsible for their own condition, and the assumption that sickness and poverty were due to unalterable social or hereditarian laws weakened the social welfare capacity of the late nineteenth century polity.

The major exception was public health. The social rate of return on late nineteenth century public health expenditure appears to have been at least as great as the potential market rate of return on that investment. The health of the American people improved markedly during these years. In New York City, for example, the use of diphtheria serum, the treatment of tuberculosis as an infectious disease, a permit system for milk distribution, tenement health inspection, and medical supervision in the schools drastically reduced the infant and child mortality rate. Massachusetts's rate of infant mortality dropped from 161.3 per 1,000 in 1880–1884 to 141.4 per 1,000 in 1900–1904. In 1886 that state's Board of Health was separated from the Board of Health, Lunacy, and Charity, a tribute to the growing success of medical science.[39]

The courts posed no serious obstacles to increasingly strict state quarantine laws, nor did Congress raise the objection that they interfered with interstate commerce. But when public health policies directly clashed with individual and property rights, difficulties arose. A number of states permitted compulsory vaccination only if there was an imminent danger of epidemic. And state and city boards of health were under constant pressure to balance their power to abate nuisances and threats to public health against their obligation to respect constitutional safeguards to property. Finally, state and local interests and conflicts of government jurisdiction blocked the development of a strong federal health agency. A national Board of Health created in 1879, and an attempt to establish a federal Department of Public Health at the end of the century, ran afoul of state and local public health interests and the internecine struggles of the federal bureaucracy.[40]

39. Edward Meeker, "The Social Rate of Return on Investment in Public Health, 1880–1910," *JEH*, 34 (1974), 392–421, "The Improving Health of the United States, 1850–1915," *EEH*, 9 (1972), 353–373; "New York City," *AC* (1897); *HS*, 26; Barbara G. Rosenkrantz, *Public Health and the State: Changing Views in Massachusetts, 1842–1936* (Cambridge, 1972), 72.

40. William H. Cowles, "State Quarantine Laws and the Federal Constitution," *ALR*, 25 (1891), 45–73; "Quarantine and Health Laws and Regulations," *AStR*, 47 (1896), 533–552; G. W. Field, "Boards of Health," *ALR*,

Changing economic and social conditions produced human needs that engulfed existing welfare institutions. State welfare expenditures rose substantially in the late nineteenth century. Half of New York City's 1890 budget went for health, education, and welfare. But this was far from meeting the needs of an urban-industrial society. In 1886, New York's hospitals and welfare institutions harbored 63,335 ill, insane, poor, delinquent, or abandoned persons; another 49,144 were quartered in private homes with public aid. Lightly populated, nonindustrial states were no better off. Texas's insane asylums were filled in 1898, and a thousand additional sufferers were lodged in jails, poor farms, and private homes. Oregon's state asylum in 1896 housed a yeasty mix of drunkards, morphine addicts, paupers, the mentally disturbed, and the physically disabled—at a monthly maintenance cost of $8.58 per inmate.

Meagerly financed institutions often were crippled by politics and patronage. An investigation of Iowa's state asylums in 1898 found them to be inefficient and corrupt, costing $150,000 a year more than was necessary. But it was the pressure for economy that had the most catastrophic consequences. Annual per capita costs in the South Carolina Hospital for the Insane dropped from $133.42 in 1891 to $107.80 in 1896. Virginia reduced her appropriations for charitable institutions in 1898. As a result, insane blacks previously housed in Petersburg Central Hospital were relocated to the counties—and in many cases were lodged in those ineffable institutions the county jails.[41]

There was constant legislative tinkering with social welfare laws. By the 1890s, acts dealing with the "unfortunate" or the "depraved" were an important category of state lawmaking. But this legislation led to no significant change in public policy. California's

24 (1890), 559–579; Freund, Police Power, 478; George M. Sternberg, "A National Health Bureau," NAR, 158 (1894), 529–533; U. O. B. Wingate, "National Public Health Legislation," NAR, 167 (1898), 527–533; George E. Waring, Jr., "The National Board of Health," AM, 44 (1879), 732–738; A. Hunter Dupree, Science in the Federal Government (Cambridge, 1957), 258–263.

41. C. K. Yearley, The Money Machines (Albany, 1970), 25; AC, states and years cited. See also "Charities in the United States," AC (1899); C. R. Henderson, "Politics in Public Institutions of Charity and Correction," ASR, 4 (1898–1899), 202–234.

Pauper Act of 1901 faithfully adhered to the spirit of the Elizabethan Poor Laws. Politics and feuding agencies often affected welfare policy. New York Democrats in the mid-eighties wanted a paid superintendent of charities to replace the existing unpaid Board; the Republican legislature blocked this attempt to increase the authority of a Democratic governor. The New York Institution for the Blind and the Society for the Prevention of Cruelty to Children fiercely contested the power of the state Board of Charity to inspect private welfare institutions.

If there was any noticeable trend in the treatment of the needy, it was toward increasingly specialized classification. The physically handicapped were sorted into the deaf, the dumb, and the blind; the mentally disturbed into the insane and the idiotic; the poor into the deserving and undeserving, the resident, transient, and alien. Abandoned children increasingly were handled through a separate legal process and sent to separate institutions. This development stemmed not from any significant change in welfare concepts, but from the growing numbers of the needy and from the precepts (and self-interest) of expanding hospital and asylum bureaucracies.[42]

The treatment of two major classes of unfortunates—the insane and the poor—throws light on the character of social welfare policy in the late nineteenth century.

In theory, the law assured a substantial measure of due process to those facing commitment to mental institutions. A judicial hearing was necessary, except for the temporary restraint of a dangerous person. The Minnesota Supreme Court voided, as an unconstitutional deprivation of liberty, a state law that allowed commitment after an *ex parte* examination without a full hearing. The prevailing judicial assumption was that the state had the relationship of a guardian or a ward to the insane. Asylums were hospitals, not prisons.

42. On California, Joel F. Handler, ed., *Family Law and the Poor: Essays by Jacobus ten Broek* (Westport, Conn., 1971), 105–110; David M. Schneider and Albert Deutsch, *The History of Public Welfare in New York State 1867–1940* (Chicago, 1941), II, 31–32, 89 ff, 107 ff; Martha Branscombe, *The Courts and the Poor Laws in New York State 1784–1929* (Chicago, 1943), 390. See also Gerald N. Grob, *Mental Institutions in America: Social Policy to 1875* (New York, 1973), ch. 7.

But in practice the insane often were treated as one of the "dangerous classes" of society, a category that included drunkards, vagrants and beggars, the bearers of contagious diseases, and criminals. It was considered proper to adopt "any mode of reasonable punishment" to keep order within insane asylums. The 1883 Nebraska legislature found it necessary to pass a law allowing inmates in the state Hospital for the Insane to write one letter a week and post it without censorship. California sought to deport her Chinese insane, and thus save about $60,000 a year in maintenance costs. Occasional investigations made it clear that, however great the legal distinction, in practice mental institutions had much in common with prisons. In both cases, political corruption, popular indifference, uncertainty as to cause and cure, and a pervasive fear of social deviance stifled innovation or improvement.[43]

The industrial depression of the 1870s sharply increased (and thus made more visible) the numbers of the poor and the unemployed in America's cities. For perhaps the first time the polity had to recognize that poverty was both real and substantial in the United States.

The initial response was "outdoor" poor relief: that is, direct public doles of food, clothing, and cash without concern for the moral state or socioeconomic status of the recipient. New York City in 1877 aided over 46,000 people. Other cities provided outdoor relief on a comparable scale.

But the potential for waste and corruption in this form of assistance jarred middle class sensibilities. Seth Low, a prominent New York merchant and civic reformer, offered a typical judgment: "The 'outdoor relief' appropriations became a vast political corruption fund." What was more, the system failed to distinguish between the truly needy and those who falsified their need. The conse-

43. Thomas M. Cooley, "Confinement of the Insane," *SLR*, ns, 5 (1880), 568–585; Tiedeman, *Limitations of Police Power*, 110–114; F. H. Wines, "The Law for the Commitment of Lunatics," *JSS*, 20 (1885), 61–77; State v. Billings, 55 Minn. 467 (1893); "Due Process of Law as Applied to Insane Persons," *AStR*, 43 (1895), 531–541; Tiedeman, "Police Control of Dangerous Classes," 556; "Nebraska," *AC* (1883); "California," *AC* (1898); Dr. Henry S. Williams, "Politics and the Insane," *NAR*, 161 (1895), 394–404. See also Allen M. Hamilton, "The Legal Safeguards of Sanity and the Protection of the Insane," *NAR*, 172 (1901), 241–249.

quence was not only a waste of public funds but the moral corruption of the recipients.[44]

These attitudes spurred the Charity Organization movement of the late nineteenth century. Based on an English prototype of the 1860s, Charity Organization Societies were established in a number of American cities during the late seventies and the eighties. The American founder of the movement, Josephine Shaw Lowell, believed that charity "must tend to develop the moral nature of those it helps." That moralism was to be inculcated by planned and purposeful help to the poor. In this sense, charity was "quite a different thing from alms." She and her coadjutors argued that "the task of dealing with the poor and degraded has become a science" —"our science."[45]

Chilling social Darwinist assumptions could be derived from this approach: "If the chief reason for governmental interference lies in the failure of the struggle for existence to bring about the survival of the fittest in the moral and economical sense, then all measures which do not aim ultimately at this result are but palliatives, not remedies." True "humanity" was to be distinguished from "weak sentimentalism" when one dealt with the hereditary sources of poverty. Under the pressure of Mrs. Lowell and others, New York in 1878 opened an asylum for feebleminded women of childbearing age: the first attempt to cut off the hereditary origins of pauperism and insanity. A leading text in the field, Amos Warner's *American Charities* (1894), stressed the importance of inherited physical and mental defects.[46]

44. Leah H. Feder, *Unemployment Relief in Periods of Depression* (New York, 1936), ch. 3; Ringenbach, *Tramps and Reformers*, chs. 1–3; Low quoted in Schneider and Deutsch, *Public Welfare*, II, 48; Octave Thanet, "The Indoor Pauper: A Study," *AM*, 47 (1881), 749–764, 48 (1881), 241–252.

45. See in general David Owen, *English Philanthropy 1660–1960* (Cambridge, 1964), part three, ch. 8, Kathleen Woodroofe, *From Charity to Social Work in England and the United States* (London, 1962), and Robert H. Bremner, *From the Depths: The Discovery of Poverty in the United States* (New York, 1956); Josephine Shaw Lowell, *Public Relief and Private Charity* (New York, 1884), 110–111, 105.

46. Frank D. Watson, *The Charity Organization Movement in the United States* (New York, 1922), 264; Henry W. Farnum, "The State and the Poor," *PSQ*, 3 (1888), 297, 303; Mark H. Haller, *Eugenics: Hereditarian Attitudes in American Thought* (New Brunswick, 1963), 28 ff. See also

The eminently scientific paradigm that equated charity with disease had a strong appeal: "Charity Organization believes that pauperism is not only a disease, but a contagious one, and that like all diseases it can be materially reduced by proper treatment in a scientific way." Poverty's "presence in a well-regulated community need be no more frequent than any other contagion; . . . its causes are capable of scientific deduction, and . . . it can be materially alleviated by proper measures."

And what were those "proper measures"? Most poverty was the "result of neglect, inattention and misgovernment" by those charged with tending to it. Poverty must be treated by trained professionals. The National Conference of Charities and Corrections (organized in 1874 as an offshoot of the American Social Science Association) espoused a scientific New Charity after 1880. Investigation, statistics-gathering, lawmaking would clear the way for aid to the poor that was both effective and socially desirable. Casework began now as a way of sorting out the "deserving" from the "undeserving" poor. The Reverend H. L. Wayland compared "the Old Charity and the New" in 1886: "where the Old Charity gave a shilling and lost sight of [the poor] . . . , the New follows them, and sees where they sleep and eat, are born and die. It tries by every effort and resource at its command to reconstruct their surroundings."

It was clear that the bestowers of scientific charity had an equivocal relationship to the recipients of their largesse. Jane Addams, discussing "the subtle problems of charity" in 1899, dwelt on the clash between the middle class mores of social workers and the problems and life style of the poor. So did a charity recipient in the 1880s: "Young girls nowadays dress dowdy when they come to see us poor folks, and call it equality. If it were, they wouldn't make such a fuss to hide it. I'd like to see their silks and satins, and hear about their beaux."[47]

Marvin E. Gettleman, "Charity and Social Classes in the United States, 1874–1900," AJES, 22 (1963), 313–329, 417–426.

47. Sheldon T. Viele, "State Legislation and Charity Organization," ALJ, 24 (1881), 346–348; Wayland quoted in Watson, Charity Organization Movement, 277; Jane Addams, "The Subtle Problems of Charity," AM, 83 (1899), 163–178; Kate G. Wells, About People (Boston, 1885), 114. See also Nathan I. Huggins, Protestants against Poverty: Boston's Charities, 1870–1900 (Westport, Conn., 1971).

Science, humanitarianism, and class interest joined in the New Charity to justify reductions in relief expenditures. The New York State Board of Charities in 1877 ascribed the condition of the poor "to their own faults, to injudicious treatment by officials, or to the unwise charity of the public." It was "scientifically" calculated that not more than 10 percent of the poor were "worthy paupers reduced to that condition by causes outside of their own acts."

These attitudes had measurable consequences. Work requirements and means tests (along with the economic upswing of the late 1870s) reduced the number of aided Cleveland families from 4,590 to 1,200. Providence relief expenditures went from $150,051 in 1878 to $7,333 a year later. Outdoor relief ended in Brooklyn (1878) and Philadelphia (1879); New York City restricted its welfare to the provision of coal in the winter and cash grants to the blind. When the depression of the 1890s created massive new poverty and unemployment, work requirements for relief were far more frequent than they had been twenty years before. The New York Association for Improving the Condition of the Poor opposed soup houses in the nineties because they did not distinguish between those who deserved succor and those who did not.[48]

The twentieth century conception of professional social work as the proper mode for dealing with the poor was an outgrowth of rather than a reaction to late nineteenth century developments. Concern over housing and slums, legal aid for the poor, care for dependent children, and the active role of the caseworker had become part of the charity-social work arsenal by the 1890s.

But these approaches developed hand-in-hand with social assumptions that severely limited their utility. They included an attempt to distinguish between the deserving and the undeserving poor, a growing belief in the racial and hereditary sources of poverty, and strong public pressure to economize as much as possible on welfare expenditure. The fear of poverty as a threat to the social order stimulated public and private action; old and new beliefs as to poverty's sources severely limited the scope of that response.

48. Viele, "State Legislation," 347; ibid., *NYSBA Reports*, 5 (1881), 168; on New York City, Schneider and Deutsch, *Public Welfare*, 46–50. See also "Charities of the United States," *AC* (1899).

Public Mores

When Kansas's Populist legislature of 1897 considered a bill designed to give statutory force to the Ten Commandments, this reflected something more than rural eccentricity. An old inclination to regulate public mores found new life in the age of American industrialization. The social values of individualism and laissez-faire had worked against such controls in the middle of the century. But the persistence of religious morality, combined with the social tensions and anxieties that came with industrialism, reinvigorated the impulse to regulate individual behavior. "Moral statistics" detailed the scope and growth of intemperance, gambling, divorce; and the polity was called on to check these threats to social order.[49]

The separation of church and state and the constitutional guarantee of religious freedom generally kept the polity from interfering with religious beliefs and practices. But religious observance and social morality were intimately connected, and the distinction between the realms of church and state was not always clear.

A leading treatise of the time observed that "the law cannot but recognize the fact that Christianity is in the main the religion of this country." There still was an occasional survival of the old concern with blasphemy. The atheist lecturer Robert G. Ingersoll came before a Morristown, New Jersey court in 1887 charged with violating the state's blasphemy law. The judge gave unequivocal instructions to the jury—"I want you to see that you yourselves do not violate the law by acquitting him"—and Ingersoll was duly convicted. Senator Henry Blair of New Hampshire proposed a constitutional amendment in 1888 affirming that the United States government was established in accordance with the "principles of the Christian religion," which Congress might enforce by appropriate laws. A National Reform Association lobbied for the amendment's passage. But the effort to give official status to Christianity foundered on the strong belief in the separation of church and

49. Theodore D. Woolsey, "Moral Statistics of the United States," *JSS*, 14 (1881), 129–135; "Kansas," *AC* (1897). See also William W. Wheildon, *Blue Laws of Massachusetts Bay and Connecticut* (n.p., 1886).

state, and on the fact that the supporters of the amendment were outspokenly anti-Catholic.[50]

The resurgence of Sunday blue laws showed how traditional religiosity and new social anxieties interfused in the late nineteenth century. The ostensible purpose of this legislation was to make Sunday a national day of rest for American workingmen. The ubiquitous Blair of New Hampshire introduced a congressional bill to this effect in 1888. Organized labor lent its support. Massachusetts in 1880 reenacted its Puritan Sunday laws—with exemptions befitting an industrial, urban society. It allowed the provision of steam, gas, electricity, and water, the operation of railroads, telephones, the telegraph, and bath houses, and the sale of medicine, newspapers, milk, and bread.

The usual rationale for these laws was the state police power to safeguard the health and morals of the citizenry. But their major support came from religious spokesmen such as the American Sabbath Union. And occasionally the courts accepted them on religious grounds. The Nebraska Supreme Court, approving a ban on Sunday baseball, intoned: "From the crucifixion of Christ until the present time the contest between Christianity and wrong has been going on." In 1896 the New York Court of Appeals upheld a ban on the Sunday operation of barber shops (except in New York City and the resort town of Saratoga Springs), arguing: "It is to the interest of the state to have strong, robust, healthy citizens, capable of self-support, of bearing arms, and of adding to the resources of the country." Barbers, it noted, had particularly long working days. It seems evident that a judiciary not conspicuous for its concern over the hours of labor was approving a regulation of social mores more than a guaranty of public health.[51]

---

50. Tiedeman, *Limitations of Police Power*, 160; John D. Lawson, *American State Trials* (St. Louis, 1928), XVI, 837; on Blair amendment, Alonzo T. Jones, *Civil Government and Religion, or Christianity and the American Constitution* (Chicago, 1889), 43–64. See also Thomas M. Cooley, *A Treatise on the Constitutional Limitations which Rest upon the Legislative Power of the States* (1868; 7th ed., Boston, 1903), ch. 13; *AEEL*, IV, 580–582.

51. Manfred Jonas, "The American Sabbath in the Gilded Age," *Jahrbuch für Amerikastudien*, 6 (1961), 89–144; Raymond L. Bridgman, *Ten Years of Massachusetts* (Boston, 1888), 43–44; State v. O'Rourke, 35 Neb. 614, 623 (1892); People v. Havnor, 149 N.Y. 195, 203–204 (1896). See also Hennington v. Georgia, 163 U.S. 299 (1896); James T. Ringgold, "Sunday Laws in the United States," *ALReg*, ns, 3 (1892), 723–740; J. A. Woerner, "Sunday and Sunday Laws," *ALR*, 18 (1884), 778–800.

The courts frequently were called on to weigh the practices of religious sects against the interests and standards of the larger society. A number of states—Massachusetts, Michigan, and New York among them—allowed Jews and Sabbatarians to work on Sunday, but only if others were not disturbed. The scruples of Quakers and other religious groups against bearing arms were not accepted as grounds for avoiding militia duty. An ordinance prohibiting Salvation Army street activities was held to be a proper police regulation. And while the courts generally accorded Christian Science and other faith healing sects the constitutional protection of religious freedom, they held that a failure to call for medical aid could be a civil offense. Mormon polygamy was one of the few religious practices that became an object of legislative prohibition. The Supreme Court upheld federal and state antipolygamy statutes on the ground that "acts inimical to the peace, good order and morals of society" could not be countenanced. Opinion might run free; behavior was another matter.[52]

Gambling was widely sanctioned in early nineteenth century America. Lotteries frequently paid for college buildings and supplemented state incomes. But opposition grew on moral, religious, and social grounds, and a number of northern states banned the practice before the Civil War.

State lotteries sprang up in the postwar South, to become an important source of revenue (and, as it turned out, corruption). The Louisiana lottery was a major institution, involving the state's political and economic leaders and attracting many out-of-state players. Legislatures and courts reacted strongly against a practice that many regarded as officially sanctioned immorality. The Supreme Court in 1876 upheld an Alabama law abolishing a privately owned state lottery, Justice Field arguing that the legislature could "suppress any and all practices tending to corrupt the public morals." Chief Justice Waite, sustaining a Mississippi antilottery act, observed that gambling and lotteries "disturb the checks and balances of a well-ordered community." By 1890, forty-three of the forty-four states had antilottery laws, and in that year Congress forbade the use of the mails to send lottery announcements and prizes.

52. Freund, *Police Powers*, 498; Reynolds v. United States, 98 U.S. 145 (1878); Davis v. Beason, 133 U.S. 333, 342 (1890).

The Louisiana lottery was ended in 1892. In Champion v. Ames (1903)—a milestone in the development of Congress's power to regulate interstate commerce—the Supreme Court upheld an act that forbade lottery tickets from being sent across state lines. The lotteries' aura of immorality—of being a threat to the good order of society—made their control an important chapter in the development of modern American economic regulation.[53]

Similar constraints applied to professional sports and gambling. Antibetting laws were common in the late nineteenth century, as were acts regulating horse racing and prohibiting prize fights. Racing interests induced the New York (1887) and New Jersey (1893) legislatures to remove some of their restrictions. The antigambling reaction was strong: New York in 1893 made off-track bookmaking a felony and in 1895 put race tracks under the supervision of a State Racing Commission. New Jersey's 1894 legislature hurriedly repealed its permissive law of the previous year. Indiana severely limited the racing season at its tracks, and Missouri's Supreme Court, sustaining an 1897 act that prohibited offtrack bookmaking, declared: "Any practice, the tendency of which is to corrupt the morals of those who participate in, or witness its practice, is a proper subject of regulation by the State; and that 'book-making and pool-selling' and betting upon horse racing are demoralizing in their tendencies, and hence evils which the law may legitimately suppress, without infringing upon the constitutional rights of any citizen, is no longer an open question."[54]

The mix of old morality and new social fears that fed antigambling sentiment also stimulated efforts to prohibit or control the use of tobacco, drugs, and—most of all—alcohol.

The growth of large-scale cigarette manufacture and use led to

53. John S. Ezell, *Fortune's Merry Wheel: The Lottery in America* (Cambridge, 1960); Boyd v. Alabama, 94 U.S. 645, 650 (1876); Stone v. Mississippi, 101 U.S. 814, 821 (1880); Ex parte Rapier, 143 U.S. 110 (1892); Champion v. Ames, 188 U.S. 321 (1903).

54. Daniel J. Boorstin, *The Americans: The Democratic Experience* (New York, 1973), 72–80; McSeveney, *Politics of Depression*, 45–46; State v. Roby, 142 Ind. 168 (1895); State v. Thompson, 160 Mo. 333, 341–342 (1896). See also Anthony Comstock, "Pool Rooms and Pool Selling," *NAR*, 157 (1893), 601–610; William B. Curtis, "Increase in Gambling and Its Forms," *Forum*, 12 (1891), 281–292.

restrictive legislation. An 1881 Massachusetts law nicely linked social and political morality by prohibiting smoking in polling places during elections. A number of states in the 1890s flatly forbade the manufacture or importation of cigarettes, or set minimum age limits on its use. The Tennessee Supreme Court in 1900 upheld that state's anticigarette law, arguing with passion that cigarettes were not legitimate articles of commerce because they were "wholly noxious and deleterious to health . . . They possess no virtue, but are inherently bad, and bad only."

The late nineteenth century saw the beginnings, too, of attempts to suppress the distribution and use of narcotics. Morphine, widely used as an anesthetic during the Civil War, had an important place in the pharmacology of the time. The use of opium spread with the coming of the Chinese. Doctors used cocaine from the mid-eighties and heroin after 1898 to treat morphine and alcohol addiction (much as methadone has been used for heroin addicts in recent times). Patent medicines frequently contained substantial amounts of morphine and alcohol. It was estimated at the end of the century that between a quarter and half a million Americans were drug-addicted.

Nevada in 1877 passed the first law prohibiting the sale of opiates for nonmedical purposes: a statute directed at its Chinese residents. Michigan's Board of Health published a pioneering compilation of data on drug addiction in 1878, and state antimorphine and antiopium laws began to spread in the late eighties. But by 1900 drug regulation still was spotty and rarely enforced. Legislation (as in the case of an 1897 Pennsylvania statute) often was designed not to prohibit the sale of patent medicines containing drugs, but to prevent their adulteration. Much of the pressure for these laws came from the American Pharmaceutical Association, which sought to protect its members from the competition of free-lance patent medicine distributors rather than to shield the public from narcotics. Regulation was impeded, too, by the fact that addiction was confined to the alien and isolated Chinese, cocaine-using blacks, and social groups (morphine-addicted doctors, women taking drug-laced patent medicine at home) not likely to be regarded as appropriate subjects of social control.[55]

55. Massachusetts," *AC* (1881); Austin v. State, 101 Tenn. 563, 566 (1898); David F. Musto, *The American Disease: Origins of Narcotic Con-*

The consumption of alcohol was by far the most important object of social regulation in late nineteenth century America. The crusade against drink was complex and long-lasting. Its initial early nineteenth century goal was temperance: that is, self-restraint. But by the middle of the century outright prohibition was at least as important. Self-control merged with the regulation of others: immigrants, Catholics, blacks, city-dwellers. As in so many other areas of social control, a mix of religious moralism and fear of social disorder fed the late nineteenth century antiliquor movement. In this sense it was the most conspicuous instance of a general effort to control the mores of a society in flux.

The evolution of the Woman's Christian Temperance Union typified the course of the movement against drink. Organized in 1874, the WCTU quickly moved from temperance and strict saloon licensing to outright prohibition; from self-restraint to regulation and coercion; from its rural and small town origins in Maine and Iowa to the major industrial states. Characteristic too was the Law and Order League of the United States, a national alliance of local organizations pledged to enforce prohibition, which stemmed from the New York Society for the Prevention of Crime and in 1887 claimed over 700 chapters and 100,000 members.

On December 27, 1876, Senator Blair of New Hampshire proposed the first national prohibition amendment, to take effect in 1900. His model was the Constitution's prohibition of the slave trade. (Thereafter a prohibition amendment was continuously before Congress until the enactment of the Eighteenth Amendment in 1918.) Blair argued: "Alcohol is a political issue that more truly concerns national politics than it does the politics of the several States." He expected southern whites, fearful of the effects of drink on the black population, to support national prohibition, and generously predicted: "Upon discussion of this issue the Irishman

---

trol (New Haven, 1973), ch. 1. See also Troy Duster, *The Legislation of Morality: Law, Drugs and Moral Judgment* (New York, 1970); Richard J. Bonnie and Charles H. Whitebread II, "The Forbidden Fruit and the Tree of Knowledge: An Inquiry into the Legal History of American Marijuana Prohibition," *VaLR*, 56 (1970), 971–1203; James H. Young, *The Toadstool Millionaires: A Social History of Patent Medicines before Federal Regulation* (Princeton, 1961).

and the German will in due time demonstrate that they are Americans."[56]

But localism, hostility to government, and cultural diversity blocked federal and even state prohibition. By 1903 only Kansas, North Dakota, and Maine had such statutes. More successful was the effort to educate American children on the dangers of drink. Between 1882 and 1902, every state passed a law requiring temperance instruction in the schools, with visual aids that vividly portrayed the physiological effects of alcohol. Congress in 1886 authorized a scientific study of the effects of liquor and narcotics on human beings.

In a number of states the major antiliquor goal was "high licensing." This was a policy that enabled states or localities to control saloons and at the same time extract a substantial public revenue. Ohio's "mulct law" of 1882 imposed a heavy tax on liquor sellers and forbade sales to minors—unless they had the written consent of a parent or doctor.

Other states subscribed to local option: in Indiana by petition, in Massachusetts by the ballot. South Carolina in 1892 enacted a Dispensary Act that set up a system of state-owned liquor stores. And everywhere, statutory regulations abounded. Indiana's 1895 Nicholson temperance bill laid down the joyless conditions under which licensed saloonkeepers might operate. They could sell no more than a quart at a time, "in a room separate from any other business of any kind, and no devices for amusement or music of any . . . character . . . shall be permitted in such room." New York's Raines law of 1896 forbade restaurants from serving liquor on Sunday unless they were in hotels, a stipulation that led many saloons to add sleazy upstairs rooms and thus become houses of prostitution as well as dispensers of alcohol.[57]

56. See in general Joseph R. Gusfield, *Symbolic Crusade: Status Politics and the Temperance Movement* (Champaign-Urbana, 1963); "Law and Order League of the United States," *AC* (1887); Henry W. Blair, "Alcohol in Politics," *NAR*, 138 (1884), 54, 56. See also "Prohibition," *AC* (1883).

57. Ernest H. Cherington, *The Evolution of Prohibition in the United States of America* (Westerville, Ohio, 1920); "Temperance Instruction in Public Schools," *AC* (1891); Clement M. L. Sites, *Centralized Administration of Liquor Laws in the American Commonwealths* (New York, 1899); Charles W. Eliot, "A Study of American Liquor Laws," *AM* 79 (1897), 177–187.

This unhappy result suggests that the regulation of social mores —and particularly of drinking—was a difficult and uncertain matter at best. An 1895 Delaware antiprohibition convention declared: "We believe that our Creator endowed man with the unalterable right to eat and drink whenever his appetite requires, so that it does not interfere with his peace and happiness." Theirs was a not entirely disinterested view—this gathering of saloonkeepers and their supporters wanted the Delaware liquor laws "modified to meet the present state of society and the trade generally"—but it was calculated to evoke a sympathetic popular response. Prohibition frequently lost in state referenda: by a vote of 166,325 to 48,370 in North Carolina (1881); in Texas and Oregon (1887); in Georgia (1899), where the threatened loss of $150,000 in liquor taxes was decisive. Under Georgia's local option law the number of wet counties increased in 1888 from thirty-eight to sixty-four.

Enforcement was even more uncertain. The 1884 conviction rate under Kansas's prohibition law was 79 percent in district courts, but only 34 percent in local justice of the peace courts. When Rhode Island in 1886 passed a prohibitory Act for the Suppression of Intemperance, "clubs," "kitchen bar-rooms," and "pocket peddlars" rose up everywhere to make liquor more available than ever. The later adage that the citizenry of Mississippi would vote for prohibition as long as they could stagger to the polls summed up the ambivalent American attitude toward liquor control. The unhappy national experience with prohibition during the 1920s was amply foreshadowed several generations before.

The courts usually upheld state regulation and prohibition laws. But there were limits. Michigan's Supreme Court in 1894 voided a "jag-cure" act that gave arrested drunks the choice of going to jail or to a curative institution. And a number of Wisconsin magistrates objected to the constitutionality—and the expense—of a statute that compelled inebriates to undergo an elaborate "cold cure." While liquor prohibition had strong and growing appeal as a means of preserving a threatened social order, powerful countervalues worked against public constraints on individual behavior.[58]

The anxieties generated by rapid social change put pressure on

58. *AC*, states and years cited: "Georgia," *AC* (1888); "Kansas," *AC* (1884); "Rhode Island," *AC* (1886); Senate of Happy Home Clubs v. Board,

the polity to regulate sexual mores as well. A broad-gauged movement for what was called "social purity" took form in the late nineteenth century. For many, sexual license no less than drink stemmed from new and unwanted aspects of American life. At the same time a growing middle class (like its Victorian English counterpart) found in sexual prudery a readymade standard of morality and behavior.

The establishment of the New York Society for the Suppression of Vice in 1872 marked the beginning of the social purity crusade. From its confines Anthony Comstock sallied forth to reform the morals of a threatened American society. Comstock relied heavily on the assistance of the state. He was appointed a special agent of the Post Office Department in 1873. And in that year Congress without hearings and after minimal debate passed the Comstock Act, which banned obscene literature from the mails. New York's antiobscenity law was strengthened, and in 1875 Comstock's Society was given the authority to make arrests.[59]

State legislatures, prodded by the Society for the Suppression of Vice and after 1885 by a Social Purity Alliance, passed "little Comstock Acts" forbidding the sale of obscene literature and contraceptives. The courts were supportive. A Kansas federal district court judge in 1891 held that anything "offensive to the common sense of decency and modesty of the community" was obscene, and encouraged the government to act "in protection of the social compact and the body politic." The United States Supreme Court confirmed that Congress had the power to close the mails to "the distribution of matter deemed injurious to the public morals." An 1891 Kansas law banned newspapers that featured illicit relations between men and women. Michigan in 1897 forbade the use of

99 Mich. 117 (1894); "Wisconsin," AC (1895). See also "The American Liquor Laws," ILT, 11 (1877), 227–229, 250–252; L. M. Dorman, "The Relative Operation of Prohibition, Local Option and License Laws," CLM, 5 (1884), 190–210; Ernest H. Crosby, "The Saloon as a Political Power," Forum, 7 (1889), 323–330.

59. David J. Pivar, Purity Crusade: Sexual Morality and Social Control, 1868–1900 (Westport, Conn., 1973); Robert E. Riegel, "Changing American Attitudes toward Prostitution," JHI, 29 (1968), 437–452; Peter T. Cominos, "Late-Victorian Sexual Respectability and the Social System," IRSH, 8 (1963), 18–48, 216–250; Anthony Comstock, Traps for the Young, ed. Robert H. Bremner (1883; Cambridge, 1967); Bremner, ed., Children and Youth, II, 222 ff.

obscene or immoral language in the presence of women or children. Laws prohibited the distribution of pictures depicting fighting, violence, murder, crime, "or any representation of the human figure which would be indecent if a living person so appeared in a public street." The Social Purity Alliance lobbied for sex (or, more accurately, antisex) education in the schools.[60]

But regulation had little effect on behavior. Vice no less than gambling, smoking, and drinking was too attractive (and too profitable) to be squelched. When an 1897 New Orleans city ordinance designated a red light district, the Supreme Court upheld it. Noting that "one of the difficult social problems of the day is what shall be done in respect to those vocations which minister to and feed upon human weaknesses, appetites and passions," the Court concluded that the character of such regulation was up to the states and localities.

Purity reform at times ran afoul of American hostility to the restrictive state. A critic of Comstock observed in 1880: "Is there in this Republic such an officer as a Public Censor, clothed with dictatorial powers, and not responsible to the people?" When a Comstock agent induced a firm selling contraceptive devices to send price and other information to a fictitious potential customer, federal judge John F. Dillon quashed the resulting conviction because of the deception that secured it. The *American Law Review* criticized the barring of Tolstoy's novel *The Kreutzer Sonata* from the mails in 1891. This, it said, was dictating to the people what they might or might not read. It appears, too, that late nineteenth century juries tended to be lenient in abortion cases. They rarely convicted when the defendant was charged with murder, and generally allowed intent, not the act itself, to determine criminality.[61]

As in so many other areas of late nineteenth century social policy, the attempt to regulate public mores was caught up in a

---

60. U.S. *v.* Harmon, 45 Fed. 414, 423 (D.C. Kansas, 1891); *Ex parte* Jackson, 96 U.S. 727, 736 (1878); "Kansas," *AC* (1891); "Michigan," *AC* (1897); ABA *Reports*, 13 (1890), 160–161; Pivar, *Purity Crusade*, chs. 3–4. See also Solon D. Wilson, "Public Indecency," *CLM*, 11 (1889), 461–478.

61. L'Hote *v.* New Orleans, 177 U.S. 587, 596 (1900); *CLJ*, 10 (1880), 439; U.S. *v.* Whittier, 28 Fed. 591 (U.S. C.C.E.D. Mo. 1878), "Kreutzer Sonata," *ALR*, 25 (1891), 102–104; Edward A. Belcher, "Criminal Abortion," *CLM*, 17 (1895), 141–150.

web of varied purposes and values. To a considerable degree this effort stemmed from a religious-based morality with deep roots in the American past. It had newer sources as well. These included the belief that social science had the knowledge and government the power to purify American life, and the need of a large (and largely insecure) middle class for a publicly defined and enforced moral code. But here as elsewhere the impulse to control social behavior clashed with strong countervalues: individualism, localism, laissez-faire.

Private Rights

Voluntary associations, always significant American institutions, took on increasing importance in the late nineteenth century. Agrarian loneliness; the social and economic needs of immigrants, workers, city-dwellers; the generally unsettled character of life in a time of industrialization: all strengthened the American propensity to join. Social clubs, farmer associations, mutual benefit societies, professional, commercial, and trade associations, educational and charitable institutions, and religious sects constituted in sum a vast range of associational activity. An 1897 study estimated that 5,400,000 people belonged to secret societies, and observed that the number of such organizations had greatly increased during the past quarter of a century. This growth led to conflicts that the polity could not ignore—conflicts fought out primarily in the courts.[62]

Incorporated voluntary associations were subject to most of the ✓ constraints that the state imposed on commercial corporations. But unincorporated societies were "not known to the law." They appeared "to have no special legal *status* at all, and thus [are] not at all subject to being brought to court." Strictly speaking, they were not corporations, joint-stock companies, or even partnerships—although, for want of anything better, the courts at times used the partnership analogy.

Clubs and societies for the most part were left to enforce their own regulations. The prevailing view was that the courts "should not, as a general rule, interfere with the contentions and quarrels

62. "Clubs," *AC* (1884); W. S. Harwood, "Secret Societies in America," *NAR*, 164 (1897), 617.

of voluntary associations." Attempts to prevent societies from expelling members always failed. And judges voided the bylaws of voluntary associations only if they were clearly immoral or illegal.

But members of these associations, incorporated or not, had property rights that rested on their institutional affiliation. Mutual benefit societies and other organizations often had a "dual nature . . . in which charity and pecuniary benefits are intermingled," leading to "numerous complications . . . difficult of adjustment."[63]

Late nineteenth century courts and legislatures began to modify their hands-off policy. Increasingly they recognized that a member of an incorporated association had "a certain vested interest in the franchise which, in itself, constitutes property, and of which he cannot be deprived except for sufficient cause and in a proper manner." An 1888 California decision went further, holding that the property rights of members of an unincorporated association were equal to those of members of an incorporated society, and that the court could review the expulsion of such persons. The insurance function of fraternal and mutual benefit societies also came under growing legislative and judicial supervision. As so often was the case in the late nineteenth century, individual rights were defined and often enlarged through the ongoing interpretation of property rights.[64]

For the most part the polity steered clear of involvement in church affairs, a principle affirmed by the Supreme Court in Watson v. Jones (1872). The controlling rule was that "the right of association is enjoyed and exercised to the fullest extent without any attempt at legislative restraint and interference." It seemed to one observer in 1876 that judicial noninterference in the internal administration of religious and other voluntary associations was "fast becoming the general sentiment of the country."

63. Cooley, Torts, 9; "Note," 3 N.E. 823 (1885); Lawrence Lewis, Jr., "Disfranchisement from Private Corporations," ALReg, ns, 21 (1882), 689; Lafond v. Deems, 81 N.Y. 507 (1880); Eugene McQuillin, "By-Laws of Benefit and Voluntary Societies," ALR, 23 (1889), 898, 891. See also Louis C. Whiton, "Club Law—Particularly as to Rights of Expulsion and Liability of Members," ALJ, 27 (1883), 326–329; Seymour D. Thompson, "Expulsion of Members of Corporations and Societies," ALR, 24 (1890), 537–558; A. J. Hirschl, The Law of Fraternities and Societies (St. Louis, 1883).

64. Lewis, "Disenfranchisement," 689; Otto v. Tailors' Protective and Benevolent Union, 75 Cal. 308 (1888).

But as church property increased in value, so did the grounds for state intervention. Chartered churches were civil (not, as in England, ecclesiastical) corporations, their property subject to legislative constraint. Thus the Pennsylvania court upheld a provision in the state constitution that taxed sectarian charities. The fear of mortmain—perpetual church property-holding—led to considerable legislative action. Every state limited the maximum value of church-held real estate. An 1883 Act of Congress restricted the worth of such holdings in the territories to $50,000. The Virginia and West Virginia constitutions forbade the granting of corporate charters to churches. The 1890 Mississippi constitution flatly prohibited any church property-holdings and voided existing bequests to religious institutions.[65]

Civil liberties, a subject of substantial political and legal concern in the twentieth century, did not figure largely in the late nineteenth century polity. Individual liberty and the sanctity of private rights (at least for adult white males) were part of the prevailing value system. But they were rarely put to the test by legislatures or in the courts. As social tensions mounted from the mid-eighties on, local and state restraints on speech and assembly did grow in number and were upheld by the courts. Yet the most conspicuous of these acts, an 1887 Illinois law (in the wake of the Haymarket explosion) that penalized public incitement to riot and violence, was repealed by the state legislature in 1891. It was only with William McKinley's assassination in 1901, the suppression of strikes by large corporations in the early twentieth century, and most of all the quashing of dissent during and after World War One, that freedom of speech and press became important issues.[66]

65. Watson v. Jones, 13 Wall. 679 (1872); Mark DeWolfe Howe, *The Garden and the Wilderness: Religion and Government in American Constitutional History* (Chicago, 1965), 75–90; Isaac F. Redfield in *ALReg*, ns, 15 (1876), 282; Freund, *Police Powers*, 497; James M. Grant, "Property Relations of Religious Societies," *ALR*, 17 (1883), 186–214; William M. Meredith, "Is Sectarianism a Bar to Exemption from Taxation as 'Purely Public Charity?" *ALReg*, ns, 37 (1898), 593–607; Philadelphia v. Masonic Home, 160 Pa. 572 (1894); on mortmain, Freund, *Police Powers*, 375–376. See also W. H. Roberts, *Laws Relating to Religious Corporations* (Philadelphia, 1896); Zollman, *American Church Law*.

66. Loren P. Beth, *The Development of the American Constitution 1877–1917* (New York, 1971), 230–235; on Illinois, Spies v. People, 122 Ill.

What did concern the late nineteenth century polity was the degree to which the individual might be protected from the intrusions of modern society: more particularly, the threat to privacy and the danger of slander and libel. At the end of the century, interest grew in what Thomas M. Cooley called the right "to be let alone." An influential *Harvard Law Review* article by Louis D. Brandeis and Samuel D. Warren in 1890 argued for a right to privacy rooted in "personal feelings" and "the sanctity of private life."

The changing conditions of American life led to litigation over that right. The Supreme Court held in 1891 that a person could not be compelled to submit to a surgical examination in connection with a damage suit. New York courts granted requests for injunctions against the unauthorized reproduction of an individual's likeness in statuary or photographs. Without such restraints, warned Court of Appeals Judge Rufus W. Peckham, "vulgarity will envelop the nation."[67]

Not all agreed that the right to privacy should be rigorously enforced. One critic warned that the courts were wresting equity from its proper concern with property rights to create a new and questionable category: the privacy of personality. But most turn-of-the-century courts found it both natural and proper to analogize the sanctity of reputation with the sanctity of property. So too did legislatures. When in 1902 the New York Court of Appeals held that privacy was not a legally protected right, the state legislature quickly provided statutory protection.[68]

Similar attitudes strengthened the law of libel. The nineteenth century tendency was to give "full liberty" to the criticism of pub-

---

1 (1887); Freund, *Police Powers*, 509 ff. See also People v. Most, 171 N.Y. 423 (1902); Cooley, *Constitutional Limitations*, ch. 12; 32 *LRA* 829–834 (1896).

67. Cooley, *Torts*, 29; Samuel D. Warren and Louis D. Brandeis, "The Right to Privacy," *HLR*, 4 (1890–1891), 193–220; Union Pacific v. Botsford, 141 U.S. 250 (1891); Schuyler v. Curtis, 15 N.Y. Supp. 787 (Sup. Ct. N.Y. County 1891); Marks v. Jaffa, 26 N.Y. Supp. 908 (Super. Ct. N.Y.C. 1893); Peckham quoted in John G. Speed, "The Right of Privacy," *NAR*, 163 (1896), 74. See also William L. Prosser, *Handbook of the Law of Torts*, 2d ed. (St. Paul, 1955), 635–636; Beth, *Development*, 200–201.

68. Herbert S. Hadley, "The Right to Privacy," *NLR*, 3 (1894), 1–20; Walter F. Pratt, "The Warren and Brandeis Argument for a Right to Privacy," *PL* (Summer, 1975), 161—179.

lic men, but to allow for the defenses of falsity and malice in other cases. Thomas M. Cooley argued in his influential treatise *Constitutional Limitations* that privileged journalistic comment on political figures was proper, since a corrupt private life lessened an official's suitability for public office. The Pennsylvania Supreme Court in 1886 held that charges of dishonesty leveled against a public official were not libelous even when they turned out to be untrue, if no malicious intent could be shown. But as concern mounted in the late nineteenth century over the stability of American life and institutions, a number of courts looked less favorably on such criticism. By the early 1890s, American decisions in cases involving libels on public officials were "hopelessly irreconcilable."

In 1890—the year in which Brandeis and Warren spoke up for the right to privacy—the journalist E. L. Godkin warned of a growing assault on individual reputations in the public prints. Slander suits were declining, a reflection of the impersonal character of social relationships in an urban society. But libel actions against newspapers, Godkin thought, were increasing, and he feared that the "despotic and irresponsible power" of sensational journalism imperiled the right of citizens to a standing in the community commensurate with their worth. The frequency with which late nineteenth century courts found unflattering statements and pictures in the public prints to be libelous, and the appearance of legislation such as a turn-of-the-century California law forbidding the publication of caricatures of private citizens unless the subject consented, suggest that Godkin's was not a unique concern. We can see here the framework of the policy clash that would dominate civil liberties controversies in the twentieth century: between the desire to protect individuals and the larger society from divisive, intrusive, or "subversive" assault and the constitutional right of criticism and dissent.[69]

69. D. H. Pingrey, "The Right to Criticize Public Candidates," *ALR*, 27 (1893), 14–23; Cooley, *Constitutional Limitations*, 5th ed. (Boston, 1883), 616 ff; Briggs v. Garrett, 111 Pa. St. 404 (1886); *ALReg*, ns, 30 (1891), 565; E. L. Godkin, "The Rights of the Citizen. IV—To His Own Reputation," *SM*, 8 (1890), 58–67; "Libel and Slander," *AEEL*, XVIII, 863–994; on California law, Henry B. Brown, "The Liberty of the Press,"*ALR*, 34 (1900), 329. See also John Proffatt, "The Law of Newspaper Libel," *NAR*, 131 (1880), 109–127; Norman L. Rosenberg, "The Law of Political Libel and Freedom of Press in Nineteenth Century America: An Interpretation," *AJLH*, 17 (1973), 336–352.

CHAPTER 14

The Politics of an Industrial Society

THE MOST DISTINCTIVE feature of late nineteenth century American politics was its domination by highly organized parties and highly professional politicians. Machines and bosses ran a pervasive, tenacious political system, as third parties and independent reformers repeatedly learned to their sorrow.

This system of organizational politics took form in the 1870s, succeeding the less structured and more explicitly ideological politics of the Civil War-Reconstruction period. It came to its full maturity in the 1880s: a mix of highly organized, professional, "modern" party machinery—and often traditional leadership styles, party ideology, and popular appeal. In this sense the party system offered the same ambivalent response to an industrial society as did the late nineteenth century governmental and legal systems, and social and economic policymaking.

The Election Process

Voting after the Civil War was open to more Americans than ever before. With the passage of the Fifteenth Amendment, most adult males had legal access to the ballot. In more than twenty states during the 1870s, aliens could vote if they had taken out their first papers. Rhode Island ended its property qualifications for native-born voters in 1888 and for the foreign born in the 1890s. There were 4,824 naturalized voters in the state in 1885, 24,615 in 1895.

Limitations on officeholding also fell away. Alabama, Missouri, Virginia, and Arkansas dropped the pre-Civil War requirement that their governors be native born. New Hampshire ended its Protestant religious qualification for state offices in 1877, as did Massachusetts (for its governor) in 1892 and Delaware (for its senators) in 1897.[1]

There still were a number of grounds for exclusion: sex, age, race (by law in the case of the Chinese, quasi-legally or by force for numbers of blacks), incarceration in a prison or asylum, lack of a fixed or legal residence. But by the standards of the late nineteenth century Western world, the United States had an electorate unique in its size and range. It was estimated that in 1880 there were 11 million legal voters, and about 1.8 million males of voting age— 14 percent of the total—who could not vote. Even after the suffrage extension of the 1880s, 40 percent of Britain's adult males were denied the ballot.[2]

Access to and control over this huge electorate was the primary concern of the late nineteenth century party system. The prevailing mode of voting before 1890 often enabled party organizations to exercise as much control as a Whig magnate in an English pocket borough. The parties prepared their own ballots and these were cast in public, practices that fostered vote buying and other forms of control. Chris Buckley, San Francisco's "Blind Boss" in the 1880s, was said to stand at polling places clad in a bulky overcoat, his pockets filled with quarter eagles (gold coins worth $2.50). He gave a rewarding handshake to each of the faithful after they voted. "Big Tim" Sullivan of Tammany once had his ballots perfumed, so that they might be tracked to the ballot box by scent as well as by size, shape, and color.[3]

1. Leon E. Aylesworth, "The Passing of Alien Suffrage," *APSR*, 25 (1931), 114–116; "Rhode Island," *AC* (1888, 1895); Frank H. Miller, "Legal Qualifications for Office in America, 1619–1899," *AHA Annual Report* (1899), I, 114, 118, 123.

2. Albert B. Hart, "The Exercise of the Suffrage," *PSQ*, 7 (1892), 313; Henry Pelling, *Social Geography of British Elections 1885–1910* (London, 1967), 6; Neal Blewett, "The Franchise in the United Kingdom 1885–1918," *PP*, no. 32 (1965), 27–56.

3. On Buckley, Joseph Hutchinson, "Corrupt Practices Acts," *ALR*, 27 (1893), 351–352; on Sullivan, Marcus R. Werner, *Tammany Hall* (Garden City, 1928), 439. See also Alexander Callow, "San Francisco's Blind Boss," *PHR*, 25 (1956), 266–267.

Casual methods of voter identification and a transient, anonymous urban population made it easy to use "floaters" and "repeaters" (Americanisms that date from before the Civil War) in the larger cities. The Philadelphia Republican machine had tens of thousands of such voters—enough to export large numbers in a "pipeline" operation to aid New York City's Republicans, who needed all the help they could get. One observer thought that 20 percent of New York City's voters got cash payments in 1877. Voting was halted and the ballots counted every few hours during Philadelphia elections in the 1870s, ostensibly to make possible a quick tally at the end of the day, but in fact to keep the organization informed of its vote needs. Charges of fraudulent counts were frequent, as in Maryland (1887) and Indiana (1887–1888), in Chicago's Sixth Senatorial District (1884), and in the 1886 New York mayoralty election, when Henry George may well have been counted out of office.

Corrupt voting was not limited to the cities. West Virginia was supposed to have 147,408 eligible male voters in 1888. But its presidential vote total was 159,440, which gave Grover Cleveland a 506 vote margin over Benjamin Harrison. It was estimated that only 30 of 400 voters in one New York township were unbribable. Connecticut town politicians "employed" large numbers of citizens on election day to take people to the polls, run errands, or do nothing but vote. "Peddling ballots" was common. Prices ranged upward to as much as $50 per voter; the cost rose as election day wore on. Some $60,000 reportedly was spent on vote buying in Sussex County, Delaware in 1894, although the county cast only about 8,000 votes.[4]

4. William M. Ivins, *Machine Politics and Money Elections in New York City* (New York, 1887), 72; on Philadelphia counting, "The Ballot in America," *LT*, 53 (1872), 388; "Maryland," *AC* (1887); "Indiana," *AC* (1887–1888); "Illinois," *AC* (1884); "West Virginia," *AC* (1888); on New York township, Jeremiah W. Jenks, "Money in Practical Politics," *CM*, 44 (1892), 949; on Connecticut towns, F. J. Stimson, *The Methods of Bribery and Its Prevention at our National Elections* (Cambridge, 1889), 7–9; "Delaware," *AC* (1894). See also Henry R. White, "Corruptible Elements in the Suffrage," *IR*, 14 (1883), 26; "Needed Municipal Reforms," *NAR*, 158 (1894), 203–210; James Bryce, *The American Commonwealth*, 3d ed. (New York, 1898), II, 142 ff. For photographs of an urban polling place and the conduct of an election see Avery D. Andrews, "The Police Control of an Election," *SM*, 23 (1898), 131–146.

Little was done to check these abuses before the mid-1880s. Close supervision of elections was unpopular in a decentralized, organization-dominated political system. And government interference with the right to vote often was held to be a greater evil than the abuse of that right. There was much hostility to voter registration acts—especially among Democrats, whose urban constituency usually was the object of these laws. When the Democrats took control of the New Jersey legislature in 1889, they repealed a Republican registration law that applied to Newark and Jersey City, and replaced a "sunset" act with a statute that kept the polls open from 6 AM to 7 PM. The post-Reconstruction Democratic constitutions of Arkansas, Texas, and West Virginia in effect forbade voter registration, and as late as 1889 these states plus Delaware, Indiana, and Oregon had no registration statutes. A number of state supreme courts voided registration laws on the ground that they imposed unconstitutional restrictions on the right to vote.[5]

But the conduct of elections came in for increasing government attention. This was not a peculiarly American development. The expansion of the British suffrage led to regulatory measures such as the Corrupt Practices Act of 1883, which forbade candidates from hiring carriages to take voters to the polls and numbered ballots so that they could be traced and voided if the voter proved to be ineligible. British election laws reflected a strong tradition of political deference and limited popular participation. The 1885 Redistribution Act redrew Parliamentary districts to separate out "the pursuits of the population," an explicit statement of purpose not possible in the United States. American regulations had to counter the powerful democratic thrust of the mid-nineteenth century. It is revealing that while the British Corrupt Practices Act was the model for much American legislation, no state copied its provisions for the forfeiture of office and disqualification from future political contests of those who were convicted under it.[6]

5. "New Jersey," *AC* (1889); "Registry Laws," *AC* (1889); Page v. Allen, 58 Pa. 388 (1868); State v. Swift, 69 Ind. 505 (1879); Dell v. Kennedy, 49 Wis. 555 (1880); Daggett v. Hudson, 43 Ohio St. 548 (1885); Kenneen v. Wells, 144 Mass. 497 (1887).

6. Pelling, *Social Geography*, 2–3, 12–13; H. J. Hanham, *Elections and Party Management: Politics in the Time of Disraeli and Gladstone* (London, 1959), 263 ff; Robert Luce, *Legislative Principles* (Boston, 1930), 422.

Massachusetts alone passed about twenty laws designed to secure honest voting in the 1880s, an elaborate campaign spending act in 1892, and a pioneering permanent registration law in 1896. New York's Corrupt Practices Act of 1890 required that candidates file expense statements, and twenty states passed similar laws during the next fifteen years. Proportional representation schemes kept cropping up, and attempts were made to regulate the process by which candidates were chosen. Illinois in 1885 passed an act "regulating primary elections of voluntary political associations," which set up Citizens' Election Boards with duties similar to official boards of election. By 1901, nineteen states had laws requiring direct primaries to select candidates.[7]

The strength of party organizations made a mockery of these constraints. Campaign spending laws were so ineffective that six of them were repealed by 1904. But the impulse to subject the electoral process to tighter control was too firmly grounded in widespread social anxieties to be readily thrust aside. Voting abuses were linked to other threats to the social order: crime, illiteracy, racial difference, class conflict. "Scientific" studies related the venality of voters in stagnant small towns and immigrant city wards to ancestry, intemperance, crime, and poverty. Corrupt election practices were condemned because they "throw into the whole matter of government the association of chance and instability," a matter of special concern in a time of rapid social change.[8]

Late nineteenth century American efforts to purify the electoral process concentrated on voter eligibility as well as election procedure. Massachusetts and other state courts, for example, wrestled with the problem of student voting in college towns. They usually held that a student's residence was the home of his parents: "The

7. Raymond L. Bridgman, *Ten Years of Massachusetts* (Boston, 1888), 16; *Mass. Acts 1892*, ch. 416; *Mass. Acts 1896*, ch. 469; *N.Y. Laws 1890*, ch. 94; "Elections, Laws, Customs and Theories of," *AC* (1887); *Ill. Laws 1885*, pp. 188–193; Ernest C. Meyer, *Nominating Systems: Direct Primaries versus Conventions in the United States* (Madison, 1902), 92–94. See also George L. Fox, "Corrupt Practices and Election Laws in the United States since 1890," *APSA Proceedings*, 2 (1905), 171–186.

8. James K. Pollock, Jr., *Party Campaign Funds* (New York, 1926), 7 ff; J. J. McCook, "The Alarming Proportion of Venal Voters," *Forum*, 14 (1892), 1–13, "Venal Voting: Methods and Remedies," ibid., 159–177; Alexander H. Rice and others, *Biennial Elections* (Boston, 1886), 3.

student is in a preparatory condition, in a state of tutelage and nonproduction, not yet able to engage in business, or in the productive pursuits of life, nor fully prepared to assume ... civil and political rights and duties."

The expansion of the suffrage that had gone on from the 1820s to the 1870s now began to be reversed. Educational qualifications— usually the ability to read and write English—had been limited to a few New England states. They spread now to Wyoming (1889), California (where an 1894 constitutional referendum approved the requirement by a better than 5 to 1 vote), Washington (1896), and Delaware and Maine (1897). Existing literacy requirements were toughened in Connecticut (1897) and New Hampshire (1903). By the early 1900s, fewer than ten states still allowed aliens who had taken out their first papers to vote. Florida, Michigan, Minnesota, Alabama, Colorado, and North Dakota ended the practice around the turn of the century.[9]

The clash between expansive and restrictive attitudes toward voting appeared in the debate over the Federal Elections Act of 1889–1890. The key element in the bill was that federal circuit courts, not state governors or certifying boards, would oversee congressional and other federal elections if one hundred or more voters in a district so requested. Federal marshals would supervise the balloting and counting. This was the final Republican effort to protect black voting in the South. Kansas Senator John J. Ingalls called it "the last opportunity that will be afforded us in this generation" to redeem "the pledges of the past twenty years." But the pervasive belief in black inferiority, the widespread indifference over what was happening in the South, and a definition of political purity that led to the reduction rather than the protection of black voting blocked passage of the bill.[10]

Instead, a movement within the South itself all but eliminated

9. O. W. Aldrich, "Residence as a Qualification for Voting," *AmLJ*, 1 (1884), 129–130; George H. Haynes, "Educational Qualifications for the Suffrage of the United States," *PSQ*, 13 (1898), 495–513, Samuel E. Moffett, "The Constitutional Referendum in California," ibid., 1–18; *Conn. Laws* 1897, ch. 233; Aylsworth, "Passing of Alien Suffrage," 114–116.

10. Richard E. Welch, Jr., "The Federal Elections Bill of 1890: Postscripts and Prelude," *JAH*, 52 (1965), 511–526; Sen. John J. Ingalls to Lewis T. Michener, July 31, 1890, Michener Mss, WSHS; Welch, *George Frisbie Hoar and the Half-Breed Republicans* (Cambridge, 1971), 146–148.

black voting as a political factor by the turn of the century and severely restricted the poor white electorate as well. Negro voting had persisted through the 1880s and remained a force to be reckoned with in states such as Tennessee, Florida, and North Carolina. But the increasingly shrill racism of southern public life and the rise of Populism and other forms of political unrest in the 1890s led to a major Democratic effort to suppress black suffrage. The devices used included the traditional ones of threats and violence, fraudulent vote counts, and cooptation. More and more, however, state Democratic organizations relied on a variety of laws. These included literacy tests; periodic voter registration made more difficult by the hostility or the inaccessibility of registrars; separate ballots (and ballot boxes) for the several state and federal offices; and poll taxes and other constitutional suffrage restrictions.

The Democratic primary was turned by law (as it was in practice) into a white-only institution. Rule Two of South Carolina's Democratic party, enacted in 1894, stated: "every negro applying to vote in a Democratic primary election, must produce a written statement of ten reputable white men who shall swear that the applicant or voter cast his ballot for General [Wade] Hampton in 1876, and had voted the Democratic ticket continuously since." It was an ironic commentary that the first statewide primary—that favored device of electoral "reform"—occurred in Louisiana in 1892, when the contesting factions in the Democratic party agreed to a pre-election white primary in order to fashion a united front against the Republican-Populist opposition.[11]

The courts added their weight to this movement. Tennessee's tribunal upheld the state law prohibiting assistance to illiterate voters, arguing: "The inconvenience to a part of the community must yield to the good of the whole." Delaware's Supreme Court in 1892 struck down the custom whereby politicos paid for poll tax receipts and distributed them to voters.

The consequence was a massive, dramatic decline in southern voting. A sampling of southern elections during the 1880s reveals that about 38 percent of the electorate voted Democratic, 26 per-

11. J. Morgan Kousser, *The Shaping of Southern Politics: Suffrage Restriction and the Establishment of the One-Party South, 1880–1910* (New Haven, 1974); on South Carolina primary, Meyers, *Nominating Systems,* 124.

cent for other parties, and 36 percent did not vote. The figures for 1902 to 1910 were 20 percent Democratic, 10 percent other, and 70 percent not voting. The South's turnout in presidential elections went from 64 percent of eligibles in 1880 to 56 percent in 1896, and then dropped precipitously to 43 percent in 1900 and 29 percent in 1904.[12]

Northern fears of an immigrant, working class electorate came to a head in close correspondence with the southern Democratic assault on black and poor white voting. A statement typical of the time—"I earnestly desire that our institutions may continue in substance unchanged, but this end cannot be obtained save through an increasing intelligence and virtue, which shall overcome the influence of that great mass of ignorant and vicious voters, on whom we have so thoughtlessly conferred the right of suffrage"—could have been aimed at southern blacks; in fact it was directed at immigrant voters in northern cities.

Late nineteenth century voting reform reached its peak with the sweeping adoption of the Australian ballot around 1890. This was an electoral method in which uniform ballots were prepared and distributed by the state and were cast in secret. The Australian ballot was first used in Louisville in 1888; thirty-five states required it in 1891; by 1910 only North and South Carolina and Georgia were without it. The new procedure was supposed to deal a devastating blow to vote buying and machine control of elections. It was not without effect. Republican votes sharply increased and Democratic voting declined in New York City's Eighth Congressional District, and it appeared that far less money was spent on election day.[13]

But the Australian ballot did not substantially change electoral patterns. Split ticket voting remained low, averaging 5 to 8 percent

12. Cook v. State, 90 Tenn. 407, 412 (1891); "Delaware," *AC* (1892); on decline, Kousser, *Shaping of Southern Politics*, 225, 12. See also Kousser, "Post-Reconstruction Suffrage Restriction in Tennessee: A New Look at the V. O. Key Thesis," *PSQ*, 88 (1973), 655–683.

13. C. A. Kent, "Political Reform in this Country," *MLJ*, 2 (1893), 459; L. E. Fredman, *The Australian Ballot: The Story of an American Reform* (East Lansing, Michigan, 1968); on Eighth District, John E. Milholland, "The Danger Point in American Politics," *NAR*, 165 (1897), 94. See also Joseph B. Bishop, "The Secret Ballot in Thirty-Three States," *Forum*, 12 (1892), 589–598.

in the 1890s. The party machines quickly adapted to the new system. They spent more money on propaganda and bringing out friendly voters, less on the mechanics of balloting and outright vote buying. Most industrial states arranged their ballots by party slates rather than by offices, which encouraged straight party voting. As Pat Maguire of the Boston Democratic organization explained: "A man who goes to the polls has his mind made up on the question of how he is to vote. He ought not to be compelled by the state to hunt for his candidates. Their names and their political affiliations should be before him in an orderly, plain and systematic manner." Until the mid-nineties New York allowed a "plaster ballot" to be prepared beforehand, brought in to the polling booth by the voter, and pasted on the official ballot. In Maryland and other states, voters who spoke no English were allowed to bring a "helper" to the polls.

Another, longer range consequence was that the regular parties gained greater legal recognition. It became more difficult for independent candidates and extra-party slates to win a place on the official ballot. Thus 1895 "antifusion" laws in Michigan and Oregon, directed at the Populists, did not allow the name of a candidate nominated by several parties to appear on more than one ballot line. The Michigan Supreme Court upheld this rule, arguing that it would "secure a more intelligent vote." Official ballots made possible a form of political control that would not have been feasible before.[14]

It has been argued that these voting constraints were part of a national effort at the turn of the century to secure elite hegemony by reducing the size of the electorate. Certainly the falloff in voting that occurred in the South had its milder counterpart in the rest of the country. Indeed, since 1900 the national secular voting trend

14. Jerrold G. Rusk, "The Effect of the Australian Ballot Reform on Split Ticket Voting: 1876–1908," *APSR*, 64 (1970), 1226; George F. Edmunds, "Perils of Our National Elections," *Forum*, 12 (1892), 691–701; Maguire quoted in Geoffrey Blodgett, *The Gentle Reformers: Massachusetts Democrats in the Cleveland Era* (Cambridge, 1966), 116; on "plaster ballots," Fredman, *Australian Ballot*, 85; Charles C. Binney, "American Secret Ballot Decisions," *ALReg*, ns, 32 (1893), 104–115; Todd v. Election Commissioners, 104 Mich. 474, 486 (1895). See also Frank J. Goodnow, *Politics and Administration: A Study in Government* (New York, 1900), 209 ff.

has been downward. But this decline was related to more profound social and cultural forces than manipulation by elites. And while restrictions on voting at the end of the nineteenth century reflected widespread social anxieties, they also may be seen as responses to a more particular development: the rise of organizational politics to its full power and maturity.[15]

The Party System

The size and variety of the American electorate, the large number of elections, and the high stakes of patronage and power that went with public office gave American politics a quality all its own. Its scale and articulation required hundreds of thousands of functionaries, more than "all other political machinery in the rest of the civilized world." Joseph Chamberlain, the major innovator of political techniques in late nineteenth century England, borrowed much from the American party system. When Max Weber discussed "politics as a vocation" in 1918, he recognized that professionally organized mass politics had come first, and gone furthest, in the United States.[16]

Contemporary observers discussed the virtues and vices of that system. Defenders pointed out that it was a nationalizing force, a check to tyranny, an institution with deep popular roots, a primary device for "assimilating ... heterogeneous peoples to American usages and American ideas." Far from being handmaidens of the corporations, the parties were a counterpoise: "As industrial organization has become more complete, increased attention has been directed in every State to the organization of the political

15. See Philip E. Converse, "Change in the American Electorate," in Angus Cambell and Phillip E. Converse, eds., *The Human Meaning of Social Change* (New York, 1972), 263–337; Walter D. Burnham, "Theory and Voting Research: Some Reflections on Converse's 'Change in the American Electorate,'" *APSR*, 68 (1974), 1002–1023.

16. Henry J. Ford, *The Rise and Growth of American Politics* (New York, 1898), 312; Joseph Chamberlain, "The Caucus," *FRev*, ns, 24 (1878), 721–741; Max Weber, "Politics as a Vocation," in H. H. Gerth and C. Wright Mills, eds., *From Max Weber: Essays in Sociology* (New York, 1940), 107 ff. See also Anson D. Morse, "Party in the Political System," *AAPSS Annals*, 2 (1890), 13; Horace E. Deming, "Political Party Organization in the United States," *WR*, 28 (1887), 174–180; and the brilliant discussion of "The Party System" in Bryce, *American Commonwealth*, II, part III.

parties." One student of the political system concluded: "Nowhere else in the world, at any period, has party organization had to cope with such enormous tasks as in this country, and its efficiency in dealing with them is the true glory of our political system."[17]

Party politics and professional politicians met a distinct social need in the late nineteenth century United States. The unsettling consequences of industrialism were spreading through American life. Bureaucracy and the welfare state, labor unions, and mass popular culture still were in their formative stages. As the legal system filled part of the void in late nineteenth century governance, so did the party system respond to changing needs of political representation.

But for all their power, the parties had an ambiguous place in the American polity. The Michigan Supreme Court observed in 1885: "parties, however powerful and unavoidable they may be, and however inseparable from popular government, are not and cannot be recognized as having a legal authority as such." There were warnings against making parties incorporated associations, for this would give them a dangerous aura of legitimacy. State regulation was minimal; and most early laws empowered party officials to prescribe membership requirements and conduct primaries and conventions. It was only in the twentieth century that parties came to be recognized in most states as instruments of government subject to public control.

There was substantial cause for discontent with the system. The parties were all too responsive (if not subservient) to vested interests. Their organizations often were "clannish, selfish, and exclusive to a marked degree." Extensive corruption and maladministration went with party government. No one questioned the pervasiveness of the party system. Many took issue with the quality of its performance.[18]

The close national balance between the major parties during the 1880s made it necessary to bring out the votes of the largest pos-

17. Levi Parsons, "The Use of Political Parties," *NPR*, 3 (1887), 348; Andrew C. McLaughlin, "The Significance of Political Parties," *AM*, 101 (1908), 145–146; Ford, *Rise and Growth*, 310. See also Allen Johnson, "The Nationalizing Influence of Party," *YR*, 15 (1906–1907), 283–292.

18. Attorney General v. Detroit, 58 Mich. 213, 218 (1885); Herbert Tuttle, "The Despotism of Party," *AM*, 54 (1884), 374; Charles N. Forten-

sible number of potential supporters. In part this was done by appeals to the emotion, ideology, and self-interest of varied groups of voters. Detailed and intensive organization was at least as important. This was especially so where the party balance was very close. Indiana, New York, Connecticut, and New Jersey were the most evenly divided states of the period. But interparty competition was keen in New Hampshire, Pennsylvania, Maryland, North Carolina, Ohio, Illinois, Michigan, Wisconsin, Minnesota, Wyoming, Montana, Oregon, and California as well. Even the solidly Democratic areas of the South and the staunchly Republican portions of New England and the upper Midwest were beset by intraparty factionalism, which put a premium on organizational skills.

Despite the seeming lack of issues, the highest mean turnouts of voters in American history—78.5 percent of eligibles—occurred during the 1876–1896 period. (If the South is excluded, the average rises to 85 percent.) When issues were strong and feelings ran deep, the vote totals were extraordinary. It is estimated that in the 1896 presidential election more than 95 percent of the eligible voters in the Midwest cast ballots. State and local election turnouts consistently were in the 60 to 80 percent range. In the 1885 New York City municipal election, of an estimated pool of 266,000 eligibles 216,000 (81.2 percent) registered and 201,000 (75.6 percent) voted. The lowest vote levels occurred in school board elections, which usually were furthest removed from party politics in issues and timing.[19]

While politicos tried to maximize election turnouts, they sought

berry, "Legal Regulation of Political Party Organization in the United States," Ph.D. diss., University of Illinois, 1937. See also Alonzo H. Tuttle, "Limitations upon the Power of the Legislature to Control Political Parties and their Primaries," *MLR*, 1 (1903), 466–495; James S. Brown, *Partisan Politics: The Evil and the Remedy* (Philadelphia, 1897), 114.

19. Paul T. David, *Party Strength in the United States 1872–1970* (Charlottesville, 1972), 43, 50; Walter D. Burnham, "The Changing Shape of the American Political Universe," *APSR*, 59 (1965), 10; Richard Jensen, *The Winning of the Midwest: Social and Political Conflict, 1888–1896* (Chicago, 1971), 2; on 1885 New York election, David D. Field, "Our Political Methods," *Forum*, 2 (1886–1887), 215; Jesse Macy, *Party Organization and Machinery* (London, 1905), 8. See also Daryl Fair, "Turnout for Presidential Elections in Lancaster and York Counties: 1876–1960," *LCHS Journal*, 67 (1963), 48–55.

to minimize voter participation in the selection of candidates. Ostensibly, party organizations were highly representative. Indiana Republican precinct meetings (there were about 250 voters in each precinct) chose committeemen and delegates to the district congressional nominating conventions; precinct committeemen composed the county committees that selected the party's county chairmen; district conventions elected district chairmen, who in turn made up the state committee and named the state chairman. Other conventions or primaries chose delegates to county, district, and state nominating conventions.

But the scale of the system put a premium on political professionalism. John Jay Chapman observed in 1890: "Our system of party government has been developed . . . to keep the control in the hands of professionals by multiplying technicalities and increasing the complexity of the rules of the game." In 1888 between 5 and 10 percent of eligible voters participated in party primaries. Much was made of the Pennsylvania Democrats' Crawford County plan, in which party members elected the state committee, and large numbers of voters (over 90 percent of those registered in some areas) directly chose county organizations. But most convention delegates were chosen through primaries and caucuses controlled by insiders. New York City Republicans selected local candidates and convention delegates in "little evening clubs" of the sort that the aspiring young Theodore Roosevelt joined in 1880. By one account there were 1,007 primaries and caucuses held by New York City's parties to select candidates and convention delegates in 1884. Of these, 633 took place in saloons.[20]

Insider control was only one aspect of the system. Party loyalty was fostered by costly, elaborate conventions and electioneering. Handkerchiefs, playing cards, mugs, posters, buttons emblazoned with candidates' names and party symbols poured forth in an unending stream. In 1888, twenty-five presidential possibilities were

20. Macy, *Party Organization*, 168–172; John Jay Chapman, "Between Elections," *AM*, 85 (1900), 26; A. C. Bernheim, "Party Organizations and their Nominations to Public Office in New York City," *PSQ*, 3 (1888), 114–116; on Crawford County plan, Talcott Williams, "Party Organization in the United States," in John J. Lalor, ed., *Cyclopaedia of Political Science* (New York, 1888), III, 120, George W. Green, "Facts about the Caucus and the Primary," *NAR*, 137 (1883), 257; Bryce, *American Commonwealth*, II, 114.

pictured on cards packed into Honest Long Cut tobacco, to be collected and traded as were baseball players and other popular heroes. The intense campaign symbology led William Graham Sumner to observe: "the popular notion of elections is superstitious."[21]

This was organized, packaged campaigning. Orators and marchers were paid for their services; observers thought that the hoopla was increasingly contrived and mechanical. But it tapped real feelings, met a real social need. With the memory of the Civil War fading and the divisive forces of an industrial order growing, elections provided the excitement, the social and psychological bonding, of war itself. The novelist Brand Whitlock described a political parade—"the smell of saltpeter, the snorts of horses, the shouts of men, the red and white ripple of the flags that went careering by in smoke and flame"—and found in this "some strange suggestion of the war our political contests typify, in spirit and symbol at least." An Indiana politician observed of the 1888 Republican convention: "The excitement, the mental and physical strains, the conflicting emotions in the hope of victory and the fear of defeat, in such a convention as that was, are surpassed only by a prolonged battle in actual warfare, as I have been told by officers of the Civil War who later engaged in convention struggles." The very vocabulary of politics lent strength to the metaphor of politics as war, as this pastiche put together by the historian Richard Jensen suggests:

> From the *opening gun* of the *campaign* the *standard bearer*, along with other *war-horses fielded* by the party, *rallied* the *rank* and *file* around the party *standard*, the *bloody shirt*, and other *slogans*. Precinct *captains aligned* their *phalanxes shoulder-to-shoulder* to mobilize votes for the *Old Guard* . . . Finally the *well-drilled fugelmen* in the *last ditch* closed *ranks*, overwhelmed the enemy *camp*, and divided the *spoils* of victory.

Nevertheless, this was not the ideological politics of the 1860s. The imagery was martial, but the needs to be serviced were economic or social interest, or mass entertainment. It is revealing that the major political journals of the 1880s, *Judge* and *Puck*, and their

21. Political History Collection, Smithsonian Institution, Item 51150C; William G. Sumner, "The Theory and Practice of Elections," in *Collected Essays in Political and Social Science* (New York, 1885), 133.

political cartoonists Joseph Keppler and Bernard Gillam, did not have the power, passion and commitment displayed by *Harper's Weekly* and Thomas Nast in the Civil War-Reconstruction generation.[22]

While party politics had a distinctly national character in the 1880s, important local, state, and regional differences existed. The increasingly one-party South, the immigrant-working class city machines of the East and the Midwest, and the state Republican organizations of the North had their particular qualities, their special needs. The population of a city—predominantly Protestant and native born, such as Republican Philadelphia and Cincinnati, or heavily Catholic and immigrant, such as Democratic New York —affected the style as well as the party affiliation of the dominant political organization.

State party machines also were varied. One observer thought that in its size and strength the Pennsylvania Republican machine resembled—and could deal on equal terms with—the large business corporations so conspicuous in that commonwealth. Highly responsive to the state's coal, iron, steel, and railroad interests, the organization at the same time exploited those interests (through such devices as the threat of hostile state legislation) in order to cover its increasingly expensive operating costs. At its turn-of-the-century peak, the Pennsylvania GOP was reputed to have lists of more than 800,000 party voters, each carefully classified as habitual, reliable, doubtful, wavering, accustomed to "fumble in the booth," and so on. The sequence of Pennsylvania Republican leaders—from the rough-hewn founder Simon Cameron to the smoother but no less venal Matthew Quay and the well-born, cynical Boies Penrose—reflected an organization that in half a century went from youth to maturity (and perhaps overripeness), "the strongest and most enduring state-wide party organization that has yet appeared in America."[23]

22. Sumner, *Theory and Practice*, 114; James Parton, "The Power of Public Plunder," *NAR*, 133 (1881), 45; Brand Whitlock, *The 13th District* (New York, 1902), 161; "1888 Folder," Michener Mss; Jensen, *Winning of the Midwest*, 11; Frank L. Mott, *A History of American Magazines* (Cambridge, 1967), III, 520–532, 552–556. See also Oliver McKee, *U.S. "Snap Shots"* (Boston, 1892), 412–418.

23. Macy, *Party Organization*, 120, 156–159. See also Walter Davenport,

The New York Republican machine, led from the late 1880s to 1902 by Thomas C. Platt—"lean rat Platt," in poet Vachel Lindsay's phrase—was similar in character (if not in the scale and success of its operation) to its Pennsylvania counterpart. Here, too, large corporate contributions replaced contractor kickbacks and officeholder levies as the major source of income. Again, a rich and varied state fostered a complex and costly party organization.

Massachusetts Republicans faced different conditions: a strong state tradition of ideological Republicanism, a persisting strain of antiparty independent politics, a unique body of state law regulating party conventions, caucuses, and committees. Not surprisingly, there was no Massachusetts state boss comparable to Quay in Pennsylvania or Platt in New York.[24]

The closeness of Indiana's party balance made it the most intensely contested state in presidential elections. This led to incredibly detailed local party organization. Lewis T. Michener became chairman of the Shelby County Republican Committee in 1882. He appointed 165 "district men," who were expected to know the "social and political affiliation" of each voter. Michener conducted frequent precinct meetings at which individual voters were thoroughly discussed. The result was that (in a Democratic year) the normal Democratic county majority of eight hundred was replaced by a Republican majority of four hundred. Michener in 1884 moved up to be secretary of the Republican State Committee. In that year state chairman John C. New put Michener's Shelby County plan into operation throughout the state: 10,000 district men were appointed. In 1888 Indiana national committeeman William W. Dudley wrote a letter, published by the Democrats, calling on county chairmen to organize and pay for votes in "blocks of five": this in a state with a quarter of a million Republican voters.

Francis E. Warren headed the Republican organization as Wyoming moved from territory to state. The source of his power lay not in his subservience to major economic interests such as the

---

Power and Glory: The Life of Boies Penrose (New York, 1931); Matthew Josephson, The Politicos 1865–1896 (New York, 1938), 407–409.

24. Harold F. Gosnell, Boss Platt and His New York Machine (Chicago, 1924); Josephson, Politicos, 409–411; on Massachusetts, Macy, Party Organization, 136–140.

Union Pacific and the Wyoming Stock Growers' Association, but rather in his ability to extract federal subsidies and in the party's stress on land reform, irrigation, and the expansion of military and Indian trading posts.[25]

There were strong Democratic state machines and leaders as well. Samuel J. Tilden's successor David J. Hill controlled the New York state party organization. Senator Arthur Pue Gorman dominated the Maryland Democracy. But immigrant-Catholic cities had the most distinctive and powerful Democratic organizations in the 1880s. Tammany Hall, the most famous of these, underwent a process of maturation not unlike that of the Pennsylvania Republican organization. Tweed's successor John Kelley systematized candidate assessments and salary percentage kickbacks from small officeholders. Richard Croker in the 1890s and Charles F. Murphy in the early twentieth century regularized the collection of funds from city businesses, both licit and illicit.

The character of the turn-of-the-century city machine appears in the recollections of George Washington Plunkitt, a Tammany man whose "very plain talks on very practical politics" were published (presumably with some literary license) by a reporter in 1905. What emerges from Plunkitt's remarks is an assured and easy view of the city as an endless source of graft, a sense of the machine as the provider of necessary comforts and services to the urban poor, and an identification with Tammany's leaders as patrons and the organization as a cross between church and corporation. In this sense his view of things was accurate. For the political machine of the late nineteenth century serviced the transition from the individualized, small-unit society of the past to the organizational society of the future.[26]

Most of all, the party boss caught the imagination of observers of late nineteenth century American politics. Political novels dwelt not so much on corrupt congressmen—the favorite theme of the 1870s—as on local (usually city) bosses. Typical of the genre was

25. "1886 Campaign Statement," Michener Mss; Robert D. Marcus, *Grand Old Party: Political Structure in the Gilded Age, 1880–1896* (New York, 1971), 143–144; Lewis L. Gould, *Wyoming: A Political History, 1868–1896* (New Haven, 1968).

26. Werner, *Tammany Hall*, 291–292, 420; William L. Riordon, *Plunkitt of Tammany Hall* (New York, 1948).

Rufus E. Shapley's *Solid for Mulhooly* (1881), which told of Michael Mulhooly's rise to control of "a political machine as complicated, as ingenious, as perfect as the works of a watch."

A stereotypical party boss emerged in the fiction and reformist writing of the time: cunning but gross and uneducated, profane and brutal—

> Skilled to pull wires, he baffles Nature's hope,
> Who sure intended him to stretch a rope.

—and thus well suited to the rough-hewn character of political life. Finley Peter Dunne's comic character Mr. Dooley observed: "Polytics ain't bean bag. 'Tis a man's game; an' women, childher an' pro-hybitionists do well to keep out iv it."[27]

In fact its practitioners were more complex than the standard view allowed for. A study of the first generation of Irish ward leaders in Boston during the 1870s and 1880s shows that a number of them were young, college- and law school-educated men for whom politics was the first step in a career that went on to law, real estate, and the like. Given its methods of organization and mass persuasion, party politics was one of the more sophisticated and successful occupations of the late nineteenth century: "a definite profession," concluded James Bryce. He noticed that Americans spoke of "the politicians," not (as in England) of "politicians," an indication that they were a distinct social group. "What characterizes them as compared with the corresponding class in Europe," he concluded, "is that their whole time is more frequently given to political work, that most of them draw an income from politics and the rest hope to do so, that they come more largely from the poorer and less cultivated than from the higher ranks of society, and that . . . many are proficients in the arts of popular oratory, of electioneering, and of party management."[28]

These "majority manufacturers" were skilled professionals in an

27. Gordon Milne, *The American Political Novel* (Norman, Okla., 1966), chs. 3–4; Rufus E. Shapley, *Solid for Mulhooly: A Political Satire* (Philadelphia, 1881, 1889), 61–62; James Russell Lowell, *Poems* (Boston, 1890), IV, 261; Philip Dunne, ed., *Mr. Dooley Remembers: The Informal Memoirs of Finley Peter Dunne* (Boston, 1963), 106.

28. Jack Larkin, " 'They Was Born to Rule': Boston's Irish Politicians, 1870–1890," unpublished seminar paper, Brandeis University, 1966; Bryce, *American Commonwealth*, II, 68, 55n, 65.

exacting trade. But at the same time the business of politics put a premium on other traits: fierce competitiveness, clanlike loyalties and hatreds, a constant trafficking with the illegal and the socially marginal. Theodore Roosevelt observed in 1886 that "a professional politician is much less apt to be swayed by the fact of a man's being a Democrat or a Republican than he is by his being a personal friend or foe."

This attitude did not foster an issue-oriented politics. Tammany's Croker, pressed on the currency issue of the 1890s, supposedly replied: "What's the use discussing what's the best kind of money? I'm in favor of all kinds of money—the more the better." Big John Kennedy in Alfred H. Lewis's novel *The Boss and How He Came to Rule* (1903) handed down some professional advice from his deathbed: "An' th' last of it is, don't get sentimental—don't take politics to heart. Politics is only worth while so long as it fills your pockets. Don't tie yourself to anything. A political party is like a street car; stay with it only while it goes your way. A great partisan can never be a great Boss."

During the troubled years at the end of the century this attitude worked against economic and social polarization. Boies Penrose told Henry C. Frick of Carnegie Steel: "What is the use of shooting a man for striking? Compromise with him. Give him half what he demands. That will be twice as much as he expects to get." Mark Hanna, the businessman-boss first of the Ohio GOP and then of the 1896 McKinley campaign, contemptuously said of George Pullman, whose obduracy touched off the massive, destructive railroad strike of 1894: "A man who won't meet his men half-way is a God-damn fool!"[29]

The prevailing style of political bossism cut across party and ethnic lines. There were Protestant Republican city bosses such as "Doc" Ames in Minneapolis or George B. Cox in Cincinnati. But it was the Irish who scored the most notable success in urban machine politics. A worried observer concluded in 1894 that they ran

29. James Russell Lowell quoted in George F. Howe, *Chester A. Arthur* (New York, 1934), 204; Theodore Roosevelt, "Machine Politics in New York City," *CM*, 33 (1886–1887), 79; Croker quoted in Werner, *Tammany*, 441; Alfred H. Lewis, *The Boss and How He Came to Rule* (New York, 1903), 210; Penrose quoted in Davenport, *Power and Glory*, 95–96; Thomas Beer, *Hanna, Crane, and the Mauve Decade* (New York, 1941), 498.

New York, Brooklyn, Jersey City, Hoboken, Albany, Troy, Buffalo, Pittsburgh, St. Paul, St. Louis, Kansas City, New Orleans, Omaha, and San Francisco. The clannishness, the barroom bonding, the arts of organization and manipulation that flourished in Ireland under British rule traveled well to the teeming cities of the New World.

In many ways the Irish were outlanders in Protestant, rural and small town-dominated American politics. Brooklyn Congressman William E. Robinson met Chicago Representative John F. Finerty on the Capitol steps one day in the early 1880s, and asked him: "Anything going on inside, Jawn?" "No, nothing but some damned American business." Tammany's Plunkitt spoke of Protestant-Republican Philadelphia as being "ruled almost entirely by Americans." This outsider's quality helped the Irish to lead the urban immigrant masses, most of whom were even less attuned to the mainstream of American life. Tammany boss Richard Croker was aware of that role: "Think what New York is and what the people of New York are. One half, more than one half, are of foreign birth ... They do not speak our language, they do not know our laws, they are the raw material with which we have to build up the State. How are you to do it on mugwump methods? ... There is not a mugwump in the city who would shake hands with them."

Croker, who in manner and appearance fit the stereotype of the late nineteenth century boss, compared the leaders of the party machines to the molders of modern American banking, railroads, and industry. They too were skilled professionals, who deserved just compensation for large and demanding work. But the metaphor that most readily came to Croker's mind was martial, not professional: "Chess is war; business is war; the rivalry of students and of athletes is war. Everything is war in which men strive for mastery and power as against other men, and this is one of the essential conditions of progress."[30]

Part skilled professional, part tribal chieftain, the boss flourished

---

30. John P. Bocock, "The Irish Conquest of Our Cities," *Forum*, 17 (1894), 186–195; Daniel J. Boorstin, *The Americans: The Democratic Experience* (New York, 1973), 252–261; Dunne, ed., *Mr. Dooley Remembers*, 87–88; Riordon, *Plunkitt*, 41; Werner, *Tammany*, 449–450; Richard Croker, "Tammany Hall and the Democracy," *NAR*, 154 (1892), 227. See also Samuel P. Orth, *The Boss and the Machine* (New Haven, 1919).

in that transitional time when a complex industrial society out-stripped the instruments of governance. On the state and national level, he mediated between vested economic interests and a demo-cratic political system; in the immigrant-worker cities, he main-tained social order and met basic social needs: all this, of course, at a steep cost in money and morality. His relative importance would decline in the twentieth century, with the coming of a more ma-ture and systematized economic order and the rise of bureaucratic public services.

It would be a mistake to view this late nineteenth century politi-cal system solely in terms of its strength and success. Fraud and corruption, and a debilitating factionalism, were among its integral components. This was particularly evident in the cities. Their large, poor populations, their ethnic cleavages and fragmented political power, their social disorganization smoothed the way for political arrivistes and eased the path of corruption.

The importance of money grew as politics became less explicitly ideological and more highly organized. By one estimate about $700,000 was spent on a typical New York City election in the 1880s. Connecticut Republicans reportedly spent $200,000 in the 1888 election, the Democrats $50,000. In New York's Thirteenth Congressional District (embracing Dutchess, Putnam, and Colum-bia counties) a congressional candidate in the mid-eighties sup-posedly spent $150,000, his opponent $75,000.

In the 1870s and the early 1880s, contractor kickbacks and assess-ments from officeholders provided the lion's share of funds. These continued, despite legislation such as an 1876 act of Congress that forbade federal employees from contributing money for political purposes. Nominations to Congress, state legislatures, and judge-ships had their price. Tammany's take in kickbacks from liquor dealers alone at the turn of the century was between $2.5 and $10 million.[31]

31. Werner, *Tammany*, 293; on Connecticut, Stimson, *Methods of Bribery*, 10; on 13th District, Henry George, "Money in Elections," *NAR*, 136 (1883), 202–203; "Political Assessments," *AC* (1882); Bryce, *American Commonwealth*, II, 117–119; on Tammany, C. K. Yearley, *The Money Machines* (Albany, 1970), 116. See also Eric McKitrick, "The Study of Corruption," *PSQ*, 72 (1957), 502–514; James C. Scott, "Corruption, Ma-chine Politics, and Political Change," *APSR*, 63 (1969), 1142–1158.

During the latter part of the century, corporate contributions became an increasingly important source of revenue. The railroads were the leading corporate contributors after the Civil War. By 1900 the large life insurance companies, coal and oil firms, and hundreds of other businesses provided funds to political organizations. The Bryan scare in 1896 substantially expanded this source. But it was growing in any event, in pace with the number, size, and needs of interstate business. This was a mutually exploitative relationship. The politicians extorted money from the companies by threats of hostile legislation, the companies sought favors and services from the politicos. The boss in David Graham Phillips's *The Plum Tree* (1905) complained of this corporate pressure: "They make bigger and bigger, and more and more unreasonable, demands on us, and so undermine our popularity . . . And thus, year by year, it takes more and more money to keep us in control." A business donor had a different perspective: "I've no time to go into politics, . . . and I don't know anything about it—don't want to know. It's a low business, . . . ignorance, corruption, filthiness."[32]

The substantial political stakes of jobs, money, and influence, and the lack of sharp ideological conflict, fed another characteristic of the system: an endless, pervasive factionalism. The Stalwart-Half Breed division rent the Republican party in the late 1870s and early 1880s. Democratic factionalism was no less keen. New York Democratic politics was kept in constant turmoil by a complex and intense struggle between Tammany and David Hill's upstate organization, and by the conflict among three New York City factions: Tammany Hall, Irving Hall, and the County Democracy. Tammany boss John Kelly's hatred of Tilden and Cleveland cost the one the 1880 presidential nomination and seriously damaged the other in his 1888 bid for reelection. Republican party divisions helped the Democrats to win Rhode Island in 1887. Democratic rule in Maryland was threatened in that year by intraparty factionalism.

Beneath the surface of powerful machines and bosses lay a reality of harried uncertainty, shifting circumstance: an instability as great of that of the society itself. "Bull" Andrews of the Pennsyl-

32. Morton Keller, *The Life Insurance Enterprise, 1885–1910* (Cambridge, 1964), 228–229; Marcus, *Grand Old Party*, 246–249; David G. Phillips, *The Plum Tree* (Indianapolis, 1905), 111, 72.

vania Republican machine struck a note that rang deep and true when he was asked what Boss Quay and his associates discussed in their frequent secret meetings: "Most always the only thing they can think to talk about is what the hell to do next."[33]

The Politics of the Eighties

When Thomas Wolfe sought to portray the gulf between his and his father's generations, he used the image of "The Four Lost Men":

> Garfield, Arthur, Harrison, and Hayes—time of my father's time, blood of his blood, life of his life, had been living, real, and actual people in all the passion, power, and feeling of my father's youth. And for me they were the lost Americans: their gravely vacant and bewhiskered faces mixed, melted, swam together in the sea-depths of a past intangible, immeasurable, and unknowable as the buried city of Persepolis.
>
> And they were lost.
>
> For who was Garfield, martyred man, and who had seen him in the streets of life? Who could believe his footfalls ever sounded on a lonely pavement? Who had heard the casual and familiar tones of Chester Arthur? And where was Harrison? Where was Hayes? Which had the whiskers, which the burnsides: which was which?
>
> Were they not lost?[34]

Which, indeed, was which? Between the sharp-edged politics of Reconstruction and the bitter Bryan-McKinley contest of 1896 lay a time when the issues, the very shape of American politics were fuzzy and indistinct. The brittle, mechanical devices of organizational politics prevailed over major national issues. As James Bryce put it, "neither party has any principles, any distinctive tenets. Both have traditions. Both claim to have tendencies . . . All has been lost, except office or the hope of it."

33. "New York," *AC* (1880 ff); Leonard Dinnerstein, "The Impact of Tammany Hall on State and National Politics in the Eighteen-Eighties," *NYH*, 42 (1961), 237–252; Werner, *Tammany*, 440–441; "Rhode Island," "Maryland," *AC* (1887); Andrews quoted in Davenport, *Power and Glory*, 45.

34. Thomas Wolfe, "The Four Lost Men," in *From Death to Morning* (New York, 1932–1935), 121. Used with permission of Charles Scribner's Sons, New York, and William Heinemann, Ltd., London.

The "proposition that in a free state, political parties are constantly tending to an equilibrium" now had its fullest confirmation. The national party balance in presidential elections became strikingly close between 1876 and 1896 (table 3).

TABLE 3. National party balance in presidential elections, 1868–1900

Year	Republican and Democratic vote	Margin	Margin as percent of Republican–Democratic total
1868	5,717,246	309,380 (R)	5.0
1872	6,431,086	763,664 (R)	11.9
1876	9,412,860	251,476 (D)[a]	2.7
1880	8,899,409	9,457 (R)	.1
1884	9,728,205	23,737 (D)	.2
1888	10,985,634	95,096 (D)[a]	.9
1892	10,748,448	365,516 (D)	3.4
1896	13,630,456	597,012 (R)	4.4
1900	13,577,988	861,668 (R)	6.0

Source: Svend Peterson, *A Statistical History of the American Presidential Elections* (New York, 1963), 42–43, 46, 49, 52, 55, 60, 64, 67.

[a] Republican electoral victory.

Congress also reflected the close party balance. The Republicans controlled the Senate for seven of the ten sessions between 1875 and 1895, the Democrats controlled the House in eight of the ten.

This was a time of electoral equipoise; it was also a time of stable voting patterns. The percentage of the Democratic vote from 1860 to 1892 correlated at .772 in Michigan and Ohio, at .762 in Wisconsin. In ten states with more than 40 percent of the electoral vote, neither party was able to win much more than half of the total, thus adding to the importance of third parties, voter defections, and the level of turnout (table 4).[35]

The closeness of the party balance gave a special character to the presidential elections of the 1880s. These were not grand confronta-

35. Bryce, *American Commonwealth*, II, 21; Ford, *Rise and Growth*, 12; on Democratic vote, Paul Kleppner, *The Cross of Culture: A Social Analysis of Midwestern Politics 1850–1900* (New York, 1970), 13.

TABLE 4. Party percentages in presidential elections, 1876–1888

State	1876 R	1876 D	1880 R	1880 D	1884 R	1884 D	1888 R	1888 D
California	50.9	49.1	48.9	49.0	52.1	45.4	50.0	47.1
Connecticut	48.3	50.7	50.5	48.5	48.0	49.0	48.4	48.7
Illinois	50.1	46.6	51.1	44.6	50.2	46.4	49.5	46.6
Indiana	48.3	49.5	49.3	47.9	48.2	49.5	49.1	48.6
Michigan	52.5	44.4	52.5	37.3	47.8	37.2	49.7	44.9
New Jersey	47.0	52.7	49.1	49.8	47.3	49.0	47.5	49.9
New York	48.1	51.3	50.3	48.4	48.2	48.3	49.2	48.1
Ohio	50.2	49.1	51.4	47.0	51.0	46.9	49.5	47.2
Pennsylvania	50.6	48.3	50.8	46.6	52.7	43.7	52.7	44.8
Wisconsin	50.9	48.5	54.0	42.9	50.3	45.8	49.8	43.8

Source: Peterson, Statistical History, 47, 50, 53, 56.

tions over national issues so much as contests for control of the federal patronage that might go either way. Thus the razor-close 1880 contest between the Republicans' James A. Garfield and Democratic candidate Winfield Scott Hancock had much less ideological bitterness than the Hayes-Tilden election of 1876. Tilden was identified with the Peace Democrats during the Civil War; Hancock was a Union army general.

Grover Cleveland's victory over James G. Blaine in 1884, the first by a Democrat since 1856, confirmed that the post-Civil War political order would not be upset by a Democratic President. An 1885 analysis concluded: "the result of the election settles the question that one of the two great parties will continue to control the government, and that there will be no new national party for a generation to come that will have any considerable influence in politics."[36]

The distinctive qualities of party politics in the eighties—a close balance, highly organized campaigning, fuzzy issues—were most evident in the 1888 election. The Democratic incumbent Cleveland and the Republican Benjamin Harrison were uncharismatic

36. Lee Benson, "Research Problems in American Political Historiography," in Mirra Komarovsky, ed., Common Frontiers of the Social Sciences (Glencoe, 1957), 123–146; Adin Thayer, The Political Situation (Worcester, 1885), 4.

figures, heavily relying on their respective parties' organizations and traditional appeals. Neither proposed to set out on a new course: "It is the old names, 'the party of Jefferson,' 'the party of the Union,' . . . that holds." Cleveland won a narrow popular victory but lost in the electoral count, which underlined the fact that chance, money, organization, local factors and issues—not sweeping national causes—were determining. "The spirit of provincialism," said one observer, "reaches it[s] greatest expression at times like the present, when the balance between the two great theories of nationalism and individualism is nearly evenly maintained."[37]

It was as though the eighties were a respite between the passionate and divisive politics of the Civil War and Reconstruction and the emergence in the 1890s of a politics more directly concerned with the consequences of American industrialization. But the equipoise of the 1880s reflected the stasis of conflicting social forces, not the calm of social harmony. There was no sudden shift from the political ambiance of Hayes and Tilden to that of Bryan and McKinley, but rather a continuing process of electoral, ideological, and organizational evolution.

One of the indices of change was third or extraparty politics. Dissent from the Republican-Democratic hegemony was minute, except for the Populist outburst of the early 1890s (table 5).

The Greenback-Union Labor and Prohibition movements generated the largest blocs of extraparty votes in the 1880s. They did not upset the party equilibrium because their vote totals were small and tended to cancel each other out. The Prohibitionists drew most strongly from normal (or potential) Republican voters, the Greenbackers and Union Laborites primarily from Democratic sources. But they were "symptomatic parties" in the sense that they brought out in bold relief issues and anxieties that the major parties tended to repress.[38]

Kentucky's Prohibitionists declared in 1881 that they "renounce

37. Charles W. Clark, "The Spirit of American Politics as Shown in the Late Election," AM, 63 (1889), 228, 230. See also H. Wayne Morgan, From Hayes to McKinley: National Party Politics, 1877–1896 (Syracuse, 1969), chs. 5, 7.

38. Kleppner, Cross of Culture, 15; Henry W. Wilbur, "Symptomatic Parties," GM, 24 (1903), 119–121.

TABLE 5. Minor party votes, 1868–1900

Year	Combined minor party vote	Percent of total vote
1868	0	0
1872	35,052	.09
1876	94,935	1.12
1880	320,058	3.47
1884	326,023	3.24
1888	404,205	3.55
1892	1,322,632	10.96
1896	317,219	2.27
1900	396,200	2.83

Source: Peterson, Statistical History, 42–43, 46, 49, 52, 55, 60, 64, 67.

connections with the old parties, full of dead issues, and declare for a new era, full of living virtues." But state Prohibition parties often identified with the old Republican equal rights doctrine. Maine Prohibitionists in 1886 sought the "application of Christian principles to politics, . . . the abolition of polygamy, the better condition of Indians, and of the colored people of the South." The Pennsylvania party ran a black candidate for congressman-at-large, and Prohibition platforms endorsed women's suffrage, compulsory education, and the direct election of senators and the President.

Prohibition candidates for President also came from this political tradition. John P. St. John, who ran in 1884, had been the Republican governor of Kansas in the late seventies and early eighties. Clinton B. Fisk, the 1888 candidate, had a distinguished Civil War record (as did St. John), and served after the war as assistant commissioner of the Freedmen's Bureau for Kentucky and Tennessee. Fisk University, a leading postwar school for blacks, bore his name. He also was a member of Grant's Board of Indian Commissioners. John Bidwell, the 1892 nominee, had a third party career dating back to an Antimonopoly candidacy for governor of California in 1875, and also had a continuing concern for Indian rights.[39]

39. "Kentucky," AC (1881); "Maine," AC (1886); "Pennsylvania," AC (1886); "Ohio," AC (1881); on candidates, DAB. See also George L. Case, "The Prohibition Party: Its Origin, Purpose and Growth," MWH, 9 (1888–1889), 705–714; Paul Kleppner, "The Greenback and Prohibition Parties," in Arthur M. Schlesinger, Jr., ed., History of U.S. Political Parties (New York, 1973), II, 1566–1581.

At the same time, by the very nature of their primary issue the Prohibitionists reflected the anxieties of many Americans facing social change. The Pennsylvania party in 1886 wanted a Christian Sabbath instead of a Continental Sunday and a federal marriage and divorce statute "conformable to the divine law." Ohio Prohibitionists called for the outlawing of speculation in gold, stocks, and agricultural futures, and in 1887 they condemned the spread of anarchism. Immigration restriction, the prohibition of state aid to sectarian schools, and common school teaching in English only (so that Americans might "become and remain a homogeneous and harmonious people") were other Prohibitionist goals. The national party's 1888 suffrage clause, adopted after sharp debate, nicely summed up the mix of old ideals and new anxieties that fed the movement: "the right of suffrage rests on no mere circumstances of race, color, sex, or nationality, and . . . where, from any cause, it has been withheld from citizens who are of suitable age and mentality and morally qualified for the exercise of an intelligent ballot, it should be restored by the people through the Legislatures of the several States, on such educational basis as they may deem wise."

The party won more than a quarter of a million votes in the national elections of 1888 and 1892. It exerted strong pressure on Republican platforms and candidates throughout the Midwest. And its cause struck a responsive chord among churchgoing rural and small town people in the North and among middle class urban southerners fearful of liquor's effect on blacks and poor whites. But it was too narrowly based to become a major political force in its own right, and would be decimated in the 1890s by the rise of the Populists and William Jennings Bryan, who appealed to many of Prohibitionism's people and concerns.[40]

Other recurrent sources of extraparty politics, fed by the dis-

---

40. "Pennsylvania," AC (1886); "Ohio," AC (1881, 1887); "Indiana," "Massachusetts," "Connecticut," AC (1892); Kirk H. Porter and Donald B. Johnson, National Party Platforms 1840–1960 (Urbana, 1961), 79; on impact, Kleppner, Cross of Culture, 138, Jensen, Winning of Midwest, ch. 4; Robert A. Hohner, "The Prohibitionists: Who Were They?" SAQ, 68 (1969), 491–505; John H. Moore, "The Negro and Prohibition in Atlanta, 1885–1887," SAQ, 69 (1970), 38–57; "Growing Power of the Prohibitionists," Nation, 42 (1886), 462–463; David P. Thelen, "La Follette and the Temperance Crusade," WMH, 47 (1964), 291–300; Kleppner, "Greenback and Prohibition Parties," 1578.

contents that came with industrialism and agricultural change, were antimonopoly and currency inflation. The postwar Greenback movement reached its peak in 1878, but continued on into the 1880s. Although it appears to have drawn more from Democratic than from Republican sources—typically, Greenbackers fused with Democrats in Iowa and Minnesota—the movement was an eclectic one. The 1881 Greenback Labor nominee for secretary of state in Rhode Island was black; so was a Kansas congressional candidate in 1882. Party platforms called not only for currency expansion but also for railroad regulation, a graduated income tax, and the protection of American workingmen through restrictions on immigration and child and prison labor.

The movement split into labor and agrarian wings during the 1880s. Ben Butler ran as an Antimonopoly candidate for governor of Massachusetts in 1882, and there were numerous municipal labor parties, culminating in Henry George's New York City mayoralty candidacy in 1886. But the Union Labor party of the late 1880s was strongest in the agrarian South and West. The bulk of its nearly 150,000 votes in 1888 came from Kansas, Texas, Missouri, Arkansas, Iowa, Wisconsin, and Illinois.[41]

The Mugwumps of the 1880s, like the Prohibitionists and the Greenbackers and Union Laborites, belonged to an established tradition of political dissent. Antiorganization Republican journalists and professionals were conspicuous in the Liberal Republican movement of 1872. Then in 1884 a number of them bolted the GOP on the ground that James G. Blaine was the quintessential spoils politician, while Democratic candidate Cleveland championed civil service reform. They won the popular name of Mugwumps, a word supposedly of Indian origin that was applied derisively to the pompous and self-important.

The Mugwump movement attracted those who wanted a more purposeful politics: "If we must have parties, it is highly desirable

41. Ibid., 1562–1565; Kleppner, *Cross of Culture*, 120–123; "Rhode Island," *AC* (1881); "Kansas," *AC* (1882); "Iowa," *AC* (1883); on Butler, "Massachusetts," *AC* (1882); Thomas J. Condon, "Politics, Reform, and the New York City Election of 1886," *NYHS Quarterly*, 44 (1960), 363–393; on Union Labor party, Fred E. Haynes, *Third Party Movements since the Civil War* (Iowa City, 1916), 206–217, Clifton Paisley, "The Political Wheelers and Arkansas' Election of 1888," *ArkHQ*, 25 (1966), 3–21.

that they should arise spontaneously, on clearly formulated principles and with definite objects; that they should cease to exist as soon as possible after these objects have been attained; . . . that we should not go on stupidly transmitting from sire to son the antipathy begotten by obsolete party differences which have been outlasted by party names." As in 1872, journalists—who keenly felt the replacement of a politics of ideology by a politics of organization —were conspicuous in the movement. Seven of New York City's leading newspapers, including the *Times*, the *Post*, and the *World*, swung from Garfield in 1880 to Cleveland in 1884.[42]

Political independence met a need for commitment that led many to equate the struggle for honest government with the antislavery crusade. James Russell Lowell declared: "A moral purpose multiplies us by ten, as it multiplied the early abolitionists. They emancipated the negro; and we mean to emancipate the respectable white man." It attracted those who were psychologically disposed to dissent. One Mugwump, William Everett of Boston, said: "When I am in a small minority I believe I am right. When I am in a minority of one, I know I am right." The lawyers, businessmen, and professionals who joined the Mugwump movement in Boston and New York were not fearful of the threat that machine politics posed to their status and power. Rather, they were secure, well-established citizens sufficiently free from other concerns to turn their attention to the issue of political morality. Jurist Thomas M. Cooley wrote in 1884: "I have long been tired of the assumptions of politicians who have held the reins of power until they have come to look upon the government as an appurtenance to a political party, & any attempt at a change of rules as a sort of treason."[43]

42. Hans Sperber and Travis Trittschuh, *Dictionary of American Political Terms* (New York, 1964), 276–277; Wendell P. Garrison, "The Reform of the Senate," *AM*, 68 (1891), 228; Mark D. Hirsch, "The New York Times and the Election of 1884," *NYH*, 29 (1948), 301–308. See also John G. Sproat, *"The Best Men": Liberal Reformers in the Gilded Age* (New York, 1968), ch. 5.

43. Lowell, "The Place of the Independent in Politics," *Literary and Political Addresses* (Boston, 1886–1890), 201; Blodgett, *Gentle Reformers*, 42; John M. Dobson, "George William Curtis and the Election of 1884: The Dilemma of the New York Mugwumps," *NYHS Quarterly*, 52 (1968), 215–234; Gerald W. McFarland, "The New York Mugwumps of 1884: A Profile," *PSQ*, 78 (1963), 40–58; Gordon S. Wood, "The Massachusetts Mug-

Some hoped that a party of independents might emerge from the 1884 experience: "political parties must face the future not the past; and if neither of the existing parties is able or willing to do this, it is certain that from the power of self-organization, which is proved by the history of this campaign to be a characteristic of the American people, there will arise a new party to answer to the new development of the nation." But many Mugwumps were deeply conservative men, fearful of the social and economic changes transforming the nation. And there was an insurmountable ambiguity in the very concept of a party of independents. Mugwumpery was "not an organization but a mood"; it would persist as a state of mind rather than a concrete alternative to the major parties.[44]

A common theme of extraparty advocates was the claim that the major parties lacked content or purpose. But were they in fact so devoid of social meaning? Certainly they appealed to distinct and distinguishable segments of the population. Each had its own web of affiliations based on location and region, class and family, ideology, ethnicity, and religion. Thus in Indiana, small-town voters were more likely than farmers to be Republicans; teachers, railroad hands, and company agents tended to be independents, traders to be Democrats. Studies of late nineteenth century voting behavior are in accord that religious differences in particular correlated closely with party preferences. Catholics customarily were Democrats whether they were rich or poor, urban or rural, German or Irish. Quakers, Congregationalists, Disciples of Christ as frequently were Republican. Within the major Protestant sects, those who inclined to a pietistic theology—such as Missouri Synod Lutherans—tended to Republicanism; those who were more ritualistic in matters of faith—such as Wisconsin Synod Lutherans—were likely to be Democrats.

A study of Nebraska politics in the 1880s demonstrates the sa-

---

wumps," NEQ, 33 (1960), 435–451; Geoffrey T. Blodgett, "The Mind of the Boston Mugwump," MVHR, 48 (1962), 614–634; Thomas M. Cooley to Thomas A. Hendricks, Nov. 17, 1884, Cooley Mss, MichHS.

44. Report of the National Executive Committee of Republicans and Independents (New York, 1885; NYPL), 23; Blodgett, "Boston Mugwump," 614.

liency of these distinctions. Platte County was evenly divided between the major parties in 1880. But that balance was the sum of extremes such as German Catholic St. Bernard Township, which went 88 percent Democratic in that year, and native American Monroe Township, which went 92 percent Republican. As the decade progressed, religious and ethnic group differences grew over issues such as temperance, Sabbatarianism, and education. Democratic strength in Nebraska, small to begin with, increased primarily because of these sociocultural issues. As the Republican party responded to its pietistic elements by taking a stronger stand on temperance and woman's suffrage, more ritualistic Lutherans and Methodists switched to the Democrats. A similar development apparently occurred throughout the Midwest, as a Republican "politics of piety" gained force everywhere and evoked a correspondingly strong Democratic reaction.[45]

The distinctive character of the parties emerged in their ideology as well as in their popular support. The Democrats of the 1880s retained their traditional hostility to active, centralized government. Their 1880 platform pledged the party "anew" to "opposition to centralization and to that dangerous spirit of encroachment which tends to consolidate the powers of all the departments in one." New York Democrats in 1881 were "unalterably opposed to centralization of power in either state or federal governments." They proposed that those who were "performing executive service for the state or General Government" be "deprived of elective franchise for such period of service." State platforms often dwelt on the need to reduce taxes and give home rule to cities.

The Democrats of the eighties frequently condemned the rise of monopolies and trusts. They called for the safeguarding of workingmen's interests through the prohibition of Chinese or contract labor, bans on the use of convict labor, and laws regulating the payment of wages and the hours of work. Tariff reduction, which nicely summed up the party's laissez-faire, free market inclinations, came to be the major Democratic economic policy. There

45. Melvin Hammarberg, "Indiana Farmers and the Group Basis of the Late Nineteenth-Century Political Parties," *JAH*, 61 (1974), 91–115; Kleppner, *Cross of Culture*, 25, 43; Jensen, *Winning of Midwest*, ch. 3; Frederick C. Luebke, *Immigrants and Politics: The Germans of Nebraska, 1880–1900* (Lincoln, Neb., 1969), 50–51, 79.

was only a passing reference to "a tariff for revenue only" in the 1880 national platform, but in 1884 and 1888 there were extended discussions of the links between the tariff, taxation, and government spending.[46]

There was also a distinctive Democratic social policy. As the 1881 Ohio platform put it, the party was "in favor of the largest individual liberty consistent with public order, and . . . opposed to legislation merely sumptuary." Democrats were against prohibition, coercive laws, police regulation "opposed to [the] plainest principles of sound government." It was not the business of government to control public tastes and habits as long as they were peaceable.

But this libertarianism had limits, which grew stronger as American social anxieties mounted in the eighties. Democratic state platforms denounced polygamy and Mormon political control. There was some criticism of state aid to religious schools and concern lest the public schools be "poisoned by [the] breath of sectarianism." Indiana Democrats in 1886 approved a ban on alien-held real estate. Ohio Democrats supported immigration restriction. Hostility to Negro, Indian, and Chinese equality was common. There were calls for an immediate end to Chinese immigration and the deportation of all Chinese resident in the United States; for the exclusive use of white labor; for the breakup of the remaining Indian reservations by "fair purchase" or by seizure.[47]

Democratic party organization in the eighties also had a characteristic style, that of the "Bourbon" Democracy. Implying as it did a political attitude that forgot nothing and learned nothing, the label nicely evoked the traditionalist strain evident in the party's rhetoric.

Southern Democratic organizations steadily grew in confidence and power. Freed from the constraints of Reconstruction, Democrats faced a substantial (though minority) Republican opposition only in the upper South and border states of Maryland, Missouri,

46. "New York," *AC* (1881); "Minnesota," *AC* (1886); Porter and Johnson, *Platforms*, 56, 65, 77–78.

47. "Ohio," *AC* (1881); "Connecticut," "Illinois," *AC* (1882); "Idaho," *AC* (1886); "Indiana," "Ohio," *AC* (1886); "Nebraska," "Colorado," "Idaho," *AC* (1886).

North Carolina, Tennessee, and West Virginia. The primary danger was factional division or political independency. Mississippi's Democrats warned in 1877: "All independent candidates are dangerous to the integrity of party organization; . . . they shall be treated as common enemies to the welfare of the people."

Virginia's Readjusters, dedicated to scaling down the state's debt obligations, threatened the Democratic leadership during the 1870s and early 1880s. Southside Virginia farmers supported the Readjusters, as did Richmond business and mercantile interests opposed to the growing control of the state's railroads by the Pennsylvania and Baltimore & Ohio lines. In 1883 Virginia Conservatives formally took on the Democratic party name, pegged their campaign to the need to preserve white supremacy, and in an election scarred by fraud and violence defeated the Readjusters. A wave of statutory changes—offices were vacated, town charters altered, congressional districts redrawn, new election laws passed— assured unbroken Bourbon Democratic rule thereafter.

Bourbon Democracy also came to power in Louisiana. The post-Reconstruction administration of Governor Francis T. Nicholls appointed some Negroes to minor offices "where . . . they were powerless to do harm," and pursued relatively moderate racial policies. But more conservative Democrats, in Louisiana as elsewhere strong in the plantation-cotton areas of high black density, condemned this policy as "rampant pseudo-liberalism." Under the state's 1879 constitution a combine of the planter parishes and the directors of the powerful state lottery took control of the party. Their political leader Samuel D. McEnery was governor from 1881 to 1888. The Louisiana Bourbon Democrats maintained their supremacy by large votes in the cotton parishes, a product of fraud and the cooptation of black votes. The opposing Nicholls faction drew its strength from small farmers and sugar planters; the balance of power lay in New Orleans. Nicholls won the governorship in 1888, and state treasurer Edward Burke, who also headed the lottery, fled the state, leaving fiscal irregularities totaling more than $12,000,000 behind him.[48]

48. "Mississippi," *AC* (1877); on Virginia, Raymond H. Pulley, *Old Virginia Restored* (Charlottesville, 1968), chs. 2–4, and C. Vann Woodward, *Origins of the New South 1877–1913* (Baton Rouge, 1951), 77–84; on Louisiana, William I. Hair, *Bourbonism and Agrarian Protest: Louisiana Politics, 1877–1900* (Baton Rouge, 1969), 22–23, 30, 109, 114–116 ff.

Similar Bourbon Democratic regimes flourished elsewhere in the South. Their rhetoric of Jeffersonian Democracy, free trade, hard money, limited government, and personal (white) freedom accorded with the views of their northern party counterparts, and appealed to many genteel reformers as well. Thomas F. Bayard, senator from Delaware and secretary of state in Cleveland's first administration, was admired by Henry Adams, David Ames Wells, and Charles W. Eliot; he was the presidential choice of the Harvard student body in 1880. This dignified, Old School Democrat, an apostle of free trade (except when it came to the protection of DuPont gunpowder from foreign competition), warned of the "spirit of centralization," of "centripetal forces at work that ... the people of this country would be most wise to check, ... in order that the orderly distribution of power intended by those who founded this government should once more prevail." It is understandable that Henry Adams spoke of the Democrats as "the last remnants of the eighteenth century; ... the sole remaining protestants against a bankers' Olympus."[49]

The character of the northern state Democratic leadership in the 1880s was very similar. Midwestern state organizations came under the control of a new generation of leaders, less involved than their predecessors in the issues of the Civil War and Reconstruction, more attuned to substantial business and financial interests. Among them were the banker-politician J. Sterling Morton of Nebraska, and banker Alexander Mitchell and millionaire lumberman William F. Vilas of Wisconsin. A triumvirate consisting of Northern Pacific magnate James J. Hill and two St. Paul Irish Catholic businessmen, Patrick H. Kelly and Michael Doran, ran the Minnesota Democracy.

The iron manufacturer and former Democratic National Chairman William H. Barnum dominated the Connecticut party in the 1880s. Low tariff, laissez-faire, Jeffersonian rhetoric provided the ideological glue for a Yankee-Irish alliance. Barnum's chief lieu-

---

49. Charles C. Tansill, *The Congressional Career of Thomas Francis Bayard 1869–1885* (Washington, 1946), 340, 250, 308, 257; Henry Adams, *The Education of Henry Adams* (Boston, 1918), 321. See also William J. Cooper, Jr., *The Conservative Regime: South Carolina, 1877–1890* (Baltimore, 1968); Allen J. Going, *Bourbon Democracy in Alabama 1874–1890* (University, Ala., 1951); Dewey W. Grantham, Jr., "The Southern Bourbons Revisited," *SAQ*, 40 (1961), 286–295.

tenant was Alexander Troup, editor of the *New Haven Union* and an Irish immigrant. Among those prominent in the party were the tariff reformer David Ames Wells and James P. Pigott, an Irish Catholic graduate of Yale who was active in the good government movement. A similar stress on the themes of economy and reform helped Democrat Robert E. Pattison win the Pennsylvania governorship in 1882 and again in 1890.

The Massachusetts Democracy flourished in the eighties, as oldtime Yankee Democrats, Mugwump reformers, and the Irish found common cause. William E. Russell won the governorship in 1890 with the help of labor, the Mugwumps, and a new generation of respectable, conservative Irish leaders such as Congressman Patrick Collins and Boston boss Pat Maguire. Again, the free trade theme, with its intonations of laissez-faire, antimonopoly, and competition with British industry, smoothed the way: "Tariff agitation in Massachusetts helped to unify party factions where civil service agitation had divided them."[50]

An intricate network of family connections, as well as shared policy and ideology, gave cohesion to the Bourbon Democracy of the 1880s. Senator Henry G. Davis of West Virginia was a first cousin of the Maryland Democratic leader Senator Arthur Pue Gorman. William C. Whitney came from an old Antifederalist Massachusetts family. His father and brother were prominent in Massachusetts Democratic politics, and his father-in-law, Henry B. Payne of Ohio, was a Democratic United States senator and Standard Oil magnate. Whitney became a corporation lawyer and a leading figure in the New York Democracy. He directed Cleveland's 1892 campaign and went to the cabinet as secretary of the navy.

Grover Cleveland was the preeminent Bourbon Democrat. The son of an upstate New York Presbyterian minister, who adhered to the ritualistic rather than the pietistic branch of the sect, he had an unspectacular career as a Buffalo lawyer until the city's Democrats, "cater[ing] to the better class," nominated him for mayor in

50. Horace S. Merrill, *Bourbon Democracy of the Middle West, 1865–1896* (Baton Rouge, 1953); Gerald W. McFarland, "The Breakdown of Deadlock: The Cleveland Democracy in Connecticut, 1884–1894," *Hist,* 31 (1969), 381–397; on Pattison, *DAB,* VII, 313–314; Blodgett, *Gentle Reformers,* viii et passim.

1881. Cleveland vaulted to the governorship of New York in 1882 and to the presidency in 1884 and again in 1892. His appeal lay in a "stubborn honesty" which usually took negative forms: resisting the more outrageous demands of David Hill's state Democratic machine, vetoing a five-cent fare bill for New York City, opposing a high tariff and soft money, vetoing Republican pension bills. Cleveland embodied the traditionalism and solidity of the Bourbon Democratic political style. He has been compared to Britain's William Gladstone in that his, too, was an intensely moralistic response to the problems of governance posed by industrialism and social change. And it is true that Cleveland's Democrats, like Gladstone's Liberals, won the support of genteel reformers and the Irish alike. But Cleveland had none of Gladstone's Whig-gentry background, and he was far less inclined to foster the active state either in domestic or foreign policy.[51]

The relationship of the Republican party to late nineteenth century American industrial capitalism was close but complex. The party's earlier social function, representing the solid core of (northern) American society, did not fade. It continued to be made up (in the words of Massachusetts Senator George Frisbie Hoar) of "the men who do the work of piety and charity in our churches, the men who administer our school systems, the men who own and till their own farms, the men who perform the skilled labor in the shops." The problem was to square the party's individualistic, Puritan, liberal composite of ideals with the realities of an increasingly polyglot, urban-industrial society. The ideological response of the Republicans was to become not only the "party of piety" but also the "party of prosperity."[52]

51. On Davis, *DAB*, III, 117–118; Mark D. Hirsch, *William C. Whitney: Modern Warwick* (New York, 1948); Blodgett, *Gentle Reformers*, 12–14; on Cleveland, *DAB*, II, 205–212, Robert Kelley, "Presbyterianism, Jacksonianism, and Grover Cleveland," *AQ*, 18 (1966), 615–636, and Kelley, *The Transatlantic Persuasion: The Liberal-Democratic Mind in the Age of Gladstone* (New York, 1969), ch. 8. See also Allan Nevins, *Grover Cleveland: A Study in Courage* (New York, 1932); Horace S. Merrill, *Bourbon Leader: Grover Cleveland and the Democratic Party* (Boston, 1957).

52. Milton Viorst, *Fall from Grace: The Republican Party and the Puritan Ethic* (New York, 1968), 65 et passim; Kleppner, *Cross of Culture*, ch. 9. See also George H. Mayer, *The Republican Party 1854–1964* (New York, 1964), ch. 7.

One way of doing so was to reiterate the Republican identification with themes of broad appeal: national progress, social stability, economic well-being. Typically, the 1881 Maryland GOP platform spoke of the "indissoluble nature of the Union," the "promotion of national industry," the "development of national power, wealth, and independence." Brand Whitlock recalled that the Ohio Republican party of his youth was "a fundamental and self-evident thing . . . It was elemental . . . It was merely a synonym for patriotism, another name for the nation . . . It was inconceivable that any self-respecting person should be a Democrat." Party spokesmen continued to "wave the bloody shirt" in the 1880s, dismissing the Democrats as an "alliance between the embittered South and the slums of Northern cities," the party of "the old slave owner and slave driver, the saloon keeper, the ballot box stuffer, the Ku Klux Klan, the criminal class of the great cities, the men who cannot read or write."[53]

GOP platforms continued to give lip service to the ideal of equal rights. Maryland Republicans insisted in 1895 that black schools were entitled to the same support as white ones. The 1891 Louisiana party declared "white supremacy, as an article of faith, to be rank political heresy, destructive of the rule of the majority." Northern state platforms spoke out for Indian rights; sympathized with oppressed people seeking liberty, as in Ireland; condemned the persecution of Jews in Russia; expressed vague sympathy with the cause of women's suffrage and called for equal compensation for equal work by men and women.

As the social strains of industrialism grew in intensity, the Republican appeal became more protective, more preservative. Various forms of social control—prohibition, Sabbatarianism, hostility to polygamy, the restriction of Chinese and other immigrants—won increasing support. In the late 1880s, after the Haymarket incident, a new theme appeared: antiradicalism. The 1887 New York platform called for laws excluding immigrants who threatened good government, disturbed social peace and order, or de-

53. "Maryland," AC (1881); Brand Whitlock, Forty Years Of It (New York, 1916), 27; Viorst, Fall from Grace, 65. See also [Alexander Bliss], Republican or Democrat? A Retrospect with Its Lesson for the Citizen of 1880 (New York, 1880); George S. Boutwell, Why I Am A Republican (Hartford, 1884); Green B. Raum, The Existing Conflict between Republican Government and Southern Oligarchy (Cleveland, 1884).

meaned the dignity and rewards of honest labor. Anarchists, communists, paupers, criminals, the insane, and contract labor were unwanted. But honest fugitives from Old World oppression and victims of "the crushing force of free-trade policies" were welcome.[54]

A protective tariff was the keystone of Republican economic policy. The party's national platforms during the 1880s (like their Democratic counterparts) made the issue an increasingly important one:

> *1880:* We affirm the belief . . . that the duties levied for the purpose of revenue should so discriminate as to favor American labor.

> *1884:* It is the first duty of a good government to protect the rights and promote the interests of its own people . . . We, therefore, demand that the imposition of duties on foreign imports shall be made, not "for revenue only," but that in raising the requisite revenue for the government, such duties shall be levied as to afford security to our diversified industries and protection of the rights and wages of the laborer; to the end that active and intelligent labor, as well as capital, may have its just reward, and the laboring man his full share in the national prosperity.

> *1888:* We are uncompromisingly in favor of the American system of protection; we protest against its destruction as proposed by the President and his party. They serve the interests of Europe; we will support the interests of America. We accept the issue, and confidently appeal to the people for their judgment. The protective system must be maintained.

The theme of protection embraced more than the tariff. Connecticut Republicans spoke in 1882 of the need to guard against the growing influence of corporations. State platforms frequently called for laws protecting workingmen from the harsher consequences of industrialism: uncompensated injuries, overlong working days, dangerous factory conditions. Contract, pauper, coolie, criminal, and prison labor were threats to the American workingman which should be ended by exclusion or prohibition. The Iowa

54. "Maryland," *AC* (1895); "Louisiana," *AC* (1891); "Illinois," "Indiana," "Ohio," "Kansas," *AC* (1892), "Minnesota," *AC* (1886); on social control, "Massachusetts," *AC* (1886), "Iowa," *AC* (1883), "California," *AC* (1888); "New York," *AC* (1887).

party platform of 1885 proposed a Board of Arbitration to settle industrial disputes and thus protect both labor and capital. Pennsylvania Republicans sought to shield the state's dairy farmers from the threat of oleomargarine: "both national and state legislation should protect them from dangerous and unjust competition and from any and all adulterations or counterfeits."[55]

Republican platform rhetoric in the 1880s often differed from the Democrats more in tone and emphasis than in content. But there were real and persisting differences on issues such as the tariff and the forms and degree of social control. The Republicans like the Democrats responded to social change in terms conditioned by the special character of their party tradition.

By the 1880s, both the ideological imperatives of the Reconstruction years and the fierce factional division between Stalwarts and Half-Breeds had faded in the GOP. We enter a "more amorphous political world." The dominant party figures of the decade were congressional leaders such as James G. Blaine and John Sherman, and state bosses such as Matt Quay of Pennsylvania and Tom Platt of New York. Factionalism was rife, but there was no sharp, bipolar division within the party until the rise of the silver issue in the 1890s.

Blaine and Sherman aptly represented the character of Republicanism in the 1880s. Blaine was the classic organization politician: a brilliant tactician, a dedicated party man who won the intense loyalty of those who shared his fealty to the GOP. These qualities (plus the taint of corruption that clung to him) made Blaine distasteful to independents and reformers. Sherman, the party's senior statesman on fiscal matters in the 1880s, had little of Blaine's flamboyance. But he shared the other's commitment to the details of organization politics, and was as loyal to the party. Blaine embodied the Republican party as a professional political organization, Sherman was the great exemplar of the GOP as an instrument of government.[56]

55. Porter and Johnson, *Platforms*, 61, 72–73, 80; "Connecticut," *AC* (1882); "Massachusetts," "Maine," *AC* (1886); "Ohio," "Iowa," *AC* (1887); "Iowa," *AC* (1885); "Pennsylvania," *AC* (1886).

56. Marcus, *Grand Old Party*, 59; on Blaine, David S. Muzzey, *James G. Blaine: A Political Idol of Other Days* (New York, 1934), Gama-

Men of wealth had a growing role in Republican as in Democratic party affairs. Stephen B. Elkins, who managed Blaine's 1884 campaign, made large sums of money in New Mexico land and minerals and West Virginia coal, lumber, and railroads. His close associate Jerome B. Chaffee (whose daughter married Grant's son) had extensive political and entrepreneurial ties with Republican leaders. The money of Elkins, or *New York Tribune* publisher Whitelaw Reid, or Philadelphia department store magnate John Wanamaker (who ran GOP fund-raising in the 1888 campaign) of course added to their power. But it was power that came at a price: their ability to help meet the rising costs of the party.[57]

The characteristic qualities of Republicanism in the 1880s are evident in the 1888 campaign. There was no leading candidate for the nomination, no distinct ideological division within the party. The choice of Benjamin Harrison of Indiana (rather than Blaine or Sherman) was dictated by the importance of his state's electoral votes and his general acceptability. He was not the candidate of leading capitalists. A Harrison supporter from Wisconsin "stood practically alone against the assaults of the most powerful business and professional interests in Illinois, Wisconsin, and Minnesota, to say nothing of certain influences centering in New York City." This was the last election of the century in which traditional party loyalty and campaign devices—parades, clubs, and the like—were dominant.[58]

Issues and ideology did not give way entirely to faction and organization within the GOP of the eighties. A constant tension prevailed between those who wished to maintain the party's traditional commitments and those who wished to strike out on new paths. Chester Arthur, who assumed the presidency in 1881 when Garfield was assassinated, persisted in the effort initiated by Rutherford Hayes to encourage white southern Republicanism. He supported the Virginia Readjusters and other independent move-

---

liel Bradford, *American Portraits 1875–1900* (Boston, 1922), 115 ff; on Sherman, Theodore E. Burton, *John Sherman* (Boston, 1906). See also Thomas W. Knox, *The Republican Party and Its Leaders* (New York, 1892).

57. Marcus, *Grand Old Party*, 64, 66, 132–134.

58. Ibid., 101 ff; Lewis T. Michener to Mrs. Henry C. Payne, Sept. 5, 1907, Henry C. Payne Mss, WSHS; Harry J. Sievers, *Benjamin Harrison, Hoosier Statesman: From the Civil War to the White House 1865–1888* (New York, 1959), chs. 20–21; Jensen, *Winning of Midwest*, ch. 1.

ments during the early 1880s, to the dismay of the already weakened black Republican organizations. Benjamin Harrison at the end of the decade also favored white over black Republicans in the South.

At the same time a number of party regulars sought to ensure the sanctity of southern black voting. Iowa Republican leader James S. Clarkson wrote of the 1890 Federal Elections Bill: "There is no other real question in present politics but this. Civil service is the toy of a child . . . thrust in to keep the Republican party away from its duty . . . of settling this great overshadowing question." Joseph B. Foraker of Ohio, another organization leader, argued: "the question of a free ballot and a fair count has so much of patriotism, Christianity, and human rights involved that the people of this country are determined to have it settled." And George Frisbie Hoar of Massachusetts, for whom the protection of Negro rights and the protection of American industry were parts of a single political ideology, intoned: "The struggle for this bill is a struggle for the last step toward establishing a doctrine to which the American people are pledged by their history, their Constitution, their opinions, and their interests."[59]

This effort failed; public opinion was at best indifferent to black voting in the South. New issues—the economic concerns of farmers, the social anxieties of native-born Americans confronting factories, cities, and immigrants—worked on the Republicans as well as the Democratic party. The Massachusetts GOP—the ideological bastion of postwar Radical Republicanism—found it necessary in the 1880s to pay increasing attention to labor legislation, prohibition, corporation control, and Catholicism and the public schools. The dominant Iowa Republican triumvirate of Senator William B. Allison, Burlington Railroad president Charles E. Perkins, and *Iowa State Register* editor James S. Clarkson struggled (with diminishing success) to meet the dual threats of the party's

59. George F. Howe, *Chester A. Arthur* (Indianapolis, 1935), 197; Vincent P. De Santis, "President Arthur and the Independent Movements in the South in 1882," *JSH*, 19 (1953), 346–363; De Santis, "Negro Dissatisfaction with Republican Policy in the South, 1882–1884," *JNH*, 36 (1951), 148–159; De Santis, "Benjamin Harrison and the Republican Party in the South, 1889–1893," *IMH*, 51 (1955), 279–302; Clarkson quoted in Leland Sage, *William Boyd Allison: A Study in Practical Politics* (Iowa City, 1956), 245; Foraker and Hoar quoted in Welch, *Hoar*, 144n, 156.

identification with corporate interests and the divisive effects of the prohibition and education issues. From the late 1880s on, both regular Republicanism and the Bourbon Democracy faced challenges that transformed the style and content of American politics.[60]

60. Richard Harmond, "Troubles of Massachusetts Republicans during the 1880s," *MAm*, 56 (1974), 85–99; Sage, *Allison*, 188 ff.

CHAPTER 15

The Crisis
of the Nineties

THE SOCIAL AND economic strains incident to industrialism reached a political flash point in the 1890s. Cultural conflict over religion, education, mores, and race relations came to dominate the politics of a number of states by the early years of the decade. Major economic dislocations—a severe agricultural price and credit squeeze, industrial depression, large-scale unemployment, labor strife—had important political repercussions in the mid-nineties.

The party system was severely shaken by popular discontent. The electoral equilibrium of the 1880s shattered. The rise of Populism posed the most important third party challenge since the Civil War. And the election of 1896 turned out to be one of the great polarizing—and realigning—national contests in American political history.

By the end of the 1890s, important changes had occurred in party loyalties, organization, ideology, and issues. But more significant was the fact that the post-Civil War American party system had faced and mastered the first major political crisis of the industrial era.

The Politics of Disequilibrium

While the political events of the 1890s had immediate social and economic causes, they reflected also the impact of longer term

565

changes. The massive flow of immigrants and the enormous internal mobility of the late nineteenth century had important political consequences. Relative Democratic strength in the Northeast and the Midwest increased during the 1880s because of the steady entry of immigrants. Urban Republicans generally benefited from the internal migration from farm to city. The uniform character of city machines was in part a function of their need to deal with neighborhoods which maintained their ethnic cohesion but whose populations turned over at a very high rate.[1]

Another source of change was the growth of a new, better informed, less parochial political public. A "magazine revolution" occurred during the last ten or fifteen years of the century. A new breed of mass circulation magazines—among them *Munsey's, McClure's, Scribner's,* and the appropriately named *Cosmopolitan* and *Everybody's*—did much to foster a national public opinion. Their readership was far larger and more eclectic than those of older opinion molders such as the *Nation,* the *Atlantic, Harper's Weekly,* and the *North American Review.* A periodical with the revealing name of *Public Opinion,* compiling newspaper comments on a variety of topics, appeared in 1886. The similar *Literary Digest* followed in 1890 and had a circulation of 63,000 by 1900. The concurrent revolution in American newspaper journalism wrought by Joseph Pulitzer and William Randolph Hearst produced a better informed newspaper readership, much more varied in its class, ethnic, and locational backgrounds than had been the case before, when newspapers aimed at narrower audiences.[2]

The rise of a national public opinion coincided with increasingly severe structural defects in the political system. One indicator was

1. Paul Kleppner, *The Cross of Culture* (New York, 1970), ch. 3; Samuel T. McSeveney, *The Politics of Depression: Political Behavior in the Northeast, 1893–1896* (New York, 1972), ch. 1; Stephan Thernstrom, *The Other Bostonians: Poverty and Progress in the American Metropolis, 1880–1970* (Cambridge, 1973), 231–232.

2. Frank L. Mott, "The Magazine Revolution and Popular Ideas in the Nineties," *AAS Proceedings,* 64 (1954), 195–214; Mott, *A History of American Magazines* (Cambridge, 1967), IV, 649–651; George Juergens, *Joseph Pulitzer and the New York World* (Princeton, 1966). See also John Higham, "The Reorientation of American Culture in the 1890s," in John Weiss, ed., *The Origins of Modern Consciousness* (Detroit, 1965), 25–48; E. L. Godkin, "The New Political Force," *Nation,* 66 (1898), 336–337.

the apparent growth in the number of substantial defalcations by state treasurers in the South and West. It was as though the increasing revenue coming into government coffers overstrained the existing system of public accountability (and standards of public morality). In 1890 alone, the treasurers of Colorado, Louisiana, Maryland, Mississippi, and Missouri stood accused of large discrepancies in their accounts. "Honest Dick" Tate, Kentucky's state treasurer for twenty years, was found in 1888 to have incurred a $230,000 shortage. About $140,000 of Arkansas's assets were missing in 1891; Arizona's former treasurer was dunned (unsuccessfully) for $16,700 in 1894; a Nebraska treasury deficit of more than half a million dollars in 1897 earned its ex-treasurer a twenty-year prison term. The Holt County, Nebraska treasurer, accused of embezzling $32,000 in 1894, was seized by a gang at night and hanged; his body then was thrown into a river.[3]

From the late 1880s on the number of contested elections sharply rose. There was a veritable epidemic of challenges to congressional seats and deadlocks over the selection of United States senators and the organization of state legislatures and governments. The 1887 Indiana legislature argued for months over the validity of a special election to choose a lieutenant governor. Two rival bodies, each with its own speaker, vied to be recognized as the legitimate Colorado assembly in 1891. The New Jersey Supreme Court resolved a similar situation in favor of the Republican claimants in 1894. The Democratic winner of the 1890 Nebraska gubernatorial election was challenged by the Republican incumbent on the ground that he was not an American citizen. The state court upheld this contention, but was reversed by the United States Supreme Court. A dispute over the Connecticut gubernatorial election of 1890 led to "an entire collapse of the legislative department." Incumbent governor Morgan J. Bulkeley, who also was president of the Aetna Life Insurance Company, remained in office until the 1892 election. When the legislature refused to pass appropriations bills, he had the Aetna underwrite the state's fiscal obligations.[4]

3. States cited, AC (1890); "Kentucky," AC (1889); "Arkansas," AC (1891); "Arizona," AC (1894); "Nebraska," AC (1897, 1894).
4. Louis A. Coolidge, An Old-Fashioned Senator: Orville H. Platt (New York, 1910), 46; "Indiana," AC (1889); "Colorado," AC (1891); State v.

The most significant expression of a growing political instability was the breakdown of the electoral equilibrium that had prevailed through the 1880s. There were warning signs of Republican weakness in 1889, when Joseph B. Foraker lost the Ohio governorship, Iowa and Rhode Island elected their first Democratic chief executives since the Civil War, the Democrats won in New York, and Massachusetts barely went Republican. The shift became a landslide in the congressional elections of 1890. The Democrats increased their House membership from 159 to 235. The party took the governorships of Massachusetts and Pennsylvania, and won state offices in Illinois, Wisconsin, California, New York, New Jersey, Connecticut, and Indiana, states that long had been Republican or divided.[5]

In the presidential election of 1892 Grover Cleveland defeated Benjamin Harrison by more than 365,000 votes, the largest margin since 1872. Harrison conducted, as Mark Hanna expected him to, "the most lifeless campaign for half a century." But Cleveland was hardly more charismatic. In 1892 as in 1890, Republican factionalism and the disaffection of important blocs of voters combined with a rare period of Democratic unity to shatter the party balance of the eighties. The *Nation* spoke of "the close of an epoch," of "the rise, the gradual demoralization, and the fall of a most powerful political organization," and predicted "a new 'era of good feeling,' out of which are to come new parties, whether or not the old ones survive."

The Populist party won a million popular and twenty-two electoral votes in 1892, ensuring Cleveland's victories in California, Illinois, and Wisconsin. The Democratic vote was only 18,300 more than in 1888; the Republican tally was 264,639 less. But the chief source of Republican weakness, and of Democratic cohesion that allowed Bourbon Democrats, Illinois governor-elect John P.

Rogers, 56 N.J.L. 480 (1894); State v. Boyd, 31 Neb. 682 (1891), Boyd v. Thayer, 143 U.S. 135 (1892); "Connecticut," AC (1891–1892); Morris v. Bulkeley, 61 Conn. 287, 372 (1892).

5. Robert D. Marcus, *Grand Old Party* (New York, 1971), 151–152, 159; J. Rogers Hollingsworth, *The Whirligig of Politics: The Democracy of Cleveland and Bryan* (Chicago, 1963), 1; *World Almanac* (New York, 1891), 275 ff. See also Franklin H. Giddings, "The Nature and Conduct of Political Majorities," *PSQ*, 7 (1892), 116–132, for an analysis of the 1890 Pennsylvania vote.

Altgeld, Congressman William Jennings Bryan of Nebraska, Henry George, and Eugene V. Debs to support Cleveland in 1892, was the politics of cultural conflict.[6]

In a number of midwestern and eastern states, cultural issues had been eroding Republican strength. Prohibition was one of these. As prohibitionist sentiment grew in places and among people fearful of social change, the GOP came under increasing pressure to lend its support. Party leaders such as Foraker in Ohio and Nils Haugen in Wisconsin did so. In reaction, German voters in particular either voted Democratic or abstained.

Similar in its impact was the movement for laws such as Wisconsin's Bennett Law and Illinois's Edwards Act, both passed in 1889, which required private as well as public schools to teach major subjects in the English language. Similar laws were proposed but defeated in Nebraska and Massachusetts. Along with compulsory education and restrictions on child labor, this requirement was regarded by many Catholics, German and Scandinavian Lutherans, and others to be an assault on their religious and social beliefs.

The Republicans paid a substantial political price for these policies. In Iowa, Horace Boies (whose father was of French ancestry) switched from the GOP to the Democrats over the prohibition issue. In 1889 he became the state's first Democratic governor. Prohibition hurt the Republicans as well in Wisconsin, Illinois, Michigan, Indiana, and Ohio. The new school laws were major contributors to the 1890 Republican defeats in Illinois and Wisconsin. Senator John Spooner said of his party's Wisconsin loss: "The school law did it—a silly, sentimental and damned useless abstraction."

Cultural issues had an important impact in the East as well. Controversies over liquor control played an important part in New York and New Jersey politics in the late eighties, and cost the Republicans dearly in the industrial cities. Issues such as women voting in liquor licensing and school board elections (Massachusetts), property qualifications for voting by naturalized citizens (Rhode Island), and sectarian restrictions on officeholding (New

6. Richard Jensen, *The Winning of the Midwest* (Chicago, 1971), 168–169, 171–172; "The Close of an Epoch," *Nation*, 106 (1893), 172; Marcus, *Grand Old Party*, 190–191, 194.

Hampshire) also strengthened the Democrats' appeal as the party of personal freedom.[7]

This cultural politics was intensified by the emergence of overtly nativist, anti-Catholic organizations: the American party, which began in California in 1886, and the American Protective Association, which reached its peak during the early nineties in a number of midwestern and far western states. In places such as Michigan and Wisconsin the APA was a response to rather than a cause of the rise of Catholic (and Democratic) political strength. It withered away with the coming of hard times in the mid-1890s. But organized nativism added to the pressure on Republicans to take stands on cultural issues which repelled more voters than they attracted, and which smoothed the path of a Catholic-Bourbon-reformer alliance within the Democratic party.[8]

Republican politicians soon responded to the threat. The party won in Iowa and Ohio in 1890 by downplaying prohibition in favor of other issues. Half of Wisconsin's Republican legislators joined the Democrats to repeal the Bennett Law in 1891. Party professionals inclined to avoid polarization, such as McKinley in Ohio, took control from their more ideological fellows throughout the Midwest.

When depression followed on the panic of 1893, the Republican stress on prosperity and protection led to a political landslide even more dramatic than the Democratic triumph of 1890. The Democrats lost 113 seats in the 1894 congressional elections, a falloff of 32 percent from their 1892 level and the largest shift since the Civil War. Missouri Democrat Champ Clark called it the greatest slaughter of the innocents since Herod. The Democrats failed to

7. Jensen, Winning of Midwest, ch. 5; Kleppner, Cross of Culture, ch. 4; Spooner quoted in Jensen, Winning of Midwest, 122; on the East, Mc-Seveney, Politics of Depression, 23–24; Geoffrey Blodgett, The Gentle Reformers (Cambridge, 1966), chs. 3–4.

8. John Higham, "The American Party, 1886–1891," PHR, 19 (1950), 37–46; Donald L. Kinzer, An Episode in Anti-Catholicism: The American Protective Association (Seattle, 1964), "Political Uses of Anti-Catholicism: Michigan and Wisconsin, 1890–1894," MH, 39 (1955), 312–326; Seymour M. Lipset and Earl Rabb, The Politics of Unreason (New York, 1970), 79–92. See also "This Mischief of the A.P.A.," CM, 52 (1896), 156–157.

elect a single member of Congress in twenty-four states and elected only one congressman in six others. "Honey Fitz" Fitzgerald, John F. Kennedy's grandfather, was the only New England Democratic congressman to survive. David J. Hill lost the New York governorship; the Republicans carried state offices in West Virginia, Missouri, Maryland, and Delaware. New York City's Fourteenth Congressional District, which had elected a Democrat by 8,825 votes in 1892, gave the Republican candidate a 5,977 vote majority in 1894.[9]

The political equilibrium of the eighties was a thing of the past. The congressional elections of 1890 and 1894 and the presidential election of 1892 involved shifts in electoral patterns of a sort that had not been seen since the era of the Civil War. And the rise of a new third party, the Populists, who won a million votes (almost 11 percent of the total) in 1892 and a million and a half votes in 1894, underlined the fact that the major party system faced its greatest challenge since the 1860s.

Populism

Populism swept onto the American political scene in the 1890s for two major reasons. The first of these was economic. Southern and western farmers in particular felt the effects of rising productivity, falling prices, and relatively higher fixed costs for land, machinery, seed, and (most of all) credit. Railroad freight charges, at least in the West, appear to have been stable or even declining, but they were widely perceived as one of the heaviest of the farmers' burdens. More special economic problems beset particular groups: overseas wheat and cotton competition; drought in the Plains; the oppressive weight of tenantry in the South; the high production and falling prices of the silver mining industry. The Populist movement had also a broader, cultural dimension. It was fed by, and gave voice to, widespread anxiety over the place of the farmer and

9. Jensen, *Winning of Midwest*, 153–159; on Clark, Allan Nevins, *Grover Cleveland* (New York, 1932), 651; Hollingsworth, *Whirligig*, 28–29; Marcus, *Grand Old Party*, 196–197.

occasionally the worker in an increasingly urban, industrial, corporation-dominated society.[10]

These economic and cultural grievances were decades old; and so were political palliatives, such as the Granger and Greenback movements of the 1870s and the Union Labor party of the 1880s. Perpetual third party men like Ignatius Donnelly of Minnesota played important roles in the development of Populist organization and ideology. Free silver fit into an established tradition of monetary inflation schemes. Attacks on railroads and monopolies, proposals for an income tax and the direct election of senators had long been part of the politics of protest. The preamble of the 1892 Populist platform, which stirringly condemned the polarization of American society into the rich and the poor, bore a close resemblance to the Union Labor party platform of 1888.

Most of all, an elaborate web of farmers' organizations set the stage for the Populist movement. The massive Farmers' Alliances— they claimed millions of members by the late 1880s—provided an infrastructure of organization, ideas, and personnel that made possible the rapid rise of Populism as a political force. Journalists— Milton George in the North, Leonidas Polk in the South—were among the leading organizers of the Alliances. Just as new types of magazines and newspapers developed a changing public opinion in urban America, so did third party ideologies and Farmers' Alliance organizers help to mold a culture of agrarian political protest.[11]

Populism was as diverse as the disaffection to which it appealed. Its core was agrarian. But it embraced more than that (and less, in the sense that it failed to win the majority of American farmers). Populism had a nativist and anti-Semitic strain, because this was a way of expressing social anxiety. It appealed as well to many immigrants, because they too shared the grievances to which Populism spoke. Populism had its socialist-oriented elements;

10. See in general John D. Hicks, *The Populist Revolt* (Minneapolis, 1931). Robert Higgs, "Railroad Rates and the Populist Uprising," *AH*, 44 (1970), 291–298, and Stanley B. Parsons, *The Populist Context* (Westport, Conn., 1973), 24, 27, argue that freight rates were stable or declining during this period, in adjusted as well as constant dollars.

11. Hicks, *Populist Revolt*, 98–100, 117, 144. See also Martin Ridge; *Ignatius Donnelly: The Portrait of a Politician* (Chicago, 1962); Roy V. Scott, *The Agrarian Movement in Illinois 1880–1896* (Urbana, 1962).

it had also a larger component of agrarian entrepreneurs who rejected socialism as readily as they condemned corporate capitalism.

Agrarian crisis at the end of the nineteenth century was not unique to the United States. A farmers' movement appeared in Germany as well during the 1890s. Like its American counterpart it indulged in a rich rhetoric of hostility to industrial capitalism and distinguished between *schaffende* (creative) and *raffende* (exploitative) work. But the differences between the two Populisms were profound. German agrarianism rested on an alliance of large estate-owning Junkers and peasant farmers that had no American analogue. Nor did American Populism match the overt anti-Semitism that had a central place in the German movement.[12]

The broad-gauged Populist program of political and economic reform coexisted with a powerful, almost evangelical moralism. Kansas Populist leader Frank Doster called on the 1894 state party convention "to make a platform that talks less about free silver and more about salvation; less about finance and more about religion." Both the initial appeal and the ultimate weakness of Populism lay in the fact that it was a movement more than a party. The longest demonstration at the 1892 Omaha convention came not with the selection of the presidential candidate but after the reading of the platform. The convention chairman told the delegates: "the old parties go wild over their candidates. We go wild over our principles." Women orators—a phenomenon profoundly at odds with the style of mainstream American politics—had a conspicuous place in the Populist movement. Mary Elizabeth Lease of Kansas was only the best known of many. The novelist Hamlin Garland observed: "No other movement in history—not even the anti-slavery cause—appealed to the women like this movement here in Kansas." That state's Populist ticket of 1890 included a woman, a Negro, a minister, a farmer, and a schoolteacher: hardly the normal

12. Norman Pollack, *The Populist Response to Industrial America* (Cambridge, 1962); Hicks, *Populist Revolt*, Richard Hofstadter, *The Age of Reform: From Bryan to FDR* (New York, 1955), ch. 2; Kenneth Barkin, "A Case Study in Comparative History: Populism in Germany and America," in Herbert Bass, ed., *The State of American History* (New York, 1970), 373–404. See also Walter T. K. Nugent, *The Tolerant Populists* (Chicago, 1963), part I, and *AH*, 39 (1965), 59–80, *AH*, 40 (1966), 235–254.

run of officeseekers. In style as well as content, Populism challenged the prevailing political culture of late nineteenth century America.[13]

These qualities characterized the substantial Kansas and Nebraska Populist movements. By 1890, after the boom years of the early and mid-eighties gave way to drought and crop failure, 60 percent of Kansas's taxed acres were mortgaged. The state's per capita debt of $347 was four times the national average. A number of other aggrieved groups found common cause with the farmers. At the Farmers' Alliance convention of 1890—which gave birth to the Kansas People's party—Grangers, Greenbackers, Single Taxers, Bellamy Nationalists, Prohibitionists, women's suffragists, the Knights of Labor, railroad workers, and miners also were represented. It is estimated that 36 percent of the 1890 Kansas Populist vote consisted of former Republicans, 31 percent were ex-Democrats, 29 percent had previously voted Union Labor, and 4 percent were Prohibitionists.

Kansas Populist strength was concentrated in the state's central counties, as distinct from the more settled and urbanized eastern part and the less developed west. In Nebraska, too, the northeastern part of the state, with a substantial Catholic-German population, and the western portion, still hungry for railroads and irrigation projects, were most resistant to Populism. The evangelical strain in the movement, and its flirtation with causes such as prohibition and women's suffrage, lessened its appeal to Catholic farmers. In both states Populism drew far more heavily from farms than from towns and cities. The most significant county correlates for the Nebraska Populist vote were percent of Protestant affiliation and improved land in wheat; in Kansas, the percentage of farm-owning families living on mortgaged farms. A comparison of Kansas Populist and Republican legislators and county candidates reveals

13. Michael J. Brodhead, *Persevering Populist: The Life of Frank Doster* (Reno, Nev., 1969), 89–90; Paul W. Glad, *McKinley, Bryan, and the People* (Philadelphia, 1964), 67; Hamlin Garland, *A Spoil of Office* (Boston, 1892), 352; on 1890 Kansas slate, Peter H. Argersinger, *Populism and Politics: William Alfred Peffer and the People's Party* (Lexington, Ky., 1974), 39. See also O. Gene Clanton, *Kansas Populism: Ideas and Men* (Lawrence, Kan., 1969); William E. Lyons, "Populism in Pennsylvania, 1892–1901," *PH*, 32 (1965), 49–65.

more similarities than differences, except that the Populists tended to have less capital and to be less involved in speculative ventures. The determinants of Populism in the heartland of the movement included subtle, marginal factors as well as the obvious ones of location and economic activity.[14]

Further west, Populism had a different face. Utah and Montana farmers grew primarily for local markets and were less concerned over credit and freight rates. In these states, Populism flourished primarily in the towns, and labor issues had a more prominent place. In sparsely populated Nevada, free silver was the central issue, and a Silver party which had little rapport with Populism elsewhere swept the state in 1892. The Colorado People's party, led by Davis H. Waite, who became governor in 1892, also was more responsive to silver and labor than to agrarian interests. In Wyoming, cattle raising was more important than crop prices, silver, or labor, and Populism there took up the cause of small ranchers and homesteaders against large stockmen. New Mexico Populism included opponents of the Santa Fe and cattle and land monopolies, oppressed Spanish-Americans, and the Knights of Labor; free silver was a late and relatively minor part of the movement.

Pacific coast Populism was no less varied. Land monopoly was the chief concern of John R. Rogers, Washington's Populist governor in 1896. He sought aid to homesteaders and a general return to the land, and had little interest in urban or labor problems. California Populism fed on the insecurities that came with that state's rapid growth in the 1880s. In Los Angeles the movement attracted Bellamy Nationalists and APA nativists. The People's party won 22 percent of the 1892 vote in California's Tulare County. Its backbone consisted of small farmers, old and settled as well as newer and marginal. But it embraced also a diverse band of Prohibition-

14. See in general Argersinger, *Populism and Politics* and Clanton, *Kansas Populism;* on 1890 vote estimate, Argersinger, *Populism and Politics,* 73; on sources of Populist strength, Argersinger, *Populism and Politics,* ch. 3, Parsons, *Populist Context,* ch. 8; on legislators, Walter T. K. Nugent, "Some Parameters of Populism," *AH,* 40 (1966), 255–270; Luebke, *Immigrants and Politics,* ch. 8. David H. Trask, "A Note on the Politics of Populism," *NH,* 46 (1965), 157–161, argues that there was a significant Populist town-country alliance in Nebraska; Frederick H. Luebke, "Main Street and the Countryside: Patterns of Voting in Nebraska during the Populist Era," *NH,* 50 (1969), 257–275, finds no evidence that such an alliance existed.

ists, Greenbackers, Christian Socialists, Single Taxers, nativists, and other dissenters.[15]

The Southern Farmers' Alliance was more militant than its northern counterpart. And the 1892 Populist vote in the South was considerable: 37 percent of the Alabama total, 24 percent in Texas, 19 percent in Georgia and Mississippi, 16 percent in North Carolina, 14 percent in Florida. Southern Populism was a sizable political force, with a distinctive character determined by the region's special factors of cotton, tenantry, poverty, race, and one-party domination.

Blacks had an ambiguous place in southern Populism. Certainly there were numerous instances of Populist deviance from the white supremacist norm. A Colored Farmers' Alliance was affiliated with the Southern Alliance. Georgia Populist leader Tom Watson made some attempt at biracial political cooperation. There were more than twenty black delegates to the 1892 Louisiana Populist convention, and a Negro was nominated for state treasurer (but quickly withdrew). In Grimes and other East Texas counties, the People's party rested on a black-white political coalition that had roots in the Greenback movement. An estimated 30 percent of the white and more than 80 percent of the black electorate in Grimes County voted Populist until the party was crushed by the Democratic White Man's Union in 1900.[16]

15. David B. Griffiths, "Far Western Populism: The Case of Utah, 1893–1900," *UHQ*, 37 (1969), 396–407; Thomas A. Clinch, *Urban Populism and Free Silver in Montana* (Missoula, Mont. 1970); Mary E. Glass, *Silver and Politics in Nevada: 1892–1902* (Reno, 1969); Griffiths, "Far Western Populist Thought: A Comparative Study of John R. Rogers and Davis H. Waite," *PNQ*, 60 (1969), 183–192; G. Michael McCarthy, "The People's Party in Colorado: A Profile of Populist Leadership," *AH*, 47 (1973), 146–155; Griffiths, "Populism in Wyoming," *AW*, 40 (1968), 57–71; Robert W. Larson, *New Mexico Populism* (Boulder, 1974); Michael P. Rogin, "California Populism and the 'System of 1896,'" *WPQ*, 22 (1969), 179–196; Tom G. Hall, "California Populism at the Grass-Roots: The Case of Tulare County, 1892," *SCQ*, 49 (1967), 193–204. See also James E. Wright, *The Politics of Populism: Dissent in Colorado* (New Haven, 1974).

16. See in general C. Vann Woodward, *Origins of the New South* (Baton Rouge, 1951), ch. 9; Lucia E. Daniel, "The Louisiana People's Party," *LaHQ*, 26 (1943), 1080; Lawrence C. Goodwyn, "Populist Dreams and Negro Rights: East Texas as a Case Study," *AHR*, 76 (1971), 1435–1456. See also William I. Hair, *Bourbonism and Agrarian Protest* (Baton Rouge, 1969), ch. 9.

Elsewhere, Populists generally adhered to prevailing racial mores. In North Carolina they supported the division of school funds on the basis of the taxes paid by each race. The state's leading Populist journal was called *The Caucasian*. Alliance men in Georgia and Alabama supported laws directed against blacks in 1891, and the Southern and Colored Farmers' Alliances divided on issues such as federal aid to education and the Federal Elections Law. Outside of Louisiana, it appears that few if any Negroes attended Populist state conventions. Tom Watson criticized President Grover Cleveland for appointing a black diplomat to Bolivia. More important, Negroes voted for Populists in only a few areas: in part, no doubt, because of traditional Republican commitments and Democratic threats, violence, and fraud, but in part also because the Populist stress on free silver and railroad regulation had little appeal to black farmers who lived in or near tenantry.[17]

This is not to say that southern Populism was without its more radical side. The rhetoric of the Alabama Populists consisted of "a belief in the moral superiority of rural life, a call for various forms of monetary inflation, an intense antagonism toward organized wealth, a conspiracy theory of history, and a firm belief that the voice of the people is the voice of God." The People's party of that state was strongest in those areas with the highest rate of farm tenancy. The movement attracted marginal men, protestants against the established order, across the South. Cuthbert Vincent, the leading Louisiana Populist editor, called his journal *The American Non-Conformist*; Hardy Lee Brian, the head of the state party, was said to have been "rocked in an 'Independent' cradle."[18]

But southern Populism ultimately was blunted by the region's ideological, racial, and political norms. Alabama Populists in 1894 took up the cause of striking miners. Yet their commitment to

17. Joseph F. Steelman, "Republican Party Strategists and the Issue of Fusion with Populists in North Carolina, 1893–1894," *NCHR*, 47 (1970), 244–269; Charles Crowe, "Tom Watson, Populists, and Blacks Reconsidered," *JNH*, 55 (1970), 99–116; Robert Saunders, "Southern Populists and the Negro, 1893–1895," *JNH*, 54 (1969), 240–261. See also William H. Chafe, "The Negro and Populism: A Kansas Case Study," *JSH*, 34 (1968), 402–419; C. J. Reinhart, "Populism and the Black," Ph.D. diss., University of Oklahoma, 1972.

18. Sheldon Hackney, *Populism to Progressivism in Alabama* (Princeton, 1969), 50, 25; Hair, *Bourbonism and Agrarian Protest*, 204–206.

Jeffersonian, minimum-government principles led them to oppose tax reform, child labor laws, and abolition of the convict lease system. Winnfield Parish in northern Louisiana, the birthplace of Huey Long and later a center of southern socialism, was a Populist stronghold, and its People's party newspaper had the provocative name of *Comrade*—but this was an anagram of "Democrat," not a sign of incipient Marxism.[19]

Populism varied over time as well as space. It evolved from a popular movement headed by ideologues to a political organization whose middle-level leaders accepted fusion with the Democrats. Western Populism's dependence on the money and literature of the well-financed silver interests dulled its edge in the mid-nineties. In Virginia, the Farmers' Alliance found itself cooperating with the Richmond Chamber of Commerce in behalf of railroad rate regulation. Louisiana sugar planters aggrieved over Democratic tariff policy rallied with the Populists in 1896, and the party's candidate for governor that year was John N. Pharr, one of the state's largest sugar planters. The Kansas People's party's stress on free silver and its fusion with the Democrats drove many ex-Republican supporters back to the GOP. By 1894, according to one estimate, the Kansas Populist vote was 57 percent ex-Democratic, 30 percent ex-Union Labor, and only 12 percent ex-Republican. By 1896, most western Populists were former Democrats or traditional third party voters.[20]

The consequent ambivalence toward the active state became evident when Populists attained state power. Colorado's Governor Waite reduced state spending by 15 percent. Nebraska Populist legislators opposed state indebtedness, and in 1891 cut expenditures on asylums, prisons, industrial schools, and homes for the aged. Frank Doster ran for chief justice of the Kansas Supreme Court in 1894 with the promise: "If elected, though hampered by technical decisions in the interest of wealth, I will diligently search through the books to find some law through which the interests of the common people may be subserved." But when he came on the

19. Hackney, *Populism to Progressivism*, 60–62, 71 ff; Hair, *Bourbonism and Agrarian Protest*, 210.

20. On Virginia, Robert M. Saunders, "Progressive Historians and the Late Nineteenth-Century Agrarian Revolt: Virginia as a Historiographical Test Case," *VMHB*, 79 (1971), 487; Hair, *Bourbonism and Agrarian Protest*, 248 ff; Argersinger, *Populism and Politics*, 128, 141, 181–188.

bench he differed little from his Republican fellow-justices and adhered to the major common law precedents.

Populist-labor alliances broke down—or never took place—because of profound and irreconcilable differences. Farmers wanted higher crop prices and cheaper money. Workingmen wanted low food prices, and most feared the effect of currency inflation on the real value of their wages. AFL president Samuel Gompers argued that the Populist party was composed "mainly of *employing* farmers without any regard to the interest of the *employed* farmers of the country districts or the mechanics and laborers of the industrial centres."

Factionalism also worked against the party's success. There was great inherent instability in a movement composed of former Democrats, former Republicans, and traditional third-party supporters. Prohibition, women's suffrage, and a host of other issues were sore points. No substantial infrastructure of organization and tradition, of money and patronage, exerted a countervailing force. The major parties had these strengths, which proved decisive. Force and fraud played their part as well. Alabama People's party candidate Reuben Kolb may well have been counted out of the governorship in 1892, and Kansas Populists charged in 1893 that they had been fraudulently deprived of a legislative majority.[21]

After the Populists endorsed Bryan in 1896, the disintegration of the movement was rapid. Some leaders continued in radical third-party politics; the most conspicuous ones returned to the major parties. Senator William A. Peffer of Kansas decided that "as between the Democratic and Republican parties, with respect to their foundation beliefs concerning the powers and duties of our government, the Republican idea is much broader." He campaigned for McKinley in 1900. Governors Waite of Colorado and Rogers of Washington were imperialists by 1898. Tom Watson of Georgia turned to a virulently Negrophobic Democratic politics after 1900. Frank Doster's Kansas Supreme Court term ended in 1901, and he became an attorney for the Missouri Pacific Railroad. Mary Lease

21. On Waite, Karel D. Prucha, "A Further Reconsideration of American Populism," *MAm*, 53 (1971), 3–11; on Nebraska, Parsons, *Populist Context*, 73–74, 139; Brodhead, *Doster*, 94, 102, 114, 121; Samuel Gompers, "Organized Labor in the Campaign," *NAR*, 115 (1892), 93; on Kolb, Hackney, *Populism to Progressivism*, 67–68; "Kansas," *AC* (1893).

spoke against Bryan in Nebraska during the 1900 campaign, her efforts paid for by Republican national boss Mark Hanna. The regular party system had met, mastered, and absorbed its greatest challenge since the 1860s.[22]

1896

The currents of political change stirred by social and economic unrest converged in the electoral maelstrom of 1896. This was one of those rare presidential contests in which the character of the parties and their electorates palpably shifted, with consequences that affected American politics for a generation to come.

Depression-fed discontent with Grover Cleveland, and indeed with the Bourbon Democracy at large, led to the emergence of new and very different Democratic leaders in 1896. Illinois Governor John Peter Altgeld was the *eminence grise* of the party's 1896 convention and the campaign that followed. Wherein lay his power? In the fact that he was the chief executive of a major state, of course. But also because of his personal gifts and the new political style for which he was the spokesman. Altgeld was a dedicated politician: "Other men get recreation from playing cards. Or they bet on horse races. Or they have their children. Politics is my recreation . . . Politics has a strong fascination for me, just as gambling has for some men." But he also was the first important Democrat of his time to depart from the Bourbon mode. He pardoned the surviving Haymarket anarchists and sought to keep Grover Cleveland from sending in the federal troops that broke the great railroad strike of 1894. Altgeld took on for conservatives something of the threatening quality of Franklin D. Roosevelt in the 1930s or Andrew Jackson in the 1830s. In fact he was no more radical than FDR or Jackson. But this lawyer and real estate man turned politician was responding to new anxieties and desires stirring in the urban electorate. In this sense he was the true pre-

22. Argersinger, *Populism and Politics*, 299–301; Griffiths, "Populist Thought," 190–192; Woodward, *Origins*, 352, 393; Brodhead, *Doster*, 137; O. Gene Clanton, "Intolerant Populist? The Disaffection of Mary Elizabeth Lease," *KHQ*, 34 (1968), 199–200.

cursor of the northern, city-oriented Democratic liberalism of the twentieth century.

Beatrice Webb concluded that Altgeld was "a metaphysician and not a statesman." She was ill at ease with the blend of Jeffersonian individualism and German collectivism that seemed to shape his views. Certainly that mix had its limits as a source of new Democratic party ideology in the nineties. While the 1896 party platform bore Altgeld's mark in its strong commitment to free silver and in its assault on presidential and judicial power, his managerial skill was most important in 1896.[23]

Altgeld loosened the national party from its dependence on the Bourbon Democratic machines. William Jennings Bryan was the great spokesman for the new course. Bryan's career was not without its ironies. Although he spoke for the agrarian South and West, he was not a farmer but a lawyer, had come to Nebraska from Illinois only in 1887, and was elected to Congress in 1890 from the state's urban First District, embracing Lincoln and Omaha. He won his first national reputation for his assaults on the McKinley tariff. But he skillfully responded to the growing agrarian discontent, made the cause of free silver his own, and by 1896 was the leading champion of aggrieved farmers. His "Cross of Gold" speech at the Chicago Democratic convention was superbly tuned to those grievances and projected an evangelical fervor new to national politics. Bryan's oratory and Altgeld's platform and organizing powers abruptly transformed the Democratic party.[24]

Mark Hanna and William McKinley sharply differed from Altgeld and Bryan in their political ideology. But they played very similar roles in Republican politics. Altgeld rode to power on the first wave of urban Democratic liberalism; Hanna represented the

23. Harry Barnard, *Eagle Forgotten: The Life of John Peter Altgeld* (Indianapolis, 1938), 64 et passim; David A. Shannon, ed., *Beatrice Webb's American Diary: 1898* (Madison, 1963), 10. See also Harvey Wish, "John Peter Altgeld and the Background of the Campaign of 1896," MVHR, 24 (1938), 505–518; Henry M. Christman, ed., *The Mind and Spirit of John Peter Altgeld* (Urbana, 1960).

24. Paolo E. Coletta, "Bryan, Cleveland, and the Disrupted Democracy," NH, 41 (1960), 1–27, *William Jennings Bryan* (Lincoln, Neb., 1964), I; Glad, *McKinley, Bryan, and the People*, ch. 6; Hollingsworth, *Whirligig*, chs. 2–3.

political power of the new industrial capitalism now entrenched in the GOP. Like his Democratic counterpart Altgeld, Hanna was drawn to President-making by his organizing talent, his taste for political power, and his belief that important issues were at stake. Hanna was by no means the first businessman turned national party leader. But he brought to his work a largeness of style and purpose that had not been seen before.

Hanna's chosen candidate William McKinley had none of Bryan's charismatic quality. But he had personal gifts—solid middle class virtues, a distinguished Civil War record, an air of quiet dignity—that corresponded closely to the Republican party's core ideals. McKinley's northeast Ohio congressional district, no less than his own character, schooled him in the arts of compromise and moderation. His constituency was a mix of industrial, labor, and farming interests. The protective tariff, benefiting producers and shielding American wage scales, was his great theme. But just as Altgeld and Bryan came by 1896 to rely on free silver as the major issue of their new brand of Democratic politics, so did Hanna and McKinley accept the challenge and make a gold-backed currency the heart of their response.[25]

The campaign that followed was sharp-edged and innovative. Bryan's speaking tours had no precedent in presidential politics. He covered some 18,000 miles by train, speaking as many as thirty-six times a day, and reached an estimated five million people in twenty-seven states. At times his campaigning took on a messianic quality. It was reported that at one meeting late in the campaign the lighting was so arranged as to cast an aureole around his head, and the crowd pressed forward to touch his clothes: "it is not alone the rôle of social reformer which he fills—there is the flavor of a wider promise in his utterances, and this it is that gives him . . . his peculiar hold."

Bryan's opponents came to see him as a political antichrist, a harbinger of anarchy and revolution. "Bryanism" came under

25. Thomas Beer, *Hanna* (New York, 1929); Herbert D. Croly, *Marcus Alonzo Hanna* (New York, 1923); Marcus, *Grand Old Party*, ch. 6; Margaret Leech, *In the Days of McKinley* (New York, 1959), chs. 2–4; H. Wayne Morgan, "William McKinley and the Tariff," *OH*, 74 (1965), 215–231, *William McKinley and His America* (Syracuse, 1963).

assault as the cause of "social misfits who have almost nothing in common but opposition to the existing order and institutions." A more perceptive analysis of Bryan's appeal was that in his candidacy "the ominous social side of politics presents itself." The polity now served a complex industrial society. But there was still a substantial preindustrial sector of American life which felt keenly the loss of representation. "It is this feeling that in some way the government has ceased to be his, as it was his in a time nearer to the town-meeting, that has aroused the suspicion of the isolated man. It is in fact a contest between the isolated and the organized."[26]

The Republican campaign was no less distinctive. As Bryan came to be the personification of a cause more than the candidate of a party, so did McKinley exemplify the values of solid working-men and the middle class. He did no traveling, but received massive delegations each day from the front porch of his Canton, Ohio home: as many as 80,000 on September 18 alone. Hanna, meanwhile, geared up an "educational" effort that had no parallel in American political history. As McKinley observed, "this is a year for press and pen." Hundreds of millions of pamphlets, fliers, leaflets, and books flooded the country, 1,400 orators spoke for the cause, opinion polls of substantial scope and accuracy pinpointed trouble spots for the Republican managers. The national campaign committee reportedly spent about $4 million; clearly far more was expended. Large corporations contributed on a scale unmatched before. John McCall, president of the New York Life, explained, "I consented to a payment [of $50,000] ... not to defeat the Democratic Party, [but] to defeat the Free Silver heresy, and I thank God I did it." The directors of the Metropolitan Life held that their contribution was "more a matter of morals than it was of policy."[27]

Along with new levels of spending and propaganda, old standards

26. On Bryan campaign, Stanley L. Jones, *The Presidential Election of 1896* (Madison, 1964), ch. 21; Glad, *McKinley, Bryan, and the People*, ch. 8; Lloyd Brice, "A Study of Campaign Audiences," *NAR*, 164 (1897), 84; "Meaning of Bryanism in American Politics," *GM*, 11 (1896), 388; "The Political Menace of the Discontented," *AM*, 78 (1896), 447–451.

27. On McKinley campaign, Jones, *Presidential Election*, ch. 20; Marcus, *Grand Old Party*, ch. 7; McKinley quoted in Jensen, *Winning of Midwest*, 288; on spending, Jones, *Presidential Election*, 280–283; Morton Keller, *The Life Insurance Enterprise, 1885–1910* (Cambridge, 1963), 228–230.

of organizational intensity were maintained. The chairman of the Ohio Republican Executive Committee passed on instructions to the county chairman. Each precinct committeeman was to appoint a Sub-District Rallying Committee composed of one member for every six Republican and doubtful voters. There were also to be county committees on organization, finance, speakers, doubtful voters, registration, naturalization, messengers, and transportation. Finally, a warning: "It is not wise to send out cartoons or literary matter if it contains any suggestion of race, creed or nationality to an offensive degree. Pictures should always portray the elevation of American workingmen through Protection, their degradation through Free Trade, etc."

Protection—through a high tariff and a gold-backed currency—of jobs and wage scales, of pensions and life insurance policies and property values, was a major Republican theme. Another was an appeal to patriotism (the national flag was the McKinley campaign banner) that spoke to old memories of the Civil War and to the assimilating aspirations of new Americans.

On the surface the campaign seemed, more than any in memory, to have become a form of class conflict. Mugwumps and many Cleveland Democrats fled to a Gold Democratic third party or to the Republicans. A number of silver Republicans in the West bolted to Bryan. The Populists endorsed Bryan and everywhere fused with the Democratic cause. Yet, as a German observer noted, both parties were for artificially stimulating prices and reversing the long secular deflation, the Democrats through free silver, the Republicans through protection. Nor did the rhetoric of the two parties clearly break along class lines. Both spoke to what they took to be a broad spectrum of voters. If anything, the Republicans cast their net more widely.[28]

The election results confirmed the fact that this was a changing political order. Regional differences in party strength were dramatic. Southern Republicans won 35 percent of the vote, compared

28. Thomas E. Felt, ed., "Suggestions for a Plan of County Organization: Charles Dick Lays the Groundwork for the Campaign of 1896," *OHQ*, 69 (1960), 367–378; on patriotism, Jones, *Presidential Election*, 291–292; "The Literature of the Campaign," *YR*, 5 (1896–1897), 235–238; "European Comments on American Politics," ibid., 233–235. See also Robert F. Durden, *The Climax of Populism: The Election of 1896* (Lexington, Ky., 1965).

TABLE 6. Democratic and Republican margins, selected cities, 1892 and 1896

City	1892 majority party margin	1896 majority party margin
Boston	(D) 10,376	(R) 18,296
New York	(D) 76,300	(R) 21,997
Brooklyn	(D) 25,595	(R) 32,253
Philadelphia	(R) 32,215	(R) 113,999
Baltimore	(D) 14,606	(R) 21,109
Louisville	(D) 5,816	(R) 11,608
Chicago	(D) 35,625	(R) 56,543
St. Louis	(R) 359	(R) 15,805
Minneapolis	(D) 9,429	(R) 5,454

Source: "Influence of Issues on Parties," GM, 12 (1897), 51.

to 54 percent outside of the South. Bryan's strength fell off sharply outside of the South, the silver states, and the Plains. He carried no state north of the Mason Dixon line or east of the Mississippi. He did poorly in the prairie states and the Midwest, where diversified farming and relative closeness to markets lessened his appeal. Bryan carried only seventeen of ninety-nine Iowa counties, only seventeen of eighty-one in Minnesota.

Equally significant for the future was the voting pattern in the cities. Bryan carried a few southern and western towns—New Orleans, Denver, Salt Lake City—by hefty margins. But otherwise he fared poorly in urban America (table 6).[29]

Not all of this could be blamed on Bryan. Hard times after 1893 cut into the 1894 Democratic city vote, and the shift to the Republicans in a number of midwestern cities had been going on since the 1880s. But McKinley ran particularly well in eastern urban centers. He won more than 60 percent of the vote in Boston and Newark, more than 70 percent in Philadelphia and Pittsburg. New York City and Jersey City went against the Democrats for the first

29. J. Morgan Kousser, The Shaping of Southern Politics (New Haven, 1974), 12; Glad, McKinley, Bryan, and the People, 197–205; Jones, Presidential Election, ch. 23; on Iowa and Minnesota, Gilbert C. Fite, "Republican Strategy and the Farm Vote in the Presidential Campaign of 1896," AHR, 65 (1960), 803–804; William Diamond, "Urban and Rural Voting in 1896," AHR, 46 (1941), 281–305.

time since 1848. Bryan's heaviest New York losses came in the more comfortable, old-stock upper west side, and in the new-immigrant lower east side. His agrarian rhetoric and fundamentalist style had little appeal for new urban immigrants. He fared somewhat better among the Irish: the Democratic city machines reluctantly went along with the national ticket, and Irish party loyalty was strong. At the same time, Bryan made inroads in pietistic, traditionally Republican rural areas such as the "Burned-Over District" of western New York and parts of Michigan. He ran well too in small towns in the Midwest and in traditional Democratic rural enclaves in the East.[30]

But the net result was to solidify the gains that the Republicans had made in 1894 and to assure GOP national political supremacy for a generation. Usually Democratic states such as Delaware, West Virginia, Kentucky, and Missouri became competitive; New Hampshire, Pennsylvania, Illinois, Michigan, Wisconsin, Oregon, and California became normally Republican. The GOP after 1896 regained its position as the dominant voice of industrial, middle class America.

The Democratic legacy was more varied. Irish machine politicians who stayed with the party assumed all but uncontested control of the Democracy in many cities, as Bourbon Democrats and Mugwumps moved into the GOP. In the South, too, a new breed of Democratic leaders, often more unregenerate on black voting and other race issues than their Bourbon predecessors, came into power. In national Democratic politics, Altgeld's northern urban liberalism and Bryan's western and southern agrarianism would coexist uncomfortably for decades to come.[31]

30. On longer term shift, Carl N. Degler, "American Political Parties and the Rise of the City: An Interpretation," *JAH*, 51 (1964), 49; on East, McSeveney, *Politics of Depression*, 198 ff, 213, 205; on Midwest, Kleppner, *Cross of Culture*, ch. 8; Jensen, *Winning of Midwest*, 280. J. Rogers Hollingsworth, "The Historian, Presidential Elections, and 1896," *MAm*, 45 (1963), 185–192, argues that Bryan's poor showing with some immigrant groups (Italians, Germans, and Scandinavians in particular) was the result of economic rather than cultural factors. See also Hollingsworth, *Whirligig*, 95–98.

31. Paul T. David, *Party Strength* (Charlottesville, 1972), 53; on Irish, Jensen, *Winning of Midwest*, 299, McSeveney, *Politics of Depression*, 173 ff, Blodgett, *Gentle Reformers*, ch. 8; on South, Woodward, *Origins*, ch. 12, Kousser, *Shaping of Southern Politics*, chs. 8–9, William C. Wooldridge,

The larger meaning of 1896 transcended party differences. The election was the high water mark of political discontent in the nineties. Yet its most striking consequence was the extent to which the party system absorbed that discontent, rather than as in 1860 being overwhelmed by it. Party politics like late nineteenth century government, law, and public administration went some way to adapt to the forces of socioeconomic change. But that adaptation was subordinate to the inertial force of existing values, interests, and institutions.

"The Sound and Fury of 1896: Virginia Democrats Face Free Silver," *VMHB*, 75 (1967), 97–108.

CHAPTER 16

The Twentieth Century Polity

A NEW ISSUE—imperialism—briefly dominated the nation's public life at the very end of the nineteenth century. The imperialist controversy had a special, emblematic quality. The issue and the rhetoric that surrounded it serve as a transition from the political ambiance of late nineteenth century America to the quite different one of the early twentieth century.

Imperialism and Anti-Imperialism

Once before, foreign policy had taken center stage in American political life. During the 1790s, Federalists dwelt on the violent and anarchic nature of the French Revolution, and identified with the stability and order that they saw in the British system of government. Their Jeffersonian Republican opponents celebrated the French Revolution as a compliment by imitation to its American forerunner, and defined the ensuing Franco-English war as one between the advocates of liberty and republicanism and the advocates of monarchy, aristocracy, and privilege. But in fact the controversy had less to do with the French Revolution than with clashing views on the character of American society itself. The domestic hopes and fears of Federalists and Republicans found an outlet in foreign policy.[1]

1. Richard Buel, Jr., *Saving the Revolution: Ideology in American Politics, 1789–1815* (Ithaca, 1972); Marshall Smelser, "The Federalist Period as

588

Precisely a century later, a comparable public controversy rose in the wake of the Spanish-American War. Once again, foreign policy was a medium for the expression of strongly held domestic attitudes. Colonies overseas served as a symbol both for those who welcomed the growing power of the United States and those who looked with foreboding on the rise of an industrial society.

American foreign policy in the 1880s had modest goals and limited resources. The lightly manned Department of State and its often nondescript emissaries abroad were adequate to the minimal demands made upon them. The representation of foreign-born United States citizens who fell into difficulty with authorities in their native lands was the largest single category of American diplomatic activity.[2]

It is true that the expansion of agricultural exports led to growing demands for the protection of American economic interests abroad. The access of American cotton, wheat, corn, pork, and beef to European markets was a matter of constant concern during the 1880s. Farm journals of the period were filled with discussions of the need to enhance the overseas market for American staples. Pressure also mounted for overseas outlets for American industrial products. Overproduction was a fashionable topic of discussion from the late 1870s on. Secretary of State William M. Evarts (1877–1881) prodded American consuls to prepare reports "calculated to advance the commercial and industrial interests of the United States." Their "principal efforts must be directed to the introduction of American trade into, and the enlargement thereof in, your several districts." Evarts's Republican successors Frederick T. Frelinghuysen (1881–1885) and James G. Blaine (1881, 1889–1892) had similar interests, and sought reciprocity treaties with other

an Age of Passion," *AQ*, 10 (1958), 391–419; Jerald A. Combs, *The Jay Treaty: Political Battleground of the Founding Fathers* (Berkeley and Los Angeles, 1970).

2. David M. Pletcher, *The Awkward Years: American Foreign Relations under Garfield and Arthur* (Columbia, Mo., 1962), ch. 13; Milton Plesur, *America's Outward Thrust: Approaches to Foreign Affairs 1865–1890* (De Kalb, Ill., 1971), ch. 5; U.S., Department of State, *General Index to the Published Volumes of the Diplomatic Correspondence and Foreign Relations of the United States. 1861–1899* (Washington, 1902), for estimate of diplomatic activities.

TABLE 7.   American exports, 1880–1896

Year	Value of exports (millions)	Exports as percent of GNP
1880	583	
1877–1881		8.2
1885	784	
1882–1886		6.6
1890	910	
1887–1891		6.3
1895	921	
1892–1896		6.6

Source: HS, 537–538, 542.

nations in order to broaden the market for American agricultural and industrial products.[3]

It is easy to exaggerate the scale and importance of a market-oriented American foreign policy during the 1880s, and much recent historical writing has done just that. The American economy was overwhelmingly pegged to domestic consumption, and this did not change in the late nineteenth century (table 7). Nor was market-oriented diplomacy noticeably successful. A general hostility toward foreign entanglements and clashing domestic interests constantly blocked reciprocity treaties. Neither the shape of the economy, the character of public opinion, nor the structure of government gave much substance to the ambitions of secretaries of state or the advocates of commercial expansionism in the 1880s.[4]

Domestic developments during the 1890s coincided with international changes to make foreign affairs a more important part of American public life. Brief but intense war scares—after a couple

3. William A. Williams, *The Roots of the Modern American Empire: A Study of the Growth and Shaping of Social Consciousness in a Marketplace Society* (New York, 1969); Walter LaFeber, *The New Empire: An Interpretation of American Expansion 1860–1898* (Ithaca, 1963); Evarts to Consuls, July 1, 1880, FR (1880), 3, FR (1877), 2–4; Pletcher, *Awkward Years*, chs. 1, 10; Tom E. Terrill, *The Tariff, Politics, and American Foreign Policy* (Westport, Conn., 1973), chs. 2, 6.

4. Pletcher, *Awkward Years*, ch. 18. See also Robert Zevin, "An Interpretation of American Imperialism," *JEH*, 32 (1972), 316–360.

of American sailors were killed by a Valparaiso, Chile mob in 1891, and a dispute with Great Britain over the Venezuela-British Guiana boundary in 1895—showed how readily public opinion might be stirred. President Harrison in the first case and President Cleveland in the second used an excited public opinion and bellicose messages to Congress to obtain their policy objectives—and to strengthen themselves in domestic politics.

The issue of Hawaiian annexation in 1893–1894 revealed the forces that were reshaping American foreign policy—and the strength of the forces opposing change. American sugar planters in Hawaii had been protected for years by a reciprocity arrangement that freed them from United States customs duties. Now they suffered from the fact that mainland sugar producers enjoyed a bounty under the McKinley Tariff Act. The planters sought to improve their lot by overthrowing the native regime on the islands and petitioning to become a protectorate of the United States. A substantial debate over annexation took place in Congress and the public prints, prefiguring the larger imperialism controversy later in the decade. Jurist Thomas M. Cooley questioned the constitutionality of annexation, and *Nation* editor E. L. Godkin argued against its social desirability. Democratic opposition (fueled by Louisiana beet sugar growers and eastern sugar refiners) was strong, and Cleveland withdrew the treaty in 1894.[5]

The full potential of foreign affairs as an issue in American public life emerged after the outbreak of Cuban rebellion against Spanish rule in 1895. The island's closeness to the United States and the intrinsic appeal of a struggle for national independence made this a prime story for the new American journalism. Highly colored reportage glorified the revolutionaries and, with considerable help from the realities of Spanish policy, painted a picture of brutal repression which was readily accepted by a people nurtured on tales of the Inquisition.

More than anti-Catholicism fed the American response to the

5. Julius W. Pratt, *Expansionists of 1898: The Acquisition of Hawaii and the Spanish Islands* (Baltimore, 1936), chs. 1–5; Cooley, "Grave Obstacles to Hawaiian Annexation," *Forum*, 15 (1893), 389–406; William M. Armstrong, *E. L. Godkin and American Foreign Policy 1865–1900* (New York, 1957), 177. See also Donald M. Dozer, "The Opposition to Hawaiian Reciprocity, 1876–1888," *PHR*, 14 (1945), 157–183.

Cuban rebellion. The Catholic immigrant readers of the Hearst and Pulitzer press were no less aroused. In part the Cuban cause met the need—a particularly keen one in the strife-torn nineties—for the reaffirmation of national unity. In part, too, it satisfied a vague but real desire for adventure, a cause. When Carl Schurz spoke out against a declaration of war against Spain, Theodore Roosevelt chided him: "you and your generation have had your chance from 1861 to 1865. Now let us of this generation have ours!" There was a powerful surge of public opinion when Redfield Proctor of Vermont, newly returned from Cuba, gave the Senate an affecting account of Cuban heroism and Spanish brutality. House Speaker Thomas B. Reed sardonically observed, apropos of the fact that the senator owned the Vermont Marble Company, "Proctor's position might have been expected. A war will make a large market for gravestones." But such skepticism was out of place at a time when sentimentality was pervasive in popular culture and when economic and social tensions were high.

Certainly there was no enthusiasm for war on the part of McKinley, Hanna, Reed, and other leading Republicans. They remembered the horrors of the Civil War all too well, and they expected hostilities to disrupt business. Leading bankers were more interested in the security of Spanish war bonds than in the uncertain prospect of gain in a free Cuba. They were roundly criticized for this by eastern hotbloods like Theodore Roosevelt and Henry Cabot Lodge, and by westerners anxious to compensate for the failures of Populism and the Bryan campaign. One historian has argued: "The verdict of [the election of] 1896 was . . . appealed, and in its probusiness aspect, symbolically overturned in the preliminaries to the Spanish-American War."[6]

But in fact the war and its aftereffects strengthened the hand of those who celebrated the power of the new industrial society, who saw the United States as "the most stupendous reservoir of seething energy to be found on any continent." The Spanish-American

6. Roosevelt quoted in John W. Burgess, *Reminiscences of an American Scholar* (New York, 1934), 315; on Reed, Gerald F. Linderman, *The Mirror of War: American Society and the Spanish-American War* (Ann Arbor, 1974), 39; Paul S. Holbo, "The Convergence of Moods and the Cuban Bond 'Conspiracy' of 1898," *JAH*, 55 (1968), 54–72; Linderman, *Mirror of War*, 6. See also Ernest R. May, *Imperial Democracy: The Emergence of the United States as a Great Power* (New York, 1961); Pratt, *Expansionists of 1898*, chs. 7–9.

War, brief as it was, stirred a new sense of national strength and purpose, much as the Civil War had done more than thirty years before. Harvard President Charles W. Eliot praised "the organization and disciplined skill which makes possible the equipment of great bodies of soldiers within a few weeks, and their transportation to distant lands with incredible speed and safety, . . . the same sort of organization and skills needed in every great productive industry." The scale and frequency of corporate consolidation increased dramatically in the years following the war, as did American enterprise and investment abroad. By the turn of the century, London publishers offered books with titles such as *The American Invasion, The American Invaders,* and *The Americanization of the World.*[7]

The most direct consequence of the war was the emergence of a demand, ultimately successful, that the United States hold the territory (save Cuba) wrested from Spain. Advocates of imperialism included theorists of an American *Realpolitik* such as Brooks Adams, Homer Lea, and the naval officer Alfred Thayer Mahan, as well as ambitious young Republican politicians Theodore Roosevelt of New York, Henry Cabot Lodge of Massachusetts, Albert J. Beveridge of Indiana, and Robert M. LaFollette of Wisconsin. Aggressive younger businessmen—New York Life Insurance Company executive George W. Perkins, publisher Frank A. Munsey—joined them. These men found in an American empire an evocative expression of the new, powerful society that they were ready to lead. They identified colonies with American strength, progress, national (and racial) fulfillment. Imperialism in this sense was both the moral equivalent and the logical outgrowth of war: a unifying enterprise that promised to offset class conflict, counter a crass and emasculating materialism, and elevate the national character.[8]

7. Franklin H. Giddings, "Imperialism?" *PSQ*, 13 (1898), 590; Eliot, "Destructive and Constructive Energies of our Government Compared," *AM*, 83 (1899), 3; Mira Wilkins, *The Emergence of Multinational Enterprise: American Business Abroad from the Colonial Era to 1914* (Cambridge, 1970), 71 ff.

8. John P. Mallan, "Roosevelt, Brooks Adams, and Lea: The Warrior Critique of the Business Civilization," *AQ*, 8 (1956), 216–230; David H. Burton, *Theodore Roosevelt: Confident Imperialist* (Philadelphia, 1968), chs. 1, 2; David Healy, *US Expansionism: The Imperialist Urge in the 1890s* (Madison, 1970), chs. 5–7. See also Padraic C. Kennedy, "La Follette's Imperialist Flirtation," *PHR*, 26 (1957), 131–146.

Advocates of empire might be found in both parties (Democratic Senator John T. Morgan of Alabama was a staunch supporter). But the cause had a special consonance with late nineteenth century Republican ideology. Albert Beveridge celebrated the unifying effect of the Spanish-American War: "No sections any more but a Nation . . . No, not *a Nation*, but the *Nation, The Nation*, God's chosen people." Imperialism was a logical extension of that spirit and gave new life to the traditional Republican identification with nationalism and patriotism. President William McKinley in particular argued for the retention of the former Spanish colonies in these terms.

Of course imperialism had its more concrete components as well. American missionaries were a "troublesome and influential" factor in the formation of American policy toward China, and along with interested entrepreneurs fostered an involvement that culminated in United States marines joining the international army that entered Peking during the Boxer Rebellion of 1900. Military strategists wanted naval coaling stations in the Pacific and a strong American presence in the Caribbean. There was much anticipation that Puerto Rico and the Philippines as American colonies would provide markets, raw materials, and bases for further commercial expansion.

But colonialism tapped wider sources than these. A 1905 French study concluded that "American imperialism is not the invention of politicians; it is the result of the American creed." American expansionism was not new. The belief in Manifest Destiny justified the nation's inexorable spread westward; the Monroe Doctrine set the terms of a special American authority in the Western Hemisphere. Theodore Roosevelt argued: "We are making no new departures. We are not taking a single step which in any way affects our institutions or our traditional policies."[9]

Nevertheless, there were distinctive features to turn-of-the-century imperialism. Before 1900, American expansion usually had an anti-British tinge. Now a rhetoric of Anglo-Saxon world leadership justified the new colonies. The presence of Marines on

9. Beveridge to John T. Graves, July 13, 1898, Beveridge Mss, LC; Marilyn B. Young, *The Rhetoric of Empire: American China Policy 1895–1901* (Cambridge, 1968), 187; Henri Hauser, *l'Impérialisme Américain* (Paris, 1905), 64; TR quoted in Young, *Rhetoric*, 97.

the Asian mainland, the use of 70,000 troops from 1899 to 1902 to crush a Filipino insurrection against the new American rulers: these were unsettling events for a nation that claimed (the treatment of the Indians notwithstanding) to be free from the European vice of colonialism. The British historian Edward Dicey offered a discomforting explanation of "the new American imperialism": "Feeling . . . that democratic institutions are no longer a panacea for the cure of social discontents, the Americans resort most naturally to the remedies which under like circumstances have recommended themselves to their English forefathers—that is, to foreign trade, to emigration, and to the establishment of a colonial empire." Finally, the acquisition of territories with large (and heavily Catholic) native populations, remote from the continental United States, raised a flock of new problems involving church-state relations, colonial administration, and the character of American citizenship. Imperialism emerged from late nineteenth century American public life. But it bore within it the seeds of issues that would have an important place in the century to come.[10]

Anti-imperialism was no less varied in its sources and revealing in its implications. In part the opposition to colonies was political. Democrats generally opposed the Treaty of Paris with Spain that provided for the transfer of sovereignty over Puerto Rico and the Philippines. It was only when Bryan for political reasons advised against blocking the treaty that it secured the necessary two-thirds Senate majority. State Democratic platforms condemned territorial expansion as "dangerous to our free institutions" and warned that "our government can not be both republican and imperial." Cleveland Democrats—not least Cleveland himself, along with former Secretary of State Richard Olney and Nebraska Bourbon leader J. Sterling Morton—spoke out against overseas possessions. So too did Bryan and Altgeld. Even Tammany boss Richard Croker showed an uncharacteristic concern over a national issue: anti-

10. Edward P. Crapol, *America for Americans: Economic Nationalism and Anglophobia in the Late Nineteenth Century* (Westport, Conn., 1973); Dicey, "The New American Imperialism," *NC*, 44 (1898), 495; Richard Hofstadter, "Cuba, The Philippines, and Manifest Destiny," in his *The Paranoid Style in American Politics* (New York, 1965), 145–187; Frank T. Reuter, *Catholic Influence on American Colonial Policies 1898–1904* (Austin, 1967).

imperialism, he said, "is opposition to the fashion of shooting everybody who doesn't speak English."[11]

But anti-imperialism transcended partisanship. A number of leading Republicans dissented from the McKinley administration's colonial policy. They included party pioneer Carl Schurz; oldtime Stalwart George S. Boutwell, Grant's secretary of the treasury; and prominent GOP figures of the eighties and the early nineties such as John Sherman, Thomas B. Reed, George Frisbie Hoar, and former President Benjamin Harrison.

Mugwumps, independents, academics, and literary men—a persistent third force in late nineteenth century American public life —reacted against imperialism with special fervor. For the old abolitionist Moorfield Storey and the sons of Ralph Waldo Emerson and William Lloyd Garrison, this was an issue filled with echoes of an earlier struggle against an evil institution. The nation's leading writers and poets—Mark Twain, William Dean Howells, Hamlin Garland, Edwin Arlington Robinson, William Vaughn Moody— lashed out at the hypocrisy and cruelty of colonial rule. Labor leader Samuel Gompers and more radical critics of American society such as Henry Demarest Lloyd and Jane Addams'joined the anti-imperialist cause—as did industrialist Andrew Carnegie. Men of a conservative social bent such as E. L. Godkin and Charles Eliot Norton looked on imperialism as additional, indeed final, testimony to the decline of American democracy. William Graham Sumner warned: "I have no doubt that the conservative classes of this country will yet look back with great regret to their acquiescence in the events of 1898 and the doctrines and precedents which have been silently established."[12]

No issue since slavery itself brought together so diverse a band of advocates. But beneath the surface variety were certain common elements. The most noticeable of these was age. The leading

11. E. Berkeley Tompkins, *Anti-Imperialism in the United States: The Great Debate, 1890–1920* (Philadelphia, 1970); "Florida," *AC* (1898); "Ohio," *AC* (1899); Robert L. Beisner, *Twelve Against Empire: The Anti-Imperialists, 1898–1900* (New York, 1968); Croker quoted in Marcus R. Werner, *Tammany Hall* (Garden City, 1928), 441. See also Hollingsworth, *Whirligig,* ch. 8.

12. Beisner, *Twelve Against Empire,* x–xii et passim; William G. Whittaker, "Samuel Gompers, Anti-Imperialist," *PHR,* 38 (1969), 429–448; Sumner, "The Conquest of the United States by Spain," *YLJ,* 8 (1899), 271.

anti-imperialists were in their late sixties by 1900, the leading imperialists were in their forties. The values and the careers of the
anti-imperialists belonged to a past America, now rapidly changing.
Imperialism was a particularly vivid expression of that change.
The anti-imperialists made it clear that what concerned them was
the character of American society more than colonialism per se.
Many actively favored commercial expansion; most shared the
racial views of the imperialists and looked on the White Man's
Burden not as a challenge but a threat. Andrew Carnegie, at the
end of his career as an industrialist—he was on the verge of selling
out to the new United States Steel combine that J. P. Morgan was
putting together—feared that Triumphant Democracy was to be
replaced by Triumphant Despotism, that a homogeneous society
was to become "a scattered and disjointed aggregate of widely
separated and alien races." Grover Cleveland, his career also over,
summed up the central anti-imperialist theme when he warned
that "the fatal un-American idea of imperialism and expansion"
was "a new and startling phase in our national character."[13]

Both the incumbent McKinley and the Democrats (who again
nominated Bryan) expected imperialism to be the "paramount"
issue of the 1900 presidential election. The Democratic platform
(once more strongly influenced by Altgeld) was almost entirely devoted to the question of overseas colonies. It warned that "no nation can long endure half republic and half empire, . . . that
imperialism abroad will lead quickly and inevitably to despotism
at home." Bryan sought to meld anti-imperialism, free silver, and
a new stress on the dangers of big business into a concerted critique
of McKinley and the Republicans. "The issue presented in the

13. On ages, Tompkins, *Anti-Imperialism*, ch. 10, Robert L. Beisner,
"1898 and 1968: The Anti-Imperialists and the Doves," *PSQ*, 85 (1970),
187–216; on commercialism, Healy, *US Expansionism*, 54–56, Beisner,
Twelve Against Empire, 85–86 ff; on racism, ibid., 27, Christopher Lasch,
"The Anti-Imperialists, the Philippines, and the Inequality of Man," *JSH*,
24 (1958), 319–331, Philip W. Kennedy, "The Racial Overtones of Imperialism as a Campaign Issue, 1900," *MAm*, 48 (1966), 196–205; Carnegie,
"Distant Possessions—The Parting of the Ways," *NAR*, 167 (1898), 239;
George H. Knoles, ed., "Grover Cleveland on Imperialism," *MVHR*, 37
(1950), 304. See also Richard E. Welch, Jr., "Motives and Policy Objectives
of Anti-Imperialists, 1898," *MAm*, 51 (1969), 119–129.

campaign of 1900," he said, "is the issue between plutocracy and democracy."

The results of the election correlated closely with those of 1896— and of ensuing presidential contests for a quarter of a century to come. There would be no seismic electoral shift again until the time of Al Smith in 1928 and the New Deal of the 1930s. The issue of imperialism, intense as it was, did not substantially affect political alignments. Rather, it resembled the questions of the tariff and free silver in that it gave voice to ambitions and anxieties that reflected the changing character of late nineteenth century American life. Like those other issues, imperialism would lose its saliency after 1900. But the questions that it raised as to the character of the nation's past, and the shape of its future, would have a conspicuous place in the American polity during the century to come.[14]

The Twentieth Century Polity

The turn of a century is a powerful spur to the belief that one period of a nation's history is ending and another has begun. Events conspired to reinforce that view of American life around 1900. The severe depression of the 1890s was followed by a buoyant expansion of overseas sales of raw and finished products, a sharp increase in corporate consolidation, and the beginnings of a sustained price rise after decades of decline. All of this suggested that a new stage in American economic development had been reached. Henceforth the problems of agricultural and industrial maturity would command public attention.

Much the same could be said of social attitudes. The weight of public opinion increasingly favored the imposition of various forms of social control. The position of blacks in the South steadily worsened. After 1910 national prohibition and immigration restric-

14. Walter LaFeber, "The Election of 1900," in Arthur M. Schlesinger, ed., *History of American Presidential Elections 1789–1968* (New York, 1971), 1878 et passim; Porter and Johnson, *Party Platforms*, 112; Waldo R. Browne, *Altgeld of Illinois: A Record of His Life and Work* (New York, 1924), 311–312; Bryan, "The Issue in the Presidential Campaign," *NAR*, 170 (1900), 753. See also Thomas A. Bailey, "Was the Presidential Election of 1900 A Mandate on Imperialism?" *MVHR*, 24 (1937–1938), 43–52; Hollingsworth, *Whirligig*, ch. 10.

tion won growing acceptance and in the wake of the First World War were enacted into law.

The tone and texture of political life also seemed to change with the turn of the century. The issues that dominated public discourse before 1900—the tariff, the currency, imperialism—lost much of their salience. Rising farm prices and overseas exports, increasing productivity, the rapid expansion of domestic urban markets, and the growth of the money supply through an enlarged world gold stock and an increase in bank notes, made protection and free trade, gold and free silver, seem more and more to belong to an earlier economic period. The issue of imperialism, too, quickly faded. Within months after the 1900 election, those who warned that the acquisition of territories meant the end of the Republic no longer clamored in the public forum, and those who looked forward to an American Century found little interest in further territorial gain.

The sense of a changing political ambiance was fostered by the assassination of William McKinley in 1901. Once again, the act of a deranged man found justification in the current conditions of public life. Lincoln's killer Booth imagined himself to be the avenger of the defeated South. Guiteau shot Garfield at a time when party politics and organizational factionalism predominated; he claimed to be a frustrated officeseeker and an adherent of the GOP Stalwart faction. Now, at a time when the social and economic consequences of industrialism laid growing claim on the attentions of the polity, McKinley's assassin Leon Czolgosz accounted himself an anarchist. "I didn't believe one man should have so much service, and another man should have none," was his explanation for the deed. Czolgosz's father was an itinerant immigrant laborer; he grew up in the heartland industrial towns of Pittsburgh and Cleveland. This product of an industrial age frequently used the alias of Fred Nieman—Fred Nobody.[15]

Vice President Theodore Roosevelt's accession to the presidency was an equally vivid bench mark of change. McKinley, like all of his Republican predecessors since Lincoln, had been a Civil War officer; Roosevelt as a boy of seven watched Lincoln's funeral procession pass through New York in 1865. TR would bring to the

15. Margaret Leech, In the Days of McKinley (New York, 1959), 592–594.

White House a style of presidential leadership, a rhetoric of reform, and a consciousness of the nation's status as a world power that had not been seen before.

It is proper, though beyond the scope of this volume, to speak of a progressive political generation that gave the early twentieth century American polity as distinct a cast as the Civil War and industrialism had done before. The sheer scale of the post-1900 effort to control large corporations, political corruption, bossism, and machines and the range of attempts to improve the working and living conditions of the industrial population sets the period apart. So, too, does the thrust to shape the character of American society through education, racial segregation, immigration restriction, and prohibition.

But one should not overstate the degree to which the early twentieth century polity broke from its late nineteenth century predecessor. The tensions of the earlier period—between individualism and social order, localism and centralism, laissez-faire and the active state, broad and restrictive views of American citizenship—continued to be prime determinants of public life. The forms in which these concerns were expressed and acted upon changed substantially over time. Their content, the social anxieties and aspirations that they represented, remained the same.

ABBREVIATIONS

INDEX

Abbreviations

AAPS—American Academy of Political and Social Science
AAS—American Antiquarian Society
ABA—American Bar Association
ABR—American Benedictine Review
AC—*Appletons' Annual Cyclopaedia and Register of Important Events* (New York, 1862–1903)
ACHS—American Catholic Historical Society
AEEL—*The American and English Encyclopaedia of Law*, 2d ed. (Northport, L.I., 1896–1905)
AER—American Economic Review
AH—Agricultural History
AHA—American Historical Association
AHR—American Historical Review
AI—Annals of Iowa
AJES—American Journal of Economics and Sociology
ALJH—American Journal of Legal History
AJS—American Journal of Sociology
AL—American Lawyer
AlaR—Alabama Review

ALit—American Literature
ALJ—Albany Law Journal
ALR—American Law Review
ALRec—American Law Record
ALReg—American Law Register
AM—Atlantic Monthly
AmJ—American Jurist
AmLJ—American Law Journal
APSA—American Political Science Association
APSR—American Political Science Review
APTR—American Presbyterian and Theological Review
AQ—American Quarterly
Arena—The Arena Magazine
ArkHA—Arkansas Historical Association
ArkHQ—Arkansas Historical Quarterly
ArW—Arizona and the West
AS—American Scholar
ASA—American Statistical Association
ASR—American Sociological Review
AStR—American State Reports
AW—Annals of Wyoming

BAT—Bar Association of Tennessee
BHM—Bulletin of the History of

Medicine
BHR—Business History Review
BHS—B. R. Mitchell and Phyllis
  Deane, *Abstract of British
  Historical Statistics*
  (Cambridge, 1962)
BLJ—Banking Law Journal
BQR—Brownson's Quarterly
  Review
BULR—Boston University Law
  Review

CalHS—California Historical
  Society
CalLR—California Law Review
CFC—Commercial and Financial
  Quarterly
CG—Congressional Globe
CanHR—Canadian Historical
  Review
CHR—Catholic Historical Review
CincHS—Cincinnati Historical
  Society
CLJ—Central Law Journal
CLM—Criminal Law Magazine
CLN—Chicago Legal News
CLQ—Cornell Law Quarterly
CM—The Century Magazine
ColLR—Columbia Law Review
ColM—Colorado Magazine
CR—Congressional Record
CWH—Civil War History

DAB—*Dictionary of American
  Biography* (New York, 1936)

EEH—Explorations in Entrepre-
  neurial History
EHR—English Historical Review
ER—Economic Review

FlaHQ—Florida Historical
  Quarterly
FLR—Fordham Law Review
Forum—The Forum Magazine
FR—Foreign Relations of the
  United States
FRev—Fortnightly Review

FS—Furman Studies

GaBA—Georgia Bar Association
GaHQ—Georgia Historical
  Quarterly
GB—Green Bag
GM—Gunton's Magazine

HAHR—Hispanic-American
  Historical Review
HEQ—Harvard Educational
  Quarterly
HER—Harvard Educational Review
Hist—The Historian Magazine
HJ—The Historical Journal
HL—Houghton Library, Harvard
  University
HLQ—Huntington Library
  Quarterly
HLR—Harvard Law Review
HM—Harper's Magazine
HO—The Historical Outlook
HPSO—Historical and Philo-
  sophical Society of Ohio
HS—U.S., Bureau of the Census,
  *Historical Statistics of the
  United States, Colonial Times
  to 1957* (Washington, 1960)
HSC—Historical Society of
  California
HT—History Today
HW—Harper's Weekly

IJH—Iowa Journal of History
IJHP—Iowa Journal of History
  and Politics
ILJ—Intercollegiate Law Journal
ILM—Indiana Law Magazine
ILR—Illinois Law Review
ILRR—Industrial and Labor
  Relations Review
ILT—Irish Law Times
IMH—Indiana Magazine of History
IR—International Review
IRSH—International Review of
  Social History
ISHS—Illinois State Historical
  Society

JAH—Journal of American History
JAS—Journal of American Studies
JCL—Journal of Criminal Law
JEH—Journal of Economic History
JHI—Journal of the History of Ideas
JHM—Journal of the History of
  Medicine
JLE—Journal of Law and Economics
JLS—Journal of Legal Studies
JMissH—Journal of Mississippi
  History
JNH—Journal of Negro History
JPE—Journal of Political Economy
JQ—Journalism Quarterly
JSH—Journal of Southern History
JSocH—Journal of Social History
JSS—Journal of Social Science
JW—Journal of the West

KHQ—Kansas Historical Quarterly
KLJ—Kansas Law Journal

LaH—Louisiana History
LaHQ—Louisiana Historical
  Quarterly
LC—Library of Congress
LCHS—Lancaster County
  Historical Society
LCP—Law and Contemporary
  Problems
LH—Labor History
LMR—Law Magazine & Review
LQR—Law Quarterly Review
LRA—Lawyers' Reports Annotated
LT—Law Times

MA—Municipal Affairs
MacM—MacMillan's Magazine
MAm—Mid-America
MAQR—Michigan Alumnae
  Quarterly Review
MdHM—Maryland Historical
  Magazine
MH—Michigan History
MHS—Massachusetts Historical
  Society
MichHS—Michigan Historical
  Society

MinnH—Minnesota History
MinnLR—Minnesota Law Review
MissLJ—Mississippi Law Journal
MLJ—Michigan Law Journal
MLR—Michigan Law Review
MoHR—Missouri Historical
  Review
MoHS—Missouri Historical
  Society
Mont—Montana: The Magazine
  of Western History
MP—James D. Richardson, ed.,
  *Messages and Papers of the
  Presidents* (Washington, 1897)
MQ—Midwest Quarterly
MQR—Michigan Quarterly
  Review
MR—Massachusetts Review
MVHA—Mississippi Valley
  Historical Association
MVHR—Mississippi Valley
  Historical Review
MWH—Magazine of Western
  History

NA—National Archives
NAR—North American Review
Nation—The Nation Magazine
NC—Nineteenth Century
NCHR—North Carolina Historical
  Review
NDH—North Dakota History
NDL—Notre Dame Lawyer
NE—New Englander
NEQ—New England Quarterly
NH—Nebraska History
NJHS—New Jersey Historical
  Society
NJLJ—New Jersey Law Journal
NLR—Northwestern Law
  Review
NMHR—New Mexico Historical
  Review
NOQ—Northwest Ohio Quarterly
NPR—New Princeton Review
NYH—New York History
NYHQ—New York Historical
  Quarterly

NYHS—New York Historical Society
NYPL—New York Public Library
NYSBA—New York State Bar Association

OH—Ohio History
OHQ—Ohio Historical Quarterly
ON—Old and New
OSAH—Ohio State Archaeological and Historical Society

PAH—Perspectives in American History
PBA—Pennsylvania Bar Association
PCSU—Publications of the Church Social Union
PH—Pennsylvania History
PHR—Pacific Historical Review
PL—Public Law
PM—Penn Monthly
PMHB—Pennsylvania Magazine of History and Biography
PNQ—Pacific Northwest Quarterly
PP—Past and Present
PR—Princeton Review
Prol—Prologue
PSM—Popular Science Monthly
PSQ—Political Science Quarterly

QJE—Quarterly Journal of Economics

Rep—The Republic
RP—Review of Politics

SAQ—South Atlantic Quarterly
SCBM—South Carolina Bar Association
SCLR—Southern California Law Review
SCQ—Southern California Quarterly
SHQ—Southwestern Historical Quarterly

SJ—The Solicitors' Journal
SL—*The Statutes at Large of the United States of America* (Boston, 1845–)
SLR—Southern Law Review
SM—Scribners' Magazine
SPSQ—Southwestern Political Science Quarterly
SS—Science and Society
SSSQ—Southwestern Social Science Quarterly
StLR—Stanford Law Review

TBA—Texas Bar Association
TennBA—Tennessee Bar Association
TennHQ—Tennessee Historical Quarterly
THGM—Tyler's Historical and Geneological Magazine
TLR—Tulane Law Review

UCLR—University of Chicago Law Review
UHQ—Utah Historical Quarterly
U.S.—United States Reports

VaLR—Virginia Law Review
VLR—Vanderbilt Law Review
VMHB—Virginia Magazine of History and Biography
VS—Victorian Studies
VSBA—Virginia State Bar Association

Wall.—Wallace's Reports
WCR—West Coast Reporter
WMH—Wisconsin Magazine of History
WPQ—Western Political Quarterly
WR—Westminster Review
WSHS—Wisconsin State Historical Society

YR—Yale Review

Index